CW01551678

THE
BLOOD-RED
ARAB FLAG

THE
BLOOD-RED
ARAB FLAG

—

An Investigation into
Qasimi Piracy 1797–1820

CHARLES E. DAVIES

UNIVERSITY
of
EXETER
PRESS

First published in 1997 by
University of Exeter Press
Reed Hall, Streatham Drive
Exeter, Devon EX4 4QR
UK

British Library Cataloguing in Publication Data
A catalogue record of this book is
available from the British Library

ISBN 0 85989 509 2

Typeset in Goudy Old Style
by Colin Bakké Typesetting, Exeter
Printed and bound in Great Britain
by Short Run Press Ltd, Exeter

People are troubled not by things,
but by their beliefs about things.

EPICTETUS

CONTENTS

ILLUSTRATIONS

Plates

Figures

Tables

Maps

ACKNOWLEDGEMENTS

The following illustrations are reproduced by kind permission: Plates 1 (BHC 1085), 6–7, 8 (PAF6142), 9–12 and 15–16 (PAF6143, PAF6154), the National Maritime Museum, Greenwich. Plates 2 and 4–5 the British Library, London. Plates 13–14 (Oriental and India Office Collections X/3213, X/3211), the British Library, London. Plate 3 (1926–575, 1926–573, 1880–75), the Science Museum, London.

x

PREFACE

This work does not presuppose any specialized knowledge of the Persian Gulf or its history. It is the account of an historical investigation into an evocative piece of history, dark and dramatic, rich and uncertain, whose significance was disproportionate with its human scale. The Qawasim— whence the adjective Qasimi (pronounced Kawáassim and Káassimee)— were Arabs inhabiting the ports of what is today the north-western United Arab Emirates. This book examines piracy said to have been committed by them between 1797 and 1820.

The significance of these dates is that it was during this period that the Qawasim's maritime activities were of concern to the British Government of Bombay; so much so, in fact, on account of attacks on British shipping, that no less than two British military expeditions were sent against the Qawasim, in 1809/10 and 1819/20. On each occasion, the Qawasim's capital, Ras al-Khaima, was briefly overrun and many of their boats were burnt. After the second expedition a treaty was drawn up with the Arab tribes which inaugurated 150 years of regular British involvement in the Gulf. Supposed piracy by the Qawasim in 1797–1820, and Britain's response to it, helped shape not only Britain's special role in the Gulf during the nineteenth century, but also the long-term political development of the Arab Gulf states, and in particular and most directly, that of the United Arab Emirates.

For very many years, the generally accepted view was the official British one that the Qawasim had been pirates engaged in piracy. Recently some have sought to qualify or completely to refute this conception. The structure of the present work is to a large extent dictated by the problems raised by this controversy. The work falls into three parts: first, an introduction to the region; second, an examination of the evidence relating to the Qawasim's maritime activities; and thirdly, an interpretation of the results of that examination.

In addition to its historical significance, there are two further aspects to the fascination of this subject. In the first place, it has human and social interest: for this reason, as well as out of a desire for authenticity, quotations from primary and mostly contemporary sources have been wielded quite liberally in the text. In the second place, the subject as a whole constitutes an enigma and a challenging historical problem: this is true both in the concrete, for what is known, and in the abstract, for what can be known.

Despite all that has been written on this subject—and it receives a mention in almost any modern history of the Gulf—there has been no attempt to describe or evaluate the activities of the Qawasim in depth; their maritime and internal history has remained hazy and indistinct. Moreover, writers have understandably often been selective in their use of sources; and an identifiable and relatively small group of contemporary despatches, reports and books, supplemented and reinforced by the notable later works of Low and Saldanha, and often mediated through Lorimer's remarkable compendium of Gulf history and geography, has tended to define the field. Unsurprisingly, Qasimi history has sometimes been cast in the mould of Anglo–Qasimi relations. Nothing has been written about this subject on the basis of a sound and detailed chronology of events. In these circumstances, impressionistic, inductive history is potentially perilous: the enhanced receptivity of such a field to open hypothesis and manipulation is self-evident; more subtle are the effects of unwitting rationalization according to subjective, anachronistic or otherwise extraneous standards. Much of this is unavoidable, but it seems to recommend a deductive approach and a return to the original sources.

This book has been written much as it has been researched, as an investigation in succeeding stages. The scene is set in an introductory section, after which the riddle of Qasimi piracy is tackled head-on. Both historically and as a matter of evidence, the backbone of this subject is formed of a series of maritime actions, whose essentials may be readily defined in isolation. I began by rejecting what I had read, then sought, on the basis of a re-reading of the range of primary sources, to rebuild a picture of events, commencing from a core of certainty and the greatest specific historical significance and extending finally to an appraisal of the whole. The exposition of this process of discovery it is hoped conveys a sufficient panorama of the events themselves. In the more conventional concluding section of this study, the results of this analysis are put in context and tested from the most important relevant angles.

In the earlier part of this study, concerned with the evidence, an unusually stringent level of proof is employed and the definition of the results is accentuated by a search for positive statements which can be made with confidence about this subject. As the book progresses, this hard logic is eased and the approach becomes more natural; the focus broadens from the specific to the general and what started as an examination of the evidence hopefully ends up as history. Given the nature of this subject, a fundamental reappraisal of the evidence was a necessary evil, but one that throws up important results both for the richness and general worth of the sources and also, implicitly, for the nature of historical truth in this context.

Inevitably discrepancies concerning fact and interpretation have arisen with the published accounts of this episode. I have not felt it necessary or elegant to point these out. The end result of a work such as this is the overall impression of events which it leaves upon the mind of the reader, and it seemed this would be clearer and more true if the negatives and qualifications which bedevil this subject were kept to a reasonable minimum. I have felt it my duty as an historian to avoid lazy ambivalence and to be as definite as I can about things, without consciously making statements I cannot narrowly defend. In practice, of course, one can only write step-by-step what one feels to be most true at the time, and it would be insane to claim more: the ultimate judge is the reader.

The main source for this work is a collection at Exeter of some 20,000 pages of photocopied documents, relating to the Gulf and Arabia in this period, which have been collected from the state archives in Bombay. These copies are all taken from the records of the East India Company's Government of Bombay, which was responsible for British interests in the Gulf; they comprise, in the main, transcripts of letters sent and received by the Bombay Council, the most useful of which proved to be despatches sent in by political and Marine or naval officers stationed in or posted to the Gulf. The East India Company's records are the only detailed contemporary record of the events of this period. The documents at Exeter were selected so as to comprise all those known to cover Gulf piracy and related affairs, and in this respect they are probably virtually complete: the bulk of this material could well be duplicated in the India Office Library in London. The extracts from the Bombay Archives held by Exeter University's Centre for Arab Gulf Studies had originally been secured from Bombay by Shaikh Sultan Muhammad al-Qasimi of Sharja, who was later generous enough to deposit duplicates with the Centre after he had concluded his own researches. Access to this unique archive sparked the genesis of the present work.

I have supplemented the Bombay Archive material with more of a similar nature held in the India Office Library, most obviously the Bushire Residency files. I have used two interesting manuscript sources, the diaries of Captain Loch RN, in the Scottish Record Office, and notes by Captain Brucks of the Bombay Marine, in the British Library. A number of published books, especially works of travel, have been useful. Source material in Arabic on this subject is rare, that in Persian rarer still: in the former category, the most important works are those of Ibn Ruzaiq and Ibn Bishr and the anonymous *Lam' al-Shihab*. I regret much that I have not in the end found the opportunity to consult the relevant T.P. Thompson Papers at Hull University, which, though they date from 1820 and after, might well contain some useful complementary material. I am unaware of any other significant primary source which I have not consulted.

The system of Arabic transliteration employed in this book is highly simplified and, it is hoped, consistent. Diacritical marks are omitted, whilst the *hamza* is represented by ' and the *'ain* by ', unless either of these letters occurs before an initial capital, in which case it is omitted entirely; the *ta' marbuta* appears where it would generally be pronounced. Certain proper names which have familiar English spellings are left in that form. Transliteration of Persian words follows the same system as the Arabic, the Persian *idafa* being indicated by -i/yi.

It is important to note that, except for a few of the quotations from published works, the spelling of Arabic names and titles has been standardized wherever they occur. I have taken this step in order to make the work intelligible and useful to the reader; not to have done so would at times have been tiresome or mystifying, and even occasionally misleading. The British records, the major documentary source for this work, are inconsistent in this respect, with orthography and even legibility presenting difficulties, the more so since most of this material consists of Writers' copies of the original despatches. Where there is significant ambiguity, I have indicated this in a note. For many of the same reasons, I have throughout also standardized the spelling of the names of classes of Arab vessel: it should, however, be recognized that these names were by no means always used with precision, and at times they were merely generics. The nature of the Bombay documents, and a desire for simplicity, have in addition recommended the modernization of capitalization, and rarely spelling, the supplementing of punctuation where required, the elimination of blatant orthographical lapses, and the standardization of Indian place-names and terms in common Anglo-Indian usage, whilst ever remaining faithful to the sense and wording of the original manuscript.

I should like to thank Brian Pridham, former Director of Exeter University's Centre for Arab Gulf Studies, where for some years I was employed as a Research Fellow, for his vital initial encouragement and for his continuous support during the research and writing of this book: it is further most rare today to be enabled to pursue a long project such as this unimpeded in the way that I was. The resources of the Centre, and in particular the Documentation Unit, under the able management of Ruth

Butler, Parvine Foroughi and others, have made this work possible. I am grateful to Terry Bacon who produced the maps, and to Paul Auchterlonie who kindly offered to read the manuscript; also to Dr Rasheed el-Enany, Dr Adrian Gully and Dr Roger Webster. I am indebted to my publishers, the University of Exeter Press, for all that they have done. My thanks, too, to the staff of the Arabic Department for making me welcome during my time at Exeter.

I hope that this book will be adjudged by some a reasonable use of the opportunities presented to me. It has many faults: these are all mine. I leave it now in the hands of my critics, taking refuge in Time.

Charles E. Davies
Exeter, July 1996

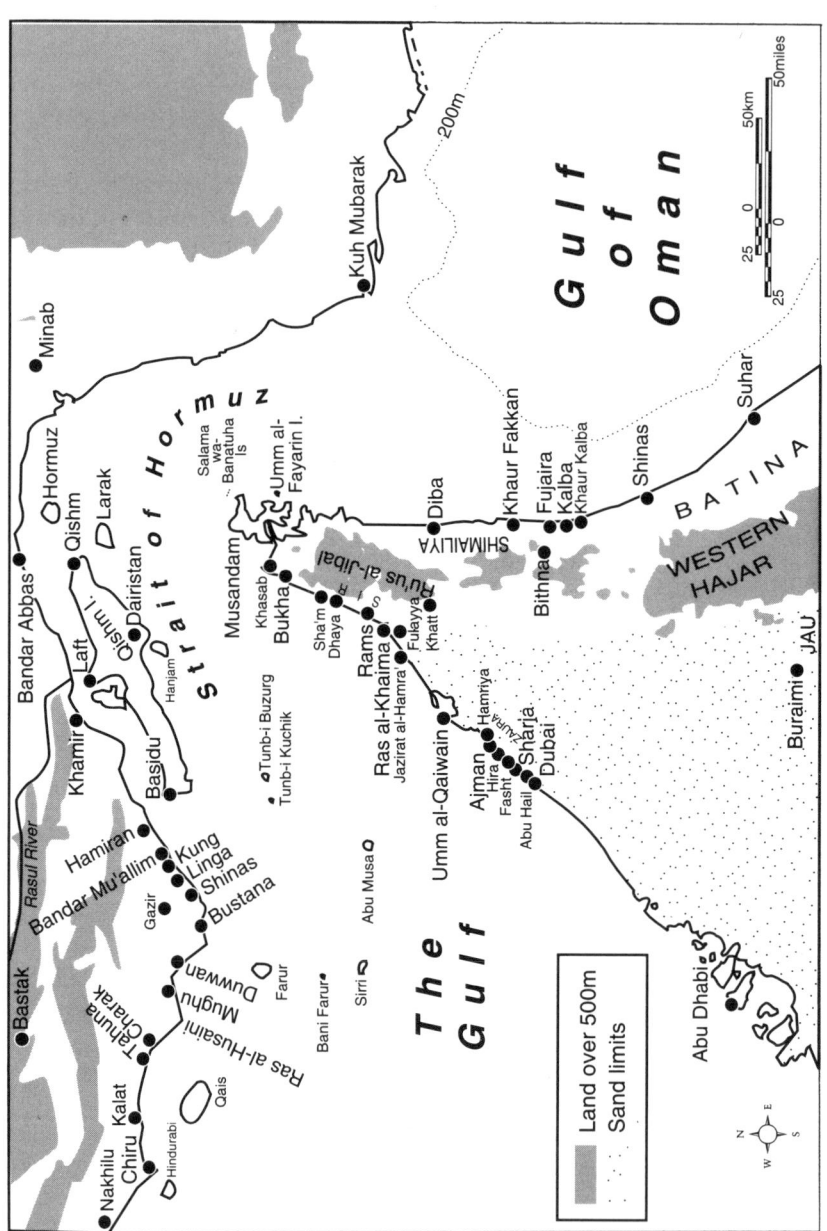

Map 1. The Arabian Peninsula and the Region.

A BRIEF CHRONOLOGY OF EVENTS

1797   *Bassein* and *Viper* incidents.

1798   Napoleon invades Egypt; British treaty with Muscat.

1800   Wahhabi penetration of south-east Arabia.

1801   Muscat's protégés, the Sudan, retire from Hormuz (c. Oct.).

1803   Sultan bin Saqr succeeds Saqr bin Rashid as ruler of Ras al-Khaima and Sharja.

1804   Sultan bin Ahmad, powerful ruler of Muscat, who had subjected Ras al-Khaima to considerable pressure, is killed (Nov.); succeeded by Badr bin Saif, inclined to the Wahhabis.

   Capture of *Trimmer* and *Shannon*; Charak and dependency of Qais sacked by Qawasim (Dec.).

1806   Suri fleet puts in at Ras al-Khaima (Jan.)

   Anglo–Qasimi agreement (Feb.).

   Young Sa'id bin Sultan assassinates and succeeds Badr at Muscat (July).

   Ras al-Khaima assumes control of Laft, on Qishm, as Muscat arrests Mulla Hasan (Nov.–Dec.).

1808   Qasimi rout of Muscat forces at Khaur Fakkan (May).

   Capture of *Darya Daulat* (July).

   Attack on HC *Sylph* (Oct.).

   Increased Wahhabi influence at Ras al-Khaima; elevation of Hasan bin Ali of Rams (c. Nov. and ff.).

1809   Persian troops occupy Linga (c. Feb.).

   Persian fleet worsted by Qawasim (April).

   Capture of *Minerva* (May).

1809/10   First Anglo–Omani expedition against Ras al-Khaima (Nov.–Jan.).

   Sultan bin Saqr detained by Wahhabis (Nov.–Jan.); leadership of Ras al-Khaima passes to his cousin Hasan bin Rahma.

1810   Britain captures Mauritius from French (Dec.).

1811   Combined Omani–Persian force defeated by Wahhabis in central Oman (c. Feb.); Wahhabi offensive there continuing since previous year.

1813	Egyptian forces take Mecca (Jan.).
	Sultan bin Saqr returns from exile and gains control of Sharja (c. Aug.); Wahhabi Ras al-Khaima remains under Hasan bin Rahma.
	Qawasim recommence activity off India (Nov.).
1814	Provisional Anglo–Qasimi agreement (Oct.).
1815	Notable encounters between Qasimi and Muscat shipping (April–May).
	Sa'id bin Sultan of Muscat's fourth expedition against Ras al-Khaima since 1811 (c. Sept.–Dec.); henceforward he turns his attentions to Bahrain.
1816	Three Surat vessels plundered at Bab al-Mandab (March).
	Rahma bin Jabir deserts Arabia and the Wahhabi cause (Oct.).
	British demonstration at Ras al-Khaima (Nov./Dec.).
1817	Capture of HCC *Darya Daulat* off Kathiawar (Jan.).
	Mughu, allied to Ras al-Khaima, burnt by Persian troops (c. Dec.).
1818	Egyptian conquest of Saudi capital Dir'iya (Sept.).
	Capture of HC military transport in or near Gulf of Cutch (Nov.).
	Captain Loch arrives in Gulf (Dec.).
1819/20	Second Anglo–Omani expedition against Ras al-Khaima (Nov.–Feb.).
1820	General Treaty between Britain and Arab rulers of Trucial States and Bahrain (Jan.–March).
	British garrison evacuates Ras al-Khaima (July).

DRAMATIS PERSONAE

Abdullah bin Ahmad	Al Khalifa (q.v.), (joint) Shaikh of Bahrain.
Abdullah bin Su'ud	Saudi ruler 1814–18.
Ahl (/Al) Ali	The Ahl (/Al) Ali were the principal tribe of Umm al-Qaiwain; the Al Ali were the principal tribe of Charak.
Al Bu Sa'id	Ruling family of Muscat and Oman.
Al Haram	Principal tribe of Asalu.
Al Khalifa	Ruling family of Bahrain.
Al Madhkur	Hereditary Shaikh–Governors of Bushire.
Al Sabah	Ruling family of Kuwait.
Al Su'ud	Ruling family in eponymous Saudi state.
Azzan bin Qais	Governor of Suhar 1808–15, son of Qais bin Ahmad (q.v.).
Badr bin Saif	Ruler of Muscat 1804–6.
Baluchis	People (Iranian) of Baluchistan.
Banu Bu Ali	Omani tribe of Ashkhira.
Banu Mu'in	(adj. Mu'ini) Ruling Arab tribe of Qishm Island.
Banu Yas	Principal tribe of Abu Dhabi, Dubai and pastoral hinterland.
Bruce, William	Official of British Residency at Bushire since turn of the century, Acting Resident at times in first decade, Resident for most of second decade, dismissed in 1822.
Elwood, C.W.	Company's Agent at Porbandar in second decade of century.
Ghafiri	One of the two divisions of the Omani tribes.
Hasan bin Ali	Shaikh of Rams and Dhaya, probably of the Tanaij tribe (q.v.); loyal Wahhabi, standing enhanced by Saudi ruler in 1808, became responsible for forwarding tribute to Dir'iya.
Hasan bin Rahma	Qasimi ruler of Ras al-Khaima 1810?–19, cousin of Sultan bin Saqr (q.v.).
Hinawi	One of the two divisions of the Omani tribes.

Huwala	Arab tribe or confederacy of lower Gulf, especially applied to southern half of Iran's Gulf coastline.
Ibrahim bin Rahma	Brother of Hasan bin Rahma (q.v.), under whom leading figure at Ras al-Khaima, sea-commander.
Ibrahim Pasha	Commander-in-Chief of Egyptian forces in Arabia (1816–19).
Jalahima	Branch of Utub (q.v.), frequently based at ports in Qatar and eastern Arabia.
Janaba	Omani tribe of Sur.
Ka'b	Tribe inhabiting eastern side of Shatt al-Arab.
Loch, Francis	Senior Royal Naval Officer in Gulf, Dec. 1818–19.
Malcolm, John	Promoted to Brigadier-General and accorded general control over Britain's affairs in Gulf 1808–9; led three missions to Persia 1800–10; (subsequently Governor of Bombay 1827).
Manesty, Samuel	British Resident at Basra 1784–1810.
Marzuq	(pl. Maraziq) Principal tribe of Mughu; (in early eighteenth century had ruled Linga).
Mir Muhanna	Ruler of Bandar Rig 1754/6–69.
Muhammad bin Abd al-Wahhab	Founder (1703/4–92) of Wahhabi religious sect synonymous with first Saudi state.
Muhammad bin Qadib	Qasimi ruler of Linga in second decade of century.
Mulla Hasan	Shaikh of Qishm, of the Banu Mu'in (q.v.), removed from office 1809/10.
Mutlaq al-Mutairi	Wahhabi military Commander-in-Chief in Oman (d. 1813).
Na'im	(adj. Nu'aimi) Principal tribe of Ajman; (also present in north-central Oman).
Nepean, Evan	Governor of Bombay 1812–19.
Qais bin Ahmad	Governor of Suhar (d. 1808), brother of Sultan bin Ahmad (q.v.).
Qawasim	(adj. Qasimi) Ruling family of Ras al-Khaima, Sharja and Linga; term applied descriptively to population of ports under their sway.
Rahma bin Jabir	Self-willed Shaikh of the Jalahima (q.v.), Wahhabi, renowned as a pirate, thorn in the side of the Al Khalifa (q.v.).
Salih bin Muhammad	Maverick Qasimi shaikh and sea-commander, responsible for *Viper* incident et al.
Saqr bin Rashid	Qasimi ruler of Ras al-Khaima and Sharja c. 1777–1803.
Sa'id bin Sultan	(Sayyid Sa'id) Ruler of Muscat 1806–56.

Seton, David — Intermittently Resident at Muscat in first decade of century until death in 1809.

Shihuh — Inhabitants of Musandam, linguistically and otherwise distinct from their neighbours.

Sudan — (adj. Suwaidi) Mobile tribal group which migrated from Ras al-Khaima to Hormuz to Qatar at turn of century; present in Sharja and Ras al-Khaima in second decade of century.

Sultan bin Ahmad — (Sayyid Sultan) Ruler of Muscat 1792/3–1804.

Sultan bin Saqr — Qasimi ruler of Ras al-Khaima and Sharja 1803–9; ruler of Sharja 1813–19; ruler of both ports 1820–66; son of Saqr bin Rashid (q.v.).

Su'ud bin Abd al-Aziz — Saudi ruler 1803–14.

Tanaij — Principal tribe of Rams.

Taylor, Robert — Bushire Residency official, Assistant there during second decade of century, posted to Basra 1818/19.

Thompson, T.P. — Commander of British garrison, and Political Agent, at Ras al-Khaima 1820.

Utub — (adj. Utbi) Tribe or confederacy of northern Gulf, whose most important branches were the (Al) Jalahima, the Al Khalifa and the Al Sabah (q.v.).

Warden, Francis — Chief Secretary to Government, Bombay, during first and second decades of century; temporary Member of Council 1819.

Za'ab — Principal tribe of Jazirat al-Hamra'.

Part One
Introductory

PROLOGUE

'Basra

29 December 1804.

Sir,

It is with regret I address you on this occasion stating the melancholy circumstance that occurred on board the brig *Shannon* under my command in the Persian Gulf on the 1st instant.

At about half an hour after noon on the aforementioned day, when the island of Farur bore south, with the wind at east south east, having all sails set, we descry'd a square-rigged vessel bearing west north west and shortly after several dows around her; the vessel appearing much like the brig *Trimmer*, Captain Cumming, made me conclude it was her and that she had been captured by the pirate dows about her. Every person on board also concurring in opinion that such a circumstance had been effected, made me resolve (being off the west extreme of Farur) to alter my course from west-by-north to south-west with the intention of avoiding them.

At a quarter of an hour before 2 o'clock I perceived that fifteen dows, and other country boats, were in chase of us, and every preparation was made to defend ourselves should they attack us. The chase was continued till between 2 and 3 o'clock, when they were within musquet-shot distance—I hoisted my ensign and hail'd in Arabic, to which they did not make any reply but continued to approach nearer. I hail'd a second time, desiring them to come no nearer, when they immediately fired a musquetoon shot on board us and which determined me to repel the attack they were about making. I consequently ordered a broadside of four guns to be discharged at them, which was repeated with the small arms. We had eight of the dows being there but a short distance off, one of which was obliged to haul her wind from us for a short time. However, soon after being 3 o'clock, the whole of them bore down and boarded us sword-in-hand, taking possession of the vessel and treating myself and crew most severely.

I am sorry to inform you that on the occasion we had one man killed and four badly wounded, besides myself being most cruelly treated, they having cut off my left hand by the wrist and wounded me in nine other places about the head and body, plundered us of everything we possessed to the very covering we had on at the time, leaving us naked and destitute of anything to eat or drink. In this inhuman manner did they oblige me to remain on the deck, unable to stir from the loss of blood I had sustained, and really should have perished was it not for a little wine and biscuit that I saved (for eight days).

The cargo that we had in was all plundered and taken away, also several stores belonging to the vessel, her guns, light sails, one anchor, one grap-nail, a new ... aft mainsail, one lower and three topgallant steering-sails, and otherwise damaged her much. The packet that I received at Bombay was also taken by them and all the letters torn, a few of which I have been able to save.

On the 11th, about 3 a.m., a boat was sent on board to tell us we were at liberty to proceed to where we chose, at the same time giving us one bag of dates only for our subsistence, a compass, part of our old ensign and two guns with their carriages. They also sent us all the Christians that were taken in the *Trimmer*, with three washermen for Mr Donald at Basra, and in this unprovided state we set sail ... with a light breeze from the north-east up the Gulf for Bushire.'[1]

Captain R. Babcock

CHAPTER ONE

Outline

Interleaved in one of the great, dusty volumes stored behind the eloquent neo-Gothic façade of Bombay's Elphinstone College Building—where the copious records of the English East India Company's, later the Imperial, Government of Bombay (7,000 stout volumes of fine longhand before 1820, a further 200,000 files by 1920) lie shelved on Victorian iron frames erected 'upon the German model' at a cost of some 80,000 rupees a century or so ago[1]—there lies a map. Or, to be more precise, Sayyid Taqi's sketch-map.[2] Although consisting of little more than two jagged lines which snake across the page to meet at right angles, the whole devoid of any bearings or compass directions, and festooned at various points and angles with notes hastily written in Persian, it is apparent that the drawing represents a coastline. But it is a stylized coastline, which appears somehow divorced from its mainland, its ports almost like islands. Beyond simple instruction, the most obvious practical use to which such a map might be put, one concludes, would be to serve as guide to a mariner willing to find his way from port to port by 'touch and smell', as it were, according to the age-old, experiential, but necessarily somewhat imperfect method of simply following up the coastline. This, in a sense, is what it is.

On 14 September 1809 an unusual scene greeted the observer who chose to look out from the Apollo Gate across Bombay's fine harbour. Beyond the strollers on the vivid green esplanade, and on past the huts and the pier, the combined vessels of the 'British Armament', a small fleet under convoy of HMS *La Chiffone*, 36 guns, their men and supplies finally aboard, had at last weighed anchor and could now be seen sailing off slowly westward, eventually to disappear over the wide, low horizon.[3]

There can have been few in the city unaware that what they were witnessing was the departure of a British expeditionary force en route to the Persian Gulf. Soon to number some 16 vessels and 1361 fighting-men,[4] it had in fact been despatched against the Qasimi confederacy,[5] an Arab naval power in the lower reaches of the Persian Gulf. The expedition had been organized by the East India Company's Government of Bombay,

5

whose Bombay Marine, forerunner of the Indian Navy, supplied the bulk of the vessels. But it was a new experience: nothing quite of this kind and scale, and at this distance, had as yet been attempted.

The force set out under the joint command of Captain John Wainwright RN and Lieutenant-Colonel Lionel Smith (of His Majesty's 65th Regiment of Foot), both of whom were new to the region and its complexities. Their instructions,[6] though not perhaps in all respects quite the model of precision, were, in their main thrust, patently straightforward: they were to proceed forthwith against the town of Ras al-Khaima and other sea ports clustered around the mouth of the Persian Gulf, such as were then controlled by the Qawasim and their allies, and lie today in the United Arab Emirates and south-east Iran, burn their ships and naval stores and, just as swiftly, retire. The rationale for this proceeding, as briefly explained in the same document, was as follows: during the past decade or more, especially since 1797, it was said, the Qawasim had carried out numerous acts of piracy in and about the Persian Gulf on British, Turkish, Arab and other shipping. Furthermore, as recently as February 1806 they had apparently pledged their word to respect the British flag—but they had subsequently broken it. Force of arms, it seemed, promised better results.

Strange as it may seem, in view of the fact that by now the British had amassed just short of two full centuries of experience in navigating the Persian Gulf, trading regularly for the most part between their settlements in India and their permanent commercial stations in the Gulf, neither the commanders of the 1809 expedition nor their masters had much beyond a rudimentary knowledge of the places they were now expected to visit. The configuration of the coastline, its navigation and even the sheer number of Qasimi-controlled ports were very inadequately known. The author of an official account of the expedition was later somewhat ruefully to recall that in respect of Qishm—the largest island in the Gulf, and hard by Bandar Abbas where for some 140 years until 1763 Britain had maintained a presence—they had not even known on what side of the island the important Qasimi fort of Laft was situated.[7]

The fact was that in general, apart from the major arteries of trade that ran up the Gulf from Muscat to Basra, much of the Gulf, and almost the whole southern, Arab, coastline, had seldom if ever been visited by European ships, still less surveyed.[8] Such vessels still entertained very justifiable fears of encountering misplaced or uncharted rocks, reefs and even islands, as the sorry fate of the injudiciously named Calcutta ship *Durable*, which foundered on a shoal en route to Bahrain in 1817, well demonstrated. In like vein, in the previous year it is recorded that whilst in the Gulf Captain Maude of HMS *Favorite* 'casually heard it mentioned that there were some unknown islands to the southward; he went in that direction and added to our knowledge no less than eight islands ... [they] were designated Maude's Islands'.[9]

It was, indeed, not solely a matter of cultural perception that one of the very few works on the navigation of the Gulf which very possibly accompanied the fleet in 1809 was a Mr Vincent's exegesis of the classical authors:[10] a later surveyor was to observe that until the Gulf visit in 1764 of the assiduous German traveller Carsten Niebuhr, Alexander's Admiral Nearchus had remained unquestionably its best guide.[11] For these reasons, when in September 1809 the British flotilla left Bombay, almost the only directly relevant maps the two commanders had to rely upon—and this was felt to be the best information then obtainable in the city—were some sketches, with brief accompanying items of intelligence, which had been drawn up by Sayyid Taqi, 'a respectable Persian merchant resident in Bombay'[12] and, it appears, the occasional supplier to Government of confidential information.[13] The sketches in question, perhaps two in number and depicting the coastline about the mouth of the Gulf,[14] were in fact very much a preliminary version of the rather fuller map, with its useful intelligence of Qasimi shipping, that introduced this chapter. It is a curious fact, however, that this latter, Sayyid Taqi's final version, with its quaint depiction of the Musandam Peninsula as the corner of some great square and its complete omission of Qatar, was only produced in mid-December. It cannot, therefore, have arrived in the Gulf before early–mid-January, by which time the expedition's main business was quite done. In more respects than one the Ras al-Khaima expedition of 1809/10 proved something of a voyage, so to speak, into the barely known.

At this point it is necessary to leap forward almost exactly ten years. On what today forms the north-western coast of the United Arab Emirates, history, in the shape of a *second* British expedition against the Qawasim, seemed to be repeating itself.

By the evening of 20 December 1819 Major Warren of HM 65th Regt of Foot, veteran of the first such expedition against Ras al-Khaima a decade before, and quite possibly also of campaigns against the Marathas, the Pindaris and Mauritius,[15] had encircled Hasan bin Ali (Chief of Rams) with his 400 or so men in the fortress of Dhaya. With six smaller guns and two mortars already in place, it took until the morning of the 21st to send to HMS *Liverpool* for two great 24-pounders, which then had to be man-handled across three miles or more of swamp and rocky ground into their position beneath the walls.[16]

At this point, responding, as he put it, to the dictates of humanity, Major Warren despatched a courier to the young Shaikh offering safe conduct for the women and children. The messenger either did not return, or, in another version, did so, but with a message of defiance and resolve:

7

'We are enduring all this, taking our stand on nothing but our religion, and preferring the death of the faithful to the life of the reverse'.[17]

The two hours of precision bombardment which ensued was such, however, that when, at 10.30 a.m., Major Warren was on the point of ordering the final assault, he observed a white flag appear above the fort. Hasan bin Ali had surrendered. In this engagement, as before, two elements seem to have been particularly decisive. The first of these was expressed ten years earlier, at Ras al-Khaima, when it was stated of the defenders that although 'brave and skilful in single combat, they were unable to withstand the shock of adversaries acting in a body'.[18] The second was, of course, the superior British artillery.[19] Major Warren summed up his capture of Dhaya in the following epigram: 'The service was short but arduous. The enemy defended themselves with an obstinacy and ability worthy of a better cause.'[20]

The fall of Dhaya marked the end of hostilities during the second British expedition against Ras al-Khaima and associated states. In January and February 1820 the Shaikhs, first of (what was to become) the United Arab Emirates, then too of Bahrain, acceded to the terms of the General Treaty with Britain. By the time the main force was withdrawn all the fortifications between Rams and Abu Hail, excepting Ras al-Khaima, had been razed, whilst about 200 of the larger vessels from these ports had been seized and many of them burnt.[21] It was decided at first to maintain a small British garrison at Ras al-Khaima. But it soon proved potentially troublesome, of too little advantage and too precarious. By July, much of the garrison had been brought low by fever.[22] The decision was therefore taken to destroy what remained of the fortifications and boats, and the town itself, and retire to Qishm:

> Houses, walls and towers have all been levelled with the dust; and the scattered fragments of buildings lie in all directions, exhibiting a most perfect scene of destruction, and the ruins are left these people as a lesson of retributive justice, as a memorial of our expedition, and a lasting testimony against them for their misdeeds.[23]

The expedition of 1819/20 had been closely modelled on that of 1809/10. It too was organized by the Government of Bombay, enjoyed Omani assistance and was ostensibly a response to piracy by the Qawasim; only this time the force employed was roughly twice the size,[24] the military achievement was more convincing and the action more geographically limited: operations were now confined to the Arabian coast, just to the south-west of the Musandam Peninsula. Whereas the first expedition had commenced in November 1809 with a land attack on Ras al-Khaima, followed over the next month and a half by others on forts at Laft, in

Qishm, and Shinas, in Oman; the second involved hostilities only at Ras al-Khaima and nearby Dhaya, in December 1819. Both expeditions were also accompanied, and, in the case of the second, to some extent preceded, by the wider, uncontested, seizure and burning of the Qawasim's vessels.

Despite the similarities between the two expeditions, there was this important difference: that of 1819/20 yielded a distinct and lasting political legacy that was embodied in the General Treaty of 8 January 1820. Drawn up between Britain and the newly 'pacificated' or 'friendly' Arabs, that is the Qawasim with their neighbours and associates, the smaller independent Arab chiefs of the Gulf, it bound these latter to abstain from piracy. But it also made Britain co-guarantor of their adherence to its terms. Thus, henceforward, with her now unrivalled ascendancy in India, Britain was to have a permanent role in the region, that of policing the waters of the Gulf.

The function that was conferred on, or assumed by, Britain in the General Treaty was to be confirmed and further developed in a series of supplements and modifications that culminated in the Perpetual Treaty of 1853, which finally outlawed all maritime hostilities between the Arab states indefinitely. From this body of the Pax Britannica there later sprang the 'Exclusive' Treaties of the 1890s, which allowed the smaller Gulf states, such as the Trucial States (later the United Arab Emirates), to become the semi-protectorates they were for much of the twentieth century. Britain's direct role in the Gulf finally came to an end in 1970/1.

A century and a half of British dominance in the Gulf had therefore in a true sense been first generated, shaped and in Britain's view even necessitated by the events of the years 1797–1820 and the experiences associated with piracy by the Qawasim. And the British response to what came to be seen as the 'problem' of maritime security in the Gulf, a response which might earlier have been seen rather more, in part, as the limited action of self-interest or self-defence, tended in later years and other hands to be presented in a grander and less compromising fashion as an example of paternalistic altruism. The Viceroy Lord Curzon, great architect of high imperialism, marked this change in his address to the Trucial Chiefs of 21 November 1903. The first of the two following excerpts from that speech is redolent of the hyperbole of hindsight, whilst the second conveys sentiments, expressive of a new imperialist ethos, which would have been wholly and completely alien in the first decades of the nineteenth century to which he largely refers:

> Chiefs, your fathers and grandfathers before you have doubtless told you of the history of the past. You know that a hundred years ago there were constant trouble and fighting in the Gulf; almost every

man was a marauder or a pirate; kidnapping and slave-trading flourished; fighting and bloodshed went on without stint or respite; no ship could put out to sea without fear of attack; the pearl fishery was a scene of annual conflict; and security of trade or peace there was none. Then it was that the British Government intervened and said that, in the interests of its own subjects and traders, and of its legitimate influence in the seas that wash the Indian coasts, this state of affairs must not continue. British flotillas appeared in these waters. British forces occupied the ports and towns on the coast that we see from this deck. The struggle was severe while it lasted but it was not long sustained. In 1820 the first general Treaty was signed between the British Government and the Chiefs; and of these or similar agreements there have been in all no fewer than eight ...

Sometimes I think that the record of the past is in danger of being forgotten, and there are persons who ask—Why should Great Britain continue to exercise these powers? The history of your States and of your families, and the present condition of the Gulf, are the answer. We were here before any other Power, in modern times, had shown its face in these waters. We found strife and we have created order. It was our commerce as well as your security that was threatened and called for protection. At every port along these coasts the subjects of the King of England still reside and trade. The great Empire of India, which it is our duty to defend, lies almost at your gates. We saved you from extinction at the hands of your neighbours. We opened these seas to the ships of all nations, and enabled their flags to fly in peace. We have not seized or held your territory. We have not destroyed your independence but have preserved it. We are not now going to throw away this century of costly and triumphant enterprise; we shall not wipe out the most unselfish page in history. The peace of these waters must still be maintained; your independence will continue to be upheld; and the influence of the British Government must remain supreme.[25]

A second, converse, consequence of these developments is one symbolized in what was, until 1971, the official designation of the United Arab Emirates, namely the 'Trucial States'. They were, in one sense, an entity as defined by (British) treaty. It was almost as if the General Treaty had been a snapshot with some of the power to freeze movement. For it is a curious accident that one effect of the British protection progressively afforded the signatories after 1820, with her increasing responsibility for inter-state relations, was the partial crystallization of what was formerly a more fluid political system in the Gulf; the gain in stability was accompanied, in effect, by insulation from important, though particular, forces for change. Without the events of 1797–1820, and without Britain's specific response to piracy, it is not inconceivable, therefore, that the present-day status of the smaller Gulf states might have been radically different.

But there is a third, elusive and less concrete consequence of the saga of Ras al-Khaima and the British. This was its complex legacy of mutual perception, the legacy of the imagination. For many years after 1820 the British continued in their official documents to describe the Trucial States (the United Arab Emirates or UAE) as the 'Pirate Coast'. And the people of the Gulf, for their part, felt too the heavy weight of emotion generated by these early years: British action is still not wholly forgotten. The legacy of these years was more, therefore, than one simply of smouldering ruins. These were years of mutual discovery, of first experience and great trauma. And already by 1820 Sayyid Taqi's naïve and tentative sketch of the pirate ports, seeming relic of a former era, had been firmly consigned to its musty obscurity.

These, then, are some of the more important results that flowed from the events of the years 1797–1820. What follows, after two further intro-ductory chapters, is an attempt to understand the central issue in this period, namely the acts of piracy which are said to have been committed by the Qawasim.

CHAPTER TWO

The Setting

Not long ago in Kuwait a new film evoked some controversy. Entitled 'Bas, Ya Bahr!', or, somewhat less elegantly in English, 'Shut up, Sea!', it set out to depict the realities of what, from ancient times until the advent of the oil industry, had been the mainstay of life in the Gulf—that is, seafaring. What so offended some amongst the older generation who still remembered those times was the seeming iconoclasm of a film that chose to represent not the heroic, idealized picture of their past, but another, in more sombre hues, that lingered on the poverty, hardship and misfortune borne by the mass of seafarers.[1] Right up until the 1930s, in the case of Bahrain, and later still elsewhere, such as the United Arab Emirates (the UAE), the dominant socio-economic and cultural life of the Arabian shores of the Gulf remained in thrall to the sea. Had the film's older and sterner critics not sensed the degree to which their lives had, as it were, formerly been moulded by the rhythms of the sea, they would not have been stung by pride into considering it both an affront to the self-sacrifices of a swiftly forgotten past and an attack upon the very soul of Kuwait.

A very large proportion of the Gulf coastline, particularly to the south, is notoriously arid and forbidding, and scarcely seems of itself to invite habitation. Most characteristic, therefore, of areas such as the Trucial States (the UAE), where the scope for settled agriculture was severely limited, were, not unnaturally, the date palm and the camel.[2] Whilst the former can, in certain oases, send its roots down to the water-table, its cultivation, like that of the other few crops that could be and were produced, was often dependent on irrigation, such as that provided in certain districts by the ancient, elaborate and laboriously constructed underground water-channels or *aflaj*—commonly some miles in length, these were designed to tap the water table where it rose above the level of the cultivated land.

To some extent this harsh physical environment was perforce met by sheer resilience: at one extreme, for example, were the bedouin of Arabia's desert hinterland, who might survive for long periods on little more than camel's milk and dates. These conditions also induced adaptability and diversity: communities, individuals, in the Trucial States not uncommonly combined a variety of pursuits such as those of pastoralism, date cultivation, fishing or pearling. But despite this, the population remained under constraint from nature and disease: at the beginning of the twentieth century the settled inhabitants of the Trucial States, which together make up over a third of the Gulf's southern coast, were estimated at 72,000; in 1968, however, the first census only recorded an indigenous population of some 120,000 in total.[3]

But it was the sea to which the coastal communities owed their existence. Wrote Lt MacIvor in 1881,

> Fish, fresh or cured, with dates, onions and a small quantity of either barley or rice, constitutes the staple food of the majority of the poorer class of natives, Arabs and Persians, inhabiting the sea-board all round the Persian Gulf, the Oman, Batina and Makran coasts.[4]

Fish are so abundant in these waters that, as in Oman and the Trucial States, dried sardines have traditionally been used as cattle feed and even fertilizer. A variety of fishing techniques were employed, ranging from the simple harpoon for turtles, porpoises and the like, through nets of different kinds, to the fish traps of Bahrain,[5] constructed of palm fronds and laid out from the shore like huge funnels so as to catch the fish at ebb tide. Almost all of this was inshore fishing and so, although the industry was probably second in scale only to pearling, it did not entail the development of quite the maritime skills, and the elements of socio-economic co-operation, that deep-sea fishing might have required. It did, however, stimulate a bulky trade: the Trucial States might typically remedy a shortfall in their date production by supplying Basra from their surplus in fish; and, certainly by 1834–5, dried shark's fins from the Gulf were in some demand in China 'where they are used for making soup, and a variety of other purposes.'[6]

Of very much greater import, however, was an activity that since ancient times had dominated life in the region, a little like the oil industry of today. Lorimer's *Gazetteer* of 1908/14, that most remarkable of works on the geography and history of the Gulf, a compendium loyally and painstakingly compiled from the rich archives of the British Government of India, puts it thus:

> Pearl-fishing is the premier industry of the Persian Gulf; it is, besides being the occupation most peculiar to that region, the principal or only source of wealth among the residents of the Arabian side. Were the supply of pearls to fail, the trade of Kuwait would be severely crippled, while that of Bahrain might—it is estimated—be reduced to

Map 2. The Persian Gulf.

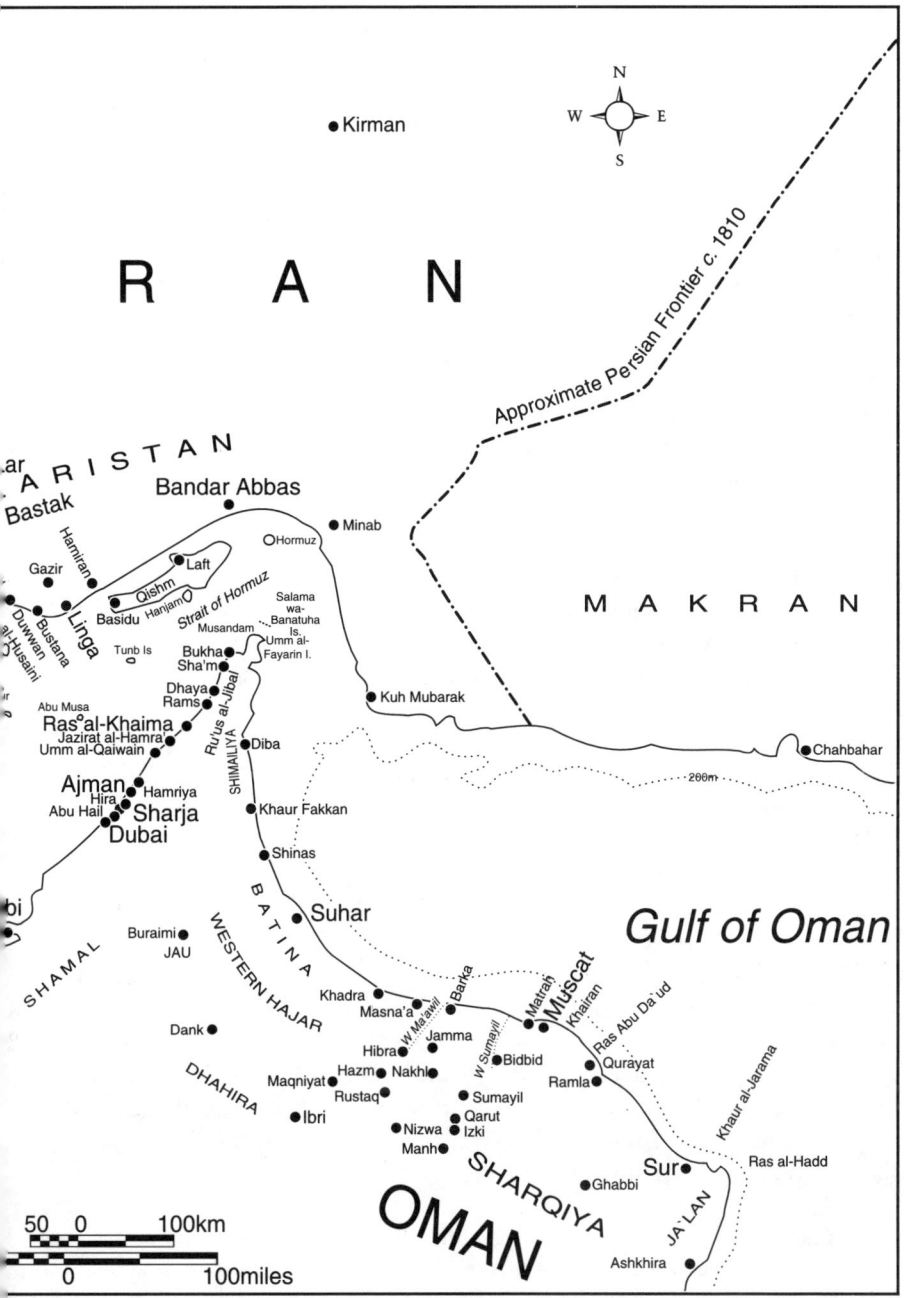

about one-fifth of its present dimensions and the ports of Trucial Oman [the UAE], which have no other resources, would practically cease to exist.[7]

Although, once again, the precise figures require severe caution, the same work later estimates the average annual export of pearls from the major Gulf ports (excluding Kuwait) in the years 1873/4–1904/5 as at least £561,353, rising to nearly £1.5 million in the year 1905/6; while the Trucial States and Bahrain were said in 1907 to be using 1,215 and 917 boats respectively in this business, together with a very high proportion of their menfolk.[8]

Not only does the Gulf provide an environment congenial to the growth of the pearl oyster, but it does so on numbers of flat beds and submarine knolls, situated especially off the Arabian shore from Kuwait in the north to near the Musandam Peninsula in the south, which lie at a depth of around 13 fathoms or less and can therefore be reached by the age-old technique of diving by means of rope and weight.[9] Archaeology has apparently uncovered pearling communities in Bahrain dating from the third millennium BC. The pearl has exerted a powerful allure: it may have inspired the Flower of Immortality which, in the Babylonian epic, the hero Gilgamesh successfully plucked from the seabed, only to lose it soon, as he slept, to the snake;[10] the pearl features in the paradise of the Koran; in classical Arabic poetry it forms the tears and teeth of the beloved; in modern times the fishermen of the Gulf held beliefs that ranged from the poetic, that the pearl was a drop of rain caught by the shell, to the anthropomorphic, claiming that the oyster had its monthly cycle.[11]

The actual procedures of diving had probably changed relatively little since early times. Although in a few locations oysters could be collected by wading, as in western Abu Dhabi, or in single-manned skiffs, off the Persian coast, the basic unit for the exploitation of the banks throughout the Gulf was the pearling-boat with its average complement at the beginning of the twentieth century of around 16 divers, pullers and others. The crew were answerable to the captain, or *nakhuda*, who might or might not be the owner of the vessel and who would navigate 'not only by the sun and stars and by bearings from the land when in sight, but also by the colour and depth of the sea and by the nature of the bottom.'[12] A naval officer witnessed the diving off Bahrain in 1834–5:

When about to proceed to business they divide themselves into two parties, one of which remains in the boat to haul up the others who are engaged in diving. The latter having provided themselves with a small basket, jump overboard, and place their feet on a stone, to which a line is attached. Upon a given signal this is let go, and they sink with it to the bottom. When the oysters are thickly clustered, eight or ten may be procured at each descent; the line is then jerked, and the person stationed in the boat hauls the diver up with as much rapidity as possible. The period during which they can remain under water has been much overrated; one minute is the average, and I never knew them, but on one occasion, to exceed a minute and a half.

Accidents do not very frequently occur from sharks, but the saw-fish ... is much dreaded. Instances were related to me where the divers had been completely cut in two by these monsters.[13]

The depths involved were, it seems, generally not great enough to induce the bends, but the monotony of the diet was not the only thing injurious to health:

It has been my observation that pearl-divers are prone to disease of the respiratory system, that may be caused by over-distension of the lungs and pressure, such as haemorrhage and pulmonary emphysema, also to deafness from perforation of the ear-drum, and to various forms of aural catarrh ... there is [also] a peculiar skin disease.[14]

The main diving season occurred during the warmth and relative calm of high summer, lasting a little over four months in all (c. June–September). Typically, therefore, a very high proportion of the menfolk in many of the coastal settlements would be away for all this period, leaving for others the tending and harvesting of the date crop.

The importance of the pearl trade lies in the fact that it gave a number of the Arab tribes settled particularly on the southern shores of the Gulf not only a livelihood, but also the capital with which to engage in large-scale trade and shipping ventures. Within the Gulf the heart of the pearl trade was Bahrain, whence pearls were eventually carried in the main to India, but also to Ottoman Iraq and Iran: the balance of the island's considerable imports was, it seems, very largely offset by remittances in pearls.[15]

This now brings us to the third branch of Gulf maritime enterprise, and that most germane to the present study, namely its seaborne trade. This commerce, near the start of the nineteenth century, may be classified on three levels: first, the small traffic that plied between the many seaboard communities, carrying local goods from one to another, articles such as dates, fish and grain, or small arms, mats and medicinal herbs; next, the medium freight and secondary distribution lines that fanned out from the handful of major international ports such as Muscat to link up with the great bulk of smaller littoral settlements; and finally, the large inter-continental carrying trade itself which ran in broad strokes between Iran,

Iraq and eastern Arabia, on the one hand, and India, the Red Sea, Africa and, though indirectly, Europe and south-east Asia on the other.[16]

The major international trade route in the Gulf between 1790 and 1820 was one that ran quite simply and directly from Muscat, the great entrepôt port at the mouth of the Gulf where very many vessels chose to load and offload their cargoes, up to Bushire (in Iran) and on a little further to Basra (in Ottoman Iraq). Certain international vessels also at times called directly at other ports, most notably, perhaps, at Bahrain, through which a good deal of the trade of eastern Arabia came to be channelled. Bushire and Basra, however, were the principal gateways of the region's most substantial economies, namely Iran and Iraq, and they therefore tended to constitute much the most powerful single determinants and barometers of Gulf trade. Imports at the Gulf ports included Indian cottons, rice and spices, Red Sea coffee, European goods and slaves from Africa. The *East India Trader's Complete Guide* of 1825 lists among the Gulf's more attractive exports items such as pearls together with Persian almonds, rose water, Shiraz wine, jujubes, lapis lazuli, arsenic, brimstone, opoponax, galbanum gum and the bezoar stone.[17] Rather more 'prosaic' items were of course exported in quantity, especially to India: horses, amongst other things, were taken from Iraq, and Muscat produced salt fish, said in the 1830s to be 'much esteemed by the lower classes of natives in India', as well as dates, large quantities of which were then required 'to make the government arrack'.[18] Nevertheless, the reports are unanimous in stating that the great bulk of returns for imports into the Gulf were made in specie, bullion and pearls. An estimate, though it was no more than that, of the Gulf's total foreign trade in 1800 reckoned it at 16 million rupees, or roughly £1.6 million.[19]

The burning summer months, when so many seafarers were exclusively engaged in pearling, also naturally coincided with the south-west monsoon in the Indian Ocean: many of the ports of western India were then effectively closed to trade on account of the rough weather and high seas. The Gulf's long-distance trading season with India, the Red Sea and Africa would therefore habitually commence in autumn and last through till the spring, taking advantage of the more favourable wind and weather patterns of the northerly monsoon (September–April). At the height of this season, a typical passage from Basra to Bombay took 26–8 days, and from Muscat, 10–12: this latter time could be reduced to 7–8 days during summer.[20]

Some Arab merchants, like the ruler of Muscat, had already begun to acquire some sailing ships of a European design, fashioned in India. But the vast majority of the Gulf's own trading vessels were still of traditional build: shaped, in the opinion of one observer, like a sharpened pear sliced in two,[21] a late commentator (c. 1905) was to remark that, 'these vessels are remarkable for the beauty of their lines, and it is probable that many of our modern yachts can hardly show more graceful curvature ... They sail well and are weatherly craft.'[22] Another naval officer, in the 1830s, was rather less charitable of a *baghla* he encountered off Muscat, describing it as

> a huge misshapen vessel, of at least four hundred tons, with a long projecting prow, and an elevated and elaborately carved and ornamented stern, having but a single mast and single sail, the latter spread on a yard one hundred and fifty feet in length, and containing more canvas than the courses of the largest first-rates in His Majesty's navy.[23]

The baghla was the largest Arab trading vessel, one in whose form traces of European ancestry were readily detectable.[24] Another important craft, held to be swifter and more elegant than the baghla, was the slightly smaller, double-ended, *battil*: it was said to have been used in pearling and in war.[25]

Looks and finish apart, there seems little doubt that these were vessels well suited to the shallow inshore waters of the Gulf and the relatively favourable winds and seas they hoped to encounter:

> The lateen is a grand pulling sail, and the dhows sail handsomely in their own conditions. There is nothing clumsy about them, though their fish-oiled hulls smell abominably and their underwater bodies are preserved by a mixture of tallow and lime, rubbed on by hand and renewed quarterly.[26]

The term 'dhow' (or dow) is now, as here in this twentieth century account, employed simply as a generic term for traditional Arab vessels; but quite often in the period 1797–1820, it indicated a specific class of vessel to be distinguished from the baghla from its having 'a long gallery projecting from the stern.'[27] What follows is an official account from 1810 of the boats then reportedly being used by the Qasimi pirates:

> The dows are vessels of peculiar form, ... so large as to be capable of carrying from three to five hundred men, ... with as high as from five to ten guns, ... yet so slightly built, and in consequence so buoyant, that a vessel in tonnage equal to a ship of war of twenty guns will not draw more than ten feet [of] water ... They take the ground well and sail rapidly, but being worked with only one immense sail cannot tack.[28]

The exploitation of the economic potential and physical resources of the Persian Gulf was naturally intimately connected with the forms of social organization prevalent on its coasts. This is best seen in relation to pearling; indeed, it is important for a proper understanding of Gulf history during the eighteenth and nineteenth centuries to recognize that a close symbiosis subsisted between this industry and the Arab tribal system which dominated the southern shores of the Gulf. In some areas, like Abu Dhabi, tribal groups fished rather in the manner of co-operatives. But very often elsewhere, as in Bahrain and the Trucial States, the later sources indicate that the divers themselves were of divers origin—slaves, manumitted Africans, poor Arabs, Persians and Baluchis: and in these cases the Arab tribesmen would typically operate as entrepreneur merchants and sea-captains. Individual tribes also tended to frequent certain pearl-banks: this was not ownership in the modern sense, but it did involve notions of territory. Usage, not Islamic law, governed the industry, and the practice over debt corresponded with tribal law. At the pinnacle of the system, the tribal rulers of Bahrain and other Gulf states during the nineteenth century helped to regulate and protect the boats of their subjects and derived a revenue from them: they even had 'first refusal' on the finest pearls that were found. Furthermore, the last option for an indebted pearl diver under pressure from his creditors or his sea-captain, a not uncommon occurrence, was to 'abscond' and take refuge with another shaikh along the coast, who would then customarily protect him and let him remain. It is not to be wondered at that disputes arising from pearling, disputes between tribes, frequently became violent before the imposition of the Pax Britannica during the nineteenth century.[29]

The pearling industry, then, was closely enmeshed with the tribal system of the Gulf's Arabian coastline. We can extend this link between society and the economy still further. The eighteenth century history of the Utub tribe or confederacy,[30] founders of modern Kuwait and Bahrain, is perhaps the most attractive demonstration of the manner in which the sea might exercise her allure over certain Arab tribal groups and allow them to exploit her potential, flourish and, if the circumstances were right, eventually to develop the maritime city-states so characteristic of the area.

The ancestors of the Utub were a group of families originally said to have inhabited the regions of northern central Arabia: it may have been drought during the late seventeenth and early eighteenth centuries that first induced them to seek a new life on the coastline of eastern Arabia. Their name conceivably derives from a root meaning 'to travel from place to place'. Much of this early history is rather hazy. Local tradition and the later accounts have it that during the first half of the eighteenth century a number of families, known collectively as the Utub, were gradually filtering northwards through Qatar and the upper reaches of the Gulf, acquiring maritime skills along the way and responding at once to political pressure and economic opportunity. Finally, under the patronage of the Banu Khalid, lords of eastern Arabia, they began to congregate in Kuwait: early in the eighteenth century it had probably been little more than a fishing village, but the site offered great commercial potential because it could supply the trade routes north into Iraq and west to Syria. The town soon began to prosper and during the 1750s one branch of the Utub, the Al Sabah, achieved pre-eminence and political primacy there, as well as a high degree of practical independence from their erstwhile overlords, the Banu Khalid. And just as the settlement grew, so too did its requirement for some form of government more elaborate and centralized than the lighter tribal consensus that had first allowed the Al Sabah to emerge as leaders: 'subjects' would need protection, municipal affairs regulating, all now upon a supra-tribal level.[31]

An almost certainly apocryphal, but telling, story relates that the three most prominent branches of the Utub had early on at Kuwait agreed to combine their efforts, but in such a way as to preserve their separate interests: the Al Sabah family was to practise the arts of government, the Al Khalifa the pursuit of commerce and the Al Jalahima the direction of shipping and matters maritime.[32] Behind the tidy *post hoc* symbolism lay this lesson: the system could not easily accommodate the ambitions of rival families. In the 1760s the Al Khalifa Shaikh chose to emigrate to the shores of Qatar whither he was drawn by the lure of the rich Bahrain pearl fisheries. Thereupon, in a later British version,

> By his talents and his treasures he soon acquired a considerable portion of the fishery, and by his prudent liberality to the neighbouring Arab chieftains, and to those of his former associates, he drew over the rest of his own tribe to the new colony, and at length ... established his independence at Zubara [in Qatar].[33]

As the settlement at Zubara throve, grew and developed, so too did the power of the Al Khalifa. Once again other prominent families, who had earlier joined the settlers, felt disappointed in the respect and favours they received. This was most notably true of the Al Jalahima:

> Urged by necessity, and a sense of wrong, the [Al] Jalahima quitted Zubara, and took up their residence at Ruwais, a barren spot at a short distance eastward of Zubara, and turned their whole attention to the increase, equipment, and preservation of their fleet, contemplating the object of revenging themselves on their proud and perfidious neighbours.[34]

A higher degree of unity, however, returned, albeit only temporarily, with the prospect of a new and glittering prize: the conquest of Bahrain island from the Persians. The military attack of the Utub, with their allies and clients, succeeded in overrunning the island in 1782 and it thereafter remained under Al Khalifa control. The old cycle of division and secession soon revived: the Al Jalahima were amongst the first to leave. In later years permanent or temporary emigration remained the final option for families, groups and individuals; but greater security and the advent of the Pax Britannica helped to sap the process of much of its eighteenth century vitality.

If the tribe seemed somehow well suited to the efficient exploitation of the Gulf's economic potential, this may in part have been on account of the flexibility it gained from being an organism that ultimately broke down into family units which could combine or act independently as circumstances required. Added to this was the special mobility and independence imparted by the ship as a mode of conveyance, together with the relative ease with which, in consequence of fishing, pearling and, finally, trade, new settlements could be planted and maintained on the shores of the Gulf. It was a fluid society. There are important parallels in all this with the situation in the desert and the Arabian interior, and the interaction there between bedouin society and the environment.

For the liberal minded in the eighteenth century there could be something strangely appealing in the tribal system of government, with its heavy overtones of almost biblical patriarchy and Rousseauesque simplicity. The system was observed at its purest amongst the bedouin:

> The most natural authority is that of a father over his family, as obedience is here founded upon the opinion of benevolence in the ruler ... The Bedouins, or pastoral Arabs, who live in tents, have many Shaikhs, each of whom governs his family with power almost absolute. All the Shaikhs, however, who belong to the same tribe, acknowledge a common chief ... whose authority is limited by custom. The dignity of Grand Shaikh is hereditary in a certain family; but the inferior Shaikhs, upon the death of a Grand Shaikh, choose the successor out of his family, without regard to age or lineal succession, or any other consideration, except superiority of abilities. This right of election, with their other privileges, obliges the Grand Shaikh to treat the inferior Shaikhs rather as associates than as subjects, sharing with them his sovereign authority. The spirit of liberty, with which this warlike nation are animated, renders them incapable of servitude.[35]

Scarce resources induce struggle; in the Gulf the sea dominated the lives of shaikh and fisherman alike. There is, perhaps, no more suggestive demonstration of the intimacy of this relationship between man and sea than a traditional ritual, with semi-magical undertones, which used to take place in Kuwait and Bahrain just prior to the long-awaited return of the pearling fleets in autumn. The women of the district would gather by the shore singing,

> Have mercy, have mercy oh Sea!
> It's already been over four months.
> Bring them [safely] back to us,
> As they hoist their jib-sails.
> Do you do not fear God, oh Sea?
> It's already been over four months.
> Have mercy, have mercy!
> Bring Sabah of the Utub . . .
> Oh Jewel!
> Give me Husain . . .
> Oh Protector!
> Give me al-Mana'i[36]

—and so on, invoking the sea under a variety of curious epithets to bring back relatives and notables. At length the women would turn from pleading to threats: one of them would 'burn' the sea with palm fronds and, listening to the mews of a kitten as they immersed it in the foam, they would imagine it the sea, replying to their imprecations 'Biyoon, biyoon', 'They are coming [home], they are coming [home].'

CHAPTER THREE

The Players

Perhaps the most surprising feature of Sayyid Taqi's map was the impression it conveyed of a Persian Gulf coastline strangely independent of its mainland, beside an equally intangible, but traversable sea. Habits of thought of this nature tend to become outmoded with 'progress', but it remains a concept perhaps more readily apprehensible to those who live in small islands and major ports. It recalls the practice of the medieval Arab geographers who were wont to describe Oman, the easternmost corner of Arabia, as an island on account of the broad swathes of desert, the Empty Quarter, which cut it off from the vast interior. And there is more to this than mere convention. In the late eighteenth and early nineteenth centuries the Persian Gulf littoral, though politically fragmented, was in reality, in a number of important ways, quite as much a single organism as any of the land-based state powers that bordered it, and of which a good deal of its coastline was nominally a part.

The strip of land that runs around, encircling, the Gulf, was dotted all along with towns and villages. Political dominance over these maritime fringes was, however, accorded one particular form of settlement, the maritime city-state, typically an Arab polis ruled by a tribal shaikh, one whose growth we have just recently been examining with the example of the Utub. It was normal for these city-states on the Arabian side to maintain a relationship with the bedouin tribes of the adjacent hinterland, and this was vital to ensure their survival,[1] but the focus of their economic and political ambitions generally lay to seaward or along the coast. At the start of the nineteenth century the Qawasim of Ras al-Khaima, for example, exerted a good deal of influence not only on the surrounding coastline, but also across the water on the opposite Persian littoral and islands. The Gulf littoral was therefore somewhat like a wheel, the ports along its rim interconnected by a maze of active sea-lanes.

And the links that bound the smaller seaboard states of the Gulf to each other were, of course, not merely economic and political but also, importantly, social and cultural. The lingua franca of the Gulf was Arabic, spoken in its distinctive Gulf accents, though Persian was naturally widely used on the northern coast. We have already seen the relative ease with which families and tribal groups were at this time able to migrate from one section of the coast to another. Exogamy in these coastal districts must indeed have been not uncommon over the long centuries. The Arab ruling families at Bandar Rig and Bushire, on the Iranian coast, both inter-married with Persians and adopted Shi'ism in the eighteenth century and so, it is said, were 'no longer counted among the Arabian nobility.'[2]

Consonant with what has been said of the Gulf as a whole, it should therefore come as no surprise that the Persian coastline was greatly more Arabicized in the years c. 1790–1820 than it is today. Iran's three most prominent ports were, like many others, still governed by Arabs who enjoyed a large measure of practical autonomy: Bushire was ruled by an Al Madhkur Shaikh, his family originally from Oman; Linga was under the sway of a Qasimi Shaikh (like Ras al-Khaima); and Bandar Abbas, after 1794, was farmed out from the Persian crown to the ruler of Oman. It was not, in fact, until 1850 that the ruling family at Bushire came to be replaced by a regular Persian governor, and some decades more until concerted efforts were made to assert the central authority at many of the other ports on the Persian littoral. Curzon, writing in 1892, was to observe that,[3]

> The change effected in the rulers of Bushire has been reflected in its population. Till the last twenty years the Arab element was largely in the ascendant, although, to a great extent, Persianised both in dress and religion. As trade, however, has increased, and purely maritime occupations have declined, the Persian ingredients have gained the upper hand, and now largely predominate, although the bulk of the people are still of Arab, or mixed Arab and Persian descent.[4]

Although the whole northern, Persian coast theoretically acknowledged the Persian crown and was liable to government taxes and customs dues, its numerous towns and villages were at this time still very much in the hands of their local ruling families, typically the tribal shaikh. The southern half of the Gulf's Iranian coastline, between Bandar Abbas and Cape Bardistan, was dominated in the later eighteenth and early nineteenth centuries by a group of ruling families generally described as belonging to the Huwala tribe, or confederacy: the Huwala also controlled the territory of the northern Trucial States on the opposite Arabian coast, their leading members being, of course, the Qawasim of Linga and Ras al-Khaima. As is possibly implicit in their name, the Huwala were popularly held to have been Arab tribesmen who had migrated from Arabia to the Iranian coast at some point in history, many of them later to return to the southern coast in the eighteenth century and thereafter. The following account is from the pen of Carsten Niebuhr, mathematician, assiduous observer and sole survivor of the King of Denmark's scientific expedition despatched to Arabia in 1760. It describes the Huwala states of the Iranian littoral in 1765:

> They live all nearly in the same manner, leading a seafaring life, and employing themselves in fishing, and in gathering pearls. They use little other food but fish and dates; and they feed also their cattle upon fish ...
>
> Almost every different town has its own Shaikh, who receives hardly any revenue from his subjects; but, if he has no private fortune, must, like his subjects, support himself by his industry, either in carrying goods, or in fishing. If the principal inhabitants happen to be dissatisfied with the reigning Shaikh, they depose him, and choose another out of the same family.
>
> Their arms are a match-firelock, a sabre, a buckler. All their fishing-boats serve occasionally as ships of war ... Their wars are mere skirmishes and inroads, never ending in any decisive action, but producing lasting quarrels, and a state of continual hostility.
>
> Their dwellings are so paltry, that an enemy would not take the pains to demolish them. And as, from this circumstance, these people have nothing to lose upon the continent, they always betake themselves to their boats at the approach of an enemy, and lie concealed in some isle in the Gulph till he have retreated. They are convinced that the Persians will never think of settling on a barren shore, where they would be infested by all the Arabs who frequent the adjacent seas.[5]

The semi-autonomy of Iran's southern littoral was a situation reinforced by its geography. A coastal plain less than 45 miles deep (often nearer 20) extends the length of the coast and is cut off from the interior of the country by mountain ranges, difficult of passage, and beyond these, in parts, by desert: the littoral tract itself is sometimes fertile and productive, sometimes barren earth and swamp. The only transport was by mule or other pack animal, the roads, such as they were, being wholly unsuitable for wheeled traffic. Transport by land was therefore slow and expensive, even along the major caravan routes, and there was frequently also the added danger of attack by robbers and refractory tribesmen. It is worth recalling that until relatively recently on the Arabian coast of the Trucial States even nearby settlements sometimes found it easier to communicate with each other by boat rather than by land.[6]

In another sense too the Persian Gulf was also something of a cultural melting-pot. Sailors were sometimes attracted thither from the Yemen, individual merchants from India lived in Muscat and other trading centres like Bahrain, whilst slaves were brought in large numbers from East

Africa,[7] often via Muscat; slave-girls received into Arab households seem not infrequently to have borne children for their Arab masters. It was observed of Muscat in 1816,

> From the preference which seems to be given here to handsome Abyssinian women over all others, there are scarcely any persons able to afford this luxury who are without an Abyssinian beauty, as a wife, a mistress, or a slave.[8]

Contact with Africa also delivered other fruit. There are probably quite pronounced indications of African influence in popular rituals such as the Zar healing ceremony, as well as in the characteristic rhythms of Gulf folk music. And once again it is quite consistent that the traditional *bandari* music of Iran's southern ports should, like their cuisine, belong so patently to this powerful Gulf tradition as opposed to that of the central Iranian plateau. Visiting Iran in the first decade of the nineteenth century, the Persophile Sir John Malcolm remarked that,

> The Persians, who have been tempted by the hope of gain to exchange the fine climate of the elevated plains of the interior for the sea-ports on the edge of the sultry desert which forms the shores of the Gulf, retain all the smooth, pliant manners of their country; and they look with disgust on what they deem the rude, barbarous habits of the Arabians, who are the great body of the inhabitants of this track, and who can scarcely be distinguished, either in look or sentiment, from their kindred on the opposite shore.[9]

It is apparent, then, that towards the end of the eighteenth century the Persian Gulf was predominantly, though by no means wholly, an Arab waterway, characterized by the maritime city-state with its constituent tribal sections. It was a situation productive of petty rivalries and shifting alliances. Another point also emerges from this: the Gulf littoral as a whole constituted an entity sufficiently distinct and cohesive of itself to merit special study and discussion; this is not simply uncalled-for academic surgery.

★　★　★

The Countries of the Region

It was only really very recently that technological development, modern communications, education and the like enabled regimes in the Gulf region to begin to effect the sort of social and political integration that has long been customary in many Western states; the first harbingers of these changes were perhaps the introduction of telegraphic and steam communications near the middle of the nineteenth century. Geography was not, therefore, the sole factor which determined the semi-autonomous status of the Gulf littoral at the turn of the nineteenth century. Hard on its heels followed the political condition of the major countries in the area: Iran, Ottoman (Turkish) Iraq, the early Saudi Arabia and Oman. The middle years of the eighteenth century were remarkable for the breakdown in authority and widespread upheaval that then occurred almost throughout the broader Gulf region. Out of this chaos were to emerge, towards the end of the eighteenth century, almost all the states, even the very regimes, that are found in the area to this day; the only true exceptions to this pattern are Qatar, a nineteenth century formation and, to some extent, Iraq, which is a special case since it then formed part of the Ottoman Empire. Nor should it be forgotten that the later eighteenth and early nineteenth centuries also witnessed the birth, or rebirth, of what was soon to become that most potent of all the regional powers: British India.

i Iran

Iran, the country with by far the longest Gulf seaboard, received few favours at the hands of the eighteenth century; indeed, it brought with it a degree of sustained violence, fragmentation and internal dissension, albeit alleviated by periods of relative peace, prosperity and even glory, that is quite unparalleled in Persian history over the last 500 years or more. The root cause of this turbulence was the dissolution of the Safavid dynasty which had ruled Iran since the late fifteenth century. This created a vacuum into which there now leapt a series of pretenders and generals at the head of tribal forces, none of whom, until the end of the eighteenth century, succeeded in establishing a dynasty with the inherent strength and direction to survive the demise of its vigorous founding member. The net effect of all this upon the ports and tribes of Iran's Gulf coast was inevitably to accord them a level of practical independence which they otherwise might not have enjoyed.

The once magnificent Safavid state had been in deep decline for over half a century when, in October 1722, it received the final, ignominious *coup de grâce* at the hands of some 20,000 Afghan tribesmen, their leader soon, it is said, a melancholy victim of tertiary syphilis,[10] who swept in and took the capital, Isfahan, after a harrowing six-month siege. Beside the artistic and intellectual achievement of their reign, the Safavid dynasty had bequeathed to Iran the religious and territorial make-up she still bears today. The physical shape of the country during the mid-eighteenth till the early nineteenth centuries was therefore roughly as it is now, though it then extended farther to the north and, as with the case of all the states in the Gulf region, her land borders were, to say the least, vague.

Out of the chaos that ensued in the 1720s there emerged the first of three strong individuals to dominate the Iranian scene during that century of strife: last of the great Asiatic conquerors, Nadir Shah the Afsharid, who seized Isfahan in 1729, the crown in 1736 and Delhi (with the Peacock Throne) in 1739, only to fall to an assassin's sword eight years later. During his lifetime Nadir became more deeply embroiled in the affairs of the lower Gulf than any subsequent Persian ruler. He conquered Oman and occupied Ras al-Khaima, though these proved of fleeting importance after his death. His great dream was to have made Iran the pre-eminent naval power in the region and to this end he caused heavy timber to be hauled at great human and financial cost from the Caspian to the southern port of Bushire. He fell back on Arab vessels belonging to the Gulf ports and on others acquired from India and the British. But the major weakness he encountered was the imperative of relying, for the manning of these ships, upon the Huwala Arabs of the lower Gulf, a people whom he could not adequately control. The British view of 1740 was that,

> Unless the Arabs are brought back to obedience, we believe it has entirely frustrated His Majesty's great scheme of a fleet, since these are the people who could only have been brought to accomplish his purpose, the Persians being entirely averse to, as well as ignorant of, sea affairs, which indeed the situation and nature of their country ... seems to disallow.[11]

With the speedy collapse of Nadir Shah's military regime following his demise, a somewhat more benign ruling family, the Zands, took its place. The leading personality of the new dynasty was the amorous and reputedly just Karim Khan-i Vakil,[12] who ruled Iran c. 1751–1779, during which time he eventually restored a measure of stability and sprightliness to the country and its economy, though he never succeeded in conquering the north. His capital, unusually, lay at Shiraz in southern Iran, near enough to the Gulf for him to show a keen concern for its politics and trade, although his emulation of Nadir Shah in this area had not that general's lustre or success. For much of his reign Karim Khan laboured to bring Iran's Gulf coast under tighter control. He eventually had some success in the northern reaches of the Gulf, with the Ka'b tribe of Dauraq and the Za'ab rulers of Bandar Rig, but the outcome was less felicitous in the lower Gulf around Bandar Abbas and Hormuz where local rulers remained strong and he tended to lose out to Oman: his threatened invasion of that country proved a damp squib. His most notable success lay therefore in the north, where the Persian occupation of Basra in 1776–9, though it proved calamitous for the city and was soon reversed, nevertheless fulfilled a longstanding ambition on the part of previous Persian rulers. At the same time, Karim Khan's relations with the British were by no means always cordial: he sought to keep them at arm's length, whilst yet desiring the help of their navy in order to bring to heel the maritime Arab city-states of Iran's Gulf littoral.

It took but 15 years following the decease of Karim Khan for the third and last of Iran's powerful eighteenth-century generals to take advantage of the disarray within the Zand family so as to extirpate both them and their rule: in the year 1794, Agha Muhammad Khan, the cruel and vindictive eunuch king and founder of the Qajar dynasty, eventually seized the last Zand stronghold of Kirman. All the adult men, it is alleged, were killed or blinded, numerous women and children enslaved, and a pyramid of some 20,000 pairs of eyeballs raised in his triumph. This act of extreme barbarism marked the end of a century of anarchy and the transition of Iran into a viable early modern state. The Qajar family was henceforth to rule a largely peaceable and steadily more unified Iran until just after the Great War.

The Qajars immediately removed the capital to Tehran in the north of the country. Regard for the affairs of the Gulf, even their own littoral, was scarcely one of their priorities. The structure of authority in the country was in theory pyramidal: at the pinnacle was the Shah in his court where he was subjected to pressures of various kinds from his entourage of ministers, courtiers, religious dignitaries, merchants and the harem. Beneath him were the provincial governors, district governors and so on, down to the locally elected village headmen and smaller tribal chiefs. The Shah who reigned for much of the period that concerns us here was Fath Ali Shah (1797–1834), remarkable, amongst other things, for his ample beard[13] and numerous offspring. One of these was Husain Ali Mirza who governed the southern province of Fars, which included most of Iran's Gulf littoral, from 1799 to 1835. In doing so he enjoyed a very high degree of independence, his court resembling that of his father at Tehran, but on a smaller scale. As Governor he was, however, never strong enough to coerce the southern ports, and, except at Bushire, no great advances in the imposition of central control over the littoral Arabs were made during these years: the dynasty was too young.

At the start of the nineteenth century Bushire was already well established as Iran's premier trading port, serving, as it did, the major route that ran north through Shiraz and Isfahan to Tehran. Bushire had received a boost under Nadir Shah, and the subsequent political turmoil in the south, together with the effect of Zand rule, both helped to foster the port's rapid growth. The British recognized its commercial potential in 1763, when they transferred their Persian factory there from Bandar Abbas. From the mid-eighteenth to the mid-nineteenth century the city was governed by one family, the aforementioned Al Madhkur.[14]

Despite the rich volume of trade passing through Bushire at the start of the nineteenth century, Europeans who visited the place were seldom anything but scathing in their description of its physical virtues. It possessed a poor harbour and the larger vessels were forced to anchor six miles offshore in the outer roads. Here it was that Abraham Parsons noted with curiosity the effects of a dry mist which blew off the Arabian desert sands from March to May:

> It is so penetrating as to insinuate itself into the skin, notwithstanding every method to prevent it. On the mahogany furniture in the ship's cabins it lay so thick, every morning, that it was usual to write devices, with the fingers, on it.[15]

The water in the town was described as so brackish, 'operating on the stranger like a dose of salts',[16] that in England it would have been considered unfit for consumption, although it was deeply esteemed locally and, after a while, began to appear strangely sweet to the palate.[17]

As to the town itself, one visitor in 1817 felt that, 'the buildings and bazars in general may be pronounced inferior to those of Muscat and Basra';[18] another decided that, 'excepting the East India Company's factory, the residence of the Governor, and a few good dwellings of the merchants, particularly the Armenians, there is scarcely one comfortable, and certainly not one handsome edifice in the place.'[19] There were in the port at this time perhaps some 500 friable stone houses, the dozen grandest supporting wind-towers, and a similar, or slightly larger, number of mean reed huts.[20] The inhabitants probably numbered no more than 10,000,[21] and were rather uncharitably described as 'a disagreeable mixture of the Arab and the Persian; in which, whatever is amiable in either character seems totally rejected, and whatever is vicious in both is retained and even cherished.'[22] Local dress, it seems, consisted of a combination of the Arab cloak and turban with the Persian outer garment, shirt and trousers.

Visitors to Bushire often remarked that the town appeared rather more attractive from the sea than it did in a state of proximity. The following account, from the 1830s, was not the first to suggest that a degree of mental adjustment was required of the newcomer:

> I am not surprised that the traveller arriving from India, with the comparative richness and verdure of its shores fresh in his memory, should feel sickened and disappointed as he gazes on the monotonous

31

aspect Persia wears ... This, however, is no bad foretaste of the shock he will receive on landing. As he enters through a dirty portal, on either side of which lounge some half-clad ragamuffins, with match-locks by their sides, and the water-pipe, with its everlasting gurgle, in their mouths, and gazes on the shapeless mass of buildings before him, on the wretched hut, on one hand, and the half-ruined graves, exposed to the footsteps of all, on the other—the dust, the dirt, the wretchedness which its narrow streets expose to view, he pauses with astonishment and enquires, 'Is this the city of thirty thousand souls [sic], the sea-port town of Persia?'[23]

It is evident from this piece that criticism was becoming harsher and more intolerant as the century proceeded, but it was not until the middle of the nineteenth century that Europeans began to be overly concerned with the question of public hygiene *per se*.[24] An English doctor in 1865 gave it as his opinion that,

> Bushire may be looked upon as a huge manufactory of foul and nox-ious gases, the pabulum for which is supplied by the filthy bodies of the inhabitants, human and brute, the decaying bodies of the dead, and excreta and refuse of all kinds.[25]

The British Residency at Bushire, built in the finest local architecture around two conjoined squares which together measured some 200–300 yards, lay situate just beyond the walls, to the south-east, opposite the beach. The four sides of the first courtyard were in 1818 arranged as fol-lows: facing you as you entered was the grandest room of all, the Resident's dining-room with its veranda reaching to the roof, flanked by his business-rooms. On the three remaining sides were first, the Resident's kitchens, next, rooms for visiting Company servants, and lastly, godowns for the Company's merchandise above which was to be found 'a remarkably nice summer-room'. The inner wall of the courtyard was constructed on the 'Chinese trellis model', and all around, behind it, were ranged a quantity of vast and curiously elegant earthenware water-jars. The second court-yard, besides containing some additional Company stores, was given over to the private apartments of the Resident's wife.[26]

During the eighteenth century the Resident's responsibilities were prim-arily commercial: his function was to manage the purchase and sale of merchandise in Persia on behalf of the East India Company. Flowing from this were other subsidiary, but nonetheless important, duties, which in-cluded the protection of British subjects and British trade, maintaining political relations between the East India Company and the local govern-ments of Bushire, Shiraz and the region, and finally, furnishing regular

reports on matters of a commercial and political nature. The precise for-
mulation of the Resident's function and status varied over the years 1790–
1820 in response to political exigency and a falling-off in the Company's
trade. His political influence in the region was hereafter to grow rapidly,
especially in the later nineteenth century, and he was eventually to earn
the sobriquet of 'uncrowned king of the Gulf'; but this, as yet, lay in the
future.

ii British India

The Resident, beneath whom there generally served an assistant, a lin-
guist, a broker and an establishment of parvoes (writers), peons et al., was
directly answerable the East India Company's Government of Bombay.
Bombay formed one of the three separate administrations, or Presidencies,
into which British India was divided, the constitution of each of which,
after a series of Acts of Parliament between 1773 and 1793, was briefly as
follows: at the head was a Governor appointed by the India Board, who
was not actually required to have had previous local experience. He
governed with the aid of 2–3 councillors, always men with a substantial
record of local service with the Company, but who could, if necessary, be
overruled by him. Beneath the Governor-in-Council there operated three
separate Boards, each normally under the supervision of a member of
Council, namely the Military Board and those of Trade and Revenue. The
Bombay Presidency was responsible for British possessions in western India,
together with the Company's trade and its factories in the Gulf and the
Red Sea. Like Madras, Bombay was now subordinate to the Supreme
Government in Bengal (Calcutta), but in practice she still exercised a very
high degree of autonomy and independence, complete with her own army
and navy. The next layer of authority above the Supreme Government was
the Court of Directors in Leadenhall Street, London: after 1784 their sway
over the Company's administration had ceased to be absolute with the
introduction of Pitt's India Act and, with it, a new Board of Control
whose function was to oversee the affairs of the Company on behalf of HM
Government.

The English East India Company, attracted by the trade of Iran, had
been active in the Gulf since near the commencement of the seventeenth
century. In 1622 they assisted Shah Abbas of Iran in ousting the Portuguese from Hormuz in return for the right to establish a commercial
station, or factory, at Bandar Abbas (Gombroon). This Agency then became the centre of the Company's trading operations in Iran and the Gulf,
and was to remain so, on and off, until 1763, when, on account of the
political turmoil and commercial uncertainty afflicting Iran, the factory

was closed and the function of Agency transferred to Basra. The Company's activities in Iran itself, by now much reduced, were, at this same juncture, shifted north to the fledgling factory at Bushire, termed a Residency, its status a step below that of Agency. Portuguese power in the Gulf, already very much on the decline in the early seventeenth century, was completely extinguished in the earlier part of the eighteenth century. The great rivals of the British in the Gulf were from the start the Dutch, but their East India Company totally relinquished the area after dismantling their colony on the island of Kharg in January 1766. From the later seventeenth century until the Napoleonic Wars, the French also, of course, from time to time presented serious competition and a threat: they destroyed the Bandar Abbas factory in 1759 and their privateers took many a British vessel in these seas. But there is little doubt that by the 1770s, at least as regards its European rivals, the English Company's position in the Gulf, confined to its two stations at Bushire and Basra, was assured. Yet, by the end of the century, the Company's operations were on such a small scale that, had not circumstance intervened, they might almost have been abandoned in their entirety.

The second of the two English factories in the Gulf in the later eighteenth century was, as we have seen, located at Basra: it was not until 1798 that a permanent Residency was opened in Baghdad, and a further twelve years until Basra was made subordinate to it. The Basra station enjoyed the status of Residency from its foundation in c. 1723 until its reduction in status in 1810, except for a brief spell as Agency, with overall control of the Company's affairs in the Gulf, from 1763 until 1778. The usual function of the Basra Residency was analogous with that of Bushire, but with the addition of one important duty at this time: the forwarding of the Company's mail in duplicate by courier along the desert route to Aleppo, then on to Constantinople and Europe, whilst the original despatches went via the Cape. This procedure was in vogue from the time of the Seven Years' War until the Napoleonic Wars, and for self-evident reasons.

iii Iraq

Basra was in these years under the control of an Ottoman governor, termed the *Mutasallim*, who was an appointee and subordinate of the *Pasha* of Baghdad. In the first decade of the eighteenth century a certain Hasan Pasha had been appointed governor of Baghdad. Thereafter, until 1831, the soon united *Wilayàt*, or province, of Iraq, was to remain practically independent of the Sublime Porte in the hands of Hasan's family and a class of Georgian slaves brought up in its service: this was Iraq's so-called Mamluk dynasty. There was apparently little stigma attached to the fact that one might originally have been purchased in the market at Tiflis. Hasan's grand-daughter herself married an ex-slave enabling him to become Pasha; though it is said an ex-slave would always, out of respect for his old master, be required to make a point of standing in his presence before strangers.[27]

Ottoman Iraq was spared the ravages that blighted Iran during the eighteenth century, but it did not escape entirely. The succession at Baghdad was not always a smooth affair—'such is the lust of dominion and authority, that there are frequently more competitors than vacancies'[28]—and a weak central government at Baghdad, or in the *Sanjaq* of Basra, ran the risk of allowing the bedouin tribes too great a latitude with which to prey on trade and settled agriculture: it was Niebuhr's contention that only a strong line of kings at Baghdad could staunch the 'anarchy of the Turks' and enable Mesopotamia to fulfil its promise.[29] There was, however, an improvement in this situation between 1780 and 1802 under the rule of Sulaiman, Pasha of three tails and 'as fine a specimen of a Turkish Pasha as ever existed.'[30]

The trade of Basra seems to have benefited in the early–mid-eighteenth century by Iran's decline and a general shift in commerce away from Bandar Abbas and the unsettled lower reaches of the Gulf. Nevertheless a number of factors were to disturb the flow of trade through Basra later in the century. A devastating outbreak of plague cut a wide swathe through Iraq in 1772–3 and severely reduced the population of Basra itself. Soon after, the long siege and rapacious Persian occupation of the city in 1775–9 brought yet further ruination and depopulation: accounts vary, but suggest that a normal population of some 40,000–50,000 before the plague may have halved by 1777, then plummeted still further to a nadir of 5,000 or so a year later.[31] One side-effect of these two calamities was to stimulate trade at the port of Kuwait, in part at the long-term expense of Basra.

There were two further factors militating against the easy prosperity of Basra in these years. Most important was the immense difficulty encountered by subsequent governors when they tried to bring the neighbouring tribes, the Muntafiq and the Ka'b, under sufficient control. In the second place, Ottoman Iraq was no longer in any sense a naval power. It is true that there was still a titular naval commander, or *Qaputan Pasha*, stationed at Basra, but his resources were meagre—'three most extraordinary-looking half ketch-, half Zubeek-rigged vessels' in 1818[32]—and his activities, such as they were, were confined to the river: if Niebuhr is to be followed, the erosion of his position had in part been a direct result of the rise of the Mamluk dynasty and their appropriation of his revenues.[33] On a number of occasions during the eighteenth century, therefore, the Mutasallim was obliged to seek British naval assistance, or commandeer their ships, so as to combat the Persians or the Ka'b. Unlike Iran, Ottoman Iraq did not even have access to the potential resources and allies of an extensive Gulf coastline.

Situated on the banks of the Shatt al-Arab 72 miles from the head of the Persian Gulf, where the river spans 600 yards and resembles a 'great beautiful lake',[34] early nineteenth-century Basra was a somewhat sprawling affair held in by eight miles or more of mud-brick fortifications built to repel marauding Arab tribesmen. Three-quarters of the space within these walls was given over to 'corn-fields, rice-grounds, date-groves, and gardens'.[35] And extending 30 miles or so downstream, as well as a considerable distance upriver and some miles inland, there were lush palm groves, and, beyond these, desert. Basra's production of dates supplied much of the Gulf region; they also, it is said, made 'exceedingly good and cheap' brandy.[36]

Basra was still, of course, one of the chief ports of the Persian Gulf, a meeting-point of the trade routes from Baghdad and Aleppo with those that came up the Gulf:

> The numbers of various descriptions of vessels passing to and fro under the walls of the Factory on the canal were far beyond what I had ever seen anywhere before, hardly two vessels being alike. This, with the constant collisions which unavoidably took place owing to the narrowness of the cut, was the cause of a universal gabble and dispute, reminding me of the voluble ribaldry of a seaport in Spain, Portugal or Italy.[37]

The population was large, with early nineteenth-century estimates apparently registering a minimum of about 50,000,[38] and, on account of the attraction exercised by commerce, mixed. Arabs were in the majority, but there was a very sizable Persian minority, together with small communities of Jews, Armenians and others such as Turks and Indians. These groups were sometimes recognizable by their dress: the Banyan merchants and brokers often wore a red turban, Jews and Armenians, some of them opulent merchants, dressed in the darker shades, and the Persians, or so it is said, favoured dark green and yellow. Of the sartorial habits of local Arab merchants it was said,

> Indian muslins and Angora shalloons are worn in the summer; but fine broad-cloths, of the brightest colours, Indian stuffs, and Cashmeer shawls, form the winter apparel; ... these are displayed in such variety as to make the wardrobe of a well-dressed man exceedingly expensive.[39]

It was also the custom to deck horses out in fine, albeit to some tastes tawdry, caparisons.[40]

Travellers who visited Basra between the mid-eighteenth and early nineteenth centuries were unimpressed by its architecture. In 1750, Bartholomew Plaisted thought it had the 'meanest aspect' and was the 'worst built' of any he had seen: 'The houses are generally two stories high, flat on top, and constructed with bricks burnt in the sun, but in such a clumsy manner that the Governor's own house was no better than a dog-hole.'[41] A quarter of a century on, Abraham Parsons reacted rather better to the richer dwellings, which seemed to him 'large and convenient'.[42] But the usual response was scathing: in 1816 Buckingham could find kind words only for the British Residency,

> which, presenting a circular brick wall toward the river with arched windows or ports, and having a large gate towards the creek, with sentries, flag-staff, & co., has all the appearance of a fortress, and is indeed by far the best building to be seen in the whole city.[43]

The second abiding impression of Basra from travellers' accounts is of its sheer filth. The seasoned voyager Niebuhr in the 1760s was not alone in thinking it the dirtiest Muslim town he had visited: houses tipped their kitchen waste directly into the streets, 'et il y en a plusieurs, qui ont même leurs commodités de ce coté la.'[44] Particularly notorious was the foul-smelling Ashar creek, of which it was reported over a century later that the poor 'use the canal from which they draw their drinking-water as a wash-tub, a bath, a dust-bin and a cesspool combined.'[45]

But in spite of this, in the eyes of European visitors, Basra had two distinct redeeming features, beside its obvious commercial attractions. The first of these was a climate which, though oppressive in the summer and autumn, was felt at other times so beneficial that invalids were brought there from India so they might ride and exercise in the open and, during the winter, enjoy the comforts of 'warm clothing, carpeted rooms, and an evening fireside'.[46] In the second place, Basra was able to afford a very fine and profuse selection of provisions, including, so we are told, a speciality of which the English and other Christians were especially fond, the 'humps' of cattle: 'in general these bunches are eaten salted, and bear a great resemblance, when cut, to a fat cow's udder, which it is so like in taste as scarcely to be distinguished from it.'[47]

iv Saudi Arabia

Saudi Arabia, as it exists today, is strictly speaking the product of form-ative events, the rise of the house of Su'ud and their conquest of Arabia in the wake of the Ottoman collapse, that occurred during the first three decades of the twentieth century. But the whole foundation for these campaigns of victory, which were fired by the ideology of *Wahhabism* and represented as the regaining of their patrimony by the Al Su'ud,[48] lay much earlier, in the experiences of the first Saudi state (1744/5–1818), of which these latter events were in many ways merely a repetition.

The years 1703–4, it is said, saw the birth into a reasonably prominent family of religious lawyers (qadis), in the central Arabian town of Uyaina, of an individual whose Islamic teaching was to transform the Peninsula before his death in 1792, and whose influence has continued strong in the region to this day; yet, consonant with his creed, no lasting monument was to mark his grave. Shaikh Muhammad bin Abd al-Wahhab set out upon his career by first undergoing the standard religious and scholarly training, initially at home, then later in the cities of Medina and Basra. He found himself particularly inspired by the somewhat severe and revivalist theology of a fourteenth-century *Hanbali* jurist, Ibn Taimiya.

Shaikh Muhammad, therefore, zealous in religion from an early age and possessed of a conviction matched only by his acute awareness of the spiritual condition of the society about him, was finally led by the ideas and experiences of these formative years nearly to this conclusion: society's ills could be remedied only by a return to the pristine Islam that had theoretically obtained during the lifetime of the Prophet, or shortly there-after, an Islam which was to be strictly interpreted, stripped of all later accretions and purged of the baneful influence of moral laxity and other corruption.[49]

The experience of a narrow escape from death, whilst in the desert on his journey home from Basra, may possibly have left Shaikh Muhammad with a more refined sense of urgency or purpose, and brought his spiritual development to a head.[50] But it was not until 1740–1, with the death of a father who had been the principal and last restraining influence upon him, that his energies at length found their release in forceful public preaching. Followers were soon roused by his words. In the town of Uyaina they helped him cut down a sacred tree and raze a saint's shrine regarded as evidence of un-islamic superstition, while they also revived the Islamic penalty of stoning for adultery. His teaching clearly began to take on weighty political implications. These were signs of foment worrying enough for the preacher to be expelled by the civil authorities. He there-fore travelled to the nearby town of Dir'iya to seek the protection of its ruling family, the Al Su'ud.[51]

It was here, in 1744–5, that Shaikh Muhammad reached an accord with the Al Su'ud, which was to last essentially till the present day and form the whole basis for the Saudi state: the Saudi *Amir*, or prince–ruler, was promised the fulfilment of his political ambitions if he agreed to abide by and help to propagate the advice and teachings of the divine. The relationship between the two families, frequently reinforced by marriage, has remained close ever since. This union of the book and the sword has proved a very powerful force.

Doctrinally there was nothing extraordinary in Shaikh Muhammad's teaching, indeed it was orthodoxy *par excellence*, of a kind which today would be classified in the West as fundamentalism. Nevertheless, it can be misleading to view theology out of context. The emphasis contained in this teaching, the nature of the society in which he lived and above all a readiness to employ political power so as to translate the abstractions of doctrine into concrete social action, all made Wahhabism into a potent revolutionary ideology. What seemed, therefore, like the artificial resurrection of a bygone era, was in fact a contemporary system adjusted to the political realities: it was almost like social comment taken to an extreme.

The Wahhabis, followers of Shaikh Muhammad's teachings, called themselves the *Muwahhidun* or Professors of Unity; theirs was the 'Summons to the Oneness of God' (al-da'wa ilal-tauhid). Belief in the Unity of God, *tauhid*, is the main pivot of Wahhabi teaching, just as it is, of course, the central tenet of Islam itself, expressed in the Muslim's attestation of faith, 'There is no god but Allah'. The converse of this profession of God's Oneness, as so often stressed in Wahhabi texts, is the sin of associating others with the One God, polytheism or *shirk*. For the Wahhabis, adherence to the doctrine of Unity took effect in at least three important areas: first, it involved a rigid and literal belief in the Unity and Omnipotence of God and His Names; second, the scrupulous, even fastidious, observance of the outward practicalities of religion, such as prayer and fasting; and third, the active elimination of polytheism and unbelief wherever they found it in so-called Muslim society. This last element is crucial. At its most extreme, Wahhabism appeared to redefine Islam within narrow limits. It was no longer sufficient merely to profess yourself a Muslim. You had actually to profess to accept certain Wahhabi principles. The Wahhabi community alone formed the true 'Abode of Islam'; beyond its frontiers lay the 'Abode of War', peopled by unbelievers against whom it was legitimate to wage Holy War. Yet it should be stressed that the Wahhabis were not always so intolerant or exclusive as this, or their reputation, might indicate. Their definition of unbelief undoubtedly varied in its direction and stringency in different hands and changing political circumstances, otherwise it should never have succeeded in the way it has. There was, although this is a social as well as a political phenomenon, a discernible hostility to things Turkish with the first Saudi state, just as, a century or so later, we find the more extreme Wahhabis attacking Western inventions such as the aeroplane and the radio.

The vehemence of the Wahhabi attack on polytheism also has to be understood within the setting of the Arabia of the day. This was not simply a reaction against the perceived excesses of Shi'ism and Sufism. It seems that un-islamic practice, saint worship and sheer superstition were prevalent amongst ordinary Sunni Muslims. Islamic law was ignored in favour of tribal codes; shrines were raised to holy men and sacrifices made there; even trees were revered, and there existed an idol, Dhal-Khilsa, against which infertile women rubbed their sides in the hope of a cure.[52] The Wahhabis saw it as their duty physically to eradicate all these manifestations of unbelief.

This crusade was an assault upon superstition, immorality and crime, but it also had even wider, political, implications, for it was at the same time an attack on factionalism and regionalism. Wahhabism, at the end of the eighteenth century, was inseparable from the Saudi state. Each in tandem required new loyalties of the individual. These were intended to supersede former local, tribal and other allegiances; though in practice the state seems to have remained little more than a vast, unwieldy tribal confederacy.[53]

When, in the late eighteenth or early nineteenth centuries, an Arabian community newly agreed to become a part of the Saudi–Wahhabi state, it typically did a number of things. Straightaway all shrines and other symbols of unbelief were torn down, the destruction of the cupolas and tombs of saints being 'the favourite taste of the Wahhabis.'[54] Wahhabi missionaries were then received, who would instruct the populace in correct practice and belief. Civil and religious dignitaries might be sent for from the capital Dir'iya, and garrisons were occasionally established. But, from one view, the most important sign of open obedience to the new rule was payment of a tax, called *zakat*, to the Public Treasury.[55] The Saudi Amir was thereby recognized as ultimate head of the new community and the individual was, in theory, henceforth obliged to respond to his summons to undertake Holy War as and when required.

The Saudi–Wahhabi armies were thus generally composed of tribesmen called to arms for a particular raid or campaign only. This extension of the traditional bedouin method of warfare, though it possessed obvious drawbacks, also brought with it a surprising degree of mobility. Service could be, and was, evaded under a variety of circumstances. Kitting oneself out could also be expensive for, besides weapons and a mount, 'One hundred pounds weight of flour, fifty or sixty pounds of dates, twenty pounds of butter, a sack of wheat or barley for the camel, and a water-skin, are the provisions of a Wahhabi soldier.'[56] The sole reward that accrued to the fighting-men, besides the spiritual, lay in their share of the plunder, four-fifths of which they were permitted to retain: 'Su'ud was often heard to say, that no Arabs had ever been staunch Wahhabis until they had suffered two or three times from the plundering of his troops.'[57] Although

Wahhabi teaching sought religiously to suppress the notion of political discord or disloyalty to the state, in practice, as we have seen, the degree of cohesion within the first Saudi state was both fluctuating and various. It was, in fact, common, though not universal, practice to leave local rulers, or at least the local power structures, in place. In outlying areas, Saudi authority could be remarkably light.

For four decades after 1744–5 the new Saudi state was steadily engaged in building up strength in its central Arabian homeland of Najd. Increasingly it began to attract the unwelcome attentions of its neighbours. It suffered invasion from the kingdom of Najran in the south-west in 1764, and later in the 1770s. But by far the most persistent and serious threat was that posed by the Banu Khalid, lords of north-eastern Arabia (Hasa), who repeatedly harried the nascent Wahhabi state and were ultimately destined to become locked with it in a duel to the death. An important milestone in the consolidation of Saudi hegemony over Najd was passed in 1773 with the eventual fall of Riyadh, a town and principality close to Dir'iya. By 1785 the Saudi state felt strong enough to commence expansionism outward from central Arabia: over the eight years that followed, a series of terrifying raids and ferocious campaigns was directed eastwards against Banu Khalid territory. In 1795, partly in consequence of these military successes, and partly on account of an adept policy of bribery and intrigue with the ruling family, Banu Khalid rule was finally extinguished and much of north-eastern Arabia fell under Saudi domination. In 1800 the important seaport of Qatif was also taken. The Saudi state was henceforward a real power in the Persian Gulf.

The decade and a half following 1795 represented a high point for the first Saudi state. Expansion was vigorous and rapid in all directions. Raiding began against Ottoman Iraq to the north, culminating in the sack of Karbala, Shi'ite Islam's holiest shrine and city, in 1802: 'I met several of the people who had been there at that period, and they all agreed in complaining most bitterly of the cruelty of the reformers.'[58] Shock waves reverberated through Iran and the Shi'ite world. Wahhabism took on connotations of evil and irreligion in the popular mind. And the *Pashalik* of Baghdad, expeditions sent against the Wahhabis in 1798 and 1802 notwithstanding, seemed for its part powerless to protect its own people. The Wahhabis likewise also despatched forays with much the same degree of impunity north-west into Syria, threatening Damascus itself in 1810. In the south-west, too, their warriors overran Asir and the coastal regions of Yemen, raiding even the secluded valleys of Hadramaut.

But the most important contest was that which had begun in the late 1780s with the Ottoman province of Hijaz in western Arabia. Ruled by the *Sharifs* of Mecca, and benefiting from the rich pilgrimage traffic and the trade of the Red Sea, the Hijaz represented the jewel of the Peninsula. But it was also the spiritual heart of the whole Islamic world, on account of Mecca and Medina, and the special pride and trust of the Ottoman Sultan himself. By the close of the century the province was on the defensive. Mecca finally fell in 1803:

> Not the slightest excess was committed ... The people of Mecca now became Wahhabis; that is, they were obliged to pray more punctually than usual, to lay aside and conceal their fine silk dresses, and to desist from smoking in public. Heaps of Persian pipes, collected from all the houses, were burnt before Su'ud's headquarters, and the sale of tobacco was forbidden. The brother of [the Sharif] was placed by Su'ud at the head of the Meccan government; and a learned man from Dir'iya ... was appointed qadi.[59]

The conquest of the Hijaz was completed in the following year with the capture of Medina:

> Su'ud soon after visited Medina, and stripped Muhammad's tomb of all the valuable articles that it still possessed ... He also endeavoured to destroy the high dome erected over the tomb, and would not allow Turkish pilgrims to approach Medina from any quarter; ... several of them, who attempted to pass ... were ill treated; their beards also were cut off, as the Wahhabis, who themselves have short scanty beards, declared, that the Prophet did not wear so long and bushy a beard as those of the northern Turks.[60]

The conquest of the twin holy cities was for many, including the Ottoman Sultan, the final provocation. Islam itself was now represented as under threat.

Virtually the whole southern, Arabian, coastline of the Gulf, and even a part of the Persian shore comprising Linga and the Huwala ports, fell under some measure of Saudi domination during the first, and to a lesser extent the second, decades of the nineteenth century. Kuwait was unusual in that, for the most part, she successfully resisted the Wahhabi onslaught throughout. Not so the Utub's possessions in Qatar and Bahrain: Saudi influence in the latter was particularly strong between December 1801, when the ruling Al Khalifa invoked their aid in order to recover the island from Oman, and mid-1810, when, curiously, Oman came to the aid of the Al Khalifa in expelling the Wahhabi garrison. Swings of allegiance and alliances of this kind were, in fact, typical of politics in the Gulf.

There was also a heavy, and for our purposes important, Saudi involvement in south-eastern Arabia, including both the Trucial States and Oman. Commencing in 1800, the base for these operations was situated at the strategically placed oasis town of Buraimi, which lay inland, on the present-day border between Oman and the United Arab Emirates. Resistance to Saudi influence and attempts at domination was strong in Oman proper, for it had its own religious, cultural and political traditions. One of the first acts of the Saudi ruler towards Oman was to despatch an important Wahhabi tract to the country in 1800, with a message for its ruler and its people to convert and show submission to Saudi rule. An Omani historian takes delight in recording that, 'The treatise contained a mass of incoherent sentences quite inconsistent with the truth, and no-one took any notice of it.'[61] An Omani religious figure was less terse regarding the Wahhabis and their tract, though no less caustic:

> It is a small book, consisting mostly of sophisms and conjectures. It legalises the murder of all Muslims who dissent from them, the appropriation of their property, the enslavement of their offspring [and] the marriage of their wives without being first divorced from their husbands ... The actuating principle in all this [is] their thirst for gain, through fraud and stratagem ... Through their doubts respecting God and their sophistical tenets they become like beasts who have no understanding—they do not know that they do not understand, for no-one knows that but the knowing.[62]

But despite the proudly defiant words of members of the ruling family in Oman—'Blood is man's only dye, and war, like the manna and quails, is as food to us'[63]—Saudi pressure on the country, both military and through the exercise of politics amongst the tribes and within the government, grew very strong in the first decade of the nineteenth century. Its rulers were, therefore, grudgingly obliged upon occasion to bow to Saudi political pressure and deliver up taxes to Dir'iya. Early in 1809 it was noted that 'six Wahhabi teachers are now at Muscat compelling the people by blows to pray in their manner, and [forcing] the merchants out of their houses to go to the mosques.'[64] But Saudi political control of Oman was never in fact consolidated. The independence of the ruler of Muscat, though severely compromised, was ultimately preserved; and after 1813, Saudi involvement in Oman receded fast.

In the Trucial States, including Ras al-Khaima and the ports associated with it, it was altogether a different story from Oman. On the face of it these states appeared far more willing and convincing parts of the Saudi state than Oman during the first two decades of the nineteenth century. But the real extent of Saudi–Wahhabi political and religious influence with the Qawasim, and the possible links between this and piracy, is a topic of such interest and uncertainty that no discussion of it can be undertaken at this point.

A strong response on the part of the Ottoman Empire to the challenge posed by the rise of the Saudi state and the taking of the holy cities was late in coming. In 1811, Muhammad Ali, the powerful and ambitious Albanian Pasha of Egypt, and the only one in a position to do so, saw fit to launch a war against the Saudi state. Within a few years Egyptian troops had retaken the Hijaz, resulting in a brief spell of peace during 1815–16. But the Egyptian power decided to recommence the struggle, and Muhammad Ali's son Ibrahim now took the fight into central and eastern Arabia. Dir'iya fell in September 1818, and with that the first Saudi state was completely extinguished. An observer at the scene of the former Saudi capital noted soon after that,

> The walls which surrounded the town, the forts, and several houses have been razed. The Pasha was determined to render this spot a wilderness, and previous to his departure caused the date plantations and gardens to be destroyed. At present there is not a single family inhabiting its ruins ... the [Egyptian] troops have been busily employed in retaliating on the Bedouin tribes. The most trifling acts of misconduct have served as a pretext for depriving them of their flocks. The defences of every village in Najd have been destroyed.[65]

The Saudi Amir himself was taken to Istanbul and decapitated.

It will have been observed that the period of Saudi domination in eastern Arabia, from the turn of the century until 1818, is roughly coterminous with the piracy and other events that form the subject of this book.

v   Oman

> 'Land from the mast-head!' 'What does it look like?' 'High land, sir, on the larboard bow, stretching away to the north-west.' 'Can you see land to starboard?' 'No.' 'Then,' says the captain, with some little swell, 'we have just hit it; the watch is a good one; and three or four hours of this will bring us into Muscat.'[66]

The reason for Muscat's existence was its harbour, the best in south-east Arabia. Its geographical location, at the crossroads of trade between East Africa, the Red Sea, western India and the Persian Gulf, made this, the chief port and city of Oman, also the key to the commerce of Persia and Arabia.[67] The approach to Muscat from the sea was 'extraordinary and romantic': seemingly quite bare of vegetation, 'the whitened surface of the houses, and turreted forts in the vicinity' contrasted 'in a singular manner with the burnt and cindery aspect of the darkened masses of rock around.'[68] The city itself nestles at the base of an inlet half a mile broad and three-quarters of a mile long. Either side of this horseshoe-shaped cove[69] rugged volcanic rocks rise up c. 350–435 feet, cradling the city and protecting it from inland.[70]Numerous fortifications were visible, the most prominent of which were the two fine Portuguese forts of Mirani (Capitan) and Jalali (San João), which stood sentinel over the entrance to the cove. Though exposed to the *shamal*, or north-west, winds and offering imperfect holding-ground, the harbour was sufficient for between 40 and 50 large vessels to anchor there in safety.[71]

A merchant traveller arriving in the early nineteenth century might, in view of Muscat's pre-eminence as an entrepôt port, have been initially unimpressed by the scenes that first greeted him:

> The Custom-House, which is opposite to the landing-place both for passengers and goods, is merely an open square of twenty feet, with benches around it, one side opening to the sea, and the roof covered in for shelter from the sun. This landing-place is also the Commercial Exchange, where it is usual, during the cool of the morning, and after al-Asr [the afternoon prayer], to see the principal merchants assembled, some sitting on old rusty cannon, others on condemned spars, and others in the midst of coils of rope, exposed on the wharf, stroking their beards, counting their beads, and seeming to be the greatest of idlers, instead of men of business; notwithstanding which, when a stranger gets among them, he finds commerce to engross all their conversation and their thoughts.[72]

For others, first impressions were more vibrant. They might carry away with them vivid and none too agreeable memories of a 'busy beach, crowded with slaves, covered with packages of dates, blackened with flies, and scented with putrid salt-fish'.[73]

The bazars themselves were crowded, filthy and, according to one Indian visitor, narrow as a prison;[74] though they perhaps made up in cosmopolitan bustle and the rich variety of goods they offered, what they lacked in architectural elegance or grandeur.[75] An English traveller in 1786 noted that, 'most of the merchants were nearly naked and each was cooled by an ingenious fan, for Muscat is the hottest place on earth. The stalls had an infinite variety of gums, grains, and medicines, and a very peculiar smell.'[76] A decade earlier it was remarked that the quantity of merchandise in the city was such that, with the warehouses overflowing, much of it was piled up in the streets.[77] Throughout this period European visitors to Muscat commonly averred that goods stored thus in the open could be left unguarded and still remain immune from theft.[78] This apparent security, and the careful regulation of the bazar and harbour by government,[79] helped to foster Muscat's reputation and, of course, her commercial prosperity.

The two most valuable items of trade at Muscat were pearls, from the Gulf, and coffee, from Mocha. But a great variety of other articles passed through the port. One important branch of trade, centred on Muscat, was the traffic in slaves. The sight of lines of slaves being paraded through the streets had the power to shock Europeans even in 1800 and caused some to leave with an unfavourable image of the place.[80] In others, the slave market, held three times weekly, had the capacity to arouse a more questionable curiosity. One rather jaded East India Company officer witnessed the spectacle in 1817:

> The sale had just commenced, as I stopped to view a scene that had at least the interest of novelty. Twenty or thirty young Africans, brought across the desert, and chiefly from the coast of Zanzibar, were ranged in rows on either side of the bazar, and according to their sex. They were, in general, handsomely trimmed (dressed is an improper term) for the occasion; and appeared in truth perfectly resigned; being certainly in as clean and sleek a condition, (with a cloth girdle round their middle, for their only covering) as their owners or purchasers could have wished. The latter, indeed, in walking between the ranks, seemed extremely particular in handling and feeling the bodies and skins of their intended purchases; extending their inspections to such minute particulars as quite astonished me; who was by no means a connoisseur, in any animal more rational than a camel or a horse.[81]

This particular visitor was somewhat bemused to find himself the object of one importunate vendor's attentions, who tried, somewhat optimistically, to sell him a young boy of ten or twelve for 40 dollars. The child was eventually purchased by an Arab senior whom he had observed 'critically nice in his selection of the young females that were exposed.'[82] One European who did, however, find himself in the unusual position of possessing a Muslim slave-girl at Muscat, was the enigmatic Italian adventurer and putative Napoleonic agent Vincenzo Maurizi, who worked for the ruler of Muscat in 1809–10 and shortly thereafter. His permitted ownership of the girl was, so he maintained, an example of the special religious tolerance practised at the port. But he did not retain her for long. Finding that 'poor Turungia was always dreadfully afraid that I should eat her', he chose to calm her fears by handing her to an Arab.[83]

It is quite suggestive, in view of Muscat's obvious cosmopolitanism, to come across a number of instances there of rumours of cannibalism in others. Black slaves whose teeth had been filed were shunned for this reason.[84] The people of Muscat muttered that it was impossible to journey thence to Mocha by land on account of the cannibals to be encountered on the way.[85] Magic and superstition were almost certainly rife both here and throughout the Gulf. The same, not always wholly trustworthy, Maurizi states out of his experience at Muscat that,

> The Arabian sorcerers pretend to have the power of changing a man into a goat; and this act of diabolic authority is supposed to be so frequently exercised, that the purchaser of a goat always takes particular notice of certain marks by which it is thought that the animals who have undergone this transformation may certainly be recognised. A servant of mine once assured me that a goat had begged his master not to kill him in very good Arabic ...[86]

The fixed population of Muscat in the early nineteenth century was estimated at 10,000, with a further 3,000 dwelling in the shanty town without the walls.[87] In addition there was, of course, a large transient population of sailors, travellers, merchants and the like. One report claims that as many as ten per cent of the population were partially blind, another that two-thirds of the inhabitants were unhealthy.[88] In the first decade of the nineteenth century Muscat gained a notorious reputation for insalubrity amongst Europeans: between 1800 and 1809 no less than four English East India Company Agents died at the port and a fifth left in 1810 for health reasons, following which he was not replaced.[89] European mortality was generally blamed on the extreme climate. One visitor agreed with a Persian poet that the summer temperature was adequate to give 'a panting sinner a lively anticipation of his future destiny.'[90] Yet, for visiting ships, these deficiencies were less noticeable than the fine provisions the port could afford. The water was good, if casks were filled at the reservoir,[91] and one naval officer maintained that the beef was the best he had tasted since leaving England.[92] Fish was especially plentiful and cheap, one speaking of 'excellent fish, of various denominations, for less than a halfpenny per pound';[93] and, amongst the wide range of fruit and vegetables produced there,[94] Muscat was especially known for its pomegranates and for its mangoes, whose stones apparently made very acceptable presents for 'those gentlemen in India' with 'gardens large enough to allow room for their growth.'[95]

European accounts of Muscat often seem to follow a pattern. Frequently they portray the inhabitants as modest by nature, sober and restrained in their social habits, and polite and tolerant in their dealings with others. No doubt part of this was somehow connected with the port's commercial prosperity. These traits were supposed then to be reflected in the city's architecture which, apart from the ruler's palace, newly built on the waterfront in the European style in the early nineteenth century, together with a handful of the houses of the rich, was felt to be uniformly meagre, bland

and unimpressive. At the turn of the century, in fact, some of the grandest and most ostentatious buildings were probably those left behind by the Portuguese, including two fine churches, one of which had been converted into the ruler's palace.[96]

Modesty and gravity were also detected by European observers in the dress worn by the inhabitants of Muscat:

> Beards are universally worn ... The dress of the men is simply a shirt and trousers of fine muslin, slightly girded round the waist, open sandals of worked leather, and a turban of small blue checked cotton, with a silk and cotton border of red and yellow, a manufacture peculiar to the town of Suhar, to the north-west of Muscat, on the coast. In the girdle is worn a crooked dagger; and over the shoulders of the merchants is thrown a purple cotton cloth of Surat; while the military, or people of government, wear a neatly made wooden shield, hung by a leathern strap over the shoulder, and either hang the sword loosely above it, or carry it in their hand. Nothing can surpass the simplicity of their appearance, or the equality of value between the dresses of the wealthiest and the lowest classes of the people.[97]

In the early nineteenth century it appears that many of the women in Muscat and nearby Matrah did without the veil, unless, if Maurizi is to be believed, they were the wives of shaikhs, or expensive courtesans from Iran and elsewhere.[98]

The judgement contained in the following piece from 1765 might almost as easily have been penned by any number of European visitors to Muscat over the course of the next half century or so. The 'Ibadis' referred to by the author are adherents of the dominant sect of Islam in Oman:

> I know of no Muslims so sober in their ways or so lacking in ostentation as these Ibadis. They smoke no tobacco and consume very little strong liquor, for the most part drinking only coffee. The man of rank and distinction does not dress any more lavishly than one of moderate means, except for sporting a slightly finer turban, a splendid sword at his side and a fine dagger at his front. They do not easily give way to violent emotion. They are polite to foreigners and allow them to live quietly in Muscat following their own laws. Whereas in Yemen Banyans [Indian Hindus] are obliged to bury their dead, in Muscat they are permitted to cremate them; and whereas in all other Muslim countries Jews are compelled to wear something to mark themselves out, in Muscat they are allowed to attire themselves in exactly the same fashion as Arabs. In Sunni Muslim countries a Banyan, a Jew or a Christian discovered with a Muslim woman has to convert, or at the very least pay a hefty fine; but, amongst the Ibadis of Muscat, the

authorities do not concern themselves with matters of this kind, provided that the foreigner only intrigues with women otherwise known to prostitute themselves to Muslims for money—and there are a large number of these dissolute women living in a separate quarter, outside the city.[99]

Muscat's Banyan, or Hindu, community was the largest of any city in Arabia and apparently made up as much as ten per cent of the population in the early nineteenth century.[100] Banyans were for the most part traders and brokers by profession and, according to one report,[101] they frequently resided in the port without their families for a period of 15–20 years, before finally returning home, mostly via Porbandar to Gujarat. One observer described the Banyans as the great bankers of Arabia,[102] and there is no doubt that they possessed a high degree of wealth and standing at Muscat. Some of the most substantial members of the mercantile community, with an especial interest in pearls, grain and cloth,[103] were Banyans. Both the ruler of Muscat and the English East India Company employed them as brokers, and the port's customs-farm at the start of the nineteenth century was in the hands of one Banyan, 'a fat cunning man and the richest subject in the place.'[104] The tolerance and encouragement Banyans enjoyed at the hands of the government of Muscat allowed them to run a small temple and tend a large herd of 'well-fed, sleek and mischievous' sacred cows.[105]

The presence of the Banyan community in Muscat was naturally a product of the close commercial ties that existed between that port and north-west India. But it does also help to substantiate frequent European claims for the practice of tolerance on the part of the government and people of Muscat. By about 1820, and in some instances much earlier, praise of the civility, honesty and sobriety of the inhabitants of Muscat seems almost to have become the norm with British travellers. It is as well to bear in mind that part of this—which is not to say all of it—was the result of borrowing from hearsay and the writings of earlier visitors: 'The people of Muscat seemed to me to be the cleanest, neatest, best dressed, and most gentlemanly of all the Arabs that I had ever yet seen, and inspired, by their first approach, a feeling of confidence, good-will, and respect.' Whilst quite possibly his true experience, this writer, for one, was not permitted to go beyond that 'first impression': he left Muscat the day he arrived.[106]

The state of Oman, whose chief port and, from the 1780s, whose capital was Muscat, has a long and rather idiosyncratic history. The widespread turmoil which seems to have transformed the Gulf region in the eighteenth century did not, however, pass it by. Indeed, Oman was peculiarly vulnerable to such vagaries of fortune because of its dependency on trade and because, unlike Iran, Iraq and Saudi Arabia, it was essentially a maritime and a seaboard power. Upheaval within the country and the prevailing weakness of Iran's position in the Gulf had important consequences for Oman in the mid–late eighteenth century: a new ruling dynasty, the Al Bu Sa'id, was born and the family soon managed to restore a greater measure of unity and strength to the country. This enabled Omani influence and commerce to expand rapidly overseas by the end of the century, making her once again unquestionably the dominant sea-power in the region. The Al Bu Sa'id have, of course, ruled the country ever since.

The country of Oman forms the south-eastern corner of Arabia and comprises a number of distinct geographical areas. Yet, despite its size, the majority of the population, estimated at half a million in the early twentieth century,[107] inhabited the north-east regions of the country: the Batina, a coastal strip some 10–20 miles wide stretching 150 miles north from Muscat to Shinas; and the middle and southern reaches of the broad mountain range that runs up behind this coastal plain from near Sur in the south to the very mouth of the Gulf in the north. Behind these mountains gravel plains, salt-flats and quicksand are soon encountered, and these in turn quickly run away into the arid expanses of the Empty Quarter.

The geography of the country has materially shaped its history: the interior, and the province of Oman proper, are cut off from the coastal areas by mountains. The numerous valleys are inhabited by a society likewise riven into some hundreds of tribes. This physical isolation has very often tended to translate into religious, cultural and political difference. Typically the heart of the country has been insular and conservative, the coastal regions more tolerant and enterprising. This is easily observed in the twentieth century when, until the 1950s, the interior of Oman maintained itself in isolation, complete with its own government and socio-religious system, independent of the Sultan of Muscat who ruled the coast.

A large proportion of the population of Oman belong to a somewhat unusual sect of Islam, called Ibadism. This break-away movement can be traced back to the eighth century AD, and it was able to survive as a religio-political system in Oman because of the country's remoteness from the traditional centres of the Islamic world and its otherwise inaccessible interior. The quality which particularly marks out Ibadism, though it also differs to a certain extent from mainstream Sunnism in its ordinary religious practice and teaching, is its distinct and developed political theory. Government of the Ibadi community was theocratic, minimalist and in theory free of despotism. At the head of the community was the Imam or leader, who was theoretically chosen by religious and tribal leaders for his moral and religious qualities:

> The Imam ... must be a mature male of outstanding intelligence, not
> blind, deaf, senile, nor lacking limbs which would prevent him from
> taking part in the obligation of *jihad* [holy war], nor should he be a
> eunuch or emasculated. He must not be mad, nor feeble-minded, nor
> should he be envious, cowardly, mean, a liar, nor a man who fails to
> keep promises and agreements, nor possess any other characteristic
> that causes concern. He must be a man of great learning for without
> learning and perception how can he carry out his duties and interpret
> the laws aright and ensure that his subordinates do so?[108]

In practice the Imamate tended to become dynastic and the Imam's real
power depended upon the support and careful management of strong tribal
leaders. Thus it is that the internal political history of Oman frequently
turns upon a kaleidoscope of shifting tribal alliances and pressures.

The history of Oman in recent centuries has often appeared to yearn to
follow a broad and repetitive 'natural' pattern, a cycle between unity and
disunity, strength and weakness, soaring ambition and troubled intro-
spection. Religiously orientated Imams have typically risen to power with
tribal support, bringing badly needed unity to the country, expelling
foreign occupiers and sometimes founding dynasties. Once successful, their
governments have gradually appeared more secular, shifting the focus of
their attentions to commerce and overseas expansion. Disunity sets in, the
tribes and the interior gain their head and foreign domination increases.
The cycle then repeats itself, or so, in recent centuries, it has seemed.[109]

The dynasty of Imams who ruled Oman in the seventeenth and earlier
eighteenth centuries was that of the Ya'ariba, whose achievement it was to
unite the country and expel the Portuguese from their fortresses at Muscat
and elsewhere on the Batina coast. The attack on Muscat was directed
by the Imam and carried with God's assistance, none of the 'beardless'
Portuguese opposing them, according to an Omani chronicler, 'but such
as were reeling drunk, incapable of firing or using their muskets, beyond
striking with them at random. These the Mussulmans dispatched with
sword and spear, and left them prostrate like the trunks of uprooted date-
trees.' Just one Portuguese commander held out, and eventually he too was
forced to flee 'as far as the cotton-market, where there was a great fight,
but they assailed him with spears and rotten eggs, and slew him and all
his followers. So God rid the Mussulmans of him and his polytheist
companions.'[110]

The Ya'ariba brought about a revival of Oman's maritime activities, to
the extent that by about the end of the seventeenth century she had come
to constitute the dominant non-European naval power in the region,
besides gaining a wide reputation for piracy. Portugal was then dispossessed
of many of her East African possessions, initiating centuries of Omani rule,

51

and her settlements even in western India were attacked. Oman also made ground in the Gulf, seizing Bahrain, for a time, from the Persians. But immediately after the high point of Omani strength under the Ya'ariba, in 1711–19, the country was plunged into three decades of debilitating anarchy, dissolution and internecine bloodshed, brought on by dynastic uncertainty and weak rule. The civil wars led directly to Persian military intervention under Nadir Shah in 1737–8 and 1742–4. They also brought about the formation of two great opposing alliances, the Ghafiri and the Hinawi, into which the tribes of Oman now variously fell: even the Trucial States were included in this scheme of things. This nationwide bipartite division of tribal allegiances, though it had much earlier roots,[111] also had important consequences for the subsequent political history of Oman. Long after this, tribes continued to be known as either Ghafiri or Hinawi by affiliation. And though the make-up of the two factions did not always remain rigid, the conceiving of local disputes as Ghafiri–Hinawi rivalry has persisted in some areas, albeit in a subdued fashion, until recent times.

The origins of the Al Bu Sa'id dynasty, who replaced the Ya'ariba in the mid-eighteenth century, are relatively obscure. The father of Ahmad bin Sa'id, founder of the new dynasty, was reportedly a coffee merchant of Suhar. Ahmad himself rose in the service of the Ya'ariba, was attached to them by marriage and appointed Governor of Suhar.[112] His reputation soared with his patriotic, though allegedly guileful and cruel, expulsion of the Persians, who had invaded the country for a second time in 1742–4. On the strength of this grand gesture, and with the particular backing of the mercantile coastal region and the Hinawi tribal division, Ahmad attained the position of *de facto* Imam in c. 1749.[113]

Imam Ahmad's relatively long reign, until his death in 1783, afforded the country sufficient unity and stability to begin to repair the damage dealt by the civil wars. Oman's fleet, from a low point in the middle of the century, began to recover and her trade seems to have prospered. Now and hereafter, the most important branch of commerce was that conducted with western India, but also significant was the annual Omani shipment of coffee from Mocha round to Basra. This latter helped in part to make Oman a natural ally of Iraq during that country's hostilities with Iran in the 1770s. But Oman was also in conflict with Iran during much of that decade in her own right, and once again the reason was predominantly commercial: each wished to dominate the lower Gulf to the detriment of the other. Oman, with the strongest single navy in the Gulf by this time, was well able to resist Iranian efforts in this regard.

By the 1760s Ahmad had largely overcome opposition within Oman, which had included lingering Ya'ariba pretensions, tribal disaffection and the threat from the Qawasim in the north. The real weakness of Al Bu Sa'idi rule only surfaced towards the very end of his reign: problems of the succession. Family rivalries crystallized in 1793 when three of Ahmad's sons finally came to an agreement to respect each other's positions, thereby dividing up power within the country. The first, Sa'id, remained at Rustaq in the interior: he was the legitimate Imam after his father and retained this religious position until his death.[114] But he was unpopular and lacked political power. The second brother, Qais, was Governor of Suhar on the coast: an abiding rivalry was to commence between Qais with his descendants, on the one hand, and the family of the third of the brothers, and the real power in Oman at this time, Sultan, on the other.

Sultan bin Ahmad, ruler of Muscat in 1792/3–1804, is an important figure in Gulf history. He is later described by an Omani historian as 'tall in stature, of a noble countenance, brave, spirited, animated, valiant, caring nothing for the number of his enemies, preferring a few select adherents to a multitude of followers and impartial in judgement.'[115] Another admirer, an English envoy who met the ruler on board his flagship in 1800, recalled that he appeared to him to inspire a certain real affection amongst the ship's crew:

> he had a shawl rolled round his head as a turban, and the Arab cloak, which hung over his plain robes, was of white broadcloth, no way ornamented; he wore no jewels, and had no arms, not even a dagger, about his person; his manner was plain and manly, and marked his active, enterprising character.[116]

Sultan was astute enough from the beginning to have taken possession of Muscat, Oman's chief port and centre of commerce, thereby overshadowing his brothers and dominating the country as a whole. From the mid-1780s it is in fact more correct to speak of the 'ruler of Muscat' than of Oman, though for practical purposes the two are nearly synonymous. An important transformation had occurred: Al Bu Sa'idi rule had become secular. It had abandoned the city of Rustaq and the interior, for Muscat and the mercantile coast. From the 1780s rulers of Muscat cease to have any pretensions to the religious office of Imam, and their attention shifts from internal Oman to commercial and political expansion overseas. This trait is very noticeable under Sultan, or to accord him his correct title, *Sayyid* Sultan, who in a short reign promoted a vigorous mercantile policy that had repercussions throughout the Gulf.

Sayyid Sultan, like other Al Bu Sa'idi rulers at this time, was essentially a merchant prince. He was himself the chief trader at Muscat and the port's customs receipts formed the principal part of his revenue. Under him the commerce of Muscat, and her shipping, continued to grow. At about the turn of the century the trade of Muscat was estimated at £1 million. She was also then said to possess 4 large square-rigged vessels, 15 ships of between 400 and 700 tons, 3 brigs, 50 dows and a similar number of large dinghies, besides some 250 dows and baghlas further south (based at Sur and Ja'lan) and a number of others which were being built and repaired in Bombay—perhaps 40,000–50,000 tons of shipping in all.[117] The growth of Omani trade and shipping began to worry certain British traders in India.

Sayyid Sultan's mercantile policy was both active and aggressive. He sought to foster diplomatic and commercial links with Mysore, Sind, British Bombay, Dutch Batavia, French Mauritius, Abyssinia, Yemen, Iran and elsewhere.[118] Early on he firmly established Omani power on the Makran coast by consolidating his position at Gwadar and annexing Chahbahar. Further west he secured from Iran the lease of the customs-farm at Bandar Abbas and apparently also gained ascendancy over nearby Iranian ports and islands:[119] this left Oman in control of the entrance to the Gulf and in a position to 'regulate' its trade.

Sayyid Sultan's ambitions occasionally brought him into conflict with Iran and Iraq, but more significant was his clash with the Utub of Bahrain: he eventually succeeded in occupying the island in 1801–2. He also continued the longstanding feud with the Qawasim of Ras al-Khaima, who threatened the country from the north and sought to compete with Oman for control over the entrance to the Gulf. And it was under Sayyid Sultan that treaty relations were, in 1798, first established with the British, who were worried at the time by the progress of French influence in the area. Following this treaty, and for much of the first decade of the nineteenth century, the English East India Company stationed a European Resident at Muscat, in addition to the Indian Broker it had long had in its employ there.

Although, by the time of Sayyid Sultan's murder in 1804, Omani shipping and commerce were pre-eminent at sea, the country was very vulnerable from inland and the north, whence, since c. 1800, the Wahhabis had been exerting pressure for the country to submit: they had raided the Batina, and Sayyid Sultan was forced to come to terms. Under Badr, who ruled briefly from 1804 till 1806, Saudi influence in Oman apparently intensified, and the ruler himself was accounted a Wahhabi.[120] Oman's power, and her control over her foreign possessions, likewise declined.

The successor to Badr in July 1806 was to remain in power for half a century: Sayyid Sa'id, protégé of the influential Mauza,[121] daughter of the first Al Bu Sa'idi ruler, was 16 when he acquired the throne by assassination:

After Saʿid and Badr, and those who were with them, had been seated in the fort for some time, the subject of swords and daggers was discussed ... Saʿid drew his sword and commenced threatening ... as if in fun. Suddenly, however, he stood up and struck Badr with it, the blow breaking the bone of his arm. Badr fled forthwith and threw himself from a window of the fort to the ground, exclaiming, 'Help, O men!' The men turned towards him, but Muhammad bin Nasir stopped them, saying, 'Let the descendants of the Imam do what they please to one another.' On hearing these words Badr mounted his horse and set off at full gallop, but on reaching the small coconut plantation of Nuʿman the wound in his arm overcame him, and he fell from his horse to the ground. The Sayyid Saʿid and his followers, who had gone in pursuit, then hurled several lances at him, one of which striking him in vital part his spirit took flight.[122]

When a child, in 1800, Sayyid Saʿid had received the model of a 74-gun ship as a present from the visiting British Envoy.[123] From the start, he recognized the importance of cultivating British friendship. It was a relationship valued too by Britain. A British naval officer was astonished to find the ruler seated on a chair behind a table when he met him at his palace in January 1819, describing him as,

extremely good-looking ... [of a] fair complexion, with dark handsome mustachios and beard, with an aquiline nose. His stature is that of about five feet ten inches in height, well made and proportioned, with the most agreeable and polite manner of any I have met with, Arabians or Persians. His dress was a white turban plain and without ornament, a white camel's hair robe not open in front, but made in the form of a long shift, his large wide white trousers of the same stuff, without any covering on his feet or ankles but his toes stuffed into a slight pair of brown slippers. The robe was bound close round the waist by a sash of fine white muslin, in which was stuck his yataghan with silver sheath and handle mounted with precious stones.[124]

Another officer in the 1830s was equally, if not more, struck by the ruler and his kind regard for the English, remarking as a further instance of the simple 'warmth of his affections', that he 'daily visits his mother, who is still alive, and pays, in all matters, implicit obedience to her wishes.'[125]

Oman under Sayyid Saʿid was still not a single nation in the modern sense of that word. Qais, and after him his son, ruled semi-independently at Suhar along the coast. Other lesser princes and tribal leaders were in a somewhat similar position each in their respective areas. Sayyid Saʿid was the legitimate successor of Sayyid Sultan, he controlled Muscat, the economic nerve centre of the country, together with its fleet and a small mercenary army, and he managed Oman's foreign relations. In terms of prestige, therefore, though early on, especially in the first decade of his rule, he may have controlled little beyond Muscat and the coast, there is no doubt that he was even then pre-eminent in Oman. His sway over the country at large was undoubtedly increased when, following the death of his self-willed relation the son of Qais in 1815, he appointed his own governor to Suhar, and likewise soon after dispossessed Imam Sa'id's family of Rustaq.

Opposition from tribal leaders and members of his own family, even the Ya'ariba, was complicated by the heavy Wahhabi involvement in the interior of Oman, which had begun at the turn of the century and which, at times, seemed to overlay pre-existing tendencies. Wahhabi influence, based at Buraimi, was strongest in the north-west of the country (the Dhahira). On a number of occasions Wahhabi forces swept through the country, raiding the Batina coast. In January 1808, it was reported that Sayyid Sa'id held little beyond the coastal territory of Muscat.[126]

The ruler, lacking the support of the interior tribes, many of whom had gone over to the Wahhabis, was generally speaking unable to combat the Saudi–Wahhabi power militarily, though on a number of occasions he tried. Ultimately, when he found himself sorely pressed, he would, like his father, come to terms with and pay contributions (zakat) to his foe. But he also reacted by seeking outside help: hence, in part, the British expedition against Ras al-Khaima in 1809–10, and a disastrous Omani–Persian joint assault on the Wahhabis in Oman in 1810–11.

But Sayyid Sa'id had a fourth option when confronted with Saudi–Wahhabi pressures, besides those of military resistance, seeking outside help and making terms; for he was generally able throughout to rely still upon Muscat's maritime supremacy. This enabled him to continue to pursue the main objectives of his father's policy in the Gulf. Sayyid Sa'id conducted expeditions against Bahrain in 1810, 1816 and 1828.[127] He intrigued amongst and repeatedly attacked the Qawasim of Ras al-Khaima, who, as before, appeared to threaten Oman's northernmost ports and her influence over the islands around the mouth of the Gulf.

Pressure from the Saudis was lifted after 1813, on account of the Egyptian expedition, and Sayyid Sa'id's control over the internal affairs of Oman seemed relatively more assured after 1816. It was not until the end of the following decade that Sayyid Sa'id diverted his main attention away from the Gulf to the development and re-establishing of Omani control in East Africa. By then, the situation in the Gulf itself had been profoundly changed.

vi The Qawasim

Lastly we come to the Qawasim, the main protagonists in this story. The intention here is not to deal at length with this people who inhabited what is today the northern United Arab Emirates. It is to be hoped that the nature of their society and their history will emerge better in the course of subsequent chapters. There are nevertheless a few points which deserve clarification at this point.

The term 'Qawasim' was employed by the British from the end of the eighteenth century to describe the total population of the seaports between Rams and Abu Hail in the present-day north-west United Arab Emirates; it was also held to embrace the population of Linga with other associated settlements and dependencies on the Persian coast and islands. Used in this broad sense, the term 'Qawasim' was strictly speaking always a mis-nomer, for the Qawasim proper are an Arab family, or small tribe, whose total numbers in all the territory of the United Arab Emirates at the start of the twentieth century amounted to just 60 individuals.[128]

The important point is that the Qawasim proper, both then and now, made up the ruling family in Ras al-Khaima and Sharja. In the late eighteenth and early nineteenth centuries these two city-states (more particularly the first) were the most powerful on the whole Rams–Abu Hail coast, and in consequence they dominated the other ports, settlements and peoples in the vicinity. Hence there arose the practice of describing the whole population of this coast as 'Qawasim', in recognition of that family's dominant political power in the area; whereas in fact they constituted but a small minority even in the two cities most closely associated with them. There are numerous examples from elsewhere of peoples eventually acquiring the name of a dominant family or tribe; though in the case of the Qawasim the process had scarcely begun when the British intervened.

The application of the term Qawasim to people who in some measure acknowledged the ascendancy of the true Qawasim who ruled the important port of Ras al-Khaima, was almost certainly not a British invention. At various times the word has certainly been used in precisely this fashion in north-west India, Iran, Iraq (?), Saudi Arabia and Oman.[129] This general usage will be followed in the present work; where it is intended to specify the true Qawasim and no others, this will be clear from the context. The term Qawasim is itself the plural noun from the adjective 'Qasimi', said to derive from the tribe's eponym, a certain Qasim. In addition to the small Qasimi family on the Rams–Abu Hail coast, there were far larger numbers of what was said to be the same tribe on the opposite Persian coast and, though the affinity is perhaps less sound, in Oman.[130] The usual pronunciation in the Gulf of the word Qawasim was Jawáassim, and this was in turn anglicized to 'the Joasmees'.

The principal seat of the Qasimi rulers during the later eighteenth and early nineteenth centuries was ever Ras al-Khaima. In the years 1797–1820 the main cities ruled directly by members of this family were Ras

al-Khaima and Sharja, on the Arabian coast, and Linga, on the Persian.
In addition, however, most of the Arabian coastal settlements between
Rams and Abu Hail were politically dominated by Ras al-Khaima, as
indeed was much of the Shimailiya,[131] although this latter was partly in
dispute with Muscat. On the Persian coast, the later important commercial
port of Linga was ruled by another branch of the Qasimi family together,
in effect, with a number of settlements in the immediate vicinity. Certain
other ports to the west, at least as far as Charak, also apparently recognized the Qawasim's preponderating influence.[132] The family likewise had
an interest in the island of Qishm.

It can be seen from this that the Qawasim, with their allies and dependants, straddled the entrance to the Gulf. All the above areas under
Qasimi influence, that is firstly the Rams–Abu Hail coast, secondly the
Shimailiya and thirdly Linga with part of the adjacent Persian coast and
islands, constituted the so-called Qasimi confederacy; but the loadstone of
this loose and elastic maritime combination was Ras al-Khaima and the
resources and close association of the seaports between Rams and Abu
Hail. It is with this 60-or-so-mile long stretch of coastline that the present
work is very largely concerned.

There is no obvious and convenient geographical name in Arabic for
the coastline between Rams and Abu Hail. At the start of the twentieth
century it seems the phrase 'Sahil Uman', or 'the coast of Oman', was
understood locally, but it probably described more of the coast than simply
that short northern stretch and, besides, contains an obvious ambiguity for
the modern reader. Another candidate might be the word 'Sir' which was
undoubtedly understood by some in the Gulf to refer precisely to this small
segment of coastline; but this meaning was probably not universal and,
moreover, runs counter to the fact that locally 'Sir' is held to describe a
twelve-mile long strip of fertile ground about Ras al-Khaima. In the present work 'Sir' will be accorded this latter meaning.[133] Other geographical
ambiguities will, it is hoped, be resolved by a glance at the maps.

The coastline between Rams and Abu Hail is low, unvaried and said to
have been 'indifferently planted with date trees.'[134] In the north, about Ras
al-Khaima, an imposing backdrop of hills follows the coastline, but these
gradually recede from view, eventually to disappear completely, as one
coasts southward. Caravan routes traced the shoreline as well as running
south to the important oasis of Buraimi and east across the mountains into
northern Oman. Otherwise the interior of this country is harsh desert,
with a few oases scattered here and there, before all is finally lost in the
unremitting Empty Quarter that opens up to the south-west.

The sea off these northern shores is shallow and, except for being
exposed to the north-west winds, not especially perilous.[135] The most

Plate 1. Engagement between a dozen or more Qasimi vessels and the Honourable Company's ship *Aurora*, which was escorting a baghla laden with treasure for Muscat, near the Tunbs about early January 1816. Oil-painting by Thomas Buttersworth (1768–1842). The design and scale of the attacking Arab vessels are not to be relied upon. For an account of this action, see note 30 on page 362.

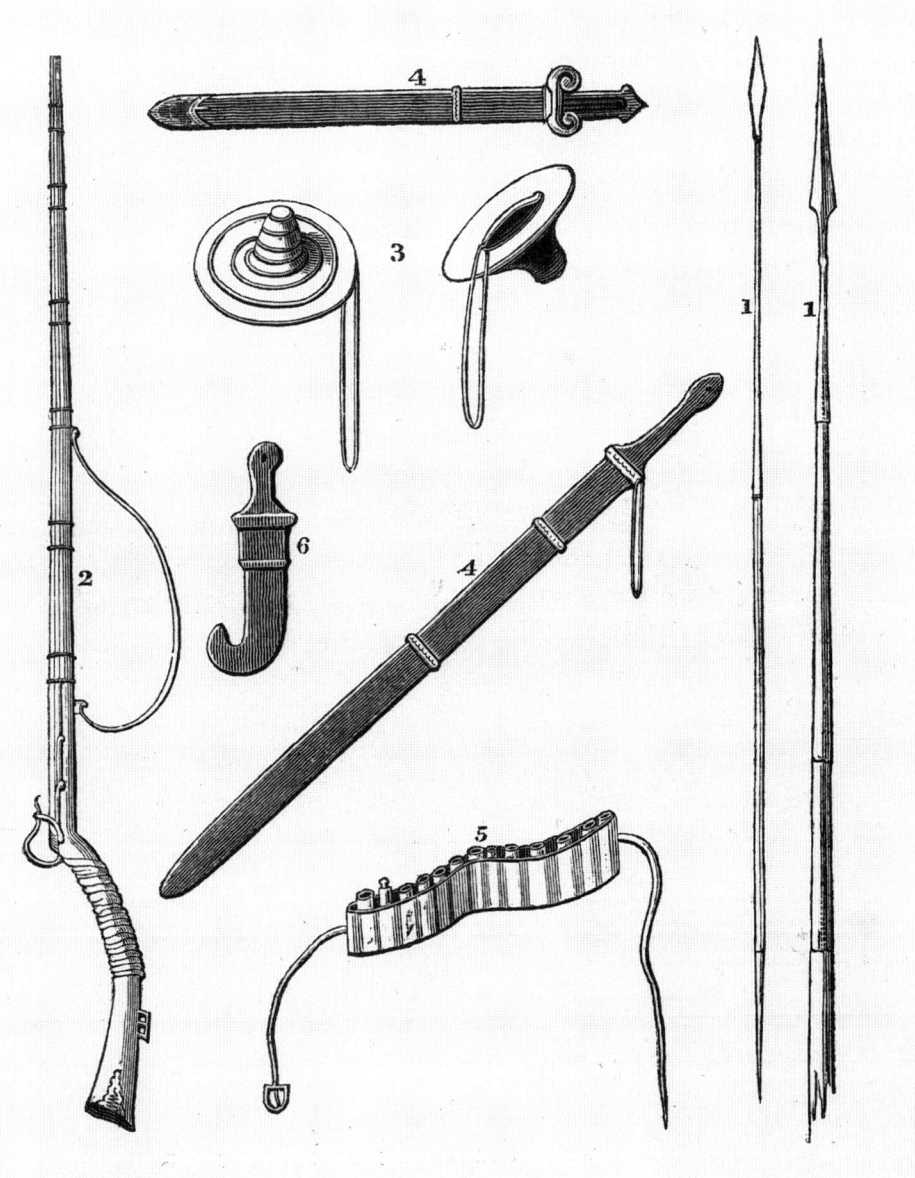

Plate 2. Arms of the Pirates in the Persian Gulf. Wood engraving of weapons carried aboard an Arab vessel in the lower Gulf in 1811: 1. Spears 2. Matchlock gun 3. Shields for the hand 4. Swords 5. Belt for cartridges 6. Khanjar or dagger. (Morier, A *Second Journey*)

Plate 3. *Top*: Model of a dow proper. *Bottom left*: A baghla (*c.* 300 tons). *Bottom right*: A battil (*c.* 70 tons). All three models exhibited at the Great Exhibition of 1851, probably constructed in the Bombay dockyard.

Plate 4. Cape Arubah (Ormara) in Makran, 1808: depiction of a dow proper. (Morier, A Journey through Persia ... in 1808 and 1809)

critical geographical feature of this stretch of coast was the frequency there of salt-water creeks and lagoons. Sometimes these creeks unite to form backwaters and mangrove swamps. Sometimes they extend to create sandspits, bars and quasi-islands. Although too shallow to afford sheltered anchorage for the larger European style of ship, these inlets were ideal for Arab vessels with their shallow draught. It was only natural, therefore, that maritime settlements should grow up along this coast, all the more important of them being situated on these advantageous creeks. Such were the cities of Ras al-Khaima, Sharja and the rest.

The Qawasim, therefore, were quintessentially a maritime power, possessed of considerable numbers of boats, and inhabiting a region strategically close to the mouth of the Persian Gulf. The general characteristics of society and life in the coastal settlements between Rams and Abu Hail were broadly speaking those described in the previous chapter: fishing, pearling and maritime commerce were the mainstays of life and the Arab city-state was the dominant political formation. The Qawasim traded widely within the Gulf, but also to western India, south Arabia and the Red Sea. Their numbers were probably small: the total settled population of the Rams–Abu Hail coast, with dependencies, was estimated at c. 50,000 at the start of the twentieth century. [136]

The headship of the individual communities on this coast tended to lie with one family or tribe, who might or might not be otherwise particularly numerous in that settlement; the tribal complexion of these parts was in fact very mixed. In practice the individual city-states, particularly the more important ones such as Ajman and Umm al-Qaiwain, were in many respects politically self-contained units despite the links between them. From Rams to Abu Hail the coast was nevertheless dominated by Ras al-Khaima. South of that, the coastline hinged about the Banu Yas rulers of Abu Dhabi who, though no match whatsoever for the Qawasim at sea, nevertheless had significant influence with the tribes of the interior. These two contiguous, but distinct, stretches of shoreline, the one centred about Ras al-Khaima, and the other about Abu Dhabi, were to act internally somewhat as counterpoise to each other: in the political language of Oman, which during this period still somehow embraced this whole area, the former were considered Ghafiri and the latter Hinawi.

Ras al-Khaima, or Julfar, as it was known until perhaps the mid-eighteenth century, [137] had been a recognized trading and maritime centre since the tenth century or before. The present site of Ras al-Khaima, occupied since the fifteenth century, may conceivably have become the chief city of Julfar around 1633 when the Portuguese were expelled thence by the Ya'ariba dynasty of Oman. [138] The Qasimi family, apparently a branch of the Huwala, begin to feature in the generally available historical sources as rulers of Ras al-Khaima in the earlier eighteenth century: most of our information, however, is confined to the second half of the century, and thereafter, when references to their activities become increasingly frequent.

During the Omani civil wars of the earlier to mid-eighteenth century, the Qawasim were, as noted, actively aligned with the Ghafiri faction. Later in the century, and during the early part of the next, Qasimi rulers continued to become involved in Oman's internal politics in support of various factions within the ruling family, and usually in opposition to the ruler of Muscat. Indeed, for much of this period, the Qawasim and Muscat were in a state of low-level undeclared war. The two powers at times came into conflict by land and frequently harassed the other's shipping. The Qawasim pursued their claims and ambitions in the Shimailiya and around the mouth of the Gulf. Muscat, in no wise less assertive and still cherishing certain old claims over much of Qasimi territory, recurrently attacked the Rams–Abu Hail coast, occasionally by land, but most often by sea. The rivalry and hostility between the two maritime powers of Muscat and the Qawasim, a contest in which Muscat always failed to subdue Ras al-Khaima though she managed the stronger hand, is a factor that lies behind much of what follows.

Qasimi influence may have been upon the ascendant in the late 1700s. At the close of the century the Qawasim of the Arabian coast succumbed to the political power and new doctrines of the Saudi–Wahhabi state. It seemed to some that during the first decade of the nineteenth century the Qasimi confederation had achieved new levels of confidence and strength. Trade and political advancement with the littoral powers and city-states of the Persian Gulf absorbed much of their energy.

They were also accused of piracy.

Part Two

Of the Evidence

CHAPTER FOUR

The Question of Piracy

We had scarcely recovered from the fright occasioned by the rocks, the insurrection, and the pirates, when early on the morning of the 28th [November 1816] we were suddenly disturbed by a loud call from our commander, to rise and defend ourselves, or we should all be murdered instantly. A summons so terrific, it may be guessed, was not long unanswered. We had always slept with loaded arms since the first alarm: but almost before I could rise and seize my pistols and my sword, (it being dark,) the door of my cabin was burst open; and, on rushing forth, I found myself attacked and grazed slightly in the side, by a sabre thrust. On closing and disarming my adversary, happily without any further hurt, he was discovered to be our unfortunate commander, who, his wits having entirely forsaken him, had imagined himself beset, and had alarmed us accordingly ... Renewed attempts of the same nature obliged us to confine him: we were not sorry, therefore, when on the 4th [December 1816] we reached Bushire, after running twice aground in the attempt.[1]

It is easy, at a space of nearly two centuries, momentarily to forget the terror which a fear of piracy, well grounded or no, could at times inspire. It is perhaps not wholly fanciful to suppose that the symptoms of melancholia so painfully manifested in the European captain of this Arab ship, as she sailed up the Gulf from Muscat and Bombay, had in part been aggravated, brought on even, by the stress of a seeming ever-present danger of attack by the Qawasim: the reality of this threat was certainly felt by the ship's company, for there had by this stage been no less than two false alarms upon the sighting of so-called 'pirate' vessels in the Gulf.

In the days of sail, and before the introduction of modern means of communication, a lone ship upon the ocean was a very vulnerable thing. Only good fortune or participation in a convoy could offer the individual, lightly armed, merchant vessel true security against the unwelcome attentions of a determined aggressor. Furthermore, prior to the spread of international law and the development of closer, more regular, contact between nation-states, there was often little chance of succour or redress for the victims of piracy after the event. The idea of Qasimi piracy in the Gulf was, at this time, especially unnerving for Europeans, Indians and certain others who sailed these waters precisely because the Qawasim, as a people, were so little known, and, moreover, because they had acquired a fearsome reputation for fanaticism and wanton cruelty: 'they were wont, after a capture,' it was subsequently asserted, 'to take the survivors to the fore part of the ship, and cut their throats upon the gunwale with their crooked knives, uttering a prayer the while'.[2]

At the same time, if piracy was terrifying for ordinary seafarers—and the more highly coloured the tales, the wider their dispersal—it was also a matter of potentially serious economic impact, and therefore all the more a matter of due state concern. Piracy had long been the subject of Britain's particular attention. In the following excerpt from a sentence reportedly delivered at a trial of English pirates on the Gold Coast in 1722, the President alludes to the special nature of the offence:

> The crime of piracy ... is of all other robberies the most aggravating and inhumane, in that being removed from the fears of surprise, in remote and distant parts, ye do in wantonness of power often add cruelty to theft.
>
> Pirates, unmoved at distress or poverty, not only spoil and rob, but do it from men needy, and who are purchasing their livelihoods thro' hazards and difficulties, which ought rather to move compassion; and what is still worse, do often, by persuasion or force, engage the inconsiderate part of them, to their own and families' ruin, removing them from their wives and children, and by that, from the means that should support them from misery and want.
>
> To a trading nation, nothing can be so destructive as piracy, or call for more exemplary punishment; besides the national reflection it infers, it cuts off the returns of industry, and those plentiful importations that alone can make an island flourishing.[3]

English law has long described the pirate as *hostis humani generis*, or 'the enemy of mankind'. Nor has it by any means been alone in this respect: the phrase itself derives from Cicero.[4] Two points arise from this. The first is the question of broad attitude: the term 'enemy of mankind' is, at its most basic, but a rhetorical device reflecting the view that the pirate is somehow execrable or 'beyond the pale'. The charge to the jury at a trial of pirates in South Carolina in 1718 maintained that,

> As to the heinousness or wickedness of the offence, it needs no aggravation, it being evident to the reason of all men. Therefore a pirate is called 'hostis humani generis', with whom neither faith nor oath is to be kept ... in our law they are termed 'brutes', and 'beasts of prey'.[5]

A second more practical issue also flows from the legal concept of *hostis humani generis*: 'that excellent civilian Dr Zouch, in his book De Jure Nautico, saith, "In detestation of piracy, besides other punishments, it is enacted, that it may be lawful for anyone to take their ships".'[6] But of course the real point about piracy here was not simply the sheer 'wickedness' of the offence, or the 'detestation' it might evoke, but the crucial fact that it was a crime commonly executed on the high seas, and so lay beyond the natural jurisdiction of any single state; this, in addition to the fact that it might often constitute a threat to trade, therefore tended to make piracy a matter of international, or at least, extra-territorial concern. Blackstone sets forth the philosophical basis for unilateral action against pirates outside a state's normal jurisdiction:

> The crime of piracy ... is an offence against the universal law of society; a pirate being ... hostis humani generis. As therefore he has renounced all the benefits of society and government, and has reduced himself afresh to the savage state of nature, by declaring war against all mankind, all mankind must declare war against him: so that every community hath a right, by the rule of self-defence, to inflict that punishment upon him, which every individual would in a state of nature have been otherwise entitled to do, for any invasion of his person or personal property.[7]

These things go toward explaining why it mattered so very much that the British had associated the Qawasim with piracy, and not some other category of behaviour. The use of the term 'pirate' was both a vilification of the Qawasim and a justification of prophylactic and punitive measures taken against them.

Yet was it actually piracy? Until recently, very few in the West, or even elsewhere, had ventured so far as to question whether it was anything but this. It was therefore almost always assumed that the standard, received version of events culled from British sources,[8] that, for example, set forth in Low's *History of the Indian Navy* (1877), was the correct one in this and other respects.[9]

But this picture has been called into question. Indeed it has become not uncommon for writers on the Gulf[10] to seek, in varying degrees, to revise the established interpretation of this episode of history. Whilst these authors tacitly concede that the Qawasim performed the acts of which they stood accused by the British—they generally do not address the issue of fact—they maintain that their motives were not piratical. In short, they argue that the Qawasim have been, at best, misunderstood by the British.

This reappraisal has not on the whole been based on a concentrated study of the whole range of primary British sources. A notable exception, and the most radical revision to date, is al-Qasimi's *The Myth of Arab*

Piracy in the Gulf: the author is himself a descendant of the original Qasimi rulers.[11] This writer has returned, as has no other for very many years, to the original British documents of the period preserved in the Bombay archives.[12] His approach is essentially to detail a number of specific acts of alleged piracy by the Qawasim, and seek to refute the evidence presented by the British regarding those individual cases. His basic contention is that the East India Company had commercial reasons for wanting to eliminate the power of the Qawasim. He alleges that the charge of piracy was consciously invoked to this end, and that the Qawasim, far from their motives simply being misunderstood by the British, were actually themselves the victims of a deliberate falsification of the truth: not solely, then, were their motives misrepresented as piratical, but *they did not actually do the acts*, the maritime attacks and incidents of sea-robbery, *of which they stood accused by the British*. This is no longer a question of interpretation, but one primarily of the evidence, and it is to this potentially serious charge that we must shortly first turn.

It seems, in fact, not unlikely that something approaching this perspective goes back some way in certain parts of the Gulf. On 13 April 1863, Lewis Pelly, British Resident in the Gulf, visited Kuwait, where, at a meeting with the shaikhs of the place, the discussion came round to Britain's anti-slaving activities in the region:

> One green young shaikh asked me why we took so much trouble to protect dows from piracy, while we ourselves took more dows than any other tribe? At this another shaikh asked if it were true that I was inquiring into the facts of our recent seizures? The old Chief sat silent, looking in at his nose with crunched features like the rings round the gnarl of an olive stump. All evidently awaited an explanation, which I did not accord.[13]

It is also worth remarking that the question of whether or not the Qawasim were pirates, as claimed by the British, besides being one of intrinsic historical interest, is also one of contemporary psychological concern in the Gulf countries where independence has so recently been achieved, and where there is still a pressing need to achieve a reconciliation with the past.

Before proceeding to the discussion of the evidence, it is as well, though we are not actually concerned here with legal niceties but with first principles, to bear in mind, as we proceed, what is taken to constitute piracy at law. At its most basic, nothing could be more straightforward: 'Piracy is only a sea term for robbery; piracy being a robbery within the jurisdiction of the Admiralty.'[14] But, as with some other aspects of the law, the certainty conveyed in this succinct definition becomes rather less marked as one delves further into the question of semantics. One point, however, is very clear: whilst a whole gamut of illegal acts of theft and violence have been at various times accounted piracy, the key linking factor in all of them has been not so much the criminal act itself, as the place where that offence is committed, or, most often, the sea.

But the most troublesome and intriguing area of the law of piracy, for our purposes, is that concerning the perpetrators themselves: what is the distinction between 'legitimate' acts during wartime and the actions of a privateer, for example, and a true act of piracy? Can, in fact, a *state* ever truly be said to have committed a piracy? There are two ways of answering this conundrum. The first is to consider the problem of motive: sometimes it is assumed by the law that a pirate true and proper must be acting out of malice and/or, more importantly, for private gain.[15] The second is to look at the issue of authority: it is sometimes said that a pirate is a ship acting without due authority from some recognized political entity. There were many, for example, who regarded the activities of German submarines during the Great War as piratical: the question of authority, however, decided the issue in their favour.[16] Still today neither of these two related points is at all clear,[17] and issues regarding the second ultimately would appear to be impossible of objective resolution in all, and particularly the more extreme, cases: who is to decide, in any given case, what is a 'legitimate' political motive, and who is to decide whether recognition should be accorded any one state or political grouping?

Although it would be very wrong to conclude from these observations that the idea of 'piracy' is purely relative—it is not, since there is probably almost universal agreement as to its basic ingredients—yet it is clear that the subject demands caution. Standards certainly do vary between individuals, peoples and different times. It is as well, then, to bear in mind Coleridge's dictum, given in response to the assertion that the privateers of Elizabeth's reign were mere pirates: 'No man is a *pirate*, unless his contemporaries agree to call him so.'[18]

★ ★ ★

It would be futile, in view of the prevailing controversy surrounding the issue of alleged Qasimi piracy in the Gulf, to embark upon a serious discussion of the events of these years, 1797–1820, without first seeking to establish what, if any, was the factual basis for those allegations. Immediately we are faced with a daunting problem: at a space of nearly two centuries, and with almost no primary sources to hand except for those produced by one party, the British, how can we be sure of establishing anything, let alone something approaching a complete picture, with true certainty and objectivity? The answer is, quite simply, that we cannot. When strictly defined, absolute certainty, like absolute truth, is seldom if ever to be encountered in matters historical. But this is very far from saying that, from a careful re-evaluation of the copious documentation that has come down to us, however imperfect that may be, nothing can be usefully achieved.

If we are to rescue anything of substance from the records as they stand, certain qualities and precepts would seem to be in order. The greater, within reason, the caution and scepticism employed in the early stages, the more convincing are likely to be the later results. Also required are certain of the attributes of the detective. The sources are there to be scoured for evidence that points to demonstrable fact, as opposed to sheer rumour, and, more important, for sound clues suggestive enough to help sketch in the inevitable remaining gaps in our knowledge: it is as if the ascertainable 'facts', such as they are, serve to supply the skeleton, whilst the clues, along with the application of simple reason, suggest the flesh, and, as for what remains, the vital outer layer of skin, hair and colouring—that tends to be left in some measure to the imagination and conjecture.

The next two chapters chronicle individual incidents at sea. They comprise an arrangement of the most certain events, supplemented by another of the most historically significant. Their aim is not, by any means, to chart every one of the large number of instances of alleged piracy in the Gulf area during these years, nor is it to attempt a broad or fundamental assessment of those events in context. It is simply to make an essay at identifying a reasonable, preliminary core of fact, almost a nucleus of certainty, for the otherwise bewildering events of these years. In the process, it may also be that a somewhat wider picture begins to emerge from the mists of obscurity and uncertainty; furthermore, if successful, the investigation may too yield a touchstone, of sorts, by which the worth of the remaining historical material may be tested. The principal sources on which this work is based are copies at Exeter University of British, or East India Company, documents relating to Gulf piracy, the originals of which are held in the Bombay Archives: much of this material is duplicated at the India Office Library in London.

There is, it should finally be said, a certain artificiality in what immediately follows. This is occasioned by the rather high level of historical proof that has been adopted, at least as regards the essentials. Most history tends quite rightly to be written on the basis of a standard of proof approximating to the 'balance of probabilities' test; it generally relates what the author regards as likely, rather than simply certain, to have been the case. To employ any more demanding standard of proof is, paradoxically, to run the risk of distortion, besides setting at naught the bulk of often precious historical sources. In the next chapter, however, a more stringent level of proof has been the guiding factor determining the selection. The result will inevitably be in one sense more, but also, it is hoped, in another sense less, partial.

A. Tableaux

CHAPTER FIVE

Incidents at Sea, in the Years 1797–1819, Which are Attested by Virtue of Admissions or Possession

One of the highest levels of historical proof is the 'admission'. The intention here is not admissions of piracy as such, which it would be most unreasonable to expect to find, but rather of some acknowledgement by its author of the material act itself; in other words, some acknowledgement of the bare bones of the incident, such as the fact that a ship was indeed attacked or its cargo seized by a particular group. This is, of course, very different from saying that the 'acknowledged act' should rightly be considered piracy or some other form of behaviour, legitimate or no: such a judgement requires consideration of the motive and the context, and these things, like the mind of a man, are seldom susceptible of rigorous proof. A second subsidiary criterion of proof that has also helped to produce the following selection is that of 'possession'. This indicates, in the main, that a ship or its contents were, or had been, in the acknowledged or proven possession of persons in the Gulf other than the obvious legal owner. This, again, is by itself no proof of piracy or otherwise.

It almost goes without saying, given the fact that communications between the British and the Qawasim in this period were so fleeting and so few, that the criteria of selection here adopted are scarcely likely to yield a great many concrete maritime incidents. Those, however, that they do are not devoid of interest.

i Vessels in Distress

(1) The *Hector*, 26 April 1803
(2) The *Ahmed Shah*, 11 July 1814

The Honourable Company's (HC) brig *Ariel*, of 10 guns and 159 tons, was built on a deep-waisted, chest-like design, of a class known in the Royal

Navy as 'coffins' or 'deaths'. Now five days out from Basra, she had encountered nothing but southerlies on her passage southward. On the night of 17 March 1820 she found herself to the south-east of Kharg Island, beating against a south-easter under double-reefed topsails. Shortly after midnight the wind shifted without warning. A terrible squall struck, accompanied by thunder and lightning.[1]

> As I looked up the vessel heeled, the water came rushing over the larboard gunwale, the launch went over the side, and at the same time I heard a crash above me, which must have been the mainmast. At this time I heard a horrid shriek, and found myself below water. All this must have taken place in less than a minute and a half from the first coming on of the squall. On coming to the surface I found myself among pieces of boards, and heard a few men around. I, however, felt myself irresistibly pulled below the water, and went to the depth of three or four fathoms. It was the vortex formed by the sinking vessel. On reaching the surface a second time, and swimming a little, I saw a canoe bottom upwards, to which I made, and got upon it ... All else was now quiet, except the tossing of the waves, and the piercing cries of a little boy.[2]

The canoe, one used by officers for duck shooting upon the Shatt al-Arab, fortunately enabled four men to reach the island of Kharg:

> After walking two or three hours along the beach, we arrived at the town, and were immediately taken to the Shaikh. He gave us a room in his house, and supplied us with what clothes and provisions he had, for the island is very poor. We remained there three days, and during that time received every attention and kindness we could expect.[3]

Out of the crew of 83 no others survived.

In accordance with standard practice in these circumstances, the kindness and liberality shown by the Shaikh of Kharg towards the crew of one of its ships was duly rewarded[4] by the Government of Bombay. It seems, in fact, to have been the norm for local shaikhs along Iran's southern coast to treat British subjects, whose vessels were not infrequently in distress in these waters, with respect and attention. The same, too, was most often the case for the ships themselves, with their sometimes valuable cargoes. Such, for example, was the exemplary conduct of Shaikh Barakat of Charak towards the country-ship *Shrewsberry*, near the turn of the century, for which service, he was suitably rewarded by her captain.[5] But in a handful of cases British vessels met with less welcome treatment on Iran's lower Gulf coast.

In the early months of 1803,[6] the HC packet *Alert* was forced by a storm onto the island of Shaikh Shu'aib. Shortly after, around 500 islanders allegedly swarmed down and made away with the treasure (pearls, specie) she had on freight, belonging to the merchants of Bushire and Basra. A few days after this, we are told that Shaikh Rahma of Nakhilu arrived at the scene and proceeded to strip the vessel of what remained, 'leaving them only two bags of their own rice as provision for 30 or 40 people'.[7]

Whatever the precise details of this incident, there is little doubt that it represents a classic instance, if not of wrecking in the grim sense in which vessels were actively lured to their doom for the purposes of plunder—there is no evidence for this practice in the Gulf at this time—but rather of the despoiling by coastal communities of wrecks that happened to come their way. It seems likely that in most cases the lion's share of this inter-mittent harvest would fall, not to villagers and minor shaikhs, but to the more powerful shaikh–governors of Iran's southern littoral, such as, in this case, the Shaikh of Nakhilu.

There is little doubt that the maltreatment of British vessels on these shores was prima facie less likely than that of other, less powerful, nations and peoples. Furthermore, according to their commercial treaty of January 1801,[8] Britain and Iran had each expressly agreed to assist damaged vessels belonging to the other, as well as to help in the recovery of goods wrecked upon their coasts. The plunder of wrecks was almost certainly therefore more common than the British records, with their emphasis on British, especially Company, property, would indicate. In 1803 Shaikh Rahma of Nakhilu is supposed to have asserted 'the right of every country to the property which might be shipwrecked on its coasts'.[9] In this he had some support from an albeit corrupt Persian official, and even the British Resident apparently questioned whether the practice could feasibly be sup-pressed on the Persian coast when it was still prevalent, despite their efforts, in north-west India.

There was a material difference between instances such as that of the *Alert*, where, before its plunder, the vessel was wrecked beyond recovery, and others where this was not the case. These latter were felt by the British to edge rather closer to the yet distinct crime of piracy.

The case of the *Ahmed Shah*,[10] like that of the *Hector*, another vessel under British colours and command, is unusually well documented because it involved the loss of a good deal of East India Company property. The *Ahmed Shah*, Captain Herriman, had been due to visit Basra and Calcutta, but plans had been unexpectedly changed so as to have her convey the ever-important Company's mail, the packet, straight to Bombay. Despite the inconvenience, this commission yielded the sum of 3,000 rupees (around £300), which compares not unfavourably with, for example, the

c. 2,000 rupees Captain Herriman received as freightage on c. 30 tons of the Company's ordinary merchandise consigned to India.[11] In consequence of this self-same decision, however, possibly less than competent Arab Seacunnies (steersmen) had been taken on in haste, and the opportunity had been lost to write to India to arrange insurance.

Soon after departing from Bushire the weather deteriorated. A violent gale set in. This began to take its toll of the mares being carried for the Company to Calcutta: everyone on board who was capable, set to in a desperate attempt to sew slings for them. Just past midnight, on 11 July, the vessel struck on the northernmost part of Qais Island. At 3 a.m., the whole crew being at prayers, the Captain could not get a man aloft to furl the topsails: 'She stove in the counter, the water then making fair breech fore and aft in the tween decks. At 5 she filled up to the tween-deck's hatches, and began to labour very hard.' Then, 'expecting she would go every moment to pieces,' the Captain had the mizen and main masts cut away: 'she now came stern to, and lay more easy.'[12]

There is no doubt, then, that when Shaikh Abdullah bin Ahmad of Charak came aboard later that day, the *Ahmed Shah* was very severely damaged. The Shaikh assured the Captain 'by his God and indeed in the strongest terms' that he would assist in any way he could. The Captain therefore entrusted him with the Bushire merchants' 38 bundles of treasure, with other articles, for 'safekeeping';

> but we soon had occasion to find out that our visitors was not so honest as we were, at first, led to expect they were; as our trunks and chests was broken open before our faces, and property of every description distributed amongst the visitors. In vain was it to remonstrate to the Shaikh; no notice whatever was taken of it.[13]

The Captain managed obstinately to retain the cherished government packet about his person. On the 13th, the Captain and crew were dropped off on the mainland and allowed to make their own way back to Bushire. The merchant passengers from Bushire, however, had been detained, and it was reported 'that the Shaikh had been beating the merchants very severely in order to make them deliver over their money to him, and that one of the merchants had been very severely cut with a cutlass.'[14]

It later appears that part of the Company's property, which included sulphur, gum ammoniac, guns and mares, was eventually recovered; so too was the Persian merchants' specie, less a present to the Shaikh and a 10 per cent reward to the Residency's negotiator, Mr Henshaw.[15] Shaikh Abdullah may have been induced to relent by the advice of Britain's sympathizer, the ruler of Asalu,[16] and by the fear of a ban on his vessels visiting British Indian ports.[17] But still not all the Company's goods were restored. In December 1816, during a visit to Charak by the Resident, the Shaikh voiced his exasperation at continued British pressure for reparation:

> he replied he had nothing more to deliver up, and if he had, should not do it, and indeed was sorry for what he had already given up; that he desired we would leave his port, nor was he at all afraid of our power.[18]

The Resident noted the presence at this meeting of envoys from Ras al-Khaima:[19] the Qawasim were also supposed, according to the Shaikh, to have visited the wreck of the *Ahmed Shah* in 1814, two days after she grounded, when they allegedly made off with part of the spoils, including some guns and 14 of the Honourable Company's mares.[20] The possibility of further squabbles over the wreck had led him to burn it as soon as they left.

The case of the *Hector*,[21] a decade earlier, in which Shaikh Rahma of Nakhilu had seized, amongst other things, 850 bales of the Company's cloth, was very similar in its general outline. But it differed in that the cargo was appropriated with less guile and more violence, when the vessel herself was almost undamaged and wanted but some assistance in getting once again afloat; though it should also be said that there was a rumour in Bombay that the ship had been purposely grounded.[22] Captain Becher recalled that,

> the Seacunnies and Topasses and servants were all turned out of the ship, who said there was then about 100 [50] Arabs, all armed, on board, plundering the ship of her cargo, stores etc. etc. they could get, and that the government despatches were cut open and thrown about my cabin ... I had the mortification to see the cargo some of it brought on shore, and some carried away in boats to other ports. Against all which plundering and loss I do hereby protest.[23]

Shaikh Rahma later allegedly proposed to the Bushire Residency Assistant to restore half the property, saying 'he would sell him the other half, on very moderate terms'.[24]

British efforts for the return of the Company's valuable shipment were unrelenting. Nakhilu was visited by three vessels of the Bombay Marine and pressure exerted on the Persian authorities at Shiraz and Bushire. But only when the Shaikh's son was taken hostage in 1806 by the Governor of Bushire, was the ruler partially forthcoming.[25]

Three things are noticeable in the *Hector* and *Ahmed Shah* incidents. In the first place the difficulties encountered in recovering British goods resulted from, and demonstrated, the very poor degree of authority and control exercised by Iran over its southern ports. In the second place, it is also apparent from these cases that the Company attached very great importance to any pecuniary loss, particularly one affecting its prestige: there were even suggestions, from Captain David Seton at Muscat, of an expedition being launched against Nakhilu to ensure reparation. Finally, though these events did not constitute piracy, they did help prejudice some British officers, such as Bruce at Bushire, against the Iranian ports of the lower Gulf, which were sometimes loosely described as 'Qasimi': the vague link between the *Ahmed Shah* incident and the Qawasim has already been mentioned. The Shaikh of Nakhilu was also believed by the British to be somehow 'connected' with Ras al-Khaima.[26]

ii   Inter-State Conflict

(3) British vessel, 8 December 1800
(4) The *Akaub*, 24 May 1801
(5) c. Nine Janaba vessels (the Suri fleet), 7 January 1806
(6) The *Shannon*, 29 October 1807
(7) The *Sultana*, c. end of September 1814
(8) The *Darabiya*, January 1815
(9) Twelve Qasimi trading-vessels, c. January 1817

At the outset of 1806, a large convoy of vessels, belonging to the Omani port of Sur, was making its way down the Gulf from Basra. This was very possibly the fleet which annually brought coffee up from Yemen to the markets of southern Iraq.[27] Approaching the mouth of the Gulf, rather than proceed upon its course to Oman, the Suri fleet was, it seems, 'persuaded' by the Qawasim, possibly with some naval assistance from Mulla Hasan,[28] Shaikh of Qishm, to put into Ras al-Khaima. Thereupon, nine[29] of the vessels, those belonging to the Janaba tribe at Sur, were plundered by the Qawasim in pursuance of a pre-existing feud.

Amongst the large amount of merchandise and treasure thereby detained at Ras al-Khaima in early 1806, was a significant amount owned by Basra merchants, together with other items, the property of British traders: this latter included some pearls belonging to an Arab merchant of Surat, which were handed back[30] in May of that year by Sultan bin Saqr, the Qasimi chief.

This detention by the Qawasim of the Omani fleet[31] was both an episode in the longstanding hostility between the two neighbouring powers, and the product of tribal feuding at Sur.[32] An event of this seriousness, though rather exceptional, clearly had the potential for disrupting the commercial life of the region. In retaliation for the detention of Basra property, the Ottoman authorities reportedly impounded 32 vessels belonging to the Qasimi port of Linga;[33] the Suri fleet hesitated, despite British mediation, to return to Oman out of fear of its ruler; and later, in 1807, we hear of a violent, but unsuccessful, assault on the Janaba at Sur by a large Qasimi fleet in furtherance of their feud.

But the real point to note here is that the detention of British goods was purely incidental to the main event. Even though the relatively speedy release of British property caught up in this seizure was the exception, and this was not the case with the other merchandise, whose fate is not recorded, yet it still seems inappropriate to describe this complex incident as piracy. It was in fact but one episode in a long-running conflict between local powers in the Gulf; only if, like Captain Seton, one was tempted to take the part of Muscat in the dispute,[34] could this episode be said to 'tell' against the Qawasim.

The Suri affair was in the first instance the result of tribal feuding at Sur. A few years earlier an interesting cluster of incidents occurred at the agency of the Suwaidi tribe (the Sudan),[35] which owed most to the commercial ambitions of the ruler of Muscat himself. In a private letter describing one of these clashes, off Ras al-Hadd, an Indian passenger on board the *Akaub* writes that,

> On the ... 19th of May [1801] we arrived at the isle of Qishm. As we had had very bad weather, the rudder required repairs, which we accordingly effected there. And, setting out again, we were soon encountered by a Suwaidi baghla, which, attacking us, one of our lascars was killed and several were wounded, of whom the Nakhuda [master], by name Qais, had six wounds ...
>
> The Suwaidis says that Sayyid Sultan [of Muscat] had ordered them to take the botella[36] and that they had accordingly done so. The Suwaidis have retained with themselves the Firinghee [European] mariner, and have by the strokes of swords driven us into the seas.[37]

The *Akaub*, en route from Bombay to Basra carrying an ever-important English packet, belonged to the Persian merchant Aqa Muhammad Nabi, though she sailed under British colours. Six months earlier a very similar incident had taken place when, off Qais, the Sudan had boarded a botella that belonged to the Bushire Resident Mehdi Ali Khan, and which was conveying Lieutenant William Bruce, with the packet, to Bombay: they 'turned Mr Bruce and the crew out of the boat with only the clothes on their backs.'[38] A third vessel, carrying British gunpowder to Basra, also reportedly fell into the hands of the Suwaidi leader, Nasir,[39] at this time and it is implied that a good many Arab and other non-European vessels shared the same fate.

When approached over the seizure of Mehdi Ali Khan's dow, the ruler of Muscat expressed regret that it had happened, 'but it was', he said, 'owing to the ignorance of the commander of the Sudan boat, who is a boy of 13 or 14 years of age':[40] the boat had been captured in the mistaken belief that she belonged to Bushire, with which port Muscat was then at odds, in part, over Bahrain.

But the underlying cause of the Sudan's seizures was a duty (of 2.5 per cent) which Muscat had 'thrust down the throats of the natives of the Gulph.'[41] Some vessels[42] understandably chose to avoid such an impost. In an attempt, therefore, to foster the customs revenues of Muscat, Sayyid Sultan had recently introduced a policy of actively compelling all non-European vessels to touch there en route from India to the Gulf; those that did not would be liable to attack by the Sudan, a tribal group of a few hundred men[43] who had attached themselves to Muscat and settled on Hormuz.[44] This practice recalls, somewhat, the compulsory 'pass' system earlier employed by the Portuguese in these seas. The British, though they understood that the Sudan were acting with the licence of their patron the ruler of Muscat, still, from their view, chose to regard them as pirates. Under pressure, the tribe quitted Hormuz with their captures and prisoners in mid-1801, when they transferred to Bida' (Doha), on the coast of Qatar, and attached themselves to the Wahhabi cause.[45] The Duncan,[46] with a small detachment of sepoys, was therefore sent in company with Sayyid Sultan and Omani troops against this port in December 1801, but the expeditionary force was militarily too weak to achieve even a successful landing.

The three remaining incidents in this category are focused acts and simple seizures: these are probably more representative of the dominant pattern of operations than the more unusual, or exaggerated, Suri and Sudan episodes. The most typical form of maritime disorder in the Gulf was arguably a form of low-level and persistent predation practised by some, upon the seaborne traffic of other, Gulf powers. Its motivation was, in varying proportions, both economic and political. An example of this would be the capture by two Qasimi vessels of the baghla Darabiya while she lay at anchor in Mughu roads:[47] it was reported that the majority of the Darabiya's crew, those who chose not to swim to safety,[48] but to remain on board and defend her, were 'all massacred'.[49] The vessel had belonged to the ruler of Muscat, the Qawasim's traditional enemies; and Hasan bin Rahma of Ras al-Khaima was later happy to release the East India Company's sulphur and horses,[50] also taken in the attack.

Sound intelligence (from the people of Mughu) was supposed to have laid the groundwork for the assault on the Darabiya, as it was in each of the following cases.

What befell the *Shannon*,[51] out from Bombay, was soon after recounted by her commander in a petition to David Seton, the Muscat Resident:[52] on 28 October 1807,

> I was obliged to come to at Shaikh Shu'aib Island, where I thought to be in quite safety, till such time the wind abated. But then we being short of water, I and the boats here went on shore to water, but, finding it very hard for us to water where there is no water to be had, we came on board again. And on the 29th, the wind and weather being the same, I did not start from my anchoring place, for I thought to be quite clear of the enemy's hands. But the same day at sunset, three boats set off from Shaikh Shu'aib Island, standing close to the wind to the northward. We then begun to weigh, but the wind and weather being very boisterous, we thought it best to remain where we were. At 6.30 p.m. they boarded us and killed nine of our men.
>
> When they were within musquet-shot, we hailed them, that the vessel was English vessel. Nor much more did we fire at them, for we being very badly armed and manned; at the same time I well knowing that they [the Qawasim] have taken their oaths at your presence never to take a vessel under English colours. Therefore we did not fire at them, nor much more make sail on account of the wind and weather; at the meantimes she being a bad sailer, for the [Qasimi] boats do outsail us with only their jibs set.
>
> On the 31st they cut the cable and made sail for Hormuz. On the 3rd Nov. we arrived there. There they landed all her cargo and plundered the vessel out of all her stores, and turned all hands of us on shore in attention for to sell. But providence being so much in our favour, that Sultan [bin Saqr al-Qasimi] having[53] arrived from Ras al-Khaima and brought a small force against them, that they were not able to do anything farther. And he took possession of us on the 15th Nov. Then we sailed for Ras al-Khaima, where we remained for some time.
>
> The Sultan wanted to lay my heart to find out if I was the son of an Englishman, and if the vessel was under English colours. I told him I really was the son of an Englishman and she being under English colours. This was the answer I first gave him and the same I last made. On the 22nd Nov., he called us on shore and said that he perfectly knows that she belongs to the Persian Embassador, but he only gives her up to us on account of I being the son of an Englishman and the word of honour they gave you, Sir.
>
> I have likewise informed you, Honoured Sir, that we are in the miserablest state that ever God has made in this world, without a single farthing, nor a stick of clothes more than what we had on.
>
> When we were near Bandar Abbas [before the attack], three boats were constantly on the same tracks that we use[d] to be in, till such time we anchored at Shaikh Shu'aib Island, and the boats anchored between the island and mainland. The same day arrived a dow from Muscat which was boarded by them, and on board the said dow was

four horse-keepers that came round with us from Bombay, which was left back. They did belong to the Persian Embassador, who, we understand by the pirates, that they gave them intelligence that the vessel and property belongs to His Excellency the Persian Embassador, and being badly armed. The pirates, they said if they have had not received that intelligence by them, they would never have had attempted to take us, for they was quite afraid.

Honoured Sir, I beg you would take it into your consideration at this present situation to assist us with little remedy. By so doing, will highly oblige your most obedient and humble servant, John Haverson.

It transpires that the three vessels which tracked the *Shannon* from Bandar Abbas and eventually took her, with another, at Shaikh Shu'aib, were under the control of Rashid bin Humaid al-Nu'aimi (of the Na'im tribe), the chief of Ajman. This appears to have been an independent venture; whilst the swift and authoritative manner in which the Qasimi leader relieved these, the original captors, of their prize, at the same time indicates that, in the event, the power of Ajman was unquestionably subordinate to that of Ras al-Khaima.[54] And a third stratum of influence was, according to Sultan bin Saqr,[55] also dimly at work here: Rashid retained the Bushire and Muscat property he captured in the vessel on account of Wahhabi support.

The case of the *Shannon* is quite revealing of contemporary official attitudes at Bombay: because the ship had had no right whatsoever to fly British colours[56]—the Na'im's intelligence was correct in this regard—and the Company property involved was negligible, the Qawasim escaped quite without censure. Another vessel, the *Sultana*, was likewise carrying a British pass to which she was in no way entitled, when she fell at the end of September 1814 to Rahma bin Jabir, the Jalahima chief.[57] The Government of Bombay therefore took the view here that it was not advisable to 'interfere between Rahma bin Jabir and those with whom he is in a state of hostility'.[58] But the case was, nonetheless, from another point of view, a serious one.

The *Sultana* belonged to the Basra merchant, Muhammad bin Rizq, an influential and successful man, whose family had long enjoyed cordial relations with the British Residency there.[59] In autumn 1814, the vessel had been hired by Dr Gideon Colquhoun, the Acting Resident and friend of Ibn Rizq, to take the belongings of 3–4 British officers thence to Bombay. At the same time, he took pains to let it generally be known that the craft was carrying British goods and would be part of a British convoy. In consequence, it is said, the usual compliment of 80 picked crew was, out of confidence in the British connection, reduced to just under 60, a circumstance allegedly made known to Rahma through his 'regular spies' in the port of Basra.[60] When the *Sultana* arrived off Hanjam Island, she became detached from the convoy and was approached by two small battils. They hailed her, and were answered, 'that the baghla belonged to Ibn Rizq and that she was laden with English horses'.[61] It may be, though accounts differ, that the *Sultana* fired first[62]—a warning shot to keep them off: Dr Colquhoun maintained that 'no person acquainted with the system of boarding practised by the Qawasim would ever allow any boats to approach too near in the Gulph. Such has at all times been my warning and advice to the commanders of merchant-ships.'[63] An engagement commencing, the two battils were reinforced by the body of Rahma's fleet. Ninety per cent, or all but six, of the *Sultana*'s crew perished in the action.

In explanation of this attack, Rahma bin Jabir wrote to Dr Colquhoun of his 'irreconcilable enmity to the Turks and those under their government'.[64] This was in keeping with the generally cool and vindictive character of the man. It also echoed the very sentiments of the Wahhabi leader, Abdullah bin Su'ud, who positively supported him in this action.[65] Of all the individual tribal leaders in the Gulf at this time, Rahma bin Jabir had the fiercest and most enduring reputation as a pirate, though he always managed, unlike the Qawasim, to avoid the wrath of the British. He first announced the fate of the *Sultana* to the Bushire Resident in the following bland terms: 'It has pleased God that I should capture the baghla belonging to Shaikh bin Rizq abreast of Ru'us al-Jibal, bound from Basra to Bombay, having on board 46 horses, but her bill of lading stated 47'.[66] As he then explained in the rest of this letter, he was careful to preserve the British horses captured in the *Sultana* and have them despatched to Bombay, though at a cost to the owners; other items, however, mathematical instruments, antiques and other paraphernalia,[67] were later somewhat curiously observed for sale in the Muscat bazar.

Rahma bin Jabir was an agile politician and his allegiances shifted wildly. The success of his efforts not to offend the British was once more demonstrated in February 1817 when, in the course of his stay at Bushire, Rahma was described by the British Resident, William Bruce, as 'much flattered' by his 'personal attention and kindness', as well as by Bombay's assurances that 'while he continues to conduct himself inoffensively, the friendly disposition of the British government will be always manifested towards him and his tribe'.[68] Rahma bin Jabir had just returned from cruising south of Bahrain, where he had attacked 12 Qasimi vessels trading with Bahrain, carrying goods that allegedly included British plunder from three Surat vessels[69] in return for dates, rice and the like. Rahma sank four of the boats, broke up another four for want of manning and finally arrived at Bushire with those that remained. He was in fact meditating a return to the same hunting grounds, just as Bruce was writing the above.

iii The Structure of Qasimi Authority

(10) Bruce's baghla, December 1814
(11) The *Omid*, or *Hubbullah*, 1815
(12) British baghla, by August 1816
(13) British vessel, *c.* early–mid-September 1819

> Yesterday, to my utter astonishment, the Nakhuda of my boat
> suddenly made his appearance in a wretched plight, without clothes
> and almost starved to death. On my asking him what was the cause of
> his being in such situation, he told me ...[70]

But before recounting the gist of what he had to say,[71] it is necessary, in
order to understand the significance of what had happened, to go back 3½
months: early in October 1814, a Qasimi envoy had arrived at the British
Residency in Bushire, bearing letters from the chief of Ras al-Khaima,
Hasan bin Rahma, and his overlord Abdullah bin Su'ud. This was the
first contact between the British and the Qawasim since their meeting,
under rather different circumstances, during the first British expedition
against Ras al-Khaima in 1809/10. The Resident, William Bruce, saw it as
an opportunity to make up for the major shortcoming of that operation by
concluding a treaty with the Qawasim. The result was a provisional
agreement, stipulating mutual respect for each other's shipping, signed at
Bushire on 6 October 1814.

But the terms had to be ratified, and Bruce had certain other business
to put before the Qawasim.[72] He therefore purchased a baghla and fitted
her out, at a cost of somewhere under 2,000 rupees (*c.* £200), with the
intention of sending her across to Ras al-Khaima. He was impelled to
this somewhat costly expedient since, out of fear of the Qawasim, no boat
could be found at Bushire willing to make the journey. In view of what
ensued, it may have been significant that there were no Europeans in
evidence on board the baghla.[73] Bruce was optimistic.

On 21 December, Bruce's craft pulled out of Bushire and, a few days
later, caught up with Sultan bin Saqr, the Qasimi ruler of Sharja—he had
lost his position at Ras al-Khaima to his half-cousin Hasan bin Rahma[74]—
at Tunb Island. An event occurred here which, though trivial, came across
as a piece of effrontery. After exchanging friendly letters, Sultan bin Saqr
forcibly abstracted 80 frazils (roughly 1 ton)[75] of dates from the baghla and
sent her on her way. Sultan bin Saqr later jocularly dismissed the occurrence as a mere nothing, which, if not purely rhetoric, might reveal something of relative attitudes: 'You call this plunder! The true plunderer does
not leave a large quantity and take only a small amount. I took this trifle
out of my high regard for you, and I am indebted to you for it.'[76]

The ill-starred vessel resumed once more her earnest mission and arrived at Ras al-Khaima on the 27th. In the evening a vessel put off from shore and suggested she stand in so as to reach a safer anchorage. Putting out a towboat, therefore, the baghla suddenly found herself boarded by 20 armed men, who proceeded to clear the decks with their sabres. The crew, or all but three lascars and two Hindus who were left behind, managed to swim to the towboat and in that small craft they now escaped northwards: they pulled along the shore to Bukha, where they were at last hospitably received, and provided for, by the Shaikh.

The captors of Bruce's baghla were, according to Hasan bin Rahma, a party from the Na'im tribe. We do not know if these were Na'im living in Ras al-Khaima, or elsewhere such as their main coastal settlements at Hira and Hamriya,[77] or even possibly whether this was merely a vessel which answered to the Nu'aimi ruler of Ajman. But although it seems improbable that the seizure was anything but the initiative of the Na'im, the captors were still under the overall authority of Hasan bin Rahma: hence his ability to restore the vessel to Bruce when required. This incident draws attention to the fact that, unlike smaller tribal leaders such as Rahma bin Jabir of the Jalahima, with their unified command, the Qawasim had varying degrees of control and authority over a number of different tribal groups. Hasan bin Rahma was avowedly responsible for this action, though he did not, we presume, order it: how, or indeed whether, he might have benefited from such an action under normal circumstances we can only surmise.

The whole incident could be described as farcical were it not so tragic: this was the last occasion before the second expedition when an agreement might easily have been achieved. It recalls an even more trivial, but almost equally ill-timed, seizure of a Company dependant's vessel[78] in 1819, only a few months before the second attack on Ras al-Khaima:[79] the capture, though soon perforce rectified, had been made by one of five vessels accompanying last-ditch envoys from Hasan bin Rahma to the British.[80] The crew of another, local, baghla also, in fact, alleged they had been run on shore near the Asses Ears by these five; though unconfirmed, their report claims the attackers were on that occasion finally beaten off with the ready assistance of neighbouring villagers.[81]

During the second decade of the nineteenth century, the Qasimi command was no longer monolithic, as it had appeared during the first. Sultan bin Saqr al-Qasimi had succeeded his father Saqr bin Rashid (ruled c. 1777–1803) as ruler of Ras al-Khaima (and Sharja) in 1803. He governed Ras al-Khaima and dominated the whole Rams–Abu Hail coast, like his father, relatively unchecked until late 1808. At this juncture, Saudi–Wahhabi influence in the country, present since the turn of the century, increased markedly, and a year later the ruler was deposed and put in confinement at Dir'iya. When next we hear of him, in 1813 and thereafter, it is simply as a much weakened ruler of Sharja, one who nevertheless maintained good relations with his first cousin,[82] the ruler Muhammad bin Qadib across the water at Linga. The principal, and third, Qasimi ruler in the second decade, was therefore Sultan bin Saqr's other cousin Hasan bin Rahma, who as ruler of Ras al-Khaima and effective candidate of the Wahhabis, easily dominated the ports north of Sharja and was the acknowledged touchstone of Qasimi power. Sultan bin Saqr remained excluded from authority and the headship of Ras al-Khaima (with the whole coast) until immediately after the British expedition of 1819/20, when he regained his patrimony once more; he retained it thenceforward unbroken until his death in 1866.

Issues concerning the structure of Qasimi authority—one ruling family, three major ports, numerous other lesser chiefs, tribal groups and settlements (on three shores) in varying degrees of subjection to them—also enter into the remaining pair of incidents in this section. In the first, members of the Sudan tribe boarded a British baghla off Kharg in 1816, and appropriated 1,515 German crowns[83] belonging to a certain Ibrahim of Constantinople.[84] One of Shaikh Muhammad bin Qadib of Linga's battils was also present at the scene. He claims that, at this point, his people ('rab'una') boarded the baghla and prevented the Sudan's seizure of the vessel herself: 'my people had not agreed to the attack on the baghla, since she was British'.[85] The Sudan allegedly made off with another vessel on the same occasion. It is difficult to evaluate quite the nature of the relationship between the Qasimi Shaikh and the Sudan. He is very clear that they were not 'his people' and were 'attached to another'.[86] At the very least it would appear that, before encountering the British baghla, his vessel had been sailing with, or engaged in some form of joint enterprise with, the Sudan. We have no means of determining whether, as seems perhaps unlikely, the Sudan were left to enjoy the fruits of their other captures alone.

This incident bears comparison with another, in 1815, which began as the seizure by a party of Sudan tribesmen of a British baghla, the *Omid* or *Hubbullah*, after she had put into Linga harbour to water.[87] Thereafter the Sudan returned, with their prize, to Sharja, where they then resided. The ruler of Sharja, Sultan bin Saqr al-Qasimi, soon relieved the Sudan of their capture. Unhappy at the ruler's conduct toward them, one assumes, and perhaps in connection with this self-same business, the Sudan now chose to decamp *en masse* from Sharja; they switched their abode and their allegiance to Sultan's rivals at Ras al-Khaima. This, by the way, also left Sultan bin Saqr in possession of the British baghla and her contents.

Although, as was the case in the December 1814 incident, Sultan bin Saqr made no attempt at restitution, he himself acknowledged in a letter that this was a more serious affair, in which he bore some responsibility: the Sudan had been, at the time, his own people and subjects ('rab'ana wa-ra'ayana')[88], though he had naturally 'neither authorized, nor had prior knowledge of, the attack'. And as to the fate of the vessel and her cargo whilst under his care, the first had mysteriously been burnt,[89] and the latter, such as remained, had 'melted away in my hands'.[90] British claims against him were, he conceded, legitimate, though he hoped they would not be pressed. It is interesting to note that in neither this, nor any of the preceding cases in this section, is any motive for the original seizure adduced beyond that which is most obvious.

iv   Attacks on British Indian Shipping

((14) Madras schooner, mid-1818)
(15) A military transport, c. mid-November 1818
(16) The *Hurry Pussa*, 9 November 1818
(17) Four Indian vessels, December 1818

On 6 February 1819, distressing news reached William Bruce at Bushire from his Banyan correspondent in Bahrain:[91] Five Indian women, and two handsome Bengal-built palanquins, had been captured by the Qawasim off India and brought to the island for disposal. Two of the Indian women had already been publicly sold. Thirteen others, together with a European lady and her niece, all from the same pattamar ketch, were still being held in Ras al-Khaima. The Banyan offered to send thither to have them quietly ransomed.

It so happened that at that very time two ships of the Royal Navy, and three of the Bombay Marine, were congregated in Bushire harbour.[92] British attitudes had hardened over the preceding decade and a half. The chief naval officer in the Gulf, Captain Francis Erskine Loch, a 30-year old Scot, newly arrived in the Gulf in late December 1818, and as fresh and forthright a commander as might be expected, took up the challenge. He led the squadron to Bahrain and bluntly demanded that the Al Khalifa Shaikh, Abdullah bin Ahmad, hand over the women. To stress his point he forcibly, and with loss of life, seized two Arab vessels in Bahrain's harbour, which had been misidentified by the Banyan Broker as Qasimi: in fact they belonged to the Shaikh of Abu Dhabi, and this costly error would require compensation. To Loch's added chagrin the women were not finally forthcoming. Indeed everyone, including the Broker, now chose to deny their existence; and it was later maintained that a group of three women who had been sold had certainly been taken by the Qawasim, but out of a Kuwaiti vessel and were not British subjects.[93] Loch had Shaikh

Abdullah agree in future to prevent the Qawasim from selling British property on the island;[94] but all he succeeded in recovering was one palanquin.

Captain Loch therefore returned to Bushire, disappointed of his object and perplexed at the contradictory behaviour of the Broker. On his arrival, however, Loch discovered that the latter had forwarded another message to Bushire. In it, he maintained that his original story about the women had been true, but that he had, for reasons of survival, been forced to deny it in Loch's presence. This time a number of Bahraini merchant vessels were impounded at Bushire as a lever on Shaikh Abdullah, and Captain Eatwell, of the HCC *Benares*, was despatched forthwith in order to demand the release of the women now said to be concealed upon the island. The outcome of this second visit was, however, no different from the first: the officer concluded once more that the story had been without foundation and the women did not exist.[95]

And here the matter might have been laid to rest, but for the fact that in consequence of Loch's visit, a correspondence had been struck up through the medium of Shaikh Abdullah with Hasan bin Rahma of Ras al-Khaima. Shaikh Abdullah enquired of the latter, on behalf of the British, whether the Qawasim might be holding any Christian women, 'white like themselves'.[96] Hasan bin Rahma was at this time keen to reach an accommodation with Britain. He wrote acknowledging that his people had recently 'captured one woman with her niece, a child, and she says she is the wife of a Captain in the army'.[97] Captain Conyers of the HCC *Mercury*, who soon met up with Lieutenant Arthur of the HCC *Antelope*, was therefore detailed to Ras al-Khaima to seek their release: Arthur records that Hasan bin Rahma

> sent for the men who had them and purchased their freedom in my presence ..., being in all fifteen women and children. He also acknowledged there were three more in one of the distant towns [Sharja] which should be given up to any vessel that came.[98]

In return for the release of these 18 (one of whom soon died), the British returned a Sharja-owned merchant trankey recently detained to this end[99]—the Senior Officer in the Gulf had 'expressed great anxiety to get prisoners'[100]—as well as 10 sailors captured by Loch in a Qasimi vessel on 29 December 1818 and since despatched as prisoners to Bombay.[101]

This incident is important because it demonstrates the extraordinarily high-handed, even blundering, approach adopted by Captain Loch and the British in the year or so prior to the second expedition. But it is also a relatively rare piece of very clear evidence that the Qawasim seized boats off the Indian coast. The 18 British Indian women and children enslaved by the Qawasim had been seized from a transport vessel which had been carrying a detachment of the Company's 5th Regiment of Bombay Native Infantry, when, in perhaps mid-November 1818, she was taken while en route to Anjar in the Gulf of Cutch:[102] the women were mostly the wives of sepoys, and their husbands had, with the rest, all been killed in the attack. It may be curious to note that another witness of what was quite possibly this same attack surfaced at Muscat around the end of April 1819: he was a Banyan who had travelled overland from Ras al-Khaima, where he had been set free. He claimed to have been in one of three (Indian) dinghies captured off Cutch at the same time as a certain 'pattamar with sepoys on board'.[103]

One of the women who were released, a certain Mariam, apparently maintained that a number of other women taken with her, British Indian subjects, had been sold on to a Bahrain boat; possibly she was referring in part to the three taken to Sharja.[104] The women also seem to have been aware of the palanquin retrieved from Bahrain. This article of respectable and effortless movement, a reclining sedan, constitutes an important clue, since we can trace its owner and the circumstances of its loss with some precision. The palanquin belonged to Sunderjee Sewjee, the Company's Native Agent at Cutch, whose initials it even seems to have borne. Unconnected reports described how it had been removed, along with c. 20,000 rupees' (roughly £2,000) worth of merchandise from Bombay, when Sewjee's boat, the *Hurry Pussa*, was boarded by Qawasim just south of Mangrol on 9 November 1818, completely stripped, then abandoned. The circumstances of the palanquin's reappearance at Bahrain, which was often named as the principal mart for the Qawasim's booty, clearly demonstrates that they were indeed responsible for the plunder of the *Hurry Pussa*; and the evidence of the women may too suggest that her assailants were closely associated, if not identical, with those who seized the sepoys' pattamar in the same area, and at about the same time.[105]

These two captures occurred during November 1818, when there were reports of other Qasimi seizures off Kathiawar. There is good reason to credit reports of a second spate of Qasimi activity off north-west India the following month. The prime evidence consists of the testimony of the 10 sailors made prisoner by Loch on 28 December, and later exchanged for the sepoys' families. These men attested, under questioning, that their group of 2 baghlas and 2 battils from Ras al-Khaima, bearing some 11 guns and 550 men, had captured four vessels off north-west India, apparently in December; when encountered by Loch off Gwadar they had three of them in tow. There is no reason to doubt this statement.

During a subsequent visit to Bahrain in April 1819, the Company's cruiser *Vestal* discovered what was interpreted as more evidence of Qasimi attacks on the shipping of British India: 15 sheets of copper were handed over by a Banyan, who claimed to have purchased them from a Sharja vessel for 200 dollars.[106] After inspecting the copper at Bushire, the Resident William Bruce stated his opinion that it must originally have been seized by the Qawasim from a Madras brig carrying military stores which had been lost in 1818. As such the evidence is neither conclusive, nor very enlightening, but the Bombay Archives fortuitously contain a wholly separate piece of evidence which presumably points to the same incident; namely the first-hand account of one of the captured vessel's crew, her Store Lascar, the Malabari Chadayappah.[107]

Chadayappah's narrative describes how the schooner Mary[108] left Madras with military stores for the stations of Quilon and Cannanore on 18 February 1818. She carried 13 passengers and crew. But neither the Master, X.D. Rosaria, nor any of the others on board, Indian, Portuguese and British, was proficient in the art of navigation. They did not even have a compass or sextant on board. This was to have disastrous consequences.

In what seemed like a month and a half (Chadayappah had no clear recollection of dates), the ship rounded Ceylon and about five weeks later arrived at the island of Kardiva in the Maldives.

> [There] we anchored and procured a supply of coconuts and fresh water. The inhabitants told us that we were about ten days' sail from Cannanore, but the Master of the vessel said he could sail there in three days. We proceeded to sea again, and days and weeks elapsed without any appearance of land

—or rather of the mainland, for it seems they passed several islands on the way. For an unspecified time they continued like this, and were eventually reduced to eating raw rice and salt water, and sickness and dysentery became rife. The ship had in fact completely lost her course. At last they reached landfall. It may have been south Arabia. Just then, as the crew's spirits lifted and they set course for the mainland, they espied 10 strange sail approaching.

> Some of [them] soon commenced firing at us. We judged that they were pirates, and we determined to run the ship on shore and endeavoured to save our lives by getting into the country. The pirates, however, were on shore as soon as ourselves and we were all made prisoners. Mr Ross, McCarthy, Mr Ross's father-in-law, the Master of the vessel, the Mate and the Seacunny were all put to death by being shot immediately. The lives of the remainder of us—that is the five Ship Lascars, my comrade Store Lascar and myself—were spared: a young lad stabbed me in the belly and would have put me to death but that some of the pirates interfered in my behalf.

Thereupon the Mary was stripped, then scuttled. It may be interesting to note that according to a letter received by the Porbandar merchant, Narjee Vurjee, from Mocha, six Qasimi dows and two battils were active off south-east Arabia in May 1818: lying in wait at Socotra, they attacked six Arab dows from Porbandar bound for Mocha, abandoning the 32 Banyans and 75 sailors on the island, and seizing merchandise valued at 157,333 rupees (c. £16,000).[109] There may of course be no connection between this squadron and those who took the Mary.

The survivors from the Mary were put on board the attacking vessels and taken to a port termed 'Munguyma' in Chadayappah's account: by this he most probably intended Ras al-Khaima, though we perhaps cannot be certain.[110] On their arrival, all seven men were sold to different individuals, the second Store Lascar to a merchant and Chadayappah, for 150 dollars, to the 'secretary of the headman of the place'. Chadayappah was now put to work on his master's vessel, probably a 7-gun, 300-man baghla called the Su'ud,[111] where he lived on a daily ration of dates and shrimps. He was obliged to accept Islam:

> I was forced by my master to submit to the operation of circumcision and subsequently I was constrained to marry according to the rites of the Mahomedan religion a slave girl selected for me by my master.
>
> Nine days after my marriage, the vessel I was attached to and several others were directed to put to sea in order to take prizes; but, after being a long time out, we returned without meeting a single vessel. On gaining the port, the pirates were dismayed and astonished at observing an English ship-of-war at anchor.[112]

This chance encounter on 10 May 1819 proved highly fortuitous. It was in fact Captain Loch, in HMS Eden, who, when he sighted the four[113] 'pirate' vessels near the islands of Salama wa-Banatuha, set off in hot pursuit. The Eden carried 110 fit men, out of a usual total of 125, as well as 26 large-calibre guns and, in Loch's view, she had 'much the advantage in point of manoeuvre' over the three baghlas and one battil (with their 14 small-calibre guns and 630 men) which now confronted her.[114] When, after a chase of 14 hours, Loch came up with them, he somewhat lamely complains that they sought to board him. It was 11.30 p.m. and a beautiful moonlit night. A couple of damaging broadsides and a volley or two of musketry from the marines caused the two smaller vessels to sheer off, and the other two ran inshore near the islet of Umm al-Fayarin;[115] and as they did so, a small boat was observed pulling away from the Su'ud, flying the flag of truce. It was Chadayappah, who rowed towards the Eden, crying 'Captain Sahib, Captain Sahib'. The Eden stopped so as to take him on board, along with two fellow captives from Muscat, and three so-called

Qawasim; then, having done so, she hauled out at 2 a.m. on the 11th in order to avoid the rocks and shallows. The Omanis were brought in safety to Muscat and Chadayappah stayed with the *Eden* till she reached Madras. What eventually became of the three Qawasim is not related, except for one, who, en route to Muscat, threw himself overboard in an attempt to escape, when his chances of survival were, according to Loch, very slim indeed.

Other Incidents Similarly Attested, But Discussed in Chapter Six

(16) The *Bassein*, 18 May 1797
(17) The HCC *Viper*, 15 October 1797
(18) The *Trimmer*, 1 December 1804
(19) The *Shannon*, 1 December 1804
(20) The *Minerva*, 23 May 1809

CHAPTER SIX

The Most Important Cases
of Alleged Piracy by the Qawasim
Against British Vessels

i The First Period, 1797–1805

(1) The *Bassein*, 18 May 1797[1]
(2) The HCC *Viper*, 15 October 1797
(3) The *Trimmer*, 1 December 1804[2]
(4) The *Shannon*, 1 December 1804

We may now date the period when the Qawasim may be said to have
engaged in piratical depredations. Up to the close of 1804, they
committed no act of piracy; but, with the exception of the attack on
the *Bassein* snow, and the *Viper* cruiser, manifested every respect to
the British flag.[3]

We may later find cause to question this portrayal of events, concerned,
even as it is, solely with incidents involving British vessels. But it is
instructive to note that in retrospect, for a Member of the Bombay Council writing in 1819, the problem of piracy in the Gulf appeared to have
begun in 1797; and that in the whole period before the Anglo–Qasimi
accord of 6 February 1806, there had apparently been but five cases of
'piracy'. That is to say, the four under consideration here with one other of
purely passing moment, when, in December 1804, the Company's cruiser,
the ship *Mornington*, was supposedly threatened off Farur Island, by a
Qasimi fleet of over 40 dows and trankeys.[4]

The 1797 and 1804 incidents share certain characteristics: they all
involved sizable Qasimi fleets, under the personal command of members of
the Qasimi family, which were at the time engaged in operations against
Omani and other shipping. But the two pairs of cases differ markedly, not
least in this that the first had much to do with the loss of prestige and the
second with a form of loss more material. The interest of these events is all

the greater since they occurred early on, at a time when the two parties were still comparatively free of preconceptions regarding each other.

In the opinion of the Government of Bombay, the *Bassein* affair was but an 'accidental stoppage and trifling detention', that scarcely touched the national honour.[5] The facts may be briefly stated: the snow *Bassein*, a private British trading vessel conveying despatches from India, was boarded 'in a tumultuous and hostile manner' by some 250 men from the fleet of Shaikh Abdullah, brother to Shaikh Saqr, the ruler of Ras al-Khaima.[6] Abdullah, upon hearing of the capture, ordered his people to quit the snow, but he did not release her immediately: he first detained her commander on board his vessel, and on the island of Qishm, for something over 24 hours. Justly considered, the affair shows Ras al-Khaima's general regard for Britain, and appears ultimately to vindicate the conduct of Abdullah, who had presumably at the time been in quest of Omani shipping. Likewise, for his part, Samuel Manesty, the Company's senior representative in the Gulf and Basra Resident, though sensing that British prestige was at stake in the affair, yet still maintained his high opinion of Shaikh Saqr of Ras al-Khaima. He therefore readily accepted that soon after, when he despatched him with his nephew Matar to cruise once more against Muscat shipping in the vicinity of Qishm and Hormuz, Saqr had issued special instructions to Abdullah, adjuring him to respect the British flag: 'If during your cruise you should even fall in with the vessel commanded by Sayyid Sultan [of Muscat] himself, and find her under British colours, you must suffer her to continue her course without molesting her in the smallest degree.'[7]

One suspects, in fact, that the *Bassein* affair might well have been forgotten had it not been for another incident which occurred in that year. Paradoxically, the background to this event is once again a fine demonstration of the cordiality of Anglo–Qasimi relations in the Gulf at this time. Around 8 October, a squadron put into Bushire under the command of Shaikh Salih bin Muhammad (bin Salih al-Qasimi?), nephew[8] to Shaikh Saqr of Ras al-Khaima: at least 2 dows and 1–2 battils from the same fleet remained stationed at Kharg. A week later Salih visited the British Resident, Nicholas Hankey Smith, to explain what he was about: his vessels were planning to intercept the Suri (Omani) fleet, then lading dates at Basra, as it passed down the Gulf. He therefore requested the British not to ship goods with the Suri fleet, or at least to send them accompanied and well marked. Finally he craved a quantity of gunpowder and cannonballs for use in the projected ambush. In retrospect, and even at the time from the point of view of the Government of Bombay, which prized Muscat's friendship, it is quite striking that Smith should have agreed to part of this request. In consequence, a small quantity of balls,[9] though no powder, was taken out of the Company's cruiser, *Viper*, just arrived, and handed over to Salih.

> The next morning while we were at breakfast, [writes the Resident] we were alarmed by the report of guns, and, on going upon the terrace, observed the [*Viper*] surrounded by four large dows and a battil. [Captain Stephenson] wished to go on board, but, however, I could not consent to his going from the certainty of his being cut off from the vessel. The Shaikh [of Bushire] himself was not on the spot, but his brother, in charge, pretended to do a great deal, but in fact did nothing; nor could I, either by offers or any other means, get a boat to go off with provisions, which she stood in need of, and the Factory Guard and a few more men. Thus the vessel was left to fight for herself. Her men and officers were at breakfast when the largest dow fired upon them, and she immediately cut her anchor and got under way. At the same instant her crew flew to arms, when Mr Caruthers was unfortunately shot thro' the body, but refused to quit his station till another ball, [passing through Mr Salter's hat], put an end to his existence; and Mr Salter, a young volunteer, the only remaining officer, nobly continued the engagement till the dows sheered off.[10]

The *Viper* brig's casualties were reported as 'the Chief Officer and one sepoy killed, 1 European and 4 natives wounded and one supposed mortally so.'[11] The British guns inflicted heavy casualties and extensive damage on the Arab vessels: Salih himself received a flesh wound in the arm.[12]

It is difficult to account for this apparently unprovoked attack. When approached over the subject by the British, Shaikh Saqr of Ras al-Khaima distanced himself from its author:

> You must know that Salih some time ago left Ras al-Khaima and, separating himself from us, repaired to the Persian shore of the Gulf, and there established himself among the Banu Malih[13] Arabs, marrying a woman of that tribe, which is one of a villainous nature and character.
> You must also know that since the commencement of hostilities between the Qasimi Arabs and the people of Oman, Salih, accompanied by the Banu Malih Arabs, and holding himself distinct from us, has cruised with certain vessels, committing depredations according to his inclinations.[14]

One presumes, however, that Salih's quarrel with Muscat was also Ras al-Khaima's.[15] Shaikh Saqr further argues that Salih's intervention in the fracas was well intentioned: 'Your vessel was first attacked by a dow belonging to the Arabs of Suhar[16] and other vessels in company with

Salih ...: God forbid that Salih, our relation, should entertain evil intentions towards our friends'.[17] Saqr, nevertheless, appears to have summoned
his nephew, presumably for a reprimand. He was clearly embarrassed by
the whole affair. Samuel Manesty recognized this, and his esteem for
Shaikh Saqr of Ras al-Khaima was not diminished: he spoke appreciatively
of Saqr's attempts to discourage Salih's occasional acts of 'piratical de-
predation'.[18] It was otherwise with the Bombay Marine, who felt only that
the Qawasim had not been adequately punished and that they had not
themselves been compensated for this by their gallantry medals. For some
time hereafter, they continued to nurse a grievance at what above all
had seemed to them, at least, a small and isolated, but consummate act
of treachery.

It is quite ironic, almost symbolic, that Samuel Manesty, the Basra
Resident, who had in 1797 been so well disposed towards Ras al-Khaima
and the Qawasim, should, in 1804, have lost two of his ships to them.
These were more serious and more straightforward incidents. An account
of the capture of the brig *Shannon* has already been given. The *Trimmer*
brig was attacked just a few hours previous to that and by the same fleet.
Her commander, Captain Cumming, recalls what happened:

> On the 1st of December 1804 at day break, in the morning, Ras
> al-Husaini bearing east-by-south distance five or six miles, we saw two
> dows, [one] close under the Cape,[19] the other within half a mile of us.
> About 7 a.m., shoaling our water to three and a half fathoms, hauled
> inshore and deepened to nine fathoms, when it fell little wind; and
> the nearest dow then being a quarter of a mile from us, we hoisted our
> colours and the dow did the same. Supposing it to be a trading-boat,
> I sent our jolly-boat with the Serang [head of the lascar crew], who
> speaks the Arabic language, for intelligence, and to enquire if there
> was any place inshore where we could water quickly at.
>
> After the boat had been a quarter of an hour alongside of the dow,
> we fired a gun to leeward as a signal for the Serang to return, which
> they seemed to take no notice of. In ten minutes afterwards, we fired
> another gun and then perceived two men that were in the jolly boat
> go up on board the dow; at the same time she made sail and stood
> inshore, which gave me the first suspicion of his being a pirate. We
> immediately made sail after her, firing shot at first wide and afterwards
> right at her: she seemed to wish to draw us inshore.
>
> At 9 a.m., we could see a number of dows coming out of Charak
> Bay, besides others from the east and westward, to join him. We then
> steered wide of him, by which I expected he would think better of
> detaining an English boat and [let] her go; in the stead of which, he
> kept towards us.
>
> We then set all sail, and he came right after us. We got a four-
> pounder over our stern and played on the dow as fast as we could, and

began to lighten ship by heaving overboard some chests of soft sugar in order to escape. We continued firing round[?],[20] double-head and grape shot, and our small arms, (which they returned with their matchlocks) till they struck us in the larboard quarter, when they threw a shower of spears on board and instantly filled our quarter-deck with men, sword-in-hand, which was in vain for us to resist. They immediately began to plunder, having wounded the Chief Mate in the hand; we were all presently stripped of the clothes we had on, and insulted by spitting at us and pushing us from place to place, and, after, threatened putting me to death (by holding a dagger to my breast). I did not discover where treasure was hid. In a very short space of time, there was as many dows alongside as could come at us, taking out the cargo and robbing the ship's stores. Our packet was shotted and thrown overboard on their boarding.

About 12 o'clock the Shannon, Captain Babcock, hove in sight and I [saw] several dows give him chase.

They continued plundering till 5 p.m., when they towed us inshore and came to anchor. Not one of us was allowed to go below all day. In the evening, one of the Captains of the dows came on board the Trimmer, who told me they only intended to take our cargo that was the property of merchants at Bushire, and that in a day or two the brig would be given up and all the stores taken out returned. This man took me, my servant, two helmsmen and an Armenian passenger on board his dow (my officer having lost so much blood could not be removed) under pretence of looking for our clothes. When on board the dow, they gave us an old sail to lay on, and all we had to eat was a few dates, and sometimes a small piece of salt fish, all the time we were with them.

On the 2nd December, in the morning, we found the Shannon brought into the fleet, seemingly treated as we had been. I wished to go on board her, but was not allowed. About 8 a.m., the whole fleet of dows, twenty-nine in number (carrying each between one hundred and fifty and two hundred men), got under sail, the Trimmer and Shannon in company, and steered westward, and about 10 a.m. fell in with two trading-dows, which the pirates captured—one of them making some resistance, the crew was put to death. On the same day, at 11 p.m., they fell in with, and engaged, two large dows and two battils. The whole four in the action took fire and were burnt. The crews that were obliged to jump into the water, I had the shocking sight to see murdered, begging for mercy.

On the 3rd, in the morning, the Captain of the dow I was in said in two days at farthest both vessels would be given up, and keeps promising day after day we should be let go. I could never get permission to go and see either Captain Babcock or my officer till the 8th December, when me and my people were ordered into a boat and sent on board the Shannon, where I found Captain Babcock laying covered with wounds and his left hand cut off and his vessel torn to pieces.

Now I came to understand that the Shaikhs of Linja, or Linga,[21] and Ras al-Khaima were the heads of these pirates; Captain Babcock also informed me that they did not intend to give up the *Trimmer* and that they promised daily to let the *Shannon* go. On the 11th December, about 3 a.m., a boat came on board the *Shannon* bringing my officer, gunner, a helmsman, two washer-men and [a] woman—she kept a young woman and a little girl: these washing-people were passengers for Basra. After putting these people on board, they told Captain Babcock we might go, only giving us one frazil of dates for our subsistence and no water. We immediately weighed and made sail with the wind at NE for Bushire. On the 18th December, we spoke the Honourable Company's cruiser *Mornington* and Captain Babcock went on board her for assistance. And the 19th we anchored in Bushire Roads.[22]

The precise circumstances of these two captures are not in all respects clear. We know that they were perpetrated by vessels, part of the combined Qasimi fleet of Ras al-Khaima and Linga, reportedly some 21–9 boats in all, which was then seemingly out cruising against Bushire, Muscat and Basra shipping. The two overall commanders were Shaikh Qadib of Linga, and the more senior in standing, Shaikh Sultan bin Saqr of Ras al-Khaima: Captain Babcock of the *Shannon*, who seems to have spoken some Arabic, claimed to have twice interviewed the latter.

During the course of talks early in 1806, the British negotiator David Seton reports that his Qasimi counterpart, Shaikh Abdullah bin Qasim bin Qurush,

> hinted the plunder of the two vessels was brought on by an accident in which we were partly to blame, at a time that the whole of the Qawasim were in an uproar; that every one was now sorry for it and the Shaikhs would on the spot have remedied it had they had the power.[23]

It is difficult to account for the first of Ibn Qurush's partial explanations, unless it be that the *Trimmer*'s first reactions were seen as provocative. But this is speculation. Significantly more suggestive as a factor that may have contributed to these captures is the second of the points made by Ibn Qurush. There had been a number of signals for change in the politics of the lower Gulf in 1803–4. In October 1803, the Saudi ruler, Abd al-Aziz, was stabbed to death by a Kurdish dervish whilst at prayer in a mosque at Dir'iya.[24] That same year, Sultan bin Saqr had succeeded his father as ruler of Ras al-Khaima and leading light of the Qawasim. But the most immediately destabilizing development was the strange murder of Sayyid Sultan bin Ahmad of Muscat, almost as if by accident, in a skirmish at the island of Qishm *c.* 14 November 1804: 'Wonders never cease in these our times,' sang an Omani poet, 'The lion of lions is assaulted by dogs.'[25] The precise identity of the ruler's assailants is, and, one infers, was, by no means clear, though all reports concur in attributing the attack generally to the Qawasim: this was what was put about at Muscat and, on this pretext, hostilities were quickly recommenced against them by Sayyid Sultan's successor.[26]

The effect of Sayyid Sultan of Muscat's murder in the early part of 1805 was to inspire the Qawasim, in alliance with Mulla Hasan bin Muhammad, the Banu Mu'in ruler of Qishm, with some latitude and much freedom of movement in the lower Gulf. Muscat was temporarily deprived of some of her possessions about the mouth of the Gulf, and the Qawasim increased their influence on the Persian coast, as at Charak. The argument might therefore be that the capture of the two British brigs in December 1804 was the harbinger of this brief, new and more energetic period of Qasimi political activity. It is certainly highly plausible that the news of the ruler's murder, received at the least a week before the attacks,[27] had an immediate psychological impact; that it stimulated power struggles and activity of various kinds, and thereby helped loosen the Qawasim, their allies, and their shipping, from their usual constraints. This excitation may, then, have lain behind the attacks on the *Trimmer* and the *Shannon*.

But of course, irrespective of the peculiar nature of the circumstances of these seizures, they were still what they were. The booty taken out of the two brigs was distributed straightaway amongst the vessels of the fleet. Some of the *Shannon*'s cargo was soon thereafter destroyed in a fight with Shaikh Barakat of Charak, over the possession of a Basra baghla he had just captured:[28] three (or four) vessels were burnt in the action, and the Shaikh himself perished. This was presumably the heart-rending scene witnessed by Captain Cumming.

The British response to these seizures was of a rather different kind and level to that of 1797. A letter of protest went out to Su'ud bin Abd al-Aziz, the Wahhabi ruler, and, upon another suggestion of Samuel Manesty, the Qawasim were in 1805 barred from trading at British Indian ports. The Company's cruiser *Mornington* was also authorized to assist Muscat in regaining her erstwhile dominance over Bandar Abbas, Minab and the entrance to the Gulf. But hostilities were not conducted against the Qawasim: Sultan bin Saqr of Ras al-Khaima was eager to come to terms with Britain, and restored, if not the cargo, at least the hull of the *Trimmer*. David Seton, the Muscat Resident, was able to reach an accommodation with the Qawasim, formalized in February 1806, in which all British claims over the Qawasim were waived. In the restored spirit of cordial, or 'neutral', relations, the seizure of the two brigs began to seem to Seton, for a time, almost like an aberration.

ii   *The Second Period, 1806–1809*

(5) The *Darya Daulat*, 3 July 1808
(6) The HCC *Sylph*, 21 October 1808
(7) The *Minerva*, 23 May 1809

Had there been no further Qasimi attack on British shipping after 6 February 1806, it is conceivable, indeed highly probable, that neither of the two British expeditions against Ras al-Khaima would have been launched. For it was on that day, in Bandar Abbas, that Captain David Seton finally managed to conclude his agreement with the Qawasim, erasing all outstanding British claims against them. At the same time, his accord made provision for each party to afford the other's shipping all due assistance, and stated that the Qawasim were now once again at liberty to frequent British Indian ports for the purposes of trade. The prevailing British view was that the Qawasim would now readily revert to more peaceable pursuits, such as pearling and commerce. As late as March 1808, the success of the arrangement achieved by Seton is attested by the Basra Resident, Samuel Manesty, who remarked that the Qawasim had not, so far as he was aware, committed any 'piratical act' on an English vessel since the 1806 agreement 'and it may, I think, be reasonably supposed that they will adhere to their promises on that subject in future.'[29] Three months later these hopes were dashed.

Before we come to that, it is worth noticing that Manesty's was a noticeably British view of events. He meant no more or less than he said: there had been no Qasimi attack on a *British* vessel. This, despite the fact that his comments had actually been prompted by news of the attack on the *Shannon* (1807), described earlier. This severely focused attitude is important because it to a significant degree characterizes the wider range of British sources for this period and this subject. The British archives naturally concentrate, for such was their purpose, on events that affected the British, or, in the case of piracy, on incidents which involved their ships. This has the effect of making these records an accented and sometimes incomplete historical document, but still, for all that, an important one. The source of this somewhat paradoxical result is this, that the maritime incidents which the British documents do in fact record, and the manner in which they do so, are inevitably what dictated British policy. It was these incidents, in other words, and more particularly the attacks on vessels flying the British flag, which most directly determined the historical outcome of these crucial decades in the evolution of the modern Gulf.

For two and a half years after Seton's accord, then, the sources contain but a few isolated instances of alleged piracy and attempted piracy. Then suddenly, in late 1808, this apparent prevailing calm is shattered, and the records become replete with instances of attacks on ships in the Gulf and the Arabian Sea. The Qawasim figure as the principal and most consistent culprits, though others, particularly Rahma bin Jabir, are also mentioned. The bulk of this new outburst of maritime disorder is reported off the Cutch and Sind coastline in the winter season of 1808/9 (November–March), but other activity is also reported from the Gulf and south Arabia. The British regarded three of these attacks as more important than the rest. These three were probably uppermost in the minds of the planners of the first expedition against Ras al-Khaima and are the only specific captures mentioned, by way of explanation of their mission, in the instructions issued to its joint commanders.[30] It is clearly of some considerable interest to examine these incidents so as to determine the quality of the evidence and the precise circumstances of each.

The *Darya Daulat*[31] was still in sight of Muscat when she came up with her captor, a 12-gun, 250-man dow, belonging to Sultan bin Saqr of Ras al-Khaima. It would have been senseless for the small grab ketch, the property of Pestanjee Eduljee, a Parsee merchant of Bombay, with her crew of only 10 or so, even to attempt to resist. She therefore submitted and was taken to Ras al-Khaima. There followed six days of deliberations on the part of the Qawasim as to whether or not to listen to her captain's protestations that she should be released since she bore the Company's pass and flag. But the argument was eventually carried by the Wahhabi *wakil*, or agent, who persuaded the Qawasim to retain the boat until they received certification from the Governor of Bombay that she was indeed British: the passengers had apparently sworn to him that the *Darya Daulat* belonged to a *Khoja*[32] merchant of Matrah.

It seems that the vessel was never released. But her captain, a Mr Fleming, and the only European aboard, was. With the conclusion of the debate at Ras al-Khaima, he was provided with camels and permitted to travel overland to Muscat. He eventually arrived in Barka, the ruler of Muscat's summer residence, where the British Residency was then also on retreat, escaping from the searing heat of the capital, about 3 August, after a journey of *c.* 2½–3 weeks.

There seems no particular reason to doubt Mr Fleming's version of events, though we have no other.[33] The role of the Wahhabi agent in this affair echoes the *Shannon* (1807) episode. The clear respect shown towards Mr Fleming, and the general regard for British property, also recall that incident, though in the present case these were not attended by such positive results. It seems not unreasonable to imagine that the Qawasim may have taken the *Darya Daulat* supposing her to be Omani: if so, then it did not therefore signify a new departure. Indeed it is interesting to note that the Government of Bombay itself did not see this as a wholly clear-cut issue. They recognized that problems could and did arise in the Gulf when, as in the present case, the Company's flag flew on vessels manned by Arab and Persian officers, whose tribes or communities might be 'at variance with the maritime freebooters in those seas, and thence give occasion for discussions of an unpleasant nature with the Honourable Company's Government.'[34] The practice of granting the Company's pass to such vessels had in fact been specifically proscribed in a determined attempt to avoid possible clashes with the Qawasim, but the ban had been allowed to lapse, probably in February 1808.[35]

By contrast with the relatively unexceptional fate of the *Darya Daulat*, the assault on the *Sylph* was a far more sharply defined and wounding affair. She was a Company vessel, belonging to the Bombay Marine, and not simply one that sailed under British colours. Furthermore, there was heavy loss of life and the attack was seemingly unprovoked and otherwise quite inexplicable. Indeed, if this was the work of the Qawasim, it represented behaviour of a kind that was essentially new. The episode was to leave a deep mark on the perceptions of the Company and its Marine officers, as pronounced, perhaps, in its own way, as that left more generally by the *Minerva* affair the following year.

The HCC *Sylph*, an 8-gun, 78-ton schooner, was given orders on 12 September 1808 to sail with HMS *La Néréide* and *Sapphire* from Bombay to Bushire, as they carried Sir Harford Jones with his retinue on a diplomatic mission to Iran. The *Sylph* had on board Sir Harford's Persian Secretary, and son of a former Bushire Resident, Muhammad Husain Khan. It seems the squadron made absolutely no attempt to stick together. The 36-gun frigate *La Néréide* pressed ahead under her choleric disciplinarian of a commander, Captain Robert Corbett, and reached Bushire on 14 October, followed four days later by the *Sapphire*. A week or so after, there was still no sign of the *Sylph*, and fears grew at Bushire for her safety, particularly after the arrival on the 28th of the HCC *Nautilus* claiming to have been attacked off Hanjam Island by 2 dows and 2 trankeys.[36] Jones proposed sending a vessel to look for the *Sylph*.[37] As it happened, the *Néréide*, which had earlier set out on the return journey to Bombay, had already met up with her.

When the *Néréide* encountered the *Sylph*, at the Strait of Hormuz on 21 October, she was sailing in the opposite direction, up the Gulf, unharmed. As the two vessels passed each other, or shortly thereafter, the *Sylph* had for a time raised her colours. This was at noon. Somewhat earlier, two large dows, having stood out from under the Musandam Peninsula, had begun to follow at a distance in the wake of the *Néréide*. They continued on course directly at the *Sylph* until they had near'd us within a cable's length,[38] when one of them, which appeared to have the advantage in sailing, kept away for our larboard bow. But still [reported her commander Lieutenant Graham] I was determined not to commence before they attacked us, as I understood it would meet with the displeasure of Government—when I immediately bore up, and, while in the act of wearing, received a volley of small arms, which we returned with a broadside. However, from their great superiority in sailing, one boarded us on the starboard quarter, while his companion closed, and sent all his men on board . . .

As the enemy was lashed alongside, we could not depress the guns sufficiently to strike her between wind and water, or elevate them enough to destroy any part of her crew. I ordered all the crew to the small arms to prevent them from boarding, which we succeeded in until our decks were much thinn'd and, the enemy having the whole range of the starboard side, we were soon completely overpowered, and shortly after taken in tow.[39]

The attack had occurred at 1 p.m. when the *Néréide* was already four miles away. Immediately she witnessed the attack she set off to rescue the *Sylph*. It took three hours to narrow the gap to one mile, when the *Néréide* commenced firing on the two dows.

About 5 o'clock, when closed within point-blank, after hulling them both several times, the headmost was dismasted. The sternmost, with a firmness that would have honoured a better cause, ran her alongside and took out the survivors, she then sinking.

While thus employed, we passed them within the ship's length and Your Excellency may judge the effect of the broadside. You will hardly believe that even then, when repeatedly hailed in Arabic, they answered by barbarous threats of defiance and straggling musquetry. One was now abandoned and sunk; the other repaired his sail and shot away, and continued his course in a very light air, shouting and firing musquetry from loopholes and scuttles. We were upon his lee beam within two ship's lengths. It was now dark, but I plainly perceived that his hull was settling in the water and we thought we heard them bailing.

After about a quarter of an hour's firing in this position, we suddenly shot past him and lost sight of him. I hope the possibility of her escape, as I think their suffering would be better as an example than their destruction.[40]

When in the evening Captain Corbett finally came up with the *Sylph*, he found that most of the crew had been killed, 'decapitated', 30 men in all, with a further 3 wounded.[41] Lieutenant Graham's life had been saved by being 'knocked down the hatchway with an immense stone, after having received six spear and sabre wounds.'[42] A few others, including the Persian

Secretary, had managed to hide below. Casualties in the Arab dows must have been even greater: a later report suggests that the second dow also sank.[43] Each of the dows had been carrying some 150 men or more.

The Arab dows did not show their colours at any point during the attack on the *Sylph*, and neither of the two commanders actually names the aggressors. It is important, therefore, to seek to determine why the British were encouraged to believe that the Qawasim were responsible, especially since it is plain that many would have assumed from the start that this was the most likely explanation.[44] Subsequent reports refer in passing to at least four different sources of intelligence regarding the identity of the *Sylph*'s attackers: these include news from the Company's Hindu Broker and others at Muscat, the 'best informed' Arab and Persian merchants at Bombay and two vessels newly arrived there in November from the Gulf,[45] as well as information from Arab boats which called at Bushire on 9–10 November.[46] Mention of sources such as these is itself persuasive. And the plausible nature of two complementary items of intelligence supplied by these sources makes the argument for Qasimi responsibility particularly convincing: Sultan bin Saqr is reported to have conceded that although it was against his wishes, at a time when his direct authority over the 'Qawasim' had become very severely curtailed, they had indeed been the attackers; and elsewhere, possibly under the naval command of the Shaikh Salih al-Qasimi, the port of Rams is singled out as having actually carried out the assault.[47] The true significance of these circumstances will emerge later.

Just as the Arab dows omitted to hoist their colours during the engagement, so too, it seems, did the *Sylph*. Indeed it will have been observed that the schooner made herself a strangely easy prey for the attacking vessels by withholding her fire until it was too late, failing even to loose warning shots across their bows, as was the normal practice. Lieutenant Graham claimed that he had acted thus strictly in accordance with the wishes of Government.[48] But it is not clear what was the status of the orders to which he implicitly refers. The written instructions issued to him at Bombay on 12 September stipulate that, in the event of his becoming detached from the squadron, he should 'carefully avoid speaking, or communicating by signal, with any vessel you may meet with ... particularly if you are not certain of her being a friend'; he should also proceed direct to Bushire without touching at Muscat.[49] On this latter point, we know, in fact, that the *Sylph* did call at Muscat, on 15 October, though not the reason.[50] On this evidence alone, therefore, one is tempted to conclude that Lieutenant Graham's overscrupulous behaviour had been the consequence of these specific orders, perhaps reinforced, or further glossed, by verbal instructions, whose aim had simply been to protect the feeble *Sylph* from any possibly avoidable entanglement with French or Arab vessels: the *Sylph*'s vulnerability must certainly have been readily apparent, despite the qualified bravado of an earlier commander who, whilst engaged in a survey of the Kathiawar coast in the spring of 1808, had remarked of the five large Qasimi dows then said to be out cruising, 'I should be very happy to fall in with them in a commanding breeze, but in a light wind they might do me considerable mischief.'[51]

But there is a further aspect to Lieutenant Graham's exaggerated restraint in the face of aggression. Later writers have frequently stated—relying mostly, if not wholly, on allegations originally put down in c. 1816[52] by J.S. Buckingham, a sometimes less than scientific author, critical of the establishment, though not to be ignored—that the Government of Bombay had issued general instructions to its cruiser commanders not to provoke Arab vessels in any way. This is supposed to have transpired either following the attack on the HCC *Fury* in May 1808,[53] or a 'year or two' before that.[54] Buckingham, in fact, goes as far as to rebuke Jonathan Duncan, the Governor of Bombay, for his supposed unshakeable belief in the innocence and inoffensiveness of the Qawasim, saying,

> The Governor of that period, from ignorance of the character of this people, could never be persuaded that they were the aggressors, and constantly upbraided the officers of the English vessels with having in some way provoked the attacks of which they complained—continuing still to insist on the observance of the orders, in not firing on these vessels until they had first been fired at by them.[55]

The present writer has found no record of any such standing orders in the British archives for 1806–8. This of course proves nothing. On the other hand, we do possess accounts by their commanders of two similar attacks made on the HCCs *Fury* and *Nautilus* earlier in 1808. One would have expected these accounts to show some evidence of the orders in question had they existed. They do not. In the case of the HC brig *Nautilus*, attacked by 2 great dows and 2 large trankeys off Hanjam on 17 October 1808, her commander showed no scruples about hoisting his colours and firing two warning shots when he perceived he was being attacked, followed shortly after by a broadside, all before he had received a single musketball.[56] And in respect of the HC schooner *Fury*, whereas Buckingham alleges that the commander, Lieutenant Charles Gowan, received a severe reprimand from Governor Duncan in person for molesting innocent Arab traders, the records actually indicate that he and the crew were commended for exemplary behaviour.[57]

It might from this seem questionable that there were in force at this time standing orders to the effect that Bombay Marine commanders should specifically hold their fire until they were fired upon. But, giving considera-tion to the wider perspective, it would be unwise to reject the force of Buckingham's representation of government policy out of hand. General instructions to Marine commanders that they eschew hostilities unless attacked had undoubtedly been issued by Governor Duncan in 1805.[58] After Seton's accord of February 1806, the restoration of good relations with the Qawasim could hardly have encouraged a reversal of policy, and there is a dearth of incidents over the next two years. Events in late 1807 and early 1808, the advance of Wahhabi influence in the area, and a recrudes-cence of the French threat, can only have further recommended this positive exercise of caution. At the least, therefore, one concludes that Graham's exercise of restraint conformed with the spirit of government policy towards the Gulf Arabs.

Buckingham's sources probably included officers of the Bombay Marine and his comments almost certainly reflect their views.[59] There must have been deep dissatisfaction on their part at what they perceived as the supine and irresolute response of Duncan's government to the handful of attacks on Marine vessels such as the Sylph. These are the sorts of feelings that must have been aroused by the Viper incident a decade before.

Even so, the Sylph affair was too serious to be ignored. And although the Bombay Government felt itself unable to go beyond 'defensive' meas-ures, protective of British trade, it was agreed, after consultation with Fort William, that a small Royal Naval force would patrol the Gulf, while Marine cruisers were now authorized to attack Qasimi boats, as long as this did not involve their deviating from their course; and the means of restricting the Qawasim's access to Malabar and Kanara timber, which was used in shipbuilding, were reconsidered and an export ban imposed the following May.[60] Further than this, with regard to the Qawasim, Bombay was neither willing nor able to go: 'there is some danger that, by their too indiscriminate punishment, we may involve ourselves in a greater or less degree with this head of that powerful sect [the Wahhabis], such as our present circumstances with regard to the French may render it desirable as far as practicable to avoid.'[61]

There is no real doubt as to the authorship of the assault on the Minerva.[62] She was discovered in the harbour at Ras al-Khaima upon the arrival there of the British expedition in November 1809, whereupon she was immediately carried and burnt. There may also be an implicit acknow-ledgement of her capture by those under Qasimi rule in a letter from Sultan bin Saqr, in which he denies personal responsibility for the capture of British property at a time when he was absent in Dir'iya:[63] the powerless-ness of Sultan bin Saqr over his own people was noticeably also a feature of the Sylph affair.

The only direct first-hand account of this attack occurs in a letter to his friends at Surat from the Bora[64] Alimanjee, who had been taken captive in the attack. The letter was probably written at about the start of August:

> I and another Bora were passengers on board the ship *Minerva*, Captain Hopwood; on the 23rd of May 1809, [the] Qawasim captured us. They were altogether, large and small, 55 vessels and had about 5,000 Qawasim on board. They fought during 2 days, then after they captured us; the Captain and Second Officer on board were killed. 77 persons were altogether on board of the *Minerva*, of whom 45 been killed and 32 persons been saved by God's favour.
>
> After the capture of the ship, they carried us to Ras al-Khaima and kept us 33 days. They told us (i.e. to the writer of this letter and to another Bora named Baker Bye) to pay them about six or seven hundred rupees. We replied to them, 'What we had, you (the Qawasim) have taken from us; at present we have nothing, only our persons remain—if you want them take them. Instant release or detain us, or do whatever you please.' Then, after that, they released us (viz. 2 Boras and 8 lascars); then, on the 17th of July, we arrived at Muscat. And Baker Bye remained 10 days at Muscat, and then after he is gone to Basra.[65]

Not all the captives on board the *Minerva* were quite so fortunate; most notably Mrs Taylor, the young Armenian wife of Lieutenant Robert Taylor of the Bushire Residency, who was carried to Ras al-Khaima along with her infant son and servants. Their freedom was only secured in the autumn after they had been ransomed through the agency of a certain relative of Shaikh Sultan bin Saqr, one of the Resident William Bruce's confidential contacts, at a total cost of 1,400 dollars inclusive of commission.[66] The handful of Christian males on the ship were induced to renounce their religion for Islam and were forcibly circumcised.

The sufferings of the *Minerva* must have struck something of a chord in the popular imagination of the British at Bombay: sensation held a peculiar fascination then as now. The *Bombay Gazette*'s account of the attack, related upon the authority of someone on board the *Minerva* at the time, is in the high heroic vein:

> The engagement commenced in forenoon of the 29th May between the hours of ten and eleven, and after the first broadside from the *Minerva* 4 dows appeared to be in a sinking condition; a general action now took place and the havoc that was occasioned was dreadful beyond example.
>
> The crew of the *Minerva* kept up a galling and spirited fire and behaved in a most gallant manner, animated by the conduct of the Captain, who displayed uncommon intrepidity.

During the engagement, which is said to have been continued for 36 hours, no less than 16 dows went down. Such part of the crews of which, as had not been wounded, found a ready retreat on board their comrades, by which means the number of the enemy closely opposed to the Minerva was never diminished, and to this circumstance may be attributed the final surrender of the ship.

The fire of the Minerva had now slackened, from the incessant and continual exertions that had been made, and particularly in consequence of the killed and wounded of a great part of her crew. On the side of the enemy, the fire was kept briskly up. They had now apparently determined to board, as their vessels were gradually closing all round the Minerva; and having laid them close to, head and astern, these desperadoes instantly jumped on board and cut to pieces every person who came in their way.

Captain Hopwood received three severe wounds, but notwithstanding, continued to defend himself. At one time he fell insensible on the deck from the wound of a pistol shot; he again recovered and again attacked his assailants, and killed several with his own hand, till, fatigued and overpowered, he was literally cut to pieces. Mr Bejaun, an American gentleman, together with the Purser and the Supracargo, were massacred in one of the tops after all resistance had ceased. The Chief Officer, the ladies and the other survivors were permitted to live on condition of their renouncing their religion. Between 30 or 40 lascars were killed.

We have seldom heard of any vessel having made a more obstinate and determined resistance than the Minerva on this occasion; and when we consider the circumstances under which she sailed, and how slightly equipped as a fighting vessel, it would be doing injustice to the memory of Captain Hopwood[67] and his brave companions not to record the admiration which has been excited in the minds of his countrymen by this glorious, although unsuccessful, contest.[68]

The Bombay Gazette noted of Mrs Taylor only that she had rendered herself expressly useful, before the attack commenced, by the manufacture of a quantity of cartridges. A second, nearly contemporary, account of the Minerva's seizure has, by contrast, little to say of the attack itself, though it records with measured relief that there was no wanton killing after the fighting had ended. This latter version, appearing in the Asiatic Annual Register, is clearly addressed at other, strictly more gallant sensibilities (though in doing so one suspects it may exaggerate the nature of the supposed transgression). After lamenting the matter of the forced conversions, it goes on to state,

Much as the men must have suffered on this occasion, it is comparatively nothing to the distress of the three ladies who were on board; and who, consequently, fell into the hands of these lawless and unprincipled violators. The subject is too painful to enlarge on. The indignities they were compelled to undergo can be easily conceived; and must excite the strongest emotions of pity in every feeling and delicate mind.[69]

When William Bruce first learnt of the loss of the *Minerva* from the Persian Governor of Bushire, after remarking that her cargo was valued at *c.* 300,000 rupees (roughly £30,000), he exclaimed that only the largest of vessels were now capable of resisting the Qawasim since, he said, they had recently adopted a new 'system' of cruising in large fleets.[70] Although it would be unwise to place reliance on the precise figures in the above accounts, it is clear that the number of vessels engaged in the tenacious assault on the *Minerva* was exceptionally large. A number of observers similarly identified a new 'system' at work in this episode, which they put down to greatly increased Wahhabi influence over the Qawasim. One of these was the Basra Resident Samuel Manesty, who was himself principal owner of the country-ship *Minerva*. He saw the attack as evidence of 'a new and systematic plan of piracy' and concluded that there was now little chance of a return to Seton's accord of 1806.[71] He was not, of course, aware that the decision had already been taken by the Supreme Government in Calcutta, on 3 April 1809, to launch a British expedition against the Qawasim that same year.

iii   *The Third Period, 1810–1819*

(8) *c.* Seven vessels, off Sind, January 1814
(9) The *Ahmadi, c.* 19 March 1816; The *Fath Mubarak* & The *Safar Salamat, c.* 23 March 1816
(10) The HCC *Darya Daulat, c.* 7 January 1817
(11) A military transport, *c.* mid-November 1818 (see preceding Chapter Five, section iv)

In the wake of the British operations against Ras al-Khaima and associated states in November 1809 to January 1810, there ensued a period of four years during which the sources are nearly silent regarding instances of piracy and attempted piracy.[72] In the last few months of 1813, this relative silence is broken by reports of Qasimi piracy off Sind. Hereafter, and for the next six years up until the second British expedition, the general level of reported piracy appears to increase quite sharply, though not in all respects steadily. The focus of this alleged piracy occurs off the coasts of north-west India, especially Cutch and Sind, though important incidents are noted for the regions of south Arabia and the Gulf. Almost all reported occurrences still take place in the 'winter' months, between September and April, and the bulk of these maritime attacks and seizures are ascribed to the Qawasim, though Rahma bin Jabir, in particular, also achieves a degree of prominence.

Four separate instances of alleged piracy stand out in the decade leading up to the second and final British assault on Ras al-Khaima, in the same manner in which we have already seen a small number of others to have dominated British reasoning in the twelve years preceding. The earliest of these occurred at the start of 1814 off north-west India. This episode, though not quite literally the first recorded case since 1809, was felt in Bombay to represent a dangerous resurgence of an activity which the first expedition was until then believed to have eliminated, and which would therefore require, at the least, a renewed vigilance.[73] The remaining incidents would constitute graver affairs. The impact of two of these bloody clashes, those involving the Company's *Darya Daulat* and the military transport, is underlined by the fact that these alone were to be mentioned in the explanatory briefing issued to the commander of the second expedition, Major-General Keir in 1819;[74] and, a few years before, Calcutta's very decision to launch that decisive expedition had itself been precipitated by the experience and sufferings of three vessels near the mouth of the Red Sea at the start of spring 1816. But before considering these episodes, let us return to the events of 1814.

The Qawasim were alleged to have made two separate cruises to Makran and Sind in the winter season of 1813/14. Agents at Mandvi and Hyderabad indicated that during the first of these, around mid-November 1813, an 11-strong squadron of Qawasim, and possibly Jalahima, captured five Cutch merchant boats, inflicting some loss of life, off Karachi; though only two of these vessels actually proved to be loaded with merchandise.[75] Early the next year, the Muscat Broker, Sind Agent, Indian mercantile contacts at Karachi and the Company's officers at Bushire, Porbandar and at sea, together speak of a second, like cruise.[76] It is said to have lasted in all from early January until early–mid-February.[77] Fifteen Qasimi vessels were originally reported to have set sail from Ras al-Khaima, variously bound for Sind, Makran, or, so as to intercept the Basra fleet, for the Strait of Hormuz. Six to ten sail of Qawasim were soon after sighted near Karachi, where they were believed to have taken a number of trading vessels,[78] in all or part, as in November, during a relatively unopposed harbour raid:[79] these captured boats included 5 dinghies,[80] two of them Baluchi, bound from Bombay to Karachi; a baghla carrying Cutch cloth to Arabia; and an Utub vessel—out of which only one man reportedly escaped with his life to tell the tale—which had been delivering Karachi property to Muscat.[81] At least two of the Bombay dinghies that were seized, laden with grain, (or possibly two others) may have been British.

When the seizure of these *c.* 7 vessels was put to the Qasimi ruler, Hasan bin Rahma, by Bruce, it was somewhat unaccountably represented to him that all the captured vessels had been British.[82] Hasan bin Rahma took up the point in what is otherwise, for what it more positively seems to imply, an intriguing answer.

> The boats mentioned by you we never saw. Those we met had neither passes nor colours, and, when they were boarded, had no people on board but were abandoned. Our boats therefore left them in the same state. But you know the Indians and Sindians in this quarter are our enemies; so also are they yours. You do not however think them worthy [of] notice ...
>
> The boats which we fell in with belonging to Karachi and the river had nothing on board but hides and few other articles, without any Dewilla[83] rice, and were left without being touched. You may rely that all vessels that are subject to you will be respected by us, as we are very well acquainted with English ships and vessels with their crews, and it has always been our custom when we have seen them to show our colours and proceed on our voyage.[84]

And, from another letter,

> I hope you will not be too severe in scrutinising the past, and request you will point out the extent of your possessions towards Sind, and those who are your subjects, to me. I have always understood that your people go about in ships and not in dinghies etc.; these belong to Sind, Dewilla and Karachi, nor do we wish to molest your people or break our engagements.[85]

There is a possible explanation for why, assuming Hasan bin Rahma's statement to have been correct, the Sind vessels were deserted when his people boarded them: it is not infrequently recorded that Indian crews on these coasts would abandon ship when they feared they were to be attacked by pirates.[86]

As to the second point, the matter of the British pass and colours not having been in evidence, it seems that Hasan bin Rahma's observations could have been right. There is a strong suspicion that Bruce's allegations of there having been '6–8' British vessels captured off Sind, had resulted simply from his loose reading of the information relayed to him in despatches from Bombay;[87] furthermore, it seems that even in the case of the two dinghies that were positively described, by Francis Warden alone, as British, there was still no evidence that the British flag had actually been flown or the pass produced. It is suggested that it was by no means uncommon for vessels entitled to fly the British, to opt instead to hoist the ubiquitous plain red flag of the Arabs.[88]

All this was, in fact, very soon privately conceded by the British, and it was for this reason that none of these claims were pressed any further against the Qawasim. Yet the affair had raised the issue of the difficulties of mutual recognition at sea. It was proposed that the Company's pass should henceforth bear an Arabic translation on its reverse and ships be urged to use their British colours;[89] and, in October, it was provisionally agreed that the Qawasim should in future distinguish their vessels from those of other Arabs by adding to the centre of the red flag the Arabic motto, 'There is no god but Allah, and Muhammad is His Prophet.' But it appears that this provision was not, or certainly not for long, executed.

The main thrust of Hasan bin Rahma's argument to Bruce seems, then, to have been that although his people did indeed board certain vessels as was alleged—and this is the most significant fact to arise from this business—they only did so under the belief that they were Indian: hence his proposal, 'let us know what people are your subjects and have all vessels provided with passes and colours that we may be able to distinguish them.'[90] In his preliminary reply to Bruce, he is reported to have been a little more explicit, explaining that

> he could not answer my letter just now as he was on the eve of setting off for Dir'iya, the Wahhabi court: but ... he was not aware of having captured any boat under British colours or passes, but if any had been taken, such property as was forthcoming, which was only guns and anchors, he would deliver up; as for anything else, it had long been shared out and made away with.[91]

Hasan bin Rahma also alludes in these letters to a second potential area of ambiguity, namely the question of whether the boats boarded by his people had, after all, been those intended by the British.

> You mention that our vessels go towards Sind which is very right; but we have scarce brought anything from that quarter, merely a little coarse red rice, [a] small quantity of wheat, a little cotton and some iron. But other tribes also visit this quarter: the Qawasim who are subject to Sayyid Sa'id of Muscat and others, who take property and then charge us with having done it.[92]

And again,

> [You write] that some of our vessels have been cruising off Cutch and Karachi. What you say is very true. Our boats have been there; but boats belonging to other tribes have also been there, the Muscat vessels with Rahma bin Jabir etc., ... in fact everybody as well as us visit[s] this quarter.[93]

There were in fact separate reports of Rahma bin Jabir and the Jalahima at this time. The Sind Agent apparently talks generally of Qasimi and Jalahima pirates.[94] More specifically, the Muscat Broker curiously implies that 5–6 Jalahima vessels were associated, even initially sailed, with the 15 Qawasim that left Ras al-Khaima in January. But they did not, it seems, proceed to India. A subsequent report records the capture by 5 Jalahima vessels of a Baluchi baghla carrying 500 moorahs (40 tons?)[95] of rice— 'a lucky chance for the pirates'[96]—and the destruction of another baghla out of Bombay, both off Ras al-Hadd: and since these two incidents apparently occurred in January 1814, it might seem unlikely, perhaps, that the Jalahima were also active with 6–10 further vessels off Sind at the same time, though it cannot of course be ruled out.[97] The only other power which the British knew to be active in this region at the time was the port of Ormara: 'during the early part' of 1814, Ormara vessels allegedly committed several piracies, including one upon a British dinghy bearing a cargo of cotton for Karachi.[98] These activities are not, however, anywhere actually associated with the above. The specific involvement of powers other than the Qawasim in the attacks purposed by the British must ultimately, therefore, on the surviving evidence, remain conjectural.

The British response to the capture of the vessels off Sind in January 1814 took eventual cognisance of both the above areas of obscurity. Hasan bin Rahma was taken at his word when he expressed a desire to show all respect to the British flag; and, after agreeing to drop all outstanding claims, the Resident William Bruce took advantage of the renewed contact with the Qawasim to reach a provisional agreement with Hasan bin Rahma's representative at Bushire on 6 October.[99] This agreement provided for mutual respect, aid and assistance at sea, for free access to each other's ports, for the introduction of a new Qasimi flag and, finally, it included the Qawasim's promise that, in the future, they would return immediately whatever British property they might incidentally discover on board vessels they captured from their enemies. As we have already seen, however, the opportunity to have these initial engagements made firmer and more full was, with damaging consequences, very soon lost: the boat sent by Bruce to Ras al-Khaima in order to convey the Qasimi representative on his way to Bombay for this very purpose, was not allowed to fulfil her mission.

A second, in itself inconsequential, result of January's attacks was the decision, on the part of Bombay, to adopt mild prophylactic measures on the northern coasts that winter: Captain Prior of HMS Acorn was ordered in October, in company with the HCCs Mercury and Sylph, to patrol the Diu–Gwadar coast, with orders to warn off any armed boats or pirates from the Gulf, of whatever tribe, who appeared to be threatening the trade.

Captain Prior was expressly ordered to prevent the interruption of all vessels trading with the Bombay Presidency 'whether they may be navigating under the British colours or not'.[100] This offers a contrast to all William Bruce's communications with the Qawasim, where concern is only manifested for British vessels. The preoccupations of the Government, however, were becoming less narrowly defined.

At this juncture, let us turn to the consideration of an affair of a little greater clarity and moment.[101]

> The widespreading shadow of the well-known power and majesty of the Honourable Company is the sacred asylum and sanctuary of every dweller on earth, and every traveller by sea and land, especially persons[?] who are sitting under the umbrage and security of the protection and defence of Your Government.

So commences a petition of July 1816, signed by 33 Indian merchants in the port of Surat, and addressed to Sir Evan Nepean, Governor of Bombay since 1812.[102] The letter continues,

> As no enmity or hostility existed between [us and] the Qasimi and Wahhabi tribes, or any other Arab sect, in confidence thereof, none of us hesitated to despatch our vessels or merchandise to the ports of Mocha and Jeddah, and we did so with tranquillity and peace of mind. We entertained no apprehension or suspicion of violence and outrage, or of plunder and tyranny from the tribe in question—in this assurance, we did not solicit a vessel from Government for their protection and security at sea. Satisfied with the Honourable Company's passes and colours, we confidently put our merchandise, to the values of about ten or twelve lacs of rupees [1–1.2 million Rs], consisting of coarse piece-goods and sundries etc., on board of three vessels, which we despatched from Surat to Mocha and Jeddah.[103]

The grab *Ahmadi*, owned by Diaram Laldass Cheeneewalla and carrying Surat, Gujarat and Patan-owned goods—'shawls, kincobs, embroidered cloths manufactured at Surat, chintzes, palempores, humbroos, Gujarati dooputties, Cambay cloths for females, and piece-goods, together with various other descriptions of cloths'[104]—set sail from Surat on *c.* 22 February 1816. The snow *Fath Mubarak* and the pattamar *Safar Salamat*, belonging to a second Surat merchant Mulla Abu al-Fath, must have departed at roughly the same time. The value of their cargoes, 1–1.2 million rupees, if correct, was roughly equivalent to £100,000–120,000 sterling;[105] the monthly salary of a Bombay lascar serving on a European ship at this time was around 12 rupees.[106]

Three and a half weeks after she set out, then, the *Ahmadi* had just passed through the Bab al-Mandab, when her crew descried 4 baghlas, 2 dows and 2 battils lying at anchor under the highlands. Almost immediately the vessels were observed to get underway and set course directly for the *Ahmadi*.

Remarking that 'the strangers appeared to be pirates',[107] the Nakhuda and the Native Officer, then seated upon the quarter-deck, summoned the Portuguese Gunner, conjured him to 'dress himself properly',[108] then stationed him on the quarter-deck, British pass in hand, so as to demonstrate under whose protection she sailed. At the same time, British colours were hoisted. Neither of these precautions had the desired effect, and within an hour of her first sighting, the *Ahmadi* was surrounded. The Second Nakhuda hailed from close quarters. The Portuguese Gunner 'stretched forth his arm, and showed them her British pass',[109] and, as Shaikh Tahir, one of the Tindals, watched the scene from the masthead, a spear was flung and struck the Gunner dead.

Hereupon, at least 40–50 men with drawn swords, possibly many more, boarded the *Ahmadi* on all sides from the attacking vessels.[110] There is no record of any resistance being offered. The next half-hour was chaos. As soon as the Gunner had fallen, the Head Nakhuda and the Native Officer retreated to the cabin; others now hurried below or tried to escape by climbing up the rigging. The attackers rushed straight for the cabin and 'began to massacre all who were in it'.[111] The Tindal Shaikh Tahir, from his perch on the masthead, claims to have witnessed the invaders remove the British flag and 'cut down ten or twelve with sabres and throw them overboard'; after this, 'seeing one of the pirates coming up the rigging to kill him, he was about to plunge into the water'—when it was ordered that no-one further should be harmed.[112] The ship, in danger of going over from the lascars having severed her braces as they scaled the rigging, was brought under control, and those in hiding below now began to emerge.

When the Native Steward came up on deck, he saw 'about ten or twelve dead bodies, some of them with the heads severed off, ... lying about the deck ... the remainder had been thrown overboard.'[113] These deaths were later presented in the Surat merchants' petition in rather more emotive terms: 'this cruel sect, feeling neither reverence, respect, nor regard for the Honourable Company, but stimulated by their own contumacious and presumptuous dispositions, ... slaughtered, like sheep, 56 persons who were on board the *Ahmadi*'.[114] Of the near correctness of this figure for the victims, which included crew, merchants and pilgrims, male and female, there is little doubt, for they are, many of them, named.[115] A similar number were in addition left unharmed.

During the next four days, those who had seized the *Ahmadi* were engaged in offloading the grab's cargo and supplies. Anxiety increased. At this point two merchantmen hove in sight. The *Ahmadi*'s captors, learning from one of her passengers 'what vessels they were and whether they were armed and capable of resistance',[116] directed four of their boats to over-power them. The *Safar Salamat* and the *Fath Mubarak* were swiftly brought to without a fight and without bloodshed. For something approaching a week, the three Surat ships and their captors remained at anchor as the unloading of their goods and merchandise was being completed. There-upon, first the *Safar Salamat* and the *Fath Mubarak*, then, a few days later, the *Ahmadi* (with provisions for 15 days), were all released and enabled soon to reach the port of Mocha. The detention of the *Ahmadi* had lasted a total of around 18 days.

We have seen that the Surat merchants were in no doubt as to the identity of those who had plundered their three ships. They even went as far as to postulate that the attackers could have gleaned foreknowledge of their sailing from clandestine 'emissaries' in the Arab dows that visited Surat.[117] The Bombay Council, however, on receiving the very first, sketchy accounts of these seizures, noted that the Qawasim were by no means the only conceivable culprits and desired that proper enquiries be made before finally apportioning blame.[118] It is fitting, therefore, that we too should respond to this cue and seek to ascertain what light the surviving accounts may shed on the matter.

We are fortunate in possessing three separate declarations on oath, executed before a Bombay Justice of the Peace in August 1816, in which the *Ahmadi*'s Second Nakhuda, her Native Steward and one of her Tindals each relate what they recall of their capture.[119] There is no evidence of conscious collusion in the production of these unpolished narratives. They unite in testifying that the eight vessels which attacked them belonged to the Qawasim of Ras al-Khaima; one of them[120] also names as their overall commander a certain 'Amir Ibrahim', who is later identified, by Rahma bin Jabir[121] and the British, as brother to Hasan bin Rahma of Ras al-Khaima. They claim to have learnt these matters either from their adversaries themselves or from captives serving with them. Certain aspects of this information are quite intriguing.

The Second Nakhuda mentions three of his assailants' principal officers by name. The first, one Sa'id, described as a 'Jemadar' and Amir Ibrahim's Deputy, was he who gave the order that the killing on board the *Ahmadi* should stop, and very soon after interrogated the Second Nakhuda as to her contents and ownership. Thereafter, he remained to superintend the transhipment of her cargo until the capture of the two other Surat ships four days later, at which point he was replaced by a certain Rashid. The Second Nakhuda states that he personally enjoyed 3–4 interviews with the overall commander, Amir Ibrahim; during one of these sessions he was quizzed on 'the conquest of Cutch by the British government, as well as for information on other matters connected with India.'[122]

Shaikh Tahir, the Tindal, could only recollect the name of one of his assailants, a Hindustani-speaking Baluchi named Musa, who, it was, ordered him down from the masthead. Yet he did recognize one other, a Gogha[123] lascar of about 16 years, whom he had first met when they were both serving on the ships of the ruler of Muscat. The lascar now related to Shaikh Tahir, that a couple of years earlier, shortly after they last saw each other, he had been returning to Bombay in a Muscat merchant's baghla when he had been captured by the Qawasim off Ras al-Hadd; after this he had been taken, along with the Bombay wife of a Muscat Serang, to Ras al-Khaima, and had remained in their hands ever since.

The lascar's tale is interesting because it confirmed what Shaikh Tahir had heard long before. A rather more striking piece of outside corroboration for the identity of the *Ahmadi*'s assailants arises out of the report of the Second Nakhuda: one of the sailors he discovered serving his captors was an Abyssinian called Mubarak, an experienced seaman and the former slave of one Bu Abid,[124] Mocha merchant. Mubarak was made the custodian of the *Ahmadi*'s captured crew, and hence found the opportunity to recount to the Second Nakhuda the manner in which he had fallen into the hands of his captors. He had, he said, been captured by Amir Ibrahim in one of Bu Abid's ships between Bengal and Mocha the previous year. His master's son, then also serving alongside him, had been taken in the same assault. Somehow this latter even managed to deliver the Second Nakhuda a letter to transmit to his distraught father at Mocha.

The important point about this claim regarding the loss of Bu Abid's vessel to the Qawasim in 1815 is that it provides us with a cross-reference. The event in question had in fact been recorded in three quite separate sources shortly after it had occurred. The Naqib, ruler, of the Yemeni port of Mukalla, a somewhat unlikely source for such intelligence, one who then sought the benefit of good relations with Britain, wrote early in 1815 that six Wahhabi vessels from Ras al-Khaima had recently captured a dow belonging to Bu Abid, with Bengal cargo, in the harbour of Shihr; they had also taken a Suri dow, bearing Indian cloth, off Qishn and burnt her with the loss of all but 12 of her crew; and although an attempt by the Qawasim on Shihr itself had been beaten off, they had managed to seize one of her merchantmen, the property of a Suri and bearing a cargo of oil.[125]

The capture of Bu Abid's ship by six Qawasim is also recorded in a despatch from the Company's Broker at Muscat, dated 10 April 1815. In his account, however, the capture occurs off Mukalla and he confuses the name of the ship for that of the owner: he puts a value of 200,000 French crowns, about £50,000,[126] on her cargo of rice, sugar, cloth and shawls. And at the same time he records other captures by the six off south Arabia and Oman, including a particularly bloody attack on a well-armed and stoutly defended Suri dow bearing Cutch cloth for Mocha and Jeddah; 'hundreds' perished on both sides, to no avail, and the vessel was eventually said to have been set on fire by her owner. This was presumably the second of the occurrences also recorded by the Naqib. Finally, the Broker remarks upon certain other boats recently seized by the Qawasim, which included a large Muscat dinghy and numbers of unspecified smaller craft.[127]

The third of these sources is the Mocha Agent Forbes. He wrote a month after the event, when reports first arrived of the capture by six Ras al-Khaima Qawasim of both the Suri dow and the 600-ton ship *Fath al-Rahman*, belonging to Abd al-Rahman Bu Abid, which had been taken on 24 February with the loss of most of her crew; immediate alarm spread at Mocha at this seeming resurgence of Qasimi activity.[128]

The existence of four such distinct sources for the story of the capture of Bu Abid's ship is quite a strong indication of the Qawasim's responsibility for that action. The presence of Bu Abid's son and former slave on board the vessels that later took the *Ahmadi* lends credence, therefore, to the proposition that the Qawasim were likewise the authors of this second attack. A further letter from the Naqib of Mukalla, dated 5 May 1816, apparently says as much, though he does not choose to distinguish between the vessels belonging to Rahma bin Jabir and the Ras al-Khaima Qawasim, 15 in all, which he said were then cruising off Yemen. He also adds that before the seizure of the three Surat vessels, they had launched attacks and been repelled, both at Burum, where they had temporarily gained a foothold, and later on at Aden.[129]

As to the presence of Rahma bin Jabir in the area at this time, there is little doubt. He himself indicated this much to the British Resident after his arrival at Bushire in October.[130] Reports from Mocha had stated that soon after early April 1816 he had captured two of Sharif Hamud[131] of Tihama's coffee dows and one Abyssinian vessel off Luhayya, then left the Red Sea for Saihut(?) where he seized the Mangalore merchant Moorarjee Culianjee's grab, laden with cotton for Mocha, with the loss of almost all her crew.[132]

In short, therefore, it seems not unreasonable to suppose that the captors of the three Surat vessels were indeed the Qawasim of Ras al-Khaima; that this took place during a cruise by at least eight Qasimi boats round south Arabia in the early months of 1816; and that something similar, involving half a dozen vessels, had occurred in the same season the previous year.

Let us return, at this point, to the main purpose of the Surat merchants' petition:

Your Excellency must reflect that it is not in our power to bear such severe losses. Our only means of subsistence is our mercantile dealings with Mocha and Jeddah; indeed, upon that commerce depends the livelihood of the greater part of the inhabitants of Surat. We are the Honourable Company's subjects. Our peace of mind and our fortunes are ruined and destroyed. This event must tend to the depopulation of the city of Surat. Under these circumstances, if Your Excellency, who is the Governor and protector of your subjects, with your sympathising feelings, should not afford us redress and listen to our petitions, we are hopeless and ruined. To whom else can we resort, or where else seek refuge? Your Excellency is our only asylum and retreat. We therefore hope that, in your exalted dispositions, you will so effectually chastise and punish these barbarous and cruel Qawasim, as to ensure the restitution of our properties, stores etc.: this circumstance will redound to your credit, and create an universal terror of the Honourable Company, as well by sea as by land.[133]

The Government of Bombay felt constrained to act. Captain Bridges of HM sloop *Challenger*, 18 guns, was directed in company with the Bushire Resident William Bruce, and the HC cruisers *Mercury*, *Vestal* and *Ariel*, to Ras al-Khaima, where they were to demand that the property from the Surat vessels be restored and Ibrahim bin Rahma be suitably punished. But Hasan bin Rahma, chief of Ras al-Khaima, rejected these demands with a denial of Qasimi complicity; though it is alleged his negotiators privately conceded the truth of the British allegations. And interestingly enough, the Wahhabi leader, Abdullah bin Su'ud, shortly after this wrote Bruce a letter—ultimately perhaps the most striking piece of evidence in this regard —in which, before suggesting that the matter were best passed over, he makes the following defence of his subjects' seizure of the Surat vessels:

If the Qawasim have taken any property belonging to an Englishman, prove it, then we will set to and have them restore the same; but as to goods owned by anyone else, we are under absolutely no such obligation. How can we return the property of our enemies? We have ascertained that most of the goods taken [on this occasion] belonged to the people of Egypt, and the rest to those of Jeddah and the ports of [Sharif Hamud bin Muhammad] Abu Mismar.[134]

Bruce claimed, in fact, to have received sound intelligence that the customary one-fifth of this booty had previously been forwarded to the Wahhabi capital at Dir'iya, and the rest of it dispersed locally:[135] hence, he explained, the Qawasim's incapacity to make a restitution.

The upshot of the brief Anglo–Qasimi negotiations at Ras al-Khaima on 26–7 Nov. and 30 Nov.–1 Dec. 1816, was immediate failure and a lasting rupture in relations. The outcome might not perhaps have been so disastrous but for British impetuosity. Exasperated by their failure to elicit either a restitution of the Surat merchants' property or the punishment of Ibrahim bin Rahma, Captain Bridges' squadron was determined not to quit the harbour of Ras al-Khaima without a show of displeasure. A barrage of fire was opened up at four Qasimi vessels which happened to be moored inshore, but, unable on account of their draught to approach within a mile of the coast, the few hundred or so shot all dropped short: this was hardly the 'universal terror' desired by the Surat merchants. The Qawasim replied by hoisting their flags in defiance, as they crowded on the beach and returned the incoming fire, possibly to slightly more effect.[136] The British squadron, therefore, having achieved little beyond its own discomfiture, was obliged to abandon the attempt and sailed away.[137]

On 22 February 1817, the Supreme Government at Fort William responded to this news by informing Bombay of the Governor-General's 'conviction of the absolute necessity of destroying the power of the pirates'; a second expedition was therefore to be launched against Ras al-Khaima whenever it became practicable.[138]

Even before this date, unbeknown as yet to Government, though the first suspicions had been aired, another ship, this time the Company's own, had allegedly been taken by the Qawasim, at the Gulf of Cutch: this seizure of the *Darya Daulat* was, in fact, one of a number of captures said to have been made by the Qawasim off north-west India between November 1816 and February 1817.[139] Qasimi activity of this kind in these waters is also recorded for each of the winter seasons between 1813/14 and 1819/20, apart from 1815/16 when the sources appear silent on the matter.

Commencing in mid-November 1816, there was talk of the approach of an unspecified number of Qawasim as far east as Sind, where soon after they were said to have taken and burnt an empty Porbandar craft, as well as another from Sind carrying rice to Mandvi.[140]

The following month reports from various British and Indian sources at Mandvi and Porbandar claimed that by the middle or end of January 1817 a group of 8–11 Qasimi vessels, half dows and half 'jymers' (a smaller craft), had taken about 14 prizes off Cutch, between Lakhpat and Mandvi; and that an attempt to cut out a further 3–5 vessels from this last port had at length been frustrated by the Raja of Cutch.[141]

These 14 captured vessels, almost all relatively small Cutch trading-craft, are said to have included the following: 8 small Mandvi vessels trading with Lakhpat; 2 of Sunderjee Sewjee's larger botellas, similarly bound and valued at 10,000 rupees;[142] the Cambay merchant Eduljee Curretjee's botella carrying tobacco via Dwarka to Cutch; and finally two Porbandar vessels, one of them the *Luckmee Pussaud*.

This 255-candy (71-ton)[143] dinghy, owned by the Porbandar and Bombay merchant Sewjee Govindjee and valued with her cargo at 13,000 rupees, had been taken at the very end of her long voyage from Mangalore via Porbandar to Lakhpat. The joyless petition addressed by her owner to Governor Nepean recollects that her 30 crewmen, being well armed with 8 cannon, 15 handguns and 20 swords, 'fought gallantly' before they were defeated; 6 were captured and 17 killed, whilst the others managed to swim to safety.[144] The *Luckmee Pussaud* was the only vessel amongst these 14 explicitly stated to have borne the British flag and pass, although Sewjee and Curretjee presumably had this right.[145] She was also very possibly the most valuable; though it should be remarked that the combined value of all these seizures must have fallen very far short of the great 1–1.2 million rupees of loss suffered by the owners of the three Surat ships in 1816.[146]

Bombay's reaction to these captures was distinctly low-key. Captain Hill of HMS *Towey*[147] had been due to set sail for the Gulf, where he was to replace Captain Bridges RN as Senior Naval Officer, at the start of February: after November's debacle at Ras al-Khaima, a ship of the Royal Navy and 3 or 4 Company cruisers came to be stationed in the Gulf so as to protect the trade. Captain Hill was now simply requested, therefore, to alter his course so as to take in the coasts of Cutch and Sind, where it was predicted he might encounter the pirates. But neither he, nor the HCC *Prince of Wales* and two pattamars that supported him, had any effective contact with the supposed offenders.[148] Interestingly, when he left Muscat for Bushire in mid-March 1817, he brought with him a list purporting to show 18 recent captures by the Qawasim, largely off Cutch, Sind and Makran, together with the statement that by then most of these prizes had been brought to Ras al-Khaima.[149] If there was any true substance to this report, it might at first sight seem to have involved a second group of Qasimi vessels, since that responsible for the 14 earlier seizures had left Makran for the Gulf at the end of the first week of February.[150] Early that month there had, in fact, been rumours of the departure of two further squadrons from Ras al-Khaima, one, of 15, bound for Cutch and Gujarat, the other, of 12, directed east of Ras al-Hadd 'to intercept the trade from the Malabar coast to Muscat'.[151] Unfortunately there is no direct means of cross-checking the news of these additional captures, and it would probably be wrong to take it at face value, since it could well have been neither fresh nor accurate. Indeed the only one of all this season's attacks off north-west India about which, and about the identity of whose perpetrators, we can be more than a little critical is that which involved the HC pattamar *Darya Daulat*.

The *Darya Daulat* was one of two armed pattamars, under the control of Captain Elwood, the Company's Agent at Porbandar, charged with protecting the Kathiawar coast between Mandvi and Diu Head. The vessel was of a class common on the west coast of India, and Elwood, yet unaware of the irony, boasted that seven years of experience at this posting had taught him 'there were no pirates which visited it, that were half the force of a single armed pattamar.'[152]

The *Darya Daulat* set sail from Porbandar on 27 December 1816, bearing instructions from Bombay which she was to deliver to the commander of the HCC *Psyche*, then detailed to Sind. Upon touching at Karachi and Sonmiani a week later, it was discovered that the *Psyche* had already parted, and so the *Darya Daulat* immediately commenced her return journey southward. At daybreak on 7 January, 20 leagues off Dwarka, or half that according to Shaikh Husain the Serang (commander), 'a baghla was seen on the lee bow, full of men. The pattamar's colours were immediately hoisted, when instantly the baghla fired into her.'[153] The Serang, confident in his superiority, preferred resistance over flight and commenced a brisk fire.

But very soon thick fog lifted to reveal two more large baghlas, which then joined the fight. The Serang 'fought his boat'[154] for three hours, but at 8 a.m. he was incapacitated by a ball that lodged in his hip, and was taken below.

> At 9 a.m. the Tindal was killed by a ball through his body, at which time one of the baghlas boarded the pattamar to windward, when from the number of the pirates that got on board, the crew finding all further resistance in vain, many of them got below, and others jumped overboard clinging to the vessel's side: the whole of those found on deck were immediately massacred by the pirates, as were those clinging to the outside [of] the vessel, to the number of 17 persons, among whom were the Havildar [Sergeant], Naik [Corporal] and 5 sepoys and 9 lascars. The pirates immediately dragged those from below, among whom was the Serang, who had been placed there by his own crew after being wounded: he was very closely questioned whether there were any Europeans concealed, threatening a deadly vengeance to such if found.[155] They took out the arms, and gunpowder, with the sails, then scuttled the pattamar and sunk her.[156]

The three attacking baghlas are each said to have had a burden of between 300 and 400 candies (110–150 tons?)[157] and held 100, or, in the case of the third, 150 men: 'It was impossible to fight such a force: they boarded without any trouble.' According to Dewarjee, the Pilot, 'Their dows were so high above us, that had there been three armed-boats, we could not have beat them off: nothing but ships can contend with such boats, so full of men and so high out of the water.' Of the killing itself, it was said, 'The enemy had a great number of Seedees, or Africans, who did more execution, on boarding, than the Qawasim.'[158]

After taking the survivors from the *Darya Daulat* down into the hold of one of their baghlas, the captors now made a feint towards the ports further south. When they arrived in 40 fathoms off his home port of Porbandar, the captured Pilot maintains they became

> very anxious that I should show them into this port; but, I passed myself off as a sail-maker, and told them, 'I knew nothing about the navigation of Porbandar.' Almost immediately after, they talked of visiting Surat and Bombay, but I regarded this language merely as threats.[159]

At about this time, the three baghlas are said to have fallen in with, and taken, an Arab dow of *c.* 400 candies from Surat, bound possibly for Muscat.[160]

After this, the three baghlas seem to have retracked northward, where we find them putting in at a small creek, one day's sail south of Karachi, in order to take on water. They remained here for two days, and it is stated that the spot also served as a rendezvous where they were now reunited with seven smaller 50–80-man trankeys (battils), in whose company, according to Captain Elwood, the baghlas had originally set sail from Ras al-Khaima, and which had then, prior to this meeting, been detached against the Cutch trade:[161] these, in theory, had been responsible for the 14 or so seizures in January.

Hereafter, the captors resumed their westerly voyage along the coastline until, about 4 February, or shortly thereafter,[162] they touched at a spot near Pasni in Makran; here they abandoned the sick and wounded from amongst the *Darya Daulat*'s captive crew, before finally they took off in the direction of the Persian Gulf. A few weeks later, on the 23rd, a Baluchi dinghy was by chance encountered by the HCC *Sylph* midway between Pasni and Porbandar, and was found to be carrying the liberated survivors from the *Darya Daulat*, in straitened circumstances.[163] Of the armed pattamar's total crew of 33, 8 had eventually been released, 8 taken captive and 17 killed.[164]

The Government of Bombay responded vigorously to these reports of the *Darya Daulat*'s capture by the Qawasim, in a manner that contrasts with the restraint of the previous month when Captain Hill had been directed to scour the northern coasts for pirates. Cruiser commanders were now ordered to attack, and endeavour to take or destroy, any vessel they met with that belonged to the 'Arab piratical tribes' of the Persian Gulf and the Arabian Gulf, or Red Sea. From this casually broad designation the state of Muscat, in particular, was excepted, its assistance in the accomplishment of this task being expected to be readily forthcoming.[165]

The interviewed survivors from the *Darya Daulat* maintained that their captors had been the Qawasim of Ras al-Khaima, and this view gained immediate currency; besides, as we have demonstrated, the statement seemed to correspond with what was already held to be known of contemporaneous Qasimi activities on these coasts. The matter was, in fact, simply not called into question; and it arises, therefore, whether any further evidence for the authorship of this attack cannot be teased out of the sources.

The path of the captors' homeward journey to Pasni, and beyond to the west, is helpful in so far as it rules out the possibility of the three baghlas having belonged to Gujarat or Sind. Most useful of all, however, are the later independent accounts of their experiences by the lascars Ibrahim Bawa bin Abd al-Karim Dholkey and Shaikh Muhammad, two of those eight *Darya Daulat* crew members who had failed to be released at Pasni in February 1817. Both men related a very similar fate: they were taken to Ras al-Khaima, sold and put to work on Qasimi boats, until they managed to effect their escape in *c.* September 1817 and *c.* March 1819 respectively.[166]

Dholkey's deposition states that 'while he was among the pirates, they seemed to cruise with fleets of 8 or 10 sail: two or three larger vessels, and six or seven smaller.'[167] His is seemingly a valuable portrait of the pattern of seven months' service with the Qawasim. Three days after his arrival at Ras al-Khaima, he was sold to an Arab crewman from the boat which had originally taken the *Darya Daulat*. A fortnight later, he was sent on board a 300-man, 9-gun dow or baghla, and set out on a successful cruise in which they managed to capture and bring back a Bhavnagar grab ketch, whose crew escaped to the shore.[168]

Next, after a month's sojourn at Ras al-Khaima, Dholkey asserts that he and his master re-embarked for a second voyage: in company with five others, their baghla sailed round to Ras al-Hadd, where they 'fell in with two Arab ships, with whom they had an action, but were beaten off with a loss of about 40 or 50 of their crews, among whom was one of the *Darya Daulat*'s sepoys.'[169] There may, if we adopt a tight construction on Dholkey's dates up to this point, possibly be separate confirmation of this incident in two letters despatched by the Company's Muscat Broker, Goolab Anundass, in May 1817.[170] In these, he reports that in about the second week of that month, seven Qasimi vessels fought a 'severe contest' with Gopal Mowjee's baghla, which was carrying ivory and slaves from Zanzibar to Muscat and was valued at *c.* 200,000 rupees, as she rounded

Plate 5. Island of Ashtola (Astola) in Makran, 1808: depiction of a battil. (Morier, *A Journey through Persia . . . in 1808 and 1809*)

Plate 6. Baghlas in the port of Muscat in the 1830s. (Paris, *Essai*)

Plate 7. Top: Battil under full sail, Muscat 1830s.   *Bottom*: Fishing badans, a baghla (*left*) and a dungiyah (*background*), Muscat 1830s. (Paris, *Essai*)

Plate 8.   Ras al-Khaima, chief port of the Wahhabi pirates. (Watercolour, Lt Col. Charles Hamilton Smith 1776–1859)

Ras al-Hadd in the company of a second baghla owned by a Qasim bin Sa'id. This attack was, he says, beaten off at the cost of 12 of Mowjee's men to '200' Qasimi dead. The following week, he also records two other, this time successful, attacks on a pair of small vessels out of Bombay, one of them near Qurayat,[171] as well as a brush with the HCC Vestal; but these last incidents find no mention in Dholkey's deposition.

Dholkey was not to attain his freedom before he had undertaken a third voyage. A month or so after his return from Ras al-Hadd, he accompanied his owner on board a 2-gun, 80-man battil; and they set off, with four others, across the Gulf to Linga, 'where they had a skirmish on shore with the people of that place'.[172] After this, as they were watering at somewhere called 'Jassam', which might well have been the island of Qishm, Dholkey contrived to evade his captors. He was well received by the local chief, who was attached to Muscat, and by this means, after some two months, he was assisted in his passage to Muscat and thence, finally, to Bombay.

Dholkey mentions that whilst he was still at 'Jassam', another of the Darya Daulat's lascars managed to flee and join him. This left five of the eight original captives still alive and unaccounted for. According to the lascar Shaikh Muhammad, who himself escaped only in c. March 1819, one of these, a Marine Battalion sepoy, had died in late 1818, but the other three, to the best of his knowledge, remained in the hands of the Qawasim. The manner of Shaikh Muhammad's escape was rather different from that of Dholkey: two years after his original capture, he regained his freedom when the Qasimi baghla in which he had been serving was forcibly taken by a Muscat vessel.[173]

The accounts given by the two escaped lascars from the Darya Daulat are consistent. There can be very little doubt that the first reports, which maintained that the Darya Daulat had been captured by the Qawasim, were accurate.

★　★　★

The 27 major incidents, which have now been examined in Chapters Five and Six, must represent the starting-point for any close investigation of Persian Gulf piracy at the start of the nineteenth century; for they are, of all the instances of alleged piracy in this period, the most detailed, the most certain and the most historically important.

Two criteria have dictated this selection, the first evidential and the second historical. Chapter Five comprised a loose categorization of most, or all, the instances of alleged piracy and seizure at the hands of the peoples of the Gulf in the years 1797–1819, such as are supported by 'admissions', or in a very few cases, 'possession'. This means that the bare essentials of all these 22 cases are, for most purposes, certain beyond any reasonable doubt; in other respects these incidents were not necessarily homogeneous. Chapter Six was an appraisal of the 11 separate incidents which Britain regarded as the gravest or most important. In fact, just over half these examples also met the exacting standard of proof adopted for Chapter Five; and, as for the remaining five, the evidence was really very convincing in all but one, or conceivably two, cases where it was still suggestive.[174] This positive result was fortuitous, since the incidents in Chapter Six had been assembled not because the evidence for them was, in any way distinctive, but because they were, for their effect on British policy and the final outcome of these years, the most historically significant.

The most striking aspect of the examples discussed hitherto is that they comprise all the major British grievances, and the heart of the Company's case against the Qawasim. All but two or three of these 27 events were accompanied by the seizure of British property; indeed, four-fifths of these incidents actually involved attacks on British vessels—nearly the same proportion of these seizures as are to be associated with the Qawasim.[175]

The importance attached by Britain to the principal examples in Chapters Five and Six, is demonstrated by the fact that, apart from these, she only chose to make representations to the Qawasim on two further occasions.[176]

The first of these concerned two seizures that had occurred around September/October 1805, off the coast of Makran. The eight attackers (1 baghla, 2 dows, 4 battils and 2 baqqaras) were reported to have been Qawasim: their victims, carrying Muscat and Bombay property, some of it British, consisted of one or more dinghies from Sind with a nauri from Bombay. The only response to the relatively mild British protest in this case, came not from the Qawasim, but from the Shaikh of Qishm, who was then negotiating with Captain Seton: his is, however, a curiously oblique letter, which most probably seeks to affix the blame on the Qawasim's southern neighbours, the people of Shaikh Hazza' (bin Za'al?) of Dubai—'they are independent and lawless, you need not doubt what I write'—though the argument he employs to this end might appear some-what misdirected; alternatively he might also conceivably imply that if the Qawasim were implicated in these seizures, then it was out of hostility to Muscat and therefore legitimate.[177]

The only other incident which Britain put before the Qawasim in these two decades was one that took place in 1816. On 4 January, the *Salamat Savoy*, carrying British property and belonging to Jadowjee Naran, was apparently taken whilst prosecuting her passage from Bombay to Muscat.

The Qawasim were supposed responsible. Hasan bin Rahma strenuously denied all knowledge of the incident, and the matter was perforce allowed to drop.[178]

If we include these two events, as well as the small number of others that have been mentioned incidentally during the course of the above discussions, it becomes clear that the greater, and without question the most significant, part of all the recorded seizures by the Qawasim of British vessels and property, has already been described. In order to make this picture complete one would need only to take note of one more capture in the Gulf and another off south Arabia,[179] together with a fair number of important seizures off north-west India, particularly in the 'winter' seasons of 1808/9, 1814/15 (?), 1817/18 and 1818/19: during the year before the first expedition, and the three years preceding the second, Britain could very seldom muster the will to protest about such losses to the Qawasim. No other seizures or successful attacks on British vessels—though there were reportedly a fair number of inconclusive or unproductive clashes—by the Qawasim, and very few indeed by any other Gulf power,[180] are recorded for these years.

The formal British case against the Qawasim rested essentially on the events hitherto described; these provided much of the justification for the two assaults on Ras al-Khaima. This group of examples also represents a reliable and valuable, though for all that a partial, cross-section of Qasimi activities in the years 1797–1819. It is crucial to recognize that, in the matter of shipping and trade as in any other, the British would seek to amass intelligence on things which most nearly affected them; and it is this which has survived to form the basis of almost all our knowledge of this subject. This explains why the information we possess of the activities of the Qawasim is fullest where their actions impinged on British concerns. This does not, of course, in any way mean that this formed the largest, or necessarily the most characteristic, part of their activities.

The heavily cautious approach to the sources employed throughout Chapters Five and Six, enables us now to assert the following: virtually all the most important specific accusations of seizure made by Britain against the Qawasim were, at their most basic level, demonstrably justified; and, for whatever reason and under whatever circumstances, the very great bulk of successful attacks by the peoples of the Gulf upon British vessels between 1797 and 1819, may be attributed with certainty only to one power, the Qawasim. This is, of course, but one aspect to this story; we must now proceed towards a somewhat broader consideration of events.

B. Perspectives

CHAPTER SEVEN

Local Opinion

No man is a pirate, unless his contemporaries agree to call him so.

An Arab fisherman ... who lived in a village on the Persian Gulf, not far from Gombroon [Bandar Abbas], being one day busy at his usual occupation, found his net so heavy that he could hardly drag it on shore. Exulting in his good fortune, he exerted all his strength: but judge of his astonishment when, instead of a shoal of fish, he saw in his net an animal of the shape of a man, but covered with hair. He approached it with caution; but finding it harmless, carried it to his house, where it soon became a favourite; for, though it could speak no language, and utter no sound except 'Haul, haul' (from whence it took its name), it was extremely docile and intelligent; and the fisherman, who possessed some property, employed it to guard his flocks.

One day, so the tale goes, whilst the Haul was thus engaged, alone and armed only with a club, a band of 100 Persian horsemen decked out in full armour appeared from the interior, and began to drive off the sheep from under his care. At first they scoffed at the Haul on account of his strange appearance, ignoring his marks of protest. But the Haul was not as he had seemed; leaping into a frenzy of activity as they attacked, aiming blows to right and left, he soon not only beat off the marauding Persian knights but, in doing so, slew half their number.

The fisherman and his neighbours, when they heard of the battle, hastened to the aid of the faithful Haul, whom they found in possession of the horses, clothes, and arms of the vanquished Persians. An Arab of the village, struck with his valour, and casting an eye of cupidity at the wealth he had acquired, offered him the hand of his daughter, who was very beautiful, and she, preferring good qualities to outward appearance, showed no reluctance to become the bride of this kind and gallant monster. Their marriage was celebrated with more pomp than was ever before known in the village; and the Haul, who was dressed in one of the richest suits of the Persians he had slain, and mounted on one of their finest horses, looked surprisingly well. He was quite beside himself with joy, playing such antics, and exhibiting such good humour, strength, and agility, that his bride, who had at first been pitied, became the envy of every fisherman's daughter. She would have been more so, could they have foreseen the fame to which she was destined.

She had four sons, from whom are descended the four tribes of Banu Qasim, Banu Ahmad, Banu Nasir and Banu Sabuhil, who are to this day known by the general name of Banu Haul, or the children of Haul.[1] They are all fisherman, boatmen, and pirates, and live chiefly at sea, inheriting, it is believed, the amphibious nature of their common ancestor.[2]

This fabled account of the origins of the Huwala Arabs of the lower Gulf, whose leading branch was the Qawasim (erroneously referred to here as the Banu Qasim), is attributed by Sir John Malcolm to 'an Arabian servant' called Khudadad, in whose company, during the first decade of the nineteenth century,[3] he had sailed from Muscat to Bushire. The fictionalized setting in which he recounts this legend is as follows: sailing through the Strait of Hormuz, Malcolm recalls observing the coast of Arabia trailing away to southward, whereupon he summoned Khudadad, and enquired of him what manner of people lived there—

They are of the sect of Wahhabis, and are called Qawasim; but God preserve us from them, for they are monsters. Their occupation is piracy, and their delight murder; and to make it worse, they give you the most pious reasons for every villainy they commit.

But, continues Khudadad, they are not wholly to blame for their excesses since they only act according to their nature; a nature, that is, which they have inherited from their monstrous ancestor, the Haul.

Now there is obviously a good deal of Malcolm in all this, and the character of Khudadad, who is soon apparently transformed into a Persian, may well, like the setting, be little more than the stock of literary convention. But it seems quite possible that the story of the Haul was one of those which Malcolm had recorded in the Gulf and preserved in the 'real, well-made, strong, iron-clamped boxes' he brought with him for the purpose;[4] nor do the comments on the proceedings of the 'Qasimi pirates' seem in general terms extraordinary. If this is a correct judgement, then it might suggest that in parts of the Gulf, such as perhaps the harbour at Bushire, a composite popular view of the Qawasim was current: the eighteenth century perception of the Qawasim, represented in the legend of the Haul, one which depicted the Qawasim as fine seafarers and gallant Arab warriors, had been overlaid in the first decade of the nineteenth by another, which described the Qawasim as ruthless sea-robbers acting in the name of Wahhabism.

In a similar fashion, an unnamed educated Arab writing at Bushire in January 1817, possibly a Sunni merchant, one who was certainly well acquainted with Bahrain, the Qawasim and commercial matters, observed that,

> The condition of the Qawasim and their subjects is quite different from what it was before. Nowadays they do not undertake commercial voyages, they do not engage in trade and they do not fish for pearls. On the contrary, their whole business has become that of disruption, corruption and piracy [sadd tariq al-'ibad]; indeed they have completely abandoned all that is legitimate and in every instance donned the mantle of vice.[5]

It should be said that these comments occur in the course of a confidential report on the economy of Bahrain and the Qawasim, which was supplied at the behest of the British Residency; but, despite that, this moral condemnation is essentially gratuitous. It is becoming clear that others in the Gulf besides the British disapproved of the maritime activities of the Qawasim in these two decades, and sensed that they were both new and extraordinary.

Given the paucity of Arabic sources for this subject, it is only to be expected that glimpses of this kind should be rare. The most extensive contemporary account in Arabic of the Qawasim during this period, occurs in an anonymous book completed in 1817 and entitled the 'Refulgent Meteor Illuminating the Biography of Muhammad bin Abd al-Wahhab', the *Lam' al-Shihab*. This unusually detached work appears to have been composed by a scholar in, and of, the northern Gulf, quite possibly at the behest of the British:[6] it sets out the history and tenets of Wahhabism.

The *Lam' al-Shihab* gives a schematic, but explicit account of the Qawasim's descent into a life of marauding, a transformation which began unwillingly at the turn of the century, and was later transfused with enthusiasm after the accession of Shaikh Sultan bin Saqr of Ras al-Khaima in 1803. Under constraint from the Wahhabis,

> the Qawasim put to sea in order to plunder people's property and to kill them in the pursuit of this aim. The Za'ab [tribe of Jazirat al-Hamra'][7] and the Tanaij [tribe of Rams] also embarked in their ships upon the Holy War; indeed, [at this stage], they executed more acts of plunder than the Qawasim, since the Qawasim initially shrank from assaults on people's life and property.

For three years, relates this author, the Qawasim perforce continued reluctant partners in this enterprise. Then Sultan bin Saqr succeeded his father in the government of Ras al-Khaima, and instituted a new and genuinely responsive policy towards the Wahhabi rulers, the Al Su'ud—

> Sultan bin Saqr ... [now] commenced plundering at sea: he himself (and this is a credited fact) used to sail on these voyages. The same year in which he became ruler, he plundered 37 vessels, both dows and baghlas. ...[8]

The author of the *Lam' al-Shihab* asserts that the decisive change in the reputation and fortunes of the Qawasim came with the Suri episode of January 1806, which is rumoured to have yielded up 600,000 riyals (roughly £150,000) or more in booty seized from the Janaba;[9] and the only other specific capture which he highlights appears to be that of the *Minerva*— though curiously he says she was known as 'the Jew's ship'—a crime (jinaya) which he argues had provoked the first British expedition against Ras al-Khaima.[10] This, in itself, is an interesting piece of rationalization.

There is probably no case for arguing that this account of the Qawasim was significantly disingenuous, despite the fact that the *Lam' al-Shihab* may well have been commissioned by the British, possibly by Lieutenant Robert Taylor, who appears to have owned the only known copy of the work, and consulted it whilst compiling his 1818 report on the history and geography of the Gulf.[11] The work as a whole does not at all readily betray its putative British connection, although its structure and style are unusually clear, objective and informative;[12] there is, as one might also expect given its likely purpose, no evidence of priming by the British.[13] One passage which, exceptionally, feels unnaturally favourable to Britain (though these are still essentially nuances in an otherwise cropped, dispassionate and not inelegantly constructed narrative) is the author's account of the first expedition against the Qawasim: but this is portrayed by him as a curiously self-contained affair only between Britain and the Qawasim, and the separate elements of the account, for the most part, still appear to reflect unmediated popular observation and speculation in the Gulf.[14] Elsewhere in the *Lam' al-Shihab*, the author's general account of the Qawasim and their activities at sea, which was detailed above, hinges about Wahhabism and is of a piece with the body of the work.

One of the simpler indications that the reputation of the Qawasim for maritime plundering was thus one indigenous to the Gulf is a brief and unprompted remark by the same author concerning the Qawasim's southern neighbours:

> These people [the Banu Yas] do not engage in plunder at sea—but if a vessel happens to fall within their grasp, then they seize her. They have indeed committed a number of acts of maritime plunder, but

only under the cover of secrecy and deception, and for this reason they have not gained the same reputation as the rest of the inhabitants of Sir.[15]

We may probably therefore conclude from this discussion of the *Lam' al-Shihab*, that there was a class of educated, moderate Arab opinion in the northern Gulf, which independently believed the Qawasim to have become active maritime plunderers under the Wahhabi aegis.

It seems reasonable to assume that those who suffered most at the hands of the Qawasim were those most likely to be aggrieved at and therefore to condemn them. The manner in which they might do so would have depended very largely on the measure of understanding and proximity between the two parties: the views on the Qawasim's maritime activities current in the Muscat bazar, for example, were likely to have been a good deal more complex, and at least as vehemently held, perhaps, as those which might be encountered round the dinner-tables of Bombay. Dominant opinion in Muscat, whose shipping was often most frequently engaged in clashes with the Qawasim, would doubtless have considered them one, if not the major prevailing source of maritime disruption.

A comparison of two standard Omani histories[16] suggests once again that the particular reputation of the Qawasim for maritime predation was one that emerged in the Gulf at the start of the nineteenth century. Writing half a century later, Ibn Ruzaiq chose to highlight two episodes in the relations between the Qawasim and his own country of Oman: both turn upon the issue in hand.[17] The first concerned the Qasimi ruler Sultan bin Saqr's establishment of Khaur Fakkan as a maritime base for sanguinary predation ('fasad al-bahr bil-nahb wal-qatl') against Omani shipping; in this and his land-based operations he was, he claims, supported by the Wahhabis, the Tanaij and Za'ab tribes (whose principal settlements were Rams and Jazirat al-Hamra') and the Jalahima leader Muhammad bin Jabir. The second episode described by this author is the 1809/10 expedition against the Qawasim: it is an imperfect account, written very much from the Omani perspective, which appears to stand for both the joint Anglo–Omani expeditions; but his explanation of the cause of these operations is unequivocal and broad—'Hasan bin Rahma's maritime disruption [had] increased: he [had] killed a number of Sayyid Sa'id [of Muscat's] subjects and those of Britain, and seized a number of Omani and Indian ships.'

The contemporary attitudes of the cosmopolitan mercantile community at Muscat are difficult to judge: despite his connections with the British, the Company's Banyan Broker Goolab Anundass was still a part of that community. The following insistent aside regarding the Qawasim and Rahma bin Jabir appears to reflect his private view: 'They will swallow down whatever may come into their possession if it possess any value, without consideration to who it may belong. Their bad faith is known to all the world.'[18] But for some of the most virulent outbursts on the subject of the Qawasim's maritime activities, and not unnaturally in view of the fact that for most of this period he was locked with them in a state of hostility, intrigue and rivalry, one must look to the ruler of Muscat himself. In a number of his letters to Bombay there is much wild talk of piracy, violence and villainy, tyranny, treachery and hardened ways; the Qawasim, with the Wahhabis, are at one point described as 'adherents of the Devil and ... enemies of our most merciful God';[19] and he urges the chastisement of these pirates for the benefit of the commercial community at large[20]—but there is more than a suspicion that, as in 1816 when he described Bahrain as a potential nest of pirates which might be averted by Omani hegemony, understanding the British position as he did, he deliberately chose to harp upon the concept of piracy for his own hoped-for political advantage.[21]

It is difficult to glean much concerning the views of another more far-flung Arabian ruler, the Naqib of Mukalla. Like the ruler of Muscat, he was hostile to the Wahhabis and had suffered losses at the hands of Rahma bin Jabir and the 'Ras al-Khaima Qawasim'. In 1816, he wrote of them: 'They are robbers and pirates who create disturbances at sea. They plunder whoever falls in their way and even commit murder. Their successes have carried ruin on the ocean, as well as on shore.'[22]

We can gain a measure of the official Persian view of the maritime activities of the Qawasim from the local historian Fasa'i, who wrote at Shiraz towards the end of the nineteenth century; his account, such as it is, is even more idiosyncratic than that of the Omani historian. Fasa'i relates that in 1813 a Bahraini envoy visited Tehran in order to petition against the Utub, who had ruled the island since Iran had lost control three decades before; he also purportedly complained to the Shah that, 'some Qawasim tribesmen, inhabitants of the island of Qishm and of Bandar Ras al-Khaima belonging to Oman, have taken to piracy on the sea, plundering the ships of Persian merchants and killing the passengers and crews.'[23] This complaint was supposedly met with positive action: 'When the friendship between Persia and England was firmly established, the Persian ministers considered it advisable for both sides to undertake the extermination of the Qawasim, who had become a nuisance on the sea'; this, at any rate, is how Fasa'i chooses to explain the British expedition(s) and a certain amount of activity on the part of the Iranian government in the south of the country.

Fasa'i's account of the Bahraini legation and its result is highly stylized and should be understood as such;[24] the envoy with his plea for government assistance is something of a literary–historical trope with him. The provincial government at Shiraz did undertake positive action against the Qawasim, but it was independently motivated and unco-ordinated with that of Britain; in so far as it was an issue, though she was suspicious, Iran condoned British measures taken against the Qawasim as long as there was no infringement of Persian sovereignty, a condition not always met.

In c. February 1809 a Persian force from Lar, or Shiraz, seized Bastak, then successfully attacked the Qawasim at Linga, and possibly at Charak and Nakhilu, driving some to seek a temporary island refuge at Basidu;[25] several heads were also sent to Shiraz in consequence. As well as evincing a desire to collect taxes and assert central authority on the southern littoral, this campaign appears to have been part of wider operations against the Wahhabi powers in the Gulf. Plans were ambitious enough for the Persian Governor of Bushire, Iran's titular Admiral of the Gulf fleet, to urge two ships of the British Navy to assist by attacking vessels assembled at Linga and other southern ports—the same Governor whose deputy we find two years later readily furnishing the Bombay Marine with intelligence on Qasimi shipping;[26] then, in c. April 1809, a fleet sailed from Bushire carrying 4,000 men with the purpose of joining up with a second force from Muscat for a joint attack upon the Jalahima at Khaur Hassan, to be followed, perhaps, if successful, by another upon the Qawasim of Ras al-Khaima. But the project lacked sufficient ships and planning; the Persian fleet soon fell in with a superior force of 22 Qasimi dows, lost six large vessels and returned, defeated, to Bushire,[27] where a counter-attack was soon anticipated.[28] Iran only seriously attempted to combat the Wahhabis overseas on one other occasion in these years, this time in even closer alliance with Muscat: a detachment of around 1500 horsemen, including 42 Russian prisoners of war, was despatched from Shiraz to Oman in 1810; after landing at Barka on 1 December, the force soon joined the army of Muscat, but despite early victories against the Wahhabis at Nakhl and Sumayil, this enterprise too ended in ignominious defeat near Izki, in or before March 1811.[29]

The government of Shiraz was in fact to clash once more with Qasimi forces, in the winter of 1817/18. The nature of this conflict seems to reflect that of nine years before, since it appears to have been motivated by a desire to assert Persian sovereignty over the Shibkuh coastline[30] which, in the official version, is described as refractory and professing Wahhabism. If this version is reliable, it would appear that when Persian forces advanced against the Shaikh of Mughu, the Qawasim of Ras al-Khaima came to his aid, helping to evacuate the women and children, whilst the men remained behind to resist. This is said to have been in vain: the Prince–Governor of Shiraz later boasted that his forces had despatched large numbers of Qawasim 'to the shades of eternal darkness and purgatory';[31] another account tells of the erection of a pyramid of the skulls of the vanquished on the shore at Mughu.[32]

The Prince–Governor of Shiraz, terming the Qawasim, and the Jal-ahima, pirates and the common enemies of Iran and Britain, declared his 'infinite satisfaction and joy' at the outcome of the first British expedi-tion.[33] The nature of his own transactions with these powers in that year suggests that there was more to this statement than mere rhetoric; he was nevertheless concerned about the infringement of Persian sovereignty by the British. Similarly, but more adamantly, the Shah agreed in 1820 to introduce measures at the southern ports to avert piracy, whilst rejecting out of hand any British involvement in these arrangements or presence on Persian soil.[34]

A further point needs to be made about the Persian government's senti-ments, such as they may be discerned, towards the Qawasim. In the second decade of the century, when the Qasimi confederacy split into two powers, one aligned with the Wahhabis and based at Ras al-Khaima, and the other under Sultan bin Saqr (of Sharja) supported by his cousin the Shaikh of Linga, the Persian government was apparently ready to respond to and cultivate the latter: Sultan bin Saqr received a robe of honour from Shiraz in late 1814[35] and the Mughu campaign was allegedly undertaken at the behest of, or somehow in support for, Shaikh Muhammad bin Qadib of Linga. Nevertheless, it seems that Sultan bin Saqr's attachment to the hereditary Arab Shaikh–Governor of Bushire was closer and deeper than any connection he may have had with the distant Persian administration in Shiraz. The status of the Al Madhkur, the shaikhly ruling family of Bushire, was being eroded in these years. In 1808–14 they had been totally excluded from power and position in favour of the Persian appointees of the government of Shiraz.[36] In 1815, when the same thing threatened to recur, the fortunes of the family were redeemed partly by the timely assist-ance of a force of Qawasim under Shaikh Muhammad bin Qadib: five vessels carrying 800 men, sent by Sultan bin Saqr from Sharja, arrived at Bushire in the last week of August and plundered the Bihbihani quarter of the town, that which had principally opposed the Al Madhkur; 'every house and caravanserai belonging to them [the Bihbihanis] was emptied, besides several of their women and children carried off with their slaves, male and female.'[37] Some months later, the government of Shiraz was obliged to back off, and Shaikh Abd al-Rasul of the Al Madhkur was reinstated in his hereditary governorship: the 'universal joy' of the inhabit-ants of Bushire at the return of the Al Madhkur, wrote the Resident two days later, 'is scarcely to be expressed nor have the rejoicings as yet ceased'; 'the Bushire Shaikhs ... have made the Shiraz government feel their power and to learn that they are determined to defend their natural rights.'[38] Sultan bin Saqr subsequently brought military assistance to the Shaikhs of Bushire in order to counter the machinations of Shiraz on at least one other occasion, in 1832.[39] It is also worth noting that in so far as we can judge, Bushire vessels seem generally to have suffered comparatively little at the hands of the Qawasim.

So much for the official Persian view of the Qawasim. There is evidence that the people of Bushire regarded Ras al-Khaima with some awe. Direct communications between the two ports were probably disrupted for much of this period; in spring 1815 the Bushire Resident, referring to the Qawasim, wrote 'such indeed is the dread of these banditti at this place that no boat or native is to be prevailed upon on any consideration to convey a letter over to the other coast.'[40] In late December 1817, news arrived that a 25- or 40-strong Qasimi fleet had seized 3–5 baghlas valued at up to 300,000 rupees (c. £30,000) in the harbour at Asalu, murdering their crews, and now intended coming north to attack Bushire and Basra: the population of Bushire was thrown into panic and only forcibly prevented from fleeing inland by the Governor's timely deployment of 1,000 Arab musketeers.[41] Finally, a small point: one of the more emotive allegations against the Qawasim can be traced back to a Persian resident of Bushire, albeit a close connection of the British; soon after the attack on the *Sylph*, one of the passengers, Muhammad Husain Khan, wrote to the Bombay President that the 'pirates' had 'exulted and even performed a religious ceremony in thanks for their having had an opportunity to put so many Christians to death.'[42] Colouring such as this had a tendency to circulate; in a later history we read of a 'wholesale massacre' on board the *Sylph* by 'a host of desperadoes ... with the name of the Prophet on their lips and a thirst for Christian blood in their hearts.'[43]

But the opinions of the Qawasim prevalent in the Gulf about which we can perhaps be most confident are those of the mercantile (and seafaring) community in ports such as Bushire; these, one suspects, may often have paralleled the stance commonly adopted in the British primary sources. The reason for this was not simply that sheer commercial considerations weighed heavily with both parties, nor only that local merchants in these ports valued trade with British India and appreciated Britain's naval strength, but something further: the merchants controlled the most extensive system of communications, and this facilitated the efficient gathering and transmission of public news, particularly when it had a bearing on trade. One of our main sources for these years, the British Resident at Bushire, like his counterpart at Basra who modestly claimed 'My friendship and influence with all the neighbouring governors and shaikhs, and with the distant shaikhs in the desert, enable me to command their services on all occasions',[44] maintained a correspondence with the rulers in a number of the Gulf ports;[45] he also had private correspondents in different parts of the Gulf such as Ras al-Khaima, Bahrain, Qatif, Kangan and Muscat, some of whom we have already encountered;[46] sometimes he despatched messengers to collect news;[47] and sometimes he employed secret sources whom we can never hope to identify.[48] But more often than not, the Resident's news of recent Qasimi activities was clearly common knowledge.[49] It was brought in merchants' letters and by ship's captains from different parts of the Gulf.[50] It was, in effect, very often intelligence gleaned from the broad commercial community. Where it is possible to cross-check these reports, they appear on the whole reliable in their simple factual reporting of Qasimi maritime activities. The same is probably true of much of the British reporting regarding this sort of activity in the Persian Gulf itself, which mirrors these sources; though it should be borne in mind that the reports submitted by the Broker at Muscat were less careful or accurate than those from Bushire, and, moreover, that all of this reporting tended to approach the subject of Qasimi activity from a particular angle. To view the British source material which emanated from Bushire, Muscat and Basra out of context, is, in short, to undervalue it.

CHAPTER EIGHT

Cruiser Commanders' Blunders

The British reporting from Bushire, Muscat and Basra, which provided most of the raw material for the deliberations of the Bombay Council, was squarely founded on local intelligence. Company cruiser commanders serving in the Gulf, with the few Royal Naval officers who were in times of heightened tension also posted there, were in varying degrees not so well informed. Their sailing instructions were brief, and whilst they often communicated with political officers in the main Gulf ports, it would appear that much of their background knowledge must have been acquired in an unofficial fashion.[1] Sometimes commanders made mistakes: it is important to discover whether these were of a nature or frequency sufficient to distort the emerging picture of Qasimi activities.

The mistakes in question did not consist in erroneous reporting of Qasimi activities, for generally speaking commanders were simply not involved in gathering intelligence. These, by contrast, were practical errors which arose at sea where there was contact between Arab and British vessels. The behaviour of commanders in these situations was delimited by any special orders, or general practice, then being followed in the Gulf. These orders were modified over the years as British confidence grew and in response, as we have seen, to particular Qasimi attacks. Even in 1805, when Captain Seton had at first suggested limited direct action against the Qawasim, cruiser commanders had remained under strict instructions to avoid all possible entanglements with them for fear of provoking the Wahhabi power.[2] But on five subsequent occasions, in theory at least, their orders invoked a posture that was more than simply defensive.

In the year preceding the first expedition, commanders were authorized to attack Qasimi boats, provided they did not deviate from their course or risk the annoyance of local merchantmen.[3]

In February 1811, in response to the eight-hour attack by 4 large and 17 small boats on the English trader *Macaulay* off Farur, supposedly by Qawasim based on Abu Musa, and on the principle that no terms of peace had been reached following the first expedition, two cruisers were sent to the Gulf; they had the vague and impractical mission of ridding the Gulf of 'every notoriously piratical vessel and particularly every Qasimi', those who molested British trade.[4] These orders were specific and short-lived; as were the similar, but more restrained, instructions issued to two cruisers in January 1813 after attacks upon the *Moholar* and the *Duncan*.[5]

From October 1814, but only on the Diu–Gwadar Indian coastline, commanders were instructed to advise 'pirate' vessels to quit these coasts, failing which, if they continued to disturb the trade, and only if the British vessel was certain of her superiority, they were to be taken or destroyed.[6] These orders, like those of 1809, 1811 and 1813, failed to stimulate any significant offensive action.[7]

Finally, two and a half years before the second expedition, all commanders were ordered to take, or failing that destroy, any Arab 'pirate' ship they encountered.[8] This time, the general authorization to attack Qasimi vessels may have remained in force until the start of the second expedition; but still the only significant offensive action which resulted was of a restricted kind beginning in December 1818.[9]

There was some modification in the attitude and behaviour of commanders over these two decades: earlier they tended to be evasive and defensive, later more simply defensive, with occasional examples, at the very end, of aggression. Especially before the Qawasim had been tested with the first expedition, the avoidance of confrontation seemed to have much to recommend it. The instructions given to Lieutenant Daniel Ross of the HC ketch *Queen* in March 1805 were clear: 'you are ... not only to abstain from aggression, but to avoid putting yourself in the way of interruption by any of [the Gulf pirates]; at the same time that if attacked, you will use your utmost endeavour for the annoyance of the enemy.'[10] There were sound reasons for this line of conduct: Qasimi vessels were numerous, large and well-manned, could very often outsail British cruisers, had a shallower draught and knew the waters better.[11] As Captain William Hill, the Senior Naval Officer in the Gulf, who then had HMS *Towey* and four Company cruisers (av. 178 tons/13 guns) at his disposal, noted in April 1817, the available resources were not adequate to do more than operate the convoy system:[12] of the Bombay Marine's 14 regular cruisers at this time, all of them under 257 tons, six were then in service in the east and only one minor schooner was not actually under orders.[13] Except very rarely, therefore, although the situation was slightly different off India where the coastline was patrolled, British ships did not cruise idly or seek out reported pirates. Apart from occasional special errands, Marine and naval commanders simply went about their business of convoying merchantmen and carrying despatches between Basra, Bushire, Muscat and the Bombay Presidency.[14] If they came upon Qasimi ships, it was by accident along the major trade routes, or occasionally in port.[15] In 1817–19, these meetings might provoke a response; but in other years, the encounter would pass off quite without note or consequence, unless, that is, the commander sensed he or his companions were under assault.

Under these circumstances, commanders stood in need of three classes of knowledge and expertise. In the first place they needed a working understanding of the sometimes bewildering politics of the Gulf. A lack of this led Lieutenant James Arthur of the HC brig *Antelope* into error in 1818; his mistake was embarrassing rather than costly.[16] On 23 August off Bani Farur, with the country-ship *Ahmadi*[17] under convoy and in the company of a Muscat war battil, he had observed a lone Bahraini trading baqqara of 28 tons; she was then on her way home from Asalu where she had taken on a cargo including rice, planks and rose petals.[18] Arthur fired a shot to bring her to, then sent the jolly-boat over to inspect her. The 2nd Lieutenant, with the Serang as interpreter, soon reported that the craft was carrying 47 armed men and was evidently a pirate. So Arthur ordered the removal of her arms and papers, deciding that it was best to bring the baqqara to Muscat where her guilt or otherwise could be properly established. But he chose to put her under the control of the Muscat battil; and within a few days the Muscat vessel had terrified many of the Bahrainis,[19] casually offloaded the baqqara's cargo and finally set her adrift. Some months later, on an application from the Shaikh of Bahrain, most of the plundered goods were returned.[20]

Arthur was censured for his unassertive conduct: contrary to statute and an article of war, he appeared to have allowed the plunder of an innocent and friendly vessel when she was under his protection. As he himself retorted,[21] there was clearly an omission on the part of the Company whereby officers such as he had not received due guidance on the correct procedure in cases of this kind; and it was equally surprising that Arthur should have been unaware of Bruce's July 1816 agreement of friendship with the Shaikh of Bahrain. Arthur's original judgement had understandably been superficial; and he had possibly been overly receptive to the opinions of the captains of the two vessels which accompanied him, the one an Omani, whose ruler was then at war with Bahrain, the other a Kuwaiti, who maintained that the Bahraini Nakhuda had personally slain the Shaikh of Kuwait's brother. Without denying that the baqqara was at the time innocently trading, these not unnaturally encouraged Arthur in his suspicions, claiming, possibly with justification, that she had been captured from Kuwait two years before. Arthur's principal mistake, however, the product of political naïvety, was to have so completely identified his own with Muscat's actually quite separate interests in this case, that he effectively lost sight of his independent duty and responsibilities.

Cruiser commanders also laboured under other difficulties. The most constant problem was the need to be able to interpret the movements of Arab vessels correctly so as to recognize a hostile action. Failure to mark the signs had brought about the *Sylph* incident. Over-enthusiasm was occasionally also a problem. A month later, off the Indian port of Mangrol, four merchant dows were sailing on course for Surat. They observed two vessels sailing directly at them, became alarmed and for some reason let off a volley of musketry. This, and the failure of the dows to alter their course, convinced Lieutenant Macdonald of the HC schooner *Lively*, who had sent the pattamar ahead to investigate, that he was being attacked. The dows nearly exhausted the *Lively's* shot and only managed to escape in a 'shattered state' when a light sea-breeze set in nearly two hours later. Their troubles were not yet over: when they arrived at Surat, they were put in detention. The matter was investigated by a committee of enquiry in Bombay and one of the three committee members was inclined to exonerate the dows. The results of the enquiry, with a protest from the ruler of Muscat, caused their begrudging release in c. June 1809: the Bombay Government had initially felt that the dignity of the Company's flag required an example be made by burning them in the harbour.[22]

The following two accounts of attacks upon the *Fury* and the *Nautilus*, taken from the same year, are probably quite representative of the sort of response that was normally to be expected of cruiser commanders up until 1809, or even late 1818. Neither of the two commanders identifies his aggressors and it is noticeable that nothing further, by way of protest or otherwise, seems to be heard of either incident. The Qawasim are the most likely candidates in the case of the *Nautilus*, especially in view of their probable attack on the *Sylph* close to the same spot only four days later. The identity of those who chased the schooner *Fury*, out from Muscat en route to Bombay, is uncertain. Her commander, Lieutenant Charles Gowan, recalls how the action unfolded:[23]

> In the morning of 2nd of May, having a light breeze from the westward, I perceived two dows in chase of us.
>
> At 3 p.m. the dows still continuing the chase and coming up very fast, I fired two shot across them, showing our colours at the same time, which they taking no notice of, I thought it was their intention to attack us. At half past 3 the dows coming up fast, I fired another shot across them, which they returned by a discharge of as many guns as they could get to bear on us.
>
> At ¼ after 4 p.m. the dows still continuing their fire on us, being within musket-shot, I commenced a heavy fire on them, which did not prevent them from attempting to board us.
>
> At ½ past 4 p.m. the dows shot up on our starboard quarter, heaving spears and large stones into us, immediately after which, their

crews attempted to jump on our decks, but were repulsed, with great loss, by the continued fire from our stern guns and musketry; on which, they backed their sails and dropped astern, in a very shattered condition, getting their sweeps out and pulling away, as fast as possible, under a heavy fire from our stern guns.[24]

Although in some circumstances potentially ambiguous, there is no reason to suppose that the usual British signal of hoisting colours and firing across a ship's bows was an expression ill-understood in the Gulf. As the following passage from Lieutenant Richard Bennett of the *Nautilus* demonstrates, this means of communication was also current in the Gulf:[25]

At noon on [17 October 1808], being off the island of Hanjam, saw three boats ahead apparently standing in for the land. At 2 p.m. perceived them firing guns, as signals to each other. At 2.50, another boat having joined them, the whole stood in towards the island of Qishm. At 3, when to windward, they wore round, and stood towards, two of them the largest-sized dows, and two large trankeys, the former keeping for our weather bow, and the latter for the quarter. About ½ past 4 could discover that they were full of men, [armed] with spears and swords, which they were shaking at us, at the same time making great shouting. It was now apparent they intended attacking us; shortened sail and cleared for action.

About 4.40 finding them well within reach of our cannonades, hoisted Company's colours and fired two shot ahead of the largest dow, which she did not appear to notice, but kept pulling and sailing towards, having her boat ahead towing her. It being evident they intended boarding us, fired our broadside at them, which was returned, and the action continued for about 25 to 30 minutes, when they stood from us close hauled on the larboard tack; immediately wore and stood after them, and kept occasionally firing at them till 6.10, at which time perceiving the shot to fall short, and it being nearly calm, resumed our course up the Gulph. At the beginning of the action Mr John Dennis Boatswain was killed by a cannon-shot, that first penetrated the vessel's side, and afterwards struck him on the breast; this is the only casualty we met with.[26]

There is a possible argument here that Lieutenant Bennett had misread the signs, and the Arab vessels were only reacting to a perceived attack. This is unlikely in the context of the time. These issues are nevertheless quite subtle. We know of one minor case from 1819 when part of the crew of a Linga trader were interviewed after their boat had been captured by the British.[27] They describe their reactions when they realized the British vessel meant to take them: first they ran in towards the shore in order to escape; next, believing they were now in a position to resist capture, they hoisted their red colours in order to summon aid, primed their guns and even loosed off a few shots.[28] Resistance, therefore, was a possibility in such cases.[29] But this explanation does not square with the movements of vessels in the *Nautilus* incident. If the reports of Gowan and Bennett were truthful, therefore, we can surmise that both commanders probably acted reasonably—each apparently had a well-founded belief that he was being attacked—though Gowan undoubtedly showed the greater nerve and restraint.[30]

The third and perhaps the greatest problem faced by commanders was the difficulty of identifying the craft they met at sea.[31] In the short periods when British ships were authorized, if necessary, to take the offensive, real and unpleasant consequences could result from a mistaken identification of this kind. Regular passes were apparently not yet used by local shipping and the papers carried by Arab ships were 'in a character with which naval officers are ... unacquainted.'[32] Arab colours seem to have been largely uniform, and one Marine officer believed that if 'piratical' boats were once overtaken, they would resort to 'lowering their sails, hoisting their colours and hail[ing] from a friendly port.'[33] Nor was it unheard of for British Indian craft bearing the Company's pass to hoist a 'plain red flag such as the Arabs use'.[34] The *Lively* incident had impressed the desirability of Muscat issuing passes to her vessels, and following the unfortunate *Vestal* affair (below), a code of signals was actually drawn up in order to distinguish them.[35] The Qawasim were also urged to adopt distinctive passes and flags, but without, it seems, great practical result.[36]

When required, pilots who knew the sea routes leading to the ports on the Gulf's southern shores could generally be found at Bushire and Muscat.[37] An unusual step was taken in May 1811 when, as part of Government's response to the *Macaulay* incident, Captain C. Sealy of the HC ship *Benares*, calling at Bushire, took on board a certain Haji Jabir who was reputedly 'well acquainted with the boats belonging to the different tribes'.[38] Later some officers may have accumulated greater confidence in their ability to recognize local vessels. But it was still not without surprise, and presumably disapproval, that Captain Hill RN remarked in April 1817 of a Marine officer under his command, 'Lieutenant Tanner[39] of the *Psyche* fired on three boats passing Kuh Mubarak; but I cannot learn that they were pirates, his only reason for supposing them such was that they endeavoured to avoid him.'[40] A more serious incident occurred on the seventh of the following month, when Lieutenant F. Faithful of the HC brig *Vestal* opened fire on up to a dozen Muscat vessels drawn up peacefully in a crescent ahead of him.[41] Mistakenly he had believed they were threatening him and the two English traders he was escorting: before the incident there had been a number of confused sightings and an alleged pursuit involving 15 or more Qawasim. So convinced was he, and so alarmed perhaps, that he regarded the Muscatis' professions of friendship and lack of any resistance in the darkness as a pretence: two men and two women were reported killed in the incident. A court of enquiry was proposed, but Faithful's justification was eventually accepted.[42]

Mistakes by cruiser commanders before December 1818 deserve to be recognized, but they do not in any real degree invalidate the emerging picture of Qasimi activities in these years. In the first place, these mistakes had little direct bearing on the validity of British reporting of Qasimi doings: commanders rarely identified their alleged aggressors and general intelligence was the preserve of the political officer. In the second place, these mistakes were few in number. Apart from those already mentioned, only one other can be certainly ascertained before December 1818: this concerned the simple pursuit of a Bahraini boat by a British brig around early 1809, a matter that provoked a mild protest and was met with an apology.[43]

A year before the second expedition, a new chief naval officer assumed overall command in the Gulf and there was a shift in the tone and behaviour of British commanders. This short period possesses intrinsic interest and merits a separate treatment.

When Captain Francis Loch of HMS *Eden* neared the Gulf in December 1818, he had been six months out from Portsmouth, and there was only one man out of the *Eden's* complement of 125 who had any prior experience of the Gulf. On Christmas Eve the crew feasted on turtle picked off Astola Island. The following morning, the *Eden*, a newly commissioned ship of *c.* 500–600 tons burden, mounting 26 guns, and the HC brig *Psyche*, 12 guns and 180 tons, sighted two battils to windward, with a third vessel in tow. Loch recalls that,

> The superior manner in which the sails were cut and set, as well as the rig of the masts and form of the hull of the two [battils], to any of the sort I had ever observed among the many country vessels I had seen, bespoke them at once to be pirate vessels. All sail was now crowded in chase.[44]

This eager self-assurance was characteristic of Loch. The Bombay Marine, subordinate to the Royal Navy, but with long experience of the Gulf, thought him arrogant and self-willed. He was said to have been 'the only officer of His Majesty's or the Honourable Company's cruisers who ... had the good fortune to effect the destruction of any of the pirate vessels.'[45] Seeing they were being pursued, the three vessels strove to run across the *Eden's* bow and get before the wind, when the battil's great shoulder-of-mutton sail operated to such effect. To increase their speed, the third vessel, supposed by Loch to have been a prize, was cut away and overtaken by the *Psyche*.[46] Aided by light winds and darkness, the two battils then outstripped Loch after a pursuit of 13 hours, leaving him to comment: 'The force of the vessels chased is but trifling, but their coolness, courage and manoeuvring required every exertion to gain the smallest advantage, and that only while the breeze was too fresh for their sweeps.'[47]

At daybreak on 28 December, seven boats were sighted off Gwatar Bay, three of them slower vessels that were soon taken in tow. There is strong evidence on this occasion that Loch was right in supposing these to have been Ras al-Khaima boats, carrying home three out of four prizes they had taken off India since first setting out 1½ months earlier.[48] Their force—whose names have been poorly transcribed—consisted of two baghlas, the *Shuma*, Sa'id bin Hasan, 4 guns and 150 men, and the *Tomashe*, Thabit bin Jum'a (?), 4 guns and 130 men; with two battils, the *Awadh*, Hamad, 2 guns and 110 men, and the *Swaybuts*, Salim, 1 gun and 160 men.[49]

A 16-hour chase began. Careful manoeuvring, light winds, the use of sweeps and at length nightfall once again gave the Arab boats the advantage: they used fire-buckets to wet the sails so as to catch every breath of air. Two of the prizes were, nevertheless, set loose and overtaken by Loch. In one of these were 16 men, who, it seems, had been unable to escape to their parent-ship owing to the *Eden*'s sudden heavy fire: Loch had finally slid to half a musket-shot's distance of the vessels under cover of darkness before loosing his starboard broadside. He describes the action:

> The moon had just risen, which enabled me to observe every man-oeuvre of theirs, they being between the moon and the *Eden*, she (the latter) being in a degree hid from them.
>
> In their dream of thorough and perfect security in our having totally and entirely lost sight of them, we heard as we drew up with the chase the tom-tom (drum), as if muffled, and an undertoned monotonous song. Thus we slipped through the water, the sails just full and the sea so smooth that there was hardly a ripple to be observed, yet the ship went along as if she knew she must exert her sailing.
>
> All was so still, everyone sitting or lying at their quarters, that the officers' feet in walking the quarter-deck was all the sound to be distinguished, until we shot up abreast of the vessel having the other in tow—[50]

and opened fire. The 16 men, four of them enslaved Muscatis, were taken on board the *Eden* at dawn, in a state of abject terror:

> Nothing can efface from my memory the grasp one of the oldest of these people took of my legs, with an imploring look and gesture, as if I had it in my power to save his soul from perdition, far less his mind from the present miserably agonising state. The face was distorted and

the muscles literally quivering with agitation; nor was it for a considerable time these poor wretches could be persuaded or made to understand that their lives were perfectly secure; but they were no sooner made to be certain of this, than their extravagance of joy was equal to their former despondency.[51]

The *Eden* spent three days at Muscat, then left for Bushire. On the morning of 10 January, 7–8 supposed Qawasim were surprised at anchor under the lee of Hanjam Island.[52] The approach of the *Eden* forced them at 11 a.m. to run further into the harbour. At 2 p.m., as one of the battils sailed out and away past the *Eden*, she received the latter's starboard broadside. The remaining 6–7 were trapped in towards the shore. At 11.30 p.m. the tide turned and three of them got underway: one, carrying rice,[53] was driven on shore, where she was abandoned, and later burnt by Loch; one, a battil, attempted to run out past the *Eden*, but being defeated by wind, swell and the *Eden*'s fire, she swamped; the third, a baghla,[54] had made the same attempt, but was beached at 12.30 a.m. after being subjected to the *Eden*'s fire between wind and water, the shot passing 'from stem to stern'. The next morning, a party was sent ashore to burn her and discovered three survivors, two men and a boy, the boy badly wounded by grape-shot. The beach was reported to be strewn with dead.[55]

The four remaining vessels all appear to have escaped during the course of that day. Two of them, battils, were pursued in vain by Loch in light winds: they first worked along the shore to windward with the aid of long sweeps, then as the tide turned, each put a towing-party ashore with a long rope, until finally at 7 p.m. they lost him. Loch maintains these were Qawasim who had intended establishing themselves at Basidu.[56] The prisoners seem to have been acknowledged by Hasan bin Rahma as his people. Their condition, when found, was poor:

> One of the men had taken poison, so that he died shortly after having been brought on board, his corpse turning a pale livid blue. The other man when found was half-suffocated by tow which he had stuffed into his mouth and throat, and which was pulled out much to the amusement and surprise of one of the boatswain's mates (Jennings), rolling out 'Damn my eyes, here's a bloody fellow been caulking up his throat with oakum', at the same time as he called it, roused it out of his mouth. The boy's wounds were dressed and did well.[57]

Loch released these two off Ras al-Khaima on 16 January, along with two others from his earlier capture and a warning addressed to Hasan bin Rahma against any further maltreatment of British subjects.[58] The four Muscatis had been liberated in Muscat. What became of the ten remaining Qasimi prisoners taken on 28 December has been alluded to already.[59]

Loch anchored at Bushire on 23 January. While he was there he would stay with the Resident, Captain William Bruce, with whom he worked quite closely and for whom he evidently developed a real affection.[60] The *Eden* was now refitted and painted, and Loch paid a short visit to the archaeological remains at Rishahr. During February and part of March, with the aid of one naval vessel and three or more Company cruisers, Loch was occupied with managing the affair of the Qawasim's British captives. This business touched his national pride and called forth the knight-errant in him. His heavy-handed approach to the problem certainly brought about the swift release of the captives; but not without the seizure of a Sharja vessel for the purposes of exchange, the temporary and unjustified detention of three Bahraini merchantmen at Bushire and, most costly since it involved casualties, Loch's violent seizure of two innocent Abu Dhabi vessels at Bahrain, on 12/13 February, under the obstinate misapprehension that they were Qawasim.[61] After this episode, Loch paid a short ceremonial visit to Basra to attend the installation of the new Resident, then spent six weeks at Bushire, allowing him to make a brief sightseeing excursion inland, before weighing for Muscat on 2 May, arriving at Bombay on the 24th. On his way down the Gulf, as we have already seen, he had one last engagement with Qasimi boats hard by the Musandam Peninsula.[62] Loch's vivacious and combative first tour of the Gulf therefore ended much as it had begun. Despite the unprecedented atmosphere of destruction that colours this tour, the only certain fatal mistake was that which occurred at Bahrain in February. It is something of a surprise to find that, in so far as we can tell, Loch's major engagements at sea do not appear to have involved misidentification.

Loch's second tour in the Gulf began on 30 September 1819, when he dropped anchor at Muscat, and was to last 7½ months. The *Eden* had arrived direct from Trincomalee (and Madras), having sailed 4,199 miles in 31 days, or an average of 135 miles a day.[63] Loch was now to spend a colourful month at Bushire before joining the expedition against the Qawasim in November. He was personally less active and, come November, less circumspect than before. There were in fact only a few maritime incidents of any note until November,[64] when the expected arrival of the British force stimulated a flurry of rather misdirected activity on the part of Loch and his subordinate officers: this consisted in the main of detaining vessels, many of them at Bushire, which were suspected of supplying or aiding the Qawasim.[65] Some of this activity encroached on Persian friendship and sovereignty. None of it seems to have produced any casualties. But these last minute seizures should really be regarded as a part of the British expedition, and as such they are not representative of regular contact, even at this late stage, between British and Arab shipping.

These same incidents do nevertheless underline the unprecedented degree to which Loch, as naval officer, had been directing the practicalities of British policy towards the Qawasim at this late stage. It is true that he almost always acted in concert with his host and political mentor, the experienced Bushire Resident William Bruce; but the contrast with his predecessors, who had been as deferent to the Company's local officers in political matters as they had been loathe to engage the Qawasim, is hard to mistake.[66] Loch's behaviour was partly occasioned by the situation in 1819, but more so perhaps by his character. When publicly confronted by an anxious Shaikh–Governor of Bushire protesting at his disrespectful detention of a Dubai vessel at Bushire, Loch curtly responded that he had acted on government orders; 'I then left him and walked up to the Residency as if nothing had happened.'[67] Earlier in the year, upon learning that Captain Conyers had conducted informal discussions with the Shaikh of Ras al-Khaima, Loch likewise brusquely ordered him to avoid all such communications in future, continuing, 'You are not to consider that you have entered into any agreement as to a cessation of hostilities: on the contrary, you are ... to do your utmost to destroy any of the Qasimi vessels you may meet with'.[68]

After his second tour, Loch sailed once more as far as Madras, returned briefly to the Gulf in August and September 1820, then made a voyage round to Calcutta before calling at Trincomalee in March, bound finally for England.[69] Between the Eden's first touching at Trincomalee on 7 October 1818, and her last on 13 March 1821, 21 of her complement of 125 had died of disease, a further two through accident.[70] This figure does not include others such as marines who died while on board the Eden, and it omits those men who died before the vessel made England. At least 10 of the 21 died during the Eden's 13 months in the Gulf. But the most lamentable casualties occurred during one week in May/June 1819, when cholera struck the ship at Bombay: eight men died, and 'the main deck was lined with the hammocks of invalids, besides numbers lying on deck in a dreadful state of agony from the spasms most of them were suffering under.'[71] It does not appear that any of the Eden's crew received serious injury during her engagements with Arab vessels.[72]

Captain Loch's period of command in the Gulf before the second expedition, whose salient features have been described here, was exceptional. Prior to this, naval and especially, perhaps, Marine commanders had been far more cautious in their dealings with Arab shipping. But there had still been a discernible trend over these two decades towards a more assertive approach, one that burgeoned, so to speak, with Loch's tempestuous arrival in December 1818. This was a process, therefore, whereby some of the earlier subtleties were supplanted by something bolder and less questioning.

The original proposition was that British commanders in the Gulf some-times made mistakes. These were not especially frequent, even arguably in the case of Loch, though a number of them were serious. The theme is an important one in so far as it illustrates the behaviour of British commanders, as well as some of the practical difficulties which arose at sea out of the peculiar situation in the Gulf. But it is now clear that these mistakes do not call into question the contemporary evidence for Qasimi activities in the Gulf. We can therefore proceed with our investigation.

CHAPTER NINE

Off the Indian Coast

A curious mode of gambling was prevalent in Mandvi, the rich and insanitary first port of the Indian state of Cutch.[1] Anticipating the arrival of their trading vessels, the Banyans who controlled the port would receive word immediately an approaching ship was sighted from the watchtower. The merchants would then place bets amongst themselves, wagering, it is said, a million rupees a year on whose the ship would prove to be.

That the Qawasim captured certain vessels off Cutch, Sind and neighbouring coasts is, by now, indisputable. But we cannot leap from this to conclude that they necessarily took all the boats they were said to have taken off north-west India. Qasimi activity in this area, by contrast with that in the Gulf and off south Arabia, where Arabic was the lingua franca and Islam the dominant religion, occurred in territory which was politically and culturally distinct from their own: the Qawasim were essentially strangers in Indian waters.[2] For this reason, we have to subject reporting of Qasimi doings from north-west India to greater scrutiny. By the same token, however, the resultant picture of Qasimi behaviour, being starker, may prove all the more revealing: the canvas was barer and we can therefore see the brush strokes left by them the better.

There are three possible fundamental objections to the Indian evidence. The first two are hypothetical and were not expressed at the time.

On one occasion the Superintendent of Marine voiced his suspicion that three lascars who claimed to have been run aground by the Qawasim near Muscat in February 1818, were fabricating the story in order to conceal their own desertion.[3] The records at Exeter do not otherwise speak of deception of any kind. This suggests very strongly that major fraud, of the kind practised wholesale by a ship's Master against the owners of his vessel or her cargo, was, at most, rare.[4] The pattern and fluctuations of recorded incidents,[5] and the whole weight of the evidence, are in fact against such an hypothesis.

Similar objections work even more strongly against the suggestion that local pirates from Kathiawar and Cutch were the true culprits in most of the cases ascribed to the Qawasim.[6] Certainly there was still some trouble with ports such as Beyt and Poseitra in the second decade of the nineteenth century, despite the continuing efforts of the Company. But the activities assigned to the Qawasim were now out of their league. The sources in fact seem to have had no essential difficulty in identifying local pirates where appropriate, and, in some cases, the circumstances of their captures clearly marked them out as such;[7] just as, in others, the vessels and observed passage of the Qawasim, prima facie, did for them. Yet the most compelling argument against the implication of local pirates is really the most self-evident: those with the greatest interest and ability to detect pirates, the local merchants, did not believe it to be so.

The third possible fundamental objection to the Indian evidence cannot be given such short shrift. News of Qasimi depredations mostly originated with the crews of Indian coasting vessels, whether they were themselves the victims or merely witnesses. Their reporting was most informative when crews were captured and released. This did not, however, guarantee positive identification. The Gujarati-speaker could presumably be expected to recognize a fellow Gujarati, and the Sindi, a neighbouring Baluchi; but there is something unsatisfactory about the four wounded Porbandar sailors who, after their release, recalled hearing the words 'Ras al-Khaima' repeatedly spoken by their captors, 'from which they conclude that the pirates were from that port'.[8] Escaped captives could be still less forthcoming: of one such Tindal it was recorded, 'the only information he can give is that the pirate's crew were Mussulmen, with very long beards and do not know to what place they belong to.'[9] It is clear, then, that identification was a problem. Recognizing this does not of course invalidate the evidence per se, but it should at least make us cautious.

The difficulty of identifying strange craft is the major qualifying factor to set against the Indian evidence, but there are two others also to bear in mind. The first has to do with exaggeration in the reports, the second with the manner in which vessels were lost. These two points go not to the essence of the subject, but to the matter of detail.

As reports of Qasimi sightings and news of their depredations circulated in the northern ports, it was only to be expected that the numbers of victims and assailants should sometimes be inflated, and thereby gain the greater resonance. This simple numerical exaggeration was a phenomenon reasonably well understood by the British officials who mediated these reports.[10]

Allowance occasionally needed to be made for other forms of exaggeration. It seems that Indian vessels rarely resisted even minor local freebooters, still less the Qawasim, a 'description of men whom all sailors dread to approach.'[11] Exceptionally, in December 1814, a Supercargo swore

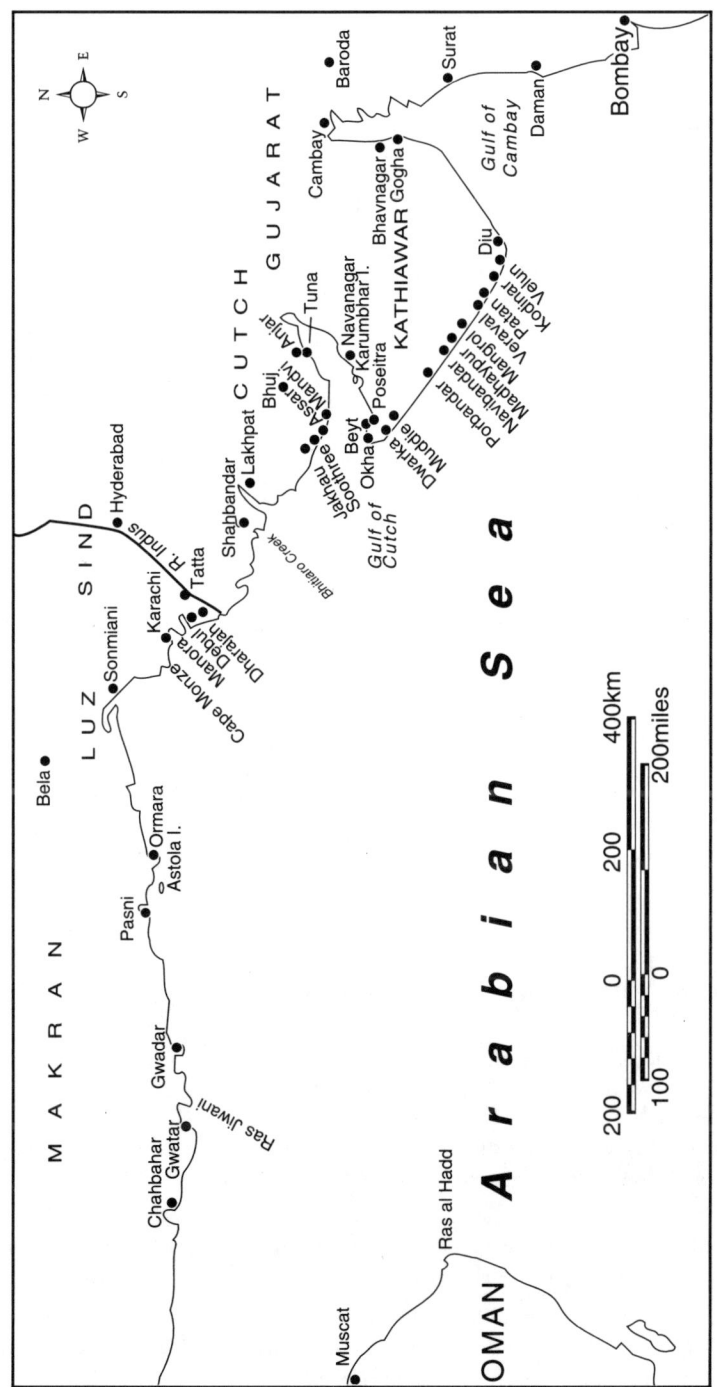

Map 3. The North-West Coast of India.

that he had sustained a 12-hour running fight off Karachi with one of four Qawasim. The Porbandar Agent thought him a Falstaff:

> I think it not improbable that the boat in question fell in with four pirate boats (for there were several reports at the time of such being in that direction) and was allowed to proceed unmolested, from having British colours flying. The merchant-boat may have expended much ammunition throughout the day very unnecessarily, through fear, and the enemy may have been at a considerable distance out of shot; for under such circumstances, a Hindu Supercargo would not hesitate to declare that he had fought the enemy, and his vanity might lead him to suppose that the noise of his guns had intimidated, or kept off (beat off he would say), his opponent.[12]

British officials reporting from the northern coasts were, it should be remarked, not always so discerning in their handling of raw intelligence. Initially they were ill-informed on Gulf affairs and they seldom received adequate information from Makran and Sind.[13] Soon after his appointment, the same Porbandar Agent, C.W. Elwood, confidently described the Makrani 'jymer' as a form of vessel which only sailed from the Gulf,[14] and gave credit to the report that a group of Qasimi pirates active off Sind in December 1813 had broken off to celebrate the Shi'ite festival of Ashura, which would surely have been anathema to the Qawasim as ardent Sunnis.[15]

A peculiar feature of many of the incidents off the Indian coast is that the plundered vessel was run on shore, or otherwise abandoned, prior to capture. At the least this would suggest that some of the Qawasim's Indian captures were, as Hasan bin Rahma seemed to say in mid-1814, unopposed.[16] It also might vindicate the other arm of Hasan bin Rahma's argument: crews in these circumstances could be expected to pay little attention to hoisting British colours; moreover,

> the panic of the crew of these boats is so great when they fall in with the Qawasim, that they seldom recollect to hoist their colours, and the attack made on them is so sudden and furious, that there is no opportunity of mentioning or showing a pass, every man being intent only on saving his life by jumping overboard.[17]

When this is added to the fact that some British Indian vessels, it is said, actively chose not to hoist their true colours, then it seems not unreasonable to speculate that a fair number of British Indian vessels may have been captured by the Qawasim in the belief that they did not enjoy British protection, and were therefore legitimate targets.

The reason why vessels were abandoned, was the ferocious reputation which the Qawasim so swiftly managed to acquire amongst seafaring, and mercantile, circles in Bombay, Gujarat and the north. It is most probable that the c. 36 Indian merchants of Bombay, protesting at current Qasimi depredations in November 1817, expressed commonly-held beliefs and fears when they wrote,

> The usual horrible practice of that pirate, that is of killing and murdering people when taken up, has thrown an apprehension, that no-one dares to undertake the speculation to [the ports of Muscat, Cutch, Veraval, Mangrol, Porbandar, Karachi etc.], nor a soul they can get to go into their vessels.[18]

It is likely that still more lurid tales of Qasimi brutality circulated at a popular level in the Indian ports. A Tindal, said to have been confined on board a Qasimi dow for ten days, gave one such account in Mandvi to Lieutenant George Grant of the Guicowar's naval service:

> From this person's statement, it appears that the Qawasim put their Mahometan prisoners to death by knocking out their brains with a hatchet or with a hammer; they cut the flesh off the bones into small pieces, break the bones and then ... [text illegible] ... amidst the blood of those they inhumanly butcher, rejoicing in having killed so many of the followers of Mahomet.
>
> I hope, sir, you will excuse the disgusting terms which I use: I am sorry that the subject requires them.[19]

Lieutenant Grant understood that quarter was given to those Muslim captives who embraced Wahhabism.

The reputation of the Qawasim therefore bolstered the natural logic of self-preservation. But there was a danger here of overreaction by panicked crews, particularly in the last years, 1817–19, when reports of Qasimi activity off India came in thick and fast. Lieutenant Guy of the HCC *Psyche*, an officer employed on the northern coasts, reported back in February 1819 from his investigative mission to Sind,

> I am happy in having it in my power to contradict the vague reports circulated of the mischief done by these marauders: that they have succeeded in destroying much valuable property is clear, but not to one-tenth of that reported; and that half the small trading-vessels have been wantonly run on shore on the appearance of any other, and the cargo if so lost, which I am convinced has often been the case, is

said to have been done by the pirates ... Indeed, were all the boats said to be captured taken in total, they would amount to more than each port has respectively.[20]

These comments should probably be taken to apply more to popular report than to the incidents which found their way into the British records, and they will not explain offshore captures. But it is still quite conceivable that the precipitate flight of Indian crews may have significantly distorted some of the surviving figures for Qasimi captures off India. This re-emphasizes the need for a cautious approach to the sources.

Two important conclusions arise from this discussion of the weaknesses of the Indian evidence. Firstly, a fair number of the Qawasim's Indian captures may have been unopposed and their British Indian victims sometimes indistinguishable from other craft. Secondly, numbers were sometimes exaggerated and certain individual incidents incorrectly reported. But the broad framework of events still stands. There are in fact persuasive positive arguments that this should be so: these include the nucleus of incidents demonstrable by reason of admission or possession; the pattern, breadth and complementariness of the evidence; and the fact that it was in the interests of the locally well-informed merchants, as of the British, to discover the truth.

A narrative of the Qawasim's seizures off the coast of India has been reconstructed in Appendix A, and the results displayed in Figure 1. This is only an approximate guide: few of the figures are likely to be precisely accurate, and there may be omissions, especially for events off Makran and Sind.

It appears to be the case that the first time the Qawasim took vessels off Cutch, and possibly east of Makran, was in early 1808. It is also evident that their activity was abated during the four years following the first British expedition against Ras al-Khaima, and it seems finally to have ceased with the second; the two years after the disastrous British demonstration at Ras al-Khaima in late 1816 were also those of the heaviest activity.[21]

The underlying pattern of captures is one of uneven growth, with most takings concentrated in the second decade. This same decade also witnessed the gradual encroachment of this activity southward: it reached Karachi in late 1813, Dwarka in early 1816, and finally Kodinar in late 1818. In connection with the late commencement of Qasimi activity off Kathiawar, it is worth noting that one of the belated peace proposals entertained by Hasan bin Rahma in 1819 was to limit Qasimi activity to the north, recognizing British preponderance 'from Cutch to the extremes to the southward.'[22] Just over two years earlier, his negotiator had been rather

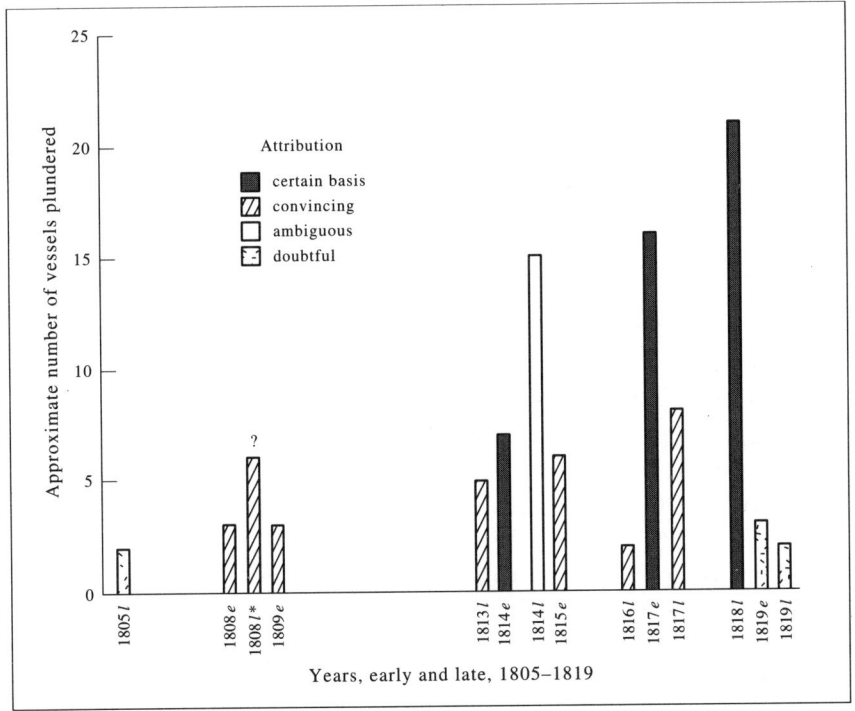

Figure 1. Qasimi Seizures off the Coast of India According to
Contemporary Records.

* Adjusted figure.

less acquiescing in his discussions with the British; stating, according to
Bruce, that

> he was much surprised at the demand we made on them, as they had
> not broken the engagements they were authorised to respect with us,
> but had only taken property belonging to the Hindus and other un-
> believers of India; that they did not consider any part of western India
> as ours besides Bombay and Mangalore; that at this rate we might go
> on and take all India and Muscat also, when nothing would be left
> for them to plunder. What was they then to do?—that in fact only
> English property of the sect of Jesus could be respected, and none
> other would be.[23]

The Qawasim visited India between October and March. In some years
they made 2–3 cruises in one 'winter' season. A typical cruise was one such
as that made by four Ras al-Khaima boats in the two months commencing

in mid-November 1818, which yielded four captures. During their return journey, part of the Qasimi crew were taken prisoner by Captain Loch, off Gwatar Bay on 28 December 1818.[24] The record of their interrogation, though clearly not taken down verbatim, is the only account we have from the Qawasim of one of these Indian voyages. There is no reason to doubt its substance:[25]

Questions Put To and Answered by the Qawasim

At what time did they sail, and what number?
Four vessels sailed at the same time, 45 days out.

Where did they first go to, and after that, the names and number of places that they touched at?
They first touched at Muctar, which is not inhabited belonging to the Baluchis, from thence to Devil[26] and to Mangrol Patan[?].[27]

The names of the places from whence they can get pilots?
Sind is the only place that they can get pilots, after they have given a promise of safety.

How many prizes have been taken altogether this year?
The four sail have taken this year three prizes which they were going to Ras al-Khaima with, and one which they were forced to abandon from her being leaky.

What places do they go to for wood and water, and how do they procure provisions?
They take with them wood enough for the time they mean to remain out. They go to the islands of Hanjam and Sirri for water, which they procure by making excavations.

Is there a great feast at Ras al-Khaima on the 11th of January, and if they were going there to be present at it?
No particular feast in January. It is the Ramadan this year.[28]

At what time do they return to the Indian coast for prizes?
No particular time for going to the coast of India, or returning home.

Is there any set of people in particular that assists them, or that they depend on more than others for information or assistance?
The Na'im, near Ras al-Khaima, and the Ahl Ali give from 3,000 to 4,000 men to assist the Qawasim, who can together raise from 15,000 to 17,000 men.[29]

How far past the Sind do they go?
They never go further than Devil or Mangrol Patan[?], in which places they have no communication, being on unfriendly terms.

What trade at Sind?
Rice and corn is the trade of Sind.

Do the Qawasim take or destroy the trading-vessels belonging to Sind?
They destroy all trading-vessels of Sind, and take them to Umm al-
Geiull[30] and put the people to death.

Do they go to (Gwatar) Ras Jiwani?
They go to Ras Jiwani sometimes.

Where is the plunder sold, and to whom?
The plunder is sold to the inhabitants of Bahrain, at Ras al-Khaima,
who take it for disposal; they being in alliance with the people of
Bahrain.

Are they in friendship with, or do they receive assistance from,
the Baluchis?
On the contrary, they are at war with all that coast and would kill
them with more pleasure than any other set of people.

Do the inhabitants of Bahrain assist the Qawasim; if so with what number
of men, and boats?
Yes, they give between 12,000 to 13,000 men and 20 or 30 boats.[31]

How much water do the baghlas draw?
The largest 18 feet, the smallest 13 feet; the largest, in going into Ras
al-Khaima, take everything out before going over the bar, where there
is at low water 2½ fathoms and at high 3½.[32]

How many boats are from Ras al-Khaima?
From 30 to 35.

How many from the Ahl Ali and the Na'im?
Thirty.

The vessels employed by the Qawasim on the north-western coast of
India, were the baghla and the battil. These are described by Elwood, the
Company's Agent at Porbandar:[33]

The Baghla, is a vessel with a square stern, and an elevated poop,
rising gradually aft towards the tafferel, much in the same manner as a
grab. Her prow projects forward in a considerable elevation, and is
nearly one third of the vessel's length, but not so high as the tafferel:
She is generally decked, fore and aft; has one mast, which stands perfectly upright, nearly in the centre of the vessel: In general she has no
mizen, tho' sometimes she is seen to use a small one, with a sail which
is hoisted in moderate weather only. Her mainsail is large, and spread
on a yard of great length, but the sail does not peak so much as that of
a pattamar's. Her tonnage is various, from 100 to 150 tons: some have

been seen in the Persian Gulph, as large as 450 tons burthen. The first class, or those from 350 to 450 tons, carry from 12 to 16 guns, and from 300 to 350 men. The depredations of this class is confined to the Arabian and Persian shores. The second class, or those from 100 to 300 tons, carry from 4 to 8 guns, and from 150 to 250 men. It is this description of boat which has appeared off Cutch and Okhamandal during the present month [of November 1818]. The guns of both classes are of iron and of various calibre, from 6 to 12 pounds.

The Trankey, or battil, is nearly of the same construction as the baghla, and is to be distinguished from such vessel, by a conspicuous curl, or fiddle head, placed on a low prow. She is seldom decked, is of a light draught of water, sails remarkably well; lays close to the wind, and pulls fast with her numerous paddles: She generally mounts a few swivels, but seldom any cannon: Her tonnage is from 40 to 120 tons, and carries from 150 to 200 men: Her sail, for the size of the boat, is larger in proportion, than that of the baghla: She has three of different sizes, for various winds, which she shifts, as occasions require; but never reefs her sail: She is steered by a high curved rudder, the tiller projecting abaft, with ropes on either side, leading to an outrigger.

The crews of the baghla and trankey, consist of stout, powerful Coffrees,[34] in the proportion of 2/3 rds.; the remaining third, are Arabs ... [They[35] are] chiefly armed with swords and spears. They have some matchlocks at times, in an half proportion ...

It is the trankey which has committed the greatest depredations on this, and the Gujarat coast.

There is no doubt as to the ability of the Qawasim as mariners. If their speed under sail, combined with discipline, nerve and a knowledge of the sea, did not defeat the efforts of the Company's cruisers to track, come up with and overpower them, then their shallow draught and use of sweeps almost always did. Even the Company's armed Indian pattamars, which often accompanied cruisers operating in these waters, proved unable to match the battil's performance:[36] it was finally concluded by one observer that the only way for the Company to meet the challenge presented by the Qawasim's superior sailing, was to build fine battils of its own, as close as possible to the Qasimi model, since, he argued, 'any attempt to improve on the trankey's build, would probably defeat the object sought for.'[37]

Although very many of the Indian captures were made after crews had abandoned ship, in some cases attacks were prosecuted at sea. These, it was said, depended for their success upon boarding, which was skilfully executed by large numbers of men from the stern. The precautionary measures recommended to British merchantmen against this form of assault were stern-chasers, boarding-nets and musketry. One 'officer of rank and great experience' added his own lethal expedient in case of attack by a multitude at close-quarters, namely the loading of a few smaller balls over the cartridge in a musket so as to multiply its fire: this was supposed to operate against the occasionally successful Qasimi practice of throwing large numbers into the rigging of the ship attacked.[38]

A third class of vessel, in addition to the baghla and the battil, is mentioned in a number of the reports of Qasimi activity off India from the second decade. This was the jymer, a small, fast, but undistinguished Makrani vessel, of between 15 and 20 tons, with one mast and a sail 'not unlike that of the trankey's'.[39] Her crew was Baluchi, and she was observed carrying others, up to a total of 60–160 men.

Jymers were sometimes seen off Cutch and Kathiawar apparently in company with Qawasim. The correct interpretation of these sightings is uncertain. Some were led to believe that the two groups of vessels acted in concert: Elwood, in particular, maintained that jymers often preceded Qasimi boats at a distance of two miles to act as pilots.[40] The only seeming test-case, however, suggests that here the two Makrani craft went before the Qawasim not because they were acting as pilots, but because they were trying to escape.[41] Whatever the case more generally, it is worth bearing in mind that Makrani vessels did visit these coasts in their own right, though whether these would have been classed as jymers is something of a mute point:[42] in addition to merchandise they sometimes carried passengers, which, since these included mercenaries, may of itself have excited suspicion; they may too have been independently responsible for cattle-raiding and small attacks on boats along these coasts.

Despite the doubtful nature of the connection between jymers and the Qawasim, Makran itself did feature in their voyages. There is good evidence that the Qawasim called at Pasni, where they replenished their supplies of water, and perhaps took the opportunity to collect wood and repair their boats. The local fishermen were left unmolested during their stay.[43] Whether Makran's role was any more that this, and in particular whether, as was believed in Porbandar, the Qawasim managed to dispose of part of the cargo they captured somewhere between Sonmiani and Ormara, is questionable: the evidence for this was slight and all that seems likely is that Bahrain was the principal mart for this merchandise.[44]

The ruler of Makran argued, perhaps with reason, that there was little either he or the local inhabitants could do about the fact that the Qawasim got supplies at Pasni: he himself professed to share his overlord, the ruler of Muscat's enmity towards the Qawasim. His neighbours to the east, the Chief of Luz and the Amirs of Sind, expressed a similar hostility.[45] They had some grounds for true feelings of this sort. The trade and shipping of Sind often suffered at the hands of the Qawasim: as early as 1809 the local authorities at Karachi had been obliged to requisition ships and institute naval action in order to repel Qawasim in the vicinity; four years later the harbour itself was raided under cover of darkness, before the attackers were beaten off by fire from Manora fort.[46] The Chief of Luz, whose territory included Sonmiani and Ormara, was most forthright in his condemnation of the Qawasim: in response to British insinuations he wrote,[47]

> I have no wish, and never have had any to extend countenance or asylum to these piratical wretches, who will no doubt receive the punishment of their crimes. Does it not seem strange, that in a state of hostility as they are with this country, I should have any leaning towards them? ... We are mountaineers, and being without vessels are unable to destroy the pirates, whose element is the sea ... It behoves you to undertake the punishment and annihilation of these wretches, who by an indiscriminate system of plunder and murder are the common enemies of mankind.

Evidence of Qasimi activity off this coast is scanty. When questioned in January 1819, the local people at Ormara revealed that relations with the Qawasim, such as they were, were unfriendly: shortly before, the Qawasim had seized a man and four boys from a small fishing-boat just outside the bay.[48] At the same time, the Chief of Luz wrote that Sonmiani itself had recently been plundered and burnt by the Qawasim, which had prompted him to despatch a force to assist the ruler of Muscat in attacking 'the town of the Qawasim'.[49]

News of the approach of the Qawasim could also stimulate limited defensive measures on the part of the local authorities further south, as at Mandvi and Porbandar; and in addition, the Cutch Raja's fleet, like that of the Guicowar of Baroda, and even a Portuguese corvette, occasionally co-operated in the attendant operations of the Bombay Marine. The efficacy of all this was slight.

The number of vessels which suffered in one way or another as a consequence of Qasimi activities, was in some years reasonably large, although many of these may have been of medium and smaller size; certain individual losses were undoubtedly great. More readily identifiable is the disruption of trade which resulted: when the Qawasim appeared off these coasts, shipping might be thrown into confusion or halted for up to a month, whilst the inconvenience of convoys lasted longer.

The victims of the Qawasim's depredations were those engaged in the coastal trade of Sind, Cutch and Kathiawar. A significant minority of those directly affected were British Indian merchants; no Europeans were ever involved. Individually, British Indian merchants were wont to petition the Governor of Bombay for help in recovering their lost goods and vessels. Collectively, on at least two occasions, the British Indian merchants of Bombay protested at the interruption of trade: 'the pirate Jasmy', they complained of the Qawasim in November 1817, 'has this year caused such depredations in sea to the vessels belonging to your petitioners and others, as has rendered your petitioners inactive to have any trade to the ports of Muscat, Cutch, Veraval, Mangrol, Porbandar, Karachi etc.'[50] Together they urged Government to take the appropriate action to curb these activities. It is striking that by 1819, the Porbandar Agent was able to write quite coolly of the local merchants, who were not even British subjects,

> Witnessing the superiority which the Qawasim possess in sailing, the native community entertain no hope of their depredations being put a stop to, but by destroying their port of Ras al-Khaima; an undertaking, which they earnestly hope, it will be convenient to Government to carry into execution at no distant period.[51]

Part Three

Interpretation

CHAPTER TEN

Preliminary Sketch

The reader may suppose I am describing the mimic wars of a panto-
mime, yet all that I relate is strictly conformable to truth.

Maurizi, on the 'bloody tragedy' of Qasimi successes
off the Muscat coast in 1815[1]

Enough has been said *per se* of the evidence for Qasimi activity. Liberated
from the strictures of undue scepticism, the way is now clear to go in quest
of the meaning of those acts. In order to do so, we must first bring the
depiction of Qasimi depredations to its summation. Figure 2, when taken
with that already given for Indian waters, represents as complete as
possible a catalogue of recorded Qasimi captures for the years 1797–1819.
The figures that produced these patterns are a distillation from a detailed
chronology, compiled from the available primary sources, which, whilst
being too lengthy to include in the present work, has in addition provided
the factual basis upon which the next chapter is constructed.[2]

The attribution of the overwhelming majority of incidents within the
Gulf and off Oman is sound, and besides imprecision, the main weakness
of the reporting is unevenness. Cases in the early years, and those involving Arab and Persian shipping unconnected with Britain and the three
principal Gulf ports are least likely to feature. Until the attacks on the
Trimmer and the *Shannon* in December 1804, scant attention was paid to
the Qawasim's maritime activities; and during the second decade, when
the reporting became often broader and more assiduous, it is unfortunate
that the otherwise rich seam of commentating provided by the East India
Company's Broker at Muscat is little in evidence in 1810–13 and 1816.

These deficiencies do not render the surviving account nugatory, though
they may make it incomplete. For all that, as a depiction of Qasimi activity in these years, more simply than as a pictorial representation of the
surviving knowledge, the graph yet retains some historical validity and will
bear discussion.

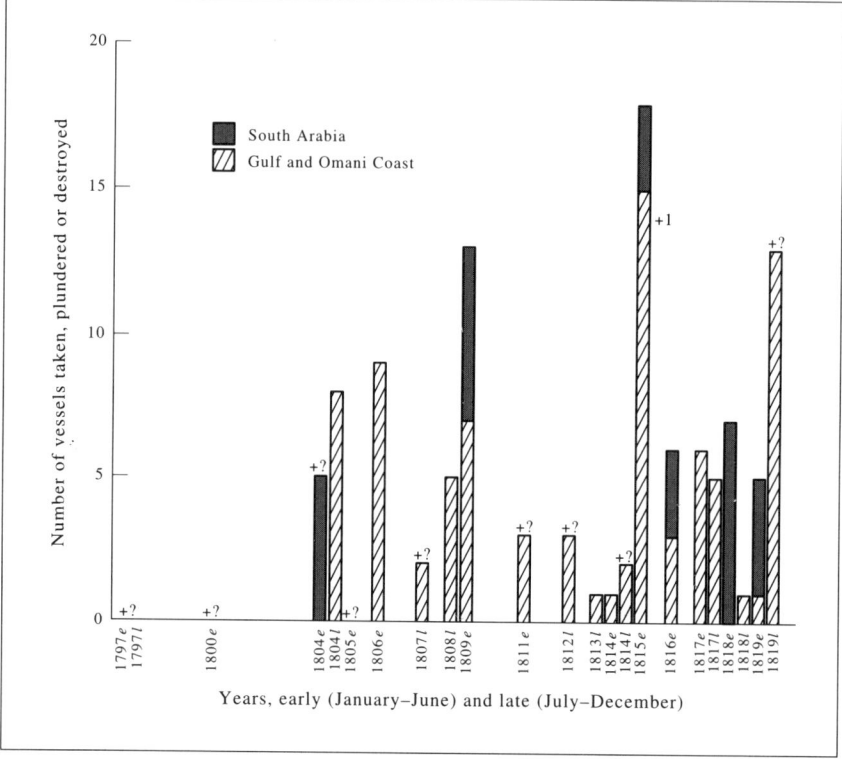

Figure 2. Recorded Captures by the Qawasim in the Gulf, and off the Coasts of Oman and South Arabia.

(a) The identification of the captors off south Arabia in 1804e is defective.
(b) Two further captures should be added before 1810.

Note: the symbol '+?' indicates that captures are referred to, in the Gulf area except in 1804e, but their number is not specified. The 'coast of Oman' here extends south to Ras al-Hadd. The term 'captures' includes incidents of boarding with plunder, but not attacks which were repulsed.

Figure 2 illustrates 87 specific incidents in the Gulf and off Oman, and alludes to others.[3] Eighty-seven should be regarded as a minimum. Without wishing to give undue prominence to the precise proportions, which inevitably reflect the nature of the reporting, the breakdown by victim before the two expeditions is set out in Table 1.

The most noticeable feature of this list, besides its breadth, is the central position of Muscat and her dependencies, which accords with expectation. Only the figures for British vessels are likely to be exhaustive. An alternative means of quantifying Qasimi captures would be by value, and this is discussed later.

The location of these captures—the term here being taken to include incidents of boarding with plunder, but not attacks which were repulsed—contains few surprises, though it is striking that almost all the attacks in the lower Gulf, for the most part between the Strait of Hormuz and Qais, were effected against ships passing up, not down, the Gulf. This circumstance might have been dictated by their likely cargoes, but more so, perhaps, by the greater possibilities of observation and tracking from vantage-points near the mouth of the Gulf. Another favourite haunt was the coastal water south from Muscat to Ras al-Hadd: repeated attacks on Muscat trade passing to and from India, and round south Arabia, were specifically recorded here after 1814.

The remaining 29 (+?) incidents in Figure 2 occurred off south Arabia. Many of the same comments apply here as to the Gulf. Although as a

Table 1: The Affiliation of Vessels Recorded Captured by the Qawasim in the Gulf and off Oman.

	1797–1809	1810–1819
Britain	6	6
India (Bhavnagar)	—	1
France	1	1
Kuwait	—	3
Basra	—	2
Basra and Kangan	—	— (+?)
Persia	7	1
Bushire	—	1
Rig (?)	—	1
Charak	3	—
Al Haram (Asalu) and Banu Mu'in	—	4
Muscat	1 (+?)	22 (+?)
Batina	—	— (+?)
Sur	—	3
Janaba of Sur	9	—
Trade of Muscat	— (+?)	2
Gulf shipping and unspecified	5 (+?)	8 (+?)
Total	32 (+?)	55 (+?)

Location of Seizures, Where Certain.*

	Upper Gulf	Lower Gulf	Coast of Oman
1797–1809	6	23	2
1810–1819	13	12	27

* Upper Gulf = north of Shaikh Shu'aib; lower Gulf = Shaikh Shu'aib to Strait of Hormuz; coast of Oman = Musandam to Ras al-Hadd.

Table 2: *The Affiliation of Vessels Recorded Captured by the Qawasim off South Arabia.*

Bombay	1
Madras	1
Surat (British)	4
India	4
Porbandar	6
Sur	1
Sayyid Muhammad Aqil (Dhufar)	1
Socotra	2
Shihr	1
Mukalla	(1?)
Mocha	1
Trade of Mocha with Berbera and Zeila	— (+?)
Unspecified	6
Total	29 (+?)

Location of Seizures.

Between Qishn and Mocha	18 (+?)
Socotra	6 (+2?)
Masira	1
Uncertain	2

group marginally less well attested than captures in the Gulf area, the activity off south Arabia is still firmly grounded. The central focus of these attacks was the trade between Mocha and north-west India, taking in that of Aden, Mukalla and Shihr. Activity was concentrated about Shihr and Mukalla, the Bab al-Mandab and Socotra, the two last presenting naturally advantageous spots for, in effect, ambush. The breadth of the recorded captures, seen in Table 2, is again striking.

Statistics can only convey so much. It is noticeable from Figure 2 that peaks and troughs in the first decade broadly correspond with ups and downs and lulls in the Qawasim's perennial tussle with Muscat. Clearly an understanding of the mechanism of the Qawasim's maritime acts requires a knowledge of their corresponding political history.

CHAPTER ELEVEN

Political History

From this narrative, [wrote the traveller Carsten Niebuhr of the Gulf in 1765,] the reader may form an idea of the continual revolutions which take place among this multitude of petty princes. At Basra I learned some particulars concerning their complicated quarrels, which I could not well comprehend: I was told, that every Arab Prince was always at open war with two or three others of his own nation.

The navigation is continually disturbed and interrupted by these strong quarrels. On board any Arabian vessel, passengers are always in danger of falling into the hands of one enemy or another. It is only on board a European ship, which the Arabian small craft dare not attack, that one can perform this voyage in safety.[1]

i The Eighteenth Century and the Emergence of the Qasimi Confederation

The main constant in the external political history of Ras al-Khaima in the early nineteenth century, and the principal constraint upon her ambitions in the lower Gulf, was the struggle with Muscat. This seemingly relentless duelling, and the dynamics it stimulated, was not a fleeting thing. It can be traced back to the middle years of the eighteenth century, when Ras al-Khaima, hitherto a limb of the enfeebled Omani state, first emerged under the Qawasim as a vital and independent entity. In the second half of that century, the contest between successive Omani rulers and the Qawasim was waged, no doubt intermittently, on different fronts: politically, through the medium of Oman's internal tribal politics, territorially in the north of the country and about Qishm, and militarily, of course, by land and sea. At the turn of the century, the encounter with her adversary and erstwhile overlord had, for Ras al-Khaima, long since ceased to be a matter of survival, and was now one of prosperity and freedom of action: for Muscat, under the vigorous and enterprising Sayyid Sultan, it was one part of the quest for Gulf dominance. The Qasimi shaikh, Matar bin Rahma, did not speak idly when in 1806 he rejected David Seton's attempt to include Muscat, under Badr, in the proposed Anglo–Qasimi peace. Ras al-Khaima's dispute with Britain seemed a straightforward, almost trivial, one by comparison:

> With regard to peace with Sayyid Badr, I hope you will not interfere. As the Arabs are in many tribes and have many quarrels amongst themselves. It is now three generations we have been at war with Muscat, and have both blood and property to settle; and we should be brought to shame were we to fix peace with the English, on the same basis as that with Sayyid Badr, as none can be lasting between us and him.[2]

An alternative translation of these same words holds added nuances:

> I hope you will not interfere in the peace between the Arabs, because we are many families and chance causes many disagreements amongst us. At present it is three generations we have been at war with Muscat, and having quarrels to settle with extent to boats, blood and property.[3]

For almost a century after her capture from the Portuguese in 1632 by the rising Ya'ariba dynasty of Oman, little is recorded of Julfar, the earlier incarnation of Ras al-Khaima, beyond intimations that she continued to be a regional and trade centre of some note.[4] The earliest at present known Qasimi Amir of Julfar was Shaikh Rahma bin Matar bin Rahma bin Muhammad al-Hauli, first referred to in Dutch sources in 1718 and thereafter more frequently.[5] Julfar and her dependent territory of Sir were at this time still accounted part of Ya'ariba Oman. Whilst this northern region had not yet actively sought to detach itself from the parent state, it was already separated by reason of geography and religion. Omani–Persian conflict in the Gulf during the second decade of the eighteenth century, followed much more importantly by the highly destructive and debilitating Omani civil war which commenced in 1719, developed this rift; and by the late 1720s, Qasimi Julfar evidently enjoyed a practical, if opportunistic, autonomy.[6]

Regional governor, merchant and military commander, Rahma bin Matar emerges through the records with a chameleon-like personality—which is perhaps to say no more than that he was an adept politician. What we know of him allows a degree of speculation on the source and nature of his position. He was reputedly one of the wealthiest of Gulf merchants, and this must have supported and guided his interests: the soon-to-be-founded Al Bu Sa'id dynasty of Oman, to name but one, similarly had something of a mercantile background. The economic strength of Julfar, situated as it was, controlling alongside Bahrain the pearling of the Gulf and exercising long-distance trade, for example with Kanara, was self-evident. Early on, under Rahma bin Matar, Julfar was not idle in safeguarding and seeking to develop this position by extending influence in the lower Gulf. By the late 1720s close links had been forged through emigration and political alliance with the new commercial centre of Basidu. In 1728, Rahma bin Matar made a bid to gain sovereignty over Hormuz, loosed from the collapsed Safavid state, but was outpaced by the Dutch.[7]

Rahma bin Matar's power was regional not tribal. He was not the hereditary Shaikh of a powerful tribe. His power was therefore supra-tribal and based on patronage and alliances. When, in his guise as a Ghafiri general in the Omani civil war, he led a force against Barka in 1723, it was said to have consisted of 5,000 bedouin and members of the settled population, 'amongst whom were some who did not understand Arabic and were unable to distinguish friend from foe':[8] this is generally taken to indicate that the force, which was alien to the folk of central Oman, included Shihuh from Musandam, or Ru'us al-Jibal.[9] Julfar, then, already had a distinctive character. As a mixed and long-established maritime centre, it differed markedly from tribal foundations in this era, such as those of the Banu Yas and the Utub.

When the Persians under Nadir Shah invaded Oman in 1737, they did so via the strategically inviting ports of Julfar and Khaur Fakkan.[10] Julfar thereafter seems to have remained in Persian hands, supporting a some-times large Persian garrison, despite serious reverses in the rest of Oman, until the assassination of Nadir Shah in June 1747 and the consequent Per-sian withdrawal from Oman. After his initial arrest by the occupying forces, Rahma bin Matar had in 1740 been reinstated as Persian 'Governor' of Julfar.[11] The power vacuum created in 1747 immediately catapulted Rahma bin Matar into asserting his independence; this, at a time when a Dutch observer in the Gulf noted that 'every Arab lord has become an independent ruler'.[12] The same process occurred simultaneously in Oman, where Ahmad bin Sa'id, the Governor of Suhar, founded the Al Bu Sa'id dynasty. The new Imam Ahmad set about reuniting the country, but despite efforts in that direction he was too weak to re-establish control over Qasimi Julfar; and if Miles is at all to be believed, he may have recog-nized its independence about 1763.[13] Just earlier, in 1756, the situation of the Qasimi capital ('Zur')[14] was described by Baron Van Kniphausen in the following terms:

> Zur is a reasonably large town which is fortified in the local manner and which has some pieces of artillery. It is inhabited by a tribe of Huwala called Qawasim. These have been in earlier times subject to the Imam of Muscat, but they do not recognise his authority anymore

and several expeditions by the Imam to bring this place under his obedience have been in vain, because he cannot achieve anything against the Shaikh of the Qawasim called Tschaid[15] or Rahma bin Matar, who is supported by several Bedu tribes from the desert. This Shaikh Rahma is at present the most powerful among the Huwala rulers, having of his own people 400 well-armed men with firearms in Zur, which has a good harbour where the largest ships can find shelter. There may be about 60 vessels there of which the most are large and well-provided and navigate down to Mocha. In this place itself there is a rather considerable trade as well of pearls as of some merchandise and provisions which are carried into the desert.[16]

The report continues,

A great piece of land, which near Zur protrudes into the sea and which becomes an island with high tide and which therefore is called the Red Island [Jazirat al-Hamra'] by the Arabs is inhabited by a caste [tribe] who carry the name of Saabs [Za'ab], who live from pearl-diving. They are numerous and have many small vessels. They have to obey the Shaikh of the Qawasim and have to pay him no small contribution.[17]

This early observation of the relationship between the Qasimi ruler and the Za'ab is noteworthy since it was to be an important factor in the upheavals half a century later.

The centuries-old experience of the venerable kingdom of Hormuz had shown that the mouth of the Gulf was ideally suited to forming the nub of a maritime commercial empire, founded upon exclusive control of the principal Gulf ports within a wide radius, and deriving its wealth from the regulation of pearling and international trade: naval supremacy had given merchants security and allowed the enforcement of obligatory shipping-tolls and customs-dues. Julfar and the ports of eastern Oman had been an integral part of this state and its successor, the Portuguese *Estado da India*. This legacy had, of course, long since been whittled away and the residue, such as it was, divided between Bandar Abbas, Muscat, Julfar and the rest. Grand ambition apart, which was not realistically in play until the activities of Sayyid Sultan bin Ahmad of Muscat at the turn of the century, there was still much unclaimed potential to squabble over. Nor was there, in the second half of the eighteenth century, any shortage of competitors for control of the ports, secure islands and narrow shipping-lanes in the region of Hormuz.

The Qasimi ruler Rahma bin Matar and his successor sought to expand their influence in this region during the 1750s and early 1760s. The tactic adopted by Rahma bin Matar was a reciprocal alliance with Mulla Ali

Shah, commander of the eastern squadron of Nadir Shah's navy and for much of this time Governor of Bandar Abbas. Besides the political advantage inherent in this axis, Mulla Ali Shah thereby profited from Qasimi manpower and Rahma bin Matar had access to his partner's ships and wealth.[18] The combination was sealed by Rahma bin Matar's marriage to the other's daughter. It was an increasingly unequal relationship. By 1760, when Rashid bin Matar replaced his brother as ruler of Julfar, Mulla Ali Shah had already expended most of his store of strength in the struggle with his adversaries; divested of his ships, he was now ousted from Bandar Abbas to the island of Hormuz, and after the middle 1760s disappeared from the scene altogether.

The alliance between Qasimi Julfar and Mulla Ali Shah was assisted by tribal allies on the Persian coast, notably the Maraziq and Al Haram. It was chiefly opposed by the Banu Mu'in of Qishm with their ally Nasir Khan of Lar; these were sometimes joined by Imam Ahmad of Oman and aided by the Al Ali of Charak. The Banu Mu'in were for the time being, perhaps, gainers, and by late 1765 possessed Larak and Bandar Abbas and were soon to acquire Hormuz. The most significant results for the Qawasim seem to have been their establishment at Laft, which they captured with Mulla Ali Shah in 1755, and their somehow gaining ascendancy a little to the west at Linga: this last seems to have occurred after 1756, when the port was still governed by Maraziq.[19]

Despite evidence of partial crystallization in the early 1760s, the situation at the mouth of the Gulf was to remain highly volatile into the next century. It was also complex. In 1765, for example, we learn that the Banu Mu'in held Basidu and the villages of Qishm, the Qawasim shared Laft with Mulla Ali Shah of Hormuz, and Mulla Ali Shah owned the old naval station of Qishm besides exacting protection money from the shipping of Khamir. Linga, Kung and Ras al-Hiti, all of which it is noted produced firewood and charcoal in small quantities, were by now Qasimi.[20] This snapshot was captured by the traveller Carsten Niebuhr. His accompanying delineation of the Qasimi state in 1765 is worth citing as almost the last such to reach us before the nineteenth century:

> The country of Sir extends along the coast from Khaur Fakkan in the north, as far as Ras Musandam, and into the Persian Gulf in the west, as far as the small island of Sharja [near where, he adds, there was rich pearling.] Up until a few years ago, these Arabs continued to recognise the authority of the Imam; at present they are independent and often at war with their erstwhile overlords. Because they are too weak to resist them [the Omanis], they as a rule maintain good relations with other small independent Shaikhs, and above all with the Shaikh of Jau in the west of Oman. The Shaikh of Sir belongs to the Huwala

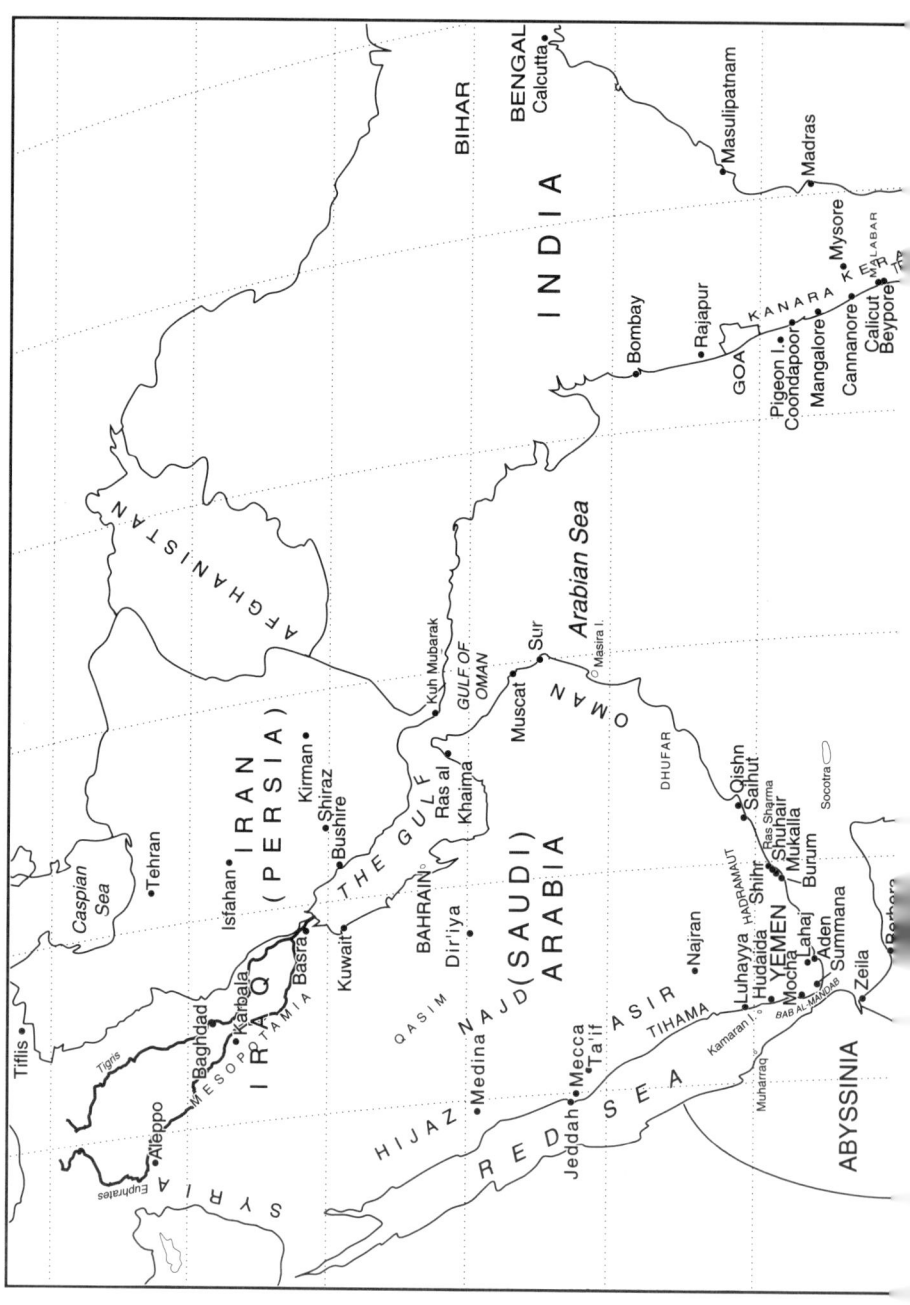

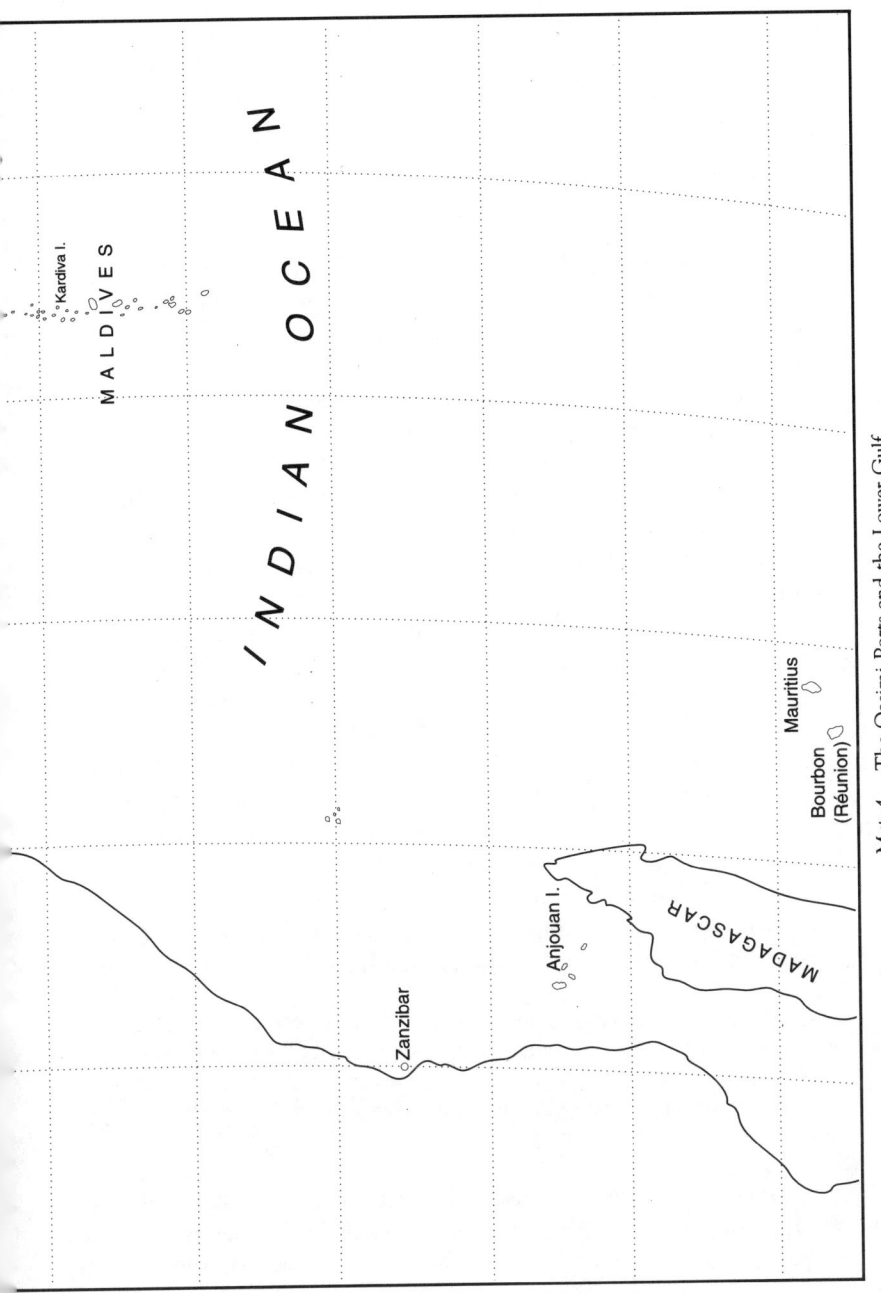

Map 4. The Qasimi Ports and the Lower Gulf.

family and in 1765 was called Rashid bin Matar al-Qasimi. Outside Arabia, he also owns part of Qishm island, as well as Ras al-Hiti, Linga and Kung on the Persian coast. His navy commands respect in this quarter, and the merchant-shipping of these Arabs is responsible for quite a sizable trade[21] within and beyond the confines of Persian Gulf.

The subjects of the Imam for the most part adhere to the Ibadi sect, but those attached to the Shaikh of Sir are Sunnis and almost all of Hanbali persuasion. Hence you find two Muslim sects in Oman, each of whom accuses the other of heresy.[22]

After 1763, when the English East India Company followed the lead of the Dutch in abandoning Bandar Abbas for Basra, Bushire and the head of the Gulf, European reporting on the events of the lower Gulf almost dried up. Knowledge of Qasimi history over the next 30 years is very patchy. It must be assumed that the preoccupation with the region of Hormuz and with Muscat both continued. The train of events made a brief, to some extent random, appearance in the records in 1778–81. This glimpse also allows a degree of speculation on the health of the Qasimi state at the end of Imam Ahmad of Oman's three and a half decades of rule.

Around September 1778, war broke out between Muscat and Julfar, and an expedition was soon led against the latter. It consisted of 10–12 ships with over 100 gallivats, dinghies and suchlike, but was unable to do anything, so before the year was up had returned to Muscat. The impasse is said to have resulted from Julfar's impregnability and relative strength. Though 'miserably poor', she was populous and owned 3–4 gallivats and over 100 dows and trankeys, in addition to which her ruler, Rashid bin Matar, was reportedly 'very powerful by land'.[23] In a by now familiar pattern, the military and political stalemate between the two neighbours, Julfar and Muscat, immediately deteriorated into a persistent state of hostility at sea.[24] The attacks on merchant shipping which characterized this skirmishing were not confined to the immediate disputants. In March 1779, the British Resident, in a sardonic mood, observed,

> Shaikh Rashid's fleet being continually on the cruise has roused almost every petty shaikh in the Gulph to fit out armed boats manned by a lawless set of barbarians under no command, who, receiving no pay but depending solely upon plunder, rob without distinction everything they can.[25]

The state of hostility with Muscat was felt to justify taking not only Muscat shipping, but also, for example, a number of small Bushire boats, on the pretext that their cargoes belonged to Muscat. Another casualty was an 8-gun British twin-master, carrying rice, china, packets and some silver from Bombay to Bushire, with a crew of lascars and two Europeans:

she had been captured whilst becalmed about 3 December 1778 by six dows under Rashid bin Matar's son (Saqr) and was subsequently brought into Julfar during the absence of the father, who was then up-country campaigning against Muscat. It was alleged that she had been flying Muscat colours until the time she was boarded, conceivably out of fear of French privateers. Rashid bin Matar agreed to let the British Resident ransom her for 4,000 rupees, but this sum was thought twice what was acceptable and a 'disgraceful compromise'.[26] It seems, in fact, that Rashid bin Matar wanted to employ her in his efforts against Muscat. He does not seem to have sacrificed British goodwill by this episode, for the Resident readily attested that 'Shaikh Rashid, who 20 years ago was Governor of Gombroon [Bandar Abbas: sic?][27] and as strong as he is at present, has always been in friendship with us, and never committed any robberies till within these four months since his being at war with the Imam of Muscat.'[28]

The Qasimi position around 1780, which was doubtless accompanied by commercial success,[29] thus appears to have been reasonably strong. There are further indications that this was so. In 1782, Khasab had seized from a Bushire dow cargo belonging to the merchants of Muscat, Bushire and Basra. Saqr bin Rashid's ability to restore part of these goods, with Muscat's desire to call in British help against Khasab, strongly suggest that the port was at this time under the sway of Julfar. Saqr bin Rashid also felt confident enough to pledge the restoration of any Basra property that might be taken by 'the peoples at the southern end of the Gulph':[30] if the apparent force of these words is to be credited, and there was some evidence in Saqr's demonstration at Basra pointing in that direction, it would suggest that Julfar had achieved a measure of pre-eminence in the lower Gulf. A contributing factor must have been the rapprochement with the Banu Mu'in, following the disappearance of Mulla Ali Shah, which may be inferred from Saqr bin Rashid's marriage to the Banu Mu'in Shaikh Abdullah's daughter. Likewise also, dynastic weakness in Oman in the early 1780s must have assisted the consolidation of the Qawasim. It was characteristic that Rashid bin Matar should at first have acted as implicitly respected and influential mediator in the dispute between Bushire and the Utub over Bahrain. But it was ultimately far more significant that the Qawasim should so soon have switched over to active support of Bushire and the Persian coast in their hostilities against the new Utbi conquerors of Bahrain.[31] There had been a long-term shift in commercial activity to the north of the Gulf, where the Utub of Bahrain and Kuwait now presented the Qawasim and their neighbours with competition, and a new political pattern was emerging out of the turmoil of the eighteenth century. Qasimi Julfar was beginning, perhaps, to sense the precariousness of her new-won position.

ii   1797–1804: the Primacy of Sayyid Sultan and the Arrival of the Wahhabis

If we are to identify the prime cause of maritime disturbance in the Gulf between 1797 and 1804, then it would have to have been Sayyid Sultan of Muscat's ambition to dominate it.[32] His grandiose plan was motivated by the wish to safeguard and promote the shipping and international trade of Muscat. To this end Sayyid Sultan (regn. 1792/3–1804) cultivated diplomatic and commercial links with trading partners outside the Gulf. He found himself courted by Afghan and Abyssinian alike, as well as by Tipu Sultan and the European powers. Closer to home, within the Gulf, he relied in part upon well-constructed commercial arrangements such as a drastic reduction in customs-dues at Bandar Abbas and reciprocal rates at Muscat and Basra; but, confident in his unrivalled navy, he also did not baulk at the use or threat of force to achieve his ends, even against a comparable state like Basra. He was especially concerned with uncompliant and enterprising commercial rivals such as the Bahrain Utub, and any threat to his position at the entrance to the Gulf. By late 1801 his power had reached its apogee. He momentarily held Bahrain, was able to call upon the services of Persian ports like Nakhilu, Asalu and Kangan and even demanded the obeisance of Kuwait. His position in the lower Gulf was likewise secure: the Banu Mu'in had been brought to heel, Bandar Abbas and her dependencies were held in farm, and his proxies, the Sudan tribe, attacked incoming ships which did not pay customs at Muscat. Still further east, both Gwadar and Chahbahar in Makran were his.

The Qawasim did not escape the consequences of all this. One of Sayyid Sultan's first acts was to make war upon them; but lacking the power to conquer Ras al-Khaima, the hostilities soon deteriorated into the pernicious stalemate so familiar from the eighteenth century. The context of the attacks upon the *Bassein* and *Viper* in 1797 fits squarely into that pattern. Qasimi retaliation, in the form that was available to them of attacks upon Muscat trade, was successful enough by February 1800 for Malcolm to christen them pirates.[33] This apart, their fifty 'small' vessels were ultimately in many circumstances no match for Sayyid Sultan's modern-equipped navy. Seton's later, albeit unduly approving, appraisal of the situation around 1800–2, presents a starker picture: whenever the Qawasim 'sent out a fleet of any force, a ship or two from Muscat drove them again within their ports and this method was continued till they were reduced to the greatest distress. Occasional truces were made with them but no lasting peace'.[34]

Pressure on the Qawasim must have been especially close at this time since it was also the period when the Sudan tribe were based on Hormuz. Having fallen out with the ruler of Ras al-Khaima, they had emigrated and been settled by Sayyid Sultan upon the island with express instructions to harry Qasimi and Utbi shipping. Their removal thence at the end of 1801, to the presumed if limited relief of Ras al-Khaima, came as the un-intended result of British protests. When Sayyid Sultan thought it import-ant, he could also take direct action against Ras al-Khaima. His blockade of 1803–4, motivated by the Qawasim's sheltering of his rebellious nephew Badr, was tight enough to reduce the Qawasim to desperate straits.

The Qawasim's mobility suffered through this conflict, as no doubt did their trade. This is suggested by Seton's comment in 1801 that Ras al-Khaima was already no longer the rich and powerful maritime state she had been formerly.[35] They were also squeezed by Sayyid Sultan on land. The brother of Shaikh Saqr bin Rashid ruled over Linga and Shinas on the Persian coast, but Laft now supported a Muscat garrison, as did Khasab in Musandam, and in 1799 the port of Diba fell and was annexed to Suhar.

There are faint indications that as Sayyid Sultan waxed strong, the Qawasim grew occasionally weary of the incessant disruption. They readily embraced his offers of peace in 1798, even if not in 1802. At all events, pearling took precedence over warfare, as the Wahhabis discovered when they failed to instigate the Qawasim to attack Muscat shipping during the summer of 1803. But the Wahhabis, who wanted a different sort of war, would not be deterred, and it took the concrete effects of the 1803–4 blockade to convince them that the Qawasim should after all be permitted to reach an interim peace with Muscat.[36]

Pressure upon the Qawasim to make war upon Muscat was a telling manifestation of the new Wahhabi presence in the eastern corner of Arabia. Precisely when Ras al-Khaima had been overrun by Wahhabi forces is unclear, but the first wave had certainly reached there by early 1800 when there was an attempt, from their forward and permanent base at Buraimi, to invade the Batina via Ras al-Khaima. The Wahhabi con-quest by land, on top of maritime pressure from Muscat, initially had a dispiriting and depressing effect upon Ras al-Khaima, beyond the mere fact of being made tributary. The *Lam' al-Shihab* suggests that Saqr bin Rashid had done his best to repel the attack by force of arms, but in an effort of self-preservation had capitulated when he understood the odds. Spiritual resistance amongst some of the Qawasim could not so easily be overcome and the diehard, such as Saqr's Sufi father, chose to emigrate to Linga.[37] The Wahhabi directives of 1803 seemed more insistent than before, and the following year may possibly have witnessed the first cruise, to south Arabia, imbued with Wahhabi overtones. It may be that greater pragmat-ism entered the Qawasim's relationship with their new overlords after the accession of Sultan bin Saqr at Ras al-Khaima in 1803. It was a testing time for a new young ruler.

iii *November 1804–1807: the Collapse of Muscat's Authority*

Sayyid Sultan was killed in a trivial skirmish near Qishm about 14 November 1804, and with that accident much of the influence he had built up for Muscat in the Gulf evaporated, as did his country's semblance of internal unity. Immediately fired with a spark of anarchic exuberance at this sudden turn of events, the combined navy of Linga and Ras al-Khaima put to sea against the trade of Bushire, Muscat and Basra, mopping up such vessels as they happened upon: the *Trimmer* and the *Shannon* were sorry witness to this. In early–mid December, although the extent to which this was premeditated is unclear, the Shaikh of Charak was killed in a sea-fight, and his dependency of Qais was ravaged and burnt.[38] Henceforth Charak, which had generally been at variance with Julfar in the contests of the mid-eighteenth century, remained under Qasimi domination, paying tribute to Linga and the Wahhabis, until the 1809/10 expedition.

In the Hormuz region, the vacuum created by Sayyid Sultan's decease was simultaneously occupied by Mulla Hasan of the Banu Mu'in who, on top of Qishm and Hormuz, rapidly took charge of his cherished Bandar Abbas and set about besieging his imbecile cousin at Minab. During the six months it took for Muscat to re-establish control of Bandar Abbas, and to an extent thereafter, the Qawasim held the respect and friendship of Mulla Hasan, and hence achieved loose mastery of the coast and islands between Hormuz and Charak. Since the mid-eighteenth century, the power of the Banu Mu'in had become etiolated, and despite strong vestigial aspirations, they were after the late 1770s obliged to face the reality of being ultimately at the mercy of the rivals Muscat and the Qawasim.[39] The Qasimi ruler Saqr bin Rashid and his son Sultan had both strengthened their hand by marrying into the Banu Mu'in, and when Muscat control lapsed reactivated an alliance with them:[40] at other times, as *c.* 1798–9, this did not prevent the Qawasim raiding Qishm, but when in play, it was a far more equal relationship than that usually imposed by Muscat.

In addition to their augmented position on the northern shore, it seems the Qawasim may have been strong just north of Ras al-Khaima. There is possibly a suggestion that Bukha owed allegiance to them even in early November 1804.[41] This is not as unlikely as it may appear in retrospect. In 1782 Khasab had been in just this situation, and the link to the Shihuh went back to the 1720s. Indeed the ruler of Muscat was himself to bracket Bukha and Sha'm with the Qawasim in May 1819, though one suspects it might have been a case of intermittent or adverse possession, since we know that Bukha was laid waste by the Qawasim at some period before the second expedition.[42]

Within a month or so of Sayyid Sultan's demise, his renegade nephew Badr, instigator of the unsuccessful 1803 coup, sailed into Muscat and laid claim to the throne. For the duration of his year and a half's reign, Oman was riven by a bitter contest fought for supremacy between Badr and his uncle Qais, the Governor of Suhar. As early as the beginning of 1805, the Qawasim were drawn in on the Ghafiri side, in opposition to Qais, whose territories in the Shimailiya they probably coveted. There was also another aspect to this civil war, which partly explains the Qawasim's superficial involvement in support of Muscat, namely Badr's open espousal of the Wahhabi cause. His appeals to Su'ud for assistance elicited the despatch of large numbers of Wahhabi troops, besides the issuance of orders to the Bahrain Utub (who were perhaps his soundest such allies) and to the Qawasim that they offer assistance. When in May 1805, 15 Utbi vessels sailed into Muscat harbour, they did so remarkably

> with pieces of the winding-sheet plundered from the tomb at Karbala flying for colours, and firing guns, which set the women in the late Imam's zenana a-crying and their screams were heard in the streets. In the evening when they called to prayers not a soul was in the streets and in the following night the Utub called in the old way which relieved the alarm.[43]

Unpalatable as it was, this help was tactically vital to Badr's survival. It carried a high level of risk, however, as became clear at the start of 1806 when, at a time of greatest peril for Badr as Qais's men reached the suburbs of Muscat, his negotiations with the Qawasim and appeal to Su'ud caused the Qawasim to attack Qais's rear; they now seized the important ports of Diba, Khaur Fakkan and Khaur Kalba[44] and held them one way or another until after the first expedition.

Badr privately represented his relationship with the Wahhabis as one of alliance not subjection, and he probably gambled upon being able to deal with the Qawasim once his position was assured. In matters unconnected with his survival he put Muscat's interests first. Thus, like any other Muscat ruler, he proceeded when he was able, but with Utbi and a veneer of British support, to recover Bandar Abbas and, which was the best he could hope for, to seek to neutralize Mulla Hasan of the Banu Mu'in, who was again made tributary and optimistically forbidden from assisting either Qais or the Qawasim. Badr applied other pressure to the Qawasim, notably by seeking to exclude them from the Basra date market in the winter season 1805/6. Following hard upon a ban on their visiting British India, imposed at the beginning of the year after the *Trimmer* and the *Shannon* were taken, Badr's action was nicely calculated to injure a 'people whose country afforded nothing but fish and a few dates, and who existed by carrying freight for others [and whose Shaikh was not more than the other heads of families, who obeyed him, or not, as they pleased]'.[45] Not surprisingly, Sultan bin Saqr had made access to British ports a priority in the discussions leading to the restoration of amicable relations with Britain in the accord of February 1806. If anything, though the rift on both sides ran to the marrow and each continued to plunder the other's shipping, one suspects that the Qawasim may have been slightly more inclined to peace than Badr.

An important episode during this period, described by Seton and the *Lam' al-Shihab* as a milestone or turning-point for the Qawasim, was the Suri affair. The Janaba and the Suri Qawasim were feuding Omani tribes inhabiting the maritime centre of Sur, to the south-east of Muscat. The Janaba had the backing of Muscat, while the Suri Qawasim engaged the support of their supposed cousins the Qasimi family of Ras al-Khaima. The two tribes separately owned and sailed a significant proportion of Oman's annual Basra fleet. In January 1806, as this fleet was returning down the Gulf, the Suri Qawasim put into Ras al-Khaima and brought the Janaba forcibly with them; the Janaba were immediately plundered and detained. This was a wounding loss to the economy of Muscat, and brought Ras al-Khaima a windfall in men, money and ships: the value of the plunder was estimated at 600,000 riyals (c. £150,000) or more, while the Janaba brought with them 13 dows and the Suri Qawasim 23.[46] The Janaba at Sur retaliated by putting the wives and children of the Suri Qawasim under detention, and an expedition from Ras al-Khaima in 1807 to rescue them was beaten off with heavy losses. The Suri Qawasim crews were still at Ras al-Khaima at the end of 1808.[47]

Ras al-Khaima must have witnessed an increase in Saudi–Wahhabi influence over these years, just as, in so noticeable a fashion, did Muscat. Qasimi resistance to delivering one-fifth of their plunder to the Wahhabis at the start of 1805, though evidence perhaps of unease at their situation, was more or less overcome. The Wahhabis had long entertained designs against Basra, but in spring 1805 the idea was first mooted of raids on the Indian coast or shipping. In the autumn, the Saudi ruler formally instructed Muscat to take the Holy War to India, and it seems reasonable to assume that the Qawasim received like bidding. Interestingly, the Islamic year commencing 1 April 1805 was also the first of six successive years of famine and scarcity in Najd: this encouraged some movement of population outward from central Arabia to places such as Yemen, Syria and Oman, and had an observable impact upon the pattern of Wahhabi raiding.[48]

During his first year and a half of office, which began with his assassination of Badr in July 1806, the youthful Sayyid Sa'id bin Sultan made a feeble attempt to restore Muscat's authority, achieving little. By the end of 1807, having lost control of the interior of Oman to the Wahhabis, to whom he himself paid allegiance, and possessing little influence overseas, he had alienated many of his potential supporters. The port of Muscat was being deserted by some of her Arab inhabitants and her trade suffered repeated interruption at the hands of the Qawasim. These were not over-awed by Sayyid Sa'id's naval supremacy, which had been evinced in his blockade of Ras al-Khaima in mid-1806 and passing victory in spring 1807. A botched attempt by Sayyid Sa'id to discipline Mulla Hasan at the end of 1806 had actually increased the Qasimi hold on the lower Gulf by giving them Qishm and Khamir; Laft, which had been lost by Muscat to Mulla Hasan under Badr, now supported a garrison from Ras al-Khaima.[49]

iv 1808–1809: the Qawasim at their Zenith and the Rapid Increase in Saudi Control

By May 1808, Sayyid Sa'id had at last reached an accord with Qais for the purpose of pushing back Qasimi gains in the north. Their armies retook Khaur Fakkan with ease, but no sooner had they done so than the Qawasim counter-attacked. Sultan bin Saqr of Ras al-Khaima's night-ambush upon the Omani encampment turned the victory into an ignominious rout: Sayyid Sa'id personally lost his treasure and his clothes, and, as the battle raged, had to be carried off to safety with a bullet wound in the leg; Qais was killed. Over the next five months, Sultan bin Saqr, as Saudi regional governor, and a handful of powerful tribal leaders from the interior of Oman, who were now aligned with the same power, pressed home the advantage with raids towards the Batina. By the end of October, Shinas had fallen to the Wahhabis and both Qais's son Azzan and Sayyid Sa'id had capitulated. This was the high point of Qasimi power, albeit under the Wahhabi aegis.

The flavour and exhilaration of these victories is reflected in a letter written at the time by a senior member of the Qasimi family, Sultan bin Saqr's cousin Matar bin Rahma bin Rashid, to his brother. It is a precious document, and survives because it was intercepted by the British:

> My present letter is written from Ras al-Khaima, the events of which place are entirely favourable. I have, also, to inform you that every-thing is quiet and tranquil here, and, further, in respect to the inhabitants of Oman, that a number of people belonging to Qais bin Ahmad, and the children of Sultan bin Imam, to the number of eight thousand men, have landed from five ships, besides baghlas, dows and twenty smaller craft, at Khaur, within the territories of Shaikh Sultan bin Saqr, and seized upon Rooka,[50] and killed about sixty Muham-madans, partly inhabitants of Khaur and partly of Ras al-Khaima, in-cluding, in the former number, several slaves belonging to Surrah,[51] a

person at Sur. They were pursued by Amir Sultan bin Saqr, who over-took the inhabitants of Oman and defeated them with great slaughter. Qais was among the number of the slain, and also the adopted son of Muhammad [bin] Khalfan, together with seven persons of the tribe of Bu Sa'id, who were excellent characters, besides six thousand of the inhabitants of Oman, who fell at Khaur. Praised be the Almighty, who has rendered the faith triumphant and put its enemies to con-fusion, as the [Sur][52] and has said My [...][53] is victorious.

After this event Amir Sultan attacked several stations in the Batina or Oman territories. He had with him, the inhabitants of Dir'iya,[54] whose numbers, added to his army, made it amount to twenty thou-sand men. From Batina they passed on to Shinas, where they halted and attacked its military defences; and I have the pleasure to inform you that the garrison was completely routed, and compelled to aban-don it: a great many of them were killed, so much so as to be in fact countless. This was followed by the son of Qais coming forward, and embracing the religion of God, and the Prophet, professing[55] to abandon a course of sin, and to return to the path of virtue, giving up, at the same time, twenty thousand dollars, ten horses, and twenty camels. The army then quitted Suhar, and proceeding into the territ-ories of the son of the Sultan, subdued three of his towns; and this led to the said son of the Sultan presenting himself, and becoming a convert to the faith of God, and the Prophet: he, also, gave up forty thousand dollars, ten prime horses, and twenty camels. The son of Qais, and of the Sultan,[56] then proceeded in the direction of Dir'iya, for the purpose of acknowledging allegiance to Su'ud bin Abd al-Aziz, and of entering into engagements with him.

The inhabitants of Oman are labouring under great apprehensions, whilst the remainder of that territory has become proselytes, and their affairs are now identified;[57] but from this act is excluded the tribes of Banu Bu Ali, and Janaba of Sur, assigning as a cause, that they have been hostile to them for a long time. On the part of the Qawasim, the inhabitants of Sur are likewise converts,[58] and they will, God willing, come out to attack the Banu Bu Ali and Janaba and other infidels.[59]

It is ironic that even as Sultan bin Saqr's triumphs were being celeb-rated, at a time when Ras al-Khaima could attract a political mission from Sind,[60] his power-base was being undermined by the Saudi ruler Su'ud. His standing had for some time past been encroached upon by Wahhabi officials. In July he had very publicly been obliged to follow the diktat of one such officer in deciding the fate of the *Darya Daulat*, even though she had been captured by his own dow. More insidious was Sultan bin Saqr's gradual loss of authority over neighbouring ports like Ajman and Rams, foreshadowed in the *Shannon* affair of October 1807. In *c.* November 1808, the Saudi ruler abruptly accelerated and formalized this comminution of Sultan bin Saqr's power and status. This was part of a wider scheme of divide and rule in Oman made possible by the recent conquests, which had been made in his name and naturally required endorsement. There was also specific disquiet at Sultan bin Saqr's less than wholehearted compliance, as in the matter of tribute and the acceptance of Wahhabi officers. Sultan bin Saqr was now stripped of his nominally supreme Saudi governorship and, more important, divested of his possessions in Shimailiya. A new and wholly artificial power was created by Su'ud, geographically situated between Ras al-Khaima and Suhar and headed at first by Hasan bin Ali of Rams, chief of the Tanaij, who was soon replaced by a leader possibly associated with the Za'ab. This new state included Shinas, Khaur Fakkan, Diba, Jau and later Bithna and Fujaira, together, presumably, with Rams. By early 1809, Sultan bin Saqr found his formal power on the Arabian coast confined very largely to Ras al-Khaima.[61]

The position of the Tanaij and Za'ab tribes is central to an understanding of the transformation of the Qasimi state, under the influence of the Wahhabis, in 1808–9. The population centres of these two client-tribes of the Ras al-Khaima Qawasim were Rams and Jazirat al-Hamra'. For many years, since at least the 1750s in the case of the Za'ab, they had endured a degree of material subjection to the Qawasim and this apparently rankled. At some point after the arrival of the Wahhabis, they discovered their salvation in them: by outdoing the Qawasim in loyalty, zeal and, it is said, preparedness for maritime plunder, they appealed to the Saudi leadership as a conduit of influence, and a potential alternative to the continued centralization of power at Ras al-Khaima. Their promotion operated concurrently with the subversion of Sultan bin Saqr's authority at ports adjacent to Sir. The experiment in a detached state in Shimailiya may possibly not have lasted beyond 1809, but Hasan bin Ali of Rams remained a staunch and genuinely pious Wahhabi throughout the second decade.[62] For this reason, he was chosen during the same period to replace an unpopular outsider as local officer responsible for the transmission to the Saudi treasury of the one-fifth due from plunder.

All these developments, the war with Muscat, the breakdown of accustomed authority and the increase in Wahhabi control, had a clear impact upon the maritime activities of the Qasimi ports. A major stimulus to the Khaur Fakkan campaign on both sides had been the port's strategic importance as a Qasimi foothold east of Musandam, affording a base for attacks on Muscat shipping and a staging-point on the journey to south Arabia: when Sayyid Sa'id first took the place he discovered over 30 vessels there. The upheavals of May–October 1808 coincided with attacks on British shipping: the *Darya Daulat* was taken by Sultan bin Saqr in July during an assault on Muscat shipping, conceivably under a misapprehension, and the *Sylph* was reputedly attacked in October by Rams, which now speaks for itself. From late 1808, adjacent ports were said to send out boats independently of Sultan bin Saqr at Ras al-Khaima, something which he himself adduced in explanation of the attack on the *Sylph*; the *Minerva* was captured the following May when the ruler was physically absent from the region. The progress of the Wahhabis was also accompanied by more vociferous calls for raids on Indian shipping. These pleas were likewise addressed to the Utub who, in an attempt to secure British help in resisting these demands, pointedly informed Seton that 'the instigators to the attempts on our vessels were the Wahhabi, who were daily pressing them to proceed on schemes of piracy to India'.[63] The peace of October 1808 may have freed Qasimi shipping for cruises to India and, at the start of 1809, for a fateful cruise to south Arabia that was eventually struck low by smallpox.

A certain amount of information is available concerning the extent of Qasimi domination of the Persian coast in the run-up to the British expedition. Laft was under the direct control of the Ras al-Khaima Qawasim until October, when Mulla Hasan was reinstated as their protégé after his escape from Muscat; their garrison, however, remained and was to offer Britain stout resistance in November. The real status of the rest of Qishm island, claimed by Muscat, is unclear, but its prosperity was said to have declined from the oppression of its inhabitants by the Qawasim: in like fashion, Qais island, a dependency of Charak, was said to have become depopulated because of them. Qadib bin Su'ud bin Qadib al-Qasimi, nephew of Sultan bin Saqr, was direct ruler of Linga.[64] He had loose authority over all the coastline between Bandar Mu'allim and Kalat: ports like Mughu, Shinas and Charak were said to pay small amounts of tribute to Iran, together with something 'out of fear' to Linga.[65] The situation just to the west, at Nakhilu, was similar in that she paid 'the regulated duties on culture and captures to the Wahhabi, besides a tax of about 24 tomans yearly to the Persian government'; but although Sultan bin Saqr was married to her ruler's sister, her political alignment was more ambiguous. Seton summed up the situation thus:

> The possessions of all the Shaikhs on the Persian side extend, in some places, one day, in others two days' journey inland. As far westward as Charak, may be considered as in the possession of the Qawasim; thence to the head of the Gulf they are in general enemies or friends as necessity and their interest dictate.[66]

During 1809 there were the first stirrings of a backlash against the Wahhabi advances. Persia, the most secure, was most decisive: early in the year she drove the Qawasim temporarily out of Linga and launched a sizable expedition against the Jalahima at Khaur Hassan, which was heavily defeated in a naval battle by the Qawasim. Muscat was to have assisted, displaying, to Britain's subjective surprise, more enthusiasm to combat the Jalahima maritime menace than that of the Qawasim, but in the event stood aside.[67] Muscat made small headway in the interior of Oman and may even have mounted her own unsuccessful attack on Shinas and Khaur Kalba or Fakkan simultaneously with the British expedition.[68] Otherwise Sayyid Sa'id was too much of a realist to take on his contiguous adversaries frontally and unaided, and when he first hesitantly laid eyes upon the British armament, he was none too sanguine of its prospects: he thought its size inadequate for the task, 'and so far from a ready co-operation there was great difficulty [and] trouble in obtaining from His Highness even the assistance of the country boats'.[69]

Sultan bin Saqr had also not been idle. Supple and resourceful, he had been trying what he might to retrieve his position. In February, when he contacted Britain, he wrote to Sayyid Sa'id to enlist his support, proposing some form of alliance against the Wahhabis; a remark by Ibn Ruzaiq could suggest he was tempting Sayyid Sa'id with the cession of Khaur Fakkan and Diba, but this is very speculative.[70] The following month, accompanied by qadis, Sultan bin Saqr personally took his complaint to Dir'iya, where he hoped legal arguments might prevail upon Su'ud to reverse his political arrangements in Qasimi territory. By November, when the British arrived, Sultan bin Saqr had returned, disappointed, and had begun to prepare for the military option by gathering forces inland so as to quell tribes in opposition to him, presumably such as the Tanaij and Za'ab. As the British armament approached Ras al-Khaima with hostile intent, Sultan bin Saqr discerned a fourth window of opportunity: he may have hoped to negotiate his restoration with a promise to safeguard British shipping, but his very belated message was either ill-judged or became distorted in the charged atmosphere of the expedition. The British commander only recorded that Sultan bin Saqr had 'had, in the most insulting manner, the audacity to demand a tribute from the Government to allow British ships to navigate the Persian Gulph in safety.'[71]

For all its gusto and idiosyncrasy, the British expedition against the Qawasim, which Muscat, Persia and Basra were encouraged to assist, swam with and subtly encouraged the fairly swelling tide of reaction against the Wahhabis. It was comparable with the Persian expedition to Khaur Hassan which preceded it, and its main feature, the seizure or destruction of shipping, was not dissimilar to what Muscat had in other situations intended or accomplished.[72] British India's peculiar overriding concern was to eradicate piracy, but she had a secondary wish to strengthen Muscat in the face of Wahhabi encroachment, which if it continued, threatened a greater evil: hence the assault on Wahhabi-held Shinas, which had nothing to do with piracy. British India had imposed a ban on the export of shipbuilding timber to the Gulf and Red Sea in May, but otherwise the expedition arrived unheralded, a snap-storm of unexampled ferocity. The searing impression created by the conflagration at Ras al-Khaima was so overwhelming that when popular report reached the Wahhabi chronicler, it described how the port had been set alight by the British wielding a great crystal to focus the sun's rays upon it.[73]

The clearest result of the British expedition of November 1809–January 1810 was the physical destruction, with immediate economic and naval consequences, of much of the substantial shipping at the principal Qasimi ports of Ras al-Khaima, Linga, Laft, Rams and Jazirat al-Hamra': 60 large and 43 small vessels valued at $55,000 (c. £15,000) were burnt, half of them at Ras al-Khaima, and a further 200,000 rupees (c. £20,000) worth of supposedly captured property was restored to Muscat. The Saudi ruler affected to shrug off the results of the expedition, for which he partly blamed Muscat, advising Britain to join him in cultivating peaceful relations:

> Be not therefore [elated][74] with the conflagration of a few vessels, for they are of no estimation in my opinion, in that of their owners, or of their country … War in the first place may be assimilated to a young woman, who by her philters stimulates the exertions of the unexperienced youth until she kindles a blaze, and having succeeded in inflaming the ardour of his passions, she retires like an old woman without a husband.[75]

Su'ud's land-based military position in Oman had scarcely been affected by the expedition, and Shinas, for example, which had been taken for Muscat, was immediately overrun by Wahhabi troops. His political hold on Ras al-Khaima had, if anything, been tightened in the wake of the British attack. He had Sultan bin Saqr arrested and brought to Dir'iya. The British commanders therefore found no-one at Ras al-Khaima in January 1810 with whom to conclude a peace agreement, and carried home to Bombay nothing but passing military success.[76] Ras al-Khaima and associated Arabian ports, for their part finding themselves unarmed and weakened by the British assault, and now headless, fell henceforth more squarely and with less reserve under the authority of the central Arabian Saudi state. For a time the Qasimi ports retreated into themselves.

v 1810–1812: Recuperation

In the aftermath of the frenzied British expedition, the Qasimi ports lapse into a state of semi-obscurity which for three years is only partially and intermittently pierced by light from the surviving sources. It seems reason-able to assume that this impression is more than just a consequence of the reporting and actually reflects the dampening effect of the British expedi-tion. The burning of the capital Ras al-Khaima, with the loss of her boats, buildings, property and merchandise—'thus, in a few hours was this enter-prising and powerful people reduced to poverty and weakness'[77]—and the destruction of shipping of the five major associated ports, curtailed mercant-ile and martial pursuits: deprived of ocean-going ships, there can have been little or no trade to India and the Red Sea. The ports of the Sir coastline were obliged to pause and rebuild, when, with powerful Saudi backing and Muscat still weak, they might otherwise have achieved wealth, strength and greater cohesion.

Qasimi maritime activity began to pick up after three years and peaked in five. This is suggestive of the time it may have taken to repair the loss in shipping occasioned by the British onslaught, or a substantial part of it; and what was appreciably true of the shipping, was also true of the build-ings at Ras al-Khaima, as attested by Bruce in late 1816.[78] We can only surmise that enough capital had survived the British attack to meet the purchase or commissioning of large vessels: renewed British efforts to restrict the export of timber from Malabar continued to prove ineffective, with supplies readily procurable from Travancore, and perhaps through intermediaries. A remark by Maurizi, that the Saudi ruler Abdullah bin Su'ud commemorated the start of his reign in May 1814 by remitting $10,000 to Ras al-Khaima for the purchase of a 12-gun, 400-man cruising-dow, raises the possibility that there was some refinancing from Dir'iya.[79] Captures also helped replenish Qasimi maritime strength, something of an exponential process no doubt, which was observed in action against Basra and Kangan dows and baghlas in later 1812.[80]

There remains the possibility that a few large boats escaped the wrath of the British because they had been out at sea, holed up in creeks or in other ports like Khaur Fakkan. A detached statement from 1819, that pirates driven from the Gulf by the 1809/10 expedition had taken refuge in the Red Sea, is hard to make much of. More positive was the contempor-ary observation that a party from Ras al-Khaima had in 1810 settled on Abu Musa, whence it launched attacks on Muscat and Basra shipping.[81] Conceivably this was a group attached to Sultan bin Saqr. Equally one might speculate that it was a squadron under the self-willed adventurer Salih bin Muhammad al-Qasimi of *Viper* fame, who resurfaces for a second and last time, achieving some prominence, in the few years after the British expedition. In spring 1810, he was said to be cruising alongside the Jalahima Shaikh and then Wahhabi, Rahma bin Jabir, based at Khaur Hassan. But he was ambitious, and just over a year later he was reported to have professed a tactical allegiance to Muscat and seized control of Ras al-Khaima.[82] If this opportunistic primacy ever was, then it may have been short-lived.

Salih's challenge suggests that in the vacuum created by her legitimate Shaikh's removal, the leadership of Ras al-Khaima was prone to instability for a while. Sultan bin Saqr's place was eventually filled by his cousin:[83] Hasan bin Rahma had almost certainly become Shaikh of Ras al-Khaima and Saudi 'Amir of the Qawasim' (nominally Oman) by mid-1813, and may have attained this position as early as 1810, as later sources assume. Hasan bin Rahma's standing was felt inferior to that of his cousin since he was born of an Abyssinian, not an Arab, mother. He was chosen and kept in power by his brother shaikhs on account of his good faith and responsiveness. His character was contrasted with that of Sultan bin Saqr, regarded by his detractors as guileful and domineering: his removal by Su'ud, who had got wind of his dalliance with Muscat, may have been partly engineered, and was certainly prolonged, by fellow shaikhs angered at Sultan bin Saqr's appeal for outside assistance as a means to chastise and control them. Hasan bin Rahma remained securely in power at Ras al-Khaima until 1820. A description of him by Buckingham, who had joined a parley with him seated on the bare earth of a street in Ras al-Khaima, survives from 1816:

> The Chief, Hasan bin Rahma, whom we had seen, was a small man, apparently about forty years of age, with an expression of cunning in his looks, and something particularly sarcastic in his smile. One of his eyes had been wounded, but his other features were good, and his teeth beautifully white and regular, his complexion very dark, and his beard scanty, and chiefly confined to the chin. He was dressed in the usual Arab garments, with a cashmeer shawl turban, and a scarlet benish, of the Persian form, to distinguish him from his followers. These [fifty] were habited in the plainest garments, with long shirts and keffeas, or handkerchiefs, thrown loosely over the head; and most of them, as well as their leader, wore large swords of the old Norman form, with long straight blades of great breadth, and large cross handles, perfectly plain; short spears were also borne by some, with circular shields of tough hide, ornamented with knobs of metal and gilding.[84]

An important consequence of the British expedition was to bring out Sayyid Sa'id of Muscat openly against the Wahhabis. A touch disingenuously he complained that his co-operation with Britain had involved him in 'a perpetual and an implacable war with the Wahhabis with whom he was before at peace':[85] early in 1810 he was exposed to a tempestuous raid which penetrated to the environs of Muscat, pillaging widely and destroying date groves. This marked the start of a year and a half's violent struggle between the two parties in the interior of Oman. Sayyid Sa'id appealed in vain to Britain, Sind and the Ottomans, and actually received military assistance from Persia; but despite this, the war told heavily against Muscat and culminated in an humiliating and costly peace accord about mid-1811. The Qasimi ports may in some degree have assisted these Wahhabi campaigns, as Sayyid Sa'id pointedly alleged, but the only precise evidence of their participation relates to a party of Na'im from Ajman: there is incidental evidence too of independent cruising by the Na'im in this period.[86]

Sayyid Sa'id may have been weak and hard-pressed by the Wahhabis on land, but by sea he was now, if anything, stronger than before, as was shown by his dealings at Bahrain in 1810. He made headway against the Qawasim in the ports of Shimailiya. He had retaken Khaur Fakkan, and perhaps Diba, by mid-1813, possibly as early as 1810. In 1811 he burnt Kalba and her boats, and seems to have launched an expedition against Ras al-Khaima. This presaged forthcoming events.

vi 1813 to early 1818: Schism in the Qasimi Confederacy— the Nuclear State of Wahhabi Ras al-Khaima

Between October 1812 and January 1813, Egyptian forces despatched against the Wahhabis at the urging of the Ottoman Sultan captured the twin Holy Cities of Mecca and Medina with their Red Sea port of Jeddah. Over the next five and a half years, the Egyptian army advanced somewhat fitfully, but ever eastward, across Arabia, pushing back the Wahhabis, humbling them, to the extent that finally, in the middle of 1818, they were poised on the verge of obliteration in their very heartland of Najd. Saudi forces and attention had to be diverted from the Gulf to face the Egyptian advance; almost more damaging to their position there was the gnawing loss of prestige.

The Saudi ruler adopted a defensive diplomacy in the Gulf as early as mid-1813 when he proposed stable relations with Persia, and incidentally Britain, and likewise he soon after sought to sponsor peace between Ras al-Khaima and Muscat. Control of Oman itself was crumbling, a process accelerated by Wahhabi exactions: the last major punitive raid was despatched there in 1813, but this ended in the ignominious killing of its commander, the renowned Mutlaq al-Mutairi, and after spring 1815 no more military expeditions visited the country. Muscat increased in strength and became a focus of activity outside the Wahhabi fold. There was no clearer symbol of declining Saudi authority than the case of Rahma bin

Jabir of the Jalahima, titular Wahhabi admiral and scourge of Gulf shipping, who read the runes and defected in 1816. This left steadfast Ras
al-Khaima, joined now ambiguously by Bahrain, as the only significant
maritime power in the Gulf consistently throughout to identify itself with
the waning fortunes of Dir'iya. Wahhabi Ras al-Khaima grew stronger and
more active over this period, but it was now a circumscribed recovery, for
she did so in an atmosphere of increased isolation and shorn of half her
associated territories.

The events in Arabia allowed a schism to open within the Qasimi confederacy. How Sultan bin Saqr had been occupied since his removal in
chains to Dir'iya is unclear: Ibn Ruzaiq curiously has him assisting Wahhabi raids against Syria and Iraq.[87] Whatever the case, having judged the
time aright, he made his escape through the Hijaz and Mocha around
spring 1813 in the wake of the Egyptian advance. En route through Jeddah
he is said to have conferred with the Egyptian authorities, who gave him
their blessing and through him opened up communications with Muscat
with a view to forming a broader front against the Wahhabis.

Sayyid Sa'id of Muscat needed little prompting to take up the cudgel
on behalf of Sultan bin Saqr and in midsummer 1813 he orchestrated a
large expedition designed to reinstate him at Ras al-Khaima. Despite the
massing of impressive forces at Dubai, Sayyid Sa'id it seems conducting
40–50 sail and 5,000 men, with more promised by allies,[88] Ras al-Khaima
was preserved by the redoubtable assistance of the Wahhabi general
Mutlaq al-Mutairi. The most tangible achievement of the expedition was
to install Sultan bin Saqr at Sharja, where he would remain nursing his
sense of frustration for the rest of the decade.

The outcome of the expedition had been dictated as much by political
as military factors. The springboard for Sultan bin Saqr's attempted come-
back was de facto independent Qasimi Linga on the Persian coast. He had
made himself too unpopular at Ras al-Khaima to be invited back, but an
alliance with the Banu Yas allowed him to charm the second port of
Sharja, on their northern flank. The Banu Yas had risen against the
Wahhabis even in mid-1811 and, besides, maintained a traditional rivalry
with Ras al-Khaima: shortly after this expedition the two powers clashed,
with the result that Ras al-Khaima lost 300 men and 400 camels. Banu Yas
land forces would have been vital to the success of operations against Ras
al-Khaima, but like other participants in Muscat's makeshift albeit broad
alliance, they were unwilling to force matters to their conclusion.[89] The
instincts of self-interest and self-preservation were everywhere evident.
Muscat launched a second very similar expedition against Ras al-Khaima
the following year, 1814, which was quite as inconclusive as the first. Sayyid
Sa'id now went over the head of Sultan bin Saqr, to his dismay and that of

the Banu Yas Shaikhs of Dubai and Abu Dhabi, by concluding a seeming peace with Wahhabi Ras al-Khaima. This fragile piece of symbolism set the seal on the status quo until the British intervention of 1819/20.

The loose association of ports grouped about the Qasimi leadership was now riven as never before. Linga, dominating the adjacent Persian coastline, was now politically quite detached from the much stronger Wahhabi Ras al-Khaima, which dominated the Arabian. Sharja was but a weak outpost in very close alliance with Linga, albeit under the most senior Qasimi Shaikh, working for his return: Sultan bin Saqr immediately after his installation set about fortifying the place with help from Muscat and Linga. The returns from 1820 indicate that Sharja had a sizable fleet of 45 trankeys, suited to fishing and small trade, but with only three large dows and baghlas she was a naval weakling beside Ras al-Khaima with ten times that number.[90] Before 1816, when the group defected to Ras al-Khaima following quarrels over maritime plunder, Sultan bin Saqr must have derived additional strength from the residence at Sharja, as his 'subjects', of a group of ever-mobile Sudan. Externally, in addition to attempted intrigue at Ras al-Khaima, he acted with Linga for their fundamental mutual benefit: at the outset he cultivated Shiraz,[91] and then, paradoxically, he revived old and deep links with the ruling family of Bushire whom he and Linga helped through military assistance to keep in power in 1815. Of his other activities in this period we learn little, though his arrest of a Saudi envoy, sent in 1814 to negotiate peace with Muscat and Britain, is slightly suggestive. After his own relations with the British Resident had soured over the Sudan's activities in 1815–16 and his own lightening of Bruce's baghla in 1814, he seemed almost casual, though diplomatic in his own defence. Much of his concern was to vilify Hasan bin Rahma and Saudi Ras al-Khaima. He understood his own interests.

There is a distinct voice behind the letters addressed to the British Resident by the three cousins and principal Qasimi Shaikhs: Sultan bin Saqr is calculating and political, Muhammad bin Qadib of Linga is sincere and accommodating; both seem reasonably familiar with the conventions and realities of such diplomacy. Hasan bin Rahma's occasionally gauche letters are overridingly Wahhabi in their phraseology. As Saudi-sponsored ruler of Ras al-Khaima and leader of much the most powerful Qasimi division, he embodied a sometimes exaggerated sense of pride and pique, but he was by inclination, if nothing else, a statesman, not a politician out for himself. Hasan bin Rahma's letters match those of his overlord Imam Abdullah bin Su'ud, with whom he was certainly from time to time in close personal consultation. Correspondence from 1814–17 reveals a degree of ambiguity in their relationship: the Saudi ruler was adamant that the people of Ras al-Khaima were his subjects and therefore had not had the capacity in 1814 to frame a provisional treaty directly with Britain; Hasan bin Rahma averred that he adhered to the Anglo–Saudi agreement, but urged the British to come direct to him with their claims, without troubling Dir'iya. Hasan bin Rahma's Ras al-Khaima was self-consciously and spontaneously a part of the Wahhabi fold. This membership generated a particular tone and dictated political alignments; but the relationship was still essentially a modified form of patronage, leaving her an independent actor and no mere tool of Dir'iya.

It is worth remarking that in practical terms, apart from the Amir himself, there were always two Saudi officials at Ras al-Khaima, a qadi[92] and someone to forward tribute to Dir'iya. As Arabian shaikhly patronage customarily is, this was a two-way relationship, and no less real for that: in addition to the cloak of Saudi protection she enjoyed, Ras al-Khaima received a useful annual gift of dates from Qatif nearly equal to her own tribute.

So much for the Saudi superstructure. Hasan bin Rahma's rule was otherwise differentiated from that of his predecessor by being more consensual. He employed his brother as deputy.[93] Although Hasan bin Rahma was reportedly present at an action off Muscat in 1815,[94] his same brother Ibrahim appears to have been the principal naval commander. In particular, he it was who led two lucrative cruising-raids to south Arabia early in 1815 and 1816. In the first, half a dozen vessels made an attempt on Shihr where they captured the 600-ton Mocha ship *Fath al-Rahman*, valued at 200,000 French crowns, before returning via the coast of Muscat, where their richest prize was a baghla bringing 50,000 French crowns and 400 slaves from Zanzibar. In the second, 2 dows, 4 baghlas and 2 battils made a descent upon the territories of Mukalla and Aden, then plundered three rich Surat vessels inside the Bab al-Mandab, together valued at 1–1.2 million rupees.

In the early part of this period, the shrunken confederacy of which Ras al-Khaima remained capital was composed of five main ports along the coastal heartland, with their satellites and friends. It was at bottom an advanced maritime alliance, albeit an unequal one, which for all of Saudi nomenclature only dimly and at a distance pursued the chimera of statehood. Each of the major ports was dominated by one tribe and was self-governing under its own Shaikh: Ras al-Khaima was the exception in that its ruling family was just that and its population was very mixed. Together these ports reportedly sailed 300 assorted dows, baghlas, battils and baqqaras;[95] the vast majority of the larger, ocean-going and war, vessels were concentrated at Ras al-Khaima. The relative strength in adult males of the five dominant tribal groups, inhabiting and controlling the ports of Ajman, Umm al-Qaiwain, Jazirat al-Hamra', Ras al-Khaima and Rams, was described by an Arab source in January 1817 as follows: Na'im 400, (Al) Ali 500, Za'ab 1,000, Qawasim 70 and Tanaij 500.[96] The contingent population comprised 500 immigrants from Persia such as the Huwala, 600 black slaves and 800 Banu Kitab: these last were interior bedouin who maintained good relations with these ports and sometimes stopped in their territory.

The following remarks from 1820, by a British commentator familiar with princely rule in Persia and India, may be a little too lightly dismissive of the subtle authority of the Ras al-Khaima Shaikhs, but they stress a useful point: Sultan bin Saqr, he argues,

> never had any very great sway, nor indeed have the chiefs since had, over the other pirate ports, indeed frequent disputes and petty wars used to take place between them; each port has ever been ruled by its own chief without allowing the Ras al-Khaima chiefs to participate in any way, but the fifth for the Wahhabi, which was remitted to Hasan bin Ali as long as he resided there and afterwards to Dhaya on his removing. Boats from all the ports cruised together, when the plunder was equally shared.[97]

The final sentence implies a greater degree of practical unity between these ports than what precedes it. The explanation may be that in his mention of 'petty wars', the writer had loosely had in mind disputes such as Sultan bin Saqr's with his recalcitrant clients the Sudan, and Ras al-Khaima's with non-allied Sharja and the Banu Yas. These are of course different points altogether, with no bearing on the co-operative unity of the core allied ports. There is no contemporary evidence of serious disputes of this kind between members of the Wahhabi bloc.

These years witnessed an irrevocable breakdown in Ras al-Khaima's relations with the East India Company. In the short term this was bad for trade: 'What is in our hearts', wrote Hasan bin Rahma, 'is the best towards you, and our wishes are to be able to visit India and carry on mercantile concerns; and have to request you will favour me with pass so as to enable our vessels to go there'.[98] In the long term, the rupture caused by the failure to reach an accord and stick to it would bring ruination.

At first, when in October 1814 Hasan bin Rahma's envoy concluded a provisional treaty with Britain at Bushire, the prognosis looked sanguine. But a few months later the chances of ratifying this peace were wrecked because Hasan bin Rahma failed to prevent a party of Na'im from capturing a Residency baghla sent to Ras al-Khaima to carry negotiations on to their next stage. This diplomatic disaster was compounded by subsequent events, that is the continued impolitic depredations. The action of Hasan bin Rahma's own brother, in plundering the three Surat vessels in March

1816, soon made the loss of British goodwill irreversible. By the time of the Resident's November visit to Ras al-Khaima to demand satisfaction for these captures, British attitudes had correspondingly hardened to the extent that their demands could not at all easily have been met or deflected by even the most capable ruler; the following spring the Supreme Government signalled an end to diplomacy and gave sanction to a second expedition to crush the Qawasim.

Hasan bin Rahma's handling of affairs connected with Britain bespeaks some lack of authority, but it was symptomatic, perhaps, of a lack of timely political wisdom: almost up to the last he failed to grasp Britain's purpose, and continued until 1819 to promote a solution to their differences which turned upon his people's right to prosecute maritime hostilities in defined areas and against certain peoples. It is highly unlikely that Sultan bin Saqr would have employed self-respecting arguments so unguarded as this, or indeed that he would ever have allowed relations to deteriorate in the way they had.

Ras al-Khaima's May 1814 truce with Muscat stipulated that in the event of violation by her vessels the former should be liable for property taken, but not lives. The provision was invoked immediately, because of an unwitting infraction by half a dozen boats already at sea, and again subsequently as late as January 1815, when there could no longer be any such explanation. The agreement had allowed the resumption of direct commercial intercourse between Ras al-Khaima and Muscat, something presumably difficult, if not impossible, during the long periods of running dissension; there was by contrast regular trade in these years between Abu Dhabi and Muscat. But it had in practice already become a dead letter. Even if some of those in authority at Ras al-Khaima still hoped to salvage the peace, there were powerful forces there unwilling to be so restrained. There was now a resurgence of Qasimi depredations in the Gulf which continued almost unabated for the rest of the decade.

Most of this cruising is reported for the coastal sea-lanes leading from Ras al-Hadd to the entrepôt port of Muscat. These were the richest cruising-grounds in the Gulf area—almost all the victims were incoming merchantmen, bearing cargoes from India, and to a lesser extent East Africa—and these attacks were best calculated to injure the Qawasim's greatest ill-wisher, Muscat. These waters may have been their favourite, but they were by no means of course their only haunt. When, for instance, Resident Bruce visited Ras al-Khaima at the end of November 1816, he learnt of a local boatman that there were 45–50 vessels then laid up on shore, 4 ready to sail, and of the 20 already out at sea, a quarter were cruising in the upper Gulf between Cape Bardistan and Basra, and the rest were active south from Muscat towards Ras al-Hadd.[99]

The Muscat Broker offered a sweeping classification of the Ras al-Khaima Qawasim's victims in 1817:

> Every person dependent upon or connected with His Highness [Sayyid Sa'id], and all the inhabitants of Bushire, and Basra, are and will continue to be plundered by the Qawasim, whenever any of those so named may fall in with them; this is not, however, the case with the Banu Utba, or the inhabitants of Bahrain, and of a few other of the Persian ports, with whom the Qawasim have contracted engagements. These excepted, all others falling in with this sinful and wicked race, are plundered.[100]

Persistent hostility between Ras al-Khaima and Kuwait was noted in the upper Gulf as early as 1814, but specific clashes are not recorded until after this period.[101] In January 1816, in the release after Sayyid Sa'id's four-month blockade of Ras al-Khaima, the last such until 1819, an isolated bout of faintly anarchic incidents involving the pursuit of British and American ships occurred near the mouth of the Gulf. In later 1817, a Bourbon French two-master, temporarily separated from her stouter companion, was plundered in the approach to Muscat down to the very clothes and bedding of her crew, suggesting here an attack invited by destination, cargo and opportunity, not so much by flag.

The essence of Sayyid Sa'id's response to news of cruising in Muscat waters, though he also applied baghlas alone and as support vessels, was to despatch after the marauders one or more of his European-style ships, whose flagship after 1814 was the 36-gun, 575-ton frigate *Caroline*, newly commissioned from the Bombay shipyard: in 1819 he would receive delivery of another twice her size, the 56-gun *Shaw Allum*.[102] Rarely did the Muscat ship come up with the intruders, and still more rarely was anything actually achieved against them. These idle chases and subsequent hollow proclamations of success at Muscat became the butt of the youthful Italian Maurizi's gleeful merriment.[103] Events had their more sombre side. The most serious and dramatic of these series of manoeuvres and engagements off the Muscat coast occurred in April–May 1815. Early in April the Qawasim had captured a dinghy near Sur after a bloody combat. This had prompted Sayyid Sa'id to go after them towards the end of the month, but he had returned on 13 May with no sightings to report. That same day, however, a dozen Qawasim under the command of Hasan bin Rahma and Ibrahim bin Rahma were reported hard by. Very soon they had captured three rich baghlas, with much loss of life.[104] After a feint of sorts towards them, Sayyid Sa'id put to sea in earnest on 14 May, himself aboard the *Caroline*, accompanied by three other ships with a number of baghlas and battils. The following day the sound of cannonading reached Muscat. This signalled the start of a close engagement between the opposing squadrons off Ras Abu Da'ud, where, as the Resident related,

> a smart action ensued, in which the Qawasim attempted to board the Imam's [i.e. Sayyid Sa'id's] ship,[105] and had actually got possession of the forecastle, when they were dislodged by the guns from the poop being fired pointed forward, loaded with grape. The Imam's other vessels having fallen astern, he was obliged to bear up and run into Muscat. Two dinghies were sunk by the Imam's ship, which had been captured by the Qawasim a few days previously. His Highness, who commanded in person on board the new ship, has been slightly wounded by a musket-ball, but he has lost a great many men, as also have the Qawasim. After refitting for two days and taking on board a supply of ammunition, His Highness again put to sea with his vessels after the Qawasim, and fell in with them off Suhar, from which he chased them to Ras al-Khaima, keeping up a constant fire at them from his chase-guns. His Highness has since returned to Muscat.[106]

The Muscat Broker reported that some 500 Qawasim had died in the action.[107]

During each of the years 1813–15, Sayyid Sa'id of Muscat mounted an expedition against or blockaded Ras al-Khaima. In the three years that followed, the port was spared these attentions because Sayyid Sa'id was preoccupied with Bahrain, dominance of which had for long been a central element in Muscat's commercial and political strategy in the Gulf. Relations between Sayyid Sa'id and the ruling Al Khalifa, whom he had helped restore to power independent of the Wahhabis in 1810, deteriorated during 1815 and the following January 15 Bahraini merchant vessels were impounded at Muscat as they returned from India. With growing confidence, Sayyid Sa'id launched an attack on Bahrain in summer 1816; but despite assistance from Kangan, Asalu, Bushire and the Jalahima, he was ignominiously repulsed at Muharraq, losing his own brother to boot. He attempted a second expedition in winter 1817/18, but was forced to call this off in March, substituting a summer blockade, because promised Persian auxiliary troops, which he perceived to be the vital complement to his naval strength, failed again to materialize: attentive to her own interests in the matter, Shiraz was not playing a straight hand. Sayyid Sa'id ultimately failed against Bahrain for some of the same reasons as he had against Ras al-Khaima. His poor performance and evident lack of political wisdom cost him prestige in the Gulf; a minor clumsy attempt to alarm the Al Khalifa by falsely claiming they were allowed to trade with British India only because of his privileged intercession raised some eyebrows too in Bombay.

Muscat's designs upon Bahrain in 1816–18 had another effect upon Ras al-Khaima, for they precipitated an exchange of alliance by the Al Khalifa and their bitterest rival, Rahma bin Jabir. During the first half of this decade, the Jalahima Shaikh had been the most notable of the Qawasim's allies on the Arabian coast. Both parties were acknowledged Wahhabis and purported to cruise against Dir'iya's enemies: the true and overriding constant in Rahma bin Jabir's affairs, however, was his abiding enmity with the Al Khalifa, a virulent parallel to Ras al-Khaima's rivalry with Muscat. Rahma bin Jabir's was quintessentially a roving power. Based at Khaur Hassan, with a fort at Dammam, he had not Ras al-Khaima's resources and may have depended largely upon plunder for his finances. Around the height of his power in 1810, Khaur Hassan had been base to some 10 large dows and baghlas, and 10 trankeys; this must have included allies, for when in October 1816 he brought his whole tribe and force to Bushire, these consisted of two large baghlas, a battil and several small baqqaras, with 1,500 men. His reputation preceded him:

> His followers ... are maintained by the plunder of his prizes; and as these are most of them his own bought African slaves, and the remainder equally subject to his authority, he is sometimes as prodigal of their lives in a fit of anger, as he is of those of his enemies, whom he is not content to slay in battle only, but basely murders in cold blood, after they have submitted. An instance is related of his having recently put a great number of his own crew, who used mutinous expressions, into a tank on board, in which they usually kept their water, and this being shut close at the top, the poor wretches were all suffocated, and afterwards thrown overboard. [108]

Shaikh Salih al-Qasimi was observed cruising with Rahma bin Jabir in 1810, and it may be supposed that good relations subsisted between Ras al-Khaima and Khaur Hassan over the next few years. There are a number of references in 1814–16 to Rahma bin Jabir's use of the port of Ras al-Khaima, and to their two forces setting out together upon cruises. The impression is that they would separate before action, although a joint attack is alleged to have been carried out upon Burum and Aden in early 1816. [109] This was the last evidence of co-operation, for Rahma bin Jabir, having with an eye upon Bahrain courted Muscat since late 1814, finally joined her Bahrain expedition in the summer of 1816. Almost immediately he broke with Dir'iya, in the words of Hasan bin Rahma 'apostatised from Islam and preferred the worship of idols to the Unity of God', [110] and was obliged to quit Arabia for Bushire and another set of alliances. Thereafter Rahma bin Jabir offered to help Britain chastise the Qawasim and in 1817 plundered no less than 14 of their boats, most of them plying their trade to and from Bahrain.

As Ras al-Khaima lost one ally, she gained another. The Al Khalifa had thrown their lot in with the Wahhabis in 1815 as their best means of defence against Muscat;[111] they had been alarmed by Sayyid Sa'id's rapprochement with Rahma bin Jabir, whom he intended to use against them 'in the same manner that a huntsman takes with him a hound.'[112] The Al Khalifa Shaikh explained to the Resident, who was in vain urging him to cut links with Ras al-Khaima, how his adopted allegiance had transformed their relations:

> Initially we did not associate with [ma hina zamilin] the people of Ras al-Khaima, and there was nothing between us but fighting and plundering [al-akhdh wal-qatl]. But then God willed it that we should make an alliance with Abdullah bin Is'ud[113] and we became as one. The people of Ras al-Khaima were already his subjects; if we should set about preventing their visiting our ports, Abdullah bin Is'ud would learn of it and regard it as an infringement of our alliance, and so we cannot forbid their coming because of the injury we would suffer as a result: and likewise, were we to forbid our vessels from frequenting their ports, once again we should suffer.[114]

It was frequently observed in these later years that Ras al-Khaima boats regularly visited Bahrain to purchase dates, grain, rice and other stores, and also to use the archipelago as principal mart for her plunder. Two isolated references to the Bahrain Utub providing crews or boats to assist in Qasimi depredations can probably be disregarded unless they refer to non-contentious or private co-operation.[115] But the relationship still had some teeth, for we know that Muscat was forced to lift her 1818 blockade of Bahrain because of the approach of a sizable Qasimi fleet.

The ports and powers of the Gulf, then, gained security though alliances. They were also constructed and invoked in answer to the endemic feuds with neighbours and even, sometimes, leadership disputes. Some elements in these broad alliances, like Muscat's relationship with Kangan and Asalu, and her less dependable connection with Abu Dhabi, tended for geo-political reasons to recur. An air of continuity was also provided, conversely, by insoluble rivalries, such as Rahma bin Jabir's with Bahrain.

The rapprochement with Bahrain, coupled with the inattention of Muscat, represented a slight improvement in Ras al-Khaima's position. She exhibited a limited degree of confidence and recovered energy during 1816–17. Her main ally on the Persian coast was Wahhabi Mughu under her Marzuq Shaikh. Around early 1816, vessels from Ras al-Khaima visited Mughu's neighbour and long-established rival, Charak, forcing her Shaikh to accept a Wahhabi officer, whose duty it was to record the details of all vessels that sailed. In response to this unwelcome subjection, Charak made overtures to Shiraz and Muscat, and presumably concerted with her more usual ally, Linga. Mounting tension between the Linga and Ras al-Khaima blocs led to a small skirmish at the former in summer 1817. The tug-of-war in which Ras al-Khaima was involved on the Persian coast may thus far have seemed low-key enough, but in the autumn and winter of 1817/18 it was transformed by the entrance of Shiraz into the fray.[116] With support from Linga and Charak, Persian troops attacked and burnt Mughu, despite her receiving military assistance from Ras al-Khaima: fugitives from Mughu were found still sheltering at Ras al-Khaima in December 1819.

Ras al-Khaima thus had lost her foothold on the Persian coast. It would seem that whilst these operations were underway, she retaliated, or possibly otherwise for the sequence of cause and effect is obscure, with a series of actions directed against ports broadly aligned with Bushire and Muscat, and in Nakhilu's case conceivably also connected with Sultan bin Saqr.[117] About early October a small Qasimi force landed on Nakhilu's dependency of Shaikh Shu'aib where, in a manner recurrently seen at Qishm, they 'burnt and plundered the villages at the western part of the island, carrying off all the cattle and killing great numbers of the inhabitants.'[118] In December, 25 or 40 Qasimi dows, baghlas and battils captured 3–5 Al Haram (Asalu) and Banu Mu'in merchant baghlas, worth up to 300,000 rupees, amidst heavy bloodshed at Asalu. Two weeks later the fleet sailed from there, attempted Kangan, then put ashore at Dayyir, where they razed 150 date palms and skirmished with the inhabitants. Panic set in at Bushire, as it was feared, mistakenly, that the Qawasim would come north.

Even if Ras al-Khaima's ventures on the Persian coast ultimately foundered, she was able to take some encouragement from a small gain close to home, the first recorded since the earlier decade. In spring 1817 she bought off Muscat's deputy at Khaur Fakkan, and was soon reported to have 25 vessels based there; she was also said to have taken Khasab and had Diba under blockade. The nuclear state of Ras al-Khaima was, in short, surprisingly resilient.

vii   Mid-1818–1820: Encirclement, Destruction and Painful New Birth

About early August 1818, the associated leading shaikhs of the lower Gulf—Sultan bin Saqr, the Dubai and Abu Dhabi Banu Yas, the Sudan, the Al Khalifa, Linga, Charak and Mughu—held a conference at Ras al-Khaima. They resolved that, in the event of a second British expedition, they would mount a concerted stand at Ras al-Khaima. This is a rare indication that in popular parlance, Ras al-Khaima had become a symbol of strength and defiance in the face of British aggression. The alliance was soon blown away by winds from Najd. When it came to it only Ras al-Khaima and Dhaya did resist, and Sultan bin Saqr, for one, was not speaking wholly ironically when he would say of the British expedition, 'I thank God for everything which has taken place at Ras al-Khaima, and which was in conformity with my wishes.'[119] Yet even if, despite the rhetoric, most rulers put pragmatism before emotion, the popular feeling was undoubtedly real and heartfelt. William Richardson, Master of the private trader Cornwall, felt the pulse of the general mood when he visited the Gulf in early summer 1819.[120] He reported that the forthcoming expedition was the main topic of conversation on Bahrain. With 7,000 men-at-arms, and having repulsed Muscat in 1816, her people were determined to resist if either they or Ras al-Khaima were attacked by Britain, and were confident too of assistance from allies: 'this was the language of the principal officers of government though the Shaikh himself was very cautious in saying anything about it.' Moreover, this bravado was not confined to Bahrain; indeed

> it was the general conversation in every part of the Gulf where I had intercourse that a determination existed in all the piratical ports that on the arrival of an expedition against any of them, they should consider it a common cause, and assist in repelling it.[121]

As well as being bastion against the threat from Bombay, Muscat and the established powers, Ras al-Khaima was also the peninsula's last solid refuge of Wahhabi political authority. This came about after the fall of Dir'iya, Egypt's momentous *coup de grâce* to the Saudi state, on *c.* 10 September 1818. During the next nine months, whilst he remained at Dir'iya, Ibrahim Pasha set about extirpating the vitality and strength from the core of the fallen Saudi–Wahhabi state. With the annihilation of Imam Abdullah bin Su'ud went the heart. Within weeks, it seems, the army was sent out to begin levelling the walls and fortifications of Najd. A force was sent to confiscate Saudi wealth in Hasa. Certain leading members of the community were arrested and put to death. The Egyptian troops made their way through the Najdi countryside, feeding off the land. The people of Dir'iya and elsewhere were mulcted. For the proud and loyal chronicler Ibn Bishr, it was a time of disorder, immorality and shame.[122]

To return to Ras al-Khaima and 1818. Qatif fell to pro-Egyptian forces, which included Rahma bin Jabir, around early October. We learn that the defeated garrison included Qawasim and that a dozen of their boats, carrying reinforcements, had arrived just too late to be of assistance.[123] This is the first mention of a Qasimi presence at Qatif, and one can only speculate as to its origins. The economy of this minor port and district-centre was based on agriculture, although there was limited trade with Bahrain which supplied Indian goods and the like.[124] The strategic importance of the fortress at Qatif presumably outweighed the town's commercial significance. Conceivably the Qawasim's presence went back some time and was allied to their relationship with Bahrain, and perhaps the expulsion in 1816 of Rahma bin Jabir from nearby Dammam. No sooner had Qatif fallen, in fact, than Rahma bin Jabir set about rebuilding his demolished fort at Dammam. The Qawasim were permitted to withdraw from the area.

Ras al-Khaima remained until the end a beacon of loyalty to the Wahhabi cause. The depth of her commitment, together with the attraction of her remoteness from Ibrahim Pasha's forces, made her a natural haven for fugitives from Dir'iya. A force of 300 fighting-men made their escape to Ras al-Khaima after the Saudi capital was overrun. Although the Qawasim's special patron amongst the Al al-Shaikh suffered transportation to Egypt, a number of other prominent Wahhabis, political, military, religious leaders from Najd, Hasa and elsewhere, are recorded as having reached safety in Ras al-Khaima.[125] They were to witness the British expedition, possibly even seek admission to the General Treaty,[126] and were observed still sheltering with the ousted Hasan bin Rahma in the palm groves outside the ruins of Ras al-Khaima in the summer of 1820. This was no passing allegiance.

It had not been immediately apparent that Ras al-Khaima would so remain inviolate. With the overthrow of Dir'iya, panic set in in this corner of Arabia. There was wild talk in Muscat to the effect that Sultan bin Saqr had assassinated Hasan bin Rahma and seized power at Ras al-Khaima. It was rumoured in Hasa that a force of 6,000 was moving against Buraimi. There was undoubtedly a generalized expectation of an imminent Egyptian advance. The ruler of Muscat had already proposed to Ibrahim Pasha a joint expedition against Ras al-Khaima. In November, 100 Ottoman horsemen actually reached Buraimi, just as another officer supposedly visited Ras al-Khaima to lodge demands for the return of plundered vessels and property: one of these claims was proffered on behalf of a Bu Abid, presumably relating to the capture of February 1815. The Qawasim were alarmed, indeed apprehensive enough of an Egyptian attack to despatch men and building materials to Basidu, which they planned to fortify as a last refuge for themselves and their belongings, should the threatened storm arrive. The project was hampered by one or two violent attacks on supply-vessels by HMS *Eden*, Captain Loch, and the HCC *Antelope* at the beginning of 1819, and by March had been abandoned.

Ibrahim Pasha had written an encouraging response to Sayyid Sa'id's suggestion that they together attack Ras al-Khaima. The latter was still toying with the idea of following up his proposal in January 1819. By mid-April, however, his ardour had very much cooled: he was now worried about possible competing Egyptian designs over Bahrain, and more generally had come to perceive the danger to his own position that would result from an Egyptian advance. The East India Company also came round to the idea of courting Ibrahim Pasha, and in spring 1819 Captain George Sadleir embarked on a secret mission to secure Egyptian co-operation in the forthcoming Ras al-Khaima expedition.[127] As he passed through Muscat, the ruler sought to dissuade him. He need not have troubled, for by the time Sadleir caught up with the Pasha, at Medina in September, central and eastern Arabia had been evacuated by his troops, and with no lasting Egyptian presence, his object achieved, the remote prospect of an Egyptian attack on Ras al-Khaima had become out of the question.

Remarkably, Battal al-Mutairi, Saudi Commander-in-Chief (Amir al-Juyush)[128] in Oman, held out in the strategic fort of Buraimi, with its pair of masonry towers and deep defensive ditch, until May 1819.[129] Faced then with the alternatives of surrendering to the possibly perilous embrace of Sultan bin Saqr and his associate Rashid bin Humaid of Ajman, and laying himself at the mercy of Sayyid Sa'id, who had ordered a force against him, he chose the latter. Buraimi passed to Muscat, ending two decades of Wahhabi control. This was a blow to Ras al-Khaima. The disruption to overland routes also enabled Muscat immediately to divest her of control over Fujaira, which she had reportedly acquired not long before. This left Ras al-Khaima with only one notable port, Diba, east of Musandam, Khaur Fakkan having apparently been given up before this. On the west, although Sha'm and Bukha were still with her, Khasab, if indeed taken in 1817, was likewise now lost. The trend is clear.

Sultan bin Saqr's recovery is the major internal political theme of this period. The process was set in motion by the collapse of Dir'iya and completed by the British destruction of Ras al-Khaima. It was a sign of change that in November 1818, when expectations of further Egyptian advances were running high, an alliance was supposedly formed between Sultan bin Saqr, Ajman, Umm al-Qaiwain and the Banu Yas, to the exclusion of Ras al-Khaima. The Egyptian conquest understandably had rather the effect of atomizing the Qasimi confederacy, encouraging individual ports to act more for themselves. The lynchpin of the ports now semi-divorced from and competing politically with Ras al-Khaima was the alliance between Sultan bin Saqr of Sharja and Rashid bin Humaid of Ajman, the former supplying most of the drive and resources. Sayyid Sa'id was happy to exploit this rift, recognizing the reciprocal benefit of tactical relations with Sultan bin Saqr, whilst privately confiding to Britain that he trusted all the ports of that coast would be chastised in the same manner as Ras al-Khaima.

The possible alliance of November 1818 cannot have been quite what it seemed. A certain amount of light is shed in these years on the nature and strength of these alliances. According to the crew of a Linga battil interviewed in November 1819, all the Qasimi ports of the two shores, including Linga, Sharja and Ras al-Khaima, were bound together by a non-aggression pact renewed annually in the autumn.[130] Its purpose was to ensure free and uninterrupted commercial maritime intercourse between the various ports: docking and supplying were always unimpeded and any interference with shipping was outlawed. Commercial considerations, therefore, outdistanced political ambition. This is more evident in what emerges in these years of the erstwhile broader Wahhabi alliance. According to local sources in Qais and Charak, the ports of Linga, Mughu, Charak, Tahuna and Kalat had connected themselves with the Wahhabis for the sake of trade, which otherwise they must have abandoned, profiting by carrying goods to Ras al-Khaima which she could not by herself have procured.[131]

Loyalties were put to the test in July 1819 when Sayyid Sa'id of Muscat launched an opportunistic expedition against Ras al-Khaima. As on previous occasions, he was relying upon receiving the support of Sultan bin Saqr, the Banu Yas and others, but in the event they failed him.[132] It transpires that Sayyid Sa'id had prepared the way by paying an undisclosed sum to Sultan bin Saqr, and it is possible that the latter's change of heart was partly brought on by a similar arrangement with Ras al-Khaima. Money was virtually always an unseen player in political events and relationships in the Gulf, but one gathers it might have played an important role: the island of Qishm was regarded as Muscat's, but her Banu Mu'in Shaikh paid nothing, only received; in 1817, as noted, Ras al-Khaima was said to have bought the allegiance of Khaur Fakkan.[133] At Ras al-Khaima in September, then, finding himself thus embarrassed, Sayyid Sa'id at first sought to salvage some benefit by posing as intermediary with the East India Company. Hasan bin Rahma confidently rejected any settlement out of hand, unless (conceivably referring here to Shimailiya) Sayyid Sa'id agreed to 'restore certain places and supply us with a number of horse etc.'[134] The latter could not, calling off his blockade and returning to Muscat only weeks before the arrival of the British armament.

The year 1819 marked a new departure in Anglo–Qasimi relations. This was largely attributable to the arrival in the new year of a fresh Senior Naval Officer, Captain F.E. Loch of the *Eden*. His stance toward the Qawasim was one of bald and unquestioning scepticism, and he brought to the task of taking and destroying Qasimi vessels at sea unprecedented conviction and energy. This resulted in some half-dozen incidents in the six months from December 1818, ranging from pursuit and detention to destructive assault, the most serious of which was Loch's onslaught on 7–8 Ras al-Khaima vessels supposedly making for Basidu in January, in which nearly half were incapacitated or destroyed. Thus almost for the first time, the Qawasim became subject to directly unprovoked attack at the hands of the East India Company. Impassioned and aggravating behaviour of this kind brought Britain little benefit and its impact on the Qawasim must have been unnerving and rather baffling. The only accompanying British diplomatic approach was something of a crusade, being directed towards freeing British subjects held as slaves by the Qawasim. Contact was set up through the Shaikh of Bahrain and this led in March to the handing over of 15 Indian women and children at Ras al-Khaima, and a further three women soon after at Sharja, in exchange for the release of ten prisoners sent by Loch to Bombay and a Sharja trankey detained to this end. This liberation of British Indian subjects, whom 'some of our true believers had taken',[135] appears not to have been exhaustive, since a further 17 were freed, along with 34 Muscat subjects, following the British occupation of Ras al-Khaima.

With increased pressure on Ras al-Khaima, Hasan bin Rahma realized at the start of 1819 the need to mend fractured relations with the East India Company. The immediate stimulus was Loch's tempestuous arrival, in particular January's attack on 7–8 vessels at Qishm and his subsequent release off Ras al-Khaima on the 16th of a pair of battered survivors: with them they carried a warning note addressed to the ruler, which must have been sufficiently ambiguous, when combined with what they had to report privately, to give him the (false) impression that Britain was ready for peace. After first asking Shaikh Abdullah bin Ahmad during a visit to Bahrain to act as his intermediary, he took the opportunity of the discussions surrounding the release of captives to pursue the matter directly. All his efforts to achieve a peace both now, and again just weeks before the arrival of the British expedition, when he sent negotiators to Bushire, were rebuffed.

However sincere and insistent Hasan bin Rahma's overtures of peace in 1819, they were not especially astute. For all that, he sought to promote a maritime truce with 'the Christians', reinforced by the establishment of 'signals and boundaries';[136] that is, the proper flagging of British and Qasimi vessels, and a recognition that east of Cutch was to be deemed British territory (hauz). These proposals involve no advance in principle: if the two parties introduced mutual respect and distance into the existing order, the likelihood of conflict would recede. Hasan bin Rahma seems to have recognized two causes of his rift with Britain. For their part, the

Qawasim had become involved with vessels which they had not suspected were British. On the Company's part, there had been knowing aggression. Until Bruce's unjustifiable behaviour at Ras al-Khaima in November/December 1816, neither side had broken the existing agreement. Since then, Company vessels had on occasions been guilty of provocation:

> Up to the present date, I have not exerted myself in the war with you. We purposely allowed your vessels to escape from us, for God has said, 'Make peace with those who sue it of you, and place your dependence upon God'.[137]

Despite the worsening situation, Ras al-Khaima and neighbouring ports had not lost their vitality. In spring 1819, the usual season, a fleet of between 10 and 30 (c. 15?) vessels sailed to the Red Sea, where they were reported to have destroyed the Somali port of Berbera. They also captured a handful of boats, including the Bombay pattamar *Darya Daulat*: according to survivors, she was attacked on 17 April, one day out from Mukalla flying British colours, by Qawasim aboard 30 vessels

> who boarded the pattamar with swords and muskets. The number on board the *Darya Daulat* was 24 men. Of these, twelve men, including the Serang, Tindal and pilot, were instantly put to death, [when] remaining twelve leapt overboard. Of them one was shot in the water, the other eleven reached the shore by swimming.[138]

The hull was later abandoned after probably being stripped of the 60,000 dollars she was carrying for Bombay merchants, along with a cargo of shark's fins, coffee, gum Arabic, drugs and the like. There was also generally unexceptional activity in the Gulf. A descent by five battils on Dayyir, where date palms were destroyed and a camel caravan plundered, recalls a similar raid two years before, in December 1817. Following the collapse of Muscat's blockade of Ras al-Khaima in September 1819, there was an outbreak of disruption, notably and not unexpectedly off the Muscat coast in November. The year 1819, then, witnessed semi-neutral captures far from home, low-level warfare with Muscat, and minor feuding and victimization in the case of Dayyir.

In October 1818 it was rumoured that a group of Ras al-Khaima vessels was going to prey upon the date traffic off the Basra river. The following autumn there is evidence of a shortage of provisions along the Ras al-Khaima coast. The Muscat blockade, British cruising and the presumed exclusion of Qasimi vessels from Basra, Bushire and Muscat must all have contributed to this situation. The Shaikh of Dubai was driven in November 1819 to the subterfuge of sending his battil via Nakhilu and Asalu, acquiring passes at each, so as to evade British restrictions, visit Bushire and purchase dates. A group of five Linga baghlas and battils hoped to sell firewood and salt-fish at Basra in exchange for dates,

> the greatest portion of which [their Nakhudas] confessed would be carried over to Ras al-Khaima where the demand was very good, consequently the price very high: they all confessed they were on the best terms with the pirates, and that a regular intercourse was kept up with them; this, however, they said policy made them do as a means of safety to themselves. [139]

Another Linga battil bound for Basra with a cargo of salt-fish, cloth and dye-stuff, was sailing in the company of four Umm al-Qaiwain vessels when they attacked four Kuwaiti boats carrying dates: the Linga vessel did not assist except to take on board some captives.

By November 1819 there was a heavy accumulation of pressures bearing down upon the Qawasim. On the eve of the second British expedition, this was already very far from being the Ras al-Khaima of a decade before.

The first British forces left Bombay for the Gulf on 3 November. Major-General Keir went ahead aboard HMS *Liverpool* and commenced a blockade of Ras al-Khaima on the 25th. The expeditionary force consisted in all of three naval ships, six Company cruisers and 18 transports. These carried c. 3,000 soldiers, of whom just over half were European troops, principally of the 47th and 65th Regiments. In addition, Sayyid Sa'id of Muscat provided the services of 20 small landing-boats, and accompanied the main British flotilla to Ras al-Khaima with two warships and 600 soldiers; his 2,000-strong land force only reached Ras al-Khaima two days after it had fallen and was immediately sent home.

The attack on Ras al-Khaima began on 4 December, when a British advance enabled a battery to be erected and the siege could get underway. The focus of the action was a sturdy fortress just outside the town walls. For three days the defenders showed ingenuity and resolve, launching a number of spirited sorties against the British lines, in one of which women were said to have taken part. [140] On 8 December, however, a furious battery was opened by the remaining guns and mortars, which now included two of the *Liverpool*'s 24-pounders, and this was continued throughout the day and into the night. When at 8 a.m. the next day British forces advanced through the breaches, they were surprised to find Ras al-Khaima all but deserted by her people, who had finally been overwhelmed by the sudden violence of the most recent bombardment, fleeing across the creek, much of the town behind them in flames.

As soon as the fire was extinguished in the town I walked through it and in the embers were yet to be seen some bodies of people which had been consumed to a cinder and were now a heap of disgustingly black apparent charcoal. These poor wretches had either been so badly wounded or so old and infirm as not to be able to be moved and thus fell a sacrifice.[141]

During the siege, the British had suffered 5 killed and 51 wounded. Hasan bin Rahma put his own tribe's killed and wounded at 400 fighting-men, but Keir claims to have learnt that the true figure for Ras al-Khaima as a whole was actually approaching 1,000.[142] According to an unnamed Bombay Marine officer, this last figure comprised about 300 killed, 100 of them by a single shell burst, and 700 wounded. Ibrahim bin Rahma, brother to the ruler, is said to have lost his leg from a cannon-shot. Estimates put the original Ras al-Khaima garrison at between 3,000 and 4,000, and these are said to have included Qawasim, 'Taal' (Za'ab?), Shihuh ('Shahine'), Matarish and about 1,000 mercenaries who had been in the Maratha service.[143]

Keir now concluded that it would be well to take the fort of Dhaya, situated on a rugged and steep hill just north of Rams—whence the influential Hasan bin Ali had retired with his people—both for its own sake, since it commanded the northern approach to Ras al-Khaima, and also because it was regarded as impregnable: the kudos which might accrue would smooth Keir's task elsewhere. Needless to say, the staunch Wahhabi and erstwhile Saudi officer Hasan bin Ali would also have been the most potent remaining symbol of defiance and for this reason alone the obvious second target of operations. Keir sent Major Warren with a detachment against Dhaya on 18 December, and it fell after a stout resistance four days later: when Hasan bin Ali surrendered, he led out 398 men and 400 or more women and children. British casualties here were 4 killed and 16 wounded.

The fall of Dhaya marked the end of the fighting. Other shaikhs submitted peacefully, encouraged perhaps by Keir's policy of clemency: the only prisoners taken were Hasan bin Ali and his men, and these had all been released within a few weeks for the sake of their health, their families and the cultivation. The main body of the British force withdrew from the coast in the first week of February, leaving a garrison at Ras al-Khaima for another five and a half months. The original reason for garrisoning Ras al-Khaima, as an intermediate measure before transferring authority to Ibrahim Pasha, had been recognized as hopeless in mid-December. After that, the task became to transfer authority to trustworthy and respected local leaders, or, failing that, Muscat; and Sayyid Sa'id being happy to see the Qasimi ports destroyed, but not to govern them, the British policy practically meant a regeneration of local forces. The difference was that these shaikhs, chastened, would now be in thrall to the General Treaty of January 1820, defining acceptable maritime behaviour: piracy, the murder of captives and the maritime seizure of slaves were therein described, outlawed and made punishable through co-operation between Britain and the signatories; special passes and flags became obligatory; on these terms there would be peaceful relations and the freedom to trade at British ports.[144] The presence of the garrison at Ras al-Khaima was only intended as a temporary measure. As soon as practicable, in July 1820, it was moved to its permanent station on Qishm, where it would enable Britain to execute her self-imposed office of guarantor of the General Treaty. Sickness and Persian opposition forced the Qishm base to be abandoned in January 1823. After that Britain would depend upon sea-power alone for the maintenance of maritime peace.

These developments lie in the future. Not unexpectedly Muscat, and also Shiraz, saw the British expedition as a chance to improve their position, notably in respect of Bahrain. Iran proposed an invasion of the islands in December 1819 and, despite Keir's attempted dissuasion of him before and after February's signing of the General Treaty by the Al Khalifa, Sayyid Sa'id agreed to participate. The attack was aborted, but the Muscat ruler managed to press the advantage of his association with Britain to secure an arrangement with the Al Khalifa, in return for his release of their boats and hostages held since 1816.

Iran was suspicious of Britain's ultimate objective in invading the Gulf, recalling the manner in which her rule in India had commenced. For this reason, and because of the absence of sound cause, the expedition did not this time visit the Persian coast.[145] The only other possible target of operations was the infamous Rahma bin Jabir; yet, having made himself a Persian subject and invoked the patronage of Muscat, he successfully gained immunity from British interference and exemption too from being admitted to the General Treaty. Keir therefore judged that with operations limited to the Ras al-Khaima coast, unlike a decade before, his expedition had achieved all it could.

The number of vessels taken or destroyed by the second expedition, at about 200, 111 of them at Ras al-Khaima and 48 at Sharja, was double the number burnt by the 1809/10 expedition. This was partly because the second was more thorough than the first, which had overall been a more fleeting affair, but principally, one suspects, because in 1820 many many more of the smaller vessels, such as baqqaras, were destroyed—50 of them at Ras al-Khaima alone. Few of the larger, and perhaps none of the largest, classes of vessels can have survived, thus crippling long-distance trade:

pearling, fishing and the coasting-trade went theoretically untouched.[146] When Lieutenant Tanner revisited the coast in August 1820, he observed but two pearling-baqqaras and a pair of abandoned trankeys at Ras al-Khaima, and the picture was similar at other ports. It is conceivable, but unproved, that Sultan bin Saqr managed to preserve some of his vessels, the case for this resting upon an observation in 1823 that he already possessed '30 fine vessels, each capable of containing 50 to 100 men', some of which seemed certainly over three years old.[147] A comparison of later shipping figures for Ras al-Khaima and Sharja conveys the impression that it took in fact a whole decade before levels recovered from the British operations.[148]

During the second expedition, not only boats were destroyed, but also, less logically, fortifications.[149] The purpose was clearly symbolic rather than practical, for Britain's concern was with stability and the sea. The fortifications of all but two of the ports between Rams and Abu Hail were brought down, and their guns removed, in late January. Jazirat al-Hamra', with her 150–200 dilapidated houses, denuded of timber, protected by a ring of six circular masonry towers of one and two storeys and walls 25–35 feet high and 3–5 feet thick, had been deserted for a year and a half or more: four of the towers still were blown up in April. Ras al-Khaima was left standing until July, when the garrison pulled out. Exceptionally here the whole town was levelled and burnt:

> In the evening we embarked under the illumination of a magnificent conflagration, produced by the last seven remaining vessels of the pirate fleet, and numerous square piles of beams, rafters and cadjans, which had composed the roofs of the houses.[150]

The commander's wife Anne recalled, 'The atmosphere seemed absolutely on fire—there was no air to breathe, and I was burning with fever. I recollect the appearance of the horizon all in flames.'[151] As well as offering a 'lesson of retributive justice',[152] the razing of Ras al-Khaima was also evidence of political frustration: Captain Thompson had been unable to induce Sultan bin Saqr to accept the intact Ras al-Khaima upon any conditions. In 1823 the ruined site of Ras al-Khaima was still uninhabited, and her inhabitants occupied the mainland opposite. They moved back during the next few years. A visitor in 1828 recorded,

> A square tower, of no great strength, has been built on the mound raised by the ruins of the strong outwork destroyed after the siege in 1819. A straight stone wall nearly connects one side of the town with the backwater or harbour, but as yet there are no defences towards the sea, excepting two old guns. The ruins of the old walls and towers

serve as stone quarries, and the town of Ras al-Khaima is rapidly increasing. The houses are of stone and chunam, and, although small, are carefully built, and remarkably neat, even with some finish. Building is yet very cheap, from the old materials being so close at hand; and Shaikh Sultan [bin Saqr] is said to encourage it.[153]

The major political outcome of the British expedition was Sultan bin Saqr's reinstatement at Ras al-Khaima, giving him dominance of the coast north of Dubai. The expedition had been directed against Wahhabi Ras al-Khaima, and had delivered the *coup de grâce* to a state already undermined by the events in central Arabia. With this obstacle removed, Sultan bin Saqr's regaining of his patrimony came almost automatically. By the first week of January, in a sudden, but apparently painless, transformation, Hasan bin Rahma had reverted to being merely Shaikh of Khatt and Fulayya:

> His family connections with Sultan bin Saqr [wrote the commander of the British garrison] have facilitated his complete and voluntary submission to the authority of the latter, and there appears to be reason for concluding that he was raised and maintained in power principally by the interests of others, and not by any talent or ambition of his own. He at present holds the situation of a friendly and submissive relative to a chieftain of allowed higher descent and family honours.[154]

Sultan bin Saqr also had to deal with two important Shaikhs who had remained with Hasan bin Rahma's Ras al-Khaima till the end. Hasan bin Ali received short shrift: he was put in chains at Sharja on the pretext of a debt and before long had been replaced at Rams by another.[155] Qadib bin Ahmad and his 2,000 men-at-arms had, for presumed reasons of security as the Wahhabis found themselves beleaguered, removed from Jazirat al-Hamra' to Ras al-Khaima towards mid-1818. In the summer of 1820 his people occupied the beach near Ras al-Khaima, where, apprehensive of their defenceless position, they engaged in pearling. Despite his vulnerable strength and potential independence, Qadib bin Ahmad was felt for a Shaikh to be relatively uninterested in power politics and consequently not one to challenge Sultan bin Saqr.[156]

The only other Shaikhs of consequence on the Qasimi coast were the rulers of Ajman and Umm al-Qaiwain. Keir had initially treated them as dependent on Sultan bin Saqr and only admitted them separately to the General Treaty in March, when he perceived they enjoyed 'a certain degree' of independence from the Qasimi ruler.[157] That of Abdullah bin Rashid of Umm al-Qaiwain cannot have been very pronounced, for in August 1820 he was found living with his 400–500 men at Sharja, under the protection of Sultan bin Saqr. The situation of Rashid bin Humaid of Ajman, whose vivacity and independence had been in evidence since late 1818, may have been slightly more anomalous.

Sultan bin Saqr's consolidation of power was set to continue over the next few years. Already in mid-1820, whilst proposing to build a fortified position at Ras al-Khaima so as to assert his authority in a hitherto fractious environment, he had built a watch-tower on his southern flank where his ambitions had brought him into conflict with Dubai. By 1825 he had developed a commanding position: he had married the young Shaikh of Dubai's sister, deposed Qadib bin Ahmad's successor in favour of his own candidate and even received the submission of the Shaikh of Ajman.[158]

On the surface, it might almost have seemed that the Saudi–Wahhabi interlude, and the British operations, had not intervened. But this was the purest illusion. There had been profound, multifarious and consequential changes. The pearling port of Sharja emerged from the struggle with enhanced prestige, at the expense of Ras al-Khaima with her date groves and tradition of long-distance trade. Soon the appeal of political unity itself would decline as new realities came home. Julfar was obliged to concede that she was not destined to fulfil her earlier promise.

CHAPTER TWELVE

The Port of Ras al-Khaima, Her Society and Economy

The town of Ras al-Khaima occupied the tip of a long, thin sand spit which ran parallel with the coastline and enclosed behind it a creek which served for a harbour. The spit was three or four miles long and half-a-mile wide at its broadest point. The narrow entrance to the safety of the harbour was protected by a sandbar which at low spring tides, when much of the backwater dried up, carried only two feet of water. The largest Arab vessels had therefore to be lightened, when they reportedly attained a maximum draught of some seven feet, before being hauled over the bar.[1] Even modest European-style ships were unable to approach the town to within a mile, let alone enter the creek.[2] On the mainland opposite Ras al-Khaima there commenced the date groves of Sir, which ran some way inland and north as far as Rams, a distance of 7–8 miles. 'Wells of indifferent water are scattered about among these groves: cattle and poultry are plentiful; here we had excellent vegetables in particular carrots and turnips.'[3]

Archaeology suggests that the site of Ras al-Khaima, which had not expanded during the preceding two centuries, tripled in size during the late eighteenth and early nineteenth centuries, before 1820; this must reflect the port's prosperity and prestige under the Qasimi shaikhs of these years. The town comprised a mix both of masonry houses, otherwise exampled on this coast only at Sharja and Jazirat al-Hamra', and the common *barasti* or palm-frond huts, all separated by narrow, winding alleys. The principal buildings were perhaps three: a mosque, a storehouse and the lofty, fortified residence of the ruler.[4]

Substantial and significant modifications would be made to Ras al-Khaima's solid defences after the first British expedition. In 1809, they had consisted of an unimposing wall with square towers cutting across the tongue of land some way below the town. These were light defences suited to protecting the settlement not from determined heavy attacking armies, but from bedouin raids and like incursions. Quite unusually there was no fortress, although of course many of the buildings could be defended at will. In place of town walls, by the time the British expedition arrived, batteries and entrenchments had been thrown up along the seafront. It was surmised that these works had been constructed under the direction of a European: although it is hard to make much specifically of a background of covert and other French activity in the Gulf, which is supposed to have extended to an offer of help to Sultan bin Saqr, or of the attested presence at Ras al-Khaima now of two captive French boys, this is not the only possible explanation, but nor is it quite inconceivable.[5]

In the second decade, the principle of a single wall protecting the end portion of the spit, product of a feeling of relative security where marauding appeared the major threat, was dropped in favour of something more robust, compact and defensive. The new system evinced neat military planning and helps to explain why Wahhabi Ras al-Khaima survived and became a symbol of resistance, and also why, aside from the factor of lost surprise, she was able in 1819 to withstand a British siege for five days, when a decade before she had fallen in one. Town walls may possibly already have been under construction at the time of Bruce's ill-omened visit of November/December 1816. The ensuing rupture with Britain and pressures bearing down upon the Wahhabis must have provided an impetus to rapid building. Three years later, when the British force arrived, the town had been fully enclosed on all but the creek side by 9–14 feet high walls tapering to a thickness of 2 or 2½ feet at the top, connecting round and square towers twice their height mounted with guns. Two hundred yards outside the walls was a gurry, or fortress, which protected the main gate and the town's southern landward approaches, constituting 'no mean or insignificant work of defence.'[6] The gurry's keep was a tall square tower built of stone and lime with walls 12–15 feet thick. This fortress, constructed possibly on the site of a mid-eighteenth century Persian castle, became the focus of the fighting during the operations of December 1819.[7]

Iran seems to have been the main source of small arms.[8] Spears, swords and small shields were still widely used, along with the ubiquitous matchlock (see Plate 2). The Qawasim were not, however, deficient in artillery. When Dhaya fell in December 1819, she yielded 100 matchlocks, 40 swords and 11 cannon. The capital Ras al-Khaima was found to contain 84 cannon, between two and twelve pounders, very many of them six or nine; three-quarters of these were mounted on ships' gun-carriages. The British occupiers also uncovered 1,200 lb. of gunpowder and 2,000 rounds of shot remaining.[9]

The size of Ras al-Khaima's population at this period is most uncertain. As British forces moved in with the cessation of the bombardment on

9 December 1819, Francis Loch witnessed the flight of the populace over a ford at the northern end of the town:

> The crossing by this ford put us in mind of the passage of the Red Sea by the Israelites, the old men, women, and children were placed in front, those capable of bearing arms bringing up the rear. It was a crowd of from seven to eight thousand souls of men, women and children ... a heart-rending scene.[10]

Loch's figure is not unreasonable. Surviving estimates point roughly to a garrison of 3,000 and a total population of 8,000; as compared with a total active male strength of 6,000 and a population of 18,000–20,000 for the whole Bukha/Sha'm–Abu Hail seaboard.[11] These figures do not seem disproportionate with the number of vessels in these ports, the most pertinent but still a very rough gauge of manpower.[12] The sole estimate of the number of houses at Ras al-Khaima, 1,000 in 1818, looks improbably small by comparison with figures from 1826–36, but precisely matches that given by Lorimer a century later; most strikingly the population on the spit at Ras al-Khaima in 1959, when the settled area covered much the same area as that in 1819, was also put at 8,000.[13] The impression is that there was to be no very substantial growth in population at these ports in the nineteenth and even earlier twentieth centuries: figures on men and boats engaged in pearling in 1817 are in the same order of magnitude as those cited by Lorimer a century later, and the first census in 1968 still only put the indigenous population of the various emirates which comprise this coast, and not simply their first ports, at approximately Ras al-Khaima 22,680, Sharja 23,118, Ajman 4,246 and Umm al-Qaiwain 3,744.[14]

It is hard to be sure, but it looks as if the second port of Sharja may have been half the size of Ras al-Khaima in the first decade or so of the century, but after 1820 understandably quite rapidly outstripped her. All the other Qasimi ports on the two shores of the Gulf were smaller still. There are uncertain indications that Ajman and perhaps Jazirat al-Hamra' were quite sizable, or at least militarily strong. Linga was the largest Qasimi port on the Persian coast, with a reported 725 fighting-men in 1820.[15] The populations of these ports fluctuated wildly both seasonally and through migration: in March 1819, with the bulk of the men at sea in their 50 large vessels, Ras al-Khaima was left with a garrison of only 200–300.[16] At last, it might seem that Ras al-Khaima was small, but with a population equal to Bushire's and two-thirds that of Muscat, she in fact constituted one of the larger Gulf ports.[17]

Information on the tribal component of Ras al-Khaima's population is scant. We know of the arrival of the Za'ab of Jazirat al-Hamra' towards mid-1818 and of the Suri Qawasim's sojourn a decade before. These aside,

Plate 9. Ras al-Khaima, with the attack of the HC cruisers, on the evening of the 11th November 1809. (R. Temple, HM 65th Regt, *Sixteen Views*)

Plate 10. The storming of a large storehouse near Ras al-Khaima, where Captain Dancey, of HM 65th Regt, was killed, November 13th 1809. (R. Temple, HM 65th Regt, *Sixteen Views*)

Plate 11. Ras al-Khaima, from the south-west, and the situation of the troops at half past two p.m. November 13th 1809. (R. Temple, HM 65th Regt, *Sixteen Views*)

Plate 12. Top: A view of Linga, from the sea, during the destruction of the dows on November [17th] 1809   *Bottom*: A view of Laft, 26th November 1809. (R. Temple, HM 65th Regt, *Sixteen Views*)

apart from the possibility that there may at certain times have been parties of Tanaij, Sudan and Na'im present, the only noteworthy allusion concerns the make-up of the December 1819 garrison: besides 1,000 ex-Maratha mercenaries, it supposedly comprised Qawasim, Za'ab, Shihuh and Matarish, the same four tribes once again reportedly making up the remnant of Ras al-Khaima's population in the 1820s, in addition to 'some strangers'.[18] In fact, in common with other long-established mercantile centres like Bushire, an undetermined but large proportion of the permanent population had either lost or never had any tribal affiliation, and these bore the appellation 'Ahl Ras al-Khaima', people of Ras al-Khaima. The Resident was caustic in this regard,

> Scarcely more than a fifth of the population of Ras al-Khaima is formed of Arab tribes, or of those aboriginal classes who inhabit the greatest part of Arabia, of men swayed by one chief and united into one unconflicting mass of interest and opinion, by ties of blood, marriage, and immemorial dominions and example; the rest is made up of an unsettled band of ruined fugitives, adventurers, and exiles from every corner of the Gulf, each pursuing his interest as it may best be secured.[19]

The converse process, exampled elsewhere in the Gulf, whereby the disparate elements of the coastal population were gradually subsumed beneath the umbrella-term 'Qawasim' (from the ruling family) had begun, as attested by the Saudi ruler, but would become arrested.[20]

There was a large influx of population into the Arabian ports during the summer pearling season, especially from the interior, and there are hints that some may have sought service on board Qasimi vessels at other times. Sadleir has a startling though unverifiable note to the effect that Ajman bedouin from south of Hasa engaged on Qasimi cruisers 'for one or two voyages, according to the share of the spoil which was allotted to them.'[21] Equally hard to comment upon is the curious fact that all ten of the Ras al-Khaima crew taken prisoner by Loch on 29 December 1818, aged 14–35, apparently described their country as Yemen.[22] Enlistment by Utub on Ras al-Khaima vessels is not well attested, that by men from Linga can be discounted, except perhaps for a short time in the first decade under financial pressure, but participation by the Shihuh of the northern coast, an area connected for a time with Wahhabi Ras al-Khaima, seems well established.[23] African slaves predominated in Rahma bin Jabir's boats and they were an important element too in Qasimi sea-power. They supposedly constituted two-thirds of the large crews of baghlas and battils seen off India, whilst Buckingham carried away the impression that over half the fighting-men at Ras al-Khaima were Africans.[24] The second major category of immigrants were Huwala and others from southern Persia, who were well nigh as numerous along this coast as the slaves.[25] Temporary visitors included of course Wahhabis from central Arabia, but also individuals from as far afield as Sind and Mocha.[26]

One of the more unusual individuals residing at Ras al-Khaima in the second decade was a young Frenchman. Native of Isle de Bourbon (Réunion), his Basra-bound schooner had been captured by Ras al-Khaima vessels not long before the 1809/10 expedition. All the crew were 'murdered in cold blood and in the most cruel manner' except two boys who became Muslims and were spared. One of these, subject of our present concern and the only one whose subsequent history is known, was taken to Ras al-Khaima and put to work on cruisers. His age allowed him to adapt to the new environment. He adopted the name Abd al-Rahman and took two wives, who bore him children, 'yet he could not brook the degradation of remaining with these people longer than he had the power of making his escape', which, the opportunity presenting itself, he effected around April 1818. Late the following year he came to the notice of the British Residency at Bushire when the country-ship *William Petrie*, on which he had by then enrolled as crew, put in on her way down the Gulf. Abd al-Rahman's apparent metamorphosis drew comment: he possessed

> a remarkably fine athletic figure of six feet and in his Arab dress appeared a perfect giant. The contrast between him and the Arabs was most striking, few of them reaching the stature of five feet eight inches. He had a constant smile on his countenance and retained all the vivacity of his countrymen yet his gesture was modulated into that of an Arab. His face and hands which were naturally white according to the custom of the country were stained with henna and his eyelashes and eyebrows with antimony.

Paradoxical curiosity he might have seemed, but his situation was somewhat pathetic. Evidently torn between the bitter-sweet anguish of a decade's captivity and nostalgia for his former unformed self, he now accepted employment medial between the British expeditionary force and the Arabs, first as intelligence adviser and interpreter, later as Beach Serang at Ras al-Khaima.

> It is strange that in spite of the feeling of disgust which he had at the people, and so strong was it as to make him not only desert them but also his wives and children, yet after having mixed again with Europeans, he found his own manners and ideas so changed that he could not by any means be persuaded to return to his own native island.[27]

The ruling Qasimi family at Ras al-Khaima and Sharja was small. The only contemporary estimate seems to talk of 70 adult males, which looks high by comparison with Lorimer's 18 a century later.[28] The ruling family was connected by marriage to others in the Gulf, notably the Banu Mu'in of Qishm; which same pivotal family had also provided wives for the ruler of Nakhilu and Sayyid Salim bin Sultan of Muscat. The marital career of Sultan bin Saqr nicely demonstrates the political potential of many of these alliances. (See Figures 3–6).

It is something of a truism to state that, as in the case *par excellence* of Muscat, rulers of Gulf ports tended also to be their principal merchants. Sultan bin Saqr was in 1822 said to derive most of his wealth from commerce and in 1845 owned one-third of the tonnage in baghlas at Ras al-Khaima.[29] There is every reason to suppose that other rulers, some of whom feature as shipowners, shared similar interests. The same was indeed also true of other members of the Ras al-Khaima Qasimi family, some of whom were in 1808 based at Bhavnagar, no doubt for the purposes of trade.[30] The rulers of Ras al-Khaima and Sharja probably maintained only a small, rudimentary establishment of guards and administrators, but the hospitality, military expenditure and various subventions generally associated with shaikhly rule would have entailed significant expense.[31] The pearling industry normally supplied the major part of the official revenue. The *Diwan* or treasury traditionally received the equivalent of one diver's share of the profits from each pearling-boat, this in addition to the ruler's once jealously guarded right to purchase all large pearls, worth over 110 tomans (c. £150?), at half the market rate.[32] In 1822, by which time the tax may conceivably have been commuted into a flat rate poll-tax on operatives, Sultan bin Saqr of Sharja's annual income from pearling was put at 2,000–3,000 dollars (£450–700).[33] The share-system of taxation seems to have been applied as late as 1817 not only to pearling, but also to the seaborne trade. Each merchant vessel was required to pay the ruler one seaman's share of the profits on every voyage; for what it is worth, there is no mention of custom houses or receipts at this date. The third significant form of revenue accruing to the ruler of Ras al-Khaima was a one-tenth tithe (zakat) on the produce of her date groves, estimated in 1817 at 8,000 rupees (c. £800). Apart from these, levies on shopkeepers, fishermen and the like would have amounted to very little.[34]

Life for all classes along the Sha'm–Abu Hail coast was hard. The land was for the most part barren and unproductive, livestock were few and the only extensive cultivation was that of dates. Most of these were grown in the north, about Ras al-Khaima, where some 15,600 palms were recorded a century later.[35] The quality of this staple suffered from lack of water and its quantity fell short of demand, requiring imports from more favoured parts of the Gulf. The sea, not the land, supported most of the population, but it provided only a sparse existence. The better off were still far from enjoying sumptuous living, and the society's natural disposition to eschew self-indulgence, luxury and ostentation was at this time accentuated by the teaching of Wahhabism. In accordance with these last tenets, Hasan bin Rahma's dress in 1816 was simple, devoid of silk, and but for his head-dress, identical to that of his followers.[36] Even after this period, in 1827, an evening's hospitality accorded Lieutenant Wellsted by Sultan bin Saqr appeared honest and straightforward:

> I was received in a small room, furnished with only a rude table, two or three chairs, given him by the commanders of our vessels, and some carpets, on which, after I had declined the honour of the chairs, we all seated ourselves. Our dinner was, as usual, of the most frugal description, and, after its removal, the Sheikh's brother roasted and pounded the coffee, which the Sheikh himself made and handed round. A story-teller was then called in, whose tale, judging from the peals of laughter he drew from his hearers, must have possessed much entertainment.[37]

A more generalized picture of the standard of living at Ras al-Khaima and neighbouring ports is conveyed by the following:

> The houses of the better classes are constructed of stone with flat roofs to sleep upon, without comfort of any kind beyond mats and rude bedsteads: the poor classes live in cadjan huts.[38]
>
> Their diet is simple enough, but wholesome; dates, fish, cakes of flour, and milk, form the principal articles: rice being expensive, is an indulgence with the poor, but they are very fond of it. Pillaw made with fowls or kid, and fruit, form the evening repast with the higher orders. Coffee is drunk at all hours out of small cups of china placed in a cup or frame of silver or brass, according to the condition of the owner. Smoking is common enough, but not on this coast so much as elsewhere, as some of the Wahhabis do not use tobacco at all. They cook in earthen pots, generally placing the fish on the living embers, and so toasting it; at the same time the sides of the pot are covered with their wheaten cakes, which are soon baked: the fish cooked in this manner is very sweet. Dates are abundant and cheap, and form their chief article of food. Fruit is not produced on this coast in any quantity, but you can obtain limes and melons in the market, and sometimes grapes, which are probably brought from Linga, or from the interior.[39]

The flavour of life at Ras al-Khaima and other ports is hard to recapture. Visitors' accounts, of which there are a few examples from the 1820s and 1830s, are by their nature subjectively coloured and occasionally perilously

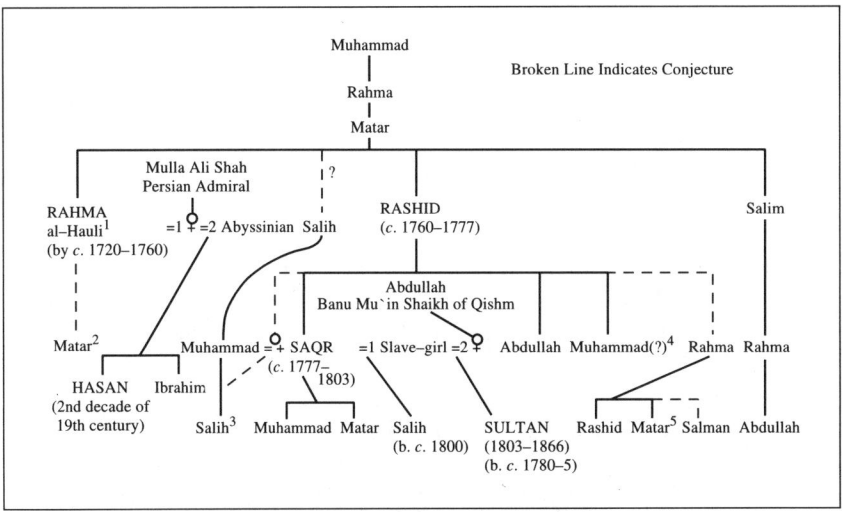

Figure 3. The Qasimi Ruling Family of Ras al-Khaima.

1. The Dutch sources contain a letter from 1718 signed by 'Shaikh Rhamha ben Mhatel ben Rhamha ben Mhamet Hoeli': Slot, *The Arabs of the Gulf*, p. 239.

2. This Matar bin Rahma is intended for the senior Qasimi who participated in the negotiations with David Seton in January–February 1806. Seton described him as Sultan bin Saqr's uncle, which need not perhaps be taken literally. Matar was then one of the three most prominent men at Ras al-Khaima and himself referred to Sultan bin Saqr as 'my son'. It seems less than likely, but not impossible, that this Matar bin Rahma was the writer of the 1808 letters, who went by the same name.

3. It is most uncertain where the maverick Salih bin Muhammad should appear in this family tree. At the time of the *Viper* affair of 1797, for which he was responsible, he was described by the Bushire and Basra Residents as Saqr bin Rashid's nephew, and by Saqr as his 'relation'. A Salih bin Muhammad bin Salih participated in the Anglo–Qasimi discussions of early 1806, when he was, with Matar bin Rahma and Sultan bin Saqr himself, one of the three leading figures at Ras al-Khaima, set to lead the fleet against Qais. Salih (bin Muhammad) bin Salih was said to be cruising with Rahma bin Jabir in 1810. In 1811, Shaikh Salih bin Muhammad al-Qasimi was rumoured to have taken control of Ras al-Khaima in Muscat's favour. Salih bin Muhammad was last referred to in late 1814, perhaps erroneously, by Maurizi, who referred to his cruising off Muscat on behalf of Su'ud.

4. The figure Muhammad bin Rashid bin Matar is taken from Lorimer's family tree. I have a suspicion that he included him in order to be able to confirm that the maverick Salih bin Muhammad was Saqr's nephew, whereas it seems likely that Salih's grandfather was one Salih. The line Abdullah bin Rahma bin Salim is also taken from Lorimer, none of these figures appearing in the contemporary sources, but seems valid since it was presumably derived from their descendants in 1907. Lorimer, *Gazetteer*, vol. 1, part 3, Table of the Ruling Qasimi Family of Sharjah in Trucial Oman.

5. Matar bin Rahma bin Rashid and his brother Rashid were respectively the writer and recipient of two letters in November 1808, Matar then apparently residing at Ras al-Khaima and Rashid in Bhavnagar. Their relationship with the rest of the Qasimi family is conjectural. It is presumed that this Matar bin Rahma was not the Matar bin Rahma, the senior figure who took part in the Anglo–Qasimi negotiations of 1806. Two letters from Matar bin Rahma to his brother, one dated 15 Nov. 1808, BA P 327/3557–66.

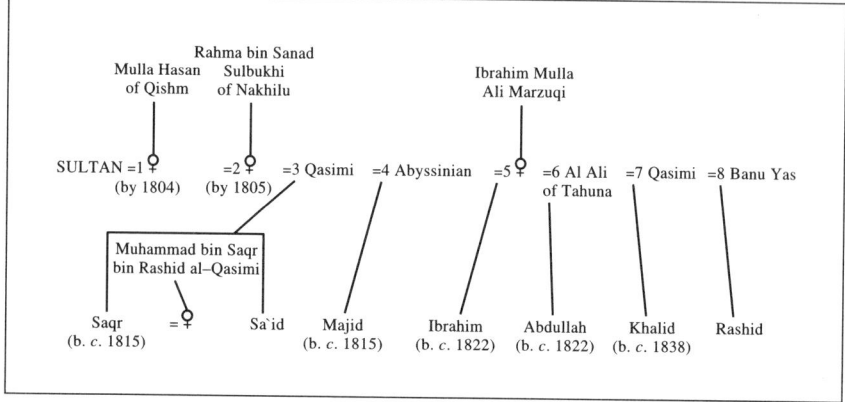

Figure 4. The Marriages of Shaikh Sultan bin Saqr bin Rashid al-Qasimi.

These birth dates are taken from a report of 1845; another of 1854 differs somewhat. Sultan bin Saqr's own date of birth is particularly uncertain. Thomas, *Arabian Gulf Intelligence*, pp. 102–4, 293–5.

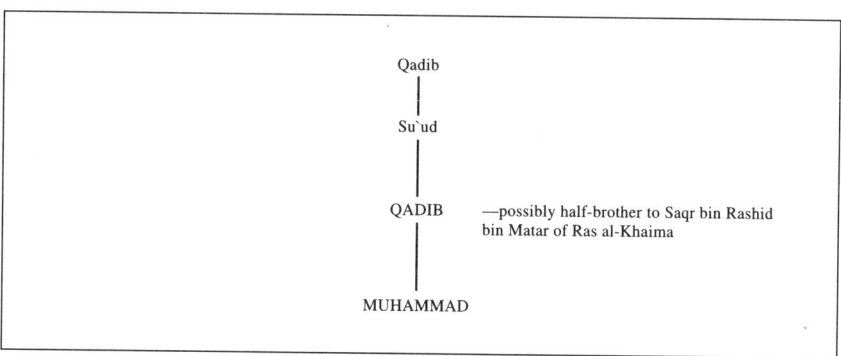

Figure 5. The Qasimi Rulers of Linga.

Qadib had probably become ruler by 1801 and was still so in 1809. By 1815 he had
been succeeded by Muhammad bin Qadib, who was still ruler in 1820 and after.
There is uncertainty over the close family relationship between this and the ruling
family of Ras al-Khaima. The Linga Shaikh was said to be Saqr bin Rashid's
brother in 1801 and Sultan bin Saqr's uncle in 1805, when he was first named.
These references are both consistent with the description in 1820 of Muhammad
bin Qadib as Sultan bin Saqr's first cousin. In 1808/9, however, David Seton gives
the full name of the Linga ruler as Qadib *bin Su'ud bin Qadib* and, surely erroneously, describes him as Sultan bin Saqr's nephew, not uncle. Lorimer must have
discounted or been unaware of this awkward reference, conceivably of course with
justification: note also the name's occurrence in the third generation of his family
tree for Sharja. Seton's intelligence, incorporated in Taylor's report, in Thomas,
Arabian Gulf Intelligence, pp. 18–19; Lorimer, *Gazetteer*, vol. 1, part 3, Table of the
Qasimi Family Formerly Ruling Lingeh, and that of the Ruling Qasimi Family
of Sharjah in Trucial Oman.

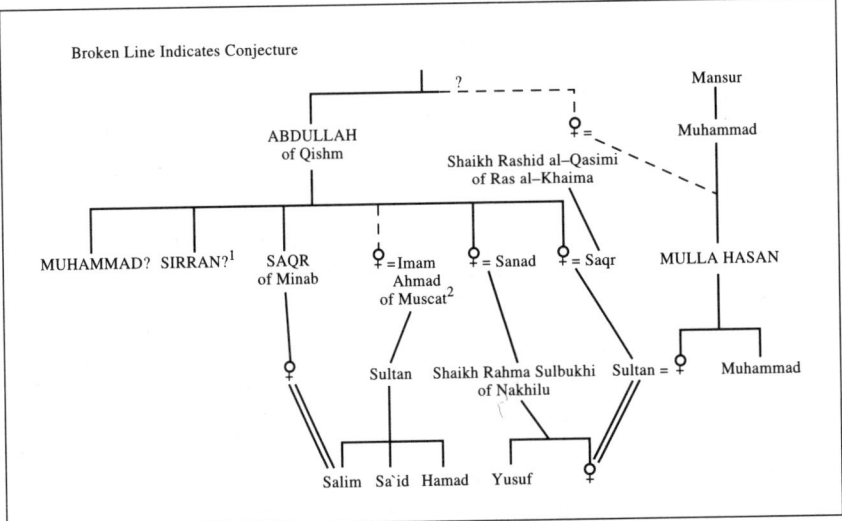

Figure 6. The Banu Mu'in Ruling Family of Qishm.

Mulla Hasan was already Shaikh of Qishm in 1797 and remained so until he was removed from office by the British expedition of 1809/10, which installed another, pro-Muscat, Banu Mu'in ruler, one Shaikh Darwish. The name of the Shaikh of Qishm does not occur again until 1819–20, when he appears as the Banu Mu'in Shaikh Hamza bin Muhammad bin Jabir whose father (died 1816) had been Governor of Bandar Abbas. Abdullah's sons may have ruled Qishm for a time, but they failed to establish themselves securely: Sirran killed Muhammad, Muhammad's mother had Sirran killed, and Saqr, being feeble-minded, succumbed to his cousin Mulla Hasan; the latter put him in chains, then turned him out on the coast of Makran, where he occupied one of Sultan bin Ahmad of Muscat's forts. Saqr was subsequently installed at Minab by Badr bin Saif of Muscat.

1. 'Seran': David Seton's Journal Sept.–Dec. 1801, BA S&P 119/77–100.

2. This seems to be implied by Perry, *Karim Khan*, p. 161.

focused and shallow. With the sea constituting the main scene of mascu-line endeavour, life ashore could strike the English visitor as somewhat slow in pace:

> They are extremely fond of coffee and smoking; the lower classes even have their coffee three or four times a day.
>
> After the afternoon prayer, they assemble together and chat over their coffee, either on business or on pressing occasion until market time. All go to market whether they wish to purchase any thing or not. It is a place for the resort of the idle, who talk over the news of the day ... They have very few amusements; frequenting the coffee-houses, and gambling, seem the only amusements they are particularly fond of ...
>
> The females on this coast are the only industrious people. They perform all the work either indoors or out. They carry water, milk the goats, spin and cook, go to market, bring fire-wood, &c. &c. while the husband is in the coffee-house.
>
> The husbandman, from the nature of his employment, is also obliged to be industrious; they water their gardens twice a day; a little before daylight, and at 3 p.m.[40]

Pearling occupied the summer months and generated the economy's lifeblood. The physical size of the industry of the Sha'm–Abu Hail coast was comparable with that a century later. At the beginning of the nine-teenth century it supposedly employed 8,000 men aboard 400 boats, who harvested a minimum of 30,000 tomans (c. £40,000?) worth of pearls annually: the Bahraini fleet was a good deal larger. The industry, here as elsewhere, was financed by means of loans advanced to individual boats at the start of each season. When the loans were repaid at the season's end, those in kind, of such as dates and rice, would bring in a profit of 50 per cent or thereabouts to the creditor. Those in cash were, in accordance with Islamic law, not subject to interest, but instead gave the financier the right to purchase a boat's catch of pearls at a 10 per cent discount. The repayment of debts could also be deferred, till at length it would be made after selling the boat, or else from the later profits of pearling or other enterprises such as fishing and commercial voyages. The financiers were substantial local merchants, some of the most important of whom were in 1817 said to be the following: Ibn Kalban, Ibn Ausiya[41] al-Za'abi, Abd al-Rahman al-Riqi of Jazirat al-Hamra' and the two Ras al-Khaima merchants, the 'well known' Ibn Qurs and one Abu Rashid Bu A'la.[42]

The fleet of sizable cruising-vessels under Ras al-Khaima was generally supposed to be in the region of fifty sail.[43] A useful breakdown of the shipping at Ras al-Khaima and dependent Arabian ports in 1807 spoke of 25 dows, some (5–15?) large baghlas, 30–40 battils and 200–300 baqqaras or intermediate-size vessels used for pearling and the coasting trade.[44] One imagines that these figures omit the smallest pearling and fishing craft, which, if added, might conceivably have doubled the total. Sharja came second to Ras al-Khaima in sheer number of vessels, presumably on account of her importance for pearling. Ras al-Khaima, however, easily dominated in large ocean-going boats like the dow and baghla, with up to two-thirds of the coast's total and perhaps all her very largest: fully half the 60 large vessels burnt by the first British expedition on both shores of the Gulf, were those at Ras al-Khaima.[45]

Estimates for the total number of cruising-vessels large and small on the Sha'm–Abu Hail coast in 1815–19, at 210–342 dows, baghlas, battils and baqqaras, look very similar to those of a decade earlier. The fact that Britain was able in 1819/20 to find around 37 dows and baghlas, 80 trankeys or battils and 60 others thought fit for destruction in these ports, leaving aside smaller pearling and fishing-boats such as the second class baqqara, lends credence to these figures. It is suggested that most of the deficiencies created by Britain's burning of 72 vessels there in 1809/10 had subsequently been made up, and that the rather misleading destruction of double the number of boats in 1819/20 can be explained by the exercise of greater thoroughness and a decision to take in slightly smaller sized vessels on the second occasion.

Ras al-Khaima was still in 1815–19 unquestionably pre-eminent amongst Qasimi ports. Sharja may have had more trankeys and possibly half the tonnage, but neither she nor any other Arabian port had more than a handful of dows and baghlas, which were almost all concentrated at Ras al-Khaima.[46] On the Persian coast, Linga's fleet of large vessels could have been roughly one-third that of Ras al-Khaima's in 1807–9: it may have been less in 1820, when the combined total of large vessels at the five Persian ports associated with the Qawasim was put at 19.[47]

The precise composition of Ras al-Khaima's fleet of large vessels is known from the British returns of January 1820.[48] There were 14 baghlas (measuring 40–120 feet long by 14–28 feet across), 5 dows (76–93 by 8–20 ft.), 10 undifferentiated moderate-sized baghlas and dows, 29 trankeys (30–70 by 8–20 ft.) and 2 cargo boats (35–42 by 11–13 ft.). Three of the baghlas must have had a cargo capacity of 350 tons or more, and a fourth cannot have been far off: an idea of the power of these vessels can be imagined from the dimensions of the mast of one such Bahraini baghla, said to have been 94 feet long and 8 feet round, supporting a yard of fully 141 feet 6 inches.[49] A quarter of the large vessels found at Ras al-Khaima were old and out of repair, and the 60 were together valued by prize agents at 136,875 rupees (c. £14,000), roughly the same as the value put upon all the vessels burnt a decade before.[50]

Calculating roughly from the dimensions of these 60 vessels, it would appear that their total cargo capacity was somewhere in the region of 6,200 tons, 1,000 of which was unusable. This is a large total. It is almost exactly the same as the tonnage in Arab-style shipping separately recorded for the leading ports of Bushire and Muscat in 1823; though of course these also operated significant numbers of European-style ships. Amongst comparable states and ports within the Gulf none in fact except Bahrain could have begun to match Ras al-Khaima's tonnage in large vessels.[51]

Confusion surrounds the nomenclature of Arab vessels. Class-names are and were not always used consistently or with precision. In the present work variations in orthography in the British sources have been eliminated for the sake of consistency of form, if not necessarily of content. Spelling must have been conditioned by Anglo-Indian usage, for there are and were vessels in use off north-west India bearing names remarkably similar to those in the Gulf; indeed this similarity extends to the vessels themselves, reflecting the fact that the two areas shared the same maritime culture.[52]

It is apparent from the few instances where this can be verified in the Arabic or Persian original, or by reference to contemporary descriptions, that the Qasimi vessels or types most frequently encountered were the dow, baghla, battil and baqqara.[53] The dow (Arabic 'dâw' pl.-ât) was at this time primarily a specific not a generic class, and a fifth term, trankey, appears from evidence in the second decade to have been another word for battil.[54] The baghla and battil seemingly conformed to the recognized types of those now extinct vessels, as no doubt broadly did the baqqara. British observers tended to highlight the battil's speed and spread of canvas, as well as the baghla's high poop, which last seems in the following description by Captain Loch of two Abu Dhabi vessels captured at Bahrain in 1819 to have been especially developed:

> One was of the largest description and called a baghla, having a crew of from 150 to 200 men on board; she was lower forward considerably than aft, having a high poop which was formed into a sort of castle and which was defended by the chiefs and principals on board, likewise when most resistance was made; this class of vessel is from two to five hundred tons burden. The other vessel taken was a battil or second in size, having a crew of from 70 to 100 men, and is from 60 to 100 tons burden, being a beautifully built vessel and sails most remarkably fast. The baghla has an enormous mast as large a small class frigate's, stepped one third from the stern, raking forward; with a mizen mast abaft. On the main mast is hoisted a prodigious sail, the yard of which is equal in size to a 36-gun frigate's main yard and requires all hands on board to manage. The sail of the battil is larger in proportion, having but one mast stepped one third from forward.[55]

Loch had models of the principal classes of Gulf vessels made for him at Bushire in 1819–20, but what subsequently became of them is unclear.[56] The three main types of vessel under discussion here are illustrated in Plates 3–7.

Maritime insecurity being so prevalent before 1820, these vessels needed to be able to defend themselves. 'An Arabian piratical vessel,' observed one cynic, 'may be considered as an armed boat which robs, and an Arabian trading vessel as an armed boat which does not rob.'[57] Swords, spears and the like were customarily to be found even in smaller vessels: a 28-ton Bahraini trading baqqara encountered in 1818 bore 47 men armed with 10 swords, 10 matchlocks and 1 shield. Larger vessels might also have cannon: a Linga-built and -owned battil taking a cargo of rice to Abu Dhabi in 1819 carried 70 men, 60 matchlocks and 3 guns. The crews of these two vessels were surprisingly large and others for the baqqara and battil respectively of 14 and 20 are also recorded.[58] Yet it does seem that boats were sometimes now more heavily manned than they would be in later more peaceful years, particularly if they expected to conduct hostilities: a group of three Ras al-Khaima baghlas and one battil which had been out cruising at this time carried 300 men and 7 guns, 150 men and 4 guns, 130 men and 3 guns, 50 men and 1 gun respectively.

An expeditionary fleet which sailed from Ras al-Khaima against Sur in April 1807 was said to have consisted of 22 dows, 2 baghlas and a number of battils.[59] This impression of a striking imbalance between the number of dows and baghlas accurately describes the overall situation throughout the first decade of the nineteenth century. When, however, Ras al-Khaima made good her losses after the destruction wrought by the first expedition, she did so overwhelmingly in baghlas, not dows: only a handful of the latter were for certain found at Ras al-Khaima in 1819/20 and some of these were old. The process of the baghla's supplanting of the dow in the Gulf was nearing completion.[60] With the demise of the specific dow class, its name would linger on as a common generic.

The transom-sterned baghla, which had become established at Muscat and elsewhere by 1801, was closer to European models than the dow, which was still reminiscent of double-ended vessels like the battil. A remark by the ruler of Mukalla in 1819 confirms the obvious impression that the baghla was generally considered the superior vessel.[61] The dow was apparently to be distinguished from it by having a long gallery projecting from the stern. The following description of the Qasimi dow and mode of attack in the first decade is now worth picking up again and completing:

> The dows are vessels of peculiar form, ... so large as to be capable of carrying from three to five hundred men, ... with as high as from five to ten guns, ... yet so slightly built, and in consequence so buoyant,

that a vessel in tonnage equal to a ship of war of twenty guns will not draw more than ten feet [of] water ... They take the ground well and sail rapidly, but being worked with only one immense sail cannot tack ... The timber with which they are built comes from the British territory, and many are launched from Cochin.

The prow and sterns of these vessels project very much and are barricadoed ... One third of the length of the vessel deck from the stern is erected a fighting-stage in height equal to the level of the upper works of a frigate, or more, ... from whence, as well as from the prow and stern, the pirates throw spears, stones and other missile[s] ... The pirates' mode of attack is generally as follows ... They surround a ship; keeping clear of the broadside if she has cannon, and begin the battle with matchlock[s,?] guns, and spears ... When a favourable opportunity offers, they run the prows over the deck of the vessel they attack, which presents an enemy well intrenched, if I may use the phrase, over the heads of the defendants who are completely exposed; and as soon as the dows swing alongside, the men from the fighting-stage board, while multitudes of men in fast sailing boats, called trankeys, rush in and overpower the unhappy people they assail.

This kind of force although truly contemptible when opposed against a ship of war, is generally irresistible to the vessels which carry on the valuable trade between the Euphrates and British India. Even if the pirates are beaten, they by rowing and swift sailing speedily retire to a coast of natural difficulties, where they are sure of support from a ferocious and armed people.

Such were the vessels of the enterprising Jowasmees.[62]

Ras al-Khaima was built on maritime commerce. At its more expansive, it was an unassured existence. The nature of trading was sensitive and competitive, prey still to political discord with fellow Gulf carriers, maritime hostilities with confirmed or opportunistic rivals and poor relations with the markets themselves. Pearls were the coastline's only valuable export, which was supplemented by relatively inconsiderable amounts of high-quality dried fish, 'aba's or cloaks, cheese and almonds etc.[63] Ras al-Khaima's geographical location and harbour were inferior to Muscat's, and she did not enjoy to the extent of Bahrain and Bushire the advantages of a populous hinterland of settled consumers. A Qasimi negotiator succinctly represented his as a 'people whose country afforded nothing but fish and a few dates, and who existed by carrying freight for others and whose Shaikh was not more than the other heads of families, who obeyed him, or not, as they pleased'.[64]

The general pattern of Ras al-Khaima's large-scale trade in normal times, following the one comprehensive account to survive, was by no means exceptional.[65] The dows and baghlas of Muscat, to cite but one example, operated along the same lines. In autumn, as the south-west monsoon fell away and the pearling season was closed, the larger vessels sailed from Ras al-Khaima to Basra where they loaded up with ripe and boiled unripe dates (*tamr* and *saluq*).[66] This prime commodity, together, perhaps, with small adventures in items such as copper, dies, drugs, beads and horses, was then shipped to a variety of destinations comprising Muscat, Sind, Cutch, western India, Yemen and the Sawahil or east coast of Africa. India was more frequented than the Red Sea.

We only know in general terms the sorts of goods which Qasimi vessels might have brought back with them to the Gulf in return for their cargoes of dates and assorted minor commodities, pearls and specie.[67] Makran supplied the Gulf with sheep, jowarree (millet) and grain, and in the 1820s or early 1830s gave Ras al-Khaima and her neighbours iron, ghee, sugar, oil and carpets. Sind was associated for the Qawasim with the trade in rice and corn,[68] but also supplied the Gulf with a range of goods such as cotton, cloth, saltpetre, tallow, ghee, oil, hides and Punjabi indigo. Cutch provided cotton, oil, silk and cotton stuffs. In Gujarat, Bhavnagar, where members of the Ras al-Khaima Qawasim lived in 1808 probably pursuing trade, was a source of oil, cotton and grain, and Surat, where they may have had contacts, of coarse piece-goods, silk and cotton stuffs, as well as bamboo and metals.[69] The emporium of Bombay was of course the principal mart for European merchandise as well as sundry goods such as sugar and spices, and in the 1820s or early 1830s Ras al-Khaima took from there iron, rice, brass, steel, cloth, thread and needles, and cotton and yarns. During this same period, Ras al-Khaima shipped large quantities of Mangalore rice, indeed it was then one of her main imports along with dates.[70] Rice and pepper were also exported to the Gulf from Malabar, as well as perhaps sugar, cloth, metal and indigo, but the region was especially important as a source of teak and other timber, as well as coir, for shipbuilding. Without Indian timber, spars and planks, Arab Gulf vessels could not be built. Strangely, however, although in later times Malabar was certainly the prime source of teak for Gulf vessels, this was reportedly not the case in 1792–1819, even before the British imposed their export ban, unless possibly this timber was purchased indirectly through Cutch, Sind, Porbandar and Mangalore. During these years the bulk of timber exports to the Gulf apparently went from Travancore, and whilst a few Arabian dows were built at Calicut, rather more were so in Cochin.[71] Daman too may perhaps have had some such role as Cochin.[72] So much for India. As for the African route, Yemen supplied Ras al-Khaima and the Gulf with coffee as well as gums, drugs and slaves, and Zanzibar exported slaves as well as cowries, rice, wood, ivory, hides, wax and ghundy(?). The trades in coffee and slaves were, however, very much the preserve of Sur and Muscat.

Exactly what became of these goods when they were brought to the Gulf is unclear. Barring the possibility of some offloading or exchange of goods at Muscat, which for much of our period must anyway have been out of the question, it is easiest to assume that incoming vessels sailed direct to Ras al-Khaima where they unloaded. Imports surplus to local requirements would presumably then have been taken on in smaller vessels like the battil and baqqara to other ports, especially perhaps those of the lower Gulf. This at least would accord with the known practice of Bahraini dows and baghlas when they returned from similar voyages; and it is also worth remarking that as early as 1790, though they were not always to adhere to the practice, Bahraini vessels returning to the Gulf preferred to bypass Muscat, much to her annoyance, so as to evade the duties levied there.[73] If this partially distributive model for Ras al-Khaima is correct, it accords her a role somewhat analogous to that assumed by Linga later in the nineteenth century. The proportion of goods re-exported through the Gulf by Ras al-Khaima is unknown. It would be unwise to underestimate the size of her local market. The roughest idea of the extent of this demand can be gained from the fact that in 1876, less vigorous days, when some 30 vessels, representing 3,480 tons of shipping, sailed between the whole Ras al-Khaima–Abu Dhabi coast and India, virtually all the imports were absorbed into the country.[74]

In addition to the prestigious ocean-going trade, Ras al-Khaima and neighbouring ports were also quite heavily involved in traffic with other Gulf ports. It is also possible that in peaceful times the Qawasim had, like the Bahrain Utub, carried a certain amount of freight up the Gulf from the entrepôt port of Muscat. The coasting-trade was, as already observed, the preserve of smaller vessels such as the battil and baqqara. As far as we can tell, Ras al-Khaima's briskest trade in these years was with Bahrain and Qatif; Bahrain was also where most of her plunder was reportedly disposed of, and a major source of provisions.[75] Qatif was the main channel of foreign imports from Bahrain to Wahhabi Hasa and Najd,[76] and as we have learnt supported a Qasimi garrison late in the second decade. The next major direct trading partner after Bahrain and Qatif was Basra. Ras al-Khaima and neighbouring ports thirdly had a more occasional trade with the Huwala ports of the Persian coast such as Kangan, Asalu, Linga and Qishm. The import of dates, from Basra, Bahrain, Minab[77] and, immediately after this period, from the Batina, was vital for her survival. In the 1820s or early 1830s, when with the re-establishment of peaceful relations trade with Muscat and the Batina had again become possible and important, Ras al-Khaima and her neighbours imported articles such as the following from other parts of the Gulf: from Basra and Bahrain, dates, horses, camel-hair or woollen abas; from Persia, [gun]powder, tobacco, carpets, cloth, sugar, swords, *janbiyas* (daggers) and matchlocks; from the coastline about Linga and Shinas, onions etc.; from the Batina, dates and ghee; and from Muscat, rice, ghee, sugar, cloth, indigo and slaves.[78]

In normal times, then, Ras al-Khaima's long-haul trade centred upon the shipment of Basra dates to India, and within the Gulf, the smaller trade of Ras al-Khaima and her neighbours was now principally with Bahrain and Qatif. The most valuable staples imported and absorbed by Ras al-Khaima and the neighbouring country may have consisted of dates, rice, grain, cotton cloth and a few other articles such as ghee and, though Wahhabism lessened the demand, coffee. Large vessels sailing outside the Gulf made one voyage each year, smaller boats engaged in the Gulf coasting-trade made two. The crews of Qasimi merchant-vessels were paid according to a share-system, which could vary from 2–3 rupees for an ordinary seaman sailing to and from the Persian coast, up to 80 rupees for the lucrative Yemen voyage: in this and other more essential characteristics, the long-haul trade recalls that of Kuwaiti dows in the 1930s.[79] It is impossible to know what the average value of Ras al-Khaima and her neighbours' trade might have been. The only estimate, in an addendum to an Arabic report from 1817 on the economy of the Qasimi ports and purportedly referring to former times when the Qawasim were most active in trade, calculates from a mean imported cargo of 50,000 piastres for each of 60 large vessels and twice 1,000 for 200 small, and arrives at an average annual total of imports of 3.4 million piastres, or perhaps £260,000; but the number and value of 'large' vessels and their cargoes could as well be quite exaggerated.[80]

As to the health in *c.* 1790–1820 of Ras al-Khaima's Indian trade, the major part of her large commerce, we have relatively little of substance to go on. There is comparative evidence that Bahraini vessels traded regularly with Surat, Bombay and Malabar, and perhaps to some extent with Sind,[81] and of course that Muscat merchants and their vessels traded extensively with much of India,[82] including, down the west coast, Cutch, Bhavnagar, Surat, Bombay, Bandar Rajapur (?), Malabar and occasionally Goa;[83] to which, following later report, one might also add Coondapoor, Mangalore, Cochin, Karachi and perhaps Tatta.[84] But if Qasimi vessels went south of the Gulf of Cambay in these years, they unfortunately left no clear trace.[85] By itself, this need not be so very significant. The presence of a possible Qasimi commercial agency at Bhavnagar in 1808, a desire on the part of Ras al-Khaima's rulers in this decade and the next to be allowed access to British Indian ports, and a likely tradition of commerce with Kanara and perhaps Malabar, the former attested in 1702 and 1835, are indicators of sorts.[86] It seems on the whole reasonable to assume from all the evidence that Ras al-Khaima's trade down the western coast of India suffered some decline at the end of the eighteenth century, but may have persisted until the middle of the first decade in the new century; thereafter Qasimi trade south of the Gulf of Cambay was probably in abeyance until the 1820s, and their maritime activities, commercial or otherwise, devoted to Sind, Cutch and Kathiawar.

The foregoing narrative of Ras al-Khaima's long-haul and coasting trades is for the most part couched in general terms. It represents the probable pattern at its most peaceful and flourishing, which may have extended from the 1750s to the 1780s. But already by 1790, her commercial status was not perhaps what it had been and this situation did not noticeably improve over the next ten years or so. During the first decade of the nineteenth century, Ras al-Khaima's trade encountered more severe obstacles than before, and in the second was sorely hamstrung and at times practically extinguished. Acknowledgement of this state of affairs, with its attendant causes and consequences, returns our attention to the primary concern of piracy, and a discussion of it is better reserved for the next chapter.

CHAPTER THIRTEEN

Some More Piquant Ingredients in Qasimi Maritime Plunder

The foregoing narrative of the Qawasim's political history offers much in the way of explanation of their maritime activities. Three pertinent themes yet await discussion, an examination of which, on top of all that has been intimated, promises to take us as close as we reasonably may, on the basis of the surviving evidence and at this interval, to an understanding of this tantalizing and involved phenomenon.

i Economic Matters Considered

It was no coincidence that the curtailment of Ras al-Khaima's long-haul trade, observed in the first two decades of the nineteenth century, should have corresponded with a gross intensification in her maritime depredations. This was an alternative use of the same resources in men and large boats. Even on the basis of known reports, the proportion of large Qasimi vessels which engaged in cruising and other warlike activities was large, particularly after 1807: in most winter seasons thereafter nearly half must have been so engaged, and in years such as 1817/18, when a large naval operation was mounted in the Gulf as well as squadrons despatched to India and south Arabia, the great bulk. Pearling, which occupied the summer months, may in contrast have been kept up relatively uninterrupted throughout this tumultuous period.[1]

At its most successful, the maritime pursuit of plunder probably yielded higher returns than trade; and, though the precise manner in which shares in the booty were soon after distributed amongst the participants in a capture is not stated, its benefits may have tended to accrue somewhat more widely.[2] The really valuable prizes were some of those vessels bringing cargo from India and Africa to Arabia: one such could conceivably have yielded as much as a whole season off north-west India, whose coasting vessels were generally far less valuable: the recorded values of Indian prizes range from a few hundred to two thousand pounds.

The amount of plunder taken by Ras al-Khaima and neighbouring states escalated after 1807, with the dramatic increase in Wahhabi political involvement. The one-fifth of booty rendered by the Qawasim to the Wahhabi treasury reportedly grew in the winter season 1808/9 from an annual $4,000 to $12,000;[3] which implies a rough total booty of £15,000 for the year to February 1809, and another of £5,000 for the few years preceding. Against this broad guide, it should be noted that on at least two occasions before 1808 larger sums were probably involved: first in late 1804, when the *Trimmer* and *Shannon* were taken and Qais and Charak pillaged, and secondly in January 1806, with the plunder of the Janaba vessels, valued by one author at 600,000 riyals (*c.* £150,000) or more.[4] Moreover, it was also not long before the capture of the *Minerva* in May 1809 would yield a cargo reportedly worth 300,000 rupees (*c.* £30,000).[5]

After a period of recuperation, the level of plunder maintained during the second decade seems to have been higher than in the first. A late source, Brucks, maintains that in 1814 and 1815 Ras al-Khaima and associated states took an annual average booty of 1 million rupees (*c.* £100,000); this fell somewhat in 1816 to 700,000–800,000 rupees (*c.* £70,000–80,000), five-eighths of it the product of the three Surat vessels plundered in the Red Sea (their owners at the time quoted a figure twice this sum);[6] then rose to its acme in 1817 and 1818, when the one-fifth of booty sent to Dir'iya averaged 93,000 German crowns plus another third in goods, now implying an annual booty of *c.* £133,000: 'I had this information while living among them from some of the principal men of the tribes when engaged in the survey of the backwaters. They were at all times ready to talk over their wars.'[7] Nor are these figures so implausible as they may at first seem. The figure for 1817 interestingly appears to correspond with that contained in the *Lam' al-Shihab*, written that very year.[8] We have some knowledge of a few other valuable individual prizes taken in these years: 3–5 Al Haram and Banu Mu'in baghlas seized at Asalu in December 1817 with cargoes from Basra, for example, were estimated to be worth 300,000 rupees (*c.* £30,000); and, more strikingly, amongst other captures off Oman and south Arabia in early 1815 was a baghla bringing 50,000 French crowns (*c.* £12,500), 400 slaves and a cargo of ivory from Zanzibar, and the 600-ton Mocha ship *Fath al-Rahman*, whose cargo was valued at 200,000 French crowns (*c.* £50,000).[9]

All this activity presupposes minimum elements of organization. Cruises required planning and co-operation. In a very few cases we learn that intelligence of prospective prizes was acquired beforehand from other vessels.[10] Bahrain was the main outlet for the sale of captured property, and must have benefited thereby. There was no mention at the time of the practice which Brucks later attributes to the Qawasim of their issuing merchants who sometimes visited the island to retrieve property with passes to protect it from capture a second time.[11]

A theoretical argument could be made out that the Qawasim were fundamentally drawn to maritime plunder in some measure as a response to the economic situation in which they found themselves. The supporting evidence for this merits examination.

The pattern of trade which evolved in the Gulf in the late eighteenth century had not favoured the continued efflorescence of Ras al-Khaima's share in it. The thorough eclipse of Bandar Abbas, which for so long had been the loadstone of trade on the Persian littoral, was already evident in 1759–63 when the European companies transferred their operations to the region of Bushire and the northern Gulf; this signified a fundamental decline in the commercial importance of the lower Gulf, which was not to be alleviated for over half a century. The need for an entrepôt near the Gulf's entrance, to receive ships from India, the Red Sea and Africa, was henceforth answered admirably by Muscat under her new and commercially ambitious rulers, the Al Bu Sa'id: the port's trade and shipping flourished, making her in 1790 the richest in the Gulf. The 1780s also saw the start of a very rapid rise in the commercial prosperity of Bahrain, buoyed up by the richest pearl fisheries in the Gulf and the advantages of an island situation well placed for commerce, in the aftermath of her conquest by the Al Khalifa in 1782; already by 1790 the enterprising Utub of Bahrain and Kuwait had reportedly engrossed the bulk of the freight trade between Muscat, eastern Arabia and Basra.[12] There may have been a remembered sense in much later Qasimi tradition that Ras al-Khaima's involvement during the earlier 1780s in the Utbi–Persian dispute over Bahrain, of obvious political and commercial moment to her and with its attendant diversion of resources away from trade, had somehow signalled the end of a brighter era and induced a lasting transformation in her psyche which ultimately contributed to what ensued.[13] Be that as it may, her position farther from the commercial centre of things confirmed, Ras al-Khaima now witnessed rising semi-competition to the west and found herself vulnerable to the economic consequences of her often fragile relations with the great port of Muscat.

After 1790, the Qawasim encountered gradually more palpable obstacles to the exercise of legitimate trade. The first test was the reign of Sultan bin Ahmad of Muscat (1792/3–1804), the effects of whose aggressive trade policy in the Gulf have already been amply illustrated. Nagging conflict between the two parties, under circumstances of Omani naval supremacy and aggravated by the arrival of the Wahhabis at the turn of the century, injured Ras al-Khaima's freedom of navigation and facility to concentrate on trade. A typical gesture was Muscat's sponsoring of attacks by a small party of Sudan, based on Hormuz up to autumn 1801, upon Qasimi and Utbi shipping; actual blockade of Ras al-Khaima by Sultan bin Ahmad in winter 1803/4 cut off imports to the extent that basic provisions grew scarce.

In the first and second decades of the nineteenth century the impediments to Ras al-Khaima's commercial prosperity became tinged with irony. An outbreak was to have been expected upon the death of Sultan bin Ahmad in November 1804; when it came, it entailed attacks on the *Trimmer* and *Shannon*, thereby invoking a reputation for piracy with the British which, later widely reinforced by their own actions, told against Qasimi trade in India.[14] The Qawasim were precluded from visiting British Indian ports as they wished to in 1804–6 and 1808–9; and, of predominantly symbolic significance, a general ban on the export of shipbuilding timber from Malabar to the Gulf was imposed in 1809. Communications were also damagingly cut with Muscat and, in concert with her in 1805/6 at least, with Basra.[15] Political, naval and military strife in four of the five winter seasons before 1809/10 absorbed the major part of Ras al-Khaima's energies, allowing little opportunity for commerce: at this point the first Anglo–Omani expedition, in burning her large boats, would have removed the means for any immediate resumption of it.

The prospects for easeful trading did not improve during the second decade. Wahhabi Ras al-Khaima was politically more isolated than before. Once her maritime strength began to return, so too did her reputation for piracy. Free access to the ports of British India and doubtless Muscat continued to be denied her. The key to Ras al-Khaima's large-scale trade would ordinarily have been Basra. References throughout this decade to isolated attacks meditated or executed against Basra shipping, or boats carrying dates from there, taken with the political rift between Wahhabi Ras al-Khaima and the ports of Basra, Kuwait and Bushire, most naturally suggest that the Qawasim did not and could not readily visit the Iraqi port. Only in 1819, however, and then on account of the new naval measures instituted by Britain, can we conclude for certain, from the evidence of a shortage of dates on the Qasimi coast, that this was the case: any converse argument, that the absence of recorded shortage before this points to ready access at Basra, can however be denied, since Ras al-Khaima then got dates from Bahrain and the lower Gulf ports, as well as receiving large quantities annually from Qatif as the gift of the Saudi ruler.[16]

There may in general have been more ambiguity about these matters than expected. Brucks alleges that there were merchants in Bahrain and Oman friendly to Ras al-Khaima who helped them acquire boats and timber from India;[17] there was frequent and unimpeded traffic between Ras al-Khaima and Bushire at the time of the attack on the *Sylph* in 1808.[18]

All else being equal, the Wahhabi Qawasim would probably have been unwelcome at Mocha and the ports of south Arabia. This was evident in the hostile reception accorded them by the ruler of Aden in January 1804, after he had been forewarned of their approach by Mukalla merchants. Once again, however, the situation was not always so clear cut: Shihr and Mukalla both suffered at the agency of the Qawasim, but in 1809, at least, their rulers were prepared to overlook their scruples, the first in order to pay the Qawasim to attack Mukalla, the second to purchase, then sequester, their prizes.[19] How, finally, the Qawasim might have fared at the ports of north-western India has already been examined.

The argument thus far demonstrates convincingly enough that the conditions under which Ras al-Khaima traded became less favourable at the end of the eighteenth century. It is attractive to postulate that this may have helped prepare the ground for what ensued. The obstacles encountered in 1804–19, although by a paradox essentially of her own making, would if anything then have tended to reinforce the assumed more predatory direction of her maritime endeavours.

It does not necessarily follow from this that Qasimi depredations in the early nineteenth century should be construed as acts of protest and constructive defiance directed against those who impeded their trade, which would be an impliedly conscious, immediate and less abstract process; and which is not of course to say that simple retaliation against aggression, and the cycle it generated, was not an important ingredient in this activity. This may be seen in relation to Muscat: Ras al-Khaima's attacks on her shipping were primarily intended to hurt her commerce much as, when the Qawasim attacked the port of Bukha, they cut down her palm trees[20]— in both cases the economic damage inflicted was an end in itself and a weapon in a political quarrel; in Muscat's case the quarrel was an ancient one, where the distinction between economic and other grievances had long since become blurred. The case with British India was different. Hasan bin Rahma would, like his predecessor, have liked authorization to trade at British Indian ports; it also evidently rankled in the second decade that the expansion of British authority had restricted the arena in which the Qawasim were free to capture vessels at will.[21] Yet attacks on European British vessels cannot have been much inspired by these feelings, since the relevant restrictions postdated the worst of them. The only other obvious irritant, the rise in customs charges for non-subjects which accompanied British control, such as the increase from three to seven and eight per cent at Surat and Mangalore in 1799–1800, would have affected the Qawasim no more than any others in the Gulf.[22] It is extremely difficult to know what manner of resentment, if any, may have helped inspire attacks on Indian British vessels. Harassment of the shipping of an important trading partner like Basra, whilst showing no doubt that shortage from lack of access invited direct action, indicates nevertheless that these inclinations were not brought in check by any overriding policy or authority: after 1807 Ras al-Khaima conspicuously failed to demonstrate a clear and unequivocal commitment to devote herself to peaceful trading.

For all its spontaneous appeal, the theory that Qasimi activity in the early nineteenth century may be explained as a series of attacks on rivals in trade has nothing to recommend it; this, assuming a working definition of trade rivalry as two or more parties carrying similar goods from, but more especially to, the same market. There could certainly have been wide competition in the export of Gulf produce to India, from Muscat and elsewhere, but this need not be accorded such great significance here. If anywhere might have been described as weighty overall competitor of Ras al-Khaima, and then none too satisfactorily, it would have been Bahrain; yet, like many smaller ports of the lower Gulf whose trade was also close to Ras al-Khaima's, Bahrain was for much of the time her ally. Victims of the Qawasim such as Surat vessels trading to Mocha and French boats coming to Muscat from Bourbon[23] clearly could not have been perceived as trade competitors; and much the same strictly goes for the many others such as Bombay craft bound for Kathiawar and Cutch, British vessels trading between Bombay and Basra and even a Muscat ship returning from Calcutta. It is in particular hard to see that there can have been any direct competition between Ras al-Khaima and the coasting vessels of north-west India which so often fell victim to her; exclusion from Indian supply-marts, with the general loss of trade, could conceivably have been one factor here, rather as shortage from lack of access to Basra may sometimes have encouraged assaults on the Iraqi date traffic.

Although it constituted a spirited defence of her maritime interests, for her part the key to Ras al-Khaima's abiding conflict with Muscat was politics. The myriad Qasimi captures off north-west India were reasonably simple acts and no part of this central duel, but it is worth briefly examining Muscat's relationship with this region to establish whether there could still have been any correlation of the most distant kind between the two arenas. An ancient relationship of commercial symbiosis subsisted between Oman and this part of India, and all Muscat's relations therewith were mercantile or mercantile in origin.

Apart from her alliance with British India, Muscat's only political links in the first two decades of the nineteenth century were with Makran and Sind. The powerful Sultan bin Ahmad (1792/3–1804) was responsible for acquiring Gwadar and Chahbahar in Makran and he was also accorded an annual gift of saltpetre by a ruler of Sind. Western Makran remained aligned with Muscat during the reign of Sultan's son Sa'id: in 1819 the ruler spoke of Sa'id bin Sultan as his overlord and averred that he had assisted him in troops against Ras al-Khaima, recalling the fact that Omani rulers had a tradition of employing Baluchi and Sindi mercenaries extensively in their armies. To the east, Sa'id bin Sultan failed to recoup his father's influence: the ruler of Bela complained bitterly to Bombay in 1815 of his hostile actions[24] and an appeal to Hyderabad in 1810 for assistance against the Wahhabis went unheeded;[25] both these regions incidentally suffered at the hands of the Qawasim, dispelling the notion that they could have been attacked for their political association with Muscat.[26] On the subject of Makran's and Sind's obvious commercial links with Muscat, however, it is relevant to note that, according to an observation at the turn of the century, Muscat merchants each year freighted large numbers of small dinghies belonging to these places for voyages to Bombay and Cutch.[27]

Muscat had ceased to enjoy any commercial privileges at Surat when the port passed wholly under the East India Company's jurisdiction in 1800, just as had occurred at Mangalore a year previous; she also had no formal relations with either Kathiawar or Cutch. Her only link with these parts, where the Qawasim were so active, was straightforward commercial intercourse, the most intriguing aspect of which was the presence at Muscat of a large Hindu merchant community. This was no recent phenomenon, indeed tradition related that one such Hindu had been instrumental in the expulsion of the Portuguese from Muscat in the mid-seventeenth century, after their commander had ill-advisedly insisted upon marrying his daughter.[28] Niebuhr recorded 1200 Hindus of all classes at Muscat in 1765 and there is no reason to suppose that this figure varied very substantially over the next 70 years.[29] According to a modern writer, however, their constitution altered during the same period from being composed principally of Sindi to Cutchi Bhattias;[30] contemporaries seldom designated their origins, although in 1816 Buckingham asserted that the Hindus of Muscat came from Gujarat and Bombay, in 1821 Fraser identified Sind, Cutch and Gujarat, and in 1835 Wellsted remarked that most embarked at Porbandar from north-west India.[31] Cutch was certainly already strongly represented at Muscat in the Bhimani family, which had reputedly begun trading there in the later eighteenth century: it was probably a member of this family, one Mowjee, who had acquired the customs-farm at Muscat by 1801[32] and two Qasimi attacks were subsequently recorded off Ras al-Hadd in 1817 and 1819 against vessels belonging to Mowjee's son Gopal importing from Zanzibar and Calcutta.[33] In 1802 Hindus at Muscat were said to own 50 large dinghies which they despatched twice yearly via Bhavnagar to Surat.[34] Unlike the Ismaili Khojas of Matrah, Hindus, it was said, usually did not bring their families with them, but returned to India after a stay in Muscat of 15–20 years.[35] It is clear from these points that there were important

Indian merchant families at Mandvi and possibly elsewhere with a private interest in Muscat's prosperity and well-being, and moreover that the commercial linkage between Muscat and north-west India had true substance.

The original question can now be addressed, as to whether any perceived association in the minds of the Qawasim between Muscat and parts of north-west India could to a degree have predisposed them, in times of extremity and heightened feeling, to regard them as unfriendly and therefore open to attack. Only western Makran was sufficiently close to Muscat for this to have been at all self-evidently the case. Elsewhere, bearing in mind that Ras al-Khaima had ancient links of her own with India, all that can be imagined is that there was potential in these times for casting up a thin shadow of popular jealousy, not enough to provoke attack.

In sum, this survey of economic factors behind Qasimi maritime activity in 1797–1819 suggests the following: worsening commercial prospects for Ras al-Khaima in the late eighteenth century may originally have made these activities more likely and the trend once established was if anything somewhat ironically reinforced by the added obstacles she encountered during these years. An indeterminate sense of frustration, shortage and lack of access to markets, as well as a desire to defend her maritime interests, could all at times have played some part in these events, but they do not explain them. Simple commercial rivalry and any theory that these activities constituted a protest against impediments to Ras al-Khaima's trade can be discounted; likewise, except possibly in relation to Makran, the close commercial links between Muscat and north-west India probably should not be considered a significant factor in explaining Qasimi captures there. The final point to observe is that maritime plunder proved in the short term more lucrative than trade.

ii Wahhabism

The degree to which Qasimi maritime depredations and other warlike activities were attributable to the political and religious impact of Wahhabism has been the subject of some disagreement. The question first arose in 1819, when it split the Bombay Council. One member, Francis Warden, argued vociferously that his researches in the Government archives showed the Qawasim and other small Gulf powers to be naturally inclined towards the peaceable mercantile life, but not in recent years free agents: the prevalence of piracy in the Gulf, he maintained, 'may be attributed wholly and exclusively to the instigation of the Wahhabi tribe. Under that impression, I feel disposed in some degree to advocate the cause, even of the Qasimi tribe, and to palliate their enormities.'[36] The Governor, Sir Evan Nepean, countered this by championing the understanding of contemporary military and naval officers with experience of the Gulf, who 'so far from thinking they are disposed to quit their present predatory habits ... consider their present habits so deeply rooted that nothing but the strong hand of power will keep them down.'[37] For the planners of the second expedition, in the wake of Dir'iya's fall, this issue was understandably important since it appeared to have a direct bearing upon the nature and extent of British measures against Ras al-Khaima deemed necessary to staunch perceived Qasimi piracy.

Inevitably Nepean's view prevailed in Council. In the long term, however, by virtue of the publication of his historical memorials, Warden's interpretation exercised the far greater sway over historians; if a little heightened, his was in any case more representative of the orthodoxy previously current in informed Company circles, particularly before the first expedition, something acknowledged in the Anglo–Qasimi negotiations of 1806 and 1814.[38] Fantastic but colourful popular tales of Qasimi religious fanaticism, which gained wide currency at the time, have also proved enduring and enticing to later writers on this subject; such, for example, as the story of ritual human sacrifice originated by the Persian Secretary on board the *Sylph*,[39] or the belief so casually expressed by the famous missionary Henry Martyn in a letter from Bombay in 1811:

> In a few days sail for the Gulf of Persia (D.V.) in a Company's sloop of war sent to cruise against the Arab pirates. Not less than 25 armed ships of these miscreant Arabs are out, taking all they meet with, and as usual murdering every Christian.[40]

Historians nevertheless by disposition also like to strike an attitude of revisionism. Lorimer and others after him have been uncomfortable with the idea that Wahhabism played a large role in events, and have reacted to the standard depiction by diminishing the emotional response and emphasizing the Qawasim's independence and responsibility for what they did.[41] The arguments of historians and later writers are, however, not our concern, which is solely with the contemporary evidence.

A good deal has already been said in earlier chapters concerning Saudi involvement in this corner of Arabia. What remains is to relate this more closely to the subject in hand. It may be observed in passing that for most of this period the prime original source of instability in the Gulf was the Saudi eruption, which first spilt into the littoral region at the end of the eighteenth century; this was the *sine qua non* of much that concerns us, including the two British expeditions.

There is at the outset a prima facie case for supposing a more direct connection between Saudi–Wahhabi involvement with Ras al-Khaima and the maritime disruption she caused. The character and extent of Qasimi maritime warfare and plunder changed dramatically in the latter part of 1808, which is precisely when Saudi policy on this coast abruptly turned more pronounced and forward—this is the symbolism of the attack by Rams upon the *Sylph*; it then retained its new form until 1820: this whole period corresponds with the lifetime of Wahhabi Ras al-Khaima *par excellence*, when the hereditary ruler, Sultan bin Saqr, was undermined and excluded from power.

The increase of Saudi political influence at Ras al-Khaima, which reached its desired conclusion between late 1808 and the start of 1810, was effected through the subversion of the unco-operative traditional leadership. A new power structure emerged, representing in part the interests of the Za'ab and the Tanaij, which saw maritime plunder as a means to demonstrate loyalty to the Saudi cause and in return received vital external support. Moreover, authority along the Ras al-Khaima coastline was less centralized than before and ports now sent boats out of their own accord. There was also a third incidental consequence of Ras al-Khaima's accession to the Wahhabi fold, which was operative almost from the first. Even if Ras al-Khaima entertained reservations about participating fully in the Saudi enterprise, she now found her formal political allegiances determined for her; at one stroke she had acquired many new and resolute enemies, and with that an increased likelihood of becoming engaged in hostilities. The political classification of the enemies of the Saudi state, reinforced at will by Wahhabi exclusivity, was a broad one, indeed it is the only one which theoretically could describe almost all the Qawasim's victims: in 1817, the Saudi ruler Abdullah bin Su'ud composed a letter to the British Resident in defence of Ras al-Khaima's plunder of the three Surat vessels, in which he enumerated his subjects' potential targets for maritime attack:

> If you choose war over peace, so be it—God is our one recourse and his will[42] be done. If you prefer peace, then I give my word that all British subjects will be free from molestation at the hands all Muslims; but as to the people of Egypt and Jeddah, Yemen, Shihr and Mukalla, Muscat, Basra and Iraq, and the Persian subjects of Sa'id bin Sultan, all these are our enemies and whenever we come across them, we seek God's help in fighting them and plundering their property: thus He has said—Glory be to Him, and after mention of His names—'Slay the idolaters wherever you find them.'[43]

The Qawasim themselves would have added 'Hindus and other unbelievers of India' to this list.[44]

It was Saudi policy to employ conquered states and peoples to attack others under the banner of jihad; success was necessary to engender success.

From early on Ras al-Khaima was instructed to carry the fight against Muscat: formal pressures combined with the general momentum of the Wahhabi advance to exacerbate the longstanding feud between them. Instructions to Ras al-Khaima in the first decade to join Bahrain and Muscat in a planned expedition against Basra bore no fruit. Most intriguing, perhaps, were the orders which must have been issued to the Qawasim, as they were to Muscat and Bahrain, to attack the Indian coast and shipping, predating the first predatory cruises thereto and providing justification for them all. These designs were mooted as early as May 1805, soon after Muscat under Badr had overtly succumbed to Saudi domination: six months later Imam Su'ud wrote to him, 'Verily thou shalt speedily proceed to the holy war in India, by which thou wilt not be fighting for me but it is incumbent on thee to be obedient to God.'[45] Now, and during the next half decade, such orders reflected the rather diffuse feeling of expansionist enthusiasm which still coursed through the veins of the victorious and self-confident Saudi state, as well no doubt as a simple desire for plunder. Renewed pressure to attack Indian shipping was brought to bear upon Muscat and Bahrain in early 1809.[46] Even as late as 1814 Muscat was secretly being urged by a Wahhabi negotiator to embark upon the 'mad project' of a lightning descent upon the coast of Malabar.[47]

Plunder mattered to the Saudi state. It was a weapon invoked against political enemies, as well as a source of revenue.[48] The appointee charged with responsibility for collecting the one-fifth of plunder due to the Saudi treasury held the most important civil office in the territory of the Amir of the Qawasim, after that ruler himself. The rendering-up of this plunder, after the process had become regular with the ousting of Sultan bin Saqr, formed an umbilical cord linking the Qasimi ports into the Saudi state. The Resident, William Bruce, was wrong to suggest that the significance of this tribute was cancelled out by the Saudi ruler's annual gift to the Qawasim of Qatif dates of nearly equal value, since it is customary in Arabia for relationships of clientship and subjectship to be reinforced by largesse.[49] The Qawasim's relationship to the Al Su'ud through presents and plunder may also, if the Lam' al-Shihab is to be believed, have had a more intimate side: some amongst Imam Su'ud bin Abd al-Aziz's ten personal Abyssinian 'maidservants' had supposedly been given him by Ras al-Khaima after they had been bought or captured.[50]

The paradigm held up for emulation by the Qawasim and their ilk was individually exemplified in the Jalahima Shaikh Rahma bin Jabir. By 1810 he had received the title 'Shaikh al-Bahr', Admiral, from the Saudi ruler:[51] a late source alleges that Hasan bin Rahma of Ras al-Khaima was given the analogous title 'Amir al-Bahr'.[52] Rahma bin Jabir is accorded special heroic mention in Ibn Bishr's Saudi chronicle:

He was the marvel of his age in fortitude, pride and courage. [Imam] Su'ud, may the Almighty have mercy upon him, had employed him in that region, installing him at the well known ports of Khuwair and Dammam in Qatar, and at Qatif, to be a warrior upon the seas, whereby he achieved power and respect. Su'ud sent men to fight alongside him and his allies increased in number. He waged war fiercely against the people of Bahrain, Muscat and others, fighting harsh battles and engagements with them.[53]

Where the Qawasim had a longstanding dispute with Muscat, Rahma bin Jabir's sole guiding passion throughout was his acrid vendetta with the Al Khalifa: in so far as was possible, these energies and propensities were harnessed to the Wahhabi cause. In practice, despite the idealization in Ibn Bishr, Rahma bin Jabir was no Saudi tool, though his depredations against Bahraini and other shipping suited their purposes and he in turn benefited from their support and protection. He was a shrewd political opportunist and deserted the Saudi cause three years before the fall of Dir'iya. His Wahhabi religious conviction nevertheless remained solid. Ibn Bishr concludes his eulogy of him by noting that he was an accomplished and prolific poet, composer of poems especially of heroism and battle, who entertained a deep love and attachment to the Wahhabi community. These are some bland lines of his composed after the fall of Dir'iya, expressive of his piety and devotion to Wahhabism:

> May God on our behalf reward the imams,
> who have summoned us to Unity from the abyss of destruction.
>
> Our shaikhs are those well versed in the religion of their Prophet,
> amongst whom is the learned ascetic Taqi al-Din.[54]
>
> There rose over his legacy a shaikh[55] who has taught us,
> an imam who expounded Unity as a science and sovereign glory.
>
> He put out the fires of polytheism which had flared up again
> in Najd, and there buried and extinguished them.
>
> His sons[56] followed in the holy path after him,
> and their followers were the people of bravery and magnanimity,
>
> God be praised, people steadfast in support of His religion,
> and they wrought judgement upon the heads of the unbelievers
>   with sharp Indian steel.[57]

Rahma bin Jabir lived by and for plunder, having little truck with commerce. He dressed with Wahhabi simplicity and in his battered person bore testimony to his mode of life. In marked contrast to the Saudi perception of him, he appeared to morbidly fascinated British observers to epitomize their conception of the Gulf pirate. The censorious traveller

Buckingham, whose disdainful moralizing was a sign of things to come, was dismayed when in 1816 Rahma bin Jabir was invited to the British Residency at the behest of naval doctors eager to inspect his arm, whence shrapnel had stripped out all the bones between elbow and shoulder. Rahma bin Jabir was clearly happy to play up to his reputation. He was

> admitted to sit at the table and take some tea, as it was breakfast-time, and some of his followers took chairs around him. They were all as disgustingly filthy in appearance as could well be imagined; and some of them did not scruple to hunt for vermin on their skin, of which there was an abundance, and throw them beside them on the floor. Rahma bin Jabir's figure presented a meagre trunk, with four lank members, all of them cut and hacked, and pierced with wounds of sabres, spears, and bullets, in every part, to the number perhaps of more than twenty different wounds. He had, besides, a face naturally ferocious and ugly, and now rendered still more so by several scars there, and by the loss of one eye.

Rahma was at this point asked 'with a tone of encouragement and familiarity' by one of the Englishmen if he could still despatch his victims with his injured right arm; whereupon he clenched his dagger in his right hand and, supporting his boneless arm at the elbow with his other hand, twirled it around in the air, vaunting the desire to cut as many throats as possible. This at least is Buckingham's colourful version of the scene, which concludes,

> Instead of being shocked at the utterance of such a brutal wish, and such a savage triumph at still possessing the power to murder un-offending victims, I know not how to describe my feeling of shame and sorrow, when a loud burst of laughter, instead of execration, escaped from nearly the whole assembly, when I ventured to express my dissent from the general feeling of admiration for such a man.[58]

Judging by the tone of the leadership, the public atmosphere at Ras al-Khaima must have become distinctly more Wahhabi in character when Sultan bin Saqr was undermined and ousted, during and after 1808. Neither Sultan bin Saqr's, or his father's, letters employ Wahhabi terminology or otherwise betray Wahhabi sentiment; in 1805 the former still signed himself in grandiose style, 'high one, magnifier of God, reliant upon the Lord' (muta'adhdhim billah, mutawakkil 'ali), and in 1806 his name appeared as 'Shaikh al-Mashayikh Amir' on an official document.[59] The case with his successor Hasan bin Rahma was very different. Referred to simply by name[60] or as 'Amir of the Qawasim' by the Saudi ruler,[61] he signed his letters with a Wahhabi flourish 'Hasan bin Rahma and his Muslim brothers'[62] or, later on at his most formal, 'Amir of the true believers'.[63] Hasan bin Rahma's letters are wholly cast in this mode, thus redolent of the Saudi–Wahhabi vision. As for his people, 'God be praised, we belong to a religious community which follows the Prophet and God's law', that is to say, the Wahhabi state ('hauzat al-muslimin al-umma al-muhammadiya') ruled by the Saudi Imam of the Muslims.[64] Those who did not belong to this ideal community, including non-Wahhabi maritime powers and, inevitably, the enemies of Ras al-Khaima, such as by late 1816 the 'apostate' Rahma bin Jabir,[65] were as a class sinners, ignorant of the faith, and enemies of the true Islam.

The religiosity of the general population of Ras al-Khaima and neighbouring ports is less easy to evaluate. The impact of the spiritual revolution which characteristically accompanied Saudi military conquest at the turn of the century must have been profound and, not unnaturally, encountered sentimental opposition. The devotional heart of this coastline, according to the Lam' al-Shihab, had been the tomb-shrine of the Sufi Sayyid Hasan at Ras al-Khaima.[66] The ruling Qasimi family had a special attachment to Sayyid Hasan, who was otherwise widely venerated, for he had been the Sufi master of the ruler Rashid bin Matar (regn. c. 1760–77): Shaikh Rashid had retired from worldly affairs in the latter part of his life in order to follow the Sufi path, and was said to have been still alive at the time of the Saudi conquest. The people of Ras al-Khaima were inevitably instructed by the conquering Saudi forces to demolish the tomb of Sayyid Hasan, which to Wahhabi purists represented a deviant accretion upon the true original Islam, in order to demonstrate their absolute transfer of loyalty to the Saudi state. They demurred. The Saudi general insisted. Finally, in what must have seemed distasteful and degrading to some, the Qawasim were obliged to dismantle the building themselves stone by stone. This was too much for Shaikh Rashid and others who now emigrated to Linga: a report circulated that just when the tomb of Sayyid Hasan was brought down at Ras al-Khaima, ten members of the Al Su'ud dropped dead.

It is likely that in subsequent years efforts were made, quite possibly involving the despatch of religious teachers, such as the six witnessed at Muscat in 1809 beating people who omitted to pray in Wahhabi fashion,[67] to reform the religious practices of the inhabitants of Ras al-Khaima and neighbouring ports. Sufi and popular tendencies apart, acceptance of this stark new version of Islam would have been facilitated by the fact that the overwhelming majority had long been of Hanbali persuasion, that school of law most in tune with Wahhabi thinking.[68] The local religious establishment did not forthwith sacrifice its identity and links with the Qasimi ruling family, for as late as 1809 Sultan bin Saqr was able to call upon local qadis to present his case at Dir'iya against recent Saudi proceedings in his territories.[69] Yet, politics apart, one infers that amongst the population at large the acceptance of Wahhabi religious teaching had from early on proceeded apace: by 1808, and conceivably long before, it had probably become more or less general. As was the case with Rahma bin Jabir, adherence to the new doctrines and practices would prove solid enough to survive dissociation from the political power which had introduced them: in 1820 and thereafter, when Saudi political pressures had subsided, the vast majority in these ports, including Sultan bin Saqr's subjects at Sharja, were still regarded as Wahhabis and dressed and lived accordingly.[70]

One of the most devout and convinced Wahhabis was, as mentioned earlier, the probable Tanaiji Shaikh Hasan bin Ali of Rams and Dhaya. Anne Thompson, wife of the commander of the British garrison at Ras al-Khaima in 1820, bore witness to the touching piety in defeat of this venerable old Shaikh, who spent his nights in prayer and his days in preaching.[71] It was for these high qualities, of course, that Hasan bin Ali had been put in charge of the collection of the one-fifth of plunder due to the Saudi treasury, and his tribe, together with the Za'ab, had since late 1808 been at the forefront of Wahhabi policy on this coastline. It may be observed that this most ardent of Wahhabis lived directly alongside the Shihuh, to the north, who were some of the least orthodox in religious matters. A later British traveller claimed that there had been ancient buildings housing 'idols' (asnam) along the coast between Rams and Khasab, until they were, like Sayyid Hasan, destroyed by the Wahhabis.[72]

There is scant, though not negligible, evidence from the first decade of the century of a connection of the most intimate kind between Wahhabism and Qasimi marine depredations. In January 1804, four Wahhabi dows cruising off south Arabia between Mukalla and Luhayya, as well as capturing vessels at sea, landed briefly near Aden in order to replenish their water-stocks: whilst ashore, they robbed passers-by indiscriminately and destroyed the tomb of a local shaikh, carrying off as spoil the copper vessels it contained. This to some sacrilegious act would, one assumes, have been unthinkable without Wahhabism and reinforces the accent of the whole expedition. Local report identified the perpetrators as Wahhabis from 'Rasul' in the Persian Gulf, which suggests Ras al-Khaima to be the most likely candidate.[73]

By far the most significant evidence of this kind, however, is confined to 1808–9. As has already been shown, this was the critical period in which both Saudi–Wahhabi influence at Ras al-Khaima and associated ports rapidly became far deeper and more assured, and when Qasimi marine depredations took on a new tone and broader scale. The driven, undauntedly expansionist and rather heedless character of the Saudi leadership at this time was apparent in a letter addressed by Imam Su'ud bin Abd al-Aziz to the British Resident at the close of 1807, in which he sought at some length to persuade him to embrace Wahhabi Islam.[74] Such an invitation when addressed to Muslim rulers would typically, if spurned, have constituted a declaration of war; though qualified by professions of good will, the letter contrasts with the more mature and diplomatic missives of Su'ud's successor. It is a matter for speculation whether the tenor of this note might have been refracted by the newly vitalized, less restrained Wahhabi enthusiasms of Rams, Ras al-Khaima and the rest, and thereby given rise to the attacks upon the *Sylph*, the *Minerva* and other British vessels in 1808–9.

Near the beginning of March 1809, an 8–10 strong Qasimi squadron, returning from a predatory cruise off Cutch and Sind, touched at Chahbahar in order to bury their dead and probably take on provisions. They delivered a letter from Hasan bin Ghaith al-Qasimi, a leading member of Ras al-Khaima's ruling family, to the local governor, demanding that he destroy all the sacred tombs in his territory on pain of declaration of war.[75] This was a fine demonstration that Ras al-Khaima now saw herself as an integral part of the Saudi enterprise and, in her belligerent activities here at least, as the agent of Saudi–Wahhabi expansionism and proselytism. This prelude would have validated later attacks on local shipping. It is not known if hostilities anywhere else were inaugurated in this way. The lesser question of agency *per se* was, however, still alive in the second decade, for around early 1816 Ras al-Khaima installed a Wahhabi officer at Charak, with responsibility for monitoring the arrivals and departures of all vessels.[76]

There is a sense in which the transformations of 1808–9 were a product of the sheer transmitted exuberance of the rapid Saudi advance, which seemed of itself the proof of God's blessing. The most precious source for a glimpse of the Qasimi psyche during this period of turmoil is two private letters, intercepted by Britain, written in late 1808 by Matar bin Rahma al-Qasimi at Ras al-Khaima to his brother Rashid at Bhavnagar. These letters, besides referring to family and commercial matters, celebrate recent Qasimi military successes in concert with the Wahhabis in Oman and express the writer's frustrated desire to undertake maritime depredations like other Qawasim. The following piece of homily projects an ardent, practical, raw-seeming attachment to the Wahhabi cause and, in context, implicitly makes the connection between Wahhabism, recent military victories and Qasimi maritime depredations:

We have no equipments for a voyage at Ras al-Khaima: from this being the religion of God, every person should join in it, until all mankind be united in our faith. The people of God fight in favour of this religion, that the Almighty may render it manifest. Several cities have submitted completely, and embraced the religion of God— Abyssinia, Syria and Oman including the whole Arabian coast, have followed the example. The Almighty bestows victory on this faith, and confounds its enemies.[77]

The special relationship between the Qasimi ports and Dir'iya, which crystallized out in 1808–9, was, with all it implied, maintained throughout the second decade. Little so well documents the symbolic importance in this connection of Qasimi maritime plunder, and the personal nature of their devotion, as a passage in the *Lam' al-Shihab* concerning Shaikh Ali bin Muhammad bin Abd al-Wahhab, son of the founder of the Wahhabi religious movement. Shaikh Ali became head of the Al al-Shaikh and overall leader of the Wahhabi religious establishment around 1811. The hostile *Lam' al-Shihab* berates Shaikh Ali for womanizing, love of luxury and limited learning, then continues of him,

He only liked social intercourse with the Al Su'ud, and he would neither visit nor entertain anyone except for the people of Ras al-Khaima. When they came on visits to see Su'ud [bin Abd al-Aziz], they ate only at his table, and he was pleased with them and honoured them. They were very attached to him and would say, if asked about the faith of the people of Dir'iya, 'We could only find one true Muslim house there', then recite the holy verse. Shaikh Ali and his family ate nothing except for gifts brought by the Qawasim, for he used to say, 'Whatever the people of Ras al-Khaima plunder is sweeter than mother's milk'. He was extremely fanatical in matters of religion, that is to say the heresy which his father had invented.[78]

The results of this discussion may be summarized in one breath: the multifarious impact and influence of Wahhabism and the Saudi state, not wholly mundane, was the prime special cause of Qasimi maritime depredations, especially those of 1808–19, lending them their unusual extent and character.

iii Social Behaviour

The dows and gallivats, belonging to the different ports, in the Persian Gulph, are vessels of very considerable force, and many of their crews, particularly those, who navigate the dows, belonging to the islands and coasts, in the vicinity of Ormus [Hormuz], are rapacious and inclined to the commission of unjustifiable acts of violence.

(Commercial report, 1790)[79]

War and plunder were ineluctable facts of life upon the waters of the Gulf, and probably had been for many centuries. The first Ibadi ruler of Oman to have undertaken naval countermeasures against piracy is said to have been the fourth Imam Ghassan bin Abdullah (c. AD 808–23), acting in response to depredations by Sindi vessels along the Omani coast and at the mouth of the Gulf. Centuries later, the kingdom of Hormuz attempted to combat similar activity by vessels from the same quarter, the Makran coast, by operating a naval patrol.[80]

It is far from surprising, given the physical shape of the Gulf and the configuration of its trade routes, that the area broadly centred about the Strait of Hormuz should for so long have exercised its allure over those in search of plunder; or, for the same reasons, that it should have been the natural heart of successive maritime commercial states. Qais, and then the independent and finally Portuguese-controlled kingdom of Hormuz, in turn dominated international trade from the twelfth to the sixteenth centuries AD. Founded on sea-power and defensively situated on the two islands, which served as emporia for the Gulf, the formation of these states was in part a response to insecurity on the mainland. Yet they themselves did not stint from the tempting exercise of maritime aggression, not merely in order to extend political control from these centres over other islands and ports in the lower Gulf and beyond, but also, characteristically, so as to compel merchant vessels to use their entrepôt and pay tolls and duties. Nor did their activities always stop at this: according to the twelfth-century geographer Idrisi, the depredations ('raiding and capturing', 'yaghzu wa-yasbi') of the ruler of Qais's unequalled fleet had struck fear on the coasts of India and Africa and, closer to home, had injured traders sufficiently to divert part of the commerce from Oman to Aden.[81]

The Portuguese carried the practice of extracting benefit from traffic through the Strait of Hormuz to its height, by means of a compulsory pass system applicable to all non-Portuguese vessels. Their expulsion from Hormuz by an Anglo–Persian expedition in 1622 marked the end of systematic forcible exactions on this scale. The Dutch and English companies, whose fortunes were now in the ascendant were, despite their naval and military capacity, primarily interested in fostering their own trade and constitutionally esteemed the ledger over the sword. Gulf states also began to adapt, but preserved the old ways in their inventory for a further two centuries. Mulla Ali Shah's levying of protection money on the shipping of Khamir in the 1760s cannot have been exceptional, and as has been seen, Sultan bin Saqr of Ras al-Khaima was even said to have proposed some such arrangement to cover British shipping in 1809. Sayyid Sultan bin Ahmad of Muscat (1792/3–1804) was, however, the last to attempt anything of this kind on the grand scale, when he sought to compel all local shipping entering the Gulf to pay customs-dues at Muscat on pain of attack. Even regardless of Muscat's subsequent loss of position in the Gulf, the East India Company's espousal of new principles of free trade and increased involvement in the Gulf meant that after the General Treaty of 1820 there could be no return to the earlier system of forcible exactions.

Great states, then, had been liberal in the use of force. For reasons of self-interest, in order to defend her trade with these parts, Muscat had assisted Mangalore in quelling local piracy in the later eighteenth century, and in 1804, under Sultan bin Ahmad, showed herself willing to join with Britain in an offensive against the pirates of Okha in Kathiawar.[82] But even at this time piracy and the use of force were not the issue of principle with Muscat that they were with Britain, as Sultan bin Ahmad's policy in the Gulf has shown. A century before, the disparity in vision had been still greater. In the late seventeenth and early eighteenth centuries, a time incidentally when European pirates operated in these seas, riding upon the crest of her earlier revanchist victories over the Portuguese, Muscat carried the fight to the coasts of India and Africa. The net result of this naval activity was commercial prosperity and territorial expansion in the lower Gulf, at the expense of the Persians, and in East Africa, at the expense of the Portuguese. In the process, however, some of Muscat's undertakings had ceased to look like legitimate war: assorted vessels were captured and plundered at large and coastal communities were raided in India, the Gulf and elsewhere. In 1695, the East India Company's Agent at Bandar Abbas, Captain Brangwin, caught the prevailing mood when he predicted that the people of Muscat 'would prove as great a plague in India as the Algerines were in Europe.'[83]

Another recurrent feature of Gulf history was the heightened use of force by small states. The events of 1797–1820 have shown that although the potential for scuffles between rival states and powers was ever present, the majority normally eschewed maritime violence in order to concentrate upon peaceable trading: the only notable exceptions in this period were Rahma bin Jabir and the Qasimi ports. A casual glance at the history of the later eighteenth century demonstrates that while regional instability could unnerve almost any state or power, only a few gained special notoriety for maritime aggression and plunder. Generalizing from the cases of the Ka'b and Bandar Rig in the 1750s and 1760s, these could be described as either tribal groups or coalitions founded on a port, in a condition of rapid expansion or at a critical stage in the defence of their own interests, under the sway of a strong and particularly energetic or ruthless leader.[84]

Shaikh Salman (c. 1737–68)[85] was responsible for the transformation of the hut-dwelling Ka'b tribe, whose affined and adscititious clans inhabited the watery fastnesses on the east of the Shatt al-Arab, from obscure agriculturalists into an amphibious trading power strong enough to block-ade Basra and boastfully lay claim to Bahrain. It was in the nature of things that such an independent newcomer should early on have attracted the hostility of the established states. The Persians were the first to move: their expedition against the Ka'b in 1757 was the immediate stimulus to Shaikh Salman's construction of a navy, which, both as a conscious defensive measure and naturally by virtue of territorial expansion em-bracing existing maritime communities, grew from nothing at this date to comprise ten gallivats, armed vessels larger than the battil, and 70 smaller trading boats in 1765.[86] During these years, the Ka'b had to weather repeated, often concerted, harassment and attacks by the Persians, the Ottomans, and their British allies, in which defence they were by and large successful, though at a cost; in the process, they carried out their own raids and other operations by land, river and sea against these powers, and plundered numbers of their vessels, for which reason they acquired a reputation for piracy.[87] Shaikh Salman gave a land dispute with East India Company representatives as the cause of his well known plunder of three British vessels on the Shatt al-Arab in 1765.[88] After Salman's death, the Ka'b entered a more peaceable phase.

Following hard upon the death of Nadir Shah in 1747, and the collapse of central Persian authority, the neighbouring ports of Rig and Bushire to-gether set out and captured Bahrain. The appearance of easy co-operation was deceptive. No sooner had they achieved their object, than the ruler of Rig denied the other ruler his share in the conquest. As it happened, they were both soon ejected, and the archipelago had to be reconquered in 1752–3 by Bushire with Utbi assistance; but the seal was now set on enmity between Rig and Bushire for the next few decades. Both ports, some 40 miles apart, were governed by Persianized Omani Arab families, and had they been situated on the Arabian shore of the Gulf, they might have preserved for longer the temporary independence they achieved in the chaos of the eighteenth century, a time when power fell more to the political system's constituent parts. The rivalry between them was intense, as each sought to become the chief commercial port of emerging post-Safavid Iran. Bushire had a better harbour and had already been favoured as a base for Nadir Shah's navy. For Rig to have won this contest, would have required a ruler with ample ability in statesmanship and diplomacy, or else a military and naval commander blessed with leadership and luck.

It was Rig's ill fortune to have had the Dutch, for their own reasons, seize her island-dependency of Kharg in 1753. This provoked a revolution in two stages, out of which, after the murder of his father, who had been accommodating towards the Dutch, and next of his elder brother, who had tried to encourage the English Company to establish itself at Rig, Mir

Muhanna emerged undisputed ruler of the port in 1756. One of his first acts was to pull down the English factory-house in order to build a defensive wall for the town:[89] during the next decade, he would have to contend not only with the Dutch, but also, like the Ka'b, with mounting pressure from the newly established Zand regime in southern Persia, which was allied with Bushire, commencing with a demand for tribute and leading eventually to concerted military action designed to crush him.

Mir Muhanna had been so poor in 1754 that he had accepted British charity. The combined pressures of his foes by land and sea, and the commercial stagnation at Rig which resulted, brought out the doggedly martial in him. He fought out by plundering caravans travelling between Bushire and Shiraz and by preying on the sea routes leading to Bushire, as well as raiding and harrying the Dutch on Kharg. By and large, he kept his enemies at bay. These activities gained Mir Muhanna a reputation for piracy. This was reinforced by a personal character, recalling a less devout, less politically adept version of Rahma bin Jabir's. The 'detestable monster'[90] Mir Muhanna—'a young indiscreet man wholly given up to the most destructive vices, and so extremely revengefull that it's dangerous to give him even the slightest occasion of offence'[91]—was supposed to have murdered both parents, a brother, two sisters, his baby daughters and other relatives, and would cut off the noses and ears of his followers when he was drunk or in order to punish them for disobedience. His triumph came in January 1766, when he retook Kharg from the Dutch. This brought him wealth and seemingly unassailable strength. It was in character that he now sought to capitalize on his new position by forcing passing shipping to pay tolls; on which pretext he looted the rich Omani coffee fleet in 1767.[92] But the Persian attacks continued, some with British assistance, and nemesis was at hand. Early in 1769 Mir Muhanna was ousted in an internal coup and, fleeing north, he was arrested and strangled on the orders of the Ottoman authorities, his body being thrown to the dogs. Whilst Bushire was soon assured as Iran's first port, Rig now became a backwater, never to recover.

It is already clear that the practice of the Ka'b on the Shatt al-Arab and Mir Muhanna at Kharg, both of whom forced passing shipping to pay tolls, had a long pedigree in the Gulf. It is also self-evident that in this harsh and competitive environment, with its readily transferable maritime resources, endemic warfare and jostling for position amongst rival groups and states necessitated the use of force.[93] Power and liberty rested in the hands of those who controlled war-boats and the men to man them. Dominant Gulf society partly acquiesced in a tyranny of violent force which allowed the measured despoiling of the weak; those who commanded warriors and the equipment of war used force not only when they had to, but also in some situations when they could. The most extreme example was the woeful plight of the indigenous Shi'ite peasantry of Bahrain, who were unremittingly exploited by their minority Arab tribal conquerors until reforms were introduced in the early twentieth century.[94] Their Shi'ite brethren in mainland Qatif were said in 1756 to share a very similar condition:

> They are ... a defenceless and a timid people. Some of them are pearl divers, while the remainder live from agriculture ... The seafaring Arabs commit many outrages there. Apart from visiting on all occasions the tammer [date] and fruit trees, often one shaikh or another comes with 3 to 4 trankeys to blockade the stream at which Qatif is situated on the basis of some frivolous pretext. There is no other remedy for these poor people than to settle the matter by payment of a few thousand rupees.[95]

This in some degree recalls the Qawasim's 'desultory attacks' upon the 'quiet, unoffensive' villagers of Qishm recorded around 1800,[96] or, in a far more restrained and only partial example of this sort of relationship, one of course where the Arab tribe was not the dominant partner, the uneasy tributary position of the Za'ab and Tanaij tribes under the Ras al-Khaima Qawasim before the Wahhabi revolution of 1808–9.

At a level immediately beneath the proto-state or stable tribal community, the field of maritime action, potentially combined with emigration and the benefits of patronage and alliance, might from time to time tempt the martially inclined ambitious leader and disaffected small tribal group with an added means of improvement; for the very many not so inclined, pearling and trade generally sufficed. Those who pursued this course to its extreme were atypical and few. Their temperament and exclusion from power and responsibility made them amongst the least discriminating in their attacks upon shipping: this, at least, judging from the prime known examples of this socio-political phenomenon in 1797–1820, from the Qasimi arena, the history of the Sudan and the important but shadowy career of Shaikh Salih bin Muhammad al-Qasimi. Poorly integrated or uprooted bands, and self-interested mavericks, operating intermittently near the fringes of their original society, though they do not loom large, constitute a lesser wild card in Gulf maritime history.

The accusation of piracy was naturally more readily levelled at smaller groups, particularly when they injured established states and Europeans, who have bequeathed records of these events. Nomenclature apart, it is clear that from the prevailing Gulf standpoint much of this was far less aberrant than might be supposed. In addition, the readiness to resort to force, to seize opportunities, goods, as they presented themselves, was a feature of social behaviour at a still more fragmented level. Wrecked vessels were habitually plundered by local communities and defenceless boats straying too near unfriendly shorelines ran the risk of capture.[97] This kind of activity was altogether less regular and less specific or exceptional than the foregoing.[98]

Relatively straightforward and self-explanatory acts of abstraction and capture practised against local vessels would similarly have been common, although such incidents seldom featured individually in the sources until later in the nineteenth century, when they became of concern to Britain.[99] Off the Qatif and Qatar coasts in the four months July–October 1878, for example, despite half a century of British efforts which had largely staunched such activity by the settled coastal communities, no less than 15 mostly small vessels were seized or plundered by local bedouin, small bands of enterprising and single-minded raiders without boats of their own, and possibly even little accustomed to the sea.[100] The permutations of these less known episodes of capture were many. A chilling piece of opportunism in 1859 concerned a Dubai boat hired to carry three cash-laden Hasa merchants over the water to Linga. On their first morning at sea, the merchants awoke to the sensation of nooses tightening about their necks; their pleas to the crew unavailing, they were summarily cast into the sea, while the boat sailed away with their belongings: one of the three was against the odds rescued by a passing vessel.[101]

The scale of things and the general lawlessness in the eighteenth century had of course been far greater, and numerous must have been the cases of greater fish devouring smaller. So it was with the British ship *Islamabad* in 1766. Some replacement Arab crew taken on at Basra mutinied when the ship anchored after a storm at Mughu. They murdered the Captain, Sutherland, and his officers, and with gunfire drove off the long-boat which had gone ashore for water, before making off with 400,000 rupees of treasure. The long-boat went for assistance to a small town nearby, but was seized and those in her stripped on the orders of the Shaikh. The mutineers for their part sped with their treasure to a nearby island, only to be fleeced by its Shaikh, who was in turn soon after obliged by the visit of the Shaikh of Hormuz to yield up his prize to this still mightier chief: a British expedition sent to discipline this last in 1767 was aborted when the lead-ship *Defiance* exploded off Qishm with the loss of 300 lives.[102]

Underlying all these different categories of behaviour at sea, from individual acts of opportunism to co-operative ventures by tribal groups and states, tolls on passing shipping, depredations, war, there lay the availability of the use of violence. If individually it was not actively intended, it was at least something to be expected. The recurring signature, and a focus for understanding, was one vessel's assault upon another in quest of plunder, a solitary act gaining applied meaning from its context and which must for a long time have occupied a recognized place in the social psyche.

In the first two decades of the nineteenth century, the Qawasim were in point of form, scale and regularity the leading exponents of this activity. It is by now clear that there were historical-geographical precedents for this. The quotation at the head of this section, though it predates their special notoriety with Britain, would have referred in particular to them; and indeed as far back as 1719 the Portuguese are said to have fallen upon Ras al-Khaima and enslaved the captives they took, in response to attacks upon their shipping.[103] What occurred in the first two decades of the nineteenth century could therefore be represented in part as an exacerbation of an earlier condition: equilibrium, thus moderation, thrown out of kilter by the arrival of Wahhabism.

The events of these years now assume the more dramatic character of a decisive duel between a maritime culture which had long incorporated violence, at this moment spearheaded in this by the Qawasim, and another, championed by the growing might of British India, which for the first time sought to engineer general, liberal trading conditions and outlaw commercially disruptive violence. The new conditions, destined to prevail later in the nineteenth century, were less likely to suit the Arabian Qasimi ports than those of the more free-spirited eighteenth. Belligerence allowed Ras al-Khaima to improve an otherwise commercially naturally disadvantageous position, and without it, it was hard to see that Ras al-Khaima would ever regain her old position. The Qawasim's activity in the first decades of the nineteenth century could thus be envisaged as a dying spasm, their crisis dimly recalling that of Mir Muhanna's Bandar Rig.

It is pertinent at this point to recount some features of a rather striking and involved tale of capture from 1804.[104] At the heart of the story was a minor, uncomplicated, opportunistic seizure by Ajman which, if allowance is made for the involvement of Europeans, helps illustrate some of the behavioural characteristics and attitudes which might customarily have been associated with these undertakings. The train of events commences with an encounter with a European privateer, whose behaviour, in its own way quite as mannered as that of the Arabs, provides an illuminating contrast therewith, something not lost on the English sailors who fell victim to both: here were two groups operating according to discrete social codes.

At daybreak on 14 October 1804, the country-ship *Shrewsbury*, which was lying at anchor in Bushire roads, observed a man-of-war some distance off under British colours. When two boats were suspiciously launched from the cruiser in her direction, the *Shrewsbury*'s treasure was sent ashore as a precaution. The cruiser was in reality the French privateer *La Fortune*,

Captain Le Meme, which in the space of a month had already captured three British vessels in the Gulf, amongst them the *Nancy* and the HCC *Fly*. The *Shrewsbury*'s chief officer, R.W. Loane, with but nine hands aboard, perforce allowed the French to board unopposed. A few hours later both he and other recent British captives were at their own request allowed to disembark at Bushire. This piece of magnanimity on the part of Le Meme earned him Loane's 'lasting gratitude and esteem', particularly since he had 'in the most polite and pleasing manner' let him remove all his personal and nautical effects.[105]

When the *Fly* had fallen to Le Meme off Qais, her captain had ordered the Company's packet to be thrown overboard. It was now jointly proposed by Flower, a passenger on board the *Fly* who had carefully recorded the bearings of the sunken packet, Captain Youl of the *Nancy* and Loane, that they return to the scene and retrieve it. Along with eleven Indian sailors and two European seamen, named Pannell and Simms, they therefore set off from Bushire on 21 October in a newly purchased baghla, equipped with a creeper, bound for Qais. Three days of arduous searching yielded up the packet. They sailed on again towards Muscat.

On 1 November, 11 leagues west of Cape Musandam, the crew became alarmed at seeing two large dows change course and bear down on them:

> Convinced by this that they were part of Joe Hassem's [supposed leader of the *Qawasim*[106]] fleet, we set every stitch of canvas we had, to get from them, but all to no purpose; for to our great mortification, we soon found they came up with us very fast, and were soon near enough for us to perceive that they were both as full of men as they could croud, armed with matchlocks, spears, and creeses.[107]

The English ensign was hoisted, then lowered, as a gesture of surrender, but it was either ill understood or ignored, for,

> to our astonishment, as soon as they came within pistol shot, about 60 of them leaped overboard, swam alongside, and boarded us in all parts of the vessel, when although we exhibited no signs whatever of resistance, these barbarians, ignorant of the laws of nations, and insensible to those of humanity, drew their creeses, and cut away in a most dreadful manner, upon those, who did not immediately jump overboard; which as we did not understand their mode of warfare, we had no idea of, until we found it was the only resource we had, to avoid instant death. But before we could accomplish this, 9 out of our little crew of 16, were severely wounded.[108]

The crew swam to their long-boat, which saved their lives, but they were almost as soon overtaken by their assailants, who by now had taken the British baghla in tow.

> As soon as we were taken on board the commodore's dow, we were stripped stark naked and thrown down in the hold, with the most opprobrious revilings the biggoted spirit of Mahometans could suggest. There we remained for several hours, before they gave us cloathing of any sort, to cover us: at length they threw us a shirt and trowsers, the only articles we could ever recover from them. In this condition we remained for 2 days and nights, with the precarious subsistence we could collect from our persecutors, which was scanty, as the bene-volence which afforded it, continually with the fear of death before our eyes. The natural terrors which our unfortunate situation instilled into our minds, and which appeared but too obvious in our counten-ances, was made a subject of derision with these wretches, who amused themselves continually, in endeavouring to heighten our fears, by bringing creeses and other weapons before us, as if they were about to execute their supposed diabolical purposes, and then laughing hear-tily at our consternation. However, we soon discovered it to be their intentions, to convert us into a more profitable commodity, and to dispose of us as slaves.[109]

The dows now returned with their prize to their home port of Ajman. There the prisoners spent the first night on the open beach.

> As soon as day broke we were surrounded by whole crouds of the inhabitants of every age and sex, and led through the hootings and abuse of this promiscuous throng to a hut about a mile on the desert, which they informed us was to be our lodging for the present: here, after having been compelled for some time to gratify the curiosity of the women and children, who seemed to look upon us all as wild beasts, and more particularly to the European part of our crew, we were left to our own reflections, which it may be supposed were not of the most pleasing sort.[110]

For much of the time the 16 British captives were now left to their own devices. They were supplied only with dates and brackish water, but they soon discovered sweeter wells in the desert and found themselves

> unregarded by the men, but compassionated by the women, who sympathising with our sufferings, frequently supplied us with a little fish, vegetables, or rice; these, with a few cockles, or other shell fish which we picked up along shore, in our rambles about the country, in which we were unmolested, afforded us generally one comfortable meal a day, which was of infinite assistance, as the dates alloted us, bad as they were, were in so small a quantity, they were actually insufficient to support nature.[111]

Three weeks or so after their arrival, Shaikh Abdullah of Ajman, their original captor, informed them they were to be sold as slaves to visiting merchants—'the horrid sensations which this diabolical declaration raised in our breasts is indescribable'[112]—and sure enough first the cook was sold for $30, then, the next day, the Gentoo[113] carpenter was mysteriously spirited away.

At this juncture, fate intervened in the shape of a Wahhabi military chief travelling through Ajman, who chanced to have a passing acquaintance with the Basra Resident Samuel Manesty. He went out of his way to intercede for the British captives, to whom this seemed 'genteel and manly behaviour' of the most welcome and unexpected kind.[114] The result was that after some four weeks of captivity[115] Shaikh Abdullah now declared he was embarking on another predatory cruise, when he would take the opportunity to release the 14 remaining prisoners on Qais island. They embarked on Shaikh Abdullah's dow. En route to Qais, the vessel chased and captured a Basra trading dow twice her size: an exchange of matchlocks proceeded to boarding and a bloody 20-minute struggle before the merchantman would surrender. After this, the 14 men were set down on Qais, barefoot, in rags, with but one bag of dates between them, thankful only to have been released from the clutches of 'a mercenary wretch, from whose avaricious machinations, nothing but a dread of future chastisement could possibly have preserved us.'[116]

This much of the story suffices to convey the flavour of Shaikh Abdullah's predatory excursions in the experience of ordinary British seamen: booty was supposedly sold in the local market. After this, during the ten days they spent on Qais c. 29 November–8 December 1804, much of it in hiding, the liberated crew were to witness larger scale and more organized violence on the part of the Qawasim, as hostility with Charak, which controlled Qais, erupted in war upon the death of Sultan bin Ahmad of Muscat: this was the disruption in which the *Trimmer* and the *Shannon* became so unfortunately entangled. Thus it was that in the first week or so of December a Qasimi fleet sacked first Qais, then Charak, the latter after defeating her Shaikh in a sea-battle.[117] The population of Qais had fled to the mainland at the fleet's first approach, which left the main town at the mercy of the Qawasim:

> About 9 o'clock in the evening, the Arabs having removed every thing of value they could find out of the town, set it on fire, as also the few boats which Sheik Useph [Shaikh Yusuf of Qais] left behind him, hauled up on the beach, which were out of repair, and unfit for their purposes, underwent the same fate. Having thus completed the destruction of the town and boats, they past the best part of the night in dancing and singing, with the most riotous noise and confusion.[118]

The Qawasim remained on Qais for a week, c. 30 November–6 December, and it struck the frightened crew, who in their fugitive ramblings came across a 'numerous quantity of slaughtered bullocks, sheep and goats', that their ravages were extended even to the island's livestock.[119]

The crew's private ordeal was by no means over. After surviving on a diet of wild figs and goat's milk and meat, dressed now in skins, they built a raft from charred timbers and in this and another craft crossed over to the Persian mainland at Kalat. Here they were taken in for a night by a poor, tender-hearted old Persian woman. The next day they began an arduous journey on foot westward, receiving scant assistance from some of the shaikhs along the way until they reached Nakhilu, where they were well received by Shaikh Rahma and given a safe passage to Muscat and Bushire, reaching the latter on 5 January 1805. When at length Loane found himself fit to depart from Bushire for India, he left Pannell seriously ill, while Flower, Simms and Youl—'a young man with a family in Bengal'[120]—had all died of a violent 'fever and ague'.[121] At least one of the nine remaining Indian sailors, a Christian Seacunny, had also died, of sickness and fatigue, in a gruelling, sheer and narrow valley through which they had passed between Kalat and Chiru. Unable to walk any further, he had been placed under the shelter of an overhanging cliff as the rest of the crew hurried on in the moonlight,

> walking, or rather crawling from rock to rock, whilst the continual cries and howlings of the jackalls and other animals, which began as soon as the sun went down, made us tremble for the fate of our unhappy companion, and indeed gave us some apprehension for our own safety, surrounded thus by innumerable beasts of prey: to dispel the anxiety and fear which began to rise in our breasts, and partly to drown their cries by our noise, we began to sing, or rather roar Rule Britannia, which I suppose was never heard before in these deserted and inhospitable regions.[122]

When a search-party was sent back for the Seacunny the next morning, they discovered only a half-eaten corpse.

There were similarities between the uses of force at sea in the Gulf and the place of plunder and violence in bedouin society. Until the early twentieth century, the active life of the camel-herding nomadic tribes of desert Arabia was constantly punctuated by raiding. Raiding and its allied pursuits represented a self-justifying socio-economic imperative, a balanced and partly formulaic tribal reaction to competitive conditions. It relieved the monotony of harsh desert life, and opened up the paths of material and social gain. Moreover, as the theme's pre-eminence in bedouin poetry and story-telling since pre-Islamic times showed, it had long since been incorporated by the society in its culture as the principal field and testing-ground of masculine endeavour.

Bedouin activities involving the use or threat of force for the sake of gain may be classed under two heads: acts directed against bedouin tribes like themselves and those directed at others.[123] Others in this instance would typically have included merchants, travellers and caravans passing through tribal territory, who might be robbed if they did not pay tolls; shepherd tribes, which became clients of the bedouin and paid them tribute; and settled communities upon the desert fringes, which were obliged to pay protection money to preserve themselves from bedouin ravages, the threat of which increased as the civil government and the protection it offered grew weak. All these groups were vulnerable and none possessed the bedouin's offensive capacity, with its overwhelming advantages in camels, horses, general mobility, knowledge of the desert, social cohesion and warlike ethic. In consequence, beyond common morals and the needs of interdependence, there were few restraints upon the bedouin when they sought to supplement the meagre resources of the desert from these groups. The exploitation took the form either of simple pillage, or in most cases resolved itself by the weaker party entering into a formal relationship of *khuwa* with the bedouin tribe: payment to one member of the tribe secured the protection and general assistance of the whole, or as the Rwala bedouin put it, 'He who eats a young goat must protect its mother.'[124] Concomitant with this power imbalance went an attitude of mind. The bedouin regarded these groups to a greater or lesser extent as inferior, and they behaved towards them as of right; difference in lifestyle and the nomad's customary swagger facilitated the required objectification.[125]

The case with inter-tribal conflict amongst the bedouin was different. Here a similar constitution and shared environment, coupled with the threat of blood feud and an expectation of retaliation, engendered mutual respect and a realization that without restraint the tribes would annihilate one another. This was prevented by common adherence to a strict etiquette of inter-tribal conflict, or raiding, which yet allowed adequate expression of a venturesome and competitive spirit: conflict with non-bedouin was by contrast neither ornate nor complex.

The system of inter-tribal raiding can be represented in a paradigm of mounting conflict between two tribes. During the initial stage, that of overt peace, when it was always in order to take possession of stray camels, surreptitious camel-lifting might also occur on a small scale. An accumulation of such minor incidents of friction would put pressure on the Shaikh to declare war formally upon the other tribe. Mutual raiding by small and large mounted parties, the *ghazw*, now ensued. The principal object in all cases was to capture camels, although horses, weapons and tent furniture would also be seized where possible, particularly in the larger raids. Prisoners were not captured and bloodshed was kept to a minimum, ingenuity and surprise being of the essence; even in defence, flight was quite honourably preferred to an unequal stand. Finally, the tribe might often move *en masse* into the territory of its enemy, motivated by claims over grazing land and water or to further its reputation (*zaud al-i'tibar*[126]), there to join a full-scale set-piece battle. This highly stylized affair sometimes began with individual combat between champions and employed a code of chivalry which safeguarded the weak, including the wounded and those who surrendered. Women were absolutely inviolable: their honour, estimation and allure were stimulus to the martial spirit such that, amongst the Rwala, beautiful girls went forward with the ranks into battle, mounted on she-camels, bare-headed and -breasted, to goad the fighters on. When at length the two warring tribes tired of conflict, their Shaikhs made peace once more.

The practical issue of inter-tribal raiding was a constant circulation of camels between the bedouin tribes, what Doughty called 'an ill exchange of cattle.'[127] Individually it offered the chance of betterment, and the successful raider might have hoped to win the heart and hand of his desiring and become a commander and even a shaikh. Plunder was ever the goal— 'He tires his mount who rides in quest of fame, Who journeys far the fairest plunder catches'[128]—but it was not simply an end in itself: in respect of the Rwala bedouin it was said,

> Without war a Rwejli could not live. War gives him an opportunity of displaying his cunning, endurance, and courage. He neither loves the shedding of blood, nor craves booty, but is allured by danger and delights in the predatory art. The booty itself he will give away without thinking much about it—even to the wife of the very man he has just robbed.[129]

Inter-tribal raiding was an honourable pursuit, elevated by and central to the culture; the thrill of it coursed through much of bedouin poetry: 'Like thieves in a dark night, like attackers after the passing of the dew, We are wont to plant ulcers in the enemy's stomach. Hey! glory!'[130]

Less honourable, but still, if the early nineteenth-century traveller Burckhardt is to be credited, an acknowledged feature of bedouin life was another form of inter-tribal raiding, committed by small irregular bands on foot.[131] This was closer to straight theft and was seemingly described as such in Arabic. If captured, the tribal robber (*harami*) was treated with far less respect than the mounted raider, being tied up and kept in a shallow pit until ransomed. This inter-tribal theft was governed still by its own more limited social conventions; but these did not signify a glorification of the pursuit of plunder, as was the case with mounted raiding, but rather a muted and disapproving acceptance of the realities inherent in a shared environment of all-pervasive want. Theft within the tribe was yet another matter; this was treated as a disgrace and a simple misdemeanour. Thus the bedouin reaction to an act of plunder could be said to have ranged widely between complex idealization and embarrassed condemnation, depending on manner and conditions, and the affiliation of the victim.

The parallels between the bedouin's use or threat of force against non-bedouin and many of the maritime activities of the Qawasim and other Gulf powers are self-apparent; suffice it to recall tolls taken from passing shipping, tribute from subordinate tribes like the Za'ab and Tanaij and protection money from communities such as the Qatif Shi'a, or ravages committed against villagers in Qishm and Qais and depredations in far-flung Indian waters. These similarities were partly the self-generated product of the two environments, but mostly the consequence of comparable societies and sets of social attitudes. This relatedness would not have been lost on those involved, for there was true overlap between the desert and the sea and their respective peoples. Inhabitants of the Gulf quite often traced their ancestry to the desert, and there was frequent contact and continuous movement of population between the two areas. Some amongst the bedouin practised not only pearling, but also occasionally maritime raiding. Ajman bedouin were, as noted, alleged to have served on Qasimi cruisers; but the most striking and detailed evidence derives from the late nineteenth century and relates to Qatar and Hasa.[132] Numerous examples were recorded then of small bands of bedouin plundering small boats inshore or commandeering them in order to commit further minor depredations, before swiftly disappearing again inland beyond the reach of the law. Casualties, occasionally fatal, were sometimes inflicted in the process and one or two prisoners were not infrequently carried off, along with the booty, as slaves. In one case from 1878, a group of bedouin innocently engaged a passage on a Ras al-Khaima baqqara, but once aboard ordered the hapless captain to rendezvous with their 17 accomplices, before setting out across the Gulf to capture a second vessel near Qais. Other operations were less subtle: in 1891, 'about 14 men supposed to belong to the Banu Hajir tribe boarded a shu'i lying in the port of Saihat. They killed one of the crew and threw the rest into the sea.'[133] Most of this was pure adventure, the same strain evident in the career of the Shaikh of Ajman in 1804.

The search for useful similarities between inter-tribal bedouin raiding and regular maritime conflict between Gulf powers and states is barren, except for generalities such as feuding, to a limited extent, and the way both systems employed plunder in the way of war and were transformed by Wahhabism. Far more striking were the profound differences.[134] There was not the differentiation of lifestyles in the Gulf to produce the cohesion and aloofness of desert society, and there is no evidence there of elaborate rules governing maritime conflict.[135] Sea-power did not, with significant exceptions, belong to uniform tribes, or even necessarily Arabs, but was the attribute of mixed ports and groupings, proto-states. The most appropriate explanation of conflict between these was overwhelmingly a socio-economic and political one. It hardly also need be observed that sea-fights were potentially very bloody affairs and large vessels implied concepts of use, ownership and manning alien to another environment. These were, then, two distinct worlds, each of which should be judged on its own terms, the one conventional and introspective, the other founded on interest. For all that, there was still one important locus where the two arenas met, through a shared culture, in the mind: it is not entirely inappropriate to imagine that as a Qasimi war-vessel set out upon a cruise, some of the same thoughts and feelings went through the minds of those on board as did so with their counterparts in the desert ghazw.

After all that has been intimated, little remains to be gleaned from the Qawasim's surviving letters and statements, limited as they are and almost all of them addressed to Britain, as to their own perception of their maritime activities. The Arabic language material in particular is not rich or necessarily representative. Hasan bin Rahma's usual descriptive term for a simple attack by one vessel upon another was the unexceptional ta'arrada, 'assault', equally applicable to people and communities;[136] Shaikh Muhammad bin Qadib of Linga, in a slightly disapproving context, preferred another, marginally more violent, such verb, sharra'a.[137] The general word for capturing a vessel (khashab, or if European-style, markab) or its contents, was the straightforward and colourless akhadha, 'take';[138] hence Shaikh Abdullah bin Ahmad of Bahrain's apt and expressive description of persistent maritime conflict between two Gulf states as a condition of 'al-akhdh wal-qatl', 'taking and killing'.[139] The technical Islamic term for lawful booty, one-fifth of which was sent to the Saudi treasury, would of course have been ghanima; whilst the everyday, and if anything pejorative, verb for 'to plunder' was the standard Arabic nahaba.[140] A similar feeling for the vocabulary of plunder was, it seems, shared by the bedouin, who commonly indicated it with nouns like kasb and faud and the above verb akhadha.[141] Those, finally, who condemned maritime assault and plunder outright might have described them in terms such as 'sadd tariq al-ibad'[142] or, in a later and more literary hand, 'fasad al-bahr bil-nahb wal-qatl',[143] both of which phrases convey similar notions to the English word piracy.

Moral standards are hard to ascertain. Having in 1878 observed from the top of his fort as his son plundered a small merchant vessel, the Shaikh of

Zubara afterwards reportedly rebuked him for not having slaughtered all on board and burnt the boat to remove the evidence.[144] This comment could be put down to a sardonic humour and the circumstances of the time, when subterfuge recommended itself, but in its implicit attitude to life it recalls an allegation made against the Qawasim and other Gulf Arabs early in the century, that they gratuitously slew captives. The Basra Resident, Gideon Colquhoun, suggested before the second expedition that rather than vainly seek to eradicate maritime conflict and piracy in their entirety, the British would better confine their efforts to halting 'that system of cool-blooded butchery' which made feuds and therefore disruption un-remitting:[145] if nothing else, this is an intriguing commentary on the natural consequences of translating the blood feud from its original environment into the inevitably far more bloody seat of maritime conflict. One Marine officer thought article seven of the General Treaty, which had outlawed the killing of those who surrendered, laudable, but unenforcible and mis-conceived since it failed to take account of standard practice amongst different nations in the region.[146]

The precise factual basis for these accusations is uncertain, although much has been said throughout this work concerning the circumstances associated with violence. Maritime fighting certainly produced heavy casu-alties and feuding did play a part in inter-state conflict. Accounts such as that of Captain Cumming who witnessed the Qawasim slaying their op-ponents in the water, 'begging for mercy', during a sea-battle with Charak, are too few to make anything of.[147] All that can be positively stated on this theme must therefore derive essentially from detailed accounts of captures outside the context of inter-state conflict, where different rules may have applied. During the frenzy of boarding it was not uncommon for all those within reach, on deck or even clinging to the side, those who did not swim or hide, to be attacked or killed.[148] Resistance invited viol-ence—there were occasional hints of retribution[149]—but in a few cases, notably that of the *Ahmadi*, its absence was no guarantee of life or limb. Once possession was assured, the violence ceased. Prisoners of all races, male and female, were regularly taken as slaves; women were sometimes wounded or killed during an attack,[150] presumably unintentionally, but were otherwise, one assumes, treated with respect. It is unlikely that the Qawasim behaved significantly differently in all this than their fellows: Rahma bin Jabir's reputation, in particular, was if anything more bloody and stony-hearted.

The Qawasim's moral and social code must naturally have embraced maritime war and plunder with all that entailed. Hasan bin Rahma's letters convey a strong sense of moral rectitude. It was a matter of honour for him to have upheld the treaty and friendship with Britain. Whereas his people had come up with vulnerable British vessels and some which had transgressed the etiquette of the sea, which circumstances would normally have invited capture, they had let them off.[151] Public ethics at Wahhabi Ras al-Khaima left a favourable impression upon Captain Thompson, Christian evangelizing commander of the British garrison at Ras al-Khaima in 1820:

> On the subject of the moral character of the Qawasim, it may be confidently urged, with the single exception of their addiction to piracy and attendant cruelty to prisoners, it is good. It may not be useless to mention, that among the hundreds of all ranks who have had access to my tent, where many articles very valuable in their opinion were within their reach, not a solitary instance of theft has been attempted. A few starving wretches are said to have picked up articles from tents which were removed; which forms but a feeble contrast with the violences which our own military discipline has been called on to repress. With respect to their public faith, you know well, that I have been unarmed with their chief, among hundreds of their armed followers; without conceiving myself in the slightest personal danger, or receiving any of these injuries and insults which it has sometimes been my misfortune to witness among individuals calling themselves civilised.[152]

For all the fundamentalist fervour of Wahhabism, it is indicative of the prevailing liberality of spirit at Ras al-Khaima that her population, encamped nearby, raised no objection to Thompson's conversion of their mosque into a chapel for his troops; this, on the basis that it had, after all, been built for prayer.[153]

The Qawasim engaged in maritime warfare and plunder not only, in their view, as of right, but also because it was expected of them. This was true both for the state as a whole and for the individual. The pressures upon Ras al-Khaima to uphold her name in the region were explained by a Qasimi negotiator in 1814, when he told the Bushire Resident that he hoped the British

> would not insist on their leaving off cruising against those states who were at enmity with them, as according to the law of nations amongst the Arabs [blood] could only be repaid by blood; that if they were not to follow this kind of warfare they would [lose] their rank amongst the Arab states; and not only that, but that those tribes who were at enmity with them would come to their very houses to attack them; besides this, they were compelled by the Wahhabi chief to wage war against the Mahomedan states of the Gulph to bring them under the yoke and religion of the Wahhabi, and only to respect the British flag and subjects.[154]

A sense of the social pressures upon the individual to maintain his honour is conveyed by the following, a unique unmediated letter from one member of the Ras al-Khaima Qasimi family to another directly concerned with maritime warfare. It was written in late 1808 against the background of heavy fighting with Muscat under the Wahhabi aegis. The author requests assistance in recovering a sum of money from one Salman bin Rahma, with which to enable him to buy a boat and join in the fray, with a view to throwing off the disgrace of inactivity:

> I have, further, to inform you, that several of our people have been killed, and that we have no dow with which we can commit depredations. The Qawasim have several of a large size, and we do not go out in company with them, because Salman sold the dows from us, which render[s] it improper in you. Should an order be issued to me, I should remain and look on. Nothing is to be expected from Salman, nor does he exert himself for those of his tribe, who have fallen. You must authorise me to interfere in respect to the money, and write a letter desiring me to receive charge, immediately, of the amount in the possession of Salman, and to purchase a dow therewith, and to prosecute hostilities with her, in the same manner as the Qawasim, for we ought not to be inferior to the rest, in as much as mankind despise us. Any letter that you may wish to send to me forward to Zubair, the son of Ibrahim bin Zubair at Surat, by whom it will be remitted to Ras al-Khaima, and desire him to keep it secret: you will, of course, send me an answer quickly, for we are in disgrace, and have lost all esteem in the opinion of the inhabitants of Ras al-Khaima and other tribes. No-one attends to us, and what may, thus, be proper in Salman, would be unworthy of you: that is to say, to submit to degradation, our advice disregarded, and we remain destitute of repute among mankind—your discernment is sufficient.[155]

This concludes the discussion of the sociology of maritime warfare and plunder. Setting aside important related matters such as tolls and tribute, which are not central to the events of 1797–1820, Qasimi activities in these years may be seen to fall into three categories: the ubiquitous opportunistic single act of plunder; inter-state conflict by sea; and the particular upsurge of maritime plunder associated with Wahhabism, which built upon these two classes of activity and was largely responsible for Ras al-Khaima's reputation. Socio-economic and political factors lay behind all the three categories of violence, but the special signature of each, respectively, was social culture, politics and religion.

This section began with an historical overview, showing that the use of maritime force had a long and broad pedigree in the Gulf and that, in its higher manifestations, it had passed through various dominant phases: the

Qawasim were obliged to recognize this in 1819/20. An examination of the constitution of two minor Gulf powers in the later eighteenth century revealed some of the conditions conducive to a heightened use of maritime force: this elicited loose resonances with Ras al-Khaima, where the necessary leadership was supplied from Dir'iya, and also with Rahma bin Jabir. Underlying this range of behaviour was a set of attitudes governing the use of force by its possessor. One of the most important constituents of the whole was the single, simple predatory act: some of the raw processes associated with this were uncovered in relation to the Shaikh of Ajman in 1804. The discussion then passed from this reductionism to a consideration of the place of plunder in bedouin society. This revealed obvious parallels between the use of force and the pursuit of plunder in the desert and the Gulf, but the most important points to arise concerned substantial social contact between the two societies and the cultural potency of the bedouin's glorification of plunder. Lastly it was noted that in the context of their society, had it not been for the great distortions introduced by the Wahhabis, there might have been little extraordinary about Ras al-Khaima's maritime activities in the years 1797–1820; and even so, it should be recognized that the Qawasim adhered to a strict ethical code and genuinely felt both entitled and required to act as they did. In this, as in so much else, even if the determinants are hard to ascertain and define, the response to even the most palpable and rational of causes was socially and culturally defined.

Conclusion

The Gulf today is worlds removed from that of the early nineteenth century. Where once, off Cape Musandam, Indian sailors would pause for the sake of a propitious voyage to cast flowers, coconuts and fruit, or launch a model boat, upon the waters, chasmous oil tankers and cargo ships now process blithely and serenely back and forth.[1] Pearling died between the world wars, and since the 1960s, in particular, oil has swept away much that remained of the old ways of life, replacing centuries of hardship and struggle with a bounty equally extreme. Lack of development and a small population before the boom have magnified and accelerated society's transformation along the Arabian littoral under a massive influx of wealth, economic activity and manpower. The centuries-old ocean-going dow trade of the Gulf ports disappeared in a single generation. At Kuwait, where in 1939 106 large ocean-going dows were based, there were none by the 1970s: in Oman, the port of Sur's 86 cargo dows in 1970 had been reduced by 1977 to a single *sambuk*.[2] The large sailing-craft which dominated the scene in the early nineteenth century, the dow proper of course, but also the battil and the baghla, had been almost completely supplanted in the Gulf by diesel and the *bum* before the Second World War. Kuwait's last surviving ocean-going bum, national symbol of the source of her existence, was destroyed during the Iraqi occupation of 1990–1. The old designs are occasionally rebuilt as luxury yachts or restaurants, but these are inevitably somewhat hollow reminders of a past that is still too close, perhaps, yet distinctly remote. Meanwhile the only tangible remains of many of the old craft are the parched bones of wrecks which lie scattered here and there, unregarded, along the coast.

Centre-stage in this composition, one performed against a backdrop of great historical movements, has been occupied by the maritime history of a community quite small in strength, and smaller still in numbers, which, but for the individual acts which punctuate the narrative, might have gone generally unnoticed. There is nothing trivial in the example of past lives. If nothing else, it is hoped that this work may have recaptured some of the

271

spirit of time and place; salvaging from the records, where such matters might have been expected to continue their repose, the documents having long since served their limited official function, glimpses of a handful of the many nameless private dramas that contributed to the patchwork of this history; revitalizing a few fleeting moments of elation, terror and despair, and some honourable and shameful acts, and the thoughts and feelings which accompanied them. A bedouin poet spoke thus of tribal history:

> History is something like a trust; it enters into one's covenant. A man who relates history must fear God and not tip the balance one way or the other ...
>
> Narratives are long and wide and raids are many and life, so the saying goes, comes your way one day and the next it goes against you. Truly, every tribe has its share of virtue.
>
> Old stories are amusing. They relate true and noble deeds, and there is nothing in them which is disparaging to anyone, not in the least.
>
> Even though we did not live in those old times, we have met and come in contact with men from Anaza and from Shammar who in turn knew men older than themselves.
>
> So, men memorise old stories. They hand them down to each other, pass them on from one to the other, the father bequeathing them to his son.[3]

For the Qasimi ports, the importance of the British expedition of 1819/20 was that it ended the experiment of Wahhabi Ras al-Khaima. Thereafter the two main themes in the internal history of what was soon designated Trucial Oman were Sultan bin Saqr of Sharja and Ras al-Khaima's efforts to recover and exercise dominance over the northern sector, and his burgeoning rivalry with the Banu Yas of Abu Dhabi who were pre-eminent in the south. As time went by it became apparent that the individual signatories of the General Treaty were not to forego their independence and that the relative fortunes of the Banu Yas, whose main strength lay not on the high seas but in the interior, were on the ascendant. Soon after the death of Sultan bin Saqr in 1866, at the legendary age of 115, more probably c. 81–6, having suffered from paralysis of the loins since his marriage to a girl of 15 the year before,[4] Ras al-Khaima formally declared her independence from the now more important Sharja. The dissolution affecting the Qawasim proceeded further still when in 1887 their cousin, the ruler of Linga, with whom they had maintained close links, was carried in chains to Tehran and replaced as Governor by a Persian appointee: the Qasimi family of Linga was henceforth obliged to live in exile on the

Arabian coast. A parallel decline affected Ras al-Khaima's arch rival in the later eighteenth and early nineteenth centuries, Muscat: on the death of Sultan bin Saqr's contemporary Sa'id bin Sultan in 1856, his realm was divided into two and Zanzibar, source of much of his wealth, became a separate Sultanate; just over a decade later, Muscat's waning was compounded by Iran's revocation of the 70-year old lease to her of Bandar Abbas, part of a wider process of consolidation of Persian rule along her Gulf littoral, often at the expense of formerly semi-independent Arab shaikhs such as those of Bushire and Linga. By the end of the nineteenth century, then, the status of the Qawasim, and of Muscat, was much reduced from what it had been a century before.

The 1819/20 expedition and its outcome in the General Treaty were symbolic of the end of an era of political turmoil and maritime disruption which had so characterized the eighteenth century. With the consolidation of authority by British India at sea and Persia on land, the independence and collective maritime freedoms of the smaller Gulf states would continue to decline, and a more stable structure would emerge. No longer could a powerful leader dream of creating a maritime empire in the Gulf, as Sultan bin Ahmad of Muscat had attempted and, in other conditions, in the lower Gulf, the Qawasim might have done. The range of political possibilities involving sea-power was ever less than it had been. The last of the free-spirited, questing maritime warrior-leaders was the redoubtable Rahma bin Jabir, whose death in 1826 fulfilled the promise of his life: in the course of a fierce duel with an Al Khalifa baghla, he perceived that he would be overwhelmed, whereupon, legend has it,

> Hastily demanding of his crew, whether they would not perish by the annihilation of their foes, and being answered by their war-cry in defiance, he rushed below, attached a match to his powder-barrel, returned on deck, and sprang upon the poop with his only son in his arms. The match ignited, and the vessels still firmly grappling, burst together into a thousand atoms, and were hurled through the air in the midst of a volcano of smoke and flames.[5]

Commerce and industry were the new gods, even if they lacked some of the glamour of past exploits. The ideas forcibly introduced by Britain in the General Treaty took root. Before the conclusion in 1835 of the first of a series of British-mediated maritime truces between the Shaikhs of Trucial Oman, representing an advance on the General Treaty which had not been concerned with legitimate war, Sharja pearl merchants had themselves volunteered to pay Britain to defend their vessels. Two years on, when Sultan bin Saqr proposed that the truces prohibiting fighting at sea during the pearling season, and at any time north of a line parallel and close to the Arabian shore, be made permanent, it was the British who demurred.[6] Although after the 1820s minor incidents of capture and looting, and occasional outbreaks of fighting, recurred throughout the century in the Gulf, large-scale plunder and persistent warfare were very much a thing of the past. In 1853 the successive maritime truces between the 'Trucial' Shaikhs were replaced unopposed by a Perpetual Treaty of Maritime Peace, of which Britain was the guarantor; and it is a small, but telling fact that hereafter British official documents tended to refer to infractions not as piracies, but as 'maritime irregularities'.[7]

One of the greatest changes in the wake of the 1819/20 expedition was the transformation of the British presence in the Gulf. In the immediate aftermath, buoyed up by new-won confidence and pride, it almost seemed that Britain was about to adopt an interventionist policy in the Gulf. Before this, news that a minor maritime tribe in eastern Oman, the Banu Bu Ali of Ashkhira, had recently plundered a small number of vessels, none of them British, would have drawn no response. In 1820, however, seduced by Muscat's preparation of an expedition to discipline this other-wise refractory tribe and incensed by the violent rebuff of a British message of protest at the seizures,[8] the hasty reaction of Captain Thompson, of the Qishm garrison, was to lead six companies of sepoys alongside the Muscat force against the tribe, and against all regular precepts. The combined force was spectacularly routed a week later, on 9 November 1820, by the poorly armed and greatly outnumbered Banu Bu Ali: Thompson lost three-quarters of his 400 or so men and was subsequently court-martialled. Bombay lost no time in sending a large force to retrieve the lost prestige; but the whole episode of foolhardy and unauthorized involvement in the interior proved a salutary lesson. For the rest of the century, British India adhered rigidly to a policy of eschewing all military and most onerous political involvement in the internal affairs of Gulf Arab states:[9] policy was founded on the general maintenance of British political influence, and the naval policing and diplomatic encouragement of acceptable and orderly maritime conditions.

British ascendancy in the Gulf, which in one form or another lasted until 1971, reaching its deepest and most involved in the first half of the twentieth century, is generally traced back to 1820. In its genesis, it was more than anything else the natural consequence of rapid expansion in India, yet it would not have taken the form it did but for the saga of Ras al-Khaima. From the 1820s, efforts were made to remedy the deficiencies in knowledge of the politics and geography of the Arabian coastline exposed during preceding decades. Marine surveying was stepped up, a British Agent was stationed at Sharja, and the Bushire Resident, with responsibility for the affairs of the Arabian coast, instituted an annual tour of the Gulf which involved visiting, making presents to and cultivating relations with the shaikhdoms.

The role of the Persian Gulf Resident quickly developed into something far removed from what it had been in the eighteenth century and even up to 1820. The Company's own trade in the Gulf was a thing of the past and Company employees were now prohibited from trading on their own behalf: their generalized consular and commercial concerns lay henceforth solely with the merchants and trade of British India. But the greatest change lay in the soon much enhanced diplomatic function and political prestige of the Resident throughout the Gulf as the representative of British India. He retained a wide degree of practical autonomy, but the importance of his position, even before the revolution in communications of the 1860s in the fields of post and telegraph—this on top of steam, which first reached the Gulf in 1838[10]—meant that public servants of a different stature and persuasion were required from the rather isolated individualists who often typified the scene before 1820. The days when the Basra Residency could be run as almost the private fiefdom of a self-important, cantankerous, tragically human, businessman and patriot like Samuel Manesty, or be left in the charge of the languid Dr Gideon Colquhoun, tormented by blinding headaches and the nocturnal caterwauling of neighbourhood cats, were over. The dismissal of the Bushire Resident William Bruce in 1822, for concluding an unauthorized agreement recognizing Persian sovereignty over Bahrain, was in its own way as much a watershed as the Banu Bu Ali debacle, or the immolation of Rahma bin Jabir.

The events of 1797–1820, the maritime activity associated with Ras al-Khaima and the two expeditions, left an indelible mark upon the British consciousness and perception of the Gulf. This was partly a matter of timing: the episode was a journey of discovery out of the dark, disorderly and foreign, archaic world of the eighteenth century, and constituted the formative first experience in a continuum which stretched well into the twentieth century. Moreover, the British were left by their experiences with the abiding impression that were it not for them the Gulf might revert to a natural condition of anarchy; hence Lord Curzon's argument to the Trucial Shaikhs in 1903, that Ras al-Khaima vindicated the British involvement in the Gulf which it had caused and shaped.[11]

Yet as much as anything, it was the power of this saga to stir the imagination, as piracy still does, which ensured it would not be forgotten. Contemporary newspapers, travellers, officers and others all felt moved to write about the Qawasim and British measures taken against them. In 1868 an article appeared in the *United Service Magazine* purporting to recount the life story of one Thomas Horton, a renegade who became pirate-king of Qishm in the first decades of the century.[12] The tale was a picaresque and romantic hoax, but in an extreme fashion it shows the ease with which the rich colours from this palette could be combined and recombined over time; the core of reality, even to the extent that it was ever truly known or understood, was very quickly hidden beneath a superstructure of perceptions. As history becomes remote it makes easier prey for legend and polemic. Lorimer, shortly before the Great War, was perhaps the last to write about these events as living history with a soul. Two of the most recent books on this subject have been written by men who served in the Gulf, one of them Charles Belgrave, important Adviser to the ruler of Bahrain from 1926 to 1957: his book is entitled simply *The Pirate Coast*, former popular name for what was successively Trucial Oman, the Trucial States and is now the United Arab Emirates.

The reaction of the Trucial Shaikhs to Lord Curzon's extraordinary, self-congratulatory speech must be imagined. The events of 1797–1820, the experiment of Wahhabi Ras al-Khaima and the British expeditions, bequeathed a different stock of memories and guiding attitudes to subsequent generations on the Trucial Coast. Stories of these times, tinged with pride and possibly nostalgia, were seemingly vibrant in the 1830s.[13] How attitudes developed later in the century, when the idea of resisting British naval-might grew inconceivable and Britain intervened in other areas of life, one can only speculate. The late twentieth century has quite rightly and understandably seen its own form of revisionism.

But what finally of the question which originally sparked off this investigation—were the Qawasim pirates? The simplest answer, if insisted upon, would have to be no, but some of what they did was piracy; but, if nothing else, it is hoped that this work will in the end have demonstrated that this is not one of the appropriate questions to ask.

The Motivation behind Britain's Two Expeditions Against Ras al-Khaima in 1809/10 and 1819/20

The causes of the East India Company's two expeditions against the Qawasim cannot so usefully be confined to the stark, material facts of the Qawasim's supposed piracy, undoubted *sine qua non* for these operations though they were: the way an issue or event is perceived can often be of greater consequence than the event itself. What follows is an attempt to sketch in some of the elements, both tangible and less concrete, which helped to shape the important, and often emotionally charged, undertakings of these years.[1]

i The Economic Background

The crime of which the Qawasim stood accused in British eyes, namely the unlawful and forcible seizure at sea of vessels or their contents, including, at times, the enslavement of those on board, was, despite the intermittent loss of life and other circumstances, essentially an economic crime. It was directed not simply at property, but, more specifically, at the very heart of international trade within the region, the marine carriers and their merchandise. It has been argued, without any supporting evidence, that the underlying cause of the two expeditions against Ras al-Khaima was the East India Company's covert desire to destroy the power of the Qawasim as rival carriers for the Gulf trade.[2] It is obviously essential to consider seriously some of the economic factors that had a bearing on the events of these years.

(A) THE EAST INDIA COMPANY'S TRADE

In the late seventeenth century the Company showed some concern for promoting its shipping activities in the region: in 1682 it experimented with a 'round voyage' direct from England to Surat via the Gulf, and soon thereafter considered means of winning over some of the Persian carrying trade, said to be so lucrative to the Dutch.[3] Such enthusiasm, however, is not to be found in the period c. 1790–1820. It is true that a trade report for 1790[4] tentatively alludes to possible advantage in the Company's participating in the India–Gulf freight trade. But the only serious, though still somewhat underemphatic, recommendation in this and another report of 1800[5] concerns the better use of the Company cruisers which visited Basra with increased frequency in the years after 1790: the suggestion was that the Company could save on freight by shipping its remittances in treasure and bulk goods back to Bombay on these vessels, and, according to the report of 1800, perhaps even a part or all of its woollens to the Gulf.

By the end of the eighteenth century any vestigial desire on the part of the Company to participate in the Gulf's carrying trade had probably vanished. It therefore requires no explanation that the dozen-or-so Company vessels reportedly exposed to Qasimi aggression were all members of the Bombay Marine, the Company's naval arm.[6] These cruisers frequented the region either to convey the packet or to protect others from French privateers, or local 'pirates', by means of cruising or convoy. It might seem reasonable to suppose that Company merchandise itself, especially the bulk variety, was now for the most part conveyed on country-vessels under British colours, whether they belonged to Europeans or to others, as was the case with the *Ahmed Shah*, wrecked in 1814.[7] Nevertheless, in relation to the question of general attitudes, it is interesting to note that a committee report for 1797 recommended, in case of need, the use of Arab over European shipping for the transmission of the packet between Bombay and Basra, a decision based on questions of economy.[8]

The Company's only real, though tangential, interest in Gulf shipping during these years has been alluded to above: a few years before the second expedition the traveller Buckingham observed that the merchants of Muscat had recently been in the habit of shipping their treasure to India in Company and naval vessels, a practice that tended to reconcile their commanders 'to all the other inconveniences of being stationed in the Persian Gulf.'[9] This procedure, occasioned, it is said, by fear of Qasimi aggression, can hardly have been very regular, although it may have been repeated off the Kathiawar coast, for similar reasons, in 1818/19.[10] Similarly, the collection of consulage and Company's duties at Bushire, credited to the Company and part-retained by its local representatives, cannot be considered an interest in shipping *per se*: the report from 1790 once again makes it clear these charges formed a levy not on British shipping but on British-subject merchants.[11]

The Company still traded to the Gulf during the period 1790–1820, and the general fortunes of this commerce, based as it was on the export of English woollens such as broad cloth and perpets, together with iron, steel, lead and tin,[12] seem well established. The Company's average annual export of woollens to the Gulf in 1753–62 was 868 bales and this rose as high as 1,407 bales per annum in 1763–7 when it formed a significant proportion of its sales in the East.[13] During the period 1780/1–1789/90, however, the yearly average had sunk to a mere 206 bales[14] and in the 1790s there even appear to have been years when the Company exported no cloth at all to the Gulf.[15] There are perhaps suggestions of a slight upturn in trade with Persia, at least, at the turn of the century,[16] but the overall trend persisted. In 1816/17 small quantities of the Company's staples were still being sent to Bushire and Basra,[17] but within a short time, possibly c. 1819, the Company had ceased altogether to trade in the Gulf.[18]

The commercial reports of 1788–90 and 1799–1801,[19] the instructions issued to Mehdi Ali Khan as Resident at Bushire in 1798,[20] and Malcolm's commercial treaty of 1801,[21] are evidence of the Company's desire to reverse this decline. But by the turn of the century it had probably been accepted by most that the Company could not hope to compete with the private merchant or seriously attempt to diversify.[22] Underlying this was the virtually unbroken unprofitability of Company trade in the Gulf in these decades, combined, perhaps, with a certain failure in the requisite commercial and political will. It is quite probable that there was no serious attempt or even, perhaps, concern to boost the Company's Gulf trade in the first two decades of the nineteenth century, and Buckingham remarked that this trade was only continued at all in order to satisfy the Company's charter requiring the proportionate export of English goods.[23]

One particular factor in the unprofitability of the Company's Gulf trade has a certain bearing on the subject of piracy. The whole structure of British trade in the Gulf was founded upon an abiding conception of the region: it was believed that foreign traders could not hope to do business in the area without protection from insecurity, be it piracy at sea or extortion on land, together with assistance in coping with the delicate and involved politics of local society.[24] In consequence, the Company, which provided these services increasingly for those under its protection rather than simply itself, assuming thereby a rather more paternal role, was burdened with huge costs. A report for c. 1790 records that the average sale of woollens at Bushire and Basra equalled £7,655, but this had to be offset against a total average annual expenditure and loss of £9,555: this latter sum comprised sheer commercial loss (13 per cent), factory expenses (59 per cent) and the cost on the two factories of the Company's cruisers and the transmission of the packet (28 per cent). This figure apparently ignores the basic cost of building, manning and maintaining the cruisers, which was borne by Bombay.[25]

But now, Sir, a Country Captain is not to be known from an ordinary man, or a Christian, by any certain mark whatever.[26]

To accept that the Company had no significant corporate interest or ambition regarding the commerce or freight-trade of the Gulf is, of course, very far from saying that it had no interest of any kind in the matter. As ruler of parts of India it had an obvious interest in fostering the trade between its territories and the Gulf in the hope of greater internal prosperity and increased revenues, while at the same time, though the subject is less straightforward, it could not wholly ignore the interests of the private merchant subject to its government or in receipt of its protection.[27] The following brief examination of Gulf trade in these years naturally reflects what contemporary British observers felt to be the case and it would be wrong to place absolute reliance on their information, particularly since accurate statistics were almost wholly lacking at the time.[28]

Of the three principal ports of the Gulf in 1790, only the entrepôt port of Muscat, whose merchants were able to deal in ready cash and derived great wealth from the coffee and sugar trades, seemed to Manesty and Jones to be flourishing.[29] Basra's international trade had received a heavy blow in the plague of 1772–3 and this had subsequently been compounded by other economic and political factors. Bushire, whose prosperity likewise principally depended on the internal condition of the country despite its large measure of effective political independence, was also languishing, most of all, it was felt, on account of the disturbances in Iran in 1779–94. Local merchants almost certainly had a very firm grip on trade at each of the three ports and it may well be that their commerce had weathered the recent storms rather better than that of others such as the British.

The fortunes of private British and Indian trade in the then recent decades are less easy to establish and the picture is perhaps most complete with regard to the trade between India and Basra. In 1763–73 it is asserted that an average of 3,000–3,500 bales of Indian piece-goods were annually brought to Basra in 10–12 vessels belonging to British subjects and to the Muslim merchants of Surat.[30] The cloth belonged to merchants of Bengal, Masulipatnam, Madras and Surat. It is also implied that in general, though the Company's trade flagged, that of private British traders was relatively sizable and profitable in the northern Gulf during much, though not all, of the 1760s and 1770s.[31] During the next decade, 1780–90, however, it is stated that 'British individuals resident in India' almost completely abandoned the Gulf trade, this commerce consequently largely falling into the hands of Armenian and Muslim merchants resident in British India.[32] These two latter were apparently for the most part also owners of the vessels in which they shipped their goods, although these had British captains and officers, and naturally went under British colours. In 1787 it is estimated that imports on vessels under British colours at Bushire and Basra amounted to nearly 2 million rupees, a very large sum if at all accurate.[33] The situation for Britain in the Red Sea had been somewhat less gratifying.[34]

The question of competition is not one that can be answered with any precision, but the information given on the Indian trade of Muscat and Mocha in 1790 might suggest the following:[35] European ships tended to import different categories of goods and from further afield, and the English not unnaturally dominated the Masulipatnam and Bengal trade. Surat shared with European vessels and those of Muscat the bulk of the trade, and, like Malabar shipping, tended to carry out the goods of its own area. The commerce between the Red Sea, Muscat and the Gulf was the preserve of Arab vessels. Muscat, however, competed directly with the Muslim merchants of India in the trade to the west coast of the sub-continent, and had even latterly opened up the route to Calcutta. Muscat shared with other Arab shipping the carrying trade of the Gulf, but it was beginning to sense competition from the Utub, who took Bahrain in 1782 and who had even begun sending vessels direct to India. An English merchant in Basra in 1790, conscious of the future potential for trade in the area, might well have sensed strong competition from Basra merchants, but his keenest and most direct rivals would have been the above-mentioned Armenian and Muslim merchants resident in British India.[36]

This depiction of Gulf trade in 1790 finds general confirmation and some elucidation in another by Malcolm in 1800.[37] The commerce of Bushire and Basra had continued to recover and these ports did an extensive trade with India, roughly 60 per cent of which, or more, may have come via Muscat, most of it freighted in Muscat boats. Indian imports to Basra are very roughly estimated at 30 lacs of rupees, to Bushire at over 17½ lacs Rs, and to Bahrain and the southern shore of the Gulf at 10 lacs Rs. Only goods from Masulipatnam and Bengal came direct to Bushire and this freight trade was, one presumes, that dominated by British vessels;[38] some corroboration of this appears in the statement that Gulf shipping charged only one-third of the freight of European vessels which were consequently reserved for long voyages.[39] The efforts of the Utub to bypass Muscat by sailing direct to India were about this time followed in part by the merchants of Bushire who began to establish agencies in Bombay.[40] Another writer also makes the rather perplexing comment that the merchants of Bushire preferred to invest in shipping rather than straight commerce due to the latter's low profitability at this time.[41]

Such figures and estimates as exist for British India and Bushire convey the impression that trade between India and the Gulf achieved a significant, though not always a steady, overall increase in the period c. 1800–20.[42] The trade of the three Presidencies, the Red Sea and the Gulf, like that between Bombay and the Gulf, seems to have approximately doubled between 1802/3 and 1817/18.[43] Most of this increase occurred after 1813/14: up to this point Bombay's trade with the Gulf had doubled, then fallen again to its starting-level at the turn of the century; over the next ten years it traced a line of rapid and unbroken increase.[44] Freight costs between Bombay and the Persian Gulf fluctuated much, but overall slipped over the same period, whilst insurance rates likewise traced a still clearer falling path, particularly in the second decade once the French threat had retreated.[45] Trade between Surat and the Persian Gulf, it should be said, was already at the turn of the century dwarfed by that of Bombay, and ceased to be of any significance in the middle of the second decade.[46]

It may be that the commerce and carrying trade of Muscat, whose ships still visited Bengal, had somewhat declined over this same period from its earlier peak, though Buckingham's observation on the matter should possibly be qualified by another report for 1823.[47] In contrast, the prosperity of Bahrain was, by now, assured and the importance and 'advantage' of its trade with India well recognized by Britain: the principal reason why Britain conceived of the trade of the Gulf with British India being so much in her favour (in 1805 for example to the tune of £500,000 with Basra alone)[48] was on account of the bulk of remittances being made in treasure, 'we only supplying the produce of our soil and labour'.[49] Given the peculiar nature of the pearl and the pearling industry, however, and the importance of pearls in the Indian trade, it would, perhaps, be wrong to overestimate the converse 'disadvantage' of this trade to the Gulf itself. Despite this, it was still undoubtedly true that the Britain–India–China trade had required huge injections of specie and this made the Gulf trade all the more attractive.

A good proportion of the trade between India and the Gulf must by 1817 have been carried in British shipping, although it should perhaps be observed that some part of this, particularly that sailing from Bombay, was Arab-built, -owned and -stocked, though commanded by European officers.[50] Whereas in 1816/17 Buckingham put the number of Muscat ships engaged in the trade to and from India and Africa at 20, he noted that in the previous year 15 ships, most or all quite possibly under British colours, had visited Basra from Bombay and Bengal.[51] This picture of the recent health of British shipping on the Gulf–Bombay, as well as the less competitive Gulf–Bengal, route is confirmed at this time, though probably with less accuracy, by the traveller Heude: using an average of 300 tons

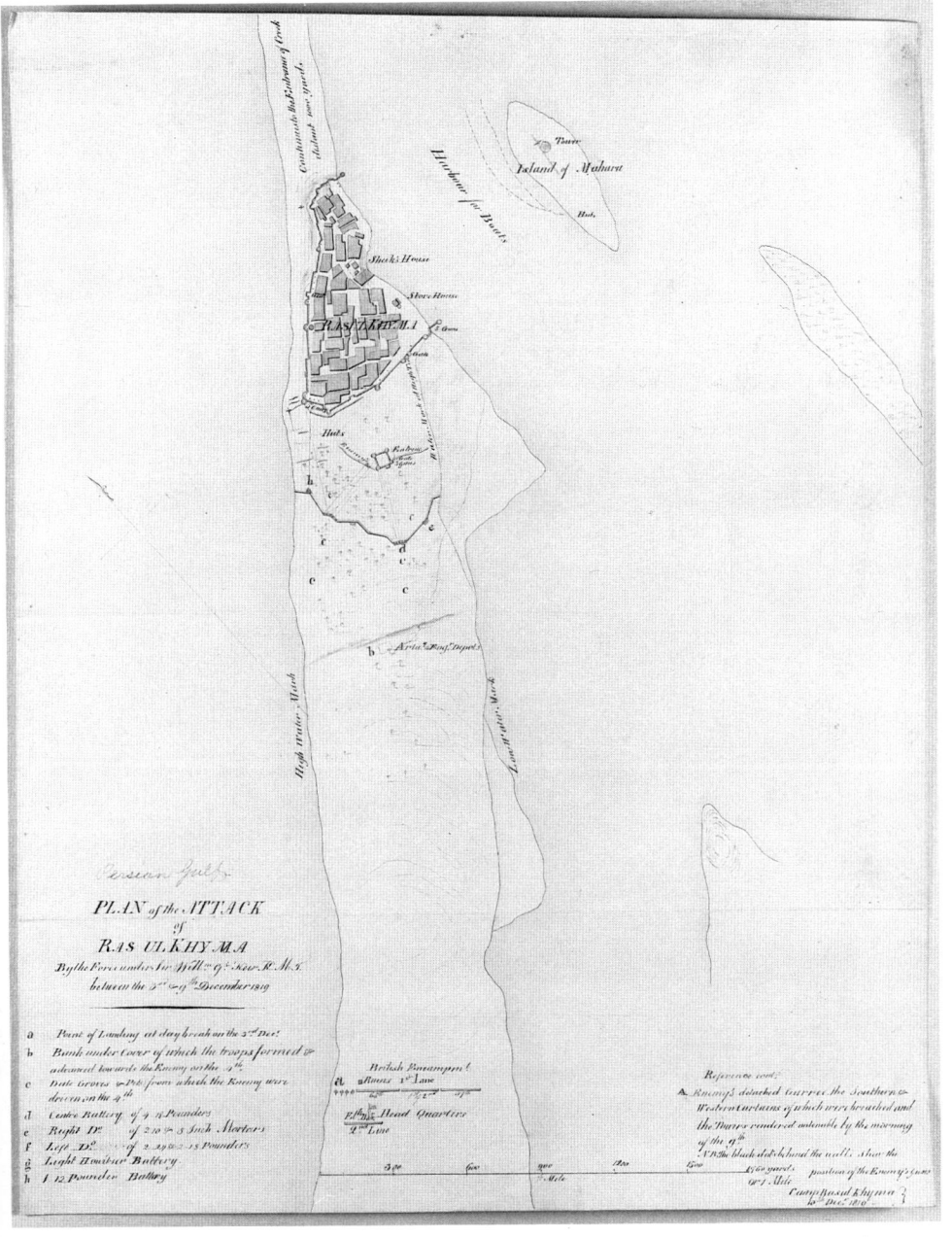

Plate 13. Plan of the attack of Ras al-Khaima by the forces under Sir Wm G. Keir between the 3rd and 9th of December 1819. (Keir)

Plate 14. View of Muscat towns and forts. Undated, delivered to East India Company Library Oct. 1811. (Watercolour, anon.)

Plate 15. Three watercolours of Muscat. 1. Jalali Castle 1822   2. Castle of Jaira 1822   3. Town of Muscat 1822. (Lt Col. Charles Hamilton Smith)

Plate 16. Bushire. (Watercolour, Lt Col. Charles Hamilton Smith)

per vessel he arrives at an annual average of 7,000 tons of outward shipping which he then roughly translates into a figure of c. 600,000 Rs or
£70,000 employed in bottomry.[52] More reliable figures exist for British
shipping at Bushire: direct imports from India on British bottoms totalled
3,003,947 New Persian Rupees (c. £225,300) in 1817 and roughly doubled
over the next five years. It may be that the quantity of Indian goods that
entered Iran through Bushire was equalled by the amount that was brought
in by Gulf shipping via Muscat at other Persian ports. Nevertheless, of
total imports at Bushire in 1817, it is estimated that three-quarters came in
on British vessels, one-quarter on non-British or Arab ships. The picture
may well have been similar at Basra.[53]

By way of comparison, recorded figures for the tonnage of vessels
employed in the trade between Bombay and the Persian Gulf present the
following pattern. In the first decade or so of the century, while the
predatory sea-war with France was at its height, Arab vessels made up
36 per cent of total tonnage, vessels under English colours the remainder;
from 1813/14 to 1820/1 inclusive, while the Qasimi question remained
unresolved, the Arab share dropped to a mere 10 per cent; and finally, in
the next four years, the Arab share again averaged 37 per cent.[54]

The foregoing account, selective and open-ended though it is, yet serves
to show that India–Gulf trade, already very sizable in 1790, may have
increased substantially over the next three decades. The proportional share
of British shipping over the same period may also have increased, more
especially, perhaps, due to the apparent expansion of the direct route from
Bombay to Bushire and Basra at the expense of Muscat. The presence of
European merchants in the Gulf in these years was quite possibly hardly
felt, except perhaps at Basra,[55] and the experiences of Bushire and Bahrain
demonstrated that rapid commercial expansion was possible, even with
Bombay, particularly once Muscat could be bypassed.

Important as the trade of the Gulf seemed to the Company in these
years, its importance was still further magnified by changes in India: in
1787 the Company had had very little territory at all outside Bengal, Bihar
and Madras (Chingleput), but by 1818 it found itself governing virtually
all the coastline from Gujarat in the north-west to Bengal in the north-
east,[56] together with Ceylon and large tracts in southern and north-eastern
India. With the exception of certain areas such as Cutch and Sind, India–
Gulf trade had therefore now become British India–Gulf trade. And, at a
level slightly removed, this transformation, which naturally entailed the
extension of the Company's pass, as is recorded of Surat in 1800,[57] must
have helped account for the increased share of British shipping in the Gulf
region at this time. It was an increase, however, that should still be set
against the general background of the primacy of British shipping in the

Indian Ocean region, one that is believed to have been achieved after the American Wars largely at the hands of the British country captain, men such as William Richardson of the ship *Cornwall*.[58]

The above narrative should furthermore be adequate to show that the two attacks on Ras al-Khaima could not have been caused by commercial rivalry between the East India Company and the Qawasim. It is also clear that commercial rivalry between the Qawasim and private British traders or shipowners was not a factor in the attacks.[59] Nowhere, indeed, in the British sources consulted are such feelings expressed, nor do the Qawasim appear as anything but small carriers and traders in these years except, perhaps, in the past tense;[60] it might also be observed that one of those who most contributed to the launching of the first expedition, the Muscat Resident David Seton, was equally a vocal proponent of free trade, including that of Arab merchants and vessels at British Indian ports.[61] The competitors were others such as Muscat, the Utub, and the merchants of Bushire and Basra who were not, of course, perceived as pirates like the Qawasim and received very different treatment.[62]

Reason alone dictates that the several-hundred reported incidents at sea in these years, ranging from threatening behaviour to the bloody seizure of ships, the bulk of which were attributed to the Qawasim, constituted a most material influence upon trade. Some, however, commencing from the premise that piracy depresses trade, express surprise that an overall increase in Gulf trade should have occurred despite the supposed piracy, and are tempted to conclude that either the premise or the piracy is a falsity.[63] The critic might, of course, simply reply that the point at issue is not the real increase in trade, or its decrease, but the hypothetical increase or decrease had that 'piracy' not existed. Amongst the many reasons why the trade figures might not so obviously register the impact of piracy are the fact that this 'piracy' was not always indiscriminate, while the figures overly reflect the health or otherwise of British trade; moreover, many of reported incidents occurred not in the Gulf, but off the coasts of Sind, Cutch and Kathiawar, and south Arabia. The principal determinant of trade volume was demand, and this was set by the internal political condition of the major nations of the region, rainfall, the incidence of epidemic and the like.

The true effects of this piracy are extremely difficult to gauge, but two consequences are self-evident: fear by others of Qasimi piracy eventually helped cause the Qawasim themselves to lose their grip on trade and, more significantly, led other shipping for a number of years prior to each expedition to depend upon Company cruisers for protection. The resultant convoys in the Gulf region and off north-west India, though apparently free, were, if used, irksome to the merchant, restrictive of his commercial freedom and may have had the net effect of reducing profitability. Without protection of this kind, merchant vessels found themselves obliged to remain in port until the danger had passed.[64] It is similarly quite possible that the actual loss of vessels would cause insurance rates in affected ports to rise, the effect of the supposed piracy on insurance being attested at Porbandar in June 1818;[65] whether the leap in rates between Bombay and Basra in 1808/9 was more than just a reaction to the activities of French privateers is a matter for speculation.[66]

Buckingham makes the intriguing statement in December 1816 that English shipping from Bombay had for a time profited from Muscat's loss while the latter was at war with the Qawasim, in the same way that Muscat shipping had earlier performed the neutral role when Britain fought France.[67] This pattern is borne out in the record of tonnage trading between Bombay and the Persian Gulf, which suggests that Arab shipping lost out to vessels sailing under British colours in the second decade of the century, when France was no longer a threat, recovering markedly only after the second Ras al-Khaima expedition.[68] It is, in fact, quite often stated both now and later, more especially at Bushire, that the continuance of supposed Qasimi piracy was actually beneficial to British shipping in the Gulf.[69] Very soon after the second expedition of 1819/20 it is, indeed, observed that Gulf shipping had expanded at the comparative expense of British shipping.[70] This effect, which benefited Arab and perhaps especially Kuwaiti shipping, reportedly persisted over the next two decades.

ii Political Factors

(A) SOME UNDERCURRENTS

> The pirate Jasmy has this year caused such depredation in sea to the vessels belonging to your petitioners and others, as has rendered your petitioners inactive to have any trade to the ports of Muscat, Cutch, Veraval, Mangrol, Porbandar, Karachi etc.

So begins a petition of 4 November 1817 addressed by c. 36 Indian merchants of Bombay to the Governor, Sir Evan Nepean.[71] One of a number of such requests for relief or protection, these documents are indicative of a certain pressure which the British Indian merchant interest sought to apply to the Bombay Council.[72] Government's perception must also have been affected, though in a wholly different fashion, by the indirect transmission of the relevant views of local merchants in Kathiawar (and Cutch) via its agents there.[73] Whilst the Council's deliberations leading up to the second expedition give distinct primacy to the Company's narrower interests, when it comes to the casus belli the Council is in no doubt at all as to who had and did suffer most by the Qawasim's alleged piracy.[74]

The character of the Government of Bombay had undergone profound and rapid change since the late eighteenth century, when this poor cousin had seemed almost ripe for closure.[75] Reprieved by the development of the cotton trade to China, the arguments of the private trader and the temporary acquisition of Malabar, its existence was assured by territorial gain in the first two decades of the nineteenth century. Events at Malabar in 1792–1800 showed the extent to which the interests of the European private merchant, whose influence was still particularly strong at Bombay, might combine with and countermine the often unwieldy efforts of the Company with its classic monopolistic tendencies.[76] But the underlying trend was by now for a separation of these interests, as exemplified in the edict of 31 August 1804 forbidding private commerce by Company servants at Bombay.[77] This divorce, however, masked a more subtle and gradual transformation: the Company was becoming the soldier and administrator financed by revenue and with crescent reciprocal duties, while the independent private merchant, buoyed up by ideas such as those of Adam Smith and the free-traders, now openly began to attack the Company's monopolies. As early as 2 July 1811, in fact, Bombay had decided in advance of the rest of India to throw open the Gulf to private trade.[78] What the free-traders wanted, however, was not just the freedom to trade, but the right conditions in which to do so. Given the circumstances of time and place, this appeared to imply the need for greater governmental intervention than the old Company's monopolies had seemed to warrant.

The Gulf was, in one respect, something of an anachronism at this time in that Company officials at Bushire and Basra were still allowed to trade on their own private account.[79] The Basra Resident, Colquhoun, was still profitably exporting horses in 1816,[80] but it was his long-serving predecessor Samuel Manesty, appointed for over a quarter of a century in 1784, who must be accounted the principal of these officials-cum-merchants at this time.[81] Manesty, in fact, suffered most particularly at the hands of the Qawasim, to whom he lost no less than three vessels in the years 1804 and 1809.[82] It is noticeable, however, that neither men were early or very great advocates of the military, as opposed to the political, solution to the Qasimi problem.[83]

Those who did so, by contrast, were the new breed of political officer, some with a military background, men like Seton and Malcolm who came to the fore in the decade before the first expedition. For Malcolm, political and strategic advantage outweighed the commercial, his imperial views in 1800 wholly new to the Gulf and, in their way, an anticipation of the future. Indeed, one of the lesser arguments which he also employed to urge upon Bombay his plan for a 'British establishment' in the Gulf was that it was for Government actively to protect private commerce and to leave the trade in Indian goods entirely in its hands; the Company, as he put it, should strive 'to excite a liberal spirit of commercial enterprise and adventure' amongst its 'numerous Indian subjects' as the means for increasing the prestige, and revenues, of 'that great empire of which they are sovereigns.'[84]

(B)   MORE IMMEDIATE CAUSES

Englishman man very good man, drinkee de punch, fire de gun, beatee de French, very good fun.[85]

Between 1798, when Napoleon invaded Egypt, and the fall of Mauritius in 1810, British policy toward the Gulf region was no longer conditioned simply by its importance for trade and as a channel of communication.[86] French maritime activity in the Indian Ocean during these years occasionally touched south Arabia, Muscat and the Gulf, enough to stimulate increased British concern for its naval strength in the region and, more specifically, for the protection of India–Gulf trade.[87] Of greater import, however, was the French diplomatic activity in Turkish Arabia, Muscat and Iran that raised for the first time the haunting spectre of a European invasion of India from the north-west, a potential scenario in which Russia was soon to assume the leading role.[88]

Muscat's abiding strategic importance was grasped earlier on in the 1790s, situated as it was at the mouth of the Gulf, holding the key to India–Gulf trade and possessing the most powerful fleet in the region. The Company's first diplomatic efforts were therefore concentrated here, activity which seemed all the more important when for a short time a French seaborne invasion via Suez seemed feasible: these approaches soon resulted in the *Qaulnama* of 1798, ratified in 1800.[89] During the next ten years, punctuated by absence and the frequent death of incumbents,[90] British interests at Muscat were represented by a series of Residents who strove, often with less than overwhelming success, to influence the ruler in their distinct favour and to the detriment of France.

The longest-serving and most influential of these men was, until his death a few months before the first expedition, the conscientious and untiring Captain Seton, an officer who during these years also undertook political work in connection with local powers, piracy and the French in Cutch, Sind and south Arabia.[91] Under the circumstances of his appointment, and given the proximity of the Qasimi coast, it was not unnatural that Seton's ample intelligence reports from Muscat should come to constitute Britain's prime source on Qasimi affairs up to the time of the first expedition. Indeed the influence of these reports upon British perception of the Qawasim was more lasting still in consequence of their priority and their detail, an outcome which served to magnify the effect of such special traits as they possess:[92] Seton was assiduous in his cultivation of friendly relations with rulers of Muscat and was, moreover, under the necessary constraint of relying upon sources there accessible. One needs no reminding of the deep mistrust and animosity that then existed between Muscat and her neighbours, the Qawasim. It is understandable, therefore, that this milieu should have been reflected at certain points in Seton's writings.[93]

Seton first became personally involved in the issue of supposed piracy by the Qawasim in 1805–6, when he successfully negotiated an agreement with them on behalf of the Company. A noticeable feature of this particular episode was his ready inclination to identify East India Company with Muscat interests, a tendency which on this occasion incurred the censure of Iran and, if pressed, would have precluded any form of dialogue with the Qawasim.[94] This regard for Muscat was also reflected in his historical sketches, implying, as they do at times, that Qasimi piracy rose and fell essentially in accordance with converse fluctuations in Omani strength.[95] By 1808–9 the focus of Anglo–French rivalry had shifted to Iran, but Muscat had by then come to be regarded as a valuable friend. When Seton returned to Muscat in February 1809 he was forcefully struck with the changes that had occurred, in particular the increase in Wahhabi activity both within the country and across its borders.[96] These, his last reports, betray an infectious anxiety, predicting as they do the imminent loss of Muscat to the Wahhabis and, with it, the extinction of British interests. It is this tone, pressing the timely need to prop up Muscat, or, as he put it, to assist in the struggles she had already begun,[97] added to the strong identification drawn between Wahhabi and Qasimi, and furthermore assuming a too literal community of interest with Muscat in suppressing 'piracy',[98] which constitutes the second of Seton's peculiar contributions to British perceptions before the first expedition: the conclusions were there to be drawn by India.[99]

In May 1807 Napoleon wrote, 'La Perse est considérée par la France sous deux points de vue: comme ennemie naturelle de la Russie et comme moyen de passage pour une expédition aux Indes.'[100] The Treaty of Finkenstein, the Peace of Tilsit and General Gardane's mission to Iran, all in 1807, caused Britain grave concern, for they seemed to imply the possibility of a fatal combination between France, Russia and Persia against her Indian possessions.[101] These fears were further fuelled by news of French naval forces being despatched eastwards from France in June 1807, and seemed perilously close to fruition when in the middle of the year the Shah was said to have reached a draft agreement with the French, in which, amongst other things, he agreed to cede to them Bandar Abbas, Hormuz and Kharg.[102]

The worried British response was energetic to the point of confusion:[103] the Foreign Office in London had Harford Jones, formerly the Resident in Baghdad, knighted and despatched him post-haste en route to Iran. Whilst India, for its own part, sensing greater urgency, sent a small naval force to the Gulf in February 1808, had Seton reopen the Muscat Residency and, following his grandiose efforts of a decade before, recruited Malcolm for a second mission to Iran. Malcolm was at the same time given overall control of Gulf affairs, and it was via him that Seton's reports now reached Bombay.

Before Jones arrived from England, Malcolm had already landed at Bushire, received a bruising rebuff from the Persian government and sailed back to India to arrange a suitably demonstrative response. Malcolm's already ambitious ideas of eight years before had by now grown more robust. His honour was also at stake in the matter, and he keenly sensed the competition between the East India Company as represented by himself and the home government as embodied in Harford Jones.[104] In the face of the European threat Malcolm lost patience with local regimes and recommended that 'the English government should instantly possess itself of means to throw those states that favoured the approach of its enemies into complete confusion and destruction'.[105] With the constant support of Minto, therefore, he immediately set about preparing an expeditionary force to seize Kharg.

What Malcolm wanted was a 'fine mess' in the Gulf.[106] But, as it turned out, the peaceable diplomatic overtures of Harford Jones, with other factors, all helped to ameliorate the British position in Iran during 1808, and therefore made such a demonstration of might both unnecessary and unjustifiable.[107] Yet passions were running high in 1808–9, and Malcolm's experiences combined with Seton's reports from Muscat to offer an outlet for these pent-up emotions: rather than abandon the expedition altogether, Ras al-Khaima now presented itself as a more politically, even 'morally', sound alternative destination. Both psychologically and in terms of planning and preparation,[108] then, the expedition of 1809/10 against the Qawasim was in essence Malcolm's Kharg expedition tempered somewhat, and with its object displaced, by circumstance.

iii   Some Questions of Perception

> There being no crime held in such general detestation as that of piracy on the high seas, such as by the laws of all countries is punished capitally ...[109]

The first expedition had set a clear pattern for the later enterprise. The latter's aims, however, namely the attainment of the semi-fulfilled literal objectives of the first, or the lasting eradication of piracy, were, by comparison, far more emphatic and explicit. In point of timing, the circumstances seemed particularly apt: Ibrahim Pasha's seemingly propitious advance against the Wahhabi power in Arabia initially suggested the possibility of some kind of military alliance with Britain.[110] At the same time, following the triumph over Napoleon in 1815, the defeat of the Marathas and the Pindaris in 1818 now afforded British India the time, confidence and resources to concentrate upon matters rather less pressing and close to home.[111]

Despite what was said above of the confluence of circumstances by which the earlier operation was eventually conditioned, there is no doubt that the theme of piracy was still its leitmotiv and a belief in Qasimi culpability its *sine qua non*. It is important to bear in mind throughout that the principal object and duty of the Bombay Marine, the Company's naval arm, was in normal times none other than the protection of trading vessels from attack.[112] It is, indeed, instructive to see the first expedition in the light of earlier moves against pirates in India. This, in fact, is how it is described in an official account of the time which begins by specifically referring to recent operations against 'freebooters' in Malabar and Sind.[113] A further connection was, as referred to above, provided by Captain Seton, who in 1802–3 was involved with plans to combat piracy in Cutch and Kathiawar said to be an obstacle to the trade of Bombay with the north, particularly the growing cotton trade: it is worth observing that Qasimi piracy was only reported in this region after Major Walker's successes of 1807.[114]

It is at this stage of some importance to attempt to consider certain aspects of the British attitude towards piracy and the Qawasim, a range of views which helped mould the character of the two expeditions. The central point at issue is naturally the relationship between pre- or otherwise-formed ideas and feelings on the part of Britain, and the real experiences she encountered in the Gulf region.

There are strong elements of morality and emotion in many of the contemporary British reports of and reactions to alleged Qasimi piracy. In an empire founded on trade and which increasingly saw its role as the protection of, rather than participation in, commerce, it is not surprising to find British observers praising 'the innocent and industrious trader',[115] attaching a moral value to trade[116] and displaying faith in its improving qualities.[117] Piracy, then, was in some sense its antithesis and its practitioners morally deficient.[118] The results of this may be seen in Taylor's historical views on past European involvement in the Gulf as, too, in Britain's generally much higher regard for and better treatment of the Utub by contrast with that afforded to the Qawasim.[119]

A second accompaniment of the growth of the administration in India, as well as of its trade, one which also perhaps owes a little more than the first to trends in British society and sentiment, was a somewhat heightened attachment to certain categories of order and authority. The Qawasim are thus at times described as 'lawless'[120] and their 'piratical' activities clearly distinguished from those who act 'with any authorised state in regular warfare according to the principles of civilised war'.[121] Concepts such as these were, of course, no absolute and they tended to presuppose some position of strength for their application, but they do possibly suggest certain parallels between British treatment of the Qawasim, on the one hand, and of other groups such as the Pindaris and Thugs, on the other.

The most powerful emotional element in the events of these years was undoubtedly the violence attributed to the Qawasim.[122] Often colouring British thinking, this theme was felt to provide Britain's strongest moral justification for its action;[123] while, in some hands, it could also, at times, give rise to certain elements of sensationalism. It was characteristic of such matters that British perception before each of the two expeditions should have focused above all upon a small number of particular, identifiable and vividly evoked maritime incidents which, as it were, stood for the whole.[124] It also seems probable that there were at the time a variety of parallel visions of the Qawasim: certain Indian mariners, for example, would tend to emphasize different maritime incidents and represented a lurid picture of wanton cruelty.[125] There is, however, no doubting the palpable reality of the fears inspired by the bloodthirsty reputation of the Qawasim, a trait felt by Colquhoun to mark them out from their counterparts in the Gulf.[126] In response to this fear, Indian sailors off Kathiawar sometimes abandoned ship at the approach of supposed Qasimi vessels. In a voyage up the Gulf in late 1816, Heude records the following incident involving the English captain of his (Arab) ship:[127]

> Early on the morning of the 28th we were suddenly disturbed by a loud call from our commander, to rise and defend ourselves, or we should all be murdered instantly ... We had always slept with loaded arms since the first alarm: ... on rushing forth, I found myself attacked and grazed ... by a sabre thrust. On closing and disarming my adversary, ... he was discovered to be our unfortunate commander who, his wits having entirely forsaken him, had imagined himself beset ... Renewed attempts of the same nature obliged us to confine him.

In varying degrees the two expeditions were, in one light, missions to retrieve a slighted British 'honour',[128] the goal being the Governor's 'atonement',[129] or the 'handsome chastisement' of the military commander.[130] The use of opprobrious epithets in relation to the Qawasim by some such

291

as the Bushire Resident Bruce, his background the Bombay Marine,[131] is evidence of a gall which seems to imply that personalization sometimes took a discernible part in this dispute. At a space of 20 years Bruce recalls with indignation the manner of his treatment at the hands of the Sudan: 'The packet taken from me, the boat's crew with myself stripped ... [they gave] me in particular a severe bastinadoing with skates' tails and cut me in the most cruel and severe manner.'[132] The state of communications and the structure of Company authority was such that individuals could still exert a significant influence upon events, even though this effect may have lessened somewhat since the later eighteenth-century heyday of Henry Moore and even the early years of Samuel Manesty.[133] The practical conduct of Anglo–Qasimi relations in the second decade of the century was often for the most part in the hands of Bruce, and it would perhaps be wrong to underestimate the importance of the forthright and irascible stance he adopted, as at Ras al-Khaima in 1816.[134] Alongside the issue of personality was that other, symbolic, repository of pride and prestige, felt at the time to be so much at stake in the issue of piracy, namely the British flag. Gone were the days when the Company's pass could, albeit temporarily, be auctioned off by a Basra Agent such as Moore.[135] Qasimi attacks were thus conceived as insults to the British flag,[136] an emblem whose 'honour and dignity'[137] was 'so sacred to every English subject.'[138] Language apart, this was a sentiment of some practical import given the nature of Britain's position in the East at this time.

During the first two decades of the century, emotion was such as to leave little room for any great display of sympathy for the Qawasim, even though it was quite common for military and naval officers to show respect for their prowess and skill.[139] Indeed the only partly 'ameliorating' factor which the British were at all regularly wont to acknowledge had some bearing on the cause of supposed Qasimi piracy, if not their culpability, was the poverty and aridity of the region they inhabited.[140] By the time of the second expedition, however, hints, at least, of a slight retraction from this hitherto overly uncompromising stance were in some quarters already partly in evidence. The main proponent of these rather more qualified views was Francis Warden, Secretary to Government and temporary member of the Bombay Council just prior to the second expedition. The gist of his arguments and testimonials, which nevertheless encountered the unyielding opposition of the Governor, Nepean, was that no fair appraisal of the acts of the Qawasim could ignore the duress under which they laboured from the Wahhabis.[141] His historical researches, in fact, had led him to the conclusion that in the less recent past Muscat, and not the Qawasim, had been the true villains of the piece, whilst his natural sympathies seemed to lie with the smaller states in the Gulf. Warden's understanding, it might be noted, was one laboriously, if swiftly, constructed from the Company's old records. Nepean's, on the other hand, less tolerant and more sweeping as it seemed, was one based by preference upon contemporary reports from the area, particularly those submitted by naval and military officers.[142]

It would, of course, be quite mistaken to seek to imply that British opinion in these matters was either unchanging or monolithic. There had been noticeable developments since the later eighteenth century. The reports of Henry Moore, for example, who was involved whilst Agent at Basra in 1767–75 in a series of events that bear some comparison with those under discussion, seldom employ the term 'pirate': when they do so of Husain Khan in 1771, it is not a descriptive term so much as a term of abuse.[143] For Moore, like others soon thereafter, the Gulf's seemingly chronic maritime insecurity often appeared to be but a product of the complexities of Gulf politics; and where Moore felt himself a part of this, others such as John Beaumont, the Resident at Bushire, stood back a little, more perplexed.[144] Some, such as Manesty, managed to preserve elements of this degree of immersion in the local environment into the early nineteenth century.[145] But the guiding forces behind policy in the Gulf in the first two decades of the nineteenth century were often now those such as the specially commissioned political officer, the military and naval officer on tour of duty, and the Company official in Bombay. These individuals were prima facie less likely to adjust so much to the circumstances of the Gulf and, moreover, entertained a sense of strength and distance that men such as Manesty, proud though they were, had lacked. The outcome of these changes was apparent on a number of levels, whether in a greater readiness to remould the status quo,[146] or in a mere increased propensity towards a form of 'moralising': there are even suggestions that Captain Thompson, framer of the General Treaty, had hopes in 1820 of converting some amongst the Qawasim to Christianity.[147]

iv Final Word

So here we are, with hareems, and the lattices, and Shiraz wine, and banks of pearl, and groves of palm, and all the rest of it—and altogether, if you will know the truth, it is but a dry and dusty view, and moreover hath an ancient and fish-like smell owing to the heaps of oyster-shells which ... can hardly be dispensed with in reality, however they may in poetry.[148]

Thus reflected Mrs Thompson as she sat in the erstwhile harem of Hasan bin Rahma at Ras al-Khaima in April 1820. In other senses, too, the sometimes heavy coloration of the British perception in recent years now subsided somewhat and, like the waters of the Gulf in which these anxieties had been reflected, grew hereafter less tempestuous and a little more secure.

The events of these years had provided British India with a role in the Gulf which she was to preserve throughout the century. From being treated more in the light of pure self-interest and a desire to avoid deeper involvement in the area, the issue of piracy came to take on heavier moral overtones: the General Treaty of 1820, unlike previous engagements, attempted to outlaw inter-state piracy, not simply attacks on British shipping, and this seemed to require some policing. Another effect of these years was the lasting impression they left upon British perception of the Qawasim, the Gulf and themselves. This impact was explicable by these events having inaugurated a century and a half of serious British involvement in the Gulf, but also, moreover, by their having delivered such a strong psychological impact, replete, as they were, with elements of sensation, horror, virtue, vice and romance: the General Treaty specified that the blood-red flag of the Arabs should henceforth be neatly enclosed in Britain's white border of peace.

Brief though it is, it is hoped that this essay will have helped to suggest certain factors that might variously have lain behind Britain's two expeditions of 1809/10 and 1819/20, resting as they both yet did upon a distinct belief in Qasimi responsibility for piracy. For all the grand considerations and ambitions rehearsed in the political discussions of the Bombay Council prior to the second expedition, when it came to it, the eventual political settlement was in many ways the extempore production of Keir and Thompson conceived in the field. It would be difficult to argue that there was any effective, overall and conscious stratagem, or concerted policy, behind Britain's experiences in the Gulf during these years: the evidence considered by and large seems to point rather to piecemeal, even *ad hoc*, development. Nor should it be forgotten that in 1800 the Qasimi coast had, for the British, been largely *terra incognita*. Even at the time of the first expedition the commanders still had few reliable charts of the area and scant political information except for Seton's earlier intelligence: the hasty sketch-map of the country, drawn up by the Persian merchant Sayyid Taqi, arrived too late for use. There was, then, a wider truth in Hasan bin Rahma's statement in a letter to Bruce that, 'neither of us is correctly informed [of] the state of the other arising from the distance of times and places.'[149]

The period c. 1790–1820 had been a hectic one in which profound changes had occurred in the make-up of the larger powers in India, Arabia and Iran. The smaller states of the Gulf were likewise struggling to emerge from the turmoil of the eighteenth century. The Qawasim were, in one sense, caught in the midst of these changes, and perhaps found themselves a little out of step with the new political expectations and alignments. There is a moment of some poignancy when, only weeks before the second and decisive attack on Ras al-Khaima, Bruce described how he dealt a heavy, impatient, even contemptuous rebuff to a final emissary from Ras al-Khaima, who now seemed to him only to be in quest of intelligence, perhaps playing for time: the envoy, he said,

> looked hard at me for a long time without replying, when at last he broke silence and said he recommended me to think well before I ventured to treat the friendly overtures of his chief with such neglect, they may not be made a second time.[150]

But the rules were changing and after 1819, upon the waters of the Gulf at least, these increasingly tended to be those devised and elaborated by Britain.

APPENDIX A

The Qawasim's Seizures off the Coast of India

The Qawasim earned part of their reputation for piracy in the waters off the coast of north-west India. These activities are of particular interest because they took place in an arena relatively free of the complexities of Gulf politics. This was evidently a more pristine class of adventure. The pattern of these seizures was by no means constant, progressing southward and peaking later in the second decade of the century. These were years when the Qawasim, adhering fast to the Wahhabi fold, laboured under mounting strictures closer to home. The evidence for these activities requires special attention. What follows is a chronological examination of documented seizures by the Qawasim in the years 1797–1820. The results of this exercise are depicted in Figure 1 and discussed in Chapter Nine.

In some of the following entries figures indicating the number of assailants are given in square brackets to signify positive doubt as to whether these were Qawasim. Few of these figures, or those for the victims, may be precisely accurate. Reporting from Kathiawar and Cutch becomes fuller during the second decade; that for Sind, and especially Makran, remains sparse.

LATE 1805

The first possible reference to Qasimi activity in this direction is the uncertain report concerning two vessels taken off Makran in c. September/October 1805: see Chapter Six, section three.

Assailants: 8.
Boats plundered: [2].

EARLY 1808

In or before mid-March 1808, five large Qasimi dows under the command of Salih bin Muhammad, the biggest of them mounting 14 guns, were reported to have visited Cutch and captured two Sindi dinghies with a Bombay vessel belonging to one Sunderjee Khitree;[1] regarding whom, see the entry for late 1808. Salih bin Muhammad was presumably the commander who had been involved in the *Viper* incident, nephew to Shaikh Saqr.

This cruise was independently attested at Muscat and Mandvi. Judging by Lieutenant Maxfield's despatch from Mandvi, its people held the Qawasim in some awe at the time.[2] Maxfield's report also suggests that this was the first time the Bombay Marine learnt that the Qawasim had made captures off Cutch (and presumably Sind);[3] whether these certainly represented the first Qasimi captures east of Makran, we cannot know.

Assailants: 5 large dows.
Boats plundered: 3.

The Qawasim appear to have captured a significant number of Indian and British Indian vessels during a cruise off Cutch and Sind in November. In February 1809, Seton wrote, no doubt loosely, that the Qawasim had been elated by the capture of 'twenty country-boats of different sizes' during their last cruise;[4] we can do no more than guess at what might have been the correct figure, though it might be worth remarking that another number in the same paragraph is inflated by a factor of four. Whatever the true figure, the impact of this cruise on the Indian mercantile community was considerable: on 1 December, 30 Parsee and Banyan merchants of Bombay united to petition the Governor for action against the Qasimi pirates in order to preserve their trade. In response, Governor Duncan instructed the Bombay Marine to take appropriate offensive action against them on the northern coasts.[5]

This season's Qasimi activity off India was interpreted by David Seton, the intermittent Muscat Resident, as a new development. In his view, at least, it represented the fulfilment of long-cherished Wahhabi designs, an event finally precipitated by the establishment of peaceful relations between Muscat and the Qawasim around the start of November 1808; this last, he argues, must have had the effect of unharnessing Qasimi shipping, leaving them free to undertake such an expedition.[6]

The Bombay merchant, Sunderjee Sewjee, claimed in a petition that his botella the *Harsingar* had been taken by the 'Jasmery' pirates during 1808,[7] at a cost to him of 5,000 rupees: the *Harsingar* could have been lost during this season; or else during the Qawasim's previous cruise, when she might also conceivably have been the vessel described as belonging to Sunderjee Khitree.[8]

A slightly more enlightening individual case concerns the British Indian merchant of Bombay, Jewraz Balloo Bhatia: he maintained that his vessel the *Rooparel*, valued with her cargo at 7,248 rupees, had been bloodily seized by the Qawasim, presumably off Cutch in c. mid–late November; this would therefore appear to have been one of the casualties of the above cruise. Jewraz Balloo Bhatia's petition and statement of loss, being delivered in late, was answered by Government with a demand for further details, to include 'positive proof' of the capture.[9] It nevertheless constitutes a not untypical example of such petitions:

> *The humble petition of Jewraz Balloo Bhatia, merchant of Bombay, inhabitant.*
> Most Humbly Sheweth,
>   That your petitioner humbly begs leave to state—that on the 7th November 1808 his certain vessel, or nundy, commonly called *Rooparel*, navigating by Tindal Hasan, sailed from this port [Bombay] with his own goods, wares and merchandises for Shahbandar under the passport and colour of Your Honour's Government: but in her way, the pirate vessels of the Wahhabi, of the place called Ras al-Khaima, came in her long side, seized, taken and carried away, after killed seven lascars, one Tindal Hasan aforesaid, and two sepoys; and two Crannies,[10] Tulloo and Nurssey, had taken, carried them to their place.
>   Your petitioner being a merchant and it is very hard on him to suffer great loss of this vessel, or nundy, together with her cargo, goods, wares and merchandises, the particular of what it will appear by the undermentioned list; and also the other merchants may have presented their applications to Your Honour relative their vessels and goods had been taken, carried away by the pirates of the said Wahhabi.

Your petitioner therefore most humbly prays to honour the premises considered, and will be pleased if think proper that the authority from Your Honour's Government may be used against the said Wahhabi for restoration her said vessel, or nundy, *Rooparel*, together with her cargo, goods, wares and merchandises, or the value thereof to this petitioner; he in hopes to be meet from Your Honour such aid and assistance in the premises, and by way as a charity to grant him due redress as your wisdom shall deem most proper etc. etc. etc.,

and your petitioner as in duty bound shall ever pray.

One vessel, or nundy, with complete furnitures, being in value of rupees . . .	2,000
Sundry goods, viz.	
31 bags of Bengal sugar	875
10 tubs of sugar candy	150
10 robins of black pepper	275
3 bales of raw silk	2,750
1 bag of tin	35
3 bags of tootnague[11]	50
1 bundle of nutmeg	30
1 piece perpet[12]	25
1 chest benjamin[13]	45
1 chest of cinnamon or tug[14]	30
7 bags of betel-nut	90
8 badras of dates	50
5 cupa of dry dates	70
1 cupa of almonds	50
1 bundle of steel	26
3 cupa of cuntho	45
8 bundos[?] of coir	22
Sundry necessaries	300
50 bags of wheat	240
24 bags of mung	90
	7,248 rupees

Lascars' articles and thing in value of about   500.

Boats plundered: up to 20 (some such figure as 6 is nevertheless conceivably more likely, though pure hypothesis).

EARLY 1809

In or by later January 1809, a party of *c.* 8–10 Qawasim[15] sailed for India. At about the start of February, an action was reported to have occurred off Karachi: two local vessels having 'sewn themselves' there, the Governor, Nur Khan's deputy Allih Ruckih, requisitioned two merchant dinghies and two small Utub vessels, put 200 sepoys on board and sent them to engage the two Qasimi vessels then in sight; these last drew their pursuers onto the rest of the squadron, which then attacked the Sindis, capturing an Utbi and a merchant boat, killing 40 of the Utub and 18 of the merchant dinghy's crew, together with all the sepoys they came upon.[16]

The Qasimi squadron now sailed on to Cutch. On *c.* 12 February off Mandvi, or nearby Assar,[17] they reportedly captured the botella *Rampasa*, causing the Bombay merchant Sunderjee Sewjee a loss of 3,000 rupees: there may too have been other attacks, possibly without success.[18] Hunsraj, at Mandvi, fitted out an 18-gun ship and 5(–6) boats in order to combat the Qawasim.[19] Lieutenant Harriott of the HCC *Zephyr*, who happened then to be blockading Poseitra, which was accused of piracy, was informed of these proceedings and set off on 14 February to chase the Qawasim in company with the Cutch Raja's fleet.[20] Feeling himself 'confident of being in their track from the pieces of wreck, bales, etc. hourly floating by us', which he interpreted as 'the effects of their devastations', Harriott continued the chase past the Indus. On the 18th, he took possession of an empty dinghy abandoned by the Qawasim: this could have been a prize. On 22 February, with the Cutch fleet left far behind, Harriott reached Sonmiani and,

> having the advantage of the wind, bore down upon [the Qawasim] with an intent to view them more closely, and to try if our single force was competent to do them any injury. On our approach, they stretched out their line on the starboard tack. Having brought them within good shot, we commenced and continued our fire upon them for near an hour; but with little other effect than their cutting away the boat from the largest of them and some shot striking her hull. Observing their decks completely crowded with men, their smaller boats with their oars all ready for boarding, in case we closed with them, and that no advantage could accrue from continuing our attack against such superior numbers, desisted from firing, but kept hovering close to them, till completely dark.

The *Zephyr* then hauled her wind and stood to the south-east, reaching Mandvi once more on the 25th.[21]

The Qasimi squadron, for its part, continued westward to Chahbahar. Once there, allegedly 'in great want of provisions and much disheartened from their bad success', they were reported to have buried some dead.[22] Some reports suggest that the Qawasim had suffered serious casualties by this stage; one sketchy remark also speaks of their raiding unprotected coastal villages, but this is not substantiated.[23] It was said that whilst at Chahbahar, the Qawasim, in a clear piece of Wahhabi propagandism, 'delivered a paper signed by Hasan bin Ghaith [al-]Qasimi recommending [Mir] Soban to destroy all tombs in his country, or, in event of his not doing it, declaring war on him.'[24] After this, the squadron returned home via Qishm, avoiding contact with HMS *La Chiffone*, possibly in the latter part of March.

This cruise is better documented than those before. The different independent reports from north-west India and the Gulf, some purporting to derive indirectly from the Qasimi crews, generally correspond well. It is, however, evident that the quality of the reports from Cutch and Sind reaching Seton in Muscat was sometimes inferior: dates, numbers and the details of engagements are at times quite wildly out.

Assailants: 8–10.
Boats plundered: 3.

LATE 1813

Two reports taken together imply the following: about the middle of November, a party of Qawasim, and possibly Jalahima, composed of 7 dows and 4 battils, slipped into Karachi harbour under cover of darkness and commenced ransacking vessels moored there. The opening-up of artillery from Manora fort, at the entrance to the creek, induced them to withdraw, but not before they had overrun five Cutch merchant vessels, only two of which were laden with cargo: one of them was allegedly abandoned, one carried off and the rest sunk.[25]

The botella *Palkee*, Tindal Musa, could have been one of these vessels.[26] According to the Bombay merchant Veerchund Sunder, she had set sail from Bombay for Cutch and Sind in November, and then fallen to the Qawasim, a loss of 8,000 rupees. The botella's Cranny, it seems, was later ransomed in Makran for a further 700 dollars; which itself could suggest that the report of the Qawasim having massacred all those crewmen at Karachi who had not managed to escape overboard was exaggerated.[27]

The Sind Agent's belated report discusses this and the subsequent cruise in one breath. Unlike the others who mention only Qasimi involvement, he speaks collectively of Qasimi and Utbi pirates, by which last he presumably intends the Jalahima. He implies that the above was the first act of Arab piracy off Sind for some time, presumably since before the 1809/10 expedition.

Assailants: 7 dows + 4 battils.
Boats plundered: 5?

EARLY 1814

This season's cruise is discussed in Chapter Six, section three. As was the case in November 1813, only the Sind Agent specifies how and where the captures took place. He writes that all seven vessels were plundered during an unopposed raid, in the latter part of Muharram (c. 8–22 January), on a port situated between Dharajah and Shahbandar; this apparently follows the pattern of November's raid on Karachi.[28] The report hastily sent by Indian mercantile contacts at Karachi on 14 January states that the Qawasim, who were then off Karachi, had already taken two Bombay grain vessels; a third having escaped after her crew had lightened her by jettisoning part of her load.[29] This seems vaguely incompatible with the description of a single harbour raid, but need not be.

These attacks had an impact on trade. Merchants at Karachi immediately reacted to the news by despatching a light dinghy to their correspondents in Porbandar,[30] advising them not to send any boats to Sind for the time being. This lends some substance to Elwood's remark soon after that 'whenever it becomes known that the Qawasim are on the Sind, all mercantile intercourse with that quarter ceases.'[31] There was a similar effect on the route to Muscat: in early February the Muscat Broker noted that there had been no arrivals from Cutch or Karachi for the past month on account of the above captures.[32]

This and the previous season's attacks prompted the Sind Amirs to consider the means of repelling the supposed pirates: it was proposed by one that the only practical solution was to appeal for the protection of British cruisers and a general hope was voiced that British efforts against piracy might prove availing; when the immediate danger passed, the matter was shelved.[33]

Assailants: 6(–10).
Boats plundered: c. 7.

LATE 1814

A number of vessels were plundered off Cutch, Sind and possibly Makran in November. Rutton Sing, apparently Sunderjee Sewjee's agent at Bombay and the only one to detail many of these cases, lists the more certain casualties as follows:[34]

Nine craft bringing gram from Sind to the Gulf of Cutch: three of these were bound to Beyt, and of the remainder, all from Dharajah, two were destined for Kumbaha and four were Mandvi vessels on their return voyage.[35] The crews of all except one of these possibly small boats swam safely ashore; the ten crew of the last, a Mandvi vessel, were reportedly murdered.

Three vessels sailing from Karachi to Muscat: the botella *Memsoor*, Nakhuda Humusa,[36] and two dinghies bearing the Company's pass, the *Dushmun Khor*, Nakhuda Buganah, and the *Radereeah*, Tindal Amind. Some doubts arose at Bombay over the existence of these passes.

Two British vessels, the (*Dungee Boresinga*)[37] and the *Khurreem Shahee*, plundered at Jakhau and Lakhpatbandar; with a third, the *Jairam Pursad*, which evaded capture at Jakhau. Like all the preceding acts, these are ascribed to the Qawasim.

The owners of this last group of British vessels each submitted petitions, which makes it possible to examine them in greater detail and to add one further victim, the *Sugand Pursad*,[38] to Sing's list:[39]

Veerchund Sunder, a Cutch merchant resident in Bombay, writes that his botella the *Dungee Boresinga*, Tindal Adam, was chased and boarded by 20 Qasimi dows near Jakhau;

> some of her crew threw themselves into the sea, in order to save their lives; in attempting which, most of them unfortunately perished and only few reached on shore. But, Right Sir, five women, three children and Cranny, who were unable to make their escape, [were] secured by the pirates: [they] put them into their own dows, with all the effects, goods, and also carried them, together with the said botella, away.

Another of his botellas, the *Sugand Pursad*, which had sailed for Cutch on 20 October, was also allegedly plundered, but the vessel was released with her crew.

Both vessels had been sailing under the British pass and colours, and Sunder claimed to have suffered a loss of 13,000 rupees by their plunder. The cargo of the first comprised: gold joys,[40] a bale of cloth, 19 bags of dates, 15 canisters of sugar, 10 tubs of sugar candy and 20,000 coconuts. That of the second consisted of: gold joys, 4 bales of tobacco, 20 bags of sugar, 15 tubs of sugar candy, 100 bags of dates and 300 bags of betel-nuts.

Pragjee Luckah Madas,[41] Porbandar merchant, asserts that during November his dinghy the *Khurreem Shahee*, Tindal Phool, had carried 2,500 rupees worth of dates, soft sugar, lead, tootnague, red lead and drugs from Bombay to Porbandar; she had then proceeded to Lakhpatbandar creek, where the crew now spied a dow and four jymers. Concluding from their composition that they were Qawasim, the crew, in fear, ran themselves ashore; whereupon, 'one of these five boats approached the *Khurreem Shahee* and anchored in deep water, and sent her men in a small boat which came near my dinghy, on seeing which the whole crew of my dinghy ran away.' The crew had omitted to hoist their British colours; consequently the merchant was refused British help in recovering his goods. The dinghy, after being stripped, was abandoned, only to be confiscated by the local chief, or Mehtar, of Koteesen, who at first refused to release her.[42]

Dyal Moolaney, Bombay merchant, records that his botella the *Jairam Pursad*, Tindal Pitambu, had sailed from Bombay for Cutch, possibly calling at Beyt en route to Lakhpatbandar. When she arrived near Jakhau on *c.* 11 November, she was chased by 'an armed vessel of the Qawasim', whereupon she escaped by putting into port and running aground.[43] Moolaney's petition, therefore, did not so much concern the Qawasim, but the Raja of Cutch, who had impounded the vessel of a British subject and would not release her. There is an obvious parallel here with the preceding case.

All these incidents appear to have occurred in November, possibly in or by around the middle of the month. Dim reports speak of those responsible sailing westward past Karachi, perhaps around late November, or possibly early December. Despite Sunder, some reports suggest that the captors consisted of up to five boats, but this is not certain. The number of boats plundered, of which 15 have been listed, seems large by comparison. Panic could have played a part in this result: almost all the plundered boats seem to have been abandoned by their crews.

There is something elusive about these events. The records appear to contain no corroboration from Gulf sources, and there is apparently no further mention of the supposed British vessels lost en route to Karachi. The Porbandar Agent, Elwood, avers that Qasimi responsibility for these acts of plunder was not certain, but likely.[44] He gives two justifications for this belief: that the jymer was a Gulf vessel, and that five vessels off Karachi, supposedly the guilty parties, may have left a boat unmolested since she flew British colours; this was supposed to reflect Hasan bin Rahma's recent promises, in October, and so to show that they were Qawasim.[45] This reasoning is very weak: the jymer seems to have been a Makrani vessel, and the other part of Elwood's argument, besides being ironic, is circular.

It might be conjectured that this season's captors, assuming they were actually all part of one group, had arrived from somewhere west of Sind. The presence of jymers could point to Makran; there may also have been one Gulf vessel involved. A good deal remains uncertain.

Assailants: [5]?
Boats plundered: 15.

EARLY 1815 [46]

It appears that a group of vessels may have left the Gulf for Sind in, or possibly by, January. There are ambiguous reports of activity off India during that month.[47] The return journey is better documented: news reached the merchants of Mangrol by 25 February that the Qawasim had quitted Sind for the Gulf, presumably a week or more before;[48] a report from Linga suggests their arrival at Ras al-Khaima in, or possibly by, the third week of March.

These vessels are alleged to have captured the following 6 boats off Karachi and Sind: three owned by Muscat and bound to Mocha, a baghla from Malabar carrying rice, planks(?) and timbers, a pattamar from Muscat bound to Bombay and a dinghy from Karachi; the majority of their crews are said to have been killed.[49] The presence of these reported Qawasim off Sind, caused a suspension of voyages between there and Kathiawar at least during the earlier part of February.[50]

Boats from Abu Dhabi, Linga and Ras al-Khaima are said to have confirmed that the Qawasim were responsible for this season's Sind cruise, although the evidence from India may have been less definite. The Muscat Broker, in a late report, claims that c. 25 assorted vessels, belonging to 'the Qawasim, and the Imanees[51] and some of the adherents of Sultan bin Saqr', had originally set off towards Karachi, Sind, and possibly Cutch; in his next despatch, he speaks of 25 Qawasim from Ras al-Khaima, and 12 of

Sultan bin Saqr's adherents.[52] It is not stated that all these 25 (or 37) eventually went to India, nor is it clear that they all sailed together or with one purpose; unfortunately there are no reports of numbers from India. The more moderate figure of 25 still looks large, though not, presumably, out of the question; a year later the Utub managed to send a group of 16 trading vessels to India, followed by another of 5.[53]

Assailants: not explicit (out of 25 or 37?).
Boats plundered: 6.

EARLY 1816

At the beginning of January it was reported that over 20 Qasimi vessels had left Ras al-Khaima, *c*. 12 of them bound for Ras al-Hadd, the remainder for the Gulf or Sind.[54] It is not apparent what followed.

LATE 1816 AND EARLY 1817

By the middle of November the Qawasim were reported to be cruising off Sind. Around the end of the first week of December, the report went out from Sind that they had burnt an empty Porbandar vessel and captured a Sind boat taking rice to Mandvi. Two weeks later 8 large and 8 small Qasimi boats were said to be cruising off Sind. On 3 January, it was believed at Sonmiani that the Qawasim had returned to Ras al-Khaima.[55] These four brief items of report, if accurate, suggest a discrete cruise of two months or so, beginning around late October. This would not have been unusual: the Qawasim were said to visit Sind in this way 'regularly every year in [the] fair season.'[56] But there is another possible interpretation, namely that the 'sixteen' Qasimi vessels were those which appeared off Cutch in January 1817: this would equally explain why they disappeared from Sind in later December. In this case, there would either have been no separate cruise in late 1816, or else one that ended rather earlier than suggested.

The events of January and February 1817 have been discussed in Chapter Six, section three. It is as well to recapitulate. As far as may be inferred, there were two groups of alleged Qawasim active off Cutch in January. The first reportedly consisted of *c*. 7 (4–11) medium size or smaller boats; these were either trankeys (battils), with crews of between 50 and 80, or alternatively, perhaps, a roughly equal mixture of dows and jymers.[57] During the first two weeks of January, this group is said to have plundered 11 vessels between Lakhpat and Mandvi: one of these was the *Luckmee Pussaud*, captured, with serious loss of life, near Lakhpat on *c*. 10 January; two belonged to Sunderjee Sewjee and were run ashore near Jakhau, the crew of one being pursued on land as far as Soothree, a Cranny perishing in the process; the remaining eight were small Mandvi craft. On 17 January, this group made an attempt on 3(–5) trading vessels in their home port of Mandvi, but were repelled by the boats of the Cutch Raja. Three additional captures are said to have been made during January: a Cambay botella taking tobacco from Dwarka to Cutch, stripped and released before 20 January, with two others, one of them a Porbandar vessel, about which details were not forthcoming. This makes a total of up to 14 alleged prizes.

The second group, about which we can be reasonably certain, consisted of 3 large baghlas, of between 300 and 400 candies, carrying a total of 350 men. These captured the HC pattamar *Darya Daulat* off Dwarka on 7 January, then briefly continued southward, capturing a 400-candy dow (baghla) from Surat, before they doubled back, out at sea, to Sind. They made land near Shahbandar. Here they took on water and sup-posedly rejoined the first group. Next they followed inshore as far as Makran. Having set down some of the *Darya Daulat*'s crew in the vicinity of Pasni around 4 February, or shortly thereafter, they sailed finally for Ras al-Khaima.

In the early part of February, fresh reports arrived at Bushire from Bahrain, Linga and Kangan, stating that 15 Qawasim had sailed for Cutch and Gujarat; something over a month later, a curious list was brought from Muscat purporting to itemize recent Qasimi captures off India. These 18 included: two pattamars and a Muscat baghla captured off Daman; four cotias[58] seized off Cutch; three dinghies carried off Karachi; four cotias and two dinghies plundered off Drawzee Sind; a dinghy taken off Makran; and a baghla from Mangalore.[59] On the face of it, these two items of intelligence would seem to point to an additional cruise.[60] But the evidence is not so easy to evalu-ate. There is no recorded direct confirmation from India of a second such cruise, and the reference to activity as far south as Daman is perplexing and superficially doubtful. There is a temptation, though it is not supported by positive evidence, to attribute some of these alleged captures to the Qawasim active before February, discounting the idea of later depredations.[61]

Much the most certain of all these episodes, therefore, is January's cruise. Three aspects of this are worth highlighting. First, the response of local governments: the Cutch authorities despatched armed vessels against those who raided Mandvi harbour, and the Minister at Porbandar, Sunderjee Sewjee's nephew, put his port's defences in readiness. Second, the effect on commerce: reports from Mandvi and Porbandar at the very end of January attest that the trade from Malabar and Bombay to Cutch, and from Porbandar to Cutch, Sind and Muscat, had been disrupted or halted for much of the month. Third, the novelty of January's cruise; this was widely believed to have been the first instance of Qasimi depredations as far east as the Gulf of Cutch; previously they had confined their attentions, it was said, to Sind.

A. *Assailants:* 8 large + 8 small?
   Boats plundered: 2.

B. *Assailants:* 3 baghlas   *Boats plundered:* 2.
   Assailants: c. 7 (4–11)   *Boats plundered:* 14.

+ up to 11 victims (alternatively: up to 15 separate assailants; 18 victims)?

LATE 1817

On 4 November 1817, *c.* 36 Indian merchants of Bombay signed a petition addressed to the Governor, Sir Evan Nepean, in which they complained that 20 Qawasim had captured 4 Bombay vessels, along with 4 others returning to their home ports of Mus-cat, Cutch, Porbandar, Mangrol and Veraval. The interest of the petitioners, whose names include some who had lost vessels in previous years, lay in their personal involvement in the northern trade.[62] Their hope was that the Company would take measures to restore the freedom of navigation along these routes.

A variety of sources from north-western India speak of Qasimi depredations off Cutch during October. Some estimates of the number of Qawasim involved ran as high as 20 and 34, prompting Elwood, the Porbandar Agent, to remark that he could not 'implicitly rely on native intelligence *as to extent of force*', on account of its being 'frequently exaggerated'.[63] The more reasonable estimates of the number of sail of

Qawasim range between 10 and 15. Elwood, the only one to attempt anything more specific, suggests a force composed of 7 dows and 5 jymers.[64]

The first recorded sighting of the Qawasim occurred off Jakhau on c. 15 October. They next appeared further south, towards Mandvi, on c. 19 October, or shortly after. They may have persisted in the Mandvi–Beyt–Dwarka area for at least a week or so. Soon after this, and certainly by mid-November, they were reported to have withdrawn northward.

Responding to these reports, Bombay despatched the HC ships *Teignmouth* and *Aurora* to Cutch and Sind in early November. The news also reached Lieutenant George Grant,[65] head of the Guicowar of Baroda's naval establishment since c. 1813, at his station, Velun, near Diu Head. He reacted with speed and initiative, by hiring and manning a brig (or grab snow), and persuading the Portuguese Governor of Diu to send out a 16-gun corvette.

All four vessels fell in with one another at Porbandar on 13 November. Their arrival enabled the Agent, Elwood, to put 20 merchant boats, which hitherto had been detained at the port for up to three weeks on account of the Qawasim, under convoy of the 24-gun *Teignmouth*, Captain Walker.[66] Grant proceeded with the Portuguese corvette only, it seems, as far as Dwarka. The *Teignmouth*, however, reached Mandvi on 19 November, then went on to Karachi. None of these vessels encountered the alleged Qawasim, who had apparently departed before the vessels sent against them had time to arrive.[67] In Elwood's view, this was typical, and demonstrated the need in future to station ships on these coasts in advance.[68]

It is interesting to note that in two letters referring to these events, Portuguese sources describe those allegedly then 'committing every sort of hostilities against the commerce of all nations' as Utub, and not Qawasim.[69] This may say something about the Portuguese contact with and knowledge of the Gulf Arabs at this time: it probably says little about the true identity of the alleged pirates active this year, since these same Portuguese sources seem to have derived all knowledge of their activities from the British who, along with all other sources bar one who speaks loosely of 'Wahhabis',[70] universally term them Qawasim.[71]

Reports of the number of captures made by the Qawasim before their departure from Cutch run as high as eight. Half of these could perhaps be more certain than the rest.

It is reasonably clear that on or shortly after 15 October, 2–4 merchant boats, possibly botellas, were run on shore near Jakhau. They are said to have been abandoned by their crews and subsequently plundered. According to Sunderjee Sewjee at Mandvi, 4 other vessels, comprising 2 dinghies and 2 pattamars, were plundered at sea before 20 October. Sewjee's total of 8 prizes matches that given by the Bombay merchants, though he does not, like them, state that half were Bombay vessels: the complementary nature of these two accounts may not be fortuitous, since all were part of one mercantile community.[72] Sources at Porbandar put the total number of captures lower, at c. 3 (2–4), since they only take account of boats run aground at Jakhau.

One of the vessels taken off Jakhau was the botella *Dojunsul*, Tindal Saō, sailing under the Company's pass and flag. She belonged to the Bombay merchant Dyal Moolaney,[73] and when captured had been proceeding from Beyt to Lakhpat, in company with seven predominantly Bombay merchantmen: her cargo was valued at 1,200 rupees. Moolaney adds that another of his vessels, the Bombay *Jairam Pursad*, Tindal Boads, carrying a British pass, was likewise pursued by the Qawasim, but managed to escape.[74]

The identity of only one other of the plundered vessels is known. The 58-candy pattamar *Sacry Sallamly*, Tindal Balloo, sailing under the British flag and pass, was allegedly stripped and abandoned near Mandvi on c. 19 October; her hull was sub-sequently recovered. The *Sacry Sallamly* had sailed from Bombay on the 5th direct for Cutch, with one Cranny and a crew of 10, and a cargo of sugar, iron, steel, copra, dates, rice and sundries worth nearly 2,000 rupees.

> It appears from the information received from the crew (4 of which are arrived at this place and the remainder 6 coming behind) [wrote her owner, the Bombay merchant Khettoo Damjee] that the pattamar, when approached near Cutch Mandvi within the distance of about 4 coss,[75] they perceived that a dow of the pirates hastening over them, when they (the crew) made possible speed to gain the shore. But when near it about 2 coss, they found it impossible to reach it before the pirates could overtake them; so they lost their spirits, and thrown themselves into the sea and reached the shore near Soothree. When they were [brought][76] deep into the water, they saw the Wahhabis first fell on the boat, and there perceiving nobody, afterwards took it along their vessel—thus all men on board saved their life.
>
> The crew, after refreshing themselves in the village, went to Mandvi where they were informed that their pattamar was lying empty on the bandar of Beyt or Dwarka. They immediately went there in a hired boat and found it was true: the Wahhabis, after unloading the pattamar, abandoned her to the sea.[77]

Assailants: 7 dows [+ 5 jymers].
Boats plundered: 8.

18[15]–18

In January 1819, Mir Muhammad Khan of Luz wrote that 'some time ago'—according to the Bombay Governor this was 'not long since'—Sonmiani was attacked by the Qawasim: 'taking advantage of the reduction of the force at Sonmiani, [they] came there and plundered the country, and when their personal safety would not permit them to remain longer, they set fire to the place.' In response, Mir Muhammad Khan says he sent a force after them, but failed to come up with them; thereupon he trans-ported the same troops to Muscat, where they assisted the ruler in an attack on 'the town of the Qawasim'.[78]

LATE 1818 (A)

In January 1819, local people at Ormara maintained that during that season, the Qawasim had taken a man and four boys out of a small boat which had been fishing outside the bay. This could have occurred as early as October 1818.[79]

An incident occurred this month which, though of fleeting importance, deserves clarification. On 26 October, just off Bhitiaro Creek, the HCCs *Thetis* and *Psyche*, with the armed pattamar *Turrarow*, encountered 4 vessels standing toward them: two smaller boats, followed some way behind by a pair of large 'war trankeys' or battils. Lieutenant Tanner concluded, from their appearance, that the trankeys were Qawasim and, from their evasive behaviour and crowded hulls, that the two smaller boats were sailing in company with them; finding the latter within range, he therefore brought them to under a cross fire and put them under detention, before setting out northward in pursuit of the trankeys, which soon escaped by 'very superior sailing.'[80]

The interrogation of the crews of the two detained boats at sea, was followed by further enquiries after they had been brought to Mandvi.[81] The larger of the two vessels had been carrying a crew of 18 and 140 passengers; the smaller, 9 crew and 29 passengers; together they were in possession of 64 matchlocks, 44 swords, 24 'waist-knives', 5 shields and a spear. Both were Gwadar vessels bound for Mandvi. Each claimed originally to have taken on board, in addition to their Baluchi passengers, cargoes, respectively, of dates and 'baskets for fish':[82] these last had allegedly been delivered to Karachi. The passengers were reportedly in search of service, presumably as mercenaries.

Keywall,[83] the Sindi Banyan Supercargo of the larger vessel, said his boat belonged to a Gwadar Banyan named Amo; he added that he had taken on his passengers at Gwadar, at the rate of one riyal per head, with the authorization of a Muscati, presumably an official. Parraree, the Muscati Nakhuda of the smaller boat, stated his vessel to be the property of a Gwadar Arab: this was, however, disputed at Mandvi by the merchant Sulaiman. According to Sulaiman, this boat had belonged to him, and had been given up for lost in September 1817, after she had been run ashore near Gwadar by 2–3 possibly Qasimi pirates. The general belief at Mandvi was that these were pirates. Keywall and Parraree were unable to find anyone in the town to act as surety for them, and it is said they 'were scoffed and spit at as pirates by many of the inhabitants'.[84]

Despite this, it is slightly easier to believe in Keywall and Parraree's innocence than otherwise. They each maintained that they had sighted the two supposedly Qasimi trankeys for the first time on the morning of the 26th: 'we know their boats and we could see they were pirates.'[85] This prompted them to fire a few warning shots and get underway, the larger Makrani boat heaving her cargo of dates overboard in order to assist her escape: hence the scene that met Tanner on that day, and hence too the disappearance of Keywall's cargo of dates.

Two minor points arise from this episode. First, the scene as it appeared on 26 October. The two detained boats are not described as jymers. Nevertheless, Tanner's first sighting appears to fit a pattern on these coasts: it is stated on a number of occasions that Qasimi trankeys cruised in company with smaller Makrani boats, called jymers, which generally preceded them and shared responsibility for their depredations. Whether or not the present episode, and its possibly innocent explanation, are typical, is unclear. Second, the identity of the trankeys: a week or so later, Qasimi vessels allegedly descended on Kathiawar; the two trankeys could in theory have been part of this group on its way southward.[86]

On 3–5 November, Lieutenant Guy of the HCC Psyche had three encounters, some or all of which could be interpreted as further evidence of the southward passage of this group: on 3 October, Guy had an engagement, near Lakhpat river, with a baghla and a trankey which he believed to be attacking him, and which resulted in the probable sinking of the trankey. The next day he sighted two baghlas and two trankeys, which he took to be pirates; they eluded him. On the evening of the 5th, just north of Mandvi, Guy heard a 'brisk fire of guns to the westward, and shortly after saw a blaze as if a vessel on fire.' The following morning, he rescued 22 Arabs clinging to a detached yard. They proved to belong to a Muscat vessel which had apparently caught fire during an engagement with two Qawasim.[87] 'Yesterday', wrote Sunderjee Sewjee on 17 November,

[I] received a letter from Porbandar learning to me the following sorrowful information of the barbarous Qawasim ... The boats of these merciless pirates are stated to be nine in number, consisting of 2 large dows and 7 boats; they are walking over the sea from Mandvi to Diu, and whenever they see any other boats going, or coming, they run immediately after them; and the boats that are unfortunately falling in their hands, they instantly massacre the crew of the captured boats, and rob the goods laden in them.[88]

A good deal of Qasimi activity is reported off the coast of Kathiawar during the first three weeks of November. The focus of these depredations begins in the north and progresses southward, but there may have been two or more groups of vessels involved.

The first reported appearance of the Qawasim off Kathiawar occurred on c. 5 November, when, according to letters from Beyt and Porbandar, two vessels were taken south of Beyt, possibly in or near the river at Dwarka.[89] There may be confirmation of maritime disruption around this spot, and conceivably of these same captures, in Lieutenant Tanner's having observed three dinghies lying stranded on the beach between Dwarka and nearby Muddie on c. 5–8 November. Tanner adds that he had then found the coast from Mandvi to Porbandar 'completely infested by a numerous horde of Qasimi pirates,' made up of 3 baghlas and 6–8 large trankeys, all of them well manned: 'we have engaged, both day and night, for this last week [4–9 Nov.] with several divisions of these marauders, in a series of rencontres and pursuits'; but on each occasion Tanner was outsailed.[90]

The alleged Qawasim next appear slightly further south. On 6 November, a boat, possibly one of 150-candies laden with timbers and other goods, was reportedly run ashore and plundered by 2 Qasimi dows and 2 trankeys six miles north-west of Porbandar. A second vessel was chased, and there may also have been a third, this time successful, attack, on a vessel bound from Porbandar to Anjar, all of whose crew, except the Cranny, managed to swim to safety. After the first of these attacks, the Raja[91] of Porbandar directed a gun be taken to the spot and unleashed against the captors, who withdrew out to sea.[92]

On 7 November, the four assailants were clearly seen from Porbandar, full of men and steering at speed in a south-easterly direction; the trankeys sailed before the dows, at a distance of two miles. On 9 November, what appeared to be a second group of Qawasim, 4 large dows and 2 small trankeys, passed Porbandar to the south-east. Four subsequent reports from Porbandar add little to this picture of the supposed Qawasim's movements, beyond further suggesting that they did not all keep together: on 11 November, within three miles of the port, two Qasimi boats reportedly attacked a pattamar carrying Lieutenant Powell with a detachment of sepoys, but were beaten off; on the same day the Raja of Porbandar warded off a supposed Qasimi by means of two shot from the cannon he had placed in defence of the creek; on 12 November, it was believed there were others still to the north-west;[93] on 15 November, in view of the shore, Lieutenant Guy set twenty-four sails aboard the HCC Psyche in an effort to come up with two supposed Qasimi trankeys, but was defeated by a poor wind and the trankeys' oars.[94]

Very shortly after 7 November, the Qawasim are said to have emptied two vessels, which had been travelling from Bombay to Cutch, in the vicinity of Madhaypur,[95] after their crews had swum to safety.

Next, the creek or port of Mangrol was reportedly raided by up to 8–9 Qawasim; a new, empty dow, the *Futeh Sawoy*, apparently a British vessel belonging to the Bombay merchant Nanjee Seazkrun, was carried off, and there may also have been successful attacks on four Mangrol merchant boats.[96]

Then, on 9 November, moving ever southward, now between Mangrol and Veraval, the Qawasim reportedly plundered the cotia *Hurry Pussa*, Tindal Isac, and made off with one of her crew; presumably a British vessel, she belonged to Sunderjee Sewjee, and had sailed from Bombay on 3 November for Porbandar and Anjar. Her cargo, all of which was abstracted, was mostly, it seems, the property of Bombay merchants,[97] and is listed as follows, beginning with Sewjee's own goods and belongings:[98]

	Value (in rupees)
10 robins of turmeric	55
10 tubs of sugar-candy	155
25 bags and 10 chests of sugar	617
1 chest of cardamoms	86
1 keg of red lead	25
11 candies of iron	528
1¼ Surat maunds (*c*. 66 lb.) cloves	141[99]
5 ps. tin	115
1 *palanquin*	500
1 bale of gunny pawls[100]	54
4 pieces of doriyas[101]	48
Boat's stores	500
Luckmedass Madowjee, gold	1,750
Mawa Umerchund Kunjee, box of jewels	1,500
Mighu Pursholum, nutmegs	10
Spices belonging to the merchants,	
Thucker Mowjee Annundjee	4,500
Bhimjee Dewray	1,400
Toolsedass Mathooradass	840
Rewajon[102] Phocarjoos	3,250
Thaker Nudoo Nazim	1,300
Mulkha Vurjee	40
Moorajee Jewram	1,160
Herjee Jyram	1,025
A chest shipped by Sir Roger de Farria(?) to Capt. Macmurdo[103] at Anjar	—
Total	19,599

In July 1819, Sewjee learnt that his palanquin was lying in the mercantile house of Messrs Stroker, Malcolm & Co. at Bombay; it had, he was informed, been recovered by a Royal Naval sloop. In fact, there is no doubt that this was the palanquin Captain Loch had managed to retrieve from Bahrain in February 1819, and which appears even to have borne Sewjee's initials. The independent report from Bahrain in February 1819 was that the palanquin had been brought for sale to the island from Ras al-Khaima.[104] This is rare and powerful evidence that those who plundered the *Hurry Pussa* on 9 November 1818 were indeed Qawasim.

Within a few days after this attack, the Qawasim reportedly captured a boat at Marwar, en route from Bombay to Veraval, and killed nine on board.

The last vessel specifically reported to have fallen to the Qawasim, and the furthest south, was another of Sunderjee Sewjee's boats, the *Tiger*, Tindal Sam. This vessel had sailed originally from Malabar to Bombay, which she had left on 10 November bound for Porbandar, with a cargo belonging to Sewjee and other merchants valued at around 5,000 rupees. On the 18th she was taken near Kodinar,[105] all her crew managing to swim to safety.

Soon after this, disruption ceased, and by the end of the month British officers felt confident that the Qawasim had vacated the coasts of Cutch and Kathiawar.[106]

Throughout these weeks, it will have become clear that the Company's cruisers were active in the vicinity of these captures. Indeed, by the middle of November, there were as many as 3 brigs, 2 ships and 2 armed pattamars busy cruising and running convoys in the area.[107] But although there were sightings, the British cruisers were almost always quite unable to come up with the supposed Qawasim on account of the latter's superior sailing, their use of oars and their ability to sail in shallow waters; only the pattamars had the requisite shallow draught, but these were by themselves weak.[108] Shipping and commerce along the coast of Kathiawar, and to Cutch, was severely disrupted during most of November; vessels remained in port, requested convoys and, if underway, took refuge in numbers and in coastal creeks.[109]

It is suggested in the sources, that the above 15 specific captures, which all took place between about 5 and 18 November, were the work of two, or possibly three, groups of Qawasim. The pattern of seizures is nevertheless apparently compatible with a voyage by one loose group of attackers from Mandvi to Kodinar. Confused sightings, and the presence of prizes with the captors, make the true number of assailants difficult to ascertain. The Porbandar Agent, Elwood, eventually puts the total at 5 Qasimi baghlas and 9 of their trankeys or battils, accompanied by 4 Makrani jymers acting as pilots.[110] Other sources speak of 8–9 Qasimi vessels, accompanied by as many as 10 prizes. The first-hand sightings at Porbandar suggest a minimum of 4 baghlas and 2 trankeys: it might perhaps be supposed that the number of trankeys at least equalled the number of baghlas; the resultant hypothetical total of roughly 4 baghlas and 4–6 trankeys looks not out of proportion, but cannot be relied upon.

All the sources speak of Qasimi responsibility for November's captures; and it is also worth noting that in mid-November the Muscat Broker wrote, no doubt loosely as regards numbers, that around 35 assorted vessels had sailed from Ras al-Khaima, Umm al-Qaiwain and Ajman for Karachi and Cutch.[111]

Besides this general evidence, there are two important specific indicators to be considered. The first of these is the business of Sunderjee Sewjee's palanquin, which, as already demonstrated, is convincing evidence that the *Hurry Pussa* was rifled by a Qasimi boat connected with, or based at Ras al-Khaima.

Before considering the final piece of evidence it is useful to return to the attack on Lieutenant Powell's pattamar off Porbandar on 11 November. Powell's brief description of this attack says very little, but is perhaps worth citing since it represents one of the few attacks on a Company vessel:

> Yesterday, between the hours of twelve and one in the forenoon, when within about three miles of Porbandar, I perceived two large pattamars[112] apparently bearing down for the purpose of attacking the boat in which I was aboard; on

nearing, they proved to be two Qasimi pirates, and when within pistol-shot opened a smart matchlock-fire, which was returned by me, and I am happy to add, that after three-quarters of an hour, I succeeded in beating them off without any loss on my side ... The whole of the sepoys behaved with the greatest coolness, and from the steady fire which was kept up by them, I am convinced that some casualties must have occurred on the side of the enemy, which was probably the cause of their not attempting to board.[113]

The real importance of this attack lies at one remove. Lieutenant Powell's sepoys belonged to the 1st/5th Native Infantry. In March 1819, a number of British Indian women were freed from captivity at Ras al-Khaima. They proved to be the wives of a body of sepoys, also from the 5th Regiment of Bombay Native Infantry; the sepoys had perished, and their families been enslaved, when their pattamar had been captured by the Qawasim some months before.

It seems likely that this second, troop-carrying Government pattamar was taken by the Qawasim, en route from Bombay to Anjar, in November.[114] On 17 November, the Porbandar Agent mentioned that two pattamars taking troops to Tuna, which had gone missing, seemed to have reappeared: the HCC *Psyche* was believed to have spoken one and sighted the other off Dwarka on 14 November. This might suggest that the pattamar in question was taken a day or so later in the Gulf of Cutch. On the other hand, the *Psyche*'s sighting may not have been reliable: it can be inferred that the pattamar in question had somehow gone missing, or astray, by 11 November or shortly after, since this is when the accompanying vessels seem to have reached Porbandar. This could imply that the pattamar was in fact captured off Kathiawar, possibly south of Porbandar, and possibly by 11 November, or shortly after. The evidence of the Indian women released from Ras al-Khaima seems to suggest an association between those who took the *Hurry Pussa* and those who took their pattamar, possibly even that the same vessel or vessels were responsible for both attacks.[115] A possible witness of the capture of the pattamar, who was himself on one of three dinghies allegedly captured by the Qawasim of Ras al-Khaima on the same occasion, may have surfaced at Muscat in May 1819.[116]

There is doubt as to the precise date and location of the attack on the troop-carrying pattamar, but no doubt as to the authorship. This, combined with the evidence of Sunderjee Sewjee's palanquin, is proof that the Qawasim attacked and plundered two British vessels here. The most reasonable explanation of the remaining captures off Cutch and Kathiawar during November is that they too were the work of the Qawasim.

LATE 1818 (B)

After leaving the coast of Kathiawar at the end of November, the Qawasim reportedly visited the area for a second time this season, in December. Lieutenant Tanner claims to have encountered 10 vessels south-west of Cape Monze on 8 December, which, if not perhaps the earlier group on their way home, might conceivably have included this second group on their way south.[117]

The first certain appearance occurred at Muddie, just south of Dwarka, on about 15 December. Twelve merchant vessels, sailing from Mandvi and Beyt to Bombay, reached Muddie only to discover 3 large and 2 small 'pirate' boats lying at anchor. They immediately turned back to Dwarka, pursued by at least the two smaller boats: eight of the merchant vessels took refuge under the fort at Dwarka, and the other four successfully resisted their pursuers further out, by a combination of their own fire and the help of a reinforcement sent out from the shore by Mr R.I. Handley of the Guicowar's service. Handley then also directed a force of 50 Arab mercenaries to Muddie, which Elwood thought judicious, 'as the pirates have more than once landed there to procure water and to seize cattle.'[118]

The Qawasim were next reported further south, at Navibandar, which they are said to have quitted about 18 December.[119] One report claimed they had captured four boats near Mangrol by about 20 December.[120] By 22 December, they were said to have made a landing near Veraval, before being beaten off by villagers in their attempt to cut three vessels out of the creek.[121] This appears to be the last sighting off Kathiawar.

The sighting near Dwarka put the number of reported Qawasim at 3 large and 2 smaller vessels. According to Elwood, the maximum number of vessels involved in this cruise was eventually put at 13 including their (4 or more?) prizes, consisting of 6 large baghlas and 7 assorted trankeys and jymers.[122] His impression was that they sailed in 2–3 divisions, attacking in different spots nearly simultaneously; the surviving evidence, such as it is, does not necessitate such an interpretation. Only four specific captures are recorded from Cutch and Kathiawar for December.

The above account of the Qawasim's reported activities during both November and December, records 20 specific captures.[123] The sources imply that this list is not exhaustive. It is best to eschew broad claims as evidence, but it is still of some interest to note that Elwood estimated the total number of Qasimi victims in these two months, between Karachi and Diu, at 35 sail: 'many of these boats', he claimed, 'were richly laden; one was valued at a lac of dollars, and some had treasure. The number of lives lost is not known'.[124]

On 26 and 28 December, British vessels had encounters with six alleged Qawasim, apparently towing four prizes, off Makran. The details of these incidents are recounted in the main text.[125] The second of these encounters is the more immediately pertinent. On this occasion, two baghlas and two battils were sighted, apparently towing three prizes. One of the prizes was captured by the British, and her crew interrogated.[126] This interrogation provides strong evidence that the four vessels did indeed belong to Ras al-Khaima, and that they were then returning home with three out of the four prizes they had recently taken off India, the fourth prize having been abandoned as unseaworthy. The crew said their voyage had taken them from a point in Makran to Sind, then south to Mangrol; and that they had set out from Ras al-Khaima 45 days earlier, or about 13 November. Although the dates look tight, it is feasible that these four vessels were those active off Kathiawar in mid-December; otherwise they may have taken their prizes slightly earlier or further north. Either way, this is convincing evidence that the Qawasim took at least four vessels off north-west India in December.

A. *Assailants*: c. 4 baghlas + 4–6 trankeys? (6–14 + 4 jymers).
   Boats plundered: 16.

B. *Assailants*: 3 baghlas + 2 trankeys (4–9).
   Boats plundered: 4.

(A + B: assailants, high figure of 35; victims, + 1 at Ormara (A?))

On 2 March, the Porbandar Agent confirmed that the Qawasim had not reappeared that year, and pronounced that there was now 'not the smallest probability that the pirates will appear before October next.'[127] Two days later, on 4 and 5 March, two Qasimi dows and two Makrani jymers were reported by him to have plundered some merchant boats off Dwarka.[128] There is no doubt that a number of vessels were plundered: cruisers found two such off Muddie on 8 March, and another, a small dinghy full of water, 25 miles WNW of Porbandar on the 10th.[129] The season was well advanced:[130] one Marine officer thought that Gulf boats were unlikely to have been responsible, since the north-west winds set in about now, making the return passage arduous; he even suggested that local pirates, from Dwarka or thereabouts, had carried out the attacks, falsely claiming to be Qawasim.[131] The Porbandar Agent, Elwood, disagreed: though he conceded that it was on the face of it improbable that they were Qawasim, he maintained that it was not impossible, since the north-westers only set in in earnest with Hoolee, on 12 March.

First-hand evidence was given by four wounded Porbandar sailors who had been captured and released by the attackers: they attested that their captors did not speak Gujarati together, and claimed they had heard them repeatedly use the words 'Ras al-Khaima', from which they presumed they were Qawasim. A fifth released captive, a Sindi, maintained that he knew there to be Baluchis among the attackers. Elwood concluded the captors were Qawasim, assisted by Baluchis: had they been local freebooters, he argued, this must have come out, 'for the trading community is greatly interested in detecting pirates.'[132]

The identity of these attackers remains uncertain; they need not have been Arabs. The evidence of the escapees suggests that they were neither Gujaratis nor Sindis, but included Baluchis from Makran.

Assailants: [2 dows + 2 jymers].
Boats plundered: c. 3?

It was reported from Linga by late September that seven Qasimi vessels from Ras al-Khaima and Dhaya had left the Gulf bound for Sind and Gujarat.[133] In about the first week of October, piracy was reported off northern Cutch. An alleged Qasimi dow and two trankeys were witnessed running a boat ashore at Jakhau on 3 October, though it is not clear whether the boat was then plundered;[134] another source spoke of four Wahhabi dows taking four Sind dinghies there.[135] Some reports put the total number of captures as high as 6–8 sail, taken, this time, in the vicinity of the Lakhpat river.[136] These last figures look superficially high, especially if there was any truth to the Bhuj Resident's apparent contention that only two, relatively small, Makran vessels were responsible, one of them carrying 62 men armed with matchlocks; strangely he even asserts they were the very same pair of vessels arrested by Tanner in 1818.[137] The counter assertion, championed by Sunderjee Sewjee, with his Mandvi contacts, and by the Porbandar Agent, was that the Qawasim were responsible. The basis for this identification is unclear.

Six weeks later, there were fresh reports of pirates. On 15 November, a group of men landed at a spot five miles north-west of Porbandar, apparently intent on stealing cattle: 'they wounded two men who were quietly cutting wood; these gave the alarm to the village, whose inhabitants assembled with their matchlocks and drove the plunderers from the shore'.[138] The next day, two boats were seen to approach to within half a mile of the port of Porbandar, then stand out to the north-west. These were evidently the disappointed cattle raiders; the Porbandar Agent had no doubt that their boats bespoke them from Makran. There is otherwise no obvious connection between this and the much earlier events of October. It may, however, constitute evidence that Makran vessels, possibly jymers, though this is not made explicit, sometimes carried out small raids along these coasts.[139]

A: *Assailants*: [1 dow + 2 trankeys (2–4)].
   Boats plundered: 1–4? (0–8).

B: *Assailants*: [2 Makran vessels].

APPENDIX B

Qasimi Voyages to South Arabia

Qasimi seizures off south Arabia bear some comparison with those in Indian waters. The two arenas were equally far-flung, the periods of recorded activity broadly correspond in time, and the nature of the enterprise was one. But there were significant differences. Qasimi activity off south Arabia was a more earnest affair, as the presence of Ibrahim bin Rahma as commander and the quality of the encounters demonstrate.

Moreover, it was often discernibly coloured or conditioned by the politics of Arabia. The trading ports and tribes of the Arabian littoral developed mutually beneficial alignments, some of which are tantalizingly visible in what follows, and in this period each was additionally required to determine its own relationship with the Saudi state: many of the ports whose trade suffered at the hands of Wahhabi Ras al-Khaima, places such as Shihr and Mukalla, came to be regarded as its natural enemies by the Saudi state.

The pickings off south Arabia were far richer than in Indian waters. The trade of India with the Red Sea suffered directly. The Government of Bombay became understandably concerned. The consequences of this, and the more material incidents, have been discussed in the body of this work, including Chapter Five, section four, and Chapter Six, section three. What follows is a chronological examination of documented seizures by the Qawasim off south Arabia in the years 1797–1820: the results are epitomized in Figure 2.

1804

According to Mocha's leading Banyan, a squadron of four Wahhabi dows from 'Rasul' anchored at 'Soo[r]meh' (Ras Sharma?[1]), near Mukalla, during Ramadan (began 15 December 1803), possibly in about the first week of January. Rasul was situated in the Persian Gulf, and the only obvious candidate with which to identify it is Ras al-Khaima.[2] The merchants of Mukalla immediately sent warning to Aden, advising them not to send ships thither, since the Wahhabi dows had already captured 4–5 prizes. On 11 January, the dows reached Aden, where they requested supplies of wood and water, and the chance to effect repairs. They met with a hostile reception, and it was rumoured they intended to seize a merchantman there belonging to the Nawab of Surat: the chief of Aden having sent word to the Sultan of 'Laz' (Lahaj?), 400 sepoys arrived overnight to resist any such attempt. In the face of this welcome, the Wahhabis sent a negotiator to see the Sultan, allegedly bearing the proposition that they would divide the spoil of their 5 prizes, together with their future spoil, if he allowed them to stay awhile in Aden. He rejected their advances, and forced them to get underway on 12 January. The next day they anchored at 'Soomar',[3] where they probably took on some water, and are said to have robbed a few people they met, besides destroying the tomb of a local shaikh, and taking off the copper vessels it contained. After this, they sailed on to an anchorage inside the Bab al-Mandab, and remained there from 15 to 22 January, 'taking and plundering a number of dows and boats bringing supplies and [sic] from Berbera and Zeila to Mocha, detaining such as suited them and releasing the rest'.[4] After this, according to the Mocha Resident, they continued to Luhayya, where they were said still to be at the time of writing, on 9 March. The number of men in their dows was put at over 500, and they were supposed to be well armed.

1809

In February,[5] 13 Qasimi dows sailed from Khaur Fakkan towards the Red Sea; in mid-March, a ship was in consequence to be despatched from Muscat to protect the Mocha and Zanzibar trade. By about the third week of March, the Qasimi squadron had report-edly run an Arab dow from Surat ashore near Shihr; next they had fought with four Shihr dows proceeding against Mukalla, before engaging with Shihr for 5,000 dollars to assist in their attack: on reaching Mukalla, however, the Qawasim were reported to have made peace with that ruler for a further like sum; after this, the Qawasim had set off with the alleged intention of intercepting the trade between Mukalla and Aden,[6] initially capturing a small vessel belonging to Sayyid Muhammad Aqil. During mid–late March or early April, the Qawasim captured four dows from India: a Muscat fleet, having sailed in early March, took sanctuary in Mukalla; and a Kuwaiti fleet, which had passed through Muscat towards the end of the month, was to report having had an engagement with 11 Qasimi dows just east of Shihr,[7] in the course of which one of the Qawasim blew up, giving the Utub the opportunity to flee, reaching Muscat once more on 5 April.[8] After this, in about early April, the Qawasim returned to Mukalla, where they sought to sell their prizes to the ruler: he agreed to the purchase, and received the vessels, but refused to pay on account of their crews being disabled by smallpox. There-after, the Qawasim reportedly returned to Ras al-Khaima via Khaur Fakkan before the end of April. Such is the account of this cruise which reached Muscat.[9]

BY 1810

Enigmatic discussions concerning Sur and Mukalla in early 1810 record in passing that a Mukalla vessel had earlier been destroyed by Ras al-Khaima; and say something, albeit obliquely, of Ras al-Khaima's relations with south Arabia and Sur.

On 31 February, Suri vessels reputedly detained three Mocha dows, one of which they stripped. In or by May, the inhabitants of Sur were said to be preparing dows to attack Mukalla. According to Sayyid Taqi, the well-informed British intelligence contact at Bombay, the cause of this lay in the previous year, when the states of Shihr and Mukalla acknowledged Su'ud, and on this account seized a dow belonging to the

Suris, as being dependants of Sayyid Sa'id of Muscat; by May 1810, these states had shaken off their Wahhabi allegiance, yet the dispute with Sur had persisted. Captain Rudland, the Agent at Mocha, offered a different explanation of this conflict, which was dismissed by Bombay as typically off-centre. He spoke of two differences: the first of these had been the destruction at Ras al-Khaima of a dow carrying 13,000 dollars in specie, the property of the ruler of Mukalla's brother; the second seems to have been Shihr and Mukalla's engaging in trade formerly dominated by Sur. He somewhat unhappily relates these two reasons by identifying the Suris' interests with those of the Qawasim.

> The Suris are looked upon as disreputable vagabonds from the vile practices which they resort to for a livelihood. For these last 15 years the Suris have been the receivers and carriers of stolen property, obtained by the Qawasim in the Gulf of Persia, and the successes of the piratical hordes in the neighbourhood of Ras al-Khaima of late years, have enriched the Suris enormously.[10]

He also suggested that they had performed a similar service for Sayyid Muhammad Aqil. The Suris, he explained, owned over 150 dows, and dominated part of the East African trade, as well as being carriers up the Red Sea. Bombay rejected Rudland's damning depiction of the Suris, which, it said, only applied to the Suri Qawasim who had abandoned Sur for Ras al-Khaima some years before. Presumably Bombay was right in this, although on the face of it Rudland's points about Mukalla's quarrel with Ras al-Khaima, and the trade conflict with Sur, taken individually seem reasonable. Rudland reflected opinion at Mocha, where he found some who expressed joy at the destruction of Ras al-Khaima; and it appears that his view of the Suris as receivers of Qasimi booty had been proposed some years before, in February 1807, by an American who had spent a year in the Red Sea.[11]

1815

In or by later February, six vessels from Ras al-Khaima were active off south Arabia. Off Qishn (?),[12] they fought with a Suri dow, said to have been carrying 100 musketeers, 20 Hindu and Muslim merchants and a cargo of cotton and cloth from Cutch for Mocha and Jeddah. The dow chose to resist, with the result that large numbers on both sides, put at 300 Qawasim and 100 of their own, were killed. The dow was burnt, possibly by her owner, and only 8–12 managed to escape: the reports from Muscat and Mukalla contradict each other as to whether the Qawasim succeeded in getting the cargo out in time.

After this, the Qasimi squadron attacked Shihr, where they encountered stout resistance. They captured a dow belonging to a Suri inhabitant of Shihr loaded with a cargo of oil, as well as the 600-ton ship *Fath al-Rahman*[13] owned by the Mocha merchant Abd al-Rahman Bu Abid: Bu Abid's ship was taken on 24 February[14] when anchored at Shihr, en route from Bengal to Mocha with a cargo of rice, sugar, piece-goods and shawls etc., valued by the Muscat Broker at 200,000 French crowns; the majority of the crew were reported killed.[15] After this, the Qawasim proceeded along the coast for a short while in order to take on water,[16] before sailing back eastwards towards Oman, at some time before mid-April.[17] The commander of this squadron appears to have been the Amir Ibrahim (bin Rahma, brother of Hasan) responsible in the following year for the attack on the *Ahmadi*.[18]

At the same time as the events near Shihr, a second party of depredators, under one Hazza', from somewhere in Oman,[19] took several small vessels within the Bab al-Mandab, sailed to Kamaran, captured some other south Arabian boats, then came to Mukalla, where they sought the protection of the Naqib; this he granted, although he was obliged to fire at them five days later when, contrary to the agreement, they had attempted to land. After this, they probably returned eastwards towards Oman, again before mid-April.[20]

In the second week of April, Qasimi vessels were said to be cruising in the vicinity of Khairan and Sur.[21] After a contest in which the Qawasim lost 46 men, and their victims all but something over a dozen, they had captured a dinghy[22] sailing from Muscat to 'Sajpoor'(?).[23]

In or by the fourth week of April, Sayyid Sa'id sailed with the ships *Caroline*, *Fyzalum* and *Salihee* towards Sur and Ras al-Hadd, following reports that a large force of Qawasim was out. On 13 May, the ruler returned with the *Caroline* to Muscat, after failing to encounter any Qawasim.

But on the same day, news arrived that twelve Qawasim, with Bu Abid's ship *Fath al-Rahman*, were hard by: Sayyid Sa'id and the *Caroline* immediately set off after them, only to come back to port that night having loosed a few shots, but judging the Qasimi force too powerful to engage. On this or the following day, the Qawasim in question reportedly captured two baghlas coming from Zanzibar off Khairan, one of which belonged to Sultan bin Abdullah Marzuqi and carried 400 male and female slaves, besides 50,000 French crowns in specie and a stock of ivory. They also captured a third baghla returning from Bombay to Muscat, which was at the time carrying 1,200 rupees worth of property belonging to the Muscat Broker; all on board were said to have been killed.[24]

On 14 May, Sayyid Sa'id put to sea once more in the *Caroline*, accompanied now by the *Fyzalum*, the *Sooleman Shah* and the *Fyzrubany*.[25] The next day, cannonading was heard at Muscat. This signalled a close engagement between the opposing squadrons off Ras Abu Da'ud, an account of which appears in Chapter Eleven, section six. The Muscat Broker asserts that Amir Hasan bin Rahma and his brother Ibrahim were present with the Ras al-Khaima fleet, and reports that the Qawasim lost 500 men in the said action.

1816

In or by early–mid March, according to the Naqib of Mukalla, 15 vessels belonging to Rahma bin Jabir and the Ras al-Khaima Qawasim descended upon Burum and subsequently Aden. At the former, a dependency of the Naqib, the attackers had overtaken the town before the arrival of his troops, who then proceeded to expel them, inflicting 30 fatalities and some damage to their ships. The attackers then had an engagement in the roads at Aden, where they were likewise repelled.[26] Hereafter the sources clearly distinguish the Qawasim and the Jalahima:

On c. 19 and 23 March, just inside the Bab al-Mandab, three rich Surat merchantmen, the *Ahmadi*, the *Fath Mubarak* and the *Safar Salamat*, were plundered by a group of 4 Qasimi baghlas, 2 dows and 2 battils. Of the three, the *Ahmadi* was detained the longest, until the end of the first week of April. This incident is recounted in Chapter Six, section three.

In or after the second week of April, Rahma bin Jabir[27] was reported to have passed Mocha en route to Luhayya, where he plundered two of Sharif Hamud's coffee dows and a vessel owned by an Abyssinian merchant; thereafter he vacated the Red Sea and next appeared off Saihut(?),[28] where he is said to have plundered and taken off a grab belonging to the Mangalore merchant Moorarjee Culianjee laden with cotton for Mocha, killing all but four or five of her crew.

1818

On 1 May, 6 Arab dows from Porbandar, bound to Mocha and not under British protection, put into Socotra for wood and water. Thereupon 6 Qasimi dows and 2 battils,[29] which had been lying at anchor in the harbour,[30] pounced upon the Porbandar dows, put ashore 32 Banyans and 75 sailors who were on board, and sailed away with their vessels. On 14 May, a Cutch nauri and a 'boombra' took off all but 15 of the abandoned passengers and crew, Banyans who had scattered to villages in the interior, and brought them to Mocha 22 days later. The captured Porbandar cargoes were valued at 157,333 rupees, and were insured.[31]

It might also have been around May, that, as described elsewhere, the Madras schooner *Mary*, which had lost her way, was run on shore, probably somewhere in south Arabia by 10 Qawasim. Though pure speculation, the possibility that her attackers were those who took the Porbandar dows cannot be ruled out.[32]

1819

By 1 March, 15 well-equipped Qawasim had reportedly sailed in the direction of Yemen and Zanzibar, intent, it was said, on plunder.[33]

A Qasimi fleet of 17 sail was briefly intimated by Sadleir to have proceeded towards the Red Sea, probably in or by April, and to have destroyed the town of Berbera;[34] they also reportedly captured two trifling Socotra boats.[35]

On 17 April, according to the survivors, the Bombay pattamar *Darya Daulat*,[36] which had left Mukalla under British colours the previous day, was attacked by about 30 supposed Qawasim

> who boarded the pattamar with swords and musquets. The number on board the *Darya Daulat* was 24 men. Of these, twelve men, including the Serang, Tindal and pilot, were instantly put to death, [when] remaining twelve leapt overboard. Of them one was shot in the water, the other eleven reached the shore by swimming;

and subsequently made their passage by way of Shihr to Bombay, where they arrived on 27 May and related what had befallen them. The vessel was owned by Jamsetjee Hirajee, and had been carrying 60,000 dollars for Bombay merchants, on top of a cargo of shark's fins, coffee, gum arabic and drugs etc. All this was presumably lost, but it appears that the pattamar herself was recovered and used by the eleven surviving crew to sail back to the Presidency.[37]

On 13 May, ten sail of Qawasim were sighted off Ras al-Hadd by one of Sayyid Sa'id's baghlas: they seemed to pursue and engage an English vessel. The following afternoon, during her passage from Bombay, the Muscat baghla *Hunnawee*[38] reported falling in with 25 dows, baghlas etc. out of sight of land between Ras al-Khairan and Ras Abu Da'ud; speaking two of them, her Serang learnt they were Qawasim: he also perceived what appeared to be the burning wreck of a square-rigged ship, with small rowing-boats from the baghlas plying about her.[39] The square-rigger had in fact belonged to one Gopal, a Hindu merchant at Muscat, and had been bringing rice from

Calcutta: eight of her crew, who afterwards made their way back to Muscat from Ras al-Khaima, maintained they had set her alight after they saw no chance of escape.[40] Sadleir hypothesized that the Qasimi fleet responsible was the same as that which had attacked Berbera, and was now returning to Ras al-Khaima. One might also posit that this fleet could perhaps have been that which captured the *Darya Daulat* in mid-April.[41]

In early–mid May, what was reported to be a second, dozen-strong Qasimi fleet was cruising to the north of Muscat.[42] This squadron had newly sailed from Ras al-Khaima, then touched at Fujaira in the first week of May for information: Fujaira had recently fallen under Qasimi control. At this period Sayyid Sa'id had vessels cruising off Cape Musandam, and on 8 May HMS *Curlew*, Captain Walpole, left Muscat in order to join them.[43]

Calling at Ras al-Khaima on 29 May, the commander of the HCC *Benares* reported seeing only ten vessels in port, asserting that their fleet had not yet returned from the Red Sea.[44]

Speculatively taking all these reports together would indicate a cruise by 10–30 (c. 15–17?) Qawasim to the Red Sea and back, perhaps lasting from about February till early June: there may have been a second fleet operating north of Muscat in early–mid May.[45]

In addition to the above captures, one further is spoken of by Loch, namely that of an Arab ship off Masira. He merely places this event within the 1818/19 season, but, for want of any other, it might seems reasonable to view this too as part of the above cruise.[46] Also no doubt referring to this cruise, the Naqib of Mukalla later recalled that the presence of Ras al-Khaima depredators had disrupted sea-traffic and prevented vessels from sailing in the vicinity of Mukalla.[47]

APPENDIX C

Ras al-Khaima's War with Muscat, and the Political Fortunes of the Za'ab and the Tanaij, 1808–1809

The events of 1808–9 had weighty consequences for Ras al-Khaima. Notable success in its war with Muscat on the eastern seaboard, at Khaur Fakkan, coincided with an abrupt marked increase in Saudi–Wahhabi political involvement in the Qasimi states. This latter increase hinged about the promotion of two tribes, the Za'ab and the Tanaij, which had formerly been dominated by the Qasimi rulers of Ras al-Khaima. A year later, in the wake of the first Anglo–Omani expedition against Ras al-Khaima, Saudi political engineering culminated in the removal of the ruler Sultan bin Saqr and his replacement by Hasan bin Rahma, thus setting the scene for the duration of the second decade when Ras al-Khaima was most securely part of the Wahhabi fold.

This political transformation is of very great importance for an understanding of the fortunes of Ras al-Khaima in this period. It had repercussions for Qasimi maritime activity, which took on a new character at around this time. The evidence for it is, however, not straightforward. What follows is a close examination of what occurred in 1808–9 from the available sources, setting Ras al-Khaima's war with Muscat in the context of the Wahhabi advances in Oman. A less detailed presentation of the results of this examination features in Chapter Eleven.

Around the start of May 1808, Sayyid Sa'id reached an accommodation with Qais whereby they both agreed to co-operate in an attack on the Qawasim in Shimailiya. They left Muscat in the first half of the month, and on their arrival in the north succeeded in taking Khaur Fakkan from the hands of the Qawasim, at a reported cost to the latter of 150–200 killed. Prior to setting out from Muscat Sayyid Sa'id had also conferred with Muhammad bin Matar of Fujaira, who had promised his assistance in the forthcoming campaign. The armies of Sayyid Sa'id and Qais were apparently encamped separately when one night in late May 1808, not long after the fall of Khaur Fakkan, they were taken by surprise, and put to flight, by a Qasimi counter-attack. The Qawasim had received reinforcements, and when it came to it, Muhammad bin Matar with his 2,000 men had stood aside and refused to intervene. In the assault, Qais was killed along with a reported 500 of Sayyid Sa'id's troops, and as for the latter, he was

> in the heat of the battle ... borne off on the shoulders of three slaves and carried to a boat whence he escaped to his ships. He lost almost the whole of his clothes and received a slight wound from a musquet-ball in his leg. He left behind him, his treasure etc. etc. etc., upwards of 30 vessels etc. of different descriptions which he had previously captured.[1]

Sayyid Sa'id reached Muscat again on 14 June. For a time he was said to be meditating a renewed attack on the Qawasim with enhanced forces including the trading ships intended for Bengal that season. Azzan bin Qais immediately succeeded his father in the government of Suhar.[2]

In the fourth week of July 1808, before proceeding to Hormuz and Bandar Abbas,[3] Sayyid Sa'id visited Suhar with three ships and some cavalry in order to strengthen it in the face of a threatened tribal incursion:[4] other sources suggest this threat arose from the Qawasim and their allies. This pressure was not, however, lifted, and in late October the Muscat Broker wrote that Wahhabi forces had appeared in great numbers in the region of Shinas,[5] obliging Azzan bin Qais to make peace with them; these forces were then expected to turn against Muscat.[6] Ten days later, the Broker reported that the Omanis at large had received the doctrines of Wahhabism, and Sayyid Sa'id had likewise felt it necessary to make a general peace with the Wahhabis and their dependants, including the Qawasim.[7] This was clearly a high point for the latter in their long tussle with Muscat.

The final outcome had, according to Seton, been precipitated by Sayyid Sa'id's failure to manage support in the interior: Hamad bin Sa'id, son of the last Imam,[8] had afforded the Wahhabis money and supplies; Humaid bin Nasir al-Ghafiri, of the Dhahira, had marched with them against Suhar; and obstruction by Muhammad bin Nasir al-Jabri, controlling the Wadi Sumayil, had limited Sayyid Sa'id to forces from the south-east and Makran, in addition to which the same Shaikh is said to have assisted the Wahhabis actively in men and money.[9]

Such is the contemporary version of events contained in the British sources, which derived from Muscat. It may be amplified by recourse to one other contemporary, and two later Arabic sources: a fourth Arabic source, the *Lam' al-Shihab*, adds nothing of value to these, and it seems to confuse later events, involving Mutlaq al-Mutairi and Muhammad bin Nasir al-Jabri, with those of 1808.[10]

Ibn Ruzaiq describes the reason for the original move against the Qawasim as a joint desire on the part of Sayyid Sa'id and Qais to diminish Sultan bin Saqr of Ras al-Khaima's naval power: Qasimi vessels attacked those of Oman, and used Khaur Fakkan, where Sultan bin Saqr had recently constructed a lofty stronghold (*burj*), to water and take shelter in rough weather. Sayyid Sa'id's forces are said to have had a backbone of Wahiba and Hajriyin,[11] some of the same forces as had supported Badr in the last stages of his conflict with Qais. Sultan bin Saqr's forces, part bedu, part settled, are said to have been twice Sayyid Sa'id's at 12,000 men. Of Qais's forces, only Za'ab are mentioned. Ibn Ruzaiq notes that among the Muscat dead was the important Muhammad bin Khalfan, who had been acting as Sayyid Sa'id's commander. Ibn Ruzaiq has the Qawasim exclaiming 'God is great', and crying out, as they descended on the Omani forces. This author not unexpectedly says nothing of the submission of Muscat beneath the Wahhabis, but he does allude to the effect this signal victory had upon the Sultan bin Saqr and the Qawasim: their depredations at sea and upon land burgeoned with the support of the Tanaij, the Za'ab and the Wahhabis; Muhammad bin Jabir, the Jalahima leader, also assisted actively. Ibn Ruzaiq acknowledges that Sultan bin Saqr now carried out more raids on the district of Suhar, and says that Azzan bin Qais received men and money from Sayyid Sa'id to help in warding off these attacks. It is clear even from this account how narrowly pressed were Muscat and Suhar.[12]

Ibn Bishr, the Saudi historian, also speaks of this affair, which he naturally puts squarely in a Saudi context: Su'ud, he says, first sent a small party to Oman to bring religious instruction. On arrival, they found Qais and Sayyid Sa'id with an army of 10,000 or more marching on 'neighbouring Omani territory subject to Su'ud'. Sultan bin Saqr, then leader of Oman on behalf of Su'ud, raised a 3,000-strong army and shattered the opposing forces, inflicting, it was said, nearly 4,000 fatalities. After this defeat, Azzan bin Qais adopted Wahhabism and allegiance to Su'ud; Sayyid Sultan also pledged allegiance to Su'ud, and, like Azzan, paid a hefty sum to him.[13] All Oman was now in theory under the tutelage of Su'ud. Sultan bin Saqr delivered one-fifth of the plunder that resulted from this campaign to Su'ud's tax-collectors, who transmitted it to Dir'iya. Ibn Bishr also notes that famine and scarcity persisted in Najd during this year, encompassing too Yemen, the Hijaz and Hasa; added to which, Najd was struck by epidemic.[14]

The last of the Arabic sources, and the most interesting, is a contemporary letter from Matar bin Rahma bin Rashid al-Qasimi, at Ras al-Khaima, to his brother Rashid, at Bhavnagar, in which he gives a first-hand account of the Khaur Fakkan campaign. This letter is cited in Chapter Eleven, section four.[15]

The attacks on the *Fury* (2 May 1808), the *Darya Daulat* (3 July), the *Nautilus* (17 October) and the *Sylph* (21 October) are described elsewhere;[16] around perhaps the beginning of the fourth week in November 1808, the country-ship *Minerva* also claimed to have been chased near Tunb-i Buzurg by 15 large Arab boats, but to have escaped with the springing up of a breeze.[17] The identity of the *Fury*'s attackers is uncertain: the captain observed, 'from the remarkable fairness of the person which I took to be her commander, I conceived he was an European': Bombay thought the possibility of French involvement worth investigating.[18] The commander of the *Darya Daulat*, Fleming, encountered two representatives from Sind, when he was brought to Ras al-Khaima in July 1808. Also apparent from his account, and bringing to mind the October 1807 *Shannon* episode, is the power there of the Wahhabi agent: he is said to have been the most vociferous in the detention of this vessel, and to have demanded an order from the Governor of Bombay before being prepared to consider her release; this, despite the fact that the captor was reportedly a dow belonging to Sultan bin Saqr himself.[19]

All accounts of the Khaur Fakkan campaign and its immediate aftermath maintain that as late as the end of October 1808 Sultan bin Saqr was the sole head of the Qawasim and their allies, as well as perhaps regional deputy on behalf of the Saudi–Wahhabi state. In early December, Seton claimed that the recent peace with Muscat had enabled the Qawasim to send boats to the coasts of India. He also reported that a recent order from Su'ud had confined the 'lawful Shaikh' Sultan bin Saqr's authority to Ras al-Khaima, whilst the other ports such as Rams, Sharja and Ajman sent out boats 'without his permission': Shaikh Qadib of Linga's subjects, he alleged, were, though averse to piracy, obliged to seek a livelihood in the vessels of others. Seton squarely ascribed these maritime activities to Wahhabi instigation.[20]

On the face of it, this intelligence points to a formal adjustment by the Wahhabis, in November 1808, of the structure of authority within the Qasimi states.[21] This is restated in a slightly later report, where Seton describes the consequences of Muscat and Suhar's peace with the Wahhabis: Muhammad bin Nasir al-Jabri, Humaid bin Nasir al-Ghafiri and Azzan bin Qais were all constituted Amirs in their own right, dependent on Su'ud, whilst Shinas, Khaur Fakkan and Diba were, he maintains, stripped from Suhar and put, with Jau, under Hasan bin Ali; the latter was one of five Saudi nominees who had assumed charge of the territories till then dependent upon Sultan bin Saqr at Ras al-Khaima.[22] It is against this background that Sultan bin Saqr later sought to distance himself from the attack on the *Sylph*, which he claimed had been made without his authorization or consent: speaking at a time when he was courting British good-will, he professed never himself to have lost sight of the 1806 treaty. The erosion of Sultan bin Saqr's position was not, it seems, completed until the following year.

Captain David Seton returned to Muscat on 1 February 1809. The Wahhabi presence in Oman was assertive. Six teachers sought to enforce attendance at prayer in Muscat; a fort was under construction at Jau, commanding the north-western approach; and a delegation to Dir'iya, which had requested the restoration of Shinas, had been rebuffed. Sayyid Sa'id was under pressure from Su'ud to attack India, or, more particularly, in the first instance, Basra. Sayyid Sa'id requested, and Seton urged, British naval assistance.[23]

By mid-February 1809 an Omani counter-reaction of sorts had manifested itself. Azzan bin Qais may have endeavoured to better his position.[24] Humaid bin Nasir al-Ghafiri, obliged to construct forts in the Dhahira for Wahhabi garrisons, was wavering. So too, apparently, was Muhammad bin Nasir al-Jabri, when he was lured into captivity by Sayyid Sa'id, who then moved against his positions in the strategic Wadi Sumayil, successfully commencing with Bidbid:[25] by early March, after the taking of Sumayil, Muhammad bin Nasir had been released and had fled to a Ghafiri fort.[26] According to Ibn Ruzaiq, he subsequently decamped to Dir'iya.[27]

Since the Wahhabi intervention of 1808, the Qawasim had taken to using Khaur Fakkan as a major maritime base. One-fifth of the Qawasim's plunder was delivered to the Wahhabi state: under Hasan bin Ali, increased depredations at sea had, according to Seton, raised the annual Qasimi tribute from 4,000 to 12,000 dollars.[28]

In February 1809, 13 Qasimi dows sailed from Khaur Fakkan towards the Red Sea: what ensued off south Arabia is described in Appendix B.

Sultan bin Saqr was reported to be absent from Ras al-Khaima at Laft in mid-February 1809, whence he had written to Seton professing adherence to the 1806 treaty, but a general incapacity.[29] It appears, in fact, that this letter was accompanied by a more weighty communication addressed to Sayyid Sa'id, reportedly proposing an alliance against the Wahhabis. Another such letter was sent to Muscat from Ras al-Khaima around the end of the month, about the same time as Sayyid Sa'id responded to the first by sending a boat with emissaries to Sultan bin Saqr: the boat visited Fujaira and was detained there awhile by a Wahhabi officer, before the garrison, which was in the pay of Sultan bin Saqr, facilitated her departure.[30] In or by about the third week of March 1809, according to Seton, Sultan bin Saqr set out with *qadis* 'to dispute with Su'ud at Dir'iya on the legality of his proceeding in Sir, the Qasimi country.'[31] It may well have been this journey to which Sultan bin Saqr himself referred when he wrote, 'When your property was seized and captured I was not present, I was at Dir'iya'; in which case, the property concerned would have been the *Minerva*, taken on 23 May 1809.[32] Sultan bin Saqr had returned to Ras al-Khaima by November 1809. Both Maurizi and Ibn Ruzaiq attest the mutual advances of Sultan bin Saqr and Sayyid Sa'id broadly at this time.[33] There is finally an intriguing suggestion that Sultan bin Saqr may conceivably have tried to approach Britain at the time of the Ras al-Khaima expedition: Captain Wainwright states that he had learnt that the ruler 'had in the most insulting manner, the audacity to demand a tribute from the Government to allow British ships to navigate the Persian Gulf in safety.'[34] The degree to which any original message had been distorted is, of course, unclear: his subsequent letter certainly laments that there had been no opportunity for negotiations.[35]

According to Seton, Su'ud had published general orders for an attack on Basra after his return to Dir'iya from pilgrimage about 5–6 March 1809.[36] At some stage formal written instructions seem to have gone out to Sayyid Sa'id, the Qawasim and the Utub to the same effect: at the beginning of May, Seton noted that the Utub had 'excused themselves',[37] the Qawasim had agreed on the condition they receive naval support, whilst Sayyid Sa'id had declared his ships ready for the undertaking. All this looks like prevarication.[38]

Around early May 1809, a somewhat increased Wahhabi pressure was felt in the region of Oman. The Wahhabi agent Muhammad bin Salama arrived in Ras al-Khaima about the start of the month with reported instructions to assert Saudi authority in Oman, and chevy them on towards attacking Basra. Sayyid Sa'id's viceregent Muhammad bin Khalfan also alleged that he bore a letter addressed to Seton asserting that Christians were not welcome in Oman: whether or not this was true is uncertain, but it should be borne in mind that Muscat felt threatened and was seeking to persuade Britain to side with her in defence; it does not appear that any such letter was received. For his part, Seton opined to Bombay that the Wahhabis were not likely to break with Britain unless Muscat fell.[39]

At about this time, Seton speaks of renewed Saudi political engineering in Qasimi territory. It was directed, it seems, towards the enhancing of the new power already elevated by the Wahhabis in 1808, hitherto governed by Hasan bin Ali, and situated on the Musandam promontory, between the powers of Muscat and the Qawasim proper. Hasan bin Ali was now summoned to Dir'iya, and his position taken by one Ahmad bin Ahmad Mu'ini.[40] The identity of this individual is unclear, although Seton asserts that by this adjustment the Za'ab tribe achieved paramountcy: one might speculate therefore that Ahmad bin Ahmad was possibly associated with the Za'ab, principally of Jazirat al-Hamra', just as Hasan bin Ali of Rams may have represented the Tanaij.[41] Concomitant with this reassignment of authority, the territory itself was given added military strength by the addition of Bithna and Fujaira, which had till then answered to the Qawasim, or presumably Sultan bin Saqr.[42] Seton ascribes Sayyid Sa'id's failure to act against the Za'ab, when it had been in his interest to do so, to a reluctance to create a rupture with the Saudi state.[43] This is the first time Seton so clearly singles out in this way any one tribe or power within the ambit of the Qawasim.

The changed status of the Tanaij and Za'ab, former clients of the Qawasim, appears central to an understanding of the political situation since 1808. They are mentioned twice more in the British sources for 1809. On the first occasion, the Basra Resident wrote in early July that Hasan bin Ali of Rams, erstwhile dependant of the Qawasim, had recently received from the Wahhabis authority over all the Qasimi states, including Ras al-Khaima and Linga, thus enabling Rams to field 70–80 dows, baghlas and trankeys etc. in association with them: they employed these in predation and transmitted one-fifth of the proceeds to Dir'iya.[44] This confirms the general thrust of Seton's earlier, more proximate and therefore preferable intelligence, by which it appears that Hasan bin Ali may have lost his prominence before this:[45] it also seems preferable to adopt Seton's implicit view that whilst Hasan bin Ali and his successor had great prestige, they represented a power separate from, and not strictly speaking inclusive of, the generality of states hitherto dependent on the Qawasim proper. The second piece of information states that at the end of October 1809, when the British expedition commenced, Sultan bin Saqr was negotiating a peace with Sayyid Sa'id conditional upon the latter's assistance in chastising his refractory clients, the Za'ab and the Tanaij:[46] it will be recalled that there had been contacts between Muscat and Ras al-Khaima earlier in the year. Sultan bin Saqr himself claimed in a letter to the British commanders, that when they attacked his capital Ras al-Khaima on 11–13 November 1809, he had been absent collecting 'troops in the country for the purpose of fighting against those who have been the cause of creating dissension between you and me ... you did not give me time to negotiate with you as we were before friends.'[47] Conceivably the adversaries he had in mind were the Za'ab and the Tanaij.

The two principal Arabic sources, Ibn Ruzaiq and the Lam' al-Shihab, both accord the Za'ab and Tanaij a significant role in the political and maritime history of the Qasimi states at this time; the Lam' al-Shihab in particular suggests an association with sea-plunder that is not made with other client tribes. Ibn Ruzaiq identifies these tribes, along with the Jalahima and the Wahhabis, as those who principally assisted the Qawasim in their maritime depredations.[48] He also notes that one Muhammad bin Ahmad al-Tanaiji was the bloodthirsty and rapacious Wahhabi Governor of Shinas at about this time.[49] In a stylized account, the Lam' al-Shihab's author argues that the Za'ab and Tanaij were instrumental in promoting Wahhabi ascendancy over the Qawasim, and in impelling the latter toward maritime predation. The political impulse this author identifies seems reasonable, though his presentation, being simplified and couched in the form of human drama, should not be relied upon implicitly for its chronology and detail.

According to this author, neighbours of the Ras al-Khaima Qawasim, such as the Za'ab of Jazirat al-Hamra', did not bow to the Wahhabis so soon as they: the Tanaij of Rams likewise held out, or 'fought', against the Al Su'ud for four years after the

Qawasim had submitted.

> And when the Za'ab accepted the creed of Muhammad bin Abd al-Wahhab, the Qawasim were thrown into confusion, and Abd al-Aziz gained total mastery of their affairs, because the Za'ab and Tanaij had been subject to Qasimi tyranny, whereas now one of their own Amirs ruled over them. So they told Mutlaq [al-Mutairi, the Saudi commander]: 'We will engage in maritime plunder, fight the idolaters and deliver one-fifth of the booty to the Imam, but we want to take over dows and baghlas from the Qawasim, because we have only got small craft such as battils and baqqaras.' Therefore Mutlaq addressed the people of Ras al-Khaima: 'The time has come to undertake cruises and kill everyone who rejects our creed. If you refuse to do this, you must deliver up twenty dows and baghlas to your brothers-in-religion, the Za'ab and the Tanaij, and they will execute it, and retain possession of your vessels and receive their share of the booty.'

This obliged the Qawasim to comply with the Saudi command and embark upon the jihad or Holy War, though for three years they were reluctant participants, and plundered less assiduously than the Za'ab and the Tanaij: these tribes used to inform the Saudi ruler if the Qawasim fell short, and he would reproach them for it. According to the author of the *Lam' al-Shihab*, this situation, whereby the Qawasim sought as far as they could to evade the Saudi injunction to plunder and kill, was reversed upon the accession of Sultan bin Saqr, following the death of his father, in 1803.[50] The Ras al-Khaima Qawasim then took the lead, and the Za'ab and Tanaij are not mentioned again.[51]

There is a final point to consider with regard to Hasan bin Ali. According to a late source, he had by 1818 become responsible for transmitting the one-fifth of plunder due from the Qawasim to the Saudi–Wahhabi treasury, after superseding in that function a Wahhabi agent imposed from outside.[52] When this happened one may only speculate. It can be explained in two ways. First, it might have been part of the Saudi ruler's plan of building up Hasan bin Ali, in which case it could have happened about now, by early 1809. Second, and following Bruce's interpretation, Hasan bin Ali's appointment to this office could actually have been a climb-down, representing the triumph of local dissatisfaction with an outsider, which, given the forward nature of Saudi involvement in 1808–9, might tend to place it in the second decade. It might then have been part of the reorganization which followed in the wake of the British expedition, or postdate the start of the Egyptian campaigns and the commencement of Wahhabi decline.

APPENDIX D

Hostilities Between Muscat and the Wahhabis in the Aftermath of the First Ras al-Khaima Expedition of 1809/10

Saudi expansionism engendered conflict with Muscat and other concerned Gulf powers, and formed the backdrop to much that occurred in the Gulf during this period. Muscat's involvement in the first Ras al-Khaima expedition was equally, then, but a part of her struggle against the Saudi–Wahhabi power. The consequences of the expedition for Muscat, at a time when Saudi power was still strong in this corner of Arabia, were predictable. As the British fleet withdrew, Oman was subjected to a series of violent Wahhabi incursions, the most serious of them in 1810–11. The last major punitive Wahhabi raid in Oman took place in 1813, after which, notably as a consequence of the Egyptian advance from western Arabia, the fire was dulled: Muscat thereafter gradually assumed more confidence, and Wahhabi Ras al-Khaima found herself increasingly isolated. What follows is an account of Muscat's struggle with the Wahhabis in the years 1810–13, the principal elements of which are alluded to in Chapter Eleven.

In or by late March 1810, a Wahhabi force fought Muscat troops hard for 13 days at Wadi Ma'awil,[1] before moving on Sumayil, in the defence of which Muscat lost some 200 men. At the end of the second week of April, the Wahhabis were said to be in the vicinity of Muscat, and had pillaged widely and destroyed date plantations.[2]

On 26 March, Sayyid Sa'id of Muscat had written to the Governor of Bombay complaining that until the recent British expedition he had kept up pretences with the Wahhabis, but that, encouraged by the British proceedings, he had initiated hostilities with them. Following the withdrawal of the British force, he had consequently fallen prey to a military onslaught directed by a force from Dir'iya, assisted by men from Ras al-Khaima, Sharja and her dependencies, and by bedouin. They had cut down date palms in Oman, and, he claimed, had twice already been seen off by him. He now requested British military assistance.[3] In August, Fort William at length instructed Bombay to advise Sayyid Sa'id that military aid would not be forthcoming and he should attempt to conclude an honourable truce with Su'ud, with whom the Company was at peace.[4] Prior to this the British had received a letter from Su'ud, stating that he was at peace with Britain, but castigating Sayyid Sa'id of Muscat for having incited Britain to launch the recent expedition and shrugging off its successes.[5]

Presumably between mid-April and the end of May 1810, according to Sayyid Sa'id, his relative Hilal bin Hamad led an expedition which captured and ravaged Zubara, then landed on Bahrain and took 16 Wahhabi officers prisoner, including the Governor's brother, Fahd (bin Sulaiman) bin Ufaisan, before proceeding against Rahma bin Jabir's base at Khaur Hassan.[6] Ibn Bishr sketches in the background to these operations: around later February 1810, members of the Al Khalifa were summoned to Dir'iya and arrested, whilst a Wahhabi financial governor, Fahd bin Sulaiman bin Ufaisan, was installed on Bahrain. Other members of the Al Khalifa fled to Muscat, where they sought Sayyid Sa'id's help. He sent an expedition to Zubara and Bahrain, with the results already described. The Wahhabi hostages were released later in the year, as were the Al Khalifa detainees at Dir'iya, after they and their people had sworn allegiance to Su'ud.[7] Muscat, in other words, had helped restore effectively independent Al Khalifa rule after a brief interlude of direct Saudi control, which had begun possibly around November 1809.[8] The Lam' al-Shihab paints a very similar account to this; though it is also prefaced by an episode concerning the Qawasim, which is not apparently confirmed in other sources.[9]

By the end of May 1810, possibly about the same time as the Zubara expedition, Sayyid Sa'id took steps to broaden his offensive capacity against the Wahhabis by sending his brother Salim bin Sultan on a mission to Persia.[10] He also turned elsewhere. In May–September a Persian envoy resided in Hyderabad, at the court of the Sind Amir; through him Sayyid Sa'id addressed a written appeal to the Amir for military assistance against the Wahhabis, noting that he had already appealed to the Shah of Iran and the Ottoman Sultan. The Amir turned him down in the autumn. On 23 November, a second letter reached the Amir from Sayyid Sa'id, stating that his agent was then at Karachi, and desiring permission to procure supplies of grain un-impeded, since supplies were needed to support his effort against the Wahhabis.[11]

The meagre contemporary accounts in the British sources of Muscat's imbroglio with the Wahhabis in Oman, accord with the Arabic sources. Malcolm attests that the Wahhabi commander at Shinas during the Anglo–Omani operations there at the start of January 1810 was Mutlaq al-Mutairi, and suggests he may have been wounded there.[12] This seems in fact to have marked the commencement of the Wahhabi milit-ary campaign which lasted until at least April. Ibn Bishr adds little of value to the above, but Ibn Ruzaiq's is a more detailed account.[13] It falls into two sections. The first of these briefly describes Mutlaq al-Mutairi's raid via Suhar, the Wadi Ma'awil and Sumayil back to Buraimi: his force comprised Na'im, Qitab, Dhawahir and other tribes from the Buraimi area;[14] he was accompanied and assisted by Muhammad bin Nasir al-Jabri, whom Ibn Ruzaiq portrays as the instigator of this business, together with Humaid bin Nasir al-Ghafiri and Malik bin Saif al-Ya'rabi.[15] The second, and much longer, section of this historian's account centres around Muhammad bin Nasir's immediately subsequent, prolonged and eventually successful siege of Sumayil. During this time, there was an amount of political manoeuvring, and a number of military engagements in or about the Wadis Sumayil and Ma'awil. Sayyid Sa'id and Azzan bin Qais twice took the field. The final outcome, the fall of Sumayil, and allegiance of the Banu Ruwaha and other tribes, to Muhammad bin Nasir, is in Ibn Ruzaiq's Omani account portrayed as the stimulus to Salim's Persian mission.[16]

Muscat's appeal to Iran was swiftly answered. On 2 December 1810, a Persian force of 1,500 horse under Sadiq Khan, having embarked at Bandar Abbas, landed at Barka. After joining up with Sayyid Sa'id, the combined forces marched on 12 December to Nakhl, which surrendered on 26 or 28 December.[17] Next Sumayil was taken. There-after, en route to Wahhabi-held Izki, they were attacked and worsted at Qarut by the Wahhabi army, the Persian cavalry fleeing via Bidbid to Barka, the Muscat infantry much of it being cut down. Of the 42 Russian prisoners-of-war included in the Persian force, half were killed. The action at Qarut seems to have occurred by mid-February 1811.[18]

This same episode also features in Ibn Ruzaiq and Ibn Bishr, who each indicate that the campaign was inaugurated by an Omani–Persian offensive against Muhammad bin Nasir al-Jabri at Nakhl and Sumayil; and that he in turn responded by invoking the aid of Mutlaq al-Mutairi from Buraimi, thereby bringing about the reversal at Qarut.[19]

Ibn Ruzaiq has Sayyid Sa'id's brother Salim as Commander-in-Chief, and says that he was joined by Azzan bin Qais, Himyar bin Muhammad bin Sulaiman al-Ya'rabi and others, including parties of Hirth and Habus. Muhammad bin Nasir is associated with Abriyin, Banu Shukail and Banu Riyam. Mutlaq al-Mutairi, in this version bribed and cajoled by Muhammad bin Nasir, raised troops from the Qitab, Banu Riyam and Dhawahir, from Dank and Ghabbi, and received support from Saif bin Thabit and the Duru'.[20]

Ibn Ruzaiq and Ibn Bishr together inflate the number of Persian horsemen to 3,000, or double the true figure.[21] Ibn Bishr notes that the Wahhabis captured over ten cannon with other supplies from the defeated army, and that the customary one-fifth of the booty was delivered to Su'ud's tax-officers.

A second distinct bout of conflict between Muscat and the Wahhabis seems to have followed very soon upon the defeat of the Omani–Persian force. The information afforded by contemporary sources on the events of February–April 1811 is sparse. In March 1811, Sayyid Sa'id is said to have attacked Kalba and burnt both town and boats.[22] In early April, the Wahhabi army was reported to be in the Wadi Ma'awil(?).[23] Sayyid Sa'id wrote that he had visited various ports in the Gulf 'in order to check and keep down, the depredations which the detestable pirates [had] committed, and in fact by suppressing the turbulent acts of that lawless banditti, restore security to mankind and to navigation in general': presumably this tour had encompassed the descent upon Kalba, and may have taken place in March–April. Whilst he was away, 'the Wahhabis and the discontented and refractory tribes' conducted an offensive, in the course of which Matrah was for a while penetrated. One might speculate this occurred around mid-April, or thereafter. By the time Sayyid Sa'id returned to Muscat, possibly by about the start of May 1811, the Wahhabis had evacuated Matrah and retreated eastwards.[24]

Maurizi too speaks of these events, though he describes Sayyid Sa'id's maritime expedition as one against not Kalba, but Ras al-Khaima. The readier explanation of this would be that he had simply confused this expedition, against Kalba, with another, against Ras al-Khaima, that may have occurred at the end of the year: Maurizi himself was absent from Muscat between 1810 and 1814. Knowledge of Sayyid Sa'id's expedition(s), however, remains slight.[25]

Ibn Bishr and Ibn Ruzaiq present a less confusing picture of events within Oman than the contemporary sources, whilst they appear to omit the descent upon Kalba.[26] Three of Su'ud's sons, aggrieved at their father, had set out from Dir'iya for Oman in January without his permission. They passed through Ajman and were thenceforth notably accompanied by the Shaikh, Rashid bin Humaid, with 100 Na'im. On arrival in Oman, they were surprised and probably worsted by people from the Batina: according to Ibn Ruzaiq these were the people of Khadra, and Su'ud's sons had the local support of Shawamis and Banu Ka'b, in addition to men they had brought from Hasa and Qasim, and the 100, but no other, Na'im.

After their defeat, Su'ud's sons appealed to Mutlaq al-Mutairi, the Wahhabi military commander in Oman, and he joined them with a large army: Ibn Ruzaiq includes in this, Na'im, Qitab and Dhawahir, with accompanying support from Muhammad bin Nasir al-Jabri who had raised levies from the Janaba, Duru', Hisham and Salim bin Ali al-Tamami.[27] The forces combined at Hazm, and moved to attack Barka via Hibra. Next they plundered Matrah, before proceeding via Ramla to Sur and Ja'lan. Much booty was taken *en passant*. Mutlaq al-Mutairi and Muhammad bin Nasir left for Izki, and the former then continued back to Buraimi.

The sequel to this extensive raid is described by Ibn Bishr. Mutlaq al-Mutairi and Su'ud's sons left Oman for Hasa whence, apparently reassured by Su'ud, they proceeded to Dir'iya. The situation for the Wahhabis in Oman deteriorated with their leaving, and the Banu Yas in particular forsook their allegiance. Su'ud despatched Abd al-Aziz bin Ghardaqa as military commander with a force to Oman. In Jumada (24 May–22 June 1811),[28] this force suffered a defeat at the hands of the Banu Yas, in which Ibn Ghardaqa, and 200 of his men, some of them from Oman, were killed. The upshot was that Wahhabi affairs in Oman became only further disturbed. Ibn Ruzaiq apparently places the said battle in Banu Yas Dhafra.[29]

One other development in relation to Muscat's relations with the Wahhabis needs to be mentioned. Ibn Ruzaiq describes a face-to-face meeting between Mutlaq al-Mutairi and Sayyid Sa'id at Masna'a, in which the two seem to have reached an accord, which was sealed by Sayyid Sa'id's delivery of 40,000 piastres (*qirsh*); just prior to this, Mutlaq had visited the country near Suhar with a large and intimidating force, as a result of which Azzan bin Qais had likewise come to terms with him. Ibn Ruzaiq places these meetings just before Mutlaq al-Mutairi's departure from Oman, apparently this year, previous to Ibn Ghardaqa's arrival. Ibn Ruzaiq's chronology cannot be relied upon, however, and whilst this dating does not seem unreasonable, especially in view of the relative peace of the next few years, it may conceivably be too early.[30]

After the death of Ibn Ghardaqa in 1811, Mutlaq al-Mutairi was sent once more to take command of Wahhabi forces in Oman. He must certainly have returned by about July 1813,[31] but when exactly is not clear: conceivably one might speculate that after Mutlaq al-Mutairi's accord with Muscat and Suhar, Su'ud had not felt the need to despatch a military commander of stature, or otherwise, to Oman until, say, early–mid 1813 when he sent Mutlaq. It seems that when he arrived Mutlaq al-Mutairi encountered widespread disaffection occasioned by the Wahhabis' financial exactions. He set to work reasserting Su'ud's authority, and he soon managed to bring the Dhahira under control, except for the refractory Banu Kilban, whom he was not strong enough militarily to coerce at Maqniyat. Returning to Buraimi, he levied the Banu Ka'b, and, marching to Dank, the Al Aziz. It appears that Wahhabi credit was low in Shamal, and he had been unable to raise troops from there: Ibn Ruzaiq refers to differences with the people of Shamal. Mutlaq al-Mutairi drew some further men from Ibri, then proceeded with his small and weak force via Manh to Hajriyin territory in Sharqiya, a day's journey from Ghabbi. Possibly intent on ravaging the district, Mutlaq al-Mutairi's force was attacked and put to flight by the Hajriyin: Mutlaq himself was killed, together with some dozen other Wahhabis and 18 Hajriyin. The sources agree that this battle took place in November 1813.[32]

Notes

Notes to Prologue

1. Capt. Babcock of the brig *Shannon* to Samuel Manesty, English East India Company (EIC) Resident at Basra and owner of the *Shannon* and the *Trimmer*, Basra 29 Dec. 1804, Bombay Archives (BA), Secret and Political (S&P) Department, vol. 164A / pp. 434–7. The *Shannon* was released at Charak bay. (Text has 'Gulph', 'top Gllt'.)

Notes to Chapter One

1. Sanjiv P. Desai, *The Hand Book of the Bombay Archives* (Dept of Archives, Government of Maharashtra, Bombay, 1978), pp. 2–3, 17. The records referred to here form only part of the total held in the Bombay Archives, which cover the period 1630–1955.
2. Board's deliberations on information supplied by Sayyid Taqi with enclosures, Bombay 6 Jan. 1810, BA Political (P) 350/122 (117–38).
3. See R. Temple's elegant depiction of the scene, Sultan Muhammad al-Qasimi, *The Myth of Arab Piracy in the Gulf* (Croom Helm, London, 1986), plate 1, p. 116.
4. There were 2 naval frigates, 9 Company cruisers, 1 bomb ketch, which quickly sank, and 4 transports: five of the vessels were already in the Gulf. The military detachment comprised about 833 Europeans, 528 sepoys and 262 followers. 'Return of a Detachment under Orders for Foreign Service ...', Bombay 7 Sept. 1809, BA P 339/8446; and Sultan Muhammad al-Qasimi, 'Arab "Piracy" and the East India Company Encroachment in the Gulf 1797–1820', PhD thesis, University of Exeter, March 1985, Appendix 2, p. 12.
5. Qasimi is the adjective corresponding to the plural noun Qawasim: pronounced Káassimee and Kawáassim. The key Qasimi ports were Ras al-Khaima, Sharja, Ajman, Umm al-Qaiwain, Jazirat al-Hamra' and Rams, on the Arabian coast, and Linga, on the Persian: Ras al-Khaima, Sharja and Linga were those directly ruled by members of the Qasimi family.
6. Chief Secretary to Government Francis Warden to Wainwright and Smith, Bombay Castle 7 Sept. 1809, BA P 339/8428–44.
7. al-Qasimi, 'Arab "Piracy"', Appendix 1, p. 7.
8. Cf. James Justinian Morier, *A Journey through Persia, Armenia, and Asia Minor to Constantinople in the Years 1808 and 1809; etc.* (Longman, Hurst etc., London, 1812), p. 9; W. Grant Keir to Warden, 1 April 1820, BA S (Secret) 316/466–7 (453–68); Capt. George Barnes Brucks, *Account of the Survey of the Persian Gulf, 1821–1835[/1837]*, British Library Add. Ms. 14,383, pp. 54–5, *passim*; Capt. J. Wainwright, Remarks on the Navigation of the Persian Gulph in 1809 and 1810, BA P 369/561–2 (552–601).
9. Capt. George Barnes Brucks, 'Draft Chapters for an Unpublished Account of the Survey of the Persian Gulf' (1835/7) (chapters 1–2 of BL Add. Ms. 14,383), in Andrew S. Cook (ed.),

Survey of the Shores and Islands of the Persian Gulf 1820–1829, 5 vols. (Archive Editions, England, 1990), vol. 1, p. 5; William Bruce, Resident, to Bombay, Bushire 31 July 1816, BA S 312/1026–35.

10. William Vincent, *The Commerce and Navigation of the Ancients in the Indian Ocean* (London, 1807). Besides this, the principal work available to Bombay Marine officers at this time was the East India Company hydrographer Alexander Dalrymple's notable compendium of 1806: see Cook, *Survey*, vol. 1, pp. xiv–vi.

11. Brucks, 'Draft Chapters', in Cook, *Survey*, vol. 1, pp. 3–5.

12. Board's deliberations, Bombay 6 Jan. 1810, BA P 350/123 (117–46).

13. Cf. two Qasimi letters intercepted and passed on to Government by Sayyid Taqi in 1809: BA P 327/3565–6 (3557–66). Sayyid Taqi was very possibly the Sayyid Muhammad Taqi bin Muhammad Hadi who became security for Nakhilu against Company claims in 1806; owned a ship which sailed between Muscat and Bombay in 1808; and acted as agent of the ruler of Muscat in 1807: BA S&P 183/5180–8, 236/7529, 202/2319–21.

14. The instructions to the two commanders of 7 September 1809 refer only to the existence of a topographical sketch by Sayyid Taqi of the Arab coast, in which are depicted the ports from Rams to Abu Hail. In al-Qasimi, 'Arab "Piracy"', Appendices 13–14, are two loose Persian maps, stylistically very close indeed to that by Sayyid Taqi at BA P 350/122. This pair of maps is presented out of context, but it does not seem unreasonable to presume that they, or something similar, were issued before the expedition sailed. One depicts part of the Arab coast and one the opposite Persian coast: the main map, however, traces the whole Arab coastline from Ras al-Hadd to Zubara, but omits the Persian.

15. This, at least, was the case with his regiment: H. Moyse-Bartlett, *The Pirates of Trucial Oman* (Macdonald, London, 1966), pp. 87–8.

16. D. Lighton, Adjutant-General of the army, to Bombay Council, with enclosures, Bombay 20 Jan. 1820, BA P 477/544–66.

17. Moyse-Bartlett, *The Pirates*, pp. 95–6. Warren's despatch of 23 Dec., in Lighton, 20 Jan. 1820, BA P 477/544–66, however, specifically states that no reply was received. Unfortunately Moyse-Bartlett does not state his source.

18. Wainwright, cited in al-Qasimi, *The Myth*, p. 137. Organization was the key. At Ras al-Khaima in 1809, the British were quite probably outnumbered; in 1819 they were not. The Ras al-Khaima garrison was estimated at 5,000 in 1809 and 3,000–4,000 in 1819: Moyse-Bartlett, *The Pirates*, p. 50; Surgeon Andrew Jukes to Keir, Muscat Cove 5 Nov. 1819, and to Bombay, Muscat 4 Nov., BA S 313/2040–3, 2055–9; Charles Rathbone Low, *History of the Indian Navy (1613–1863)*, 2 vols. (Richard Bentley, London, 1877), vol. 1, pp. 354–8.

19. A brace of naval 24-pounders were also used to great effect in breaching the walls of Shinas in January 1810 and of Ras al-Khaima in December 1819: al-Qasimi, *The Myth*, p. 143; Major-General W. Grant Keir to Bombay, Ras al-Khaima 19 Dec. 1819, BA S 312/2202–11: Return of ordnance, Ras al-Khaima 12 Dec. 1819, Dhaya 12 Jan. 1820, BA P 479/1276–8. The effectiveness of the British artillery and tactics is reflected in the generally far higher casualties suffered by the defenders during the two expeditions. At Dhaya in 1819 the British suffered 5 killed and 15 wounded, and at Ras al-Khaima in 1819 they suffered 5 killed and 51 wounded. Keir estimated the number of Qawasim killed at Ras al-Khaima in 1819 at 300, 100 the result of a single shell burst, with a further 700 wounded. Lighton, with enclosures, Bombay 20 Jan 1820, BA P 477/544–66: Return of casualties, Ras al-Khaima 10 Dec. 1819, BA S 314/2211; cf. Low, *Indian Navy*, vol. 1, p. 357. Keir to Adjutant-General, Ras al-Khaima 3 Jan. 1820, BA P 477/545–50.

20. Warren, 23 Dec. 1819, in Lighton, 20 Jan. 1820, BA P 477/544–66.

21. Major General Keir to Adjutant-General, 5 Feb. 1820, with enclosures, BA P 479/1257–78.

22. Capt. T.P. Thompson to Warden, Muscat 9 Aug. 1820, BA P 491/6132–51; Moyse-Bartlett, *The Pirates*, pp. 129–30.

23. Moyse-Bartlett, *The Pirates*, pp. 129–30, citing the *Bombay Courier*.

24. The British force consisted of 3 naval ships, 6 Company cruisers and 15(–18) transports. The land force comprised around 1,662 European troops, principally of the 47th and 65th regiments, 1,482 sepoys, the largest contingent from the 1st/2nd Bombay Native Infantry, and

1,738 followers. The ruler of Muscat provided perhaps 20 small landing-boats, and accompanied the flotilla to Ras al-Khaima with 2 warships and 600 soldiers: a perhaps 2,000-strong land force arrived two days after Ras al-Khaima fell and was directly sent home. Embarkation returns and other material, Bombay 1 Oct.–2 Nov. 1819, BA S 313/1571, 1776, 1803, 1891–1912; W. Bruce to Jukes, Bushire 26 Nov. 1819, BA S 315/68–72; Low, *Indian Navy*, vol. 1, p. 355; J.G. Lorimer, *Gazetteer of the Persian Gulf, Oman and Central Arabia*, 2 vols. (Superintendent Government Printing, Calcutta, 1915), vol. 1, p. 665.

25. Lorimer, *Gazetteer*, vol. 1, pp. 2638–9.

Notes to Chapter Two

1. The film was first shown in Kuwait on 1 April 1971. It has been released in a dubbed version entitled 'Sea of Silence'. For a trenchant critique see, Saif Marzuq al-Shamlan, *Ta'rikh al-Ghaus 'alal-Lu'lu' fil-Kuwait wal-Khalij al-Arabi*, 2 vols. (Hukumat al-Kuwait, Kuwait, 1398/1978), vol. 2, pp. 352–62: cites the other translation.

2. The camel predominated in desert regions, such as Dubai and Abu Dhabi, although goats and sheep were far more numerous in the better watered, northern Trucial States. Lorimer, *Gazetteer*, vol. 2, pp. 1425–51, entries for individual Trucial States, *passim*; Frauke Heard-Bey, *From Trucial States to United Arab Emirates: a Society in Transition* (Longman, London, 1982), chaps. 1, 5.

3. Lorimer put the number of bedouin, additional to the 72,000, at 'about 8,000 souls'. The total population in 1968 including expatriates was 180,226. Lorimer, *Gazetteer*, vol. 2, p. 1437; K.G. Fenelon, *The United Arab Emirates: an Economic and Social Survey* (Longman, London, 1973), pp. 6–8, 126.

4. 'Notes on sea-fishing in the Persian Gulf', Persian Gulf Administration Report for 1880–1, p. 54 (54–77), in *The Persian Gulf Administration Reports 1873–1947*, 10 vols. (Archive Editions, Gerrards Cross, 1986), vol. 2.

5. Fuad Khuri, *Tribe and State in Bahrain* (University of Chicago Press, Chicago, 1980), pp. 53–6.

6. J.R. Wellsted, *Travels in Arabia*, 2 vols. (John Murray, London, 1838: reprint Akademische Druck—u. Verlagsanstalt, Graz, 1978), vol. 1, p. 25.

7. 'The Pearl and Mother-of-Pearl Fisheries of the Persian Gulf', in Lorimer, *Gazetteer*, vol. 1, p. 2220 (2220–93).

8. Lorimer, *Gazetteer*, vol. 1, pp. 2252–3, 2256–8.

9. al-Shamlan, *Ta'rikh al-Ghaus*, vol. 1, pp. 370–3. For other accounts of pearling see e.g.: Lorimer, *Gazetteer*, vol. 1, pp. 2220–93; Charles Belgrave, *Personal Column* (Hutchinson, London, 1960), chap. 4; Heard-Bey, *From Trucial States*, pp. 182–8, 198–223 (and *passim*); Khuri, *Tribe and State*, pp. 56–67; S.K. Datta and J.B. Nugent, 'Bahrain's Pearling Industry: how it was, why it was that way and its implications', in J.B. Nugent and T.H. Thomas (eds), *Bahrain and the Gulf* (Croom Helm, London, 1985), pp. 25–41.

10. Geoffrey Bibby, *Looking for Dilmun* (Pelican, Harmondsworth, 1970), pp. 172–4.

11. al-Shamlan, *Ta'rikh al-Ghaus*, vol. 1, pp. 120–1, 160; Lorimer, *Gazetteer*, vol. 1, p. 2225.

12. Lorimer, *Gazetteer*, vol. 1, p. 2229.

13. Wellsted, *Travels in Arabia*, vol. 1, pp. 265–6.

14. Dr Thoms, American Missionary Hospital, Bahrain, in Lorimer, *Gazetteer*, vol. 1, p. 2231 note.

15. 'Report of Capt. Malcolm on the state of trade between Persia and India and suggestions as to the means for improving it, 1800', in J.A. Saldanha, *The Persian Gulf Précis*, 8 vols. (Superintendent Government Printing, Calcutta, 1908: reprint Archive Editions, Gerrards Cross, 1986), vol. 1, p. 445 (442–55).

16. For an account of Gulf trade at this time see: trade reports by Jones and Manesty (1790) and by Malcolm (1800) in Saldanha, *Persian Gulf Précis*, vol. 1, pp. 404–34, 442–55.

17. William Milburn, *Oriental Commerce, or the East India Trader's Complete Guide*, 2 vols. (Kingsbury, Parbury and Allen, London, 1825), vol. 1, pp. 97–106.

18. Wellsted, *Travels in Arabia*, vol. 1, p. 25.
19. 'Report of Capt. Malcolm', in Saldanha, *Persian Gulf Précis*, vol. 1, p. 445 (442–55).
20. J. Horsburgh, *India Directory, or Directions for Sailing to and from the East Indies etc.* (4th ed. 1836), in Cook, *Survey*, vol. 1, pp. 304–5.
21. Captain Colomb RN, *Slave-Catching in the Indian Ocean* (1873), cited in Arnold T. Wilson, *The Persian Gulf* (Allen and Unwin, London, 1954), pp. 225–6.
22. Commander A. Rowland, 'Sailing Craft of the Persian Gulf', in Lorimer, *Gazetteer*, vol. 1, p. 2319 (2319–32).
23. Wellsted, *Travels in Arabia*, vol. 1, p. 28.
24. Anon, *Oman, a Seafaring Nation* (Ministry of Information and Culture, Oman, 1979), p. 118; David Howarth, *Dhows* (Quartet, London, 1977), p. 33; Alan Villiers, 'Some Aspects of the Arab Dhow Trade', in Louise E. Sweet, *Peoples and Cultures of the Middle East: an Anthropological Reader*, 2 vols. (The Natural History Press, New York, 1970), vol. 1, p. 164.
25. Lorimer, *Gazetteer*, vol. 1, Annexure 2, p. 2329.
26. Villiers, 'Some Aspects', in Sweet, *Peoples and Cultures*, vol. 1, p. 165.
27. Rowand, 'Sailing Craft', in Lorimer, *Gazetteer*, vol. 1, p. 2321 (2319–32).
28. 'A Sketch of the Proceedings of the British Armament which Sailed from Bombay in September 1809 for the Purpose of Destroying the Vessels of the Jowasmee Pirates in the Gulph of Persia', in al-Qasimi, 'Arab "Piracy"', Appendix 1, p. 3 (1–11).
29. Heard-Bey, *From Trucial States*, pp. 182–223, esp. 198–200, 208–12; Khuri, *Tribe and State*, pp. 58–9, 65–7 (56–67); Lorimer, *Gazetteer*, vol. 1, pp. 2233–4, 2240–4, 2284–93.
30. See particularly B.J. Slot, *The Origins of Kuwait*(E.J. Brill, Leiden, 1991), pp. 70–2, 86–9; Ahmad M. Abu Hakima, *History of Eastern Arabia 1750–1800: the Rise and Development of Bahrain and Kuwait* (Khayats, Beirut, 1965); B.J. Slot, *The Arabs of the Gulf 1602–1784* (Leidschendam, 1993).
31. Cf. Peter Lienhardt, 'The Authority of Shaykhs in the Gulf: an Essay in Nineteenth-Century History', in *Arabian Studies* (Hurst, London, 1975), vol. 2, pp. 61–75.
32. This account is given by Warden, who took it almost word for word from a sketch-history of the Utub translated and compiled by William Bruce 'from oral communications of an Arab of intelligence'. Francis Warden, 'Historical Sketch of the Uttoobee Tribe of Arabs', in R.H. Thomas (ed.), *Arabian Gulf Intelligence: Selections from the Records of the Bombay Government* (Oleander Press, New York, 1985), pp. 362–5; W. Bruce, Resident, to Bombay, Bushire 26 Oct. 1816, BA P 432/2521–9.
33. Warden, 'Historical Sketch', in Thomas (ed.), *Arabian Gulf Intelligence*, p. 363.
34. Ibid., p. 363.
35. Carsten Niebuhr, *Travels Through Arabia, and Other Countries in the East*, translated by Robert Heron, 2 vols. (Morison and Son, Perth, etc., Edinburgh, 1792: reprint Librairie du Liban, Beirut, c. 1968), vol. 2, pp. 16–23. Cf. Kniphausen in Slot, *The Arabs of the Gulf*, pp. 354–5, note 97; and Loch: 'Every man has a slavish obedience to the Shaikh of the tribe, yet is as free in his mind as the air he roves through, he is as wild as the deserts and hills he travels over, and as high spirited as the horse he rides.' Captain Francis Erskine Loch RN, *Diaries of Captain F.E. Loch, Compiled by him in 1835*, covering the period 19 March 1818–29 March 1821, Scottish Record Office, Edinburgh, GD1/633/1&2, MS p. 236, typescript (TS) p. 212.
36. al-Shamlan, *Ta'rikh al-Ghaus*, vol. 2, p. 308 (307–12); cf. H. Jasim, 'Tub Tub Ya Bahr', in *al-Ma'thurat al-Sha'biya*, no. 21, Jan. 1991, pp. 59–67.

Notes to Chapter Three

1. A parallel situation existed on the Persian coast, although the tribes in question were, of course, not bedouin.
2. Niebuhr, *Travels through Arabia*, vol. 2, pp. 146–7; cf. J.S. Buckingham, *Travels in Assyria,*

Media, and Persia (Henry Colburn, London 1829: reprint Gregg International, Farnborough, 1971), pp. 349–50.

3. Cf. e.g. C.E. Davies, 'A History of the Province of Fars during the Later Nineteenth Century', DPhil thesis, St Antony's College, Oxford, 1985, pp. 434–41.

4. George N. Curzon, *Persia and the Persian Question*, 2 vols. (Longmans, London 1892: reprint Frank Cass, London, 1966), vol. 2, p. 233.

5. Niebuhr, *Travels through Arabia*, vol. 2, pp. 138–9. Cf. Kniphausen on the Huwala, in W. Floor, 'A Description of the Persian Gulf and Its Inhabitants in 1756', *Persica*, vol. 8 (1979), pp. 162–85.

6. Heard-Bey, *From Trucial States*, p. 11.

7. See e.g. J.B. Kelly, *Britain and the Persian Gulf 1795–1880* (Oxford University Press, Oxford, 1968), chap. 10, pp. 412–51.

8. Buckingham, *Travels in Assyria*, p. 514.

9. Sir John Malcolm, *Sketches of Persia*, 2 vols. (1815: republ. Cassell, London, 1888), vol. 1, p. 39.

10. Roger Savory, *Iran under the Safavids* (Cambridge University Press, Cambridge, 1980), p. 250.

11. *Gombroon Diary* 26 Aug.–6 Sept. 1740, cited in L. Lockhart, *Nadir Shah* (1938: reprint Al-Irfan, Lahore, 1976), p. 212.

12. See John R. Perry, *Karim Khan Zand: a History of Iran, 1747–1779* (University of Chicago Press, Chicago, 1979).

13. In Persia, 'Long beards are at the present day very fashionable—His Majesty having one (when sitting down) that reaches to his shawl and all the great men of course imitate him in everything he does as much as possible.' Lt E. Frederick, 'A Trip to the Persian Gulf in 1802', India Office Library and Records (IOR), MSS Eur. D. 109, p. 53 (40–58).

14. See e.g. Stephen Ray Grummon, 'The Rise and Fall of the Arab Shaykhdom of Bushire: 1750–1850', PhD thesis, Johns Hopkins University, 1985, (UMI, 1987).

15. Abraham Parsons, *Travels in Asia and Africa* (Longman, Hurst etc., London, 1808), p. 190.

16. Edward Scott Waring (Bengal civil), *A Tour to Sheeraz by the Route of Kazroon and Feerozabad* (Cadell and Davies, London, 1807), p. 10.

17. Loch, *Diaries*, MS p. 149, TS p. 137.

18. Lt William Heude (Madras military), *A Voyage Up the Persian Gulf, and a Journey Overland from India to England in 1817* (Longman, Hurst etc., London, 1819), p. 43.

19. Buckingham, *Travels in Assyria*, p. 347. Morier pronounced the bazars 'exactly those of a provincial town in Turkey', and noted the general absence of commercial 'bustle and movement': 'Instead of crowds of vessels at anchor ... the masts of a solitary vessel may be here and there perceived, and perhaps a single boat creeping along with a flapping sail.' Morier, *A Journey through Persia ... in 1808 and 1809*, pp. 56–8; James Justinian Morier, *A Second Journey through Persia, Armenia and Asia Minor, to Constantinople, between the Years 1810 and 1816* (Longman, Hurst etc., London, 1818), pp. 38–42.

20. Morier, *A Journey through Persia ... in 1808 and 1809*, pp. 56–8; Heude, *A Voyage*, p. 43; Buckingham, *Travels in Assyria*, p. 347; Grummon, 'The Rise', pp. 43–8.

21. Estimates for the population during this period generally lie between eight and twenty thousand, and, for the number of houses, range from 800 to 1500.

22. Buckingham, *Travels in Assyria*, p. 349.

23. Lt J.R. Wellsted (Indian Navy), *Travels to the City of the Caliphs, along the Shores of the Persian Gulf and the Mediterranean*, 2 vols. (London, 1840), vol. 1, pp. 130–1, cited in Kelly, *Britain*, p. 43. Cf. Morier, *A Second Journey*, pp. 41–2; James Baillie Fraser, *Narrative of a Journey into Khorasan in the Years 1821 and 1822* (Longman, Hurst etc., London, 1825), pp. 54–5; Lt J.E. Alexander, *Travels from India to England* (Parbury, Allen, London, 1827), p. 92.

24. Cf. The Act for Promoting Public Health of 1848.

25. Dr Adair, Medical Superintendent Indo-European Telegraph Department, report of 29 April 1865, Public Records Office, Kew, (PRO), FO 248/255.

26. Loch, *Diaries*, MS pp. 175–7, TS pp. 159–60.

27. Dr E. Ives (EIC surgeon), *A Journey from Persia to England* (London, 1773), quoted in Stephen Hemsley Longrigg, *Four Centuries of Modern Iraq* (Oxford University Press, Oxford, 1925), p. 165.
28. Heude, *A Voyage*, p. 159.
29. Niebuhr, *Travels through Arabia*, vol. 2, p. 172.
30. Sir Harford Jones Brydges, quoted in Lorimer, *Gazetteer*, vol. 1, p. 1285.
31. See Perry, *Karim Khan*, pp. 170, 195; and Carsten Niebuhr, *Voyage en Arabie et en d'Autres Pays Circonvoisins*, 2 vols. (S.J. Baalde, Amsterdam, 1780), vol. 2, pp. 179–80.
32. Loch, *Diaries*, MS p. 209, TS p. 188.
33. Niebuhr, *Voyage en Arabie*, vol. 2, p. 175.
34. Loch, *Diaries*, TS p. 188.
35. Buckingham, *Travels in Assyria*, p. 367.
36. Parsons, *Travels*, p. 159.
37. Loch, *Diaries*, TS p. 185.
38. Loch thought 50,000 grossly exaggerated, while Buckingham even thought 100,000 nearer the mark. A century later, Lorimer gives *c.* 58,000. Niebuhr remarked in the 1760s, 'si l'on veut s'en informer chés les habitans, ils parlent toujours de quelques centaines de milliers': Loch, *Diaries*, TS p. 184; Buckingham, *Travels in Assyria*, p. 369; Lorimer, *Gazetteer*, vol. 2, p. 276; Niebuhr, *Voyage en Arabie*, vol. 2, p. 179.
39. Buckingham, *Travels in Assyria*, p. 370 (370–80).
40. Loch, *Diaries*, TS p. 198.
41. Bartholomew Plaisted, 'Narrative of a Journey from Basra to Aleppo in 1750', in Douglas Carruthers (ed.), *The Desert Route to India*, series 2, vol. 63 (Hakluyt Society, 1928: reprint Kraus Reprint, Nendeln, 1967), p. 59.
42. Parsons, *Travels*, p. 156.
43. Buckingham, *Travels in Assyria*, p. 367.
44. Niebuhr, *Voyage en Arabie*, vol. 2, p. 172; cf. Buckingham, *Travels in Assyria*, p. 395.
45. Cited in Lorimer, *Gazetteer*, vol. 2, p. 271; cf. Parsons, *Travels*, p. 157.
46. Buckingham, *Travels in Assyria*, p. 395.
47. Parsons, *Travels*, p. 158: Parsons himself actually speaks of 'bison' and not cattle.
48. Christine Moss Helms, *The Cohesion of Saudi Arabia: Evolution of Political Identity* (Croom Helm, London, 1981), p. 110.
49. Shaikh Muhammad founded a knowledge of the faith on the Koran, six collections of *hadith* (especially al-Muslim and al-Bukhari) and two of *tafsir*, by Ibn Kathir and al-Baghawi. The *'ijma* of the first three generations of Islam was acceptable: Moss Helms, *The Cohesion*, p. 92.
50. See Derek Hopwood, 'The Ideological Basis: Ibn Abd al-Wahhab's Muslim Revivalism', in Tim Niblock, *State, Society and Economy in Saudi Arabia* (Croom Helm, London and Centre for Arab Gulf Studies, Exeter, 1982), chap. 2, p. 28.
51. For a general account of these events and the history of these years see e.g. A.M. Vassiliev, *Ta'rikh al-Arabiya al-Su'udiya* (Dar al-Taqaddum, Moscow, 1982).
52. Aziz al-Azmeh, 'Wahhabite Polity', in Ian Richard Netton, *Arabia and the Gulf: from Traditional Society to Modern States* (Croom Helm, London, 1986), chap. 6, p. 76.
53. See, *inter alia*, John Lewis Burckhardt, *Notes on the Bedouins and Wahabys, Collected during his Travels in the East* (Colburn and Bentley, London 1831: reprint Johnson Reprint, New York, 1967), vol. 2, p. 119.
54. Burckhardt, *Notes*, vol. 2, p. 109.
55. But, cf. Burckhardt, *Notes*, vol. 2, pp. 152–3.
56. Burckhardt, *Notes*, vol. 2, p. 165.
57. Burckhardt, *Notes*, vol. 2, p. 168.
58. Waring, *A Tour to Sheeraz*, p. 123. Cf. letter from Haji Karim Husain Ali to Harford Jones, Karbala? April/May 1802, BA S&P 123/3237–41.
59. Burckhardt, *Notes*, vol. 2, p. 195.
60. Burckhardt, *Notes*, vol. 2, pp. 199–200.
61. Humaid bin Muhammad bin Ruzaiq, *al-Fath al-Mubin fi Sirat al-Bu Sa'idiyin*, translated by George Percy Badger (chaplain, Bombay) as, *History of the Imams and Seyyids of Oman* (Hakluyt Society, series 1, no. 44, 1871: reprint Burt Franklin, New York, 1970), p. 230.

62. Ibn Ruzaiq, *Imams and Seyyids*, pp. 248–9.
63. Ibn Ruzaiq, *Imams and Seyyids*, p. 236.
64. David Seton, Resident, to J. Malcolm, HCC *Ternate*, Muscat Cove 5 Feb. 1809, BA P 325/2622–8.
65. George Forster Sadleir (47th Regt), *Diary of a Journey Across Arabia (1819)* (Falcon Press, Naples and Oleander Press, New York, 1977), pp. 90–1.
66. Malcolm, *Sketches*, p. 21.
67. Milburn, *Oriental Commerce*, vol. 1, p. 81.
68. Wellsted, *Travels in Arabia*, vol. 1, p. 12.
69. Parsons, *Travels*, p. 210.
70. Lorimer, *Gazetteer*, vol. 2, p. 1180.
71. Brucks, 'Memoir Descriptive of the Navigation of the Gulf of Persia', and Horsburgh, *India Directory*, in Cook, *Survey*, vol. 1, pp. 222, 245.
72. Re December 1816: Buckingham, *Travels in Assyria*, pp. 517–18.
73. Malcolm, *Sketches*, p. 25.
74. Khwaja Abdul Qadir (Tipu Sultan's emissary, 1786), *Waqai-i Manazil-i Rum: Diary of a Journey to Constantinople*, ed. Mohibbul Hasan (Asia Publishing House, London, 1968), Persian text p. 11.
75. E.g. Heude, *A Voyage*, pp. 22, 32; Wellsted, *Travels in Arabia*, vol. 1, pp. 12–13; Buckingham, *Travels in Assyria*, pp. 507, 518.
76. Dr John Griffiths, *Travels in Europe, Asia Minor and Arabia* (London, 1805), cited in Philip Ward, *Travels in Oman: on the Track of the Early Explorers* (Oleander, Cambridge, 1987), p. 8.
77. Parsons, *Travels*, p. 207.
78. As, Niebuhr, *Voyage*, vol. 2, pp. 67–8; Buckingham, *Travels in Assyria*, p. 519.
79. Fraser, *Narrative*, pp. 10, 6–20; Milburn, *Oriental Commerce*, vol. 1, pp. 80–1.
80. Malcolm, *Sketches*, p. 25.
81. Heude, *A Voyage*, p. 24.
82. Heude, *A Voyage*, pp. 24–5.
83. Vincenzo Maurizi, *History of Seyd Said, Sultan of Muscat* (John Booth, London, 1819: reprint Oleander, Cambridge, 1984), p. 132. Maurizi was present in Oman in 1809–10 and 1814–15.
84. Heude, *A Voyage*, p. 25. Cf. Alfred J. Swann, *Fighting the Slave-Hunters in Central Africa* (1910: republ. Frank Cass, London, 1969), p. 222.
85. Maurizi, *Seyd Said*, p. 28.
86. Maurizi, *Seyd Said*, pp. 132–3.
87. Buckingham claims these figures were supported by a recent census: Buckingham, *Travels in Assyria*, p. 507. Whilst a number of population estimates range much higher, the figure of 10,000 seems to reoccur in a significant number of early nineteenth-century reports. It slightly exceeds Lorimer's figure a century later: Ward, *Travels*, pp. 7–17; Lorimer, *Gazetteer*, vol. 2, p. 1185.
88. Capt. Hon. George Thomas Keppel, *A Personal Narrative of a Journey from India to England* (London, 1825), and Griffiths, *Travels*, cited in Ward, *Travels*, p. 13 (see also p. 9).
89. Resident Seton, who succumbed in 1809, had been under no illusions about his possible fate: David Seton to Bombay Council, Bombay 20 March 1805, BA S&P 165A/1309–12; cf. Maurizi, *Seyd Said*, p. 130 (his chronology is slightly inaccurate).
90. Malcolm, *Sketches*, p. 28.
91. Buckingham, *Travels in Assyria*, pp. 524–5.
92. Capt. W.F.W. Owen, *Narrative of Voyages to Explore the Shores of Africa, Arabia, and Madagascar: Performed in HM Ships Leven and Barracouta* (Bentley, London, 1833), cited in Ward, *Travels*, p. 13.
93. Parsons, *Travels*, p. 209.
94. Cf. Abdul Qadir, *Waqai*, Persian text p. 14.
95. One traveller, in partnership with another, bought 1,000 mangoes for this purpose: Parsons, *Travels*, p. 210.

96. E.g. Wellsted, *Travels in Arabia*, vol. 1, p. 13; Maurizi, *Seyd Said*, p. 22; Niebuhr, *Voyage*, vol. 2, p. 69; Buckingham, *Travels in Assyria*, p. 518; Malcolm, *Sketches*, pp. 25–6.

97. Buckingham, *Travels in Assyria*, pp. 515–16.

98. Maurizi, *Seyd Said*, p. 24; Wellsted, *Travels in Arabia*, vol. 1, pp. 32–3; Malcolm, *Sketches*, p. 24.

99. Niebuhr, *Voyage*, vol. 2, pp. 67–8.

100. Buckingham, *Travels in Assyria*, p. 507; Fraser, *Narrative*, pp. 6–7.

101. Wellsted, *Travels in Arabia*, vol. 1, pp. 18–21.

102. Maurizi, *Seyd Said*, p. 129.

103. Wellsted, *Travels in Arabia*, vol. 1, p. 21.

104. David Seton to Bombay, 9 Jan. 1801, cited in Patricia Risso, *Oman and Muscat: an Early Modern History* (Croom Helm, London, 1986), p. 192.

105. Wellsted, *Travels in Arabia*, vol. 1, pp. 18, 20–1.

106. Viz. 5 Dec. 1816: Buckingham, *Travels in Assyria*, p. 517. Niebuhr, in particular, was widely drawn upon by later writers of travelogues. But even Niebuhr, who apparently amassed much of his information from 'un couple d'Arabes et le Schech des Indes', only stayed at Muscat for two weeks (3–18 Jan. 1765): Niebuhr, *Voyage*, vol. 2, p. 68 (66–71).

107. Lorimer, *Gazetteer*, vol. 2, p. 1411.

108. Eighteenth century Omani source (Salim bin Sa'id al-Sa'ighi), cited in John C. Wilkinson, *The Imamate Tradition of Oman* (Cambridge University Press, Cambridge, 1987), p. 170.

109. See Wilkinson, *Imamate Tradition*.

110. Ibn Ruzaiq, *Imams and Seyyids*, p. 85.

111. Reflecting in both general and specific terms the pre-existing Adnani/Nizari-Qahtani/Yamani divisions.

112. M. Reda Bhacker, 'Roots of Domination and Dependency: British Reaction towards the Development of Omani Commerce at Muscat and Zanzibar in the Nineteenth Century', DPhil thesis, St Antony's College, Oxford, 1988, p. 31.

113. Wilkinson, *Imamate Tradition*, p. 225.

114. The date of Sa'id's death is uncertain, but it may have been before 1809: D. Seton to Malcolm, Muscat 20 Feb. 1809, BA P 325/2633–50; Maurizi, *Seyd Said*, pp. 173–4; Wilkinson, *Imamate Tradition*, pp. 352–3.

115. Ibn Ruzaiq, *Imams and Seyyids*, pp. 213–14.

116. Malcolm, *Sketches*, p. 23.

117. D. Seton to Bombay, Surat 9 July 1802, BA S&P 126/4595–612; J. Malcolm to Fort William, Bushire 1 Feb. 1800, in Saldanha, *Persian Gulf Précis*, vol. 1, pp. 376–7; Risso, *Oman*, pp. 192–3.

118. Bhacker, 'Roots of Domination', pp. 45 and ff.

119. The Bandar Abbas lease included neighbouring coastal dependencies such as Minab; Sayyid Sultan also gained control of Qishm and Hormuz, probably by subjugating the ruling Banu Mu'in Shaikh.

120. For published accounts, see e.g. Zamil Muhammad al-Rashid, *Su'udi Relations with Eastern Arabia and Uman (1800–1871)* (Luzac, London, 1981), pp. 45–71, and, as ever, Kelly, *Britain*.

121. Emily Ruete (Salma bint Sa'id bin Sultan), *Memoirs of an Arabian Princess* (Ward and Downey, London, 1888), pp. 159–62.

122. Ibn Ruzaiq, *Imams and Seyyids*, pp. 290–1.

123. Malcolm, *Sketches*, pp. 28–9.

124. Loch, *Diaries*, MS p. 110, TS pp. 103–4; cf. Fraser, *Narrative*, pp. 19–20.

125. Wellsted, *Travels in Arabia*, vol. 1, p. 7 (6–9).

126. D. Seton to Bombay, at sea 16 Jan. 1808, BA S&P 220/334–5.

127. There were also important preparations in 1817–18 and 1820.

128. Lorimer, *Gazetteer*, vol. 2, p. 1435, cf. 1547–8.

129. The Saudi Imam Abdullah bin Su'ud and Sa'id bin Sultan of Muscat both employed the term to describe those under the sway of Ras al-Khaima: three letters from Abdullah bin Su'ud to Bruce, early 1817, BA Sel. (selections on pirates) 74/411–14, 418–28,

435–8, 444–9; Sa'id bin Sultan to Bombay and Bruce, 25 May 1820, BA P 490/5830–44. See also e.g. Sayyid Taqi's map, Board's deliberations 6 Jan. 1810, BA P 350/122; Petition by c. 36 Indian merchants of Bombay, 4 Nov. 1817, BA Sel. 72/448–50; Mirza Hasan Fasa'i, *Farsnama-yi Nasiri*, translated by Heribert Busse as, *History of Persia under Qajar Rule* (Columbia University Press, New York, 1972), pp. 145, 154; Ahmad Mustafa Abu Hakima (ed.), *Lam' al-Shihab fi Sirat Muhammad bin Abd al-Wahhab* (Dar al-Thaqafa, Beirut, 1967), pp. 81, 139–40 *et passim*: the author is clear that 'Qawasim' applies only to places dependent on Ras al-Khaima and the true Qawasim. For the place of composition of this work, see Michael Cook, 'The Provenance of the Lam' al-Shihab fi Sirat Muhammad Ibn Abd al-Wahhab', *Journal of Turkish Studies*, 10 (1986), pp. 79–86; Lorimer, *Gazetteer*, vol. 2, pp. 1547–8.

130. Lorimer, *Gazetteer*, vol. 2, pp. 1547–8: at the start of the twentieth century c. 650 Qawasim tribesmen lived at Duwwan near Mughu on the Persian coast.

131. I.e. especially Diba, Fujaira, Khaur Fakkan and Khaur Kalba.

132. Saldanha, *Persian Gulf Précis*, vol. 2, pp. 46–7, 50–1.

133. Interestingly an Arabic report on the Rams–Abu Hail coast, probably written at Bushire, introduces the coastal inhabitants as 'the Qawasim of Ras al-Khaima and their subjects in Sir': Arabic report on Bahrain and the Qawasim, 22 Jan. 1817, BA Sel. 74/416–17. See also Abu Hakima (ed.), *Lam' al-Shihab*, p. 152 and *passim* re Sir; Lorimer, *Gazetteer*, vol. 2, pp. 1825–6: cf. John C. Wilkinson, *Water and Tribal Settlement in South East Arabia: a Study of the Aflaj of Oman* (Clarendon Press, Oxford, 1977), p. 33, note 5.

134. Captain Wainwright's report of 10 Jan. 1811 on the navigation of the Persian Gulf, BA P 369/5.

135. Ibid.

136. Lorimer, *Gazetteer*, vol. 2, p. 1437.

137. European sources only really take up the name Ras al-Khaima at the very end of the century. An isolated mention of the name itself occurs in the work of a sixteenth-century Venetian traveller: Slot, *The Arabs of the Gulf*, pp. 36–44.

138. John Hansman, *Julfar, an Arabian Port: its Settlement and Far Eastern Ceramic Trade from the 14th to the 18th Centuries* (Royal Asiatic Society, London, 1985), pp. 10, 21.

Notes to Chapter Four

1. Heude, *A Voyage*, pp. 39–40.

2. Fraser, *Narrative*, Appendix A, p. 4: cf. Wellsted, *Travels to the City of the Caliphs*, vol. 1, p. 101, cited in Kelly, *Britain*, p. 111, and Wellsted, *Travels in Arabia*, vol. 1, pp. 247–8.

3. Captain Mungo Herdman, Cape Corso Castle, 31 March 1722, in the version of Captain Charles Johnson, *A General History of the Pyrates* (J.M. Dent, London, 1972), pp. 263–4.

4. 'Pirata non est ex perduellium numero definitus, sed communis hostis omnium': cited in Barry Hart Dubner, *The Law of International Sea Piracy* (Martinus Nijhoff, The Hague, 1980), pp. 43–4.

5. Charge to the jury at the trials of Major Stede Bonnet and 33 others, Vice-Admiralty court, Charles-Town, 1718, cited in Dubner, *International Sea Piracy*, p. 93.

6. Ibid.

7. Sir William Blackstone, *Commentaries on the Laws of England* (Cadell and Davies, London, 1809), vol. 4, p. 70.

8. See e.g. Sir Charles Belgrave, *The Pirate Coast* (Librairie du Liban, Beirut, 1972) (1st publ. 1960); and Moyse-Bartlett, *The Pirates* (1st publ. 1966).

9. The best researched and most reliable of modern works in this broad tradition is, once again, that contained in Kelly, *Britain*.

10. Patricia R. Dubuisson has made a special study of the subject: see her article 'Qasimi Piracy and the General Treaty of Peace (1820)' in *Arabian Studies* (Hurst, London, 1978), vol. 4, pp. 47–57. Other writers who deal with this topic in passing include e.g. Heard-Bey, *From*

Trucial States; Ahmad Mustafa Abu Hakima, *Ta'rikh al-Kuwait*, 2 vols. (Hukumat al-Kuwait, Kuwait, 1970–3), vol. 2, part 1, pp. 73–91; and such as Rosemarie Said Zahlan, *The Making of the Modern Gulf States* (Unwin Hyman, London, 1989), pp. 5–7 (following al-Qasimi, *The Myth*).

11. And he is the present ruler of the state of Sharja.

12. Copies of the relevant texts are now held in the Centre for Arab Gulf Studies at the University of Exeter, and these form the prime source for the present work. Much of this material is, of course, duplicated at the India Office Library in London.

13. Lt Col. Lewis Pelly, 'Report on Tribes, Trade and Resources of Shoreline of Persian Gulf', Bushire 13 April 1863, in K. Bourne and D.C. Watt, *British Documents on Foreign Affairs: Reports and Papers from the Foreign Office Confidential Print*, part 1, series B, vol. 10 Persia 1856–1885 (University Publications of America), p. 209 (185–211). Two years later, the Saudi Imam addressed Pelly on the same subject of anti-slavery: 'He spoke of us as successful pirates; but laughed at the notion of our philanthropy.' Lt Col. Lewis Pelly, 'Report on a Journey to the Wahabee Capital of Riyadh in Central Arabia' (1866), in P. Tuson and A. Burdett (eds), *Records of Saudi Arabia, Primary Documents 1902–1960*, 10 vols. (Archive Editions, England, 1992), vol. 1, pp. 450, 443.

14. Sir Charles Hedges, judge of the court of Admiralty (1696), cited in W.S. Holdsworth, *A History of English Law*, vol. 6 (Methuen, London, 1924), p. 401.

15. I.e. as against, say, a 'political' motive. This proposition is often denied.

16. J.A. Hall, *The Law of Naval Warfare* (Chapman and Hall, London, 1921), p. 5.

17. On these and other unresolved issues, see Dubner, *International Sea Piracy*, pp. 3, 37–102, *passim*.

18. Samuel Taylor Coleridge, *Table Talk* (Routledge, London, 1884), 17 March 1832, p. 146.

Notes to Chapter Five

1. Saldanha, *Persian Gulf Précis*, vol. 2, p. 72.

2. Dr Glen, one of the four survivors of the *Ariel*, cited in Low, *Indian Navy*, vol. 1, pp. 368–9.

3. Ibid.

4. With a small gift of 500 rupees: cf. e.g. BA P 415/3819, a similar gift to Shaikh Khalfan of Asalu in 1814.

5. The ship had been grounded on Qais: 'he immediately gave all the assistance in his person, landed her cargo, got her afloat, loaded her again, and sent her away in the handsomest manner', for which he received 4,000 rupees. Shaikh Barakat was the uncle of Shaikh Abdullah bin Ahmad of Charak. Bushire Resident Lt William Bruce to Francis Warden, Chief Secretary to Government of Bombay, Bushire 24 July 1814, BA P 415/3799–800 and IOR R/15/1/14 pp. 171–5.

6. About the end of February.

7. Lovett, Bushire Resident, to Cheragh Ali Khan, Bushire 12 March 1803, BA S&P 147/5522–3. See also Saldanha, *Persian Gulf Précis*, vol. 2, p. 65.

8. See Lorimer, *Gazetteer*, vol. 1, pp. 1888–9.

9. Saldanha, *Persian Gulf Précis*, vol. 2, p. 67; and cf. Shaikh Rahma maintaining at one point that this accorded with 'British customs' and had been accepted as a principle by Seton, in H. Becher to Grant, Sec. to Govt., Bombay 20 Aug. 1803, BA S&P 151/7148. (On Rahma's talents and prestige in the Gulf: BA S&P 119/87–8.)

10. The vessel had formerly belonged to the Persian Ambassador Muhammad Nabi Khan: W. Bruce, note, Bushire 4 July 1814, IOR R/15/1/14 p. 161. For the *Ahmed Shah* affair see especially BA P 415/3795–824; 419/122–5, 128–30; and IOR R/15/1/14 pp. 152, 157–61, 168–75, 192–4.

11. The freightage on sulphur and gum ammoniac, from Bushire to Bombay, was equivalent to a little over one-third of their original purchase prices; on sulphur consigned from Bushire to Calcutta, it was somewhat over a half—viz. The freight costs on 78 bales (187 Hashim

maunds/c. 9.6 tons) of native sulphur and 60 bales (2,212 Tabriz maunds/c. 6.7 tons) of gum ammoniac consigned to Bombay, and on 100 bales of sulphur (246 Hashim maunds/ c. 12.6 tons) consigned to Calcutta, all from Bushire, were 390 Bombay rupees, 720 Bombay rupees and 800 Sicca rupees respectively. For comparison with these freight costs, it may be observed that the purchase cost of these 78 bales of sulphur had been 1,122 Bombay rupees (1,496 piastres), that of the gum ammoniac 1,866 Bombay rupees (2,488 piastres), and that of the 100 bales of sulphur 1,397 Sicca rupees (1,968 piastres). The Hashim maund was equivalent to 116 lb. avoirdupois in theory, a pound or two less in practice; the Tabriz maund has here been taken as 6.75 lb.; in Aug. 1819, the Calcutta rupee equalled 1.06827 Bombay rupees. W. Bruce, Resident, invoices of goods laden on board the ship *Ahmed Shah*, Bushire 1 and 2 July 1814, and Bruce to Bombay, 30 June, IOR R/15/1/14 pp. 157–61. Milburn, *Oriental Commerce*, vol. 1, pp. 96, 138–41.

12. Capt. S. Herriman to Bruce, Bushire 23 July 1814, BA P 415/3805–6.
13. Ibid., BA P 415/3808.
14. Ibid., BA P 415/3812; cf. IOR R/15/1/15 pp. 208–10.
15. The Shaikh received 3,375 rupees (4,500 piastres) from Bruce. When Henshaw, late Marine Agent, returned to Bushire from his mission to Charak, he had managed to secure the release of all the specie, 113 bales of HC sulphur, 4 HC (?) brood mares, 4 Bushire horses and a few ship's spars. At least 16 HC mares, 65 bales of HC sulphur and a number of guns were not recovered: a number of cattle appear to have perished, and other cargo was likewise destroyed, as a consequence of the wreck and subsequent conflagration. W. Bruce to Bombay, Bushire 8 Sept. 1814, IOR R/15/1/14 pp. 192–4.
16. Shaikh Khalfan, 'who has long been attached and shown a great friendship towards the British government. He is a very respectable old man and head of a large tribe of Arabs inhabiting the coast ... about Cape Naband and Asalu'. The Shaikh had accompanied Henshaw on his mission to Charak, and was rewarded by Bruce for his assistance with a gift of about 300 rupees' worth of Europe articles. W. Bruce to Bombay, Bushire 24 July 1814, BA P 415/3795–801.
17. Henshaw presumably also relayed to the Shaikh Bruce's argument that severe discredit would attach to him from the continued detention of the Bushire property. He was, of course, a Persian subject. Bruce supposed that Shaikh Abdullah considered he had a right to the Persian specie on the grounds that Bushire had not been a party to the new treaty between Muscat and Ras al-Khaima. W. Bruce to Bombay, Bushire 15 and 24 July, BA P 415/3793–4, 3795–801.
18. W. Bruce, Bushire 19 Dec. 1816, BA Sel. 72/180.
19. The Shaikh had allegedly promised them some sort of concord.
20. Article six of the provisional Anglo–Qasimi agreement signed in Oct. 1814 stipulated that the Qawasim would return this property: the agreement remained a dead letter. Agreement between W. Bruce and Qasimi representative, Bushire 6 Oct. 1814, BA P 419/128–30.
21. En route from Bombay to Bushire. Saldanha, *Persian Gulf Précis*, vol. 2, pp. 65–9: BA S&P 147/5519–38; 151/7142–51; 7205–57; 158/2465–71; 161/4443–5; 164A/551–95; 173/5429–57; 180/1874–7; 182/2660–3; 183/5180–92; 200/1608–21.
22. The authorities eventually discredited these rumours: Bombay Council to Court of Directors, 31 July 1805, BA S&P 199/1235 (1209–64).
23. Capt. Henry Becher, Muscat 13 May 1803, BA S&P 147/5533. The Shaikh allowed the Captain, his officer Galbraith and 12 Topasses (Portuguese) to leave, but kept the lascars behind. 'A bag of dirty linen ... is all that I have saved': H. Becher, Muscat 17 May 1803, BA S&P 147/5529.
24. Capt. H. Becher, Bombay 20 Aug. 1803, BA S&P 151/7148. The Assistant was W. Bruce.
25. 45 bales were also recovered from Hormuz by Seton with the help of the ruler of Muscat: list of woollens, Bushire 5 Oct. 1805, BA S&P 173/5488–91. The Company reluctantly ceased to pursue the case in 1810: W. Bruce to Bombay, Shiraz 1 May 1810, with Council Minute of 10 June, BA P 358/3130–2.
26. And with Zubara, Charak, Asalu and Kangan: Memorandum by Capt. D. Seton, *c.* July 1804, BA S&P 158/2468.

27. Cf. Risso, *Oman*, pp. 77–80.
28. Hasan bin Muhammad bin Mansur.
29. At first reported by Seton as 13.
30. To the Nakhuda of one of the Janaba boats.
31. For these events see: BA S&P 173/5361–4, 5391–402, 5435–45, 5684–93, 6416–20; 181/2399–430; 186/6629–43; 208/4246–8. Abu Hakima (ed.), *Lamʿ al-Shihab*, pp. 79–83.
32. Seton reports that the Qawasim were related to perhaps the dominant section in the Suri fleet, namely the Qawasim of Sur; this tribe was locked in a quarrel with its neighbours, the Janaba, a tribe which enjoyed the backing of Muscat. The Janaba had confined the wives and children of the Suri Qawasim by March 1806, conceivably in retaliation, and still held them in April 1807, when a fruitless expedition was launched from Ras al-Khaima to release them. The Suri Qawasim still remained with their dows at Ras al-Khaima, unwilling to return to Sur, in late 1808. (According to a report from 1808 the branch of Qawasim under Muscat rule lived at Sur and Khaur al-Jarama.) D. Seton to Bombay, Baroda 2 July 1807; EIC Broker at Muscat Vishandass to Bombay, Muscat 8 May 1807; D. Seton to Government, Bombay 12 Dec. 1808: BA S&P 208/4937–50, 205/3835–7, 255/14269–71. Governor Duncan's Minute, Bombay 24 Nov. 1808, BA S&P 253/13607–9.
33. According to the Shaikh of Ras al-Khaima.
34. In the latter part of 1805, according to Seton, the Qawasim once more 'began their depredations, but in a petty way until they persuaded the Sur fleet ... to go to Ras al-Khaima' etc.: D. Seton to Bombay, Baroda 2 July 1807, BA S&P 208/4946–7.
35. BA S&P 105/189–98; 112/4227–37; 116/5899–902, 5966–72, 6001–9, 6312–15; 113/4538–43, 4771–2, 4804; 119/71–100; 120/685–92; 126/4595–614. Saldanha, *Persian Gulf Précis*, vol. 1, pp. 431–2; Lorimer, *Gazetteer*, vol. 1, p. 431.
36. Presumably the Indian vessel, not the battil which this word, or a myriad of variants upon it, is often used to describe. Hereafter, when an Indian vessel is clearly intended, or when it is unclear whether the Arab battil or Indian batel or batella is intended, I will write the word as 'botella'.
37. Rejib Crany of the *Akaub*, to Aka Abul Hussein at Bombay, Muscat early June? 1801, BA S&P 112/4227–8.
38. This occurred off Qais on 8 December; from there the crew crossed over to Charak, whence the Shaikh freely transported them on his own dow to Muscat, arriving on 23 December. D. Seton to Bombay, Muscat 29 Dec. 1800, BA S&P 105/189–94.
39. 'Nasser', or 'Nasser bin Sweedee': possibly, therefore, Nasr.
40. D. Seton to Bombay, Muscat 29 Dec. 1800, BA S&P 105/189–93.
41. Ibid.
42. Such as the Utub.
43. There were later estimated to be 150–200 men in the garrison at Bidaʿ.
44. The island fell under Muscat's aegis in or shortly after 1794: Risso, *Oman*, pp. 106, 117, 175.
45. In a letter to Samuel Manesty, Mulla Hasan, the Shaikh of Qishm, claimed that the Sudan had been given the option by the ruler of Muscat of quitting Hormuz or their prize. They chose the former, and passed through Qishm en route to Bidaʿ, bearing with them the *Akaub*, her cargo and two captive mariners: S. Manesty to Bombay, Basra 31 July 1801, BA S&P 113/4771–2. The British felt the ruler of Muscat to have been remiss.
46. This vessel was probably the 450-ton *Governor Duncan*, commander John Taylor (1800, 1802: Thomas Ley 1804), which belonged to Haji Khalil, and secured a pass through his Bombay agent Aqa Muhammad Hasan Bihbihani. List of Company passes granted at Bombay to Arab and Persian vessels in 1795–1804, IOR P/343/14.
47. BA P 420/483, 619–20; 421/1059–60; 432/2441–55; Sel. 72/93–116.
48. Or were not already on shore: W. Bruce to Bombay, Bushire 29 Jan., IOR R/15/1/16, pp. 31–3.
49. Ibid., citing intelligence culled from a boat arrived from Asalu.
50. And possibly some British dates: Hasan bin Rahma, chief of Ras al-Khaima to Bruce, Arabic text, Ras al-Khaima Nov. 1816, BA Sel. 72/110.

51. BA S&P 220/139–41, 150–2; 232/5886–8.
52. Dated 8 Dec. 1807, Muscat, the brig *Shannon*, BA S&P 220/139–40.
53. Hearing?
54. Cf. the Qasimi role in the *Ahmed Shah* incident.
55. D. Seton to Bombay, Khunadee 9 Dec. 1807, BA S&P 220/139.
56. She was purchased in Bombay in 1806 and belonged to the Persian Ambassador, Aqa Muhammad Nabi: Bombay to Fort William, 12 Jan. 1808, BA S&P 220/152. Also, S. Manesty to Bombay, Basra 9 Dec. 1807, with Board's comment, BA S&P 220/324–6.
57. BA P 419/295–305; 424/2075–77; 422/1572–5; cf. 432/2521–9. The *Sultana* had been captured by 4 October.
58. Bombay Council, Minutes 13 Feb. 1815, BA P 419/304.
59. Muhammad bin Rizq, assuming the forename to be correct, was presumably of the same family as the well known Ahmad bin Rizq: see Abu Hakima, *History of Eastern Arabia*, pp. 7–8; and e.g. BA S&P 148/6314.
60. Colquhoun to Bombay, Basra 29 Dec. 1814, BA P 419/295–9.
61. Ibid.
62. As Rahma himself claimed: W. Bruce to Bombay, Bushire 15 April 1815, BA P 421/1060.
63. Ibid.
64. Ibid.
65. Abdullah bin Su'ud to Bruce, received 7 June 1815, and to Rahma bin Jabir, BA P 422/1573–5.
66. Rahma bin Jabir to Bruce, 19 Shawwal 1229/3(prob. 4) Oct. 1814, IOR R/15/1/14 pp. 226–7.
67. It has been assumed in the present account that the vessel in which Lt Macdonald, 'late surveyor of Turkey and Persia', lost his possessions was the same as that described by Colquhoun, and not a separate incident: Macdonald to Fort William, Fort St George 4 May 1815, BA P 424/2076–7.
68. Bombay was, nevertheless, still somewhat worried at Bruce's policy towards Rahma bin Jabir and enjoined caution. W. Bruce to Bombay, Bushire 8 Feb. 1817, with Minutes 14 March 1817, BA Sel. 73/337–40.
69. See Chapter Six.
70. W. Bruce to Bombay, Bushire 23 Jan. 1815, BA P 420/582–7.
71. For this incident see: BA S 312/1058–62; P 420/582–9; 421/1059–60; 432/2452–3; Sel. 72/116, 177–194; 74/430.
72. He had 'friendly' messages for Sultan bin Saqr and Hasan bin Rahma, and specifically hoped to encourage or assist the latter to send an agent to Bombay, as well as pick up any EIC horses taken off Qais following the wreck of the *Ahmed Shah* in 1814. The Governor of Bushire, Shaikh Abd al-Rasul, also had a man on board whose mission was to come to terms with Ras al-Khaima: W. Bruce to Bombay, Bushire 23 Jan. 1815, BA P 420/582–90.
73. That the apparent absence of British officers or officials on the vessel had a bearing on her treatment is, of course, pure supposition.
74. W. Bruce to Bombay, HMS *Curlew*, off Qais, 14 Feb. 1820, BA P 480/1820–35.
75. At Mocha and Jeddah there were 10 frazils to the maund, each frazil of 22 and 30 lbs respectively. Milburn, *Oriental Commerce*, vol. 1, pp. 64, 70; Yule, *Hobson-Jobson*, pp. 358–9.
76. 'Ja'altahu nahb! Walladhi yanhab, ma ya'khudh al-qalil wa-yukhalli al-kathir ...': Sultan bin Saqr bin Rashid bin Matar al-Qasimi to Bruce, 2 Safar 1232/22 Dec. 1816, BA Sel. 74/430; 312/1058–62 (translation).
77. According to a later source: Lorimer, *Gazetteer*, vol. 2, p. 1301.
78. Under British colours.
79. BA S 313/1791–8; Sel. 73/244–5.
80. The Resident, Bruce, detained the Qasimi envoy's vessel until he sent to Ras al-Khaima to have the capture released.
81. W. Bruce to Bombay, Bushire 25 Sept. 1819, BA S 313/1791–6.
82. W. Bruce to Bombay, HMS *Curlew*, off Qais, 14 Feb. 1820, BA P 480/1820–35.
83. In a Bombay assay of August 1819, the German crown is given as about 4s. 4d. sterling, or 2.1784 Bombay rupees: Milburn, *Oriental Commerce*, vol. 1, pp. 138–40.

84. BA P 434/127–34; Sel. 72/72, 177–194. There was, it seems confusion on deck, and it was unclear whether it was the Sudan or the Linga people who took the money.

85. Muhammad bin Qadib to Bruce, 20 Muharram 1232 AH/10 Dec. 1816, BA Sel. 72/184A.

86. 'Wa-hum mahsubin 'ala ahad ghairina': Muhammad bin Qadib to Bruce, 20 Muharram 1232 AH, BA Sel 72/184A.

87. BA P 434/127–34; Sel. 72/177–94; S 312/1038–62; P 480/1820–35.

88. Sultan bin Saqr to Bruce, 2 Safar 1232, BA Sel. 74/430.

89. According to Bruce, 'after taking her over to Sharja, he [Sultan bin Saqr] disputed about the division of property with the people who he had employed, a party from the Sudan tribe living with him at Sharja. The dispute became warm, when he put the torch to the vessel and burnt her': W. Bruce to Bombay, HMS *Curlew*, off Qais, 14 Feb. 1820, BA P 480/1820–35. Cf. above re the circumstances of the burning of the *Ahmed Shah* in 1814.

90. 'Dhab min aidina', been expended: Sultan bin Saqr to Bruce, 2 Safar 1232 AH, BA Sel. 74/430.

91. He was the brother of the Company's Broker at Bushire. W. Bruce to Bombay, Bushire 6 Feb. 1819, BA Sel. 73/357–9; F.E. Loch to Bombay, HMS *Eden*, off Bahrain 17 Feb. 1819, BA Sel. 73/418–27. For this whole affair, see: BA P 465/2381–94, 2592–3, 2622–4; 466/3153–4. BA Sel. 73/357 ff.

92. HMS *Eden* and *Conway*; HCC *Benares*, *Mercury* and *Antelope*.

93. Shaikh Abdullah's secretary and Bahrain's chief merchant told Eatwell they consisted of two Coffree slaves, sold and taken to Basra, and one Arab woman, sent to Qatif. Loch to Bombay, with enclosures, 28 Feb. 1819, HMS *Eden* Bushire Roads, BA P 465/2381–94.

94. Agreement between Capt. Loch and Shaikh Abdullah, Bahrain 16 Feb. 1819, BA Sel. 73/425.

95. Ibid.

96. Abdullah bin Ahmad to Hasan bin Rahma, Bahrain 19 Feb. 1819, BA P 465/2381–2.

97. The Arabic original of this particular letter is not extant. Hasan bin Rahma to Abdullah bin Ahmad, enclosed in latter's letter to Loch, received at Bushire 29 March 1819, BA Sel. 73/500–2.

98. Hasan bin Rahma at first produced only seven women. Lt Milson discovered that there were others from a Mocha merchant in Ras al-Khaima, before successfully putting the matter before the ruler. Note also that the figure 18 was that originally given by the Banyan broker, less the two Europeans, of whom, we soon find, nothing further is said: Acting Lt Joseph Milson to Capt. D.D. Conyers, HCC *Mercury*, Ras al-Khaima 14 March 1819, BA Sel. 73/458–9.

99. Seized by Lt James Arthur of the HCC *Antelope* on 1 March 1819 near Abu Musa, when out of Linga en route to Sharja, carrying rice, wheat, 3 Linga and 8 Banyan merchant-passengers (who had freighted the cargo), with a Sharja crew of 11 men and a boy: Extract of a letter from Lt Arthur, 22 March 1819, BA Sel. 73/460–3.

100. Ibid.

101. They were released on 29 May 1819: BA Sel. 73/642–3.

102. It seems likely this attack occurred in November and not the December loosely suggested by Conyers and Arthur. D.D. Conyers to Loch, HCC *Mercury*, Muscat Cove 21 March 1819, and J. Arthur to Meriton, HCC *Antelope*, 22 March 1819, BA Sel. 73/455–7, 460–3.

103. The brief report which reached Bruce at Bushire in May actually says the attack took place 'about two months since'. (Hasan bin Rahma had not specifically been asked to deliver up any except female captives): W. Bruce to Bombay, Bushire 18 May 1819, BA Sel. 73/627–33.

104. Mariam spoke of two groups of women, one of 3 and one of 6. Hasan bin Rahma denied the existence of any other women 'like these' at Bahrain, and this was apparently accepted by Britain. Capt. Conyers to Loch, HCC *Mercury*, Muscat Cove 21 March 1819, BA Sel. 73/455–7; Hasan bin Rahma to Abdullah bin Ahmad, received Bushire 10 May 1819, BA Sel. 73/632A, 637–40.

105. Sunderjee Sewjee, petition to Bombay Governor, Bombay 12 July 1819, BA Sel. 73/661–2; also S. Sewjee to Bombay Governor, Bombay 29 December 1818, BA Sel. 71/182–3.

106. F.E. Loch to Bombay, HMS *Eden*, Bushire Roads 1 May 1819, BA P 466/3154; W. Bruce to Bombay, Bushire 27 Sept., 18 May, 18 June 1819, BA Sel. 73/117–18, 627–33, 684–6.

107. Enclosed in John Sinclair to Secretary of Military Board, the Arsenal, Fort St George, 23 June 1819, BA S 313/1743–51.

108. She is described by Chadayappah and Sinclair as a schooner, but by others as a brig.

109. The Porbandar-owned cargo was insured: C.W. Elwood, Porbandar Agent, to Bombay, with enclosed translate, 23 July 1818, BA P 453/4882–5. Vurjee's name elsewhere appears as Nanjee Veerjee.

110. It must really be a port on the 'Qasimi' coast. The word sounds vaguely like Umm al-Qaiwain or Ras al-Khaima. The copper sheets came from Sharja. And Loch cites evidence that points directly, though not conclusively, to Ras al-Khaima. Further reason to suppose that Ras al-Khaima was intended lies in the recorded interrogation of a captured Linga crew: citing news brought from Ras al-Khaima, these men independently attested the *Eden's* clash with four vessels on 10 May (see text). They describe the four vessels as 'two large boats from the Red Sea and two from Ras al-Khaima', and say the surviving pair returned to Ras al-Khaima. Interrogation, dated 22 May, of the crew of a Linga battil, which had been captured by HMS *Curlew* in Mughu harbour on 21 May 1819, BA Sel. 73/651–3.

111. Capt. F.E. Loch to Bombay, HMS *Eden*, off Diba 11 May 1819, BA P 466/3161–2; Loch, *Diaries*, MS pp. 255–9, TS pp. 230–4.

112. From Loch's account it is apparent that both he and they must in fact have been at sea when they sighted each other, and he first saw the Qasimi vessels 'inshore to the SSW, the Quoins [Salama wa-Banatuha] bearing WSW': Loch, *Diaries*, MS p. 255.

113. In his dispatch of 11 May, Loch says there were four, but in his *Diaries* he adds two more battils and 170 men, makes the first sighting at 4 p.m. on the 9th and speaks of only one Qasimi prisoner. Details in the letter concerning the Qasimi vessels were almost certainly derived from Chadayappah and Co. Information in the *Diaries* regarding the later fate of the Qasimi boats and crews (the return of some by sea and most by land to Ras al-Khaima) was very probably later gained in Muscat: the addition of this later intelligence may be one part of the reason for the discrepancies. Loch to Bombay, HMS *Eden*, off Diba 11 May 1819, BA P 466/3161–2; Loch, *Diaries*, MS pp. 255–9, TS pp. 230–4.

114. Loch, *Diaries*, MS p. 237; Loch to Bombay, HMS *Eden*, off Diba 11 May 1819; BA P 466/3161–2, Sel. 73/581–4.

115. Twelve men were reported killed in the *Su'ud*, five by a single ball travelling from stern to the bow, so tightly were they packed. Casualties on the other vessels may have been higher.

Notes to Chapter Six

1. For the *Bassein* and *Viper* incidents see: BA S&P 57/1539–46, (1618–44); 59/53–73, 75–98, 115–44, 164–71, 206–20; 63/1612–20.

2. For the *Trimmer* and *Shannon* incidents see: BA S&P 164A/430–43, 602–14; 165/912–35; 170/4067–75; 173/5391–402; 181/2399–430; 186/6629–43.

3. Francis Warden, 'Historical Sketch of the Joasmee Tribe of Arabs' (1819), in Thomas, *Arabian Gulf Intelligence*, p. 303.

4. The word trankey seems often to have been an alternative for battil, although like all these words it was sometimes used as a generic. Bombay Council (J. Duncan: O. Nicolls, L. Corkran and T. Lechmere) to Court of Directors, Bombay 26 Feb. 1805, BA S&P 165/912–35; W. Bruce to Basra, Bushire 20 Dec. 1804, BA S&P 164A/606–8.

5. Bombay Council ?6 Sept., cited in S. Manesty to Court of Directors, Basra 9 Nov. 1797, BA S&P 59/115–33.

6. S. Manesty to Shaikh Saqr, 1 July 1797, BA S&P 59/133–6. Despite Manesty's comment in this letter, the *Bassein*, Captain Torrie, seems to have been a private vessel which had

entered into an arrangement with the Governor of Bombay: Manesty to Bombay, Basra 8 July 1797, BA S&P 57/1539–46; Low, *Indian Navy*, vol. 1, p. 313.

7. Information given to Manesty by Saqr's 'confidential person', Shaikh Muhammad bin Ahmad: S. Manesty to Court of Directors, Basra 9 Nov. 1797, BA S&P 59/115–33.

8. If he is the same to have written to David Seton *c*. Jan. 1806: D. Seton to Bombay, in Minutes for 21 March 1806, BA S&P 181/2399–430. S. Manesty and N.H. Smith describe Salih as Saqr's nephew; Saqr calls him only 'my relation', Salih bin Muhammad.

9. 40 three-pounders.

10. N.H. Smith to Manesty, Bushire 17 October 1797, BA S&P 59/88–93.

11. Ibid.

12. N.H. Smith to Manesty, Bushire 4 Nov. 1797, BA S&P 59/168–71.

13. ? The text reads 'Maleeh', or possibly even 'Malich': according to Manesty's investigations, Salih had during the past year been associating with the port of Asalu, after quitting Ras al-Khaima 'in disgust'. George Brucks' report of 1835 refers to a village next to Asalu which was inhabited by the 'Beni Malah tribe'; and some others nearby inhabited by the 'Beni Mullak'. Brucks, 'Memoir Descriptive of the Navigation of the Gulf of Persia', in Thomas, *Arabian Gulf Intelligence*, p. 593. S. Manesty to Court of Directors, Basra 9 Nov. 1797, BA S&P 59/115–33.

14. Shaikh Saqr bin Rashid bin Matar to Manesty, received late Nov. 1797, BA S&P 59/164–6.

15. 'Our enemies are the people of Oman': Ibid.

16. Text reads 'Shar': Suhar is the most obvious reading, but this is slightly odd, and possibly some other port or town is intended.

17. Ibid.

18. Against 'different Arab tribes': S. Manesty to Court of Directors, Basra 9 Nov. 1797, BA S&P 59/115–33.

19. Cape Certes, or Ras al-Husaini, where Mughu and Charak bays meet.

20. Reads 'pound'; possibly, therefore, '... -pound double-head'.

21. 'Linja or Lung': cf. in the transcription of Captain Babcock's letter, 'Linge Lung'.

22. Capt. J. Cumming to Manesty, Basra 29 Dec. 1804, BA S&P 164A/439–43.

23. D. Seton to Bombay, Muscat 4 March 1806, with enclosures, BA S&P 181/2399–430.

24. News had reached Muscat by 28 October. The assassin was also described as an Afghan or a Persian. Sayyid Saif to Bombay Governor, Muscat 2[8] Oct. 1803, BA S&P 150/6935–8; Uthman bin Abdullah bin Bishr, *Unwan al-Majd fi Ta'rikh Najd*, 2 vols. (Darat al-Malik Abd al-Aziz, Riyadh, 1982/1402), vol. 1, pp. 264–5; Lorimer, *Gazetteer*, vol. 1, p. 1054; Burckhardt, *Notes*, vol. 2, p. 201; Baghdad Resident Harford Jones to Court of Directors, Baghdad 30 Dec. 1803, BA S&P 156/1490–8.

25. Elegy for Sayyid Sultan by an Omani '*alim*, cited in Bhacker, 'Roots of Domination', p. 68.

26. First reports reaching Bushire termed the assailants the 'Aza' Qawasim, that is presumably the Dubai branch of the Banu Yas under Shaikh Hazza', or his dependants; Ibn Bishr much later specifies them as Ras al-Khaima Qawasim who had been unaware of their victim's identity until afterwards; Ibn Ruzaiq, presumably reflecting the later tradition in Muscat, lays the blame on a party of Ras al-Khaima Shwaihiyin. (The Shwaihiyin are described by Ibn Ruzaiq as Huwala; Lorimer records their presence in both Dubai and Sharja.) Badger's 'Shihuh' is a misunderstanding. Muscat apparently blamed the Qawasim at the time, and a member of a Qasimi detachment sent to Muscat to assist Badr early in 1805 was reputed to have arrived wearing the sword and dagger borne by Sayyid Sultan when he met his end. Ibn Ruzaiq's very late suggestion that Sayyid Sultan now enjoyed truly warm relations with Linga, where he claims he was buried, is unusual. Ibn Ruzaiq's location for the attack, off Linga, accords with that in Maurizi: a contemporary report from Muscat possibly suggests a spot near Larak. Bruce, at Bushire, has the ruler disembarking on Qishm. When he unexpectedly came up with the 3–5 vessels that attacked him, Sayyid Sultan had probably been crossing over to Hormuz or Qishm in a small, relatively defenceless boat. W. Bruce to Bombay, Bushire 12 Jan. 1805, to Basra 27 Nov. and 10 Dec. 1804, to Fort William 17 Dec. 1804, BA S&P 164A/596–606; Ibn Bishr, *Unwan al-Majd*, vol. 1, p. 281; Humaid bin Muhammad bin Ruzaiq, *al-Fath al-Mubin fi Sirat al-Bu Sa'idiyin* (Wizarat al-Turath,

Oman, 1983/1403), p. 439, *Imams and Seyyids*, pp. 238–40; Lorimer, *Gazetteer*, vol. 2, p. 1436; D. Seton to Bombay, Muscat 10 May 1805, BA S&P 168/2908–12; Maurizi, *Seyd Said*, pp. 2–3; Ibrahim Mulla Ali of Muscat to Bombay Governor, early–mid Dec.?, received 24 Dec. 1804, BA S&P 162/5090–2.

27. Viz. a boat first brought the news to Bushire from the south on 25 November: W. Bruce to Manesty, 27 Nov. 1804, BA S&P 164A/599–601.

28. The owner of the baghla was Abdullah bin Salam-[?]. W. Bruce to Manesty, Bushire 10 Dec. 1804, BA S&P 164A/602–4; Ibn Qurush in Seton to Bombay, Muscat 4 March 1806, BA S&P 181/2418 (2399–430).

29. S. Manesty to Bombay, Basra 31 March 1808, BA S&P 232/5886–8.

30. F. Warden, Chief Sec. to Government, Bombay, to Capt. J. Wainwright and Lt Col. Smith, Bombay Castle 7 Sept. 1809, BA P 339/3428–44.

31. There is no apparent consistency in the transliteration or spelling of this ship's name in the British sources; hence the adoption here of the regular form '*Darya Daulat*'.

32. 'Lotta/Lotica [Luti]' or Khoja: (originally) Ismailis, principally from Sind, living in Oman.

33. W. Watts, Assistant-in-Charge of Muscat Residency, to Bombay, enclosing protest of Capt. I/J.D. Fleming dated 3 Aug., Barka 4–6 Aug. 1808, BA S&P 243/9867–72.

34. Bombay Council, J. Duncan etc., Minutes 20 Jan. 1809, BA P 320/781 (775–847). (Also note W. Bruce to Bombay, Bushire 22 Oct. 1808, BA S&P 254/13884.)

35. When John Malcolm assumed responsibility for the affairs of the region.

36. The Boatswain had been shot dead in the attack: Morier, *A Journey through Persia . . . in 1808 and 1809*, p. 43.

37. Sir H. Jones to Bruce, Bushire 29? Oct. 1808, IOR R/15/10/374.

38. A cable measures one-tenth of a nautical mile, or *c*. 608 ft.

39. Lt W.T. Graham to W.T. Money, Superintendent of Marine, *La Néréide* Bombay 28 October 1808, BA S&P 251/12991–5.

40. Capt. R. Corbett to Sir Edward Pellew, 29 Oct. 1808, in Pellew to W.W. Pole, Secretary to Admiralty, *Culloden*, at sea, 25 June 1809: cited in Kelly, *Britain*, p. 113, and Moyse-Bartlett, *The Pirates*, pp. 39–40.

41. And another 2 'bruised'. The commander's casualty list of 28 October gives 30 dead, 13 of them lascars, that of 26 October 25 dead, 8 of them lascars: Lt Graham to W. Money, Superintendent of Marine, Bombay 26 and 28 Oct. 1808, BA S&P 251/12991–6, 13000–4.

42. Ibid.

43. Intelligence in J. Duncan's Minute, Bombay Council 26 Nov. 1808, BA S&P 253/13607–10.

44. H. Jones to Bruce, Bushire 29? Oct. 1808 and Bruce to Commander Maugham of the *Benares*, IOR R/15/10.

45. Ibid.; Bombay Council, Minute of 11 Nov. 1808, BA S&P 251/13005–6; Bombay Council to Court of Directors, Bombay Castle 15 April 1809, BA P 327/3636–41; Muscat Broker, Vishandass, to Bombay, Muscat 26 Oct. 1808, BA S&P 252/13089–92.

46. Morier's statement to this effect may conceivably imply that one of the boats had come from Ras al-Khaima: Morier, *A Journey through Persia . . . in 1808 and 1809*, p. 44.

47. The contemporary designation of Rams as source of this attack was also later confirmed by Seton, when he assigned responsibility for this spate of attacks on British vessels to Hasan bin Ali, who was himself the ruler of Rams and newly constituted Wahhabi protégé. According to Morier, report reaching Bushire in November named the commander of one or all the vessels which attacked the *Sylph* as 'one of their first chiefs, Sal ben Sal', who is then supposed to have died in the action with the *Néréide* along with a few hundred of his men. This probably refers to the maverick Shaikh Salih bin Muhammad (bin Salih) al-Qasimi, of *Viper* fame. Salih bin Muhammad may conceivably have returned to Ras al-Khaima upon the demise of Shaikh Saqr. He was reported to have led an abortive attack by three dows on the HCC *Mornington* between Chahbahar and Muscat on 1 May 1805, and to have boarded Muscat vessels at the same period. In 1805–6, he was apparently the second man at Ras al-Khaima, after Sultan bin Saqr, both politically and as military and naval commander: the next most powerful and active commander on this coast was then, as at other times during these decades, the Nu'aimi ruler of Ajman. In early 1808, Salih bin Muhammad led the

first recorded Qasimi predatory raid to Cutch. All assuming this to have been the same man, then news of Salih's death in late 1808 was premature, for he reappears in 1810 in the dubious company of Rahma bin Jabir, and soon after again perhaps at Ras al-Khaima; the implication is thus that Salih, ever the adventurer, had chosen to ally himself with the Wahhabi political faction from at least late 1808, when it first became strong and distinct. Morier, *A Journey through Persia ... in 1808 and 1809*, pp. 43–6. D. Seton, Resident, to Bombay, Muscat 10 May 1805, BA S&P 168/2908–12; Seton to Bombay, HMS *Albion* 30 March 1808, BA S&P 229/4181–4; Lt W. Maxfield to Walker, HCC *Sylph*, Mandvi Roads 14 April 1808, BA S&P 232/5613–15; Seton, Muscat, report of 19 Feb. 1809, BA P 325/2638–50; Seton to Bombay, Muscat 4 March 1806, BA S&P 181/2399–430.

48. The Persian Secretary on board the *Sylph*, who later boasted to Morier that Graham had spurned his advice that he should prevent the dows approaching the schooner purportedly declaring 'they would not touch him', was an unreliable source and witness. Morier, *A Journey through Persia ... in 1808 and 1809*, p. 45.

49. Charles Court, Assistant to Superintendent of Marine, to Lt Graham, Bombay 12 Sept. 1808, BA S&P 251/12997–8.

50. Muscat Broker to Bombay, Muscat 26 Oct. 1808, BA S&P 252/13089–92.

51. He further observed that the local inhabitants perceived the presence of the *Sylph* as 'a sort of protection' against the Qasimi pirates. The charts he was involved in producing were intended to help combat piracy issuing from that coast. He had originally set out from Bombay in company with the pattamar *Shewban*, but they had soon become separated: Lt William Maxfield to Major Alexander Walker, Baroda Resident, HCC *Sylph*, Mandvi Roads 14 April 1808, BA S&P 232/5613–15.

52. His *Travels in Assyria* covers the months Sept.–Dec. 1816.

53. According to Kelly, *Britain*, p. 113: Kelly is quite specific about these orders. It may be that he came across an explicit reference to them in the British archives, in which case that must be right. Unfortunately he does not record any source for his statement.

54. As per Buckingham, *Travels in Assyria*, p. 414.

55. Buckingham, *Travels in Assyria*, p. 415.

56. Lt Richard Bennett, Cmdr of *Nautilus*, Bombay Harbour 1 Dec. 1808, BA S&P 255/14147–50.

57. Buckingham, *Travels in Assyria*, pp. 414–15; cf. Minutes 10 May 1808, enclosing report by Lt Gowan of the *Fury*, Bombay Harbour 10 May 1808, BA S&P 232/5668–72.

58. Bombay Council to Court of Directors, Bombay Castle 26 Feb. 1805; J. Duncan to Seton, and to Lt Ross of the HCC *Queen*, Bombay 3 March 1805: BA S&P 165/912–35, 968–76, 978–80.

59. This is confirmed by Brucks, *Account of the Survey*, pp. 42–4, 57, 60–2, 65: criticism of government orders and its management and equipment of the Bombay Marine.

60. The ban would prove ineffectual. The immediate reaction in November 1808 had been to order the HCC *Teignmouth* to visit the Gulf and destroy all the Qasimi vessels she met, in order to oblige the Qawasim to relent and seek a restoration of peaceful relations, but there is no evidence that these orders bore any tangible results. Board's Resolution of 21 April 1809, Bombay Castle, BA P 327/3756–7; Bombay Council to Court of Directors, 15 April 1809, BA P 327/3636–41 and 20 Jan. 1809, BA P 320/779–82; Bombay Council, Minutes of 11 Nov. 1808, with Marine Supt's correspondence, BA S&P 251/13000–6; Bombay Council to Fort St George, 18 May 1809, BA P 330/4689–96; also 326/3251–2, 329/4392–4.

61. J. Duncan's Minute, Bombay Council 26 Nov. 1808, BA S&P 253/13607–10.

62. This was quite possibly the incident intended in the *Lam' al-Shihab*, where the violent seizure by the Qawasim of a British vessel sailing from Bombay, curiously said to have been known as 'the Jew's boat' (markab al-yahudi), is given as the principal reason for the first British expedition against Ras al-Khaima 'five months later'. The capture of the *Minerva* is also described by Maurizi, who claims to have interviewed the pilot. Abu Hakima (ed.), *Lam' al-Shihab*, p. 139: Maurizi, *Seyd Said*, pp. 51–2.

63. Sultan bin Saqr al-Qasimi to the joint commanders of the British expedition, Shawwal 1224 AH/9 Nov.–7 Dec. 1809 (enclosed in Wainwright and Smith to Bombay, HMS *La Chiffone*, Muscat Roads 19 Dec. 1809), BA P 350/48–50.

64. Yule, *Hobson-Jobson*, pp. 105–6, describes the Boras as a class of Shi'a Muslims, characteristically devoted to trading and money-lending, most numerous in the Gujarat area and with their centre at Surat.

65. Translate of a letter from Borah Alimanjee at Muscat to his friends at Surat, BA P 339/8444–5 (in Bombay Minutes for 7 Sept. 1809).

66. W. Bruce to Bombay, with enclosures, Bushire 5 Dec. 1809, BA P 351/817–20; ditto, HMS *Curlew*, off Qais 14 Feb. 1820, BA P 480/1820–35. The cost of Mrs Taylor's release had to be met by her family: Bombay Council Minute of 27 Jan. 1810, BA P 351/828.

67. According to the will he deposited with his executor on 20 April 1809, apart from some minor bequests to servants, John Hopwood of Bombay bequeathed all he owned, including a fourth share in the *Minerva* and two houses at Mazagoor (or Mazagong), to his female Muslim housekeeper Khoulsom absolutely. Hopwood's widow, Mary Elizabeth, subsequently lodged a complaint against the executor. Maria Graham described Mazagong, on Bombay island, as 'a dirty Portuguese village, putting in its claim to Christianity, chiefly from the immense number of pigs kept there.' Wills and Administrations, Bombay, 8 Jan. 1810, IOR L/AG/34/29/343; Bombay Inventories, Register for Jan.–March 1813, IOR L/AG/34/27/389. Maria Graham, *Journal of a Residence in India* (Constable, Edinburgh and Longman, London, 1812), p. 6.

68. *Bombay Gazette*, Wednesday 4 Oct. 1809, BA, cited in al-Qasimi, *The Myth*, pp. 95–7.

69. *Asiatic Annual Register*, 1809, p. 146, cited in al-Qasimi, *The Myth*, p. 97.

70. The Persian Governor's sources of information were 'written accounts from the southern ports': W. Bruce to Fort William, Bushire 30 June 1809, BA P 336/7343–4. Bruce's suspicions had, in fact, first been alerted some weeks before: W. Bruce to Fort William, Bushire 12 June 1809, BA P 335/6867–8.

71. S. Manesty to Bombay, Basra 8 July 1809, BA P 338/8088–93: cf. Remarks by D. Seton, in Bombay Council Minutes 10 Dec. 1808, BA S&P 255/14150–60.

72. During 1810–12, three British vessels reported being threatened in the Gulf, the *Macaulay* c. Jan. 1811, the *Moholar* Jan. 1812 and the *Duncan* Nov. 1812: the most significant reported activity was successful Qasimi attacks on Basra and Kangan shipping in the latter part of 1812.

73. As, Adam, Sec. to Government, to Bombay, Fort William, 1 April 1814, BA P 410/2140–3; also Governor-General Moira to Bombay, Futtyghur 20 April 1815, BA Sel. 74/372–8A.

74. Paragraph seven, Bombay Council to Major-General Sir W. Grant Keir, Bombay 27 Oct. 1819, BA Sel. 76/128–53.

75. The 11 reportedly comprised 7 dows and 4 battils. The Sind Agent, referring both to this and the January 1814 cruise, describes the perpetrators collectively, and possibly somewhat loosely, as Qawasim and Utub; by which last he presumably intends the Jalahima. Porbandar Agent to Bombay, transmitting letter from Sewjee dated 20 Nov. 1813, BA P 403/3693 ff; Muhammad Yusuf Munshi, Native Agent in Sind, to Bombay, Hyderabad 27 Aug. 1814, BA P 415/4149–63.

76. Ibid.; Company's Broker at Muscat, Cassee Goolab, to Bombay, Muscat 30 Jan., (2) and 27 Feb. 1814, BA P 408/1257–68; Capt. C.W. Elwood, Porbandar Agent, to Bombay, Porbandar 22 Jan. 1814 and F. Warden, Chief Sec. to Government, citing Capt. Davidson of the *Ternate*, to Capt. Eatwell of the HCC *Benares*, Bombay 27 Feb. 1814, IOR R/15/1/15 pp. 93–7; W. Bruce to Bombay, Bushire 7 May 1814, BA P 412/2695–7; I.(/J.) Orton, in charge Residency, to Bombay, Bushire 17 March 1814, BA P 410/1860–1; also 410/2140–5, 411/2562–4.

77. Or possibly March: Porbandar Agent C.W. Elwood to Bombay, 22 Jan. 1814, BA P 415/3788–91. The Muscat Broker relays a rumour that the Qawasim returned to Ras al-Khaima on 10 February: Muscat 27 Feb. 1814, BA P 408/1261–8.

78. Six vessels were identified by sources at Karachi and ten were sighted by Captain Davidson on his return from there: these two groups may or may not have been one and the same.

79. The precise circumstances of these captures, allegedly involving a raid on Karachi harbour in November and upon another Sindi port in January, only appear in the Sind Agent's report.

80. The dinghy was a vessel from north-west India. Numbers of dinghies were owned at Muscat,

possibly in the main by Indian shipowners. This term, like others, may not always be used precisely. Reference is made to large and small dinghies. The 'denghi' in which Maurizi departed from Muscat, bound for Cutch, in 1810 was 'in shape, like the Arabian baghla, but the stern and bows are surrounded with leather, patched like the shoe of an Indian peasant.' Maurizi, *Seyd Said*, p. 168. In modern times the dinghy has been associated with Baluchi merchants: see Hawkins, *The Dhow*, p. 105, the dhangi, a double-ender, unlike Maurizi's vessel.

81. This vessel had been freighted by the Muscat Broker on her earlier, outward voyage from Muscat to Karachi.

82. W. Bruce to Amir Su'ud, Chief of the Wahhabis, and to Shaikh Hasan bin Rahma bin Matar, Shaikh of the Qawasim, Bushire 1 May 1814, and to Rahma bin Jabir, BA P 412/2698–702. (For the reply of Abdullah bin Su'ud, received at Bushire 2 Oct. 1814, see BA P 419/125–6.)

83. Dewilla presumably stands for Sind or a port on the Indus delta. It may well be a variant of the historic Debul, which lay just south of Karachi. Yule, *Hobson-Jobson*, pp. 320–1; French Agent, Shiraz 4 March 1808, BA S&P 229/4153.

84. Translation of Hasan bin Rahma to Bruce, Dir'iya, received at Bushire 8 Sept. 1814, enclosed in W. Bruce to Bombay, 9 Sept., IOR R/15/1/14 pp. 188–91.

85. Translation of Hasan bin Rahma to Bruce, 16 Aug. 1814, received at Bushire 2 Oct., enclosed in W. Bruce to Bombay 11 Oct., BA P 419/122–30.

86. E.g. in Babington, Sec. to Government, to Capt. Prior of HMS *Acorn*, Bombay 22 October 1814, cited in al-Qasimi, *The Myth*, pp. 186–9.

87. His sources appear to have included the original information from the Porbandar Agent and the Muscat Broker cited above: W. Bruce to Bombay, Bushire 7 May 1814, BA P 412/2695–8.

88. As, W. Bruce to Bombay, Bushire 9 Sept. 1814, IOR R/15/1/14 pp. 188–9.

89. Ibid., and Babington to Prior, 22 Oct. 1814, cited in al-Qasimi, *The Myth*, pp. 186–9.

90. Hasan bin Rahma to Bruce, Dir'iya, received at Bushire 8 Sept. 1814, IOR R/15/1/14 pp. 189–91.

91. W. Bruce to Bombay, Bushire 7 Aug. 1814, BA P 415/3821–3.

92. Translation of Hasan bin Rahma to Bruce, 16 Aug. 1814, BA P 419/122–30.

93. Hasan bin Rahma to Bruce, Dir'iya, received at Bushire 8 Sept. 1814, IOR R/15/1/14 pp. 189–91.

94. Hasan bin Rahma's remarks would also appear to confirm the unlikelihood of there having been joint action.

95. Equating the moorah, not with Milburn's Bombay moorah of 864 lb., but with the Gulf qusara of 180 lb. Milburn, *Oriental Commerce*, vol. 1, p. 143; Thomas, *Arabian Gulf Intelligence*, pp. 100–1; Lorimer, *Gazetteer*, vol. 1, pp. 2328–9.

96. Muscat Broker to Bombay, Muscat 30 Jan. 1814, BA P 408/1257–60.

97. When, in October 1816, Rahma bin Jabir arrived at Bushire with 'all his boats and tribe', he apparently brought with him 'two very large baghlas, a large battil and several small baqqaras': W. Bruce to Bombay, Bushire 26 Oct. 1816, BA P 432/2521–3.

98. Babington to Prior, Bombay 22 Oct. 1814, cited in al-Qasimi, *The Myth*, pp. 186–9.

99. Article eight states that negotiations for a full treaty were intended soon to follow at Bombay. For the English and Arabic text of the agreement signed between Bruce and Hasan bin Rahma's representative Hasan bin Muhammad bin Ghaith, see IOR R/15/1/14 pp. 213–16.

100. Babington, Sec. to Government, to Capt. Prior, Bombay 22 Oct. 1814, cited in al-Qasimi, *The Myth*, pp. 186–9.

101. The bulk of the material regarding the following events may be found at: BA Sel. 72/1–63, 83–132.

102. Nepean had assumed the position in mid-1812, following a year in which authority had been exercised by George Brown, Acting Governor and successor to the long-serving Jonathan Duncan.

103. Translation of letter from Surat merchants to Nepean, Surat 26 July 1816, BA Sel. 72/4–10.

104. Kincob was a gold brocade, chintz a printed or spotted cotton cloth, palempore a kind of chintz bed-cover and dooputty a piece of stuff of 'two breadths', a sheet. First declaration of

Abd al-Razzaq bin Abd al-Hayy, Second Nakhuda of the *Ahmadi*, Bombay 24 August 1816, BA Sel. 72/11–18; q.v. Yule, *Hobson-Jobson*. Patan: text reads 'Putun' (Sel. 72/36).

105. A Bombay Assay Report of 4 August 1821 gives the Bombay rupee as 164.68 grains pure silver, plus 14.32 grains alloy, value 23.6546352 d. The Bombay rupee had been brought in line with that of Surat in 1800, before which it had weighed 178.314 grains, of which 1.24% alloy: Milburn, *Oriental Commerce*, vol. 1, pp. 137–41. There is no reason to assume that the figure of 10–12 lacs was not substantially correct, and it was readily accepted as such at the time. The Nakhuda of the *Ahmadi* even gives the value of his own ship's cargo, by itself, as *c.* 10 lacs rupees: first declaration of Abd al-Razzaq bin Abd al-Hayy, Second Nakhuda of the *Ahmadi*, Bombay 24 August 1816, BA Sel. 72/11–18.

106. A Tindal would similarly have received 20, and a Serang 30, rupees *per mensem*: Milburn's rates may refer to *c.* 1820/1. In 1812, the monthly salary of the Assistant Resident at Bushire was settled at 500 rupees. Milburn, *Oriental Commerce*, vol. 1, pp. 133–4; Saldanha, *Persian Gulf Précis*, vol. 2, pp. 82–9.

107. Information on oath of Shaikh Tahir, Tindal, Bombay 28 Aug. 1816, BA Sel. 72/36–43.

108. Ibid.

109. Ibid.

110. The Tindal, from the masthead, observed 40–50 on deck, but did not know how many had entered the cabin. The Second Nakhuda, who rushed below, asserts that they were boarded by a total of 100–200: Information on oath of Shaikh Tahir, Tindal, Bombay 28 Aug. 1816, BA Sel. 72/36–43; two declarations on oath of Second Nakhuda, Abd al-Razzaq bin Abd al-Hayy, Bombay 24 & 26 Aug. 1816, BA Sel. 72/11–27.

111. This included the Nakhuda and Native Officer: two declarations on oath of Second Nakhuda, Abd al-Razzaq bin Abd al-Hayy, Bombay 24 & 26 Aug. 1816, BA Sel. 72/11–27.

112. Information on oath of Shaikh Tahir, Tindal, Bombay 28 Aug. 1816, BA Sel. 72/36–43.

113. Information on oath of Shaikh Zia Allah of Surat, Native Steward, Bombay 27 Aug. 1816, BA Sel. 72/29–34.

114. Translation of letter from Surat merchants to Nepean, Surat 26 July 1816, BA Sel. 72/4–10.

115. The three interviewees from the *Ahmadi* each give lists: cf. list of surviving crew at Bombay. BA Sel. 72/14–15, 20, 30–1, 43.

116. Information on oath of Shaikh Tahir, Tindal, Bombay 28 Aug. 1816, BA Sel. 72/36–43.

117. Translation of letter from Surat merchants to Nepean, Surat 26 July 1816, BA Sel. 72/4–10.

118. This is the purport of the first seven paragraphs of the letter in question; but the remaining paragraphs, written two weeks later, after the arrival of the *Ahmadi* had brought fuller news to Bombay, are very far from expressing these reservations: Bombay Council to Capt. Bridges of HMS *Challenger*, Bombay [23 Aug.&] 8 Sept. 1816, BA Sel. 72/46–54.

119. Two declarations on oath of Second Nakhuda, Abd al-Razzaq bin Abd al-Hayy; one of Shaikh Zia Allah of Surat, Native Steward; one of Shaikh Tahir, Tindal: Bombay 24 & 26, 27, 28 Aug. 1816, BA Sel. 72/11–43.

120. The Second Nakhuda.

121. Rahma bin Jabir had been in the vicinity at the time of the attacks and the information he later passed on to Bruce at Bushire appears to have been quite specific: W. Bruce to Hasan bin Rahma, at sea, Ras al-Khaima 27 Nov. 1816, BA Sel. 72/99–109.

122. Two declarations on oath of Second Nakhuda, Abd al-Razzaq bin Abd al-Hayy, Bombay 24 & 26 Aug. 1816, BA Sel. 72/11–27.

123. A Company port.

124. Buabeed, Boobeed, Bhao Bhed, Baboobeed: variant such as Ba Ubaid possible.

125. Naqib of Mukalla to Governor of Bombay, Mukalla, in Minutes for 26 April 1815, BA P 421/920–1.

126. Milburn, *Oriental Commerce*, vol. 1, pp. 63 cf. 138–41. The confusion over the name of the ship and the owner could conceivably, of course, be a fault of the translation.

127. Muscat Broker to Bombay, Muscat 31 March (should probably read 10 April) 1815, BA P 421/1036–8. Although the text states that the second dow belonged to an inhabitant of 'Soohar', it is clear from the rest of the letter that this is actually a transcription of the word 'Sur', not 'Suhar'.

128. T. Forbes to Bombay, Mocha 25 March 1815, BA P 422/1337–8.
129. Naqib of Mukalla to Governor of Bombay, Mukalla 5 May 1816, BA P 430/1310–13.
130. He arrived from Qatif, en famille, on 24 Oct. 1816: W. Bruce to Bombay, Bushire 26 Oct. 1816, BA P 432/2521–3; (Rahma bin Jabir to Mr Goodwin, Bushire 9 Nov. 1816, BA Sel. 72/144).
131. Bin Muhammad Abu Mismar.
132. Two declarations on oath of Second Nakhuda, Abd al-Razzaq bin Abd al-Hayy, Bombay 24 & 26 Aug. 1816, BA Sel. 72/13–14 (11–27).
133. Translation of letter from Surat merchants to Nepean, Surat 26 July 1816, BA Sel. 72/4–10.
134. Arabic version of Abdullah bin Su'ud to Bruce, received at Bushire, via Basra, 10 April 1817, BA Sel. 74/414; (BA S 312/1084–6).
135. As, W. Bruce to Bombay, Bushire 26 Oct. 1816, BA Sel. 72/196.
136. Buckingham, Travels in Assyria, p. 496.
137. Capt. P.H. Bridges, Commander and Senior Officer Gulf of Persia, to Bombay Council, undated; W. Bruce to Bombay, with enclosures, HCC Mercury, Hanjam Sound 28 Nov. and off Sharja 2 Dec. 1816, BA Sel. 72/75–130: (also at BA P 432/2431–56).
138. Acting Chief Sec. Adam to Bombay, Fort William 22 Feb. 1817, BA Sel. 74/380–6.
139. For these incidents, with that of the Darya Daulat, see especially: BA Sel. 72/65–6, 210–46, 247–333.
140. Later in the month the Porbandar Agent received intelligence that the Qawasim had 8 large and 8 small vessels on the Sind coast. Lt F. Faithful, of HCC Psyche, to Elwood, Porbandar Agent, Mandvi 15 Dec. 1816, BA Sel. 72/253–4; C.W. Elwood to Bombay, Porbandar 26 Dec. 1816, BA Sel. 72/159–62.
141. See BA Sel. 72/210–46, especially: Agent of Sunderjee Sewjee, Mandvi 15 Jan., and 'another letter' from Porbandar, 20 Jan., in Bombay Council's Minutes of 25 Jan. 1817; Sewjee Govindjee's petition to Governor of Bombay, Bombay 5 Feb. 1817; James Macmurdo, Bhuj Resident, to Bombay, Mandvi 30 Jan. 181[7]; C.W. Elwood to Bombay, Porbandar 1 Feb. 1817; also, Capt. William Hill to Bombay, HMS Towey, off the Indus 20 Feb. 1817, BA P 435/614–15.
142. Taken near Jakhau and Soothree: the preceding eight were also reportedly lost in the same area. Agent of Sunderjee Sewjee, Mandvi 15 Jan. 1817, BA Sel. 72/210–11; and J. Macmurdo to Bombay, Feb. 1817, BA Sel. 72/241 ff.
143. There were generally 20 maunds (man) to the candy. At Bombay the maund weighed 28 lb. and the candy 560 lb. avoirdupois; i.e. there were 3.57 Bombay candies to the ton. (The Surat maund, of c. 750 lb., was equivalent to 20 Cutch maunds, each of 37.5 lb.)
144. Petition of Sewjee Govindjee to Governor of Bombay, Bombay 5 Feb. 1817, BA Sel. 72/228–9; Deposition of same, Porbandar 1 Feb. 1817, BA Sel. 72/238–9.
145. Cambay was now a Company port. All the shipping of British ports such as Bombay and Surat was equally entitled to the British flag. The pass seems to have required renewal, possibly annually. See Bombay Council to Fort William, Bombay Castle 19 Oct. 1802, BA S&P 129/6073–5. Sewjee was an important merchant with Bombay, Mandvi and Porbandar connections, who acted as a Company agent.
146. It seems to be implied that the eight Mandvi vessels were lesser craft than Sewjee's. It is unwise to speculate in this way, but if we resort to the necessarily forced recourse of hypothesizing on the basis of the values that we do know, then we arrive at a tentative figure for these c. 14 losses that is still a good way beneath one-tenth of the value of the losses of the three Surat ships in 1816.
147. The name appears thus in the Bombay records, though Fowey might seem more likely.
148. Only Lieutenant Tanner of the HCC Psyche fired on three boats near Kuh Mubarak, vessels which, according to Captain Hill, were by no means proved to have been pirates: Capt. William Hill to Bombay Council, off Bushire 11 April 1817, BA Sel. 72/362–5.
149. These seizures are listed as: 1 baghla belonging to Muscat and 2 pattamars, both captured off Daman (this location is somewhat odd); 4 cotias ('colliahs'), off Cutch; 3 dinghies, off Karachi; 1 dinghy, off Makran; 2 dinghies and 4 cotias ('colliahs'), all off 'Drawzee Sind'; and, finally, 1 baghla, coming from Mangalore. W. Bruce, to Bombay, Bushire 25 March 1817, BA S 312/1083–4.

150. Lt F.H. Guy, commander of the HCC *Sylph*, to Elwood, at sea (23°40′N, [66]°50′E), 23 Feb. 1817, BA Sel. 72/283–4.

151. According to Bruce this news had been brought to Bushire by boats from Linga and Bahrain, and 'in some measure' corresponded with accounts from Kangan and the southern ports: W. Bruce, to Bombay, Bushire 13 Feb. 1817, BA Sel. 72/341–2.

152. C.W. Elwood to Bombay, Porbandar 7 Feb. 1817, BA Sel. 72/247–52.

153. Statement of Serang Shaikh Husain, made before Meriton, and reported in Henry Meriton, Supt of Marine, Bombay, to Governor, Bombay 6 March 1817, BA Sel. 72/318–22.

154. C.W. Elwood to Bombay, Porbandar 2 March 1817, BA Sel. 72/314–16.

155. Cf. 'The Serang adds, the pirates were very inquisitive, if there was a European of any description on his boat? He cannot say what their motive was for the enquiry': C.W. Elwood to Bombay, Porbandar 2 March 1817, BA Sel. 72/314–16.

156. Statement of Serang Shaikh Husain, made before Meriton, and reported in H. Meriton to Governor, Bombay 6 March 1817, BA Sel. 72/318–22.

157. In Surat, Cambay and Cutch the candy was the Surat candy of *c.* 750 lb. avoirdupois, made up of twenty maunds at 37.5 lb. each. It seems possible that this was the weight used at Porbandar and therefore intended in this instance. This possibility appears to be strengthened by the fact that the owner of the *Luckmee Pussaud* (above) described his dinghy as of '200' (?Surat) candies, when he made his deposition at Porbandar, but of 255 (presumably Bombay) candies, when he penned his petition at Bombay. (If the figure of 200 candies was actually intended to have been precisely identical with the burden in Bombay candies, then the candy in question (that used at Porbandar) would have to have equalled 711 lb.) See including Milburn, *Oriental Commerce*, vol. 1, pp. 113, 117, 142–4.

158. Deposition of Dewarjee, a Porbandar Pilot, given before Captain Elwood this 27th day of February 1817, Porbandar, BA Sel. 72/285–9.

159. Deposition of Dewarjee, a Porbandar Pilot, given before Captain Elwood this 27th day of February 1817, Porbandar, BA Sel. 72/285–9, P 435/612–13.

160. Ibid.

161. Capt. C.W. Elwood to Bombay, Porbandar 2 March 1817, BA Sel. 72/314–16.

162. C. 4–11 Feb.

163. Lt F.H. Guy, commander of the HCC *Sylph*, to Capt. Elwood, Porbandar Agent, at sea in latitude 23°40′N, longitude [reading 66]°50′E, 23 Feb. 1817, BA Sel. 72/283–4.

164. The captives included 2 sepoys and 6 lascars; the dead, 7 sepoys and 10 lascars; the saved, 5 sepoys, 1 lascar, the Pilot and the Serang. Deposition of Dewarjee, a Porbandar Pilot, given before Captain Elwood, Porbandar 27 Feb. 1817, BA Sel. 72/285–9.

165. Bombay Council, Minutes for 10 March 1817, BA Sel. 72/325–7.

166. H. Meriton to Governor, Bombay 1 Dec. 1817, enclosing Deposition of Ibrahim Bawa bin Abd al-Karim Dholkey, BA P 439/2363–5; Meriton to Governor, 23 Aug. 1819, BA Sel. 73/1–3.

167. H. Meriton to Governor, Bombay 1 Dec. 1817, enclosing Deposition of Ibrahim Bawa bin Abd al-Karim Dholkey, BA P 439/2363–5.

168. On 7 May 1817, off Cape Musandam, Lt Faithful of the *Vestal* observed a large baghla and two trankeys towing a grab ketch, supposedly their prize: he concluded from later enquiries at Muscat that this had been a Bhavnagar vessel recently captured by the Qawasim. The dates would on the face of it preclude this having been identical with Dholkey's grab ketch, unless she was by then in service, not a prize. H. Meriton to Governor, Bombay 23 May and 10 June 1817, with Lt F. Faithful to Meriton, Bombay 5 Nov. 1817, BA Sel. 72/384–400, 470–6, P 465/2536–9.

169. Ibid.

170. Translation of Goolab Anundass to Bombay, Muscat 16 and 21 May 1817, BA Sel. 72/380–1, 401–2.

171. One of these boats was owned by a Naljee Jyram. The other, a dinghy belonging to 'Khima' and likewise en route to Muscat, had called at Sur before she was captured by the Qawasim off Qurayat. There were also more sketchy reports of two further captures, again apparently in the region of Ras al-Hadd: a 'botella' from Zanzibar, and an unidentified pattamar. All the owners of the vessels taken were Muscat subjects.

172. H. Meriton to Governor, Bombay 1 Dec. 1817, enclosing Deposition of Ibrahim Bawa bin Abd al-Karim Dholkey, BA P 439/2363–5.

173. H. Meriton to Governor, Bombay 23 Aug. 1819, BA Sel. 73/1–3.

174. Detailed evidence for the January 1814 incident off Sind was not available then or now; some aspects of this case remain unresolved. The evidence for the *Sylph* affair is a good deal fuller and appears to support the idea that the Qawasim were responsible.

175. 21–2 incidents involving British vessels, and 23 seizures ascribed to the Qawasim.

176. Strictly speaking, there was nearly a third. As a result of the annoyance of the *Duncan* in November 1812, the following January the Governor issued Lt Davidson of the HCC *Vestal* with a letter addressed to the Qasimi ruler complaining of this incident and recent assaults on non-British Basra shipping, and desiring adherence to the 1806 agreement: this letter was never delivered.

177. Mulla Hasan of Qishm responded to Seton's allegations as follows: 'You are not ignorant that the Hazza', a tribe of the Banu Yas, in the time of the late Sayyid Sultan were enemies of Muscat and plundered their property where they met it; but the Qawasim have no concern with these people whatever, they [the latter] are independent and lawless, you need not doubt what I write. War exists between Sayyid Badr and the Qawasim, and when they act contrary to agreement it is time to complain.' Sayyid Sultan had been murdered in 1804. The difficulty with this letter may lie in the translation. Seton accepted that the people of Hazza' were responsible, not the Qawasim. D. Seton, Muscat Resident, to Bombay, with enclosures, Muscat 6, 16 and 29 Nov. 1805, BA S&P 173/5684–93, 174/6349–51 and 175/6416–20: last includes Mulla Hasan to Seton, received 15 Nov., cited here.

178. W. Bruce to Bombay, Bushire 26 October 1816, BA P 434/159–160; W. Bruce to Hasan bin Rahma, Ras al-Khaima 27 Nov. 1816, and Hasan bin Rahma to Bruce, received at Bushire 12 November 1816, BA P 432/2441–8, or BA Sel. 72/93, 106–9 for Arabic versions.

179. The British baghla which went in search of the *Fly*'s packet in October 1804, and the Bombay pattamar *Darya Daulat*, seized near Mukalla on 17 April 1819. These incidents are described in later chapters.

180. The only other incidents I have found where British property was reportedly seized from vessels, or British vessels were successfully attacked, by Gulf powers other than the Qawasim in 1797–1820 number between 3 and 5, none of which receive more than a passing reference. The Kuwait Utub plundered a Bushire battil belonging to Aqa Muhammad Nabi, en route to Bushire from Basra in Dec. 1801, carrying the packet and a British flag granted her by the Basra Resident—making her strictly perhaps a Persian boat. In March 1802, Captain Cook's vessel, carrying the packet, grounded on the bar at Basra and was plundered, presumably by local Arabs. In Nov.–Jan. 1804/5, the *Zephyr*, possibly a British ship, went aground at Minab and was plundered. In May 1814 Rahma bin Jabir plundered a baghla off Ras al-Hadd carrying the property of the EIC Broker Cassee Goolab, which one might have assumed was British. Finally, the Banu Bu Ali captured a Bombay botella, the *Futih Ilahee*, off Ashkhira, en route to Muscat from Mangalore in perhaps later Nov. 1819. In addition, a British dow was temporarily boarded during the Utbi descent on Bushire in September 1798; Rahma bin Jabir is said to have burnt the British wreck 'Anan' at Khargu before late 1809; and one of Rahma bin Jabir's relations fired upon a small boat from the HCC *Mornington*, when sounding off the bar at Basra in perhaps early 1814.

Notes to Chapter Seven

1. This refers to the Huwala Arabs. The identity of these four subdivisions of the Huwala is, however, apart from the Qawasim, not really clear. Captain Brucks, in his report of 1835, describes the inhabitants of Tahiri, Parak and Nakhl-i Taqi as belonging to the [Al] Nasur, and records other members of that tribe at Kangan. He notes that there were Banu Ahmad/a in 'Jella Abade' (near Chiru) and Kangan. Lorimer later noted that the Ubaidli, of Chiru and Hindurabi, claimed to be part of a larger tribe, the Ahmada: presumably Malcolm was not

referring in this passage to the Al Hamad, whom Lorimer also records as present in Shibkuh. Lorimer nevertheless makes an interesting, and in view of the legend possibly illuminating remark about Shibkuh, the 'peculiar and important' stretch of Persian coastline between Banak and Mughu: 'the bulk of the people are of mingled Persian and Arab blood and the tribes to which they belong are of no consequence. Local patriotism is however strong among those who are subjects of the same chief, a bond which is here regarded almost as one of clanship.' Brucks, 'Memoir Descriptive of the Navigation of the Gulf of Persia', part 2, 5 Oct. 1835, in, Thomas, *Arabian Gulf Intelligence*, pp. 590–2, 596; Lorimer, *Gazetteer*, vol. 2, pp. 1779–84. (In the geographical section of his work, the *Farsnama*, the nineteenth-century Persian writer Fasa'i (1821/2–1896/7) apparently defines Shibkuh as comprising the coastline between Dayyir and Charak, but in the historical part of this work he too extends it to include Mughu: Busse (trans.), *A History of Persia*, p. 154 text and note 218.) Malcolm writes 'Ben Jouassim, Ben Ahmed, Ben Nasir, Ben Saboohil,' 'Ben Houl', and 'Houl' *passim*.

2. Malcolm, *Sketches*, pp. 32–4.
3. Possibly in 1808, but Malcolm may also have been drawing here on his other missions to the Persia in 1800–1 and 1810.
4. Malcolm, *Sketches*, p. 11.
5. Reading 'al-sau'a' for 'al-hau'a' in the last phrase. New translation of the Arabic text, which occurs at BA Sel. 74/416–17 and is dated 4 Rab. 1 1232/22 Jan. 1817; contemporary translation and enclosing letter may also be found at, W. Bruce to Bombay, Bushire 26 Jan. 1817, BA S 312/1038–58, 1064–72.
6. See Cook, 'The Provenance of the *Lam' al-Shihab*'. Cook notes the author's use of a colloquialism indicative, perhaps, of a Mesopotamian rather than an Arabian background; he also observes that the author had avowedly visited Zubair, Kuwait and perhaps, implicitly, Basra; he was not living in Hasa, though he clearly had a knowledge of that area.
7. This form of the place-name Jazirat al-Hamra', without the definite article al-, appears to have been standard in the Gulf at this time. Of the three contemporary Arabic and Persian language sources which mention it, the most authoritative of which is an anonymous report from 1817 on the Qasimi ports and Bahrain, only the *Lam' al-Shihab* is equivocal in that it employs both forms side by side. Arabic report on the Qawasim and Bahrain, (Bushire?) 22 Jan. 1817, BA Sel. 74/416–17; Abu Hakima (ed.), *Lam' al-Shihab*, pp. 81, 141; Memorandum by Sayyid Taqi, with accompanying map of the coast between Ras al-Hadd and Abu Hail, (Bombay) mid-Dec. 1809, BA P 350/122 (116–38).
8. Translation of text in Abu Hakima (ed.), *Lam' al-Shihab*, pp. 79–83.
9. Reading 'Janaba' for Abu Hakima's 'J-y-n-h'; Ibid., pp. 139–41. The riyal was presumably the dollar, which was roughly equivalent to the crown: cf. R. Bayly Winder, *Saudi Arabia in the Nineteenth Century* (Macmillan, London, 1965), p. 89 note 4, with references.
10. Abu Hakima (ed.), *Lam' al-Shihab*, p. 139. (BA S&P 208/4947, 'yeoudee' for Janaba, probably not significant.)
11. The *Lam' al-Shihab* was completed in December 1817, but much of it had been written by August. Lieutenant Taylor, of the 3rd Bombay Native Regiment, was at the time Assistant at the Bushire Residency, where he had been employed since the first decade; in 1818, promoted to Captain, he was nominated to replace Gideon Colquhoun, who was then retiring from the post of Assistant Political Agent at Basra on account of ill health. Taylor may have moved to Basra around late summer; on 22 September he was said to have been 'recently' appointed, although the formal installation only took place in March 1819, when his family came to join him, and Colquhoun at last departed for Bombay. Taylor's report on the Gulf had been received in Bombay before 22 September: most of it has been published in Thomas, *Arabian Gulf Intelligence*, pp. 1–40; the complete original is preserved at, BA Sel. 74/21–108, as enclosures in, Evan Nepean, Bombay Governor, to Marquis of Hastings, Governor-General, Bombay 22 Sept. 1818, BA Sel. 74/3–20; the published extract reproduces BA Sel. 74/31–91. For Taylor's installation see Loch, *Diaries*, TS pp. 162, 182, 204.
12. The modern Arab editor of the work did not apparently suspect any British association with the compilation of the *Lam' al-Shihab*, and for him it was simply an exceptionally valuable, and unbiased, work of Arabic history: Abu Hakima, *History of Eastern Arabia*, pp. 8–11; Abu Hakima (ed.), *Lam' al-Shihab*, pp. 9–11.

13. The only slightly odd thing is the accuracy of the numbers of ships and men used by the British in their first expedition against Ras al-Khaima, but this may not be significant: Abu Hakima (ed.), *Lam' al-Shihab*, p. 139.

14. In an otherwise valuable article, Cook's discussion of the treatment of the British expedition in the *Lam' al-Shihab* is surely misleading; it is not as biased as he suggests. The ruler of Muscat's lack of enthusiasm at joining the expedition was surely not widely known, not to be expected and hardly apparent from his actions; the quotation from Kelly should not be given exaggerated prominence; the Qasimi resistance was stout, but brief, and Britain did achieve her immediate objectives; the incident of the arrival of the Wahhabi army and the hasty departure of the British, with this interpretation of it, is, I think, less certain than might be supposed—Buckingham (*Travels in Assyria*: followed by Low, Lorimer, Moyse-Bartlett) is the only original source I have managed to identify for this episode, and I have a suspicion, though I could be wrong, that he was erroneously describing here what in fact occurred under special circumstances at Shinas. Lastly, Cook states that 'the *Lam*' gives an account of the expedition which contains nothing likely to offend an English reader—though it easily could have done': this might be said with almost equal validity of Ibn Bishr's standard Saudi-Wahhabi account of the expedition—it is a judgement based on an *a priori* assumption of what the writer felt towards Britain. What is odd about the *Lam' al-Shihab*'s discussion of the first British expedition is, one suspects, rather more a question of perspective and author-identification, and is evident perhaps most specifically in the author's attribution of moral value, also alluded to by Cook. Ultimately, of course, questions such as these will probably tend to be a matter for feeling and personal judgement. Cook, 'The Provenance of the *Lam' al-Shihab*', p. 84; Ibn Bishr, *Unwan al-Majd*, vol. 1, pp. 305–6, 450–1, re both expeditions.

15. Abu Hakima (ed.), *Lam' al-Shihab*, p. 162.

16. The eighteenth century *Kashf al-Ghumma: al-Jami' li Akhbar al-Umma*, attributed to Sirhan bin Sa'id al-Izkawi, which contains a chronicle of Omani history till 1728; and Ibn Ruzaiq's *al-Fath al-Mubin*, completed in 1857.

17. Ibn Ruzaiq, *al-Fath al-Mubin*, pp. 492–4, 517–20 ; (in Badger's translation, Ibn Ruzaiq, *Imams and Seyyids*, pp. 293–5, 320–4).

18. Muscat Broker to Bombay, Muscat 25 Feb. 1815, BA P 420/619–20.

19. Sayyid Sa'id, ruler of Muscat, to Bombay Governor Jonathan Duncan, 19 Saf. 1225/26 March 1810, received 2 April, BA S 264/1287–90.

20. 'I trust in God that the wishes of my best friends [the British] may be gratified by their success and by the chastisement of the pirates, and that the excesses of the banditti may be repressed by the sword of vengeance, in such manner that future navigation may be relieved from fear and anxiety on their account, and resume their pursuits in security': Sayyid Sa'id, ruler of Muscat, to Bombay Governor Jonathan Duncan, Muscat 28 May 1811, BA P 375/3054–8; cf. same of 28 May, 375/3095–102.

21. In 1816 he wrote to Governor Nepean in a transparent attempt to justify himself and to turn Britain against Bahrain, over which he entertained designs, after he had learnt to his chagrin that the Bushire Resident William Bruce had just concluded an agreement with the Shaikh: 'God forbid [Bahrain] should become a second Ras al-Khaima, or even worse, for at Ras al-Khaima there are only ten ports, whereas here there are fifty'. He employed similar language with regard to the Qawasim in 1820, when he backed the idea of a British military station in the Gulf, and frantically sought to persuade Britain to assume permanent responsibility for the government of Ras al-Khaima in order to prevent their recovery. Sayyid Sa'id, ruler of Muscat, to Sir Evan Nepean, Governor of Bombay, 1 Ram. 1231/27 July 1816, BA S 312/1023–6; Sayyid Sa'id to Bombay and to Bushire Resident, 25 May 1820, BA P 490/5830–44.

22. The Naqib was reporting the activities of 15 of their vessels off south Arabia. He was courting good relations with Bombay, and commended the Company's resolution to punish the Qawasim: 'I hope you will proceed against them with the utmost severity, and that you will destroy their country ... May God take vengeance of them.' Translation of letter from Naqib of Mukalla to Bombay Governor, 5 May 1816, BA P 430/1310–13: cf. another such letter of a year earlier, at BA P 421/920–1. For some idea of the view at Mocha 1807–10, see e.g. BA P 358/2898–903, 2916–23, 2976–84.

23. Spelling of names modified: Fasa'i writes Javashem for Qawasim. Busse (trans.), *A History of Persia*, pp. 144–5.

24. Nevertheless there was probably some basis to the story of the legation itself: in spring 1817, the Resident received intelligence of the presence at the Royal Court of an agent from Muscat, seeking Persian co-operation in the conquest of Bahrain, and a delegate from the (Shi'ite) 'aboriginal population' of Bahrain, imploring Persian assistance in 'relieving them from the painful supremacy of their foreign masters', or the Al Khalifa. There was reportedly much sympathy in Iran for their majority co-religionists in Bahrain. W. Bruce to Bombay, Bushire mid–late April 1817, BA S 312/1087–9.

25. Linga had captured Gazir, 12 miles inland to the north, in January, before losing it to the advancing Persian army. The people of Linga returned home from Qishm during summer. al-Qasimi, 'Arab "Piracy"', Appendix 14, sketch-map of Persian coast, seemingly from Sayyid Taqi, Persian merchant of Bombay, late 1809.

26. The Governor in question was Muhammad Nabi Khan, while his deputy, the Acting Governor of Bushire during most of Nabi Khan's period of tenure, was his brother Muhammad Ja'far Khan. On the 1811 assistance: W. Bruce to Bombay, Bushire 29 May 1811, BA P 378/4346–9.

27. Capt. David Seton, Muscat Resident, to Bombay, Muscat 20 Feb. 1809, with enclosure of 19 Feb. 1809, BA P 325/2619–50 (esp. 2648); Seton to Brig.-Gen. John Malcolm, Muscat 9 March 1809, BA P 325/2702–7; Seton to Bombay, Muscat 7 May 1809, with letter to Malcolm of 6 March (should perhaps read 16 or 26 April) 1809, BA P 329/4607–11, 4613–16; Seton, despatch of 31 March 1809, BA P 327/374[?]–3752; Charles Pasley, Political Agent in Persia, Surgeon A. Jukes and I/J. Briggs, all to Bombay Government, Bombay 5 Sept. 1809, BA P 339/8418–25.

28. Orders were issued for the fortification of Bushire at the beginning of June, in expectation of a Qasimi attack. In mid-September, Shiraz announced to the Resident an intention of preparing a military force in *c.* Ramadan (10 Oct.–8 Nov.), to be sent against the Qawasim settled on the Persian coast; this was possibly to be followed, if circumstances were favourable, by an attack on the Qawasim overseas. This announcement seems to have been a direct response to a British request for co-operation in her forthcoming expedition, and probably came to nought; although it is said rather loosely that Iran had by August already made some sort of approach along these lines to Muscat. W. Bruce to Fort William, Bushire 12 June 1809, with enclosed letter of Muhammad Husain Khan, BA P 335/6867–71; W. Bruce to Bombay, Bushire 22 Sept. 1809, BA P 347/11189–90; Bombay Council to Bruce, under date 18 Aug. 1809, BA P 338/7997–9.

29. Husain bin Hamad, Agent of ruler of Muscat, to Bombay Government, 10 April 1811, and account of four Russian soldiers, BA P 372/1741–5; Ibn Ruzaiq, *Imams and Seyyids*, pp. 306–20; Maurizi, *Seyd Said*, pp. 79–88; Kelly, *Britain*, p. 125. Whilst on the theme of Omani–Persian co-operation, it is perhaps worth adding that in autumn 1816, when the ruler of Muscat actually led an expedition against Bahrain, and again in the winter of 1817, when he made preparations to do the same, the troops promised by Shiraz, which were to be financed by Muscat, never materialized: W. Bruce to Bombay, Bushire 16 Sept. and Oct. 1816, 6 Oct. 1817, 9 and 14 April 1818; Muscat Broker to Bombay, 3 Nov. 1817, Jan. 1818; BA P 432/2171–3, 439/2284 and 2379–80, 443/834–7, 448/2884–90.

30. Shibkuh stretches from Mughu north to Banak.

31. HRH Husain Ali Mirza, Governor of Fars, to W. Bruce, received at Bushire 30 July 1819, Shiraz(?) Ram. 1234, BA P 469/4319–21. Cf., again, Husain Ali Mirza to Bruce, received at Bushire 16 Oct. 1819, BA Sel. 73/162–5: 'The Qasimi tribe are the enemies of this state: ... you must ... [have] heard that last year how many of them were destroyed by us and we now again have it under consideration.'

32. Busse (trans.), *A History of Persia*, pp. 153–5.

33. HRH Husain Ali Mirza, Governor of Fars, to Bushire Resident, Dh.Q. 1224, received 24 Jan. 1810, BA P 353/1297–8. Fath Ali Shah is also said to have approved: Bombay Governor to Ouseley, Ambassador at Tehran, Bombay Castle 25 March 1811, BA P 371/1501–3.

34. On 20 June 1805, the Persian Ambassador to India, Muhammad Nabi Khan, had told Bruce

that he 'did not suppose there would be any objection' to Britain's punishing the Banu Mu'in and the Qasimi Shaikhs of Linga and Shinas, 'if they had acted in any manner deserving of it', even though they were Persian subjects; it seems he had had in mind the Persian islands and did not envisage British operations on the mainland. Persian sensitivities seem to have been relatively greater by the time of the second expedition, but this impression may be in some part due to the development of greater consultation, and of closer contact between the two parties in Tehran, where feelings were stronger and plainer than in Shiraz. W. Bruce, Acting Bushire Resident, to Seton, Bushire 30 June 1805, BA S&P 171/4343–8. Henry Willock to Bombay, with enclosures, Tehran 11 May 1820, BA P 492/6640–57; and to Keir, 23 Dec. 1819, BA S 315/250–2.

35. This was presumably the fruit of Sultan bin Saqr's despatch to the court at Shiraz of a certain Sayyid Majid 'on some business of importance'. The delegate had set out from Linga, where Sultan bin Saqr was then residing, in mid–late July 1814; the robe of honour, according to Lorimer, arrived in about November. Sultan bin Saqr to W. Bruce, received at Bushire 30 July 1814, BA P 415/3823–4; Lorimer, Gazetteer, vol. 1, pp. 651–2. On the robe of honour, Morier, A Journey through Persia ... in 1808 and 1809, pp. 26–7.

36. Shaikh Abd al-Rasul was seized by Shiraz in October 1808, and subsequently confined. The government of Bushire now passed to Muhammad Nabi Khan, recently the Persian Ambassador to India, who soon took up high office in Shiraz, leaving his brother Muhammad Ja'far Khan as Acting Governor in Bushire until March 1813 when both brothers were stripped of position by the Prince–Governor of Fars. The government of Bushire now remained unsettled until at least July 1814, during which time it passed to Acting Governors and, for a time, to the Shah's cousin, Mahdi Quli Khan Qajar. Shaikh Abd al-Rasul had been reinstated in the Governorship of Bushire by December 1814. It is not clear when exactly the Al Madhkur family itself, which up till now had been in exile, scattered in different parts of the Gulf, had returned. Abd al-Rasul's uncle and second in rank, Shaikh Muhammad, had certainly arrived in Bushire with his numerous relations before October 1814, and possibly rather earlier; he himself spoke, perhaps rather approximately, of five years of exile. Shaikh Muhammad to Bombay, enclosed in Bombay to W. Bruce, Bushire Resident, Bombay 21 Oct. 1814, IOR R/15/1/15 pp. 191–5; Bruce to Bombay, Bushire 4 Jan. 1815 IOR R/15/1/16, pp. 10–12; also IOR R/15/1/10, Oct. 1808, pp. 348 ff.; Bruce to Bombay, Bushire 15 March 1813, IOR R/15/1/12, pp. 316–18; Bruce to Bombay, Bushire 23 Jan. 1815, BA P 420/582–90; Bruce to Bombay, Bushire 20 July 1813, BA P 399/2679–81; Saldanha, Persian Gulf Précis, vol. 2, pp. 61–4; Buckingham, Travels, pp. 350–1.

37. W. Bruce, Resident, to Bombay Governor, Bushire 3 Sept. 1815, BA P 425/2432–6.

38. W. Bruce, Resident, to Bombay, Bushire 7 Feb. 1816, BA P 428/650–1.

39. Late in 1832 Sultan bin Saqr brought a Qasimi fleet to aid the Shaikh of Bushire who was blockading the port. Sultan bin Saqr now apparently told the British Resident that the Qawasim 'had on several occasions acted as allies of the late Shaikh of Bushire [Abd al-Rasul, who ruled for most of 1807–32], of which the instance in 1815 was well known': despatch of 17 Sept. 1832 cited in Grummon, 'The Rise', p. 145. Cf. W. Bruce, Bushire Resident, to Harford Jones, Lt W. Eatwell and Capt. D. Seton, 13 and 29 Dec. 1805, IOR R/15/1/8 pp. 74–5, 78.

40. W. Bruce, Bushire Resident, to Bombay, Bushire 22 March 1815, BA P 421/1059–60.

41. Two thirds of the Qasimi fleet was reportedly composed of dows and baghlas, the rest battils. W. Bruce, Bushire Resident, to Bombay, 3 and 6 Jan. 1818, BA P 443/1124–8, Sel. 72/535–40; Broker Goolab Anundass to Bombay, Muscat (2nd or early 3rd week of Jan. 1818), BA P 443/834–7.

42. Bombay Council Minutes of 11 Nov. 1808, BA S&P 251/13005–6. Muhammad Husain Khan, eldest son of the former Bushire Resident (1798–1803) Mehdi Ali Khan, was travelling as secretary to the legation; bespectacled, and fond of the dashing costume of a Persian horseman, Muhammad Husain Khan was married to the daughter of a Zand prince. Malcolm, Sketches, pp. 79–81.

43. Low, Indian Navy, vol. 1, p. 321. Morier was the first to publish Muhammad Husain Khan's account of the attack: Morier, A Journey through Persia ... in 1808 and 1809, pp. 43–6.

44. Samuel Manesty, Basra Resident, to Bombay, Basra 24 May 1798, in Saldanha, *Persian Gulf Précis*, vol. 1, pp. 338–9.

45. William Bruce spoke of 'the good understanding and correspondence' he had established with 'the chiefs along both shores of the Gulph': Bruce was at the time holding encouraging communication with Rahma bin Jabir, Sultan bin Saqr, Hasan bin Rahma and Shaikh Khalfan of Asalu (over Charak). W. Bruce, Resident, to Bombay, Bushire 7 Aug. 1814, BA P 415/3819–23. He also, of course, gained intelligence from the Governor of Bushire: he it was who had first received 'written accounts from the southern ports' informing of the loss of the *Minerva*; so too in 1811, when he passed on to Bruce news received by express from Asalu of the sailing of nine Ajman vessels on a cruise, it was thought, towards the bar of Basra. W. Bruce to Bombay, Bushire 30 June 1809, BA P 336/7343–4; ditto, 29 May 1811, BA P 378/4346–9.

46. E.g. W. Bruce to Bombay, Bushire 19 Aug. and 24 Dec. 1818, BA S 310/280–3, P 460/483–5; ditto, 28 Nov. 1816, BA Sel. 72/83–91; ditto, 8 Feb. 1816, BA P 429/819–20. N.H. Smith, Bushire Resident, to Bombay, Bushire 24 March 1810, BA P 355/1995–2001. And see earlier concerning the release of Mrs Taylor, from the *Minerva*, and the report of Indian women captives supposedly sold on Bahrain.

47. E.g. W. Bruce to Bombay, Bushire 3 and 6 Jan. 1818, BA P 443/1124–8, regarding the five vessels seized by the Qawasim at Asalu: an express messenger from Kangan first brought the news to Bushire on 23 December, one of Bruce's own messengers arrived from Kangan on 5 January, and letters had also been received on this subject from Bahrain before 3 January.

48. E.g. W. Bruce to Bombay, Bushire 26 July 1819, BA P 469/4314–16—secret information on a Charak battil; ditto, 8 Feb. 1816, BA P 429/819–20—an unnamed informant in the confidence of the ruler of Muscat.

49. As, his statement regarding news of the movements of the Qasimi fleet, which had been brought to Bushire by boats from Linga and Bahrain: 'This information has obtained general credit here, as it has been in some measure confirmed by accounts from Kangan and the southern ports.' W. Bruce to Bombay, Bushire 13 Feb. 1817, BA Sel. 72/341–2.

50. E.g. Bruce first received news of the attacks on the *Trimmer* and the *Shannon* from the Nakhuda of a boat from Asalu on 9 December; he did not credit this merely verbal report until it was confirmed in a letter brought by cossid, or courier, from the Kangan merchant Haji Muhammad Jamal the following morning. W. Bruce to Manesty, Bushire 10 Dec. 1804, BA S&P 164A/602–4. Cf., at Muscat, Narrotum Ramchunder, Muscat Broker, to Bombay, received 6 Dec. 1797, BA S&P 59/206–9—letters from Bushire merchants; Muscat Broker to Bombay, in Minutes of 16 March 1815, BA P 420/598–9—a battil arrived from Abu Dhabi. Note also Nathan Crow's arguments on the superiority of intelligence brought by Arab vessels to Basra over that brought by them to Bombay: Committee on communications with England, 22 Aug. 1797, BA S&P 57/1637–8 (1618–44); Morier, *A Journey through Persia . . . in 1808 and 1809*, p. 44, the *Sylph*, arrivals at Bushire; and BA P 327/3638, Arab and Persian merchants at Bombay, intelligence of Qasimi politics, April 1809.

Notes to Chapter Eight

1. Note Captain William Hill's special request for information regarding the 'commercial intercourse' of the Gulf, and the policy to be observed in respect of Qasimi and Wahhabi vessels, together with Government's reply: Hill to Governor, HMS *Towey*, Bombay 26 Nov. 1817, and reply of 28 Nov., BA Sel. 72/495–9.

2. On 26 February 1805, shortly after the *Trimmer* and *Shannon* incidents, David Seton proposed assisting the ruler of Muscat in operations against the Qawasim, by offering him the support of the Company's cruiser(s) then in the Gulf. In the event, Seton preferred negotiation with the Qawasim over hostilities, and the result was his agreement with Sultan bin Saqr of February 1806. The Anglo–Omani co-operation which did result from Seton's suggestion was

directed to slightly different ends: Seton and the HCC *Mornington* attended the ruler of Muscat's 1805 operations at Bandar Abbas and Qishm, where the latter was seeking to re-establish his authority, but the cruiser did not herself engage in action. This affair recalls another of Seton's enterprises, the abortive Anglo–Omani attack on the Sudan in December 1801, which had briefly involved one cruiser, the *Duncan*. Governor Duncan to Seton; and instructions to Lt Charles Gilmour of the HCC *Mornington* and Lt Daniel Ross of the HCC *Queen*, Bombay Castle 3 March 1805, BA S&P 165/968–80. Muscat Resident D. Seton to Bombay, with enclosures, Muscat 13 Dec. 1801, BA S&P 119/71–100.

3. Orders were apparently issued at Bombay on or after 11 November 1808 in response to the attack on the *Sylph*. Similar orders were in force on the route to the Arabian Gulf, or Red Sea: F. Warden, Chief Sec. to Government, to commander of the HCC *Benares*, Bombay Castle 5 April 1809, BA P 326/3253–4.

4. In Muscat Captain Waddington of the *Macaulay* learnt that his attackers were Qawasim who had fled Ras al-Khaima and settled on Abu Musa; they were also supposed to have seized two Basra dows and a number of Muscat vessels. Bombay Board's resolution of 19(?) Feb. 1811, with Secretary in Marine Department to Chief Sec. to Government 23 Feb., BA P 370/914–22; also W. Bruce to Bombay, with enclosure, Bushire 29 May 1811, BA P 378/4346–50. Other material at BA P 371/1494–501, 1358–60, 1485–93; 370/1128–30; and Morier, *A Second Journey*, p. 27, possibly the same fleet.

5. Bombay Council to Bruce, 21 Jan. 1813, enclosing letter to Qasimi chief and instructions to Lt Davidson of the HCC *Vestal*, BA P 392/131–2, 136–7, 139–40: other material at BA P 383/394–6; 392/17–18, 131–2, 19–20; 398/2290–1.

6. S. Babington, Sec. to Government, to Capt. Prior of HMS *Acorn*, Bombay 22 Oct. 1814, cited in al-Qasimi, *The Myth*, pp. 186–8; Chief Sec. F. Warden to Supt of Marine Henry Meriton, Bombay Castle 28 Feb. 1815, BA P 420/429–30; Meriton to Lt F. Faithful of the HCC *Psyche*, Bombay 5 Dec. 1816, BA Sel. 72/171–4.

7. The 1808/9 orders conceivably had some more effect off Cutch and Sind. The one clear example of offensive action occurred there in 1809, and involved the spirited, but hopeless pursuit of 11 Qasimi vessels by the 64-ton, 7-gun schooner *Zephyr*. The HCC *Zephyr* set out from Poseitra on 14 February and called off the chase near Sonmiani on the 22nd, after firing some ineffectual shots. Lt T. Harriott, commander of the *Zephyr*, to Supt of Marine, Bombay 5 March 1809, BA P 324/2342–59.

8. These orders were issued on or by 10 March 1817, following the attack on the *Darya Daulat*.

9. The only Senior Naval Officer to take these rules seriously was Captain Loch. A sample of the orders he issued to his subordinate officers reads: 'You are hereby required and directed to do your utmost in destroying all Qasimi vessels you may fall in with, provided you cannot capture them ... You will at all times do your utmost for the protection of the British trade in the Persian Gulph.' Capt. F.E. Loch to Capt. Hall of the HCC *Teignmouth*, HMS *Eden*, Muscat Cove 16 May 1819, BA P 466/3160.

10. J. Duncan, President, to Lt Ross, Bombay 3 March 1805, BA S&P 165/978–80.

11. Brucks was very critical of Government's administration of the Bombay Marine: offensive action should have been permitted and cruisers properly equipped: 'They were to excess filled with guns—so much so indeed that there was no room to work them—deficient as they were in the number of officers and men, they sailed worse than coal barges ... cruisers of 12 or 14 guns frequently could not muster 20 Europeans ... I have frequently known the merchant vessels under their convoy far more efficient as fighting vessels than their protectors'. Brucks, *Account of the Survey*, pp. 60–1; 42–4, 60–2, 65, 70.

12. One of the four cruisers was in fact then returning to Bombay; Hill felt that 4–5 cruisers and one naval vessel were needed for a comprehensive convoy system in the Gulf. Capt. Hill to Bombay, Bushire 11 April 1817, BA Sel. 72/362–5.

13. Disposition of cruisers, 17 March 1817, BA Sel. 72/307; Moyse-Bartlett, *The Pirates*, Appendix A, pp. 232–4; Bombay Council to Fort William, 31 Dec. 1816, BA Sel. 72/151–4

14. The extent to which they did otherwise was severely limited, even really in the year preceding the second expedition: in 1813, for example, Bruce recommended that the HCC *Ternate*, on her return journey from delivering her convoy to Muscat, 'stand in towards the

coast of Ras al-Khaima and cruise off it for a short time', as a signal of the Company's continued determination to prevent a resurgence of piracy. In 1816, Captain Bridges stated that he would first attend the matter of convoys, and if the chance remained he would cruise off the Tunbs a while. W. Bruce, Resident, to Bombay, Bushire 24 April 1813, BA P 398/2290–1; Capt. Bridges to Bombay, HMS *Challenger*, Muscat 11 Dec. 1816, BA Sel. 72/198–200.

15. Before 1820, British merchantmen and cruisers rarely sailed along any but the Persian coast, a practice reinforced by insecurity and the lack of charts. Major-General Keir to Chief Sec. Warden, 1 April 1820, BA S 315/453–68.

16. Various despatches from Capt. Edward Barnard of HMS *Conway*, Bushire Resident W. Bruce, Shaikh Abdullah bin Ahmad Al Khalifa of Bahrain, Lt Arthur and others of the *Antelope*, 23 Aug. 1818–6 Feb. 1819, BA P 455/5969–73, 5854–77, 5588–600; 312/1035–8; (Sel. 73/353–5).

17. Apparently belonging to a certain Abd al-Razzaq.

18. The cargo included at least 102 bags of rice, 23 teak planks and 33 bags of dried roses, together with quantities of cloth, clothing, carpets, metalware, china and other goods, and was accompanied by an amount of pearls and specie. The planks had apparently been purchased by Shaikh Abdullah bin Ahmad Al Khalifa of Bahrain, for which purpose he claimed to have engaged the vessel—'I learned that there was plenty at Asalu for sale'—the other goods representing the purchases of Bahraini merchants. The rice had been purchased from an Al Haram (Asalu) baghla. Shaikh Abdullah bin Ahmad to W. Bruce, Bahrain 6 Sept. 1818, BA P 455/5594–8.

19. At the first, out of fear of the Muscatis, 15 men had leapt overboard and swum over to the *Antelope*.

20. 10 swords, 10 matchlocks and 1 shield with a small quantity of coins, pearls and papers had in fact been received on board the *Antelope*: these were all returned. The Muscat battil took the cargo: all of this was promised and a significant part certainly restored.

21. 'Being destitute, Sir, as we are of the smallest particle of instructions and guidance how to act with certainty, and without fear, in cases like the above, either in print or otherwise; being unfurnished with any acts of Parliament or articles of war; the Company's officers are liable to considerable error and mismanagement, particularly with regard to the pirate[s] in the Gulf of Persia. And in the above case, I thought I was acting with all caution and foresight which was requisite for, particularly with respect to the [ruler of Muscat]'. Captain Barnard supported this plaint. Lt J. Arthur to Capt. Barnard, HCC *Antelope*, and Capt. Barnard to Bombay, HMS *Conway*, both Kharg 9 Oct. 1818, BA P 455/5861–72, 5854–6.

22. The action between the *Lively* and the four dows took place on 22 November 1808. David Seton to Government, Bombay 12 Dec. 1808, BA S&P 255/14269–71; report by Money, Goodwin and Briscoe, Bombay 21 March 1809, BA P 325/2780–93; Ruler of Muscat to Chief of Surat, 21 Feb. 1809, and Bombay Governor's reply of 30 March 1809, BA P 326/3145–56; Governor Duncan to Muscat Ruler, Bombay 11 June 1809, BA P 334/6223–5. Low, *Indian Navy*, vol. 1, pp. 319–20.

23. Lt Gowan to Supt of Marine William Taylor Money, Bombay 10 May 1808, BA S&P 232/5669–70.

24. Gowan states that one of the dows mounted 10 guns, with several swivels, and carried at least 300 men; the other perhaps 6 guns, with several swivels, and at least 200 men. Neither hoisted any colours. On board the *Fury*, the Gunner, two seamen and one sepoy were seriously wounded, the Boatswain, one sepoy and one lascar slightly so; the schooner received 'a few shot holes through her sails, and some ropes cut by [the assailants].' Lt Gowan to William Taylor Money, Supt of Marine Bombay, HCC *Fury*, Bombay harbour 10 May 1808, BA S&P 232/5669–70.

25. Extract of a letter from Lt Bennett, Bombay 1 Dec. 1808, BA S&P 255/14147–50.

26. Extract from Lt Bennett to Supt of Marine, Bombay harbour 1 Dec. 1808, BA S&P 255/14147–50.

27. The large battil in question had been built at Linga and was the property of Shaikh Muhammad bin Qadib. She had set sail on 20 May bound for Abu Dhabi with a cargo of 1600 bundles of rice, a few bales of goods and a quantity of coarse earthenware. She bore 3 guns,

60 matchlocks and 70 men. Capt. Walpole, HM sloop *Curlew*, to Bombay, Bushire 7 June 1819, enclosing examination of men found on Linga battil taken in Mughu bay on 22 May 1819, BA Sel. 73/649–53. For the subsequent developments in this case, including a protest from the Shaikh of Linga and the Prince–Governor of Shiraz, see BA Sel. 73/9–38, 73–4, 91–2, 160–72, 208–15, 222, 671, 676–8.

28. The battil sought help from Charak. Real resistance, however, was slight; after one broadside from the *Curlew*, the culmination of a day's pursuit, most of the crew dived overboard and swam ashore. The behaviour and intentions of the *Curlew*, which from the very start had patently meant to detain the Linga battil, were completely different from the *Nautilus* which certainly had no such aim.

29. But not necessarily the rule: cf. the 1817 *Vestal* incident (text below); and Morier, 'merchantmen ... lower their sails upon the least appearance of danger', *A Second Journey*, p. 36, Shaikh Shu'aib Feb. 1811.

30. At this point it is useful to examine an incident involving the HC ship *Aurora* in c. early January 1816, which is depicted in two romanticized, but nonetheless noteworthy, paintings by Thomas Buttersworth. An account of the action by her then Acting Lieutenant might seem to suggest that it had more in common with the *Lively* than the *Fury* or *Nautilus* incidents: about the Tunbs en route from Bushire to Muscat, whilst towing a baghla freighted with treasure for the ruler of Muscat, the *Aurora* is said to have sighted a dozen or more vessels at anchor ahead of her and concluded that they intended cutting away the baghla; she carried on her course however, and when she came up with the dows, simply opened fire, whereupon a short and damaging action ensued that was cut short by nightfall. The problem with this account is that it is far too late for us to put any great reliance on its exactitude; a nearly contemporary report speaks of a far more trivial action. This latter report nevertheless contains an important clue. It states that at about this time, in January 1816, one British country-ship and two Americans were unsuccessfully attacked by 5–7 boats near the Tunbs and Cape Musandam. Three further incidents of this kind suggests they cannot all have been accident. No protests were lodged over these incidents. The involvement of friendly and 'politic' powers such as Muscat, Bahrain and the Jalahima can probably be ruled out. If we then take into consideration the location, and the fact that the activities of 12–25 Qasimi cruisers are independently reported in this area at this time, then the most rational explanation for this group of incidents would be one that implicates the Qawasim. The fact that the ruler of Muscat had just prior to this abandoned a four-month blockade of Ras al-Khaima, culminating in an abortive maritime expedition against Qasimi shipping in the vicinity of Ru'us al-Jibal which was terminated at around the start of January, may somehow have contributed to this apparent burst of activity. W. Bruce, Resident, to Bombay, Bushire 8 Feb. 1816, BA P 429/819–20; Muscat Broker to Bombay, 6 and 10 Jan. 1816, BA P 427/283–4, 285–7; Low, *Indian Navy*, vol. 1, pp. 340–1. This last contains the later account of the *Aurora* incident by her Acting Lieutenant at the time, and not her commander, Richard Kinchant; this account was apparently written for Low's information. The Buttersworth oil paintings are held by the National Maritime Museum at Greenwich.

31. As, Captain Wainwright's remarks in, David Seton, Muscat Resident, to Bombay, Muscat 7 May 1809, BA P 329/4607–11.

32. Senior, who maintained that spoken Arabic was equally unfamiliar to Royal Naval officers, therefore proposed a system of passes for non-square-rigged Muscat vessels, and those under Arab or Persian colours sailing thence. Capt. J.W. Senior to D. Seton, Muscat Resident, HMS *La Chiffone*, at sea 4 May 1809, BA P 333/5963–6.

33. 'None of the boats in this Gulph have passes and they all hoist the same colours in general.' Lt H. Davidson to Supt of Marine W.T. Money, HCC *Fury*, Bushire roads 22 Jan. 1809, with Minutes of 2 March, BA P 323/1956–61. Davidson was reporting the circumstances of an apparent action between unidentified vessels on 20 January 1809, which he had witnessed from afar: 'we heard a very heavy cannonading, and from the *Fury*'s masthead with a good glass, could just see over the Island [of Kharg] a square-rigged vessel and four piratical boats engaging.' The real nature of the scene he had observed is, however, with the identity of the vessels, far from clear.

34. W. Bruce, Resident, to Bombay, Bushire 9 Sept. 1814, IOR R/15/1/14 pp. 188–9; (cf. BA S&P 129/6073).

35. Bombay Council Minutes of 30 March(?) 1809, BA 326/3155–6; Six simple day and night signals submitted by Supt of Marine H. Meriton, Bombay 4 Aug. 1817, BA Sel. 72/416–19.

36. In February 1806, Seton proposed to the Qawasim that they introduce passes on vessels they sent to India. One of the provisions of Bruce's inoperative October 1814 agreement was that the Qawasim adopt the use of a red flag, to be inscribed with the motto 'There is but One God, and Muhammad is His Prophet'. During Conyers' unsanctioned discussions at Ras al-Khaima in March 1819, it was agreed that the Qawasim would fly a white flag, and bear passes with Hasan bin Rahma's seal. The matter was only settled with the General Treaty of January 1820, which made passes compulsory on all vessels and designated a red flag with white borders (white pierced red). On the Arab use of the flags cf. Loch's encounter of 10/11 May 1819, Walpole's seizure of 22 May 1819, text above, and Conyers' arrest of 1 November 1819, note below. Agreement between William Bruce, Bushire Resident, and representative of Hasan bin Rahma of Ras al-Khaima, executed Bushire 6 Oct. 1814, in Bruce to Bombay, with enclosures, Bushire 9 Oct. 1814, BA P 419/122–30; translation of letter from Hasan bin Rahma to Bombay President, Ras al-Khaima 13 March 1819, and of note from Hasan bin Rahma to Capt. F.E. Loch, received at Bushire 3 April 1819, with other enclosures in Loch to Bombay, HMS Eden, Bushire Roads 4 March 1819, BA Sel. 73/485–8, 509–21. Cf. also W. Bruce's grandiose and unrealistic scheme for the compulsory introduction of identity certificates for those on 'friendly' terms with Britain in 1805: Bruce to Bombay, Bushire 22 Nov. 1805, BA S&P 175/6807–9.

37. There was, however, some difficulty in securing pilots for Ras al-Khaima at Bushire, for which reason in the second decade the British tended to recruit the necessary assistance of Rahma bin Jabir. Pilots for the route to Basra were readily obtainable at Kharg. Various reports, e.g. BA S&P 164A/596–9; P 432/2435–9; P 412/2702–4; Sel. 72/83–91; Buckingham, Travels in Assyria, pp. 466–7; Sadleir, Journey Across Arabia, pp. 47–8; Brucks, Account of the Survey, p. 70.

38. W. Bruce, Acting Resident, to Bombay, Bushire 29 May 1811, BA P 378/4346–9.

39. Thomas Tanner joined the Royal Navy in 1801, serving on the Fisgard, before transferring to the Bombay Marine after the peace of Amiens in 1802. In later life he was elected Mayor of his native Exeter. Low, Indian Navy, vol. 1, p. 323.

40. Capt. W. Hill to Bombay, HMS Towey, off Bushire 11 April 1817, BA Sel. 72/362–5. Tanner later reported that there had been 'two large trankeys crowded with men and two of a smaller size who showed but few hands'; their 'light draught of water' and 'superiority in sailing' allowed them to escape: H. Meriton, Supt of Marine, to Governor, Bombay 5 May 1817, BA Sel. 72/367–9.

41. Cf. the recollected circumstances of the Aurora incident, note above.

42. In 1819 we learn of another incident of passing moment involving Muscat vessels: before February, a dinghy and a nauri belonging to the ruler were temporarily, but without harm, detained by the Company's cruisers on suspicion of being Qawasim. They had been carrying mercenaries in search of employment in Cutch, a practice which the ruler now agreed to prohibit. H. Meriton, Supt of Marine, to Bombay Governor, Bombay 23 May 1817, BA Sel. 72/384–7; (ditto with enclosure /389–92); Bombay Council Minute of 31 May 1817, /394–5; Meriton to Governor, 10 June 1817, with Minute of 14 June, /396–400; Faithful to Meriton, Bombay 5 Nov. 1817, with Minute of 13 Nov., /470–6. Ruler of Muscat to Bombay Governor, 18 March 1819, BA P 465/2536–9.

43. David Seton, Resident, to Brig.-Gen. Malcolm, Muscat 6 March 1809, BA P 325/2692–701.

44. This incident apparently occurred off Gwadar. Loch, Diaries, MS pp. 92–4, TS pp. 88–9.

45. Cited in Moyse-Bartlett, The Pirates, p. 80; cf. Low, Indian Navy, vol. 1, p. 347.

46. A hindrance, and of little value, she was scuttled along with her small load of wet cotton. Lt Guy in, H. Meriton, Supt of Marine, to Governor, enclosing extracts from Lt Tanner of the Thetis, and Lt Guy of the Psyche, Bombay 16 Jan. 1819, BA Sel. 73/304–12.

47. Capt. F.E. Loch to Bombay, HMS Eden, Bay of Gwatar 27 Dec. 1818, BA Sel. 73/315–16; P 460/487. Lt Guy also spoke of the 'masterly manoeuvres' which allowed them to stay just

outside the range of the *Psyche*'s broadside and cross her bows, notwithstanding her 'every exertion in pulling and sailing': report by Lt Guy of the HCC *Psyche*, in H. Meriton, Supt of Marine, to Governor, Bombay 16 Jan. 1819, BA Sel. 73/304–12.

48. The evidence for this is that of the crew themselves, some of whom were later interrogated by Loch. These same captives were later delivered to Ras al-Khaima in return for the release of the Qawasim's British Indian captives. Questions and answers put to Qasimi captives, details of Arab vessels etc., in Loch to Bombay, HMS *Eden*, Muscat 2 Jan. 1819, BA P 460/488–93.

49. The original reads, '*Shuma*, Seid Eber Hasun, *Tomashe*, Sebet Eber Yemo, *Awad*, Homett, *Swaybuts*, Salem'. An alternative for Thabit might be Suwait, perhaps suggestive of the lower Gulf. My thanks to Paul Auchterlonie and Dr Roger Webster. Loch to Bombay, HMS *Eden*, Muscat 2 Jan. 1819, BA P 460/488–93; BA Sel. 73/320–6.

50. Loch, *Diaries*, MS pp. 98–9, TS pp. 93–4.

51. Loch, *Diaries*, MS pp. 101–2, TS pp. 95–6.

52. In his *Diaries* Loch speaks of seven vessels, in a contemporary despatch of eight. Loch to Bombay, HMS *Eden*, between Hanjam and Qishm 12 Jan. 1819, BA P 462/1451–4; Loch, *Diaries*, TS pp. 120–8.

53. One of two baghlas, the rest being battils (trankeys), she carried 4,000 bags of rice, two 9-pounders and one 3-pounder. Loch supposed she was a prize. Loch to Bombay, HMS *Eden*, between Qishm and Hanjam 12 Jan. 1819, BA P 462/1451–3.

54. According to Loch she carried two 9-pounders, one 3-pounder and 120 men. Ibid.

55. Loch, *Diaries*, TS pp. 120–8; Loch to Bombay, HMS *Eden*, between Hanjam and Qishm 12 Jan. 1819, BA P 462/1451–3.

56. The Bushire Resident also claims to have received a similar report from a boat arrived from Linga. Bruce's report predates Loch's encounter (and therefore does not necessarily refer to these particular vessels), and states that the Qawasim's intention was hereby to be in a position to resist an expected Turko–Egyptian onslaught at the hands of Ibrahim Pasha. On 4 March Loch reported that the Qawasim had desisted from 'fortifying or making a lodgement at Point Basidu' on account of two interruptions of their vessels by HMS *Eden* and the HCC *Antelope*. W. Bruce, Resident, to Bombay, Bushire 5 Jan. 1819, BA P 460/484–6; Capt. D.D. Conyers to Supt of Marine, HCC *Mercury*, 22 March 1819, BA Sel. 73/453–4; Loch, *Diaries*, TS p. 124; Loch to Bombay, HMS *Eden*, Bushire Roads 4 March, BA Sel. 73/509–11.

57. Loch, *Diaries*, MS pp. 135, TS pp. 124–5.

58. Loch, *Diaries*, TS pp. 127–8; Hasan bin Rahma of Ras al-Khaima to Shaikh Abdullah bin Ahmad of Bahrain, received at Bushire 29 March 1819, BA Sel. 73/500–2.

59. They were first sent to Bombay, then on 29 May were finally liberated at Ras al-Khaima in return for the Qawasim's freeing of their British captives. See Chapter Five.

60. Loch, *Diaries*, TS pp. 133, 275–6.

61. 'I regret that the vessels were not Qawasim, as several of their men have been killed and wounded'. His original intention had been to exchange the vessels for the Qawasim's British captives, but Loch had apparently been misinformed of their identity by the Company's Broker. There had, it seems, been a total of five such vessels in the harbour, and according to Loch they belonged to Shaikh Shakhbut. Low, admittedly somewhat partisan in these matters, ascribed the mistake to Loch's 'perversity and ignorance of Persian Gulf politics, in which he was too proud to take advice from the commanders of the Company's cruisers.' Loch to Bombay, HMS *Eden*, off Bahrain 17 Feb. 1819, BA Sel. 73/418–27; Loch, *Diaries*, TS pp. 148–58; W. Bruce to Bombay, Bushire 26 Feb. 1819, BA Sel. 73/438–42; Low, *Indian Navy*, vol 1, p. 350.

62. Chapter Five.

63. In one 24-hour period during this voyage from Trincomalee, the *Eden* managed 205 miles. When she made the same voyage from Trincomalee to Ras al-Hadd the following year, it measured 4,488 miles and took 37 days; in one 24-hour period on this second occasion, the *Eden* traversed 217 miles. Loch, *Diaries*, MS pp. 301–3, 488.

64. On 7 September, Lt Guy of the HCC *Psyche* chased a Qasimi battil on shore near Kuh Mubarak, burnt her and took three prisoners; she had reportedly been three days out from Ras

al-Khaima and was towing a small prize. On 7 October, Loch claims to have chased seven Qawasim near Barka, forcing them to destroy their supposed prize; but he was again outsailed, 'the *Eden*'s sailing having a good deal fallen off in consequence of her having struck so often on the ground'. H. Meriton, Supt of Marine, to Governor, Bombay 25 Oct. 1819, BA Sel. 73/127–8; Loch, *Diaries*, MS pp. 304–5, TS p. 272.

65. On 1 November, Captain D.D. Conyers of the HCC *Mercury* overtook a baqqara, one of two vessels then three days from Abu Dhabi en route to Asalu. First she displayed white, then soon after, red colours. No shots were fired. 200 dollars were found on board, but no cargo: she was carrying 14 men armed with spears and matchlocks etc., three of whom were passengers belonging to Asalu, and the rest 'Wahhabis'. Conyers to Loch, HCC *Mercury*, Bushire Roads 9 Nov. 1819, BA Sel. 73/231–2.

On 11 November, the boats of the *Eden* captured a large battil at Bushire, without recourse to arms. The battil carried 29 men and 2 six-pound guns, and belonged to Shaikh Muhammad bin Hazza' of Dubai. He had allegedly sent her to Bushire via Nakhilu and Asalu, acquiring passes at each port, in order to circumvent the efforts of the British to prevent vessels from the 'Qasimi' coast from acquiring supplies at the three or four major Gulf ports: 'The battil has been driven to this scheme owing to the great scarcity of dates throughout the pirate coast.' Needless to say, this was a misguided capture, and one that showed disrespect towards the Shaikh of Bushire. Loch describes how he was assailed by a crowd of Bushiris protesting at his action, and records that when the Shaikh of Bushire publicly taxed him with its inappropriateness, he simply replied that he was acting upon the orders of his government, then walked away. Loch to Bombay, HMS *Eden*, Bushire Roads 11 Nov. 1819, BA Sel. 73/226–8; Loch, *Diaries*, MS pp. 311–14, TS pp. 278–81; Shaikh Abd al-Rasul, Governor of Bushire, to Bombay Governor, Bushire undated, with proposed reply of 21 Jan. 1820, BA P 477/472–8.

On 13 November, Captain Conyers of the HCC *Mercury* came up with five vessels at Khaur Musa. Giving chase, he fired a shot to bring the straggler to, then took possession of her. She proved to be a Linga battil which had left Bushire bound for Basra on the 2nd or 3rd with a cargo of salt-fish, cloth and dye-stuff. On board were 19 men, 2 boys and 2 women; the women and one of the boys did not belong to the battil. Their story, and the story of the four vessels that escaped, was reportedly as follows: the four vessels, in whose company the Linga battil had been for the last five days, belonged to Umm al-Qaiwain. They had recently attacked four Kuwait boats bound for Dailam, driving two of these on shore after heaving their loads of dates overboard, but capturing the other two and despatching them to Umm al-Qaiwain. The Linga battil took no part in these operations; her only role was to be obliged to receive on board the above three captives, and hand over her Bushire pilot. The Umm al-Qaiwain vessels, in other words, had shown respect for the Linga battil. Conyers to Loch, HCC *Mercury*, at sea 18 Nov. 1819, BA Sel. 73/239–41; W. Bruce to Bombay, Bushire 20 Nov. 1819, BA Sel. 73/201–5.

On 13 November, on the loose grounds that Linga was associated with Ras al-Khaima and should be prevented from supplying her with dates and other provisions, Loch took control of five sail newly arrived at Bushire from that port. These five had come from Linga laden with firewood and salt-fish, and were proceeding to Basra for cargoes of dates, 'the greatest portion of which [their Nakhudas] confessed would be carried over to Ras al-Khaima where the demand was very good, consequently the price very high: they all confessed they were on the best terms with the pirates, and that a regular intercourse was kept up with them; this, however, they said policy made them do as a means of safety to themselves.' The five vessels comprised the following: 1 baghla belonging to Shaikh Muhammad bin Qadib of Linga; 1 baghla belonging to a relation of his at Bustana(?); 1 baghla owned by a Bahraini, Husain Ali, resident at Linga; 1 battil sailing out of Linga, part-owned by her Nakhuda and part by another said to be living in Muscat; 1 battil the property of a Suwaidi Arab resident at Diba and Linga. Loch and Bruce seem to have acted in concert over this, and are each at some pains to justify the detention of Iranian shipping. W. Bruce to Bombay, Bushire 16 Nov. 1819, BA Sel. 73/195–9; Loch to Bombay, HMS *Eden*, Bushire Roads 18 Nov. 1819, BA Sel. 73/234–7; Loch, *Diaries*, pp. 318–20.

On 17 November, off Shaikh Shu'aib, Captain Hall of the HCC *Teignmouth* observed a trankey with 120–130 men on board. She now took her companion, a baghla, in tow. Hall concluded from her manoeuvres she was a pirate, and set off in pursuit, obliging her eventually to abandon the baghla after taking off the crew. When Hall overtook the baghla he discovered she was loaded with grain, cotton and other goods, worth as a whole perhaps 6,000 dollars: 'there was not a living soul on board nor any marks of violence.' To the disappointment of his crew, cheered by the prospect of a rich prize, Hall was soon forced to destroy her because he was carrying government despatches and was therefore in some haste. The trankey had escaped. Hall to Supt of Marine, 10 Dec. 1819, BA S 315/21–3; Loch to Bombay, HMS *Eden*, off Qishm (?) 23 Nov. 1819, BA Sel. 73/224.

Most of these vessels, together with a battil belonging to the Ras al-Khaima envoy who had arrived at Bushire on 23 September, accompanied Loch when he set out to join the British expedition on 20 November; they were apparently released just before the military operations got underway. As, Loch, *Diaries*, MS p. 361.

66. As a general rule Company cruiser commanders received running instructions from Residents, but when there was a Senior Naval Officer in the Gulf, he would have been their highest authority. Even then, as Meriton argued in respect of the Porbandar Agent, cruiser commanders would in practice be expected to respond to the informed directions of the political officer: H. Meriton, Supt of Marine, to Governor, Bombay 4 Jan. 1819, BA Sel. 72/269–73. Note e.g. S. Manesty, Basra Resident, to Bombay, Basra 31 March 1808, BA S&P 232/5886–8; W. Bruce, Resident, to Bombay, BA P 398/2290–1; and Factory records *passim*. Malcolm's period of command before the first expedition was another exception: D. Seton, Resident, to J. Malcolm, Muscat 20 Feb. 1809, BA P 325/2633–8; cf. Capt. J. Wainwright to Governor, HMS *La Chiffone*, Bombay Harbour 28 June 1809, BA P 335/6580–1.

67. Loch, *Diaries*, MS pp. 311–14, TS pp. 278–81: on the Dubai vessel seized 11 Nov. see note above.

68. Loch's tone is the important thing here; since it must be recognized that Loch's orders to Conyers as to the rejection of negotiations with the Qawasim were the only possible ones at this stage consistent with British policy, and he was of course supported by Bombay in this, as in other matters. Loch to Conyers, HMS *Eden*, Bushire Roads 3 April 1819, BA Sel. 73/523–4; Bombay Council Minutes 23 April 1819, BA Sel. 73/490–2.

69. The dates of the *Eden's* arrivals and departures from Muscat, marking the start and finish of her three visits to the Persian Gulf, were as follows: 31 Dec. 1818/16 May 1819; 30 Sept. 1819/11 May 1820; 24 Aug. 1820/30 Sept. 1820.

70. Loch, *Diaries*, MS pp. 2–3, 544–5.

71. Loch, *Diaries*, MS p. 288.

72. On 30 Nov./2 Dec. 1818 Loch took on 5 volunteers from the *Liverpool* and *Batavia* free-traders at Bombay; on 30 May 1819 he received 19 volunteers from Indiamen just arrived at Bombay in the China fleet; and on 17 May 1820 he was obliged to take on a further 7 volunteers at Bombay from the *Bolcarras* and *Thames* Indiamen. Loch, *Diaries*, TS pp. 259, 486; also 62–3, 104, 113, 116, 124, 130, 156–7, 205–6, 258–60, 266, 335, 387, 397, 400–3, 486–8.

Notes to Chapter Nine

1. 'The houses are of a mean appearance and crowded, without order or regularity. The streets are mostly shut in with gates, and extremely dirty. It is perhaps the only place in India where there are no necessaries ... And as with this they abstain from killing vermin of any kind, their houses etc. are in a sad state.' 'Some Particulars of the Countries on the Sea-coast between Cutch and Bushire' by Capt. David Seton, in al-Qasimi, 'Arab "Piracy"', Appendix 6, pp. 75–6: this part of the Appendix is badly confused; it looks as if the 'Particulars' may date to early 1806.

2. Though this was not literally the case.

3. Supt of Marine, H. Meriton, to Governor Nepean, with enclosure, Bombay 2 March 1819, BA Sel. 72/547–51.

4. Cf. Low, *Indian Navy*, vol. 1, pp. 116–17.

5. The pattern is, in the relevant sense, too erratic for such an hypothesis, and the fluctuations appear in part to respond to events in the Gulf.

6. Individual instances, as with fraud, cannot of course be ruled out.

7. E.g. Poseitra and the Qawasim distinguished: Sunderjee Sewjee to Lt J.R. Carnac, Acting Baroda Resident, Tankarra 28 Feb. 1809, BA P 324/2340–1. Three British Indian merchant petitions detailing captures by Beyt and Poseitra, in all of which the pattamars were taken to Poseitra, and the crews released, in two cases so as to reach Porbandar by begging: Three petitions dated Bombay 15 Jan. 1806, with subsequent letter of 22 Jan., BA S&P 178/486–94, 673–5. The faintly suspicious example of a merchant aware of his vessel lying at Dwarka or Beyt: Petition of Khettoo Damjee to Governor, Bombay 12 Nov. 1817, BA Sel. 72/477–8.

8. C.W. Elwood to Acting Baroda Resident, Porbandar 7 April 1819, BA Sel. 73/482–4.

9. Commodore William Mainwaring to Asst Supt of Marine Capt. Walter Hamilton, Surat 18 Jan. 1810, BA P 351/868–9.

10. 'I cannot implicitly rely on native intelligence as to extent of force, which is frequently exaggerated': C.W. Elwood to Bombay, Porbandar 21 Oct. 1817, BA Sel. 72/432–4, referring to reports of numbers of Qawasim off Cutch. (Cf. J. Macmurdo to Bombay, Anjar 25 Oct. 1817 and Elwood to Bombay, 27 Oct. 1817, BA Sel. 73/437–42; Lt Guy of the HCC *Psyche*, Porbandar 10 Feb. 1819 to Supt of Marine Meriton, BA P 462/1289–96.)

11. Porbandar Agent C.W. Elwood to Bombay, Porbandar 13 Dec. 1814, BA P 417/4998–5003.

12. Ibid. This event had occurred in the early part of November 1814, and the boat had been sailing from Porbandar to Sind with a valuable cargo.

13. In 1819, the Porbandar Agent felt he had reasonable intelligence from the ports of Sind, but not from Luz and neighbouring Makran. He therefore suggested setting up an Agency in Sonmiani, an increasingly important port in Luz and the 'key' of Baluchistan: in support of this proposal, he argued of Makran, to the west, 'The intercourse between Makran and these coasts is too trifling, and its distance and paucity of inhabitants is too great, for any authentic intelligence to be procured at this port [Porbandar] regarding the connection of the Baluchis with the Qawasim.' C.W. Elwood to Bombay, Porbandar, Agent's Office 17 April 1819, BA P 467/3180–6.

14. Porbandar Agent C.W. Elwood to Bombay, Porbandar 13 Dec. 1814, BA P 417/4998–5003. His misapprehension did not endure: Elwood to Bombay, Porbandar 24 Nov. 1818, BA Sel. 71/143B–52.

15. C.W. Elwood to Bombay, Porbandar 17 Aug. 1814, BA P 415/3788–91.

16. See Chapter Six.

17. C.W. Elwood to Bombay, Porbandar 17 Aug. 1814, BA P 415/3788–91.

18. Petition of c. 36 native merchants of Bombay to Governor Nepean, Bombay 4 Nov. 1817, BA Sel. 72/448–50.

19. The narrator is in fact Elwood, relaying information from Grant dated Mandvi 27 Jan. 1815: C.W. Elwood, Porbandar Agent, to Capt. J.R. Carnac, Baroda Resident, Porbandar 31 Jan. 1815, BA P 420/440–1.

20. Lt Guy of the HCC *Psyche*, Porbandar 10 Feb. 1819 to Supt of Marine Meriton, BA P 462/1289–96.

21. The two years following the frustrated, but not wholly unpromising, Anglo–Qasimi negotiations of late 1814 were less disturbed.

22. W. Bruce's translation of a note from Hasan bin Rahma to Capt. F.E. Loch, received at Bushire on 3 April 1819, BA Sel. 73/519–21; see also translation of Amir Hasan bin Rahma to Governor Nepean, 13 March 1819, BA Sel. 73/485–8.

23. W. Bruce, Bushire Resident, to Bombay, reporting interview held at Ras al-Khaima on 27 Nov., HCC *Mercury*, Hanjam Sound 28 Nov. 1816, BA P 432/2435–41.

24. See Chapter Eight and Appendix A.

25. In addition, there are a number of specific features in the recorded interrogation which suggest that it is genuine: these include the idle inclusion of the question about the festival, the use of Arab place-names such as Devil and the contrary reply to the question about the Baluchis. It is clear that much of the knowledge imparted would have been novel, and, barring marginal misunderstandings of a kind such as that concerning the nature of the assistance from Bahrain, it has the basic ring of truth. If there had been any doubt as to the identity of the sailors interviewed, which there is not, this would have been apparent from some of the knowledge displayed, such as that of the port of Ras al-Khaima. Brief personal details of 10 of the 12 examinees were recorded later, when they were to be delivered up to Ras al-Khaima, in final return for the release of British Indian captives: the ages of the ten men ranged between 14 and 35, averaging 23. The two others had already been set free, with a message for Hasan bin Rahma, off Ras al-Khaima on 16 January 1819. Four other men had also been found with the 12 Qasimi prisoners; these had proved to be enslaved Muscatis, and they were released at Muscat by 2 January 1819. 'A Descriptive List of the Qasimi Prisoners-of-War taken by HM Ship *Eden*' etc., Bombay 24 (?) April 1819, BA Sel. 73/545. The interrogation was possibly made on board the *Eden* at Muscat, and is recorded in, two letters from Capt. F.E. Loch to Bombay, HMS *Eden*, Muscat 2 Jan. 1819, BA Sel. 73/318–26; BA P 460/488–93.

26. This word presumably stands for a port in Sind, quite possibly the historic Debul, near Karachi, or just conceivably even Karachi itself. The name 'Diul, Debal, Dewal' etc. had been in use since the time of the early Arab geographers; it was taken up by early European writers, who sometimes, it seems, referred to the whole of the Indus delta as Diul-Sind. Yule, *Hobson-Jobson*, p. 320; French Agent, Shiraz 4 March 1808, BA S&P 229/4153.

27. Here and below, text reads 'Mangalore Feton'. Mangalore was now commonly used to indicate Mangrol in Kathiawar, as well as the city in Kanara.

28. Ramadan 1234 AH did not begin until the start of the last week in June 1819 AD. There was no obvious Muslim holiday in January, unless conceivably the birthday of the Prophet on 17 Rab. I/14 Jan.

29. The principal town governed by the Na'im was Ajman; according to Lorimer, writing of the situation nearly a century later, large numbers then also inhabited nearby settlements such as Hira and Hamriya. The principal town of the Ahl (or Al) Ali was Umm al-Qaiwain. Lorimer, *Gazetteer*, vol. 2, p. 1301. (Here and below, text reads 'Niams, Neams, Achil-Ali, Hell Ali'.)

30. ? (text reads 'Um-el Geiull').

31. The force of this reply cannot be quite what it seems, in view of the answer concerning the Na'im and the Ahl Ali, and because there is no evidence that the people of Bahrain assisted in reported Qasimi depredations. It presumably refers more generally to Bahrain's good relations with the Qawasim, and the island's maritime resources.

32. The reading of the fraction after the figure 2 is uncertain. The observation that larger vessels were obliged to unload before being hauled over the bar was correct: according to Houghton, these only drew 7 feet when lightened. The rise in tides, if this reading is correct, is reasonably accurate. The depth of the water over the bar looks unaccountably large: Houghton and Brucks give 2–(9) feet at low and high tides, Taylor 5–11 feet; it may also be noted that Sayyid Taqi, the Persian merchant and British correspondent at Bombay, referring to what he called the mouth ('dihan'), which may alternatively have lain on the other side of the spit, in 1809 reported a depth of 6–11 feet. Houghton is probably the best source, but it should be borne in mind that the sands, and hence the depth of water, were constantly shifting: the figures given by the Qasimi interviewees seem more appropriate to the depth of water within the harbour, and it is also possible that some confusion arose from the conversion of measurements. Lt M. Houghton, 'Account of Part of the Southern Coast or Arabian Side of the Persian Gulf between Ras Musandam and Dubai', dated 1822, in Cook, *Survey*, vol. 1, pp. 107–8. Brucks, 'Memoir Descriptive of the Navigation of the Gulf of Persia', 21 Aug. 1829; and Capt. Robert Taylor, 'Extracts from Brief Notes Containing Historical and Other Information Connected with ... ports and places in the Persian Gulf', in Thomas, *Arabian Gulf Intelligence*, pp. 541–2, see also p. 15. al-Qasimi, Arab "Piracy"', Appendix 13, pp. 94–5.

33. C.W. Elwood to Bombay, Porbandar 24 Nov. 1818, BA Sel. 71/143B–52.

34. Negroes.

35. Referring to the crews of baghlas, trankeys and jymers.

36. On the pattamar, see Clifford W. Hawkins, *The Dhow: an Illustrated History of the Dhow and Its World* (Nautical Publishing, Lymington, 1977).

37. C.W. Elwood to Bombay, Porbandar 12 Jan. 1819, BA Sel. 73/294–9.

38. Advice passed on to Elwood personally, and cited in C.W. Elwood to Bombay, Porbandar 25 Feb. 1817, BA Sel. 72/302–4; it later finds its way into Low, *Indian Navy*, vol. 1, p. 341.

39. C.W. Elwood to Bombay, Porbandar 24 Nov. 1818, BA Sel. 71/143B–52. 'Jymer' is the usual spelling, though Macmurdo has the variant 'jâima': Capt. Macmurdo, Bhuj Resident, to Bombay, Mandvi 30 Jan. 1817 (text reads 1816), BA Sel. 72/231–2.

40. Elwood to Bombay, Porbandar 24 Nov. 1818, BA Sel. 71/143B–52. As was noted in the text above, Elwood's understanding of the nature and role of this vessel had increased since his arrival at Porbandar; and it was probably still developing.

41. See Appendix A, late 1818.

42. Elwood actually states at one point that jymers only appeared off Kathiawar, and perhaps also Cutch, when alongside the Qawasim. There are reasons for questioning his conviction: his intelligence was imperfect; he had a less than certain theory to support; it is difficult to see how these boats could act as pilots if they were unfamiliar with the area; and, besides, as Elwood himself acknowledges, the jymer was indistinguishable from the standard, small trading-craft. This last point suggests that the classification of vessels as jymers was not always rigidly exclusive and may have been partly circumstantial; the potential for a semi-circular argument here is plain. C.W. Elwood to Bombay, Porbandar 24 Nov. 1818, BA Sel. 71/143B–52.

43. Lt Guy, a sensible reporter, ascertained this much when he visited this coast in late January and early February 1819: the Chiefs of Luz and Makran also both allude to the Qawasim's visits to Pasni; and there is further support for the belief that the Qawasim visited the area in the fortunes of the survivors of the HC pattamar *Darya Daulat*. Extract of a letter from Lt Guy of the HCC *Psyche* to Supt of Marine Meriton, with Guy's reports on Sonmiani and Ormara, Porbandar 10 Feb. 1819, BA P 462/1290–1300; Translated letter from Mir Muhammad Khan of Luz to Bombay Governor Nepean, 4 Rab. II 1234 AH/31 Jan. 1819, BA Sel. 73/614–17; Husain bin Ubaid, Chief of Makran, to Bombay Governor, 14 Rajab 1234 AH/ 9 May 1819, BA Sel. 73/694–5; Chapter Six, the *Darya Daulat*.

44. The belief that the Qawasim disposed of part of their plunder on these coasts seems to have grown up from observation: in late 1818 in particular, Qasimi boats had seemed to disappear from the coasts of Cutch and Kathiawar, only to reappear at a relatively short interval without their loads. The validity of the deduction partly rests upon the question of whether the boats seen on the two occasions were really the same; this is, however, not demonstrated, and seems merely to have been assumed, particularly by Elwood, the principal commentator. Elwood also claims that his theory was supported by intelligence from Sunderjee Sewjee, who had contacts in Luz. Elwood's interpretation of later events, and in particular his implication of the Chief of Luz in this business, was to some extent challenged by Lt Guy, who had made investigations of his own at Sonmiani and Ormara. Nevertheless, Guy himself still supported the idea that captured cargoes were somehow disposed of early on; again for the reason that he believed he had seen the same boats deeply laden, then afterwards light. Guy failed to find any evidence for this on the ground. Extract of a letter from Lt Guy of the HCC *Psyche* to Supt of Marine Meriton, with Guy's reports on Sonmiani and Ormara, Porbandar 10 Feb. 1819, BA P 462/1290–1300; C.W. Elwood to Bombay, Porbandar, Agent's Office 17 April 1819, BA P 467/3180–6, and 12 Jan. 1819, BA Sel. 73/294–9.

45. Husain bin Ubaid, Chief of Makran, to Bombay Governor, 14 Rajab 1234 AH/9 May 1819 AD, and, translated letter from Mir Muhammad Khan of Luz to Governor Nepean, 4 Rab. II 1234/31 Jan. 1819, BA Sel. 73/694–5, 614–17; Amirs of Sind to Bombay Governor, enclosed in Minutes for 27 Feb. 1819, BA P 462/1438–41.

46. See Appendix A.

47. Luz is presumably Bela in Makran. Translated letter from Mir Muhammad Khan of Luz

to Governor Nepean, 4 Rab. II 1234 AH/31 Jan. 1819 AD, BA Sel. 73/614–17. (BA P 421/1062–4).

48. Extract of a letter from Lt Guy of the HCC *Psyche* to Supt of Marine Meriton, Porbandar 10 Feb. 1819, BA P 462/1290–6.

49. Translated letter from Mir Muhammad Khan of Luz to Governor Nepean, 4 Rab. II 1234 AH/31 Jan. 1819 AD, BA Sel. 73/614–17.

50. Petition of *c.* 36 native merchants of Bombay to Governor Nepean, Bombay 4 Nov. 1817, BA Sel. 72/448–50. There had been a similar group-petition from 30 Banyan and Parsee merchants of Bombay in December 1808.

51. C.W. Elwood to Bombay, Porbandar 18 Jan. 1819, BA Sel. 74/154–7.

Notes to Chapter Ten

1. And on Muscat's futile counter-measures. Maurizi, *Seyd Said*, p. 95.

2. In compiling this chronology of known events (now deposited at Exeter University's Centre for Arab Gulf Studies), my aim was as far as possible to include the following: all recorded maritime incidents in the Gulf, and all those elsewhere related to the Gulf, including captures, fighting, loss, intimidation and the general movements of shipping; all known facts of Qasimi history; the relevant maritime history of the Gulf, including British undertakings; and finally, other history which had some bearing on the Qawasim and the matters under consideration in this book, most notably the history of Oman and the smaller Gulf states. Far and away the main source for this chronology was the Bombay records housed at Exeter: this was supplemented with a certain amount of material from the India Office; and, where it seemed reasonable, by Ibn Bishr, Ibn Ruzaiq, the *Lam' al-Shihab* and Fasa'i; Maurizi, Buckingham, Morier and a few other works. Sources such as Maurizi, in particular, but also all the published material, require caution. My guiding principle throughout was not to trust anything but con-temporary material, and for this reason I inevitably discounted some of the events, supposed facts and chronology which have found their way into the generally available published accounts: the history of the Qawasim by Warden in Thomas, *Arabian Gulf Intelligence*, for example, does not qualify as a primary source and is unreliable. The contemporary material itself has to be stripped down to its likely factual core in order to become useful. In Chapter Eleven, by contrast with others in the body of this work, where quite exhaustive references are cited, these have been kept to a minimum, particularly for the period 1797–1820.

3. Specific incidents (the bars) are those where the number of vessels captured was precisely stated; other incidents (the symbol +?) are those where vessels were reported to have been captured, but their number was not specified (e.g. some, a few, many etc.). All the incidents off south Arabia were numerically specified, except in 1804.

Notes to Chapter Eleven

1. Niebuhr, *Travels through Arabia*, vol. 2, p. 153.

2. Letter from Matar bin Rahma to Seton, received at Qishm 21 Jan. 1806, in Resident Seton to Bombay, Muscat 4 March 1806, BA S&P 181/2399–430.

3. Both translations are contemporary: the original does not survive. David Seton's journal, entry for 21 Jan. 1806, al-Qasimi, 'Arab "Piracy"', Appendix 6, pp. 56–7.

4. For an account of the early history of the Qawasim according to 'traditional legend', repres-enting in part the group memory which survived on the Trucial coast in the 1820s and early 1830s, see Brucks, *Account of the Survey*, pp. 33–40.

5. According to Slot, Rahma was first referred to as Amir of Julfar soon after 1718: Slot, *The Arabs of the Gulf*, pp. 238–9, 190.

6. Slot, *The Arabs of the Gulf*, *passim*. Slot's book is one of the more rewarding published works on the local history of the lower Gulf during the seventeenth and eighteenth centuries, since it relies extensively on hitherto underused Dutch sources. I have used Slot's book as my main source for the early history of the Qawasim throughout this section. In addition to this I have in particular consulted the British records from Gombroon and Bushire, with Saldanha's *Persian Gulf Précis*, and found Risso's *Oman* sometimes useful.

7. Slot, *The Arabs of the Gulf*, pp. 24–5, 51, 250–1, 255, 266, 296, *passim*; al-Qasimi, *The Myth*, p. 12.

8. Sirhan bin Sa'id al-Izkawi, *Kashf al-Ghumma*, partially translated by E.C. Ross as *Annals of Oman to 1728* (Oleander Press, Cambridge, 1984), p. 63.

9. In 1807, Seton somewhat loosely described Qasimi country as stretching from Khaur Fakkan to Sharja and containing 'many tribes, the Shihuh, Zohery [Dhahuriyin], Qawasim, Banu Qitab and Banu Na'im etc.' He claims that before the rise of the Qawasim, the Na'im had enjoyed ascendancy in this area. David Seton, Muscat Resident, to Bombay, Baroda 2 July 1807, BA S&P 208/4937–50. Lorimer describes the Dhahuriyin as 'practically a part of the Shihuh tribe': Lorimer, *Gazetteer*, vol. 2, p. 433.

10. Cf. Wilkinson, *Imamate Tradition*, pp. 46–7.

11. Slot, *The Arabs of the Gulf*, 295, 328–9.

12. Dutch report of 1749, cited in Slot, *The Arabs of the Gulf*, p. 331.

13. S.B. Miles, *The Countries and Tribes of the Persian Gulf* (Frank Cass, London, 1966), p. 269.

14. It might be easier to take this as a reference to Sir, rather than to the Zaura tract between Hamriya and Ajman. Lorimer, *Gazetteer*, vol. 2, pp. 1947–8.

15. On the name 'Tschaid', see Slot, *The Arabs of the Gulf*, p. 330; and note also that Lorimer's Qasimi family tree, which is incorrect for the earlier eighteenth century but probably reflects family tradition, makes the first ancestor of the Qasimi family one Kaid/Chaid; whilst Brucks gives Rahma bin 'Keyed' or 'Kyed' instead of Rahma bin Matar, and similarly makes Kyed the founder of the Ras al-Khaima dynasty: Lorimer, *Gazetteer*, vol. 1, part 3, no. 2; Brucks, *Account of the Survey*, pp. 36–9.

16. Kniphausen's 1756 report on the Gulf, cited in Slot, *The Arabs of the Gulf*, pp. 329–31. According to the same report, Imam Ahmad of Muscat's navy at this stage comprised one usable small ship, a new 600-ton vessel purchased at Bombay and two gallivats, while his standing-army consisted of up to 500 African slaves armed with flintlocks and straight swords. In 1760, Rashid bin Matar and Mulla Ali Shah led 50 trankeys carrying 800–1,000 men against Bandar Abbas: a century earlier Julfar had attacked Kung using 25 trankeys. English Gombroon Diaries, IOR G/29/12 pp. 92–3; Slot, *The Arabs of the Gulf*, p. 190.

17. Floor, 'A Description of the Persian Gulf and Its Inhabitants in 1756', pp. 162–85. Floor's translation of the immediately preceding passage differs very slightly from Slot's. Texts have 'Houlas', 'Huwala' (Slot?), 'Quassum', 'Guassums'.

18. As, Saldanha, *Persian Gulf Précis*, pp. 137, 161; Slot, *The Arabs of the Gulf*, pp. 338, 344, 382; English Gombroon Diaries, IOR G/29/12 p. 67; D. Seton, Muscat Resident, to Bombay, Baroda 2 July 1807, BA S&P 208/4937–50.

19. This last according to Kniphausen: 'The inhabitants of Lenge are called Mersousies. They are 50 large and small vessels and 700 men strong, of which 350 are armed with matchlocks. They are poor and live from firewood and charcoal, which is plentiful near them, and which they transport throughout the Gulf. Their present chief is called sjeek Saijd [Shaikh Sa'id], he keeps up a good friendship with us.' Again according to Kniphausen, it seems, the Qawasim settled Al Haram sailors and fishermen at Laft after they had captured the place. Floor, 'A Description of the Persian Gulf and Its Inhabitants in 1756', pp. 167–8; Slot, *The Arabs of the Gulf*, pp. 385–6, 343–4, 23–5, *passim*; Gombroon Diaries, IOR G/29/12 p. 97; D. Seton, Muscat Resident, to Bombay, Baroda 2 July 1807, BA S&P 208/4937–50.

20. Kung had by the 1750s declined to a faint shadow of her former self. Slot, *The Arabs of the Gulf*, p. 23. Ras al-Hiti lies just west of Linga in Niebuhr's map, and would appear to correspond roughly with Ras Bustana.

21. 'Un assez bon commerce'.

22. Carsten Niebuhr, *Description de l'Arabie* (S.J. Baalde, Amsterdam, 1774), pp. 266–7, 284, 271–83.

23. John Beaumont, Resident, to Bombay, Bushire 17 Jan. 1779, IOR R/15/1/3 pp. 10–11.

24. The war and attendant insecurity were still in evidence in July 1780: Saldanha, *Persian Gulf Précis*, p. 315.

25. J. Beaumont, Resident, to Bombay, Bushire 16 March 1779, IOR R/15/1/3 pp. 16–18.

26. Accompanying the proposed restoration of the vessel was a promise not to molest British shipping. The Resident felt sensible that had he accepted the offer he would have been purchasing not only the ship, at a high cost, but also Rashid's friendship. J. Beaumont, Resident, to Basra, Bushire 10 March 1779, IOR R/15/1/3 pp. 15–16.

27. The statement that Rashid had been Governor of Bandar Abbas (Gombroon) looks surprising, but in the absence of full records cannot perhaps be discounted. Rashid had succeeded his brother Rahma in 1760, and in the same year he and Mulla Ali Shah certainly plundered Bandar Abbas, as Rahma had done in 1759. At all events 1760 was possibly something of a high point for the Qawasim.

28. J. Beaumont, Resident, to Bombay, Bushire 17 Jan. 1779, IOR R/15/1/3 pp. 10–11.

29. Seton was referring very roughly to the last years of Imam Ahmad's rule when he wrote, 'The Cassmee [Qawasim] now appeared as traders and in a very few years by their activity attained to great riches'. D. Seton, Muscat Resident, to Bombay, Baroda 2 July 1807, BA S&P 208/4937–50.

30. William Latouche, Resident, to Bombay, Basra 4 Nov.(?) 1782, BA S&P 27/851–3; Risso, *Oman*, pp. 64–5.

31. Utub, adjective Utbi. Bushire Resident to Bombay, 28 Feb., 12 Oct., 31 Dec. 1783 and 22 Feb. 1785, and to Basra 19 Oct. 1783, IOR R/15/1/3 pp. 98–9, 107–9, 120–1.

32. It should be reiterated that henceforward, for the rest of this chapter, for reasons of space and manageability, exhaustive references will not be cited. The account is based upon the detailed chronology, compiled from the available primary sources, referred to early in the last chapter.

33. Captain John Malcolm's report on trade between Persia and India, Bushire 26 Feb. 1800, Saldanha, *Persian Gulf Précis*, vol. 1, pp. 442–55.

34. D. Seton, Muscat Resident, to Bombay, Baroda 2 July 1807, BA S&P 208/4937–50.

35. David Seton's Journal from Muscat to Bahrain and back, 31 Sept.–13 Dec. 1801, BA S&P 119/77–100.

36. The murder of the Wahhabi ruler Abd al-Aziz in perhaps October 1803, and the succession of his son Su'ud, might presumably also have been a factor.

37. Abu Hakima (ed.), *Lam' al-Shihab*, pp. 79–83.

38. As, it seems, was Charak itself: see Chapter Thirteen, section three.

39. This vulnerability was evident in 1777 when Shaikh Abdullah of the Banu Mu'in, who had been attacking Muscat merchant-shipping, was readily inveigled aboard a Muscat ship and taken prisoner. J. Beaumont, Resident, Bushire 6 Jan. 1778, IOR R/15/1/2 pp. 61–2.

40. Sultan bin Saqr was married to Mulla Hasan's daughter. In a parallel fashion, Salim bin Sultan bin Ahmad of the Al Bu Sa'id was married to the daughter of Mulla Hasan's rival cousin Saqr bin Abdullah of the Banu Mu'in, Governor of Minab.

41. W. Bruce, Acting Resident, to Bombay, 12 Jan. 1805, and to Manesty, 27 Nov. 1804, BA S&P 164A/596, 610–14: Bruce's specific statement that British captives of the Qawasim were in November 1804 taken to Bukha is, however, likely to be wrong, for Ajman appears correct; see Chapter Thirteen, section three.

42. Sadleir, *Journey Across Arabia*, p. 36; BA Sel. 74/281–303. Cf. the way in which the Shaikh of Bukha featured in the affair of Bruce's baghla in December 1814.

43. D. Seton, Resident, to Bombay, Muscat 23 May 1805, BA S&P 168/2862–73; and Bombay 20 Feb. 1805, 165/897–9.

44. D. Seton, Resident, to Bombay, Muscat 4 March 1806, BA S&P 181/2355–8. Seton speaks of Khaur Kalba, not Kalba, as do Sayyid Taqi and the commanders of the first expedition in 1809. In 1811, the ruler of Muscat's agent described an Omani expedition against Kalba.

45. These words, or at least the sentiment they convey, are probably ascribed by Seton to Sultan bin Saqr of Ras al-Khaima's negotiator, Ibn Qurush. D. Seton, Resident, to Bombay, Muscat 4 March 1806, with enclosed diary, BA S&P 181/2399–430.

46. By way of comparison, in July 1805 the projected size of the forthcoming Basra fleet had been put at 60 dows and 3,000–4,000 men.

47. Note the rather curious and hostile portrait of the Suris and their relations with Ras al-Khaima in, Henry Rudland to Henry Salt, Ambassador to Abyssinia, British Residency Mocha, 1 Jan. 1810, BA P 358/2898–903; other papers, BA P 358/2916–23, 2976–84, 379/4855–7.

48. Ibn Bishr, *Unwan al-Majd*, vol. 1, pp. 284–5, 293–4, 297–9; under years 1220, 1222, 1223 (widespread famine, with epidemic in Najd), 1224 (epidemic and flooding), 1229 AH (epidemic). D. Seton, Resident, to Bombay, Muscat 17 Nov. 1807, BA S&P 216/8228–33. (BA P 399/2679–81, southern Iran 1812–13)

49. Muscat only managed to install garrisons at Hormuz and Qishm at the end of 1807, but even then most of Qishm was under Qasimi or Wahhabi control, as were the islands of the lower Gulf.

50. This word, like a number of others in this letter, is unclear: ruq'a, raqqa, rauq etc.? or simply a corruption of Fakkan? The text used is a copy of the translation of an Arabic original, and there are spelling mistakes in the English.

51. Text reads 'Surrah': something along the lines of Surra (Sarra, Sirra), Sarra'?

52. 'Sor'. If the text is not corrupt, one imagines this to refer to the people of Sur, in particular perhaps the Janaba; it does not, from the way it is written, seem to read 'sura'. Text apart, the reading Sur is strained.

53. army? A hiatus in the text.

54. I.e. presumably Wahhabis: this appears to be the best reading, rather than, say, 'Duru''; the word in question appears to be written in the same way here as later in the letter, where it ought to signify 'Dir'iya'.

55. Text reads 'prossessing'.

56. I.e. Azzan bin Qais and Sayyid Sa'id (bin Sultan).

57. I.e., presumably, with Wahhabism and the Saudi state.

58. I.e. the Qawasim of Sur are likewise converts to Wahhabism.

59. Extract from one of two translated letters from Matar bin Rahma bin Rashid al-Qasimi to Rashid bin Rahma bin Rashid al-Qasimi at Bhavnagar, the other dated 26 Ram. 1223/ 15 Nov. 1808, entered under date 14 April 1809, BA P 327/3557–66.

60. W. Watts, Asst Resident, to Bombay, Barka 4–6 Aug. 1808, BA S&P 243/9867–72.

61. Though greatly diminished and otherwise difficult to quantify, he must still have possessed informal influence elsewhere. In February 1809, for example, there was evidence of split authority at Fujaira: a Wahhabi officer held charge over the comings and goings of boats, but his orders regarding the detention of a Muscat boat on an errand to Sultan bin Saqr were after a time circumvented by the garrison, which was still in the pay of Sultan bin Saqr.

62. Note Moyse-Bartlett, *The Pirates*, p. 107.

63. D. Seton, Resident, to Malcolm, Muscat 6 March 1809, BA P 325/2692–701.

64. It is difficult to be absolutely certain about the precise family relationship between the Linga and Ras al-Khaima branches of the family. Our information derives from Seton, who understandably displayed occasional lapses in such matters. In 1801 he said the ruler of Linga was Saqr of Ras al-Khaima's brother, and in 1805 he described Qadib of Linga as Sultan bin Saqr of Ras al-Khaima's uncle: in the first half of 1809, or perhaps 1808, he described Qadib bin Su'ud bin Qadib of Linga as nephew to Sultan bin Saqr. If these statements were all correct they would imply that Qadib I was Saqr's brother, and that he was succeeded between 1805 and 1809 by his grandson Qadib II (bin Su'ud bin Qadib), whose mother was also Sultan bin Saqr's sister. By 1815, Muhammad bin Qadib, presumably the son of Qadib II, had succeeded at Linga. (An alternative reading of Seton's information might be to assume that there was only one Qadib, possibly a half-brother of Saqr, and that the 1808/9 information was a mistake, but this is a very forced reading). BA S&P 119/77–100; 171/ 4341–3, 173/5391–402; Thomas, *Arabian Gulf Intelligence*, pp. 18–20; BA Sel. 72/76–9; BA P 425/2432–6.

65. Memorandum by Sayyid Taqi, with accompanying map of the coast between Ras al-Hadd and Abu Hail, and Board's deliberations and letter to Capt. J. Wainwright of 6 Jan. 1810,

BA P 350/116–38: the memorandum's date is given according to the corresponding entry in the catalogue of the Bombay Archives. Also loose copies of contemporary sketch-maps, which appear to derive from the same source in, al-Qasimi, 'Arab "Piracy"', Appendices 13–14 (8 and 10).

66. Memorandum by David Seton, first half of 1809, or perhaps 1808, cited in Robert Taylor's 1818 compilation on the Persian Gulf, Thomas, *Arabian Gulf Intelligence*, pp. 18–20, or BA Sel. 74/76–9.

67. When Sayyid Sa'id urged Britain to break with the Jalahima, he was told, 'it was supposed in Bombay the piracy proceeded from the Qawasim'. D. Seton, Resident, to Malcolm, Muscat 21 March 1809, BA P 326/3243–50.

68. Maurizi, *Seyd Said*, pp. 54–8; Bombay Council to Fort William, 22 Nov. 1809, BA P 346/10961–6. Cf. al-Qasimi, 'Arab "Piracy"', Appendix 1, pp. 1–10, Muscat trankeys.

69. Report of British expedition to Court of Directors, al-Qasimi, 'Arab "Piracy"', Appendix 1, pp. 1–10.

70. Ibn Ruzaiq, *Imams and Seyyids*, p. 321.

71. Capt. J. Wainwright to Bombay, HMS *Chiffone*, off Ras al-Khaima 14 Nov. 1809, BA P 347/11164–5.

72. E.g. Vishandass, Broker, to Bombay, Muscat 2 Oct. 1811, with Sayyid Sa'id's, BA P 380/4908–15.

73. Ibn Bishr, *Unwan al-Majd*, vol. 1, pp. 305–6.

74. Text reads 'stated'.

75. Translation of letter from Su'ud bin Abd al-Aziz to British Envoy, undated (probably April 1809), enclosed in Assistant Babington to Bombay, Bushire (May?), Minutes of 6 June 1809, BA P 358/3061–70.

76. 'Ras al-Khaima was found to contain goods of very considerable value ... and nothing seemed to have been removed into the interior, many warehouses being found filled with valuable goods, which were now set on fire and consumed. All these valuables might with ease have been embarked on board the captured vessels, which was suggested at the time, but the commanders acted on the principle that the British forces had come to inflict vengeance, and not acquire gain.' Looting was not therefore strictly permitted, but some treasure and jewels found by the troops were left in their possession: one soldier was famously reputed to have found 1,400 gold mohurs, worth just short of 2,000 English guineas. Low, *Indian Navy*, vol. 1, pp. 329–30; *Asiatic Annual Register*, 1809, cited in al-Qasimi, *The Myth*, p. 139.

77. Anonymous report of the expedition to Court of Directors, (Bombay Castle 1810?), al-Qasimi, 'Arab "Piracy"', Appendix 1, pp. 1–10.

78. W. Bruce to Bombay, HCC *Mercury*, Hanjam Sound 28 Nov. and off Sharja 2 Dec. 1816, BA Sel. 72/75–130; the Muscat Broker had reported fortification already in 1814, Cassee Goolab to Bombay, Muscat 14 May 1814, BA P 412/2922–6.

79. Maurizi, *Seyd Said*, p. 93.

80. There may possibly have been a Qasimi attack on Kangan itself soon after this: Edward Matson of the *Moholar* to Bombay, Bushire 9 Feb. 1812, with W. Bruce to Bombay, Bushire 1 Feb. 1812, BA P 383/394–6.

81. F. Warden's Minute of 12 Aug. 1819, BA Sel. 72/1–62. Bombay Board's resolution of 19(?) Feb. 1811, with enclosure, BA P 370/914–22. For a very late account of these matters, see Brucks, *Account of the Survey*, pp. 49–54, alleging that Qasimi vessels were laid up during the expedition at Dubai and Abu Dhabi, and Cape Musandam.

82. N.H. Smith, Resident, to Bombay, Muscat 13 April 1810, BA 355/2205–12; Vishandass, Broker, to Bombay, Muscat 18 Aug. 1811, BA P 378/4235–9; Maurizi, *Seyd Said*, pp. 92–6. Smith, like Morier in 1808, erroneously refers to 'Sauleh bin Sauleh'; the Broker identifies him correctly as Salih bin Muhammad. Maurizi's is the last reference to Salih. It seems to refer to the latter half of 1814, when he was supposedly responsible for increased predatory cruising off the Muscat coast, but erroneously portrays him as head of the Qawasim of Wahhabi Ras al-Khaima: the specific reference may therefore be unreliable, but still no doubt reflects Salih's stature in the aftermath of Sultan bin Saqr's fall. One supposes that Salih died at the latest soon after late 1814.

83. Sultan bin Saqr was Hasan bin Rahma's first cousin once removed.
84. Buckingham, *Travels in Assyria*, pp. 481–3. Cf. Loch, *Diaries*, TS p. 338, of Hasan bin Rahma in affecting defeat, 27 Dec. 1819: 'He was of middling size, his features marked, strong and prominent; replete with a restless jealousy and suspicion, having a full, brilliant, hazel eye, constantly on the enquiry of what was passing in the minds of those in his presence.' Keffeas i.e. *kufiyas*.
85. N.H. Smith, Bushire Resident, report of an interview with Sayyid Sa'id held on 13 April 1810, in Smith to Bombay, HCC *Mornington*, off Muscat 14 April 1810, BA P 355/2212–21.
86. Sayyid Sa'id to Bombay Governor, 26 March 1810, BA S 264/1287–91: Ibn Bishr, *Unwan al-Majd*, vol. 1, pp. 317–19; Ibn Ruzaiq, *Imams and Seyyids*, pp. 318–20: W. Bruce, Resident, to Bombay, Bushire Governor's intelligence from Asalu, Bushire 29 May 1811, BA P 378/4346–50.
87. Ibn Ruzaiq, *Imams and Seyyids*, pp. 320–4; *al-Fath al-Mubin*, pp. 517–20.
88. In addition to forces supplied by Sultan bin Saqr, Linga and allied Arab rulers on the Persian shore, Shaikh Shakhbut of Abu Dhabi was to have contributed 2,000 men and the Al Khalifa of Bahrain were expected to give 15–20 boats with 2,000 men. The British Resident William Bruce also accompanied Sayyid Sa'id with HMS *Hesper* and the HCC *Ternate* as far as Abu Dhabi: he had initially hoped to witness the signing of a peace and perhaps make one of his own, but in the end preferred to avoid entanglement; Sayyid Sa'id credited his presence with having encouraged the formation of a broad alliance.
89. In addition to seeking to mobilize forces under the Banu Yas rulers of Dubai and Abu Dhabi, Hazza' and Shakhbut, Sayyid Sa'id had initially appealed for assistance on as broad a front as possible, addressing invitations to Bushire, Bahrain, Britain and some of the Persian ports, but with scant positive response.
90. Keir to Adjutant-General, HMS *Liverpool*, off Sharja 5 Feb. 1820, BA P 479/1257–78. One of the few clear examples of Sultan bin Saqr using his vessels in naval action relates to an incident in April 1814, when he tried to engage Rahma bin Jabir near Sharja.
91. In response to Sultan bin Saqr's overtures in summer 1814, Shiraz bestowed a robe of honour upon him, hoping he might assist in Persian designs on Bahrain. Sultan bin Saqr also took the opportunity of his envoy passing through Bushire to offer Britain his services over the *Ahmad Shah* affair.
92. I presume: Bruce's 'mullah or chief priest'. W. Bruce, Resident, to Bombay, HMS *Curlew*, off Qais 14 Feb. 1820, BA S 315/362–73, BA P 480/1820–35. Ibn Bishr, *Unwan al-Majd*, vol. 1, pp. 362–4, 423–4. Ibn Bishr's later group-lists of Saudi officials gives three categories for Oman as a whole: the Amir (the Qasimi Shaikh); the Qadi; and the military Commander-in-Chief, who was probably generally based at Buraimi.
93. There is slight evidence from 1820 that Sultan bin Saqr may by then have begun to involve his own 20-year old brother Salih bin Saqr in government, but there is no indication that he was relatively at all as prominent as Hasan bin Rahma's brother Ibrahim had been. Lt Thomas Tanner to Maillard, Political Agent Dairistan, HCC *Antelope*, Hanjam Sound 23 Aug. 1820, BA P 492/6479–90; Thomas, *Arabian Gulf Intelligence*, pp. 293–4.
94. Cf. perhaps Capt. Edward Barnard to Bombay, HMS *Conway*, off Cape Bardistan 19 Oct. 1818, BA P 455/5969–73.
95. W. Bruce, Resident, to Bombay, Bushire 23 Jan. 1815, BA P 420/582–7, relaying information supplied by 'an intelligent native from the coast'.
96. Figures derived from the Arabic version of a report characterized by Bruce as 'the most correct information carefully compiled and communicated by a learned and intelligent Arab'. The original report reads 'Banu Bu Ali' not 'Al Ali'. The English translation gives 700 not 70 for the number of Qawasim, and the Arabic original reads literally 'seventy/0070': the latter is to be preferred. Arabic text, 22 Jan. 1817, BA Sel. 74/416–17; translation in W. Bruce, Resident, to Bombay 26 Jan. 1817, BA P 312/1038–72, (BA Sel. 74/396–409, 416–17).
97. W. Bruce, Resident, to Bombay, HMS *Curlew*, off Qais 14 Feb. 1820, BA S 315/362–73, BA P 480/1820–35.

98. Hasan bin Rahma to Resident Bruce, (Ras al-Khaima?) 26 Aug. 1814, BA P 419/126–8. Cf. Sultan bin Saqr's wishes during the 1805–6 Anglo–Qasimi negotiations, and Rahma bin Jabir's like request to the Resident in August 1814 for permission to visit British Indian ports. In 1814, Bruce proposed that a ban be imposed upon the export of timber from Bombay and Malabar, which indicates that there was none then: the idea does not seem to have been taken up. A remark by Colquhoun at about the same time seems to imply that the Qawasim were then shut out of Malabar: strictly speaking, this need not be incompatible with Bruce's statement. G. Colquhoun to Bombay, Basra 29 Dec. 1814, BA P 419/295–305; W. Bruce to Bombay, Bushire 23 Jan. 1815, BA P 420/582–7.

99. W. Bruce, Resident, to Bombay, HCC *Mercury*, Hanjam Sound 28 Nov. 1816, and off Sharja 2 Dec. 1816, BA Sel. 72/75–130.

100. Goolab Anundass, Broker, to Bombay, Muscat 16 Oct. 1817, BA Sel. 72/454–6.

101. G. Colquhoun to Bombay, Basra 29 Dec. 1814, BA P 419/295–305.

102. The 1,111-ton frigate *Shaw Allum*'s dimensions were 181 ft. 3 in. by 41 ft. 5 in. Anon, *Oman, a Seafaring Nation*, pp. 76–7.

103. Maurizi, *Seyd Said*, pp. 92–6.

104. One of the baghlas had been carrying some property belonging to the Muscat Broker.

105. I.e. the *Caroline*. The British continued to apply the title of Imam to the rulers of Muscat even after it had passed away from them.

106. W. Bruce to Bombay, Bushire 9 June 1815, BA P 422/1572–3. Text reads 'dingeys'.

107. Muscat Broker to Bombay, 26 (should probably read 25) April 1815, BA P 421/1069–70; 18 May, 422/1268–70; and 20 June, 422/1438–40. W. Bruce, Resident, to Bombay, Bushire 9 June 1815, BA P 422/1572–5.

108. Buckingham, *Travels in Assyria*, p. 356.

109. Naqib of Mukalla to Bombay Governor, 5 May 1816, BA P 430/1310–13.

110. Hasan bin Rahma to Resident Bruce, 27 Nov. 1816, Arabic text and translation, BA Sel. 72/110–15.

111. They recognized that the most potent counter-measure would have been a diversionary Wahhabi land-attack on Muscat.

112. Ruler of Muscat to Bombay Governor, 27 July 1816, BA S 312/1023–6.

113. The Saudi ruler Abdullah bin Su'ud.

114. Abdullah bin Ahmad of Bahrain to Resident Bruce, received at Bushire 12 Jan. 1817, BA Sel. 72/437.

115. W. Bruce to Bombay, Bushire 23 Jan. 1815, BA P 420/582–7; Loch to Bombay, HMS *Eden*, Muscat 2 Jan. 1819, BA Sel. 73/318–26, BA P 460/488–93. Bruce cited local intelligence to the effect that Qasimi crews were made up of '6,000 of the Utub and other tribes with a number of Coffree slaves': this might conceivably indicate that some individuals or groups from Bahrain sought service on Qasimi boats. Loch's information, to the effect that 20–30 Bahraini boats and 12,000–13,000 men 'assisted' the Qawasim, emerges from an interrogation of captured Qasimi crew: it cannot really mean quite what it seems to imply, and probably was intended as a neutral description of Bahrain's strength and her relationship of friendship with Ras al-Khaima.

116. Nasir Khan of Laristan was instrumental in this development.

117. The ruler of Nakhilu just before the first British expedition had been Yusuf bin Rahma bin Sanad Sulbukhi, whose sister, according to Seton, was married to Sultan bin Saqr. Seton's report, c. late 1808 or early 1809, cited by Taylor in 1818, Thomas, *Arabian Gulf Intelligence*, pp. 18–20, BA Sel. 74/76–9. Also at this time, or just conceivably in late 1818, the 'Wahhabis'—probably the Qawasim and their allies on the Persian coast—reportedly seized one of the Shaikh of Charak's vessels returning from Muscat, causing a state of mutual hostility to persist thereafter into 1820: John McNeill, local information, Feb. 1820, BA S 315/355–62.

118. W. Bruce, Resident, to Bombay, Bushire 16 Oct. 1817, BA Sel. 72/480–2.

119. Sultan bin Saqr to Bombay Governor, (Sharja) 22 Aug. 1820, BA P 492/6535–7.

120. The *Cornwall* sailed from Bombay on 8 April 1819, reaching Muscat on 26 April, Bushire on 14 May, Bahrain on 19 May, Bushire on 11 June, Matrah on 13 July and Bombay again

on 24 July: she took on cargo at Muscat, delivered some at Bushire and discharged 687 bags of rice at Bahrain (23 May–2 June). The *Cornwall* later participated in the 1819/20 expedition against the Qawasim. The *Cornwall* was a 423-ton ship, 116½ ft. long by 29 broad, built at Plymouth in 1794. Log of the Ship *Cornwall*, 9 November 1818 to 31 March 1821, National Library of Scotland MS 9661.

121. Richardson to Governor Nepean, Bombay 1 Sept. 1819, BA Sel. 75/100–2.

122. Ibn Bishr, *Unwan al-Majd*, vol. 1, pp. 425–30.

123. W. Bruce, Resident, to Bombay, Bushire 17 Oct. 1818, BA P 456/5978–9; Capt. E. Barnard to Bombay, HMS *Conway*, off Bardistan 19 Oct. 1818, BA P 455/5969–73; and cf. Brucks, *Account of the Survey*, pp. 68–9.

124. Uqair was by far the main channel for trade between Bahrain and the interior. Sadleir, *Journey Across Arabia*, pp. 50–3.

125. Ibn Bishr, *Unwan al-Majd*, vol. 1, pp. 431–3, 450–1; Abu Hakima (ed.), *Lam' al-Shihab*, p. 177; Sadleir, *Journey Across Arabia*, pp. 35–9, 150–4, and BA Sel. 74/281–303.

126. In March 1820, several shaikhs from Najd, who had taken refuge at Ras al-Khaima, applied to be admitted to the General Treaty, without result. Capt. Thomas Perronet Thompson to Military Secretary Wilson, Ras al-Khaima later March 1820, and Wilson to Thompson, HMS *Liverpool*, off Ras al-Khaima 25 March 1820, BA S 316/497–502, 510–15.

127. The Anglo-Irish George Forster Sadleir (1789–1859) served in HM 47th of Foot from 1805 till 1837, though for the last decade he saw no active service; in 1837 he became Sheriff of Cork, like his father before him, and subsequently he emigrated to New Zealand. Sadleir, *Journey Across Arabia*, introduction by F.M. Edwards, pp. 3–18. (Sadleir, not Sadlier, appears to be the correct spelling: e.g. also BA Sel. 74/303.)

128. Ibn Bishr, *Unwan al-Majd*, vol. 1, pp. 423–4, 362–4.

129. It is therefore not clear what, if anything, the 100 Ottoman horsemen who were said to have come to Buraimi in November 1819 achieved: Company Broker to Bombay, Muscat 25 Nov. 1818, BA P 456/6338–41.

130. Capt. Walpole to Bombay, HMS *Curlew*, Bushire 7 June 1819, BA Sel. 73/649–55.

131. These ports, lying opposite Ras al-Khaima, were also particularly susceptible to *force majeure*. The resources of the five Persian ports in armed men and large boats is given as: Linga, 725 men and 5 boats, Mughu, 142 men and 3 boats, Charak, 452 men and 5 boats, Tahuna, 70 men and 2 boats and Kalat, 490 men and 5 boats; or a total of 1879 men. The total for boats should probably come to 19, which means one of the numbers cited is out by one. Dep. Med. Storekeeper John McNeill, information collected from inhabitants of Qais and some of those from opposite shore, corroborated by shaikhs Harun and Yusuf, sons of Shaikh Barakat formerly of Charak, Feb. 1820, BA S 315/355–62. W. Bruce to Keir, HMS *Curlew*, off Qais, 20 Feb. 1820, BA S 315/350–5.

132. Umm al-Qaiwain may possibly have assisted him somewhat.

133. In 1829 Sayyid Sa'id is reported to have prepared for his absence on the African coast by settling an annual payment on the Qasimi shaikhs, including 2,000 German crowns a year for Sultan bin Saqr. Thomas, *Arabian Gulf Intelligence*, p. 324.

134. Translation and text of Hasan bin Rahma to Bruce, 8 Sept. 1819, received at Bushire 23 Sept., BA S 313/1796–8, Sel. 76/97–100.

135. Translation of Hasan bin Rahma to Loch, (mid–late March), received at Bushire 3 April 1819, BA Sel. 73/519–21.

136. Abdullah bin Ahmad to Bruce, enclosing Hasan bin Rahma to Abdullah bin Ahmad (late Feb./early March), Bahrain 23 March, received at Bushire 29 March, 1819, BA Sel. 73/498–502; translations of three letters from Hasan bin Rahma to Capt. Conyers of the HCC *Mercury*, one to his man Sulaiman, and one from Ibrahim bin Rahma to Conyers, Ras al-Khaima mid-March 1819, BA Sel. 73/597–610.

137. Translations of three letters from Hasan bin Rahma to Capt. Conyers of the HCC *Mercury*, one to his man Sulaiman, and one from Ibrahim bin Rahma to Conyers, Ras al-Khaima mid-March 1819, BA Sel. 73/597–610.

138. Junior Police Magistrate to Chief Sec., Bombay 29 May 1819, BA Sel. 73/611–12.

139. W. Bruce, Resident, to Bombay, Bushire 16 Nov. 1819, BA Sel. 73/195–9; F.E. Loch to

Bombay, HMS *Eden*, Bushire Roads 18 Nov. 1819, BA Sel. 73/234–7; Loch, *Diaries*, TS pp. 318–20.

140. A night raid on the mortar position, which was bloody on both sides. Loch, *Diaries*, TS p. 324. Cf. Journal of a Voyage from Glasgow to Bombay and the Persian Gulf, 1828, National Library of Scotland MS 9594, pp. 270–1.

141. Loch, *Diaries*, TS p. 333.

142. William Grant Keir to Adjutant-General, Ras al-Khaima 3 Jan. 1820, BA P 477/545–50.

143. Brucks was later told by shaikhs on the Trucial coast that large numbers of mercenaries had become unemployed when the Maratha wars ended in 1818, many of them finding their way to the Gulf and Ras al-Khaima; observing, 'Those engaged in the Pindarrie and Mahratta wars can bear testimony to the intrepid conduct of the [Arab] mercenaries'. It might be easiest to speculate that the mercenaries at Ras al-Khaima were local Arabs, from Greater Oman. There is separate evidence in the records of these decades for Omanis seeking military service in north-west India, while conversely rulers of Muscat employed Baluchi and other mercenaries. The Baroda Resident had in 1802 relayed disapproving reports that between 2,000 and 3,000 potential Arab mercenaries annually entered Gujarat and Cutch; 600 had arrived that same year at Surat, besides others at Bhavnagar and Cutch ports: 'All of these adventurers come from Arabia with arms in their hands and look only to their swords for a livelihood. They have no acquaintance with industry and consider India merely as a field for plunder.' Major Alexander Walker to Bombay, Baroda 9 Oct. 1802, BA S&P 129/6090–1. Brucks, *Account of the Survey*, pp. 43B; 66B. Low, *Indian Navy*, vol. 1, pp. 354–8.

144. The Banu Yas ports of Dubai and Abu Dhabi acceded to the General Treaty on 28 and 11 January respectively. Out of consideration for his loyalty to Sayyid Sa'id, the minor Muhammad bin Hazza' bin Za'al of Dubai was promised that his town would not be plundered or destroyed: a number of Dubai boats were by accident burnt. There was no destruction at Abu Dhabi. Keir had sought information on Shaikh Shakhbut of Abu Dhabi: Shaikh Hamza of Qishm reported to Surgeon Jukes that he had been a staunch supporter of Sayyid Sa'id, had acknowledged the Wahhabis but not adopted their faith, and had merely maintained friendly relations with the Qawasim and others for the sake of peace, without ever being involved in their maritime activities. The Governor of Bandar Abbas's son (or possibly the Governor himself: 'Aga Hussein Alee son of Khoja Abdul Guffoor Governor of Bunder Abbass') acknowledged Shakhbut's good relations with Sultan bin Saqr and the Qawasim, but shared the same favourable opinion of his conduct, commenting upon his intercourse with Qishm and Bandar Abbas. A separate report also spoke of Abu Dhabi's good relations with Muscat, and set her population at 9,000–10,000 who lived in huts along the beach without any wall, fished for pearls, and imported dates and rice from Bahrain and elsewhere. Reports of Shaikh Hamza and Aqa Husain Ali, Ras al-Khaima 11 Jan. 1820, BA S 315/175–6. (Cf. Thomas, *Arabian Gulf Intelligence*, p. 464.) Lt McDonald's report 24 March–3 May 1820, BA P 486/3950–8.

145. Iran promised to introduce similar arrangements at her own ports concerning papers and so forth as were envisaged in the General Treaty. Willock to Bombay, Tehran 11 May and 4 June 1820, with enclosures including letter to Keir of 10 March, BA P 492/6640–64. Chief Sec. F. Warden to Willock, Bombay Castle 15 Dec. 1819, BA S 314/2104–15.

146. Cf. Horsburgh, *India Directory*, in Cook, *Survey*, vol. 1, pp. 286–7, of Rams: 'The inhabitants were greatly distressed in 1822, by the destruction of their trading boats, which forced many of them to emigrate.'

147. Lorimer, *Gazetteer*, vol. 1, pp. 689–90; Brucks, *Account of the Survey*, pp. 79, 89, 92, and likewise in Thomas, *Arabian Gulf Intelligence*, p. 541.

148. Figures are recorded in tables for 1826, 1831 and 1845(?): Thomas, *Arabian Gulf Intelligence*, pp. 100–1, 327–8.

149. 'A square fort, with flanking round towers, built of rough stone and coarse lime, capable of containing, in case of siege, from four to six hundred men; with detached round towers for the defence of the creek and landing-place, and to cover the wells that supply the inhabitants with water (situated usually at some short distance), make up the general features of

Arab fortifications. The town consists of cadjan huts, constructed of date sticks and mats, around the fort on every side. Stone dwelling-houses are rare, and Sharja and Ras al-Khaima can alone boast of them.' Lt Kemball, Assistant Resident, 'Memoranda on the Resources, Localities, and Relations of the Tribes Inhabiting the Arabian Shores of the Persian Gulf', 6 Jan. 1845, in Thomas, *Arabian Gulf Intelligence*, p. 99.

150. Camp follower's account from *Bombay Courier*, cited in Moyse-Bartlett, *The Pirates*, pp. 129–30.
151. Mrs Thompson, cited in Moyse-Bartlett, *The Pirates*, p. 130.
152. Camp follower's account from *Bombay Courier*, cited in Moyse-Bartlett, *The Pirates*, pp. 129–30.
153. Thomas, *Arabian Gulf Intelligence*, p. 322.
154. Capt. T.P. Thompson to Bombay, Ras al-Khaima 15 May 1820, BA S 316/4280–308.
155. Lorimer, *Gazetteer*, vol. 1, pp. 689–90.
156. One speculates that the pearling was the reason for the large figure of 2,000 men, and that many of these would disperse after the season was over. Capt. T.P. Thompson, garrison commander, to Bombay, Ras al-Khaima 15 May 1820, BA P 486/4280–308.
157. W.G. Keir to Chief Sec. Warden, 1 April 1820, BA S 316/453–68.
158. Lorimer, *Gazetteer*, vol. 1, pp. 689–90.

Notes to Chapter Twelve

1. The statement that the largest vessels had a maximum draught of seven feet was made by Houghton, who surveyed this coast in 1821–2: it accords with the only contemporary estimate of the draught of large Qasimi dows, in an official account of the first expedition dating to around 1810, of ten feet when at sea. Although one report went as high as eleven feet, the best estimate of the maximum depth over the sandbar protecting the harbour at Ras al-Khaima was nine feet, which should naturally have exceeded the maximum draught of any vessel there. In the light of the few measurements and estimates that have come down to us, it is slightly surprising that baghlas over 300 tons should have drawn only seven feet unladen: Arabs vessels probably carried no ballast. The design may of course have varied. By way of comparison, Hawkins describes a 'brig' under construction at Beypore in Kerala in the early 1970s, which was planned to have a capacity of 250 tons, and to draw 8 feet and 5½ feet in ballast. Houghton, 'Account of Part of the Southern Coast', in Cook, *Survey*, vol. 1, p. 108; al-Qasimi, 'Arab "Piracy"', Appendix 1, pp. 1–10; Lorimer, *Gazetteer*, vol. 1, pp. 2321–9; Hawkins, *The Dhow*, pp. 84–5, 100, 110, 125. Cf. e.g. the ship *Fazool Kerreem* of Bombay, 358 tons, 9 feet light, 16 laden: tender, Bombay 2 Nov. 1819, BA S 314/1920–2.
2. Company cruisers preferred to anchor two or three miles offshore; the largest ships in the 1809/10 expedition had to remain four miles out. Houghton, 'Account of Part of the Southern Coast', in Cook, *Survey*, vol. 1, pp. 107–9; al-Qasimi, *The Myth*, p. 137; Buckingham, *Travels in Assyria*, p. 496; Wellsted, *Travels in Arabia*, vol. 1, pp. 262–3; Thomas, *Arabian Gulf Intelligence*, p. 15; Cook, *Survey*, vol. 1, p. 134 and *passim*; Capt. J. Wainwright, Remarks on the Navigation of the Persian Gulph in 1809 and 1810, BA P 369/569 (552–601).
3. Brucks, 'Draft chapters', 1835/7, in Cook, *Survey*, vol. 1, p. 27.
4. Hansman, *Julfar, an Arabian Port*, pp. 14–20; Buckingham, *Travels in Assyria*, pp. 483–4; Thomas, *Arabian Gulf Intelligence*, pp. 99, 327 and map facing p. 15 (also at BA Sel. 74/18–19); Capt. T.P. Thompson to Bombay, Ras al-Khaima 1 May 1820, with enclosures, BA P 484/3430–5.
5. It is worth noting that there also were significant numbers of European mariners on Arab vessels at this time, including, for example, the French gunner who in autumn 1805 was supposed to have blown up his ship at Muscat with heavy loss of life, after being punished by his master Ibn Rizq of Basra. French activity in the Gulf largely ceased with the fall of

Mauritius in December 1810. Before that French privateers had been active there, as had upon occasion French agents: two French officers inspected Bandar Abbas, Qishm and Hormuz in February 1808; a French agent was reporting from Muscat in early 1809; the well-known Vincenzo Maurizi, who on his own admission had sought to promote French interests at Muscat, was present in Oman in 1809–10 and 1814–15. The supposed French offer of assistance to Sultan bin Saqr is mentioned in the official report of the first expedition reproduced in al-Qasimi, 'Arab "Piracy"', Appendix 1, pp. 1–10. W. Bruce to Harford Jones, Bushire 26 Sept. 1805, BA S&P 173/5462–6; N.H. Smith, Resident, to Fort William, Bushire 11 March 1808, enclosing intercepted French letters, BA S&P 229/4150–4; D. Seton, Resident, to Malcolm, Muscat 31 March 1809, enclosing French agent's letter from Muscat to Tehran legation, BA P 327/3747–56. Cf. the French *Pishnamaz* of Bushire, British agent and corsair, M. Talamash, in Morier, *A Journey through Persia ... in 1808 and 1809*, pp. 33–4.

6. Loch, *Diaries*, TS pp. 328–9.

7. See plates 8–11 and 13. al-Qasimi, *The Myth*, plates 4–5, 16; Low, *Indian Navy*, vol. 1, pp. 311, 326–30, 354–62; Buckingham, *Travels in Assyria*, pp. 483–4; Taylor's report, with accompanying map, enclosure A in Evan Nepean to Hastings, Bombay 22 Sept. 1818, BA Sel. 74/21–8; Cook, *Survey*, vol. 1, p. 25; Hansman, *Julfar, an Arabian Port*, pp. 14–20.

8. Buckingham, *Travels in Assyria*, p. 384; Cook, *Survey*, vol. 1, p. 341; Saldanha, *Persian Gulf Précis*, vol. 1, pp. 425–6.

9. A very high proportion of the guns were deemed by the British unserviceable. Morley and Hardy, Returns of captured ordnance etc., Dhaya 22 Dec. and Ras al-Khaima 12 Dec. 1819, BA P 479/1276–8.

10. Loch, *Diaries*, TS pp. 331–2.

11. The single most convincing table of manpower is probably that supplied to Sadleir on 10 May 1819 by Sayyid Sa'id of Muscat. The figure of 400 fighting-men for Umm al-Qaiwain is otherwise confirmed in a number of ways; the figure for Ras al-Khaima also does not look unreasonable from what we know of the second expedition. Hasan bin Ali led out of Dhaya when he surrendered, this after the evacuation of Rams (and Ras al-Khaima), some 398 men and 400 or more women and children. Estimates of population are interspersed through the Bombay papers, including: David Seton, Muscat Resident, to Bombay, Baroda 2 July 1807, BA S&P 208/4937–50. Memorandum by Sayyid Taqi, with accompanying map of the coast between Ras al-Hadd and Abu Hail, and Board's deliberations and letter to Capt. Wainwright of 6 Jan. 1810, BA P 350/116–38: the memorandum's date is given according to the corresponding entry in the catalogue of the Bombay Archives; also BA Sel. 74/21. W. Bruce to Bombay, Bushire 23 Jan. 1815, BA P 420/582–7; Information from Arab informant, 22 Jan. 1817, BA Sel. 74/416–17, BA P 312/1064–72. Taylor's report, enclosed in Nepean to Hastings, Bombay 22 Sept. 1818, BA Sel. 74/20–110. (Brucks, *Account of the Survey*, pp. 45, 49.) Also: Various reports on the 1819/20 expedition and its aftermath; Sadleir, *A Journey across Arabia*, pp. 52–3; Cook, *Survey*, vol. 1, *passim*, reports by Houghton, Brucks, Whitelock, Horsburgh. (Cf. Sharja Agent, 20,400 in 1881, *Persian Gulf Administration Reports*, vol. 2, report for 1880–1, p. 4.)

12. Cf. Lorimer, *Gazetteer*, vol. 1, Appendix F, pp. 2319–32.

13. The only other estimates of the number of houses in Taylor's report, for Rams and Jazirat al-Hamra', also match Lorimer's. Thomas, *Arabian Gulf Intelligence*, pp. 14–16, and estimates from 1826–36, pp. 327, 101; Lorimer, *Gazetteer*, vol. 2, pp. 622–3, 1004–9, 1573; Hansman, *Julfar, an Arabian Port*, p. 16; Penelope Tuson (ed.), *Records of the Emirates, Primary Documents 1820–1960*, 12 vols. (Archive Editions, England, 1992), vol. 12, pp. 463–5.

14. Bruce's informed Arab contact stated that the Arabian Qasimi ports employed 7,000 men on 400 pearling-boats, as compared with the 9,539 men and 470 boats supposed to have been operated by these ports in 1907. Anonymous Arabic report supplied to Bushire Resident W. Bruce, dated 22 Jan. 1817, BA Sel. 74/416–17, imperfect translation at BA P 312/1064–72; Lorimer, *Gazetteer*, vol. 1, pp. 2256–7; Fenelon, *The United Arab Emirates*, pp. 6–8, 126.

15. The other main Persian ports associated with the Qawasim were Mughu, Tahuna, Charak and Kalat, the two last being sizable: altogether, including Linga, they had a fighting strength

of 1879 men and possessed 19 large sea-going vessels. Dep. Med. Storekeeper John McNeill, information collected from inhabitants of Qais and some of those from opposite shore, corroborated by shaikhs Harun and Yusuf, sons of Shaikh Barakat formerly of Charak, Feb. 1820, BA S 315/355–62.

16. Capt. D.D. Conyers to Loch, HCC *Mercury*, Muscat Cove, 21 March 1819; Acting-Lt J. Milson to Conyers, Ras al-Khaima 14 March; Lt James Arthur to Supt of Marine Meriton, HCC *Antelope* 22 March, BA Sel. 73/455–63.

17. William Bruce, long-time Resident at Bushire, estimated her population to be 'at least 8,000 souls'. Buckingham thought the figure of 10,000 often applied to Bushire uncomfortably large, but he did not have these qualms about the size of Ras al-Khaima, which he also estimated at 10,000. W. Bruce to Bombay, Bushire 5 Aug. 1815, BA P 424/2148–53; Buckingham, *Travels in Assyria*, pp. 349, 484.

18. Brucks, *Draft Chapters*, in Cook, *Survey*, vol. 1, p. 27. Also, Low, *Indian Navy*, vol. 1, pp. 354–8.

19. W. Bruce, Resident, to Bombay, Bushire 26 Jan. 1817, BA S 312/1026–58. (Cf. Lorimer, *Gazetteer*, vol. 2, p. 1008.)

20. Cf. Seton, 'Each tribe has its own shaikhs and those shaikhs elect from the most powerful tribe a shaikh who rules the whole, who all adopt the name of his tribe as a nation'. Abdullah bin Su'ud referred to Hasan bin Rahma as 'Amir of the Qawasim'. Sayyid Sa'id appears to have used the terms 'Qawasim' and 'Qasimi tribe' in a broad fashion. The term 'Qawasim' was also of course used in this way by Abu Hakima (ed.), *Lam' al-Shihab* and Fasa'i, *Farsnama-yi Nasiri*. General descriptive terms of this kind had a natural appeal to outsiders, with whom the usage was presumably generated: it was of course a major step for the population concerned to adopt it themselves. D. Seton, Muscat Resident, to Bombay, Baroda 2 July 1807, BA S&P 208/4937–50; Lorimer, *Gazetteer*, vol. 2, pp. 1782–4, on Shibkuh, and 1548; W. Bruce, Resident, to Bombay, with enclosures, Bushire 11 Oct. 1814, BA P 419/122–30; Sayyid Sa'id to Bruce, (probably Muscat) 25 May 1820, BA P 490/5835–44.

21. Sadleir, *Journey across Arabia*, p. 64.

22. 'Yamen': their average age was 23 (and adult height 5 feet 3½ inches). Descriptive List of Joasmee Prisoners, Bombay 24 April 1819, BA Sel. 73/545.

23. According to an Arabic intelligence report delivered to the Bushire Resident around January 1815, Qasimi crews consisted of '6,000 of the Utub and other tribes with a number of Coffree slaves.' W. Bruce to Bombay, Bushire 23 Jan. 1815, BA P 420/582–7: cf. Interrogation of Qasimi crew, in Capt. Loch to Bombay, HMS *Eden*, Muscat 2 Jan., BA Sel. 73/318–26, BA P 460/488–93. Enlistment by the Shaikh of Linga's subjects *c.* 1808 is indicated in, Remarks by D. Seton, Muscat Resident, introduced by Governor, Bombay Castle 10 Dec. 1808, BA S&P 255/14150–8: cf. Interrogation of Linga crew in Capt. Walpole to Bombay, HMS *Curlew*, Bushire 7 June 1819, BA Sel. 73/649–55; Bruce to Keir, HMS *Curlew*, off Qais, 20 Feb. 1820, BA S 315/350–5; Dep. Med. Storekeeper John McNeill, information collected from inhabitants of Qais and some of those from opposite shore, corroborated by shaikhs Harun and Yusuf, sons of Shaikh Barakat formerly of Charak, Feb. 1820, BA S 315/355–62. On the Shihuh, see Brucks, *Draft Chapters*, in Cook, *Survey*, vol. 1, p. 20.

24. C.W. Elwood to Bombay, Porbandar 24 Nov. 1818, BA Sel. 71/143B–52; Buckingham, *Travels in Assyria*, pp. 356, 484. Part of the negro population would presumably have been composed of manumitted slaves and the descendants of slaves.

25. Listing the population of the Rams–Abu Hail coast, Resident Bruce's Arab informant estimated the number of 'Persians from Persia [Fawaris min bilad Faris] such as the Huwala and their like' at 500 (presumably adult) men, and the number of 'black slaves' at 600. Arabic report on the Qawasim and Bahrain, (Bushire?) 22 Jan. 1817, BA Sel. 74/416–17, BA S 312/1064–72.

26. The commander of the *Darya Daulat*, Fleming, encountered two representatives from Sind, when he was brought to Ras al-Khaima in July 1808; a British officer met a Mocha merchant there when sent ashore in March 1819. W. Watts, Assistant Resident, to Bombay, Barka 4–6 Aug. 1808, BA S&P 243/9867–72; D. Conyers to Loch, HCC *Mercury*, Muscat Cove, 21 March 1819, J. Milson to Conyers, Ras al-Khaima 14 March, J. Arthur to Meriton, HCC *Antelope* 22 March, BA Sel. 73/455–63.

27. This and the preceding quotations concerning Abd al-Rahman are from Loch, *Diaries*, MS pp. 349–51, TS pp. 311–12. Loch was presumably mistaken as to his age: see W. Bruce, Resident, to Bombay, Bushire 21 Oct. 1819, BA S 314/2052–4.

28. Anonymous Arabic report on the Qawasim and Bahrain supplied to the Bushire Resident, (Bushire?) 22 Jan. 1817, BA Sel. 74/416–17, BA S 312/1064–72; Lorimer, *Gazetteer*, vol. 2, pp. 1547–8.

29. Houghton, 'Account of Part of the Southern Coast', in Cook, *Survey*, vol. 1, p. 114; Kemball's Memoranda on the Arabian coast in Thomas, *Arabian Gulf Intelligence*, pp. 100–1.

30. Two translated letters from Matar bin Rahma to Rashid bin Rahma, one dated 15 Nov. 1808, entered under date 14 April 1809, BA P 327/3557–66. Rulers who occur as shipowners included the shaikhs of Dubai, Abu Dhabi, Bushire, Bahrain, Muhammad bin Qadib of Linga and others.

31. (Cf. Heard-Bey, *From Trucial States*, pp. 85–7, 124–5.)

32. According to the Arabic report of January 1817 whence this information is derived, the toman equalled 18 Rumi piastres in Ras al-Khaima, and 12 in Bahrain. It seems that here, just as Milburn describes at Basra, the toman was not the Persian gold coin, worth according to the 1821 Bombay assay 6.5106 Bombay rupees, but an imaginary unit of accountancy. The invoices for the *Ahmed Shah* in July 1814 accord the piastre a value of 0.75 Bombay rupee: this would make the Ras al-Khaima toman equal 13.5 Bombay rupees, and the Bahrain toman 9; there were roughly 10 (9.8) Bombay rupees to the English pound in 1821. These figures for the imaginary toman do not look out of order. At Basra, according to Milburn, the toman equalled 15 rupees, and at Bandar Abbas it was roughly £2 sterling: the piastre varied as well, and at Mocha it was an imaginary unit worth 1.85 Bombay rupees. Arabic intelligence on Bahrain and the Qawasim, (Bushire?) 22 Jan. 1817, BA Sel. 74/416–17; Milburn, *Oriental Commerce*, vol. 1, pp. 70, 90, 94 and 138–41; W. Bruce, Resident, to Bombay, Bushire 30 June, with invoices of *Ahmed Shah* of 1–2 July 1814, IOR R/15/1/14 pp. 157–60; Rumi piastre/rupee rate confirmed in D. Seton's Journal, Jan.–Feb. 1806, BA S&P 181/2422 (2399–430).

33. In 1821, the Spanish dollar was worth 2.2525 Bombay rupees, the English crown 2.45101: Milburn, *Oriental Commerce*, vol. 1, pp. 138–41.

34. The contemporary description of pearling, trade and date-cultivation derives from the anonymous Arabic report on the Qawasim and Bahrain supplied to the Bushire Resident, (Bushire?) 22 Jan. 1817, BA Sel. 74/416–17, BA S 312/1064–72: partly reproduced in Thomas, *Arabian Gulf Intelligence*, pp. 22–3, 38–40. This report refers to a *naub* tax then being levied at Bahrain, which tends to confirm Lorimer's statement on this subject: Lorimer, *Gazetteer*, vol. 1, pp. 2240–2, 2284–7. See also Houghton and Whitelock in Cook, *Survey*, vol. 1, pp. 114, 342. Note the apparent absence of customs at Bahrain, Saldanha, *Persian Gulf Précis*, vol. 1, p. 408, and Thomas, *Arabian Gulf Intelligence*, p. 105; Whitelock, in Cook, *Survey*, vol. 1, p. 342, if strictly reliable, might suggest the introduction of customs on the Trucial Coast after 1820.

35. Lorimer, *Gazetteer*, vol. 2, p. 1008; Thomas, *Arabian Gulf Intelligence*, p. 327.

36. Buckingham, *Travels in Assyria*, p. 483.

37. Wellsted, *Travels in Arabia*, vol. 1, p. 261.

38. 'Cadjan' or cajan, i.e. barasti or palm-frond huts.

39. On smoking, cf. Burckhardt, *Notes*, vol. 2, p. 114. (Text has 'Wahabees' and 'Lingar'.)

40. This and the preceding quotation derive from Lt H.H. Whitelock IN, 'An Account of Arabs who Inhabit the Coast between Ras-el Kheimah and Abothubee in the Gulf of Persia, generally called the Pirate Coast', *Transactions of the Bombay Geographical Society*, vol. 1 (1835–6), in Cook, *Survey*, vol. 1, pp. 325–47.

41. Seemingly 'Ausiya as written; but Uwaisa, Uwaisiya etc. possible.

42. This account of pearling derives from the anonymous Arabic intelligence report on the Qawasim and Bahrain delivered to the Bushire Resident in January 1817. According to this report, Bahrain's pearling industry employed 32,000 men on 1,400 boats, and produced 100,000 tomans (c. £90,000?) worth of pearls each year: the figure 100,000 appears to have been emended from 200,000. The value of the pearl harvest would have fluctuated. Two

British observers in the 1820s and early 1830s wielded the more conservative figure of roughly 100,000 dollars for that specifically of Sharja, or a total annual average closer to £20,000 than £40,000. Lorimer gives the figures 9,539 men and 470 boats, and 17,633 men and 917 boats, engaged in pearling from the Rams–Khan coast and the Bahrain archipelago respectively in 1907. Anon, Arabic intelligence report, (Bushire?) 22 Jan. 1817, BA Sel. 74/416–17; BA S 312/1064–7; Thomas, *Arabian Gulf Intelligence*, pp. 22–3, 38–40. Houghton and Brucks in Cook, *Survey*, vol. 1, pp. 114, 136; Saldanha, *Persian Gulf Précis*, vol. 1, p. 407; Mehdi Ali Khan to Bombay, Bushire 12 Aug. 1802, BA S&P 128/5823–5. Lorimer, *Gazetteer*, vol. 1, pp. 2252–8.

43. References to the number of vessels at the Qasimi ports include the following: Floor, 'A Description of the Persian Gulf and Its Inhabitants in 1756'. English Gombroon Diaries, IOR G/29/12 pp. 92–3. Slot, *The Arabs of the Gulf*, p. 190. IOR R/15/1/3 pp. 10–11. Heude, *A Voyage*, pp. 36–7. Saldanha, *Persian Gulf Précis*, vol. 1, p. 451. BA S&P 208/4937–50; 253/13607–9. BA P 338/8088–93; 350/122A; 369/552–602; 420/582–7; 477/565–6; 484/3371–4; 485/3565–6; 486/4205–23, 4280–304; 492/6479–90. BA S 315/81–102, 103–10, 217–28, 355–62; 316/475–8. BA Sel. 72/75–130, 177–95; 73/455–63; 74/21–4. Sadleir, *Journey across Arabia*, p. 36. al-Qasimi, *The Myth*, pp. 137, 140–1; al-Qasimi, 'Arab "Piracy"', Appendix 1. Lorimer, *Gazetteer*, vol. 1, pp. 646–9, 669. Low, *Indian Navy*, vol. 1, chap. 10. Buckingham, *Travels in Assyria*, p. 484. Cook, *Survey*, vol. 1, p. 25; Brucks, *Account of the Survey*, pp. 44B, 49–54, 79A. Thomas, *Arabian Gulf Intelligence*, pp. 100–1, 327. *Persian Gulf Administration Reports*, vol. 1, report for 1878–9, pp. 40–2.

44. D. Seton, Muscat Resident, to Bombay, Baroda 2 July 1807, BA S&P 208/4937–50.

45. At Ras al-Khaima, over 50 dows were destroyed, 30 of them 'of very large dimensions'; at Rams, 10 large vessels; at Jazirat al-Hamra', 8 large vessels; at Mughu, 4 Sharja boats; at Laft, 11 vessels, 3 of them 'very large dows'; at Linga 20 vessels, 9 of them 'very large'. No large seaworthy craft were found at Sharja, Fasht, Ajman and Umm al-Qaiwain, or at Nakhilu, Charak, Kung, Hamiran and Mu'allim. The destruction of 'trankeys and small boats' was not insisted upon. Ras al-Khaima, Linga and Laft were visited on 11–13, 17 and 26–7 November 1809, all the other ports commencing only in mid-January 1810. Capt. Wainwright, cited in al-Qasimi, *The Myth*, pp. 137, 140–1; according with anonymous account of expedition cited in al-Qasimi, 'Arab "Piracy"', Appendix 1, pp. 1–10. Lorimer, *Gazetteer*, vol. 1, pp. 646, 648–9; Capt. Wainwright's report on navigation of Persian Gulf in 1809–10, BA P 369/552–602; Lt Col. L. Smith to Bombay, HCC *Ternate*, at sea 2 Feb. 1810, BA Sel. 71/16–23.

46. The second expedition captured perhaps 202 vessels, 177–87 of which belonged to the Rams–Abu Hail coast. Sharja yielded at least 3 dows and baghlas and 45 trankeys; Ras al-Khaima at least 30 dows and baghlas, 31 trankeys and 50 other, probably small, non-fishing boats; precise figures are not recorded for Ajman and Umm al-Qaiwain, but the number of vessels taken at these ports was small, possibly 18 or so: Ajman may have possessed a few baghlas and dows. One might hazard a guess that the total of shipping seized belonging to this coast was around 37(–9) dows and baghlas, 80(–2) trankeys and 60(–6) other vessels such as the baqqara. In addition, the expedition took at least ten Dubai, three Linga and two Charak vessels in error; the remaining ten, or perhaps eleven, are not identified. W.G. Keir to Adjutant-General, HMS *Liverpool*, off Sharja 5 Feb. 1820, BA P 479/1257–78; Keir to Bombay, HMS *Liverpool*, off Sharja 7 Feb. 1820, BA S 315/217–28. Lorimer, citing a figure of 212 captured vessels, *Gazetteer*, vol. 1, p. 669.

47. The five ports were Linga, Mughu, Charak, Tahuna and Kalat: Dep. Med. Storekeeper John McNeill, information collected from inhabitants of Qais and some of those from opposite shore, corroborated by shaikhs Harun and Yusuf, sons of Shaikh Barakat formerly of Charak, Feb. 1820, BA S 315/355–62. Also, D. Seton, Muscat Resident, to Bombay, Baroda 2 July 1807, BA S&P 208/4937–50; Seton to Bombay, Muscat 21 March 1806, BA S&P 182/2708–13; Sayyid Taqi's memorandum, Bombay 19 Dec. 1809, BA P 350/118–22A; W. Bruce, Resident, to Bombay, Bushire 19 Dec. 1819, BA Sel. 72/177–95.

48. Survey of vessels found at Ras al-Khaima, 23 Dec. 1819, with related papers, BA S 315/103–10.

49. Observed by Lt Tanner, in Horsburgh, *India Directory*, 1836, in Cook, *Survey*, vol. 1, p. 298.

50. The 60 large and 43 small vessels destroyed in 1809/10 were valued at $55,000 (c. £15,000), and, in addition, captured property restored to Muscat at 200,000 rupees (c. £20,000). The total value of boats, specie and other property seized in 1819/20 was 273,565½ rupees (c. £28,000). Court of Directors to Fort William, 23 Feb. 1813, BA P 401/3222–3; Moyse-Bartlett, *The Pirates*, p. 98. Note the significantly higher valuation of eleven additional vessels, compared with the scale employed by the 'disinterested officers' who surveyed the sixty found at Ras al-Khaima: Return of vessels captured and destroyed by the *Eden*, *Curlew* and *Nautilus*, in Collier to Bombay, HMS *Liverpool*, Trincomalee 21 June 1820, BA S 315/230–48.

51. In 1823, Muscat owned 6,175 tons of European-style ships, Bushire 1,880 tons: List of Gulf shipping in 1823, 3 June 1824, PRO FO 60/24. The tonnage of nine of the 60 vessels at Ras al-Khaima is implied, but for the rest has to be estimated on the basis of length and breadth, class and value. This overall rough calculation of tonnage takes account of Lorimer, *Gazetteer*, vol. 1, pp. 2319–32; also Hawkins, *The Dhow*, pp. 84–5, 100, 110, 125. (G. Colquhoun to Bombay, Basra 29 Dec. 1814, BA P 419/295–9, on Kuwait, is rejected.)

52. Note especially the Indian vessels the batel and batella, which are distinct from the Arab battil. The word 'battil' occurs in a bewildering variety of forms in the records of 1797–1820, apparently quite at the will of the copyist, including batill, botill, bottil, batille, battille, bottele, botella, bottela, bottella, butilla, buttilla and battilah. See, for example, Hawkins, *The Dhow*.

53. E.g. Sayyid Taqi's memorandum, Bombay 19 Dec. 1809, BA P 350/122A; W. Bruce to Bombay, Bushire 23 Jan. 1815, BA P 420/587 (582–7); Hasan bin Rahma to Bruce, received 27 Nov. 1816, BA Sel. 72/116; Arabic intelligence on the Qawasim and Bahrain, (Bushire?) 22 Jan. 1817, BA Sel. 74/416–17. The Arabic report of 1817 speaks of 'large trading-boats [khashab al-safar] like dows and baghlas ... and small ones like battils and baqqaras'. Used in this way, of course, a term like baqqara would presumably have described vessels of similar form, size and use, some of which might locally perhaps also have borne other particular names. On class-names, see Anon, *Oman, a Seafaring Nation*, pp. 117–53.

54. Loch, for example, uses the terms interchangeably. Likewise the illustrations by Temple and Thirtle of the landing-craft used in the first expedition at Ras al-Khaima, which had been loaned from Muscat and are referred to in the written sources as trankeys, sport the distinctive fiddle-head stem-piece and dog's-head stern-post of the battil: al-Qasimi, *The Myth*, plates 4, 16; 'Arab "Piracy"', Appendix 1.

55. Loch cites these two vessels as being reasonably typical of others in the Gulf; belonging to Shaikh Shakhbut of Abu Dhabi, they were captured in the evening of 11 February under the misapprehension that they belonged to the Qawasim. Loch writes 'barhalo' and 'batille'. Loch, *Diaries*, MS pp. 171–2, TS pp. 155–6. Brucks commented that the battils of Ras al-Khaima in 1835 were the largest and best sailers in the Gulf: Brucks, 'Draft Chapters', in Cook, *Survey*, vol. 1, p. 27; *Account of the Survey*, p. 43.

56. Loch wrote that he later presented these 'along with a Babylonian brick and several arms, shields etc. taken from the pirates' to the Museum of the College of Edinburgh. I have been unable to trace these interesting artefacts. Loch, *Diaries*, MS pp. 171–2.

57. Private memorandum from Capt. T.P. Thompson to Capt. Marriott, recorded in Bombay Council Minutes under date 16 Feb. 1820, BA S 315/205–9.

58. Yet another, a battil belonging to the Shaikh of Dubai encountered in November 1819, carried 29 men and two six-pound guns. For this and the other examples of crewing see: BA P 455/5861–72, 5854–6; 460/488–93. BA Sel. 73/201–5, 226–8, 231–2, 239–41, 320–6, 649–53.

59. D. Seton, Muscat Resident, to Bombay, Baroda 2 July 1807, BA S&P 208/4937–50; Broker Vishandass to Bombay, Muscat 8 May 1807, received 17 May, BA S&P 205/3835–7.

60. By 1834, the dow had ceased to exist in the Gulf, only a few examples remaining at Jeddah and elsewhere: J. Edye, 'Description of the Various Classes of Vessels Constructed and Employed by the Natives', *JRAS* (1834), cited in Low, *Indian Navy*, vol. 1, pp. 169–70.

61. Naqib of Mukalla to Bombay, Mukalla 15 Sept. 1819, BA P 473/5676–9.

62. al-Qasimi, 'Arab "Piracy"', Appendix 1, pp. 1–10: an official account of the cause and course

of the first expedition. This quotation is based upon a typescript, since the original is not available. This text contains a few inconsistencies, which have been omitted here for the sake of clarity, and which appear to represent unfinalized emendations in the original. 'Jowasmees' i.e. Qawasim. Cf. Low, *Indian Navy*, vol. 1, p. 321.

63. Whitelock, 'An Account of Arabs', Bombay 1835–6, in Cook, *Survey*, vol. 1, p. 342.

64. The negotiator, with whom Seton was suing for restoration of the cargoes of the *Trimmer* and the *Shannon*, against which this supporting plea of poverty was made, was Abdullah bin Qasim bin Qurush. D. Seton, Muscat Resident, to Bombay, Muscat 4 March 1806, enclosing Journal for Jan.–Feb., BA S&P 181/2418–19 (2399–430).

65. The account in question is dated 22 January 1817 and was written in Arabic, probably at Bushire and at the behest of the British Resident, by an anonymous author well acquainted with the Qawasim and Bahrain; it purports, doubtless with a degree of rhetoric, to describe the situation as it had been before the Qawasim abandoned mercantile and peaceable pursuits for piracy and wrongdoing. Bruce describes this four-page account of the economies of the Arabian Qasimi ports and Bahrain as 'the most correct information carefully compiled and communicated by a learned and intelligent Arab': the author was possibly a merchant, one such as the Sultan Bandar Riqi (al-Riqi?) who had assisted in the release of Mrs Taylor in 1809 and was related to Sultan bin Saqr. The Arabic original occurs at BA Sel. 74/416–17, the slightly incomplete and inaccurate translation, with a translated addendum on potential government revenue on the Qasimi coast, dated 24 Jan. at BA S 312/1064–72. Much of the information from this report was used by Robert Taylor and occurs in Thomas, *Arabian Gulf Intelligence*, pp. 22–3, 39–40. On Rigi, see W. Bruce to Bombay, HMS *Curlew*, off Qais 14 Feb. 1820, BA P 480/1820–35.

66. On saluq, in Hasa an unripe date simmered for a few days, then dried, and sometimes flavoured with aniseed, see F.S. Vidal, 'The Oasis of al-Hasa', *The Aramco Reports on al-Hasa and Oman 1950–1955*, 4 vols. (reprinted Archive Editions, England, 1990), vol. 2, pp. 164–70.

67. The general character of this trade has been constructed essentially from the following: Manesty and Jones' description in 1790 of the trade of Bahrain, Muscat and Basra; Malcolm's Gulf trade report of 1800; Seton's description of Muscat's trade in 1802; the anonymous retrospective account in Arabic of the economy of the Arabian Qasimi ports dated 22 Jan. 1817; Milburn's *East India Trader's Complete Guide* of 1825; Whitelock's account of the trade of Ras al-Khaima and her neighbours dated 1835–6, but actually the result of his experience with the Bombay Marine survey along this coast commencing in 1821; observations contained in Brucks' account of this coast and history of Qasimi piracy, also the product of his service with the survey in these years. Samuel Manesty and Harford Jones, 'Report on the Commerce of Arabia and Persia', Basra 15 Aug. 1790; Maister and Fawcett, Custom Master and Accountant General, Report on the Trade of Persia and India, Bombay 17 Dec. 1799; John Malcolm, Report on the State of Trade between Persia and India, Bushire 26 Feb. 1800: Saldanha, *Persian Gulf Précis*, vol. 1, pp. 404–55. D. Seton, Muscat Resident, to Bombay, Surat 9 July 1802, BA S&P 126/4595–612. Arabic report, (Bushire?) 22 Jan. 1817, BA Sel. 74/416–17. Milburn, *Oriental Commerce*, vol. 1, *passim*. Whitelock, 'An Account of Arabs', in Cook, *Survey*, vol. 1, pp. 325–47. Capt. G. Brucks, *Account of the Survey of the Persian Gulf, 1821–1835[/1837]*, British Library Add. Ms. 14,383: the first two chapters of this manuscript, covering the survey (the remainder is a history of Qasimi piracy) have been reproduced in Cook, *Survey*, vol. 1, pp. 1–28.

68. Interrogation of captive Ras al-Khaima crew, Capt. F.E. Loch to Bombay, HMS *Eden*, Muscat 2 Jan. 1819, BA Sel. 73/318–26, BA P 460/488–93.

69. Two letters from Matar bin Rahma to Rashid bin Rahma bin Rashid al-Qasimi at Bhavnagar, Ras al-Khaima, one dated 15 Nov. 1808, with subjoined government decision, BA P 327/3557–66; Surat merchants to Bombay Governor, Surat 26 July 1816, BA Sel. 72/4–10.

70. Brucks, 'Draft Chapters', 1835/7, in Cook, *Survey*, vol. 1, p. 27. Of the revival of Qasimi trade after 1820, ostensibly *c.* 1820–7 in his account, Brucks wrote, 'The boats which had been secreted together with many others they had purchased were employed in trade. Dates, rice and cloth to some amount found their way to Sharja and Ras al-Khaima. The larger boats went to Basra w[h]ere they loaded with dates which they carried to Bombay where they found

a ready market. Some of these boats conveyed back to the Gulf freight for the merchants while others went to Mangalore where with the price of their dates they purchased rice which they disposed of in the Gulf often to considerable advantage.' Brucks, *Account of the Survey*, pp. 92A–B.

71. A. Bell, Conservator of Forests, to Supt of Marine, Calicut 2 May 1809, with related papers, BA P 330/4689–95; Governor Nepean to Fort William, Bombay 22 Sept. 1818, BA Sel. 74/4–19. A ban on the export of timber from Malabar to Arabia was imposed for a year in May 1809, and Calcutta approved a decision to reimpose it in March 1811: this had probably been lifted before 1815. There may perhaps have been others, but none prevented the building of vessels in the Gulf: Fort William to Bombay, 22 March 1811, BA P 372/1785–6; S. Manesty to Bombay, Basra 20 March 1810, BA P 355/2045–50; W. Bruce, Resident, to Bombay, Bushire 23 Jan. 1815, BA P 420/582–7. W. Bruce, Resident, to Bombay, Bushire 26 Jan. 1817, BA S 312/1051–2. Cf. Lorimer, *Gazetteer*, vol. 1, pp. 2319–21; Anon, *Oman, a Seafaring Nation*, pp. 154–65.

72. This at least according to the later source of Brucks, who alleges that Bahraini and Omani merchants secretly friendly towards the Qawasim had vessels built for them in the first half of the second decade at Daman and Cochin, and that when completed these vessels brought thence more timber for shipbuilding in the Gulf. Brucks, *Account of the Survey*, p. 57B.

73. Note of course the Sudan episode at the start of the century. Cf. W. Bruce, Resident, to Bombay, Bushire 31 July 1816, BA S 312/1026–38.

74. *Persian Gulf Administration Reports*, vol. 1, report for 1876–7, pp. 71–5.

75. Dates and grain were reportedly got from Bahrain. The *Vestal* reported thence in April 1819 that there was constant traffic between Bahrain and Ras al-Khaima, there being always at least 15 or 20 Qasimi boats in port. Abdullah bin Ahmad of Bahrain to Bruce, received 12 Jan. 1817, BA Sel. 72/437: W. Bruce, Resident, to Bombay, Bushire 5 March 1817, BA Sel. 74/418–21; 25 March 1817, BA S 312/1083; 8 Feb. 1817, BA Sel. 72/337–40. Capt. E. Barnard to Bombay, HMS *Conway*, off Cape Bardistan 19 Oct. 1818, BA P 455/5969–73. Various reports May–Sept. 1819, BA Sel. 73/567, 117–18, 627–33, 684–6. Brucks, *Account of the Survey*, pp. 70B–71A.

76. See, for example, Sadleir, *Journey across Arabia*, pp. 51–3.

77. Seton argued that 'all the neighbouring countries, Qishm, Ras al-Khaima etc. drew their supplies of dates and grain from Minab', and hence the importance of Badr relieving the place in June 1805: D. Seton, Resident, to Bombay, Muscat 25 July 1805, BA S&P 170/4067–73.

78. Whitelock, 'An Account of Arabs', Bombay 1835–6, in Cook, *Survey*, vol. 1, pp. 341–2.

79. The anonymous Arabic report of 22 Jan. 1817, BA Sel. 74/416–17, gives the following rates for an ordinary seaman's share per round voyage: large vessels, India 50–60 rupees, Yemen 80, the Sawahil 40, Sind and Cutch 25–30, Muscat 12 and Basra nothing, since it was visited as part of the preceding voyages; small vessels, Bahrain and Qatif 6 and 4 rupees respectively, Basra (trading directly) 10 and the Huwala ports such as Kangan, Asalu, Linga and Qishm 2–3. These rates reflect profitability. On the Kuwaiti dow trade of the 1930s, see Villiers, 'Some Aspects', in Sweet, *Peoples and Cultures of the Middle East*, vol. 1.

80. These figures are appended to the translation of the anonymous Arabic report on the economy of the Arabian Qasimi ports supplied to the Bushire Residency, and their purpose is to suggest the potential revenue which might accrue to government if it possessed itself of those places, in this case by gathering customs-dues. This addendum is likewise translated and must have been written directly after by the author of the main report, or conceivably by an Arab munshi or other intermediary attached to the Residency: it shows a knowledge of government's involvement in the Ceylon pearling industry. The figure for small vessels takes account of the fact that they made two voyages a year. The Rumi piastre equalled 0.75 Bombay rupees. Translation of Arabic report on the economy of the Arabian Qasimi ports and Bahrain dated 22 Jan. 1817, with short translated addendum, BA S 312/1064–72. For loose comparison, see various estimates of Gulf trade in Saldanha, *Persian Gulf Précis*, vol. 1, pp. 411, 432, 439, 445; Thomas, *Arabian Gulf Intelligence*, pp. 104, 476, 568; *Persian Gulf Administration Reports*, various years, 1873 ff.

81. See the Manesty and Jones report of 1790, in Saldanha, *Persian Gulf Précis*, vol. 1, pp. 404–5,

407–9. In 1815/16, the Bahrain Utub reportedly sent 21 vessels via Muscat and Bombay, to Malabar for rice: Broker to Bombay, Muscat 6 and 10 Jan. 1816, BA P 427/283–8; these particular vessels were later impounded as they returned through Muscat.

82. Note that the price of Indian produce, including rice, was almost always higher in the Gulf than in other Indian ports, and that Muscat, and presumably other Arab vessels too, did not generally engage in the carriage of Indian goods from port to port in India: Remarks by David Seton, Muscat Resident, on report of Reporter General on External Commerce, 27 July 1804, IOR P/343/14, pp. 2875–84.

83. D. Seton, Muscat Resident, to Bombay, Surat 9 July 1802, BA S&P 126/4595–612.

84. Milburn, *Oriental Commerce* (1825), vol. 1, pp. 109–12, 168–77.

85. There were of course allegations that the Qawasim made captures further south during the second decade, but these are few and, though impossible to dismiss totally, appear insubstantial. The belief that the Qawasim were to a limited degree active near Bombay has found its way into secondary sources; the theory that the Qawasim made captures as far south as Mangalore and Malabar only appears in Brucks, which, though interesting for its manner of compilation, is not a contemporary source; the isolated report of a capture as far south as Pigeon Island in 1817 seems to have been discredited soon after. Low, *Indian Navy*, vol. 1, p. 346; W. Bruce, Resident, to Bombay, Bushire 13 Feb. and 25 March 1817, BA Sel. 72/341–2; Brucks, *Account of the Survey*, pp. 56B, 58A, 65B; Remington, Crawford and Co. to Warden, Bombay 2 March 1817, with other papers, BA Sel. 72/272–3, 278, 331; Supt of Marine H. Meriton to Governor, Bombay 5 May 1817, BA Sel. 72/371–2.

86. In 1701 the *Dever Salamett* was freighted from Coondapoor to Julfar: Dutch report of 1702 cited in al-Qasimi, *The Myth*, p. 12. Ras al-Khaima's heavy involvement in the Mangalore rice trade was attested by Brucks, 'Draft Chapters', in Cook, *Survey*, vol. 1, p. 27, and *Account of the Survey*, pp. 92A–B.

Notes to Chapter Thirteen

1. *Ex nihilo* one assumes this to have been the case; and Brucks, *Account of the Survey*, p. 92B. The Qawasim were resistant to Wahhabi pressure to attack Muscat shipping during the pearling season of 1803: D. Seton, Resident, to Bushire, Muscat 8 June 1803, IOR R/15/1/6 p. 178. There could have been some disruption on account of Muscat's two expeditions against the Qawasim in summer 1813 and 1814. One imagines that comments on this subject by Bruce's Arab informant were largely hyperbole: Anonymous Arabic intelligence on the Qasimi ports and Bahrain, (Bushire?) 22 Jan. 1817, BA Sel. 74/416–17.

2. On shares and profits, cf. Burckhardt, *Notes*, vol. 2, pp. 151–2; Alois Musil, *The Manners and Customs of the Rwala Bedouins* (American Geographical Society, New York 1928: reprint AMS, 1978), pp. 510–11; Villiers, 'Some Aspects', in Sweet, *Peoples and Cultures of the Middle East*, vol. 1, p. 171.

3. D. Seton, Resident, to Brig.-Gen. Malcolm, Muscat 5, 16 and 20 Feb. 1809, with general report of 19th, BA P 325/2622–50.

4. Abu Hakima (ed.), *Lam' al-Shihab*, pp. 82–3.

5. W. Bruce, Acting Resident, to Fort William, Bushire 30 June 1809, BA P 336/7343–4.

6. Translation of letter from Surat merchants to Bombay Governor, Surat 26 July 1816, BA Sel. 72/4–10; cf. first declaration of Second Nakhuda of *Ahmadi*, BA Sel. 72/11–18.

7. Brucks, *Account of the Survey*, pp. 62A; 59A, 60A.

8. The Al Su'ud 'receive each year from Ras al-Khaima in particular 120,000 riyals worth of plunder [ghana'im], in addition to gifts.' Abu Hakima (ed.), *Lam' al-Shihab*, p. 170.

9. W. Bruce, Resident, to Bombay, Bushire 3 and 6 Jan. 1818, BA P 443/1124–8 (originals at BA Sel. 72/535–40); Goolab Anundass, Broker, to Bombay, Muscat (2nd, or early 3rd, week of Jan. 1818), BA P 443/834–7. Goolab Anundass to Bombay, Muscat 18 May 1815, BA P 422/1268–70; and 10 April 1815 (dates wrongly converted: text reads 31 March), BA P 421/1036–8.

10. See, for example, the *Shannon*, October 1807, and the *Darabiya*, January 1815, Chapter Five; cf. the allegation of the Surat merchants in their letter to Governor Nepean of 26 July 1816, BA Sel. 72/4–10: in the case of the *Darabiya* the information was supposed to have been passed on by the port itself. Brucks says that the Qawasim had informants in Bombay who kept them abreast of British affairs in India and he even goes as far as to say that their agents in Indian ports forwarded them manifests of vessels destined for the Gulf: the second point looks unnecessarily formal, but there was probably some substance to the first, since Qasimi shaikhs apparently told Brucks that they had known, presumably in late 1816, about the imminence of the Pindari War of 1817–18, and had rightly concluded from this that Bombay's threat of a second expedition against Ras al-Khaima was for the time being an idle one, since she did not have any troops to spare. Brucks, *Account of the Survey*, pp. 63B–64A.

11. It seems unnecessary to credit the force of Brucks' separate assertion that the Bahraini ruler sanctioned the use of Bahrain as a mart for plundered property for a small payment. Brucks' depiction of Qasimi maritime plunder derives principally from the 1820s and early 1830s, and is an uncomfortably simplistic one of relatively straightforward, indiscriminate, but thoroughly systematic, piracy on the grand scale. Some of what he relates is, nevertheless, of the greatest interest since it derives from Brucks' long experience with the Bombay Marine, and in particular his service with the survey on this coast; this gave him the opportunity to interview the Qawasim themselves about their former condition, in an atmosphere which would not have been possible at the time. Brucks, *Account of the Survey*, pp. 55B, 70A–71A. (Cf. Note from Haji Muhammad Jamal, received Bushire 2 Dec. 1807, BA S&P 220/151–2.)

12. S. Manesty and H. Jones, 'Report on the Commerce of Arabia and Persia', Saldanha, *Persian Gulf Précis*, vol. 1, pp. 409 and *passim* 404–34.

13. Brucks, *Account of the Survey*, pp. 39A–40A.

14. During the brief period of greatest, Wahhabi-inspired, exuberance in the first decade, that is in late 1808 (time of the attack on the *Sylph* and Ras al-Khaima's victories by land against Muscat), the reputation of Linga, which even in this decade was not normally quite so closely identified with Ras al-Khaima, also became tarnished: the Qasimi Shaikh of Linga was reportedly 'averse to piracy, but his subjects cut off from trade on account of the general disrepute of their tribe, seek a livelihood in the vessels of others.' Remarks by David Seton Muscat Resident, introduced by Governor, Bombay Castle 10 Dec. 1808, BA S&P 255/14150–8.

15. On 1 June 1806, Seton wrote to Sultan bin Saqr of Ras al-Khaima that, in consequence of the recent confirmation of February's Anglo–Qasimi agreement, his vessels would now be able to frequent Indian ports as before, but recommended they should first proceed to Bombay 'to prevent your meeting any delays at the other ports and let your vessels be furnished with letters saying whose they are.' Seton had failed to induce Muscat to settle her differences with Ras al-Khaima, but opined that even without British ships to support her, Muscat was 'fully able to control the Qawasim, who having found themselves once in a perilous situation and on the brink of starvation from having interrupted their communication with India and Muscat at the same time, will now be extremely careful not to place themselves in the same predicament again by any attempt on our trade'. The Qawasim must have been able to visit Muscat in early 1805, perhaps until May, when it was recorded that the ruler Badr seized one of their boats as she loaded rice in the port. D. Seton, Resident, to Bombay, Muscat 2 and 13 June 1806, enclosing journal for May, BA S&P 186/6629–43; D. Seton to Bombay, Muscat 10 May 1805, BA S&P 168/2908–12; and, on Basra, Seton to Bombay, Muscat 16 Oct. 1805, BA S&P 173/5361–4; the Janaba affair also provoked the detention at Basra of 32 Linga vessels, clearly till then unaffected by the ban which affected Ras al-Khaima there: Seton to Bombay, Muscat 4 March 1806, BA S&P 181/2399–402.

16. W. Bruce, Resident, to Bombay, HMS *Curlew*, off Qais 14 Feb. 1820, BA S 315/362–73, BA P 480/1820–35.

17. Brucks, *Account of the Survey*, p. 57B.

18. Morier, *A Journey through Persia . . . in 1808 and 1809*, pp. 43–6.

19. Pudumul Judumul, EIC Broker, to Bombay, Muscat 21 and 24 Nov. 1804, BA S&P 162/4902–7; Dr Pringle to Bombay, Mocha 9 March 1804, with enclosures, including translated information from leading Banyan, BA S&P 157/1943–58. D. Seton, Resident, to Brig.-Gen. Malcolm, Muscat 9 and 30 March 1809, with another erroneously dated 6 March, which should perhaps read 16 or 26 April, and Seton's despatch of 7 May to Bombay, BA P 325/2702–7, 327/374(5)–9, 329/4607–16.

20. 'Destroying the date trees being a principal object in Arabian warfare' (Capt. G.B. Brucks 1827), in Thomas, *Arabian Gulf Intelligence*, pp. 539–40.

21. E.g. Hasan bin Rahma to Resident Bruce, [Ras al-Khaima?] 26 Aug. 1814, BA P 419/126–8; W. Bruce, Bushire Resident, to Bombay, HCC *Mercury*, Hanjam Sound 28 Nov. 1816, BA P 432/2435–41. On Sultan bin Saqr, see e.g. D. Seton and W. Bruce 1805, BA S&P 170/4067–75, 4090–9; 171/4341–53; 173/5361–4; 173/5391–402.

22. Bombay Governor to Fort William, Bombay Castle 19 Oct. 1802, with enclosure, BA S&P 129/6073–5; D. Seton, Muscat Resident, to Bombay, Surat 9 July 1802, BA S&P 126/4595–612; Pamela Nightingale, *Trade and Empire in Western India 1784–1806* (Cambridge University Press, Cambridge, 1970), chap. 5.

23. On 19 September 1817, a small two-masted French boat, which had temporarily been separated from her large companion vessel, and was carrying some 2,000 French crowns, 20 bags of sugar and 30 bags of cloves for disposal at Muscat, was plundered off Qurayat by a Qasimi battil ('botella'). The vessel herself, with the crew, who had lost even their bedding and clothes, were set at liberty and reached Muscat on 20 September. The two French boats, the smaller of which was called the *Lal Cuttee*(?) and the ship the *Eliza*, had come from Bourbon to purchase livestock: Muscat Broker to Bombay, 27 Sept. 1817, BA Sel. 72/422–6. The Frenchman Abd al-Rahman, mentioned in the last chapter, who escaped from Ras al-Khaima in 1818, had originally been captured in another Bourbon vessel before the 1809/10 expedition.

24. Mir Khan of Bela wrote to the Governor of Bombay around late spring, complaining that Sayyid Sa'id of Muscat was sheltering Baluch Khan ('Baloch Khan Marnamee/Merwannee'), whom he had previously chastised and expelled. He also voiced a deeper grievance that ports including Gwadar and Chahbahar, which had formerly been his, had been seized by Muscat: 'Some time ago Kuwadhur, Choupar and various other ports on the sea coast, were in our possession, but were seized upon by the ruler of Muscat. Muhammad Khan subsequently to the death of the great Khan opened a negotiation on the subject, and the consequence has been that the ruler of Muscat has taken possession of those ports, and is besides committing other excesses.' Mir Khan to Bombay Governor, undated, in Minutes of 12 May 1815, BA P 421/1062–4.

25. From May to September 1810 a Persian envoy resided in Hyderabad, at the court of the Sind Amir; through him Sayyid Sa'id of Muscat addressed a written appeal to the Amir for military assistance against the Wahhabis, noting that he had already appealed to the Shah of Iran and the Ottoman Sultan. The Amir turned him down in the autumn. On 23 November, a second letter reached the Amir from Sayyid Sa'id, stating that his agent was then at Karachi, and desiring permission to procure supplies of grain unimpeded, since supplies were needed to support his effort against the Wahhabis. Muhammad Yusuf Munshi, Native Agent Hyderabad, to Bombay, 27 July, 11 Nov., 17 Dec. 1810, BA P 374/2573–652, 2776–98.

26. Chapter Nine.

27. D. Seton, Muscat Resident, to Bombay, Surat 9 July 1802, BA S&P 126/4595–612.

28. As, Ibn Ruzaiq, *Imams and Seyyids*, pp. 81–5.

29. Niebuhr, *Voyage en Arabie*, vol. 2, p. 68. Cf. Buckingham, *Travels in Assyria*, p. 507; Fraser, *Narrative*, p. 6; Wellsted, *Travels in Arabia*, vol. 1, p. 18.

30. Calvin H. Allen, 'The Indian Merchant Community of Masqat', *Bulletin of the School of Oriental and African Studies*, vol. 44 (1981), pp. 39–53; Calvin H. Allen, 'Sayyids, Shets and Sultans: Politics and Trade in Masqat under the Al Bu Sa'id, 1785–1914', unpublished PhD thesis, University of Washington, 1978.

31. Buckingham, *Travels in Assyria*, pp. 507, 517–18; Fraser, *Narrative*, p. 7; Wellsted, *Travels*

in Arabia, vol. 1, pp. 18–25. Fraser noted the existence of a temple to Calee Devee, and that occasional visitors from India included Jains and mendicants such as Jogees, Byragees and Sanyassees.

32. D. Seton, 9 Jan. 1801, cited in Risso, *Oman*, p. 192; (Maurizi, *Seyd Said*, pp. 29, 127–30); Allen, 'The Indian Merchant Community', pp. 44–5; M. Reda Bhacker, *Trade and Empire in Muscat and Zanzibar: Roots of British Domination* (Routledge, London, 1992), pp. 71–2.

33. On the 1817 attack see Chapter Six, section three, and on that of 1819 see Appendix B.

34. D. Seton, Muscat Resident, to Bombay, Surat 9 July 1802, BA S&P 126/4595–612.

35. Wellsted, *Travels in Arabia*, vol. 1, p. 19.

36. Minute by Warden, Chief Secretary to Government and temporary Member of Council, Bombay Castle 12 Aug. 1819, BA Sel. 77/13, 2 and 1–62.

37. Governor Nepean's Minute, Bombay Castle 6 Sept. 1819, BA Sel. 75/96–9.

38. Warden's historical sketches have been published in Thomas, *Arabian Gulf Intelligence*, pp. 55–60, 167–87, 299–312, 361–72, 427–36, 521–4: BA Sel. 77 constitutes the original. D. Seton, Resident, to Bombay, Muscat 4 March 1806, BA S&P 181/2399–430; W. Bruce, Resident, to Bombay, Bushire 11 Oct. 1814, BA P 419/122–30.

39. When he reached Bushire, writes Morier, the Persian Secretary Muhammad Husain Khan related that 'as the first act of possession, the Arabs threw water on the ship to purify it; that they then proceeded to the deliberate murder of the men, who were on deck or discoverable; that they brought them one by one to the gangway, and in the spirit of barbarous fanaticism cut their throats as sacrifices; crying out before the slaughter of each victim, "Ackbar", and when the deed was done, "Allah il Allah".' Morier, *A Journey through Persia ... in 1808 and 1809*, pp. 43–6. Likewise, Bombay Council Minutes of 11 Nov. 1808, BA S&P 251/13005–6. For one later incarnation of this story see Wellsted, *Travels in Arabia*, vol. 1, p. 247.

40. Revd Henry Martyn to Revd Hitchins of Stoke, Bombay 19 Feb. 1811, IOR MSS Eur. A. 87.

41. Lorimer, *Gazetteer*, vol. 1, pp. 636, 643; Heard-Bey, *From Trucial States*, pp. 281–2.

42. Reading 'ikhtiyar' for 'ikhtibar'. The fuller sense of the first phrase is 'God is our recourse, his assistance will be enough for us whatever the circumstances.'

43. Abdullah bin Su'ud to William Bruce, received at Bushire 28 Feb. 1817, BA Sel. 74/411–14.

44. Reported words of Qasimi negotiator to Bruce at Ras al-Khaima on 27 Nov. 1816, in W. Bruce, Bushire Resident, to Bombay, HCC *Mercury*, Hanjam Sound 28 Nov. 1816, BA P 432/2435–41.

45. Sayyid Badr to Governor Duncan, Muscat? 21 Oct. 1805, enclosing undated letter from Su'ud, cited in Kelly, *Britain*, p. 108.

46. Capt. D. Seton, Resident, to Bombay, Muscat 10 and 23 May 1805, BA S&P 168/2862–73, 2908–12; various despatches from Seton Feb.–May 1809, BA P 325/2622–50, 325/2692–701, 327/324(5)–9 and 334/6478–88.

47. W. Bruce to Bombay, Bushire 8 June 1814, BA P 413/3150–1.

48. Cf. Burckhardt, *Notes*, vol. 2, pp. 151–79.

49. W. Bruce to Bombay, HMS *Curlew*, off Qais 14 Feb. 1820, BA S 315/362–73, BA P 480/1820–35.

50. Abu Hakima (ed.), *Lam' al-Shihab*, p. 175.

51. Capt. N. Warren of HM 65th Regt to N.H. Smith, Bushire 17 March 1810, BA P 355/2009–22.

52. Brucks, *Account of the Survey*, p. 56A. According to Brucks p. 93, Sultan bin Saqr received a robe of honour and the hollow title Amir al-Bahr from the Prince-Governor of Shiraz in 1823.

53. Ibn Bishr, *Unwan al-Majd*, vol. 2, p. 52. Cf. Rahma bin Jabir's own defence of his maritime depredations to Britain in 1810, 'I am only carrying on hostilities against those Muhammadans who have departed from the institutions of our Prophet and introduced innovations in our faith'; and his, 'We were originally dependants upon Ibn Su'ud, and we destroyed all the Arabs and others who were against him', in 1816. Letters from Rahma bin Jabir and

Amir Su'ud, enclosed in Assistant-in-Charge Babington to Bombay, Bushire undated, in Bombay Council Minutes of 6 June 1810, BA P 358/3061–70; Rahma bin Jabir to Bombay Governor, (Bushire) 9 Nov. 1816, BA Sel. 72/147–9. Khuwair, i.e. Khaur Hassan.

54. Taqi al-Din Ahmad bin Taimiya (AD 1263–1328), Hanbali theologian and jurisconsult, major formative influence on Muhammad bin Abd al-Wahhab.

55. Muhammad bin Abd al-Wahhab.

56. The Al al-Shaikh, descendants of Muhammad bin Abd al-Wahhab.

57. Ibn Bishr, Unwan al-Majd, vol. 2, p. 54.

58. Buckingham, Travels in Assyria, pp. 357–8.

59. Sultan bin Saqr to Mulla Hasan of Qishm, enclosed in D. Seton, Resident, to Bombay, Muscat 16 Oct. 1805, BA S&P 173/5391–5; text of Anglo–Qasimi agreement of 6 Feb. 1806, in Seton to Bombay, Muscat 4 March 1806, BA S&P 181/2399–430. Shaikh al-Mashayikh, i.e. 'Shaikh of Shaikhs'. 'Amir', commander etc., may be the Saudi title here. Text has 'Mottazim Billa, Muttiwukkeel Aaly'.

60. W. Bruce, Resident, to Bombay, enclosing letters from Abdullah bin Su'ud (texts and translations), Bushire 28 Feb., 5 March, 12 and 29 April 1817, BA Sel. 74/411–14, 418–28, 435–8, 444–9 (copied, without Arabic texts, at BA P 312/1073–94).

61. Abdullah bin Su'ud to W. Bruce, received at Bushire 2 Oct. 1814, BA P 419/125–6. Hasan bin Rahma bears the same title in the Arabic text of the provisional Anglo–Qasimi accord of 6 Oct. 1814, IOR R/15/1/14, pp. 213–16 (art. 8). 'Amir' would have been the standard official Saudi designation: Ibn Bishr, Unwan al-Majd, vol. 1, pp. 362–4, 423–4, lists the officers of the Saudi state in Oman as three, the Amir, the Amir al-Juyush and the Qadi. In his letters of early 1817 (BA Sel. 74/411–14, 418–28, 435–8, 444–9) Abdullah bin Su'ud speaks quite regularly of 'ahl Ras al-Khaima'; he also refers to 'Hasan bin Rahma wa-ikhwanih' and 'al-Qawasim'.

62. Hasan bin Rahma to W. Bruce, 6 Nov. 1816, text and translation, BA Sel. 72/93–8.

63. Bruce's translation of Hasan bin Rahma to Loch, received at Bushire 3 April 1819. Office of Country Correspondence translation of Hasan bin Rahma to Governor Nepean, Ras al-Khaima 13 March 1819, has only 'Amir'. Neither are however extant in Arabic. BA Sel. 73/485–8, 519–21.

64. Hasan bin Rahma to W. Bruce, 6 Nov. 1816/14 Dh.H. 1231, Arabic text and translation, BA Sel. 72/93–8. Abdullah bin Su'ud for his part in early 1817 described his people as 'belonging to a religious community [milla] which acted in accordance with the Book of God and the Sunna [practice] of the Prophet, upon whom be peace': Abdullah bin Su'ud to W. Bruce, received at Bushire 28 April 1817, BA Sel. 74/449.

65. Hasan bin Rahma to W. Bruce, 27 Nov. 1816, Arabic text and translation, BA Sel. 72/110–15.

66. Abu Hakima (ed.), Lam' al-Shihab, pp. 80–1.

67. D. Seton to Malcolm, HCC Ternate, Muscat Cove 5 Feb. 1809, BA P 325/2622–8.

68. Niebuhr, Description de l'Arabie, pp. 266–7.

69. D. Seton to Malcolm, Muscat 30 March 1809, BA P 327/324(5)–9.

70. Lt Thomas Tanner to Charles James Maillard, Political Agent Dairistan, HCC Antelope, Hanjam Sound 23 Aug. 1820, BA P 492/6479–90; Whitelock, 'An Account of Arabs', Bombay 1835–6, in Cook, Survey, vol. 1, pp. 325–42.

71. Moyse-Bartlett, The Pirates, p. 107.

72. Whitelock, 'An Account of Arabs', Bombay 1835–6, in Cook, Survey, vol. 1, p. 339.

73. The tomb in question was at 'Soomar': conceivably Summana? Pudumul Judumul, EIC Broker, to Bombay, Muscat 21 and 24 Nov. 1804, BA S&P 162/4902–7; Dr Pringle to Bombay, Mocha 9 March 1804, with enclosures, including translated information from leading Banyan, BA S&P 157/1943–58. It may be worth noting that an unconnected translation from Gujarati by the translator of the Muscat Broker's report, uses the name 'Rasul' to describe an island in the Gulf where Sayyid Sultan was killed: it may conceivably refer to Qishm or a neighbouring island, or to somewhere off the bar of Basra. Cf. Thomas, Arabian Gulf Intelligence, p. 577 ('Rassul'); (the modern Times Atlas of the World shows a river Rasul inland north of Laft).

74. 'Do not say that there be three Gods, discard this idea and it will be better for you' etc. Translation of Su'ud bin Abd al-Aziz to N.H. Smith, received at Bushire 16 Dec. 1808, BA S&P 222/1083–91.

75. D. Seton, Resident, to Malcolm, Muscat 22 March 1809, BA P 326/3210–12. Ibn Ghaith was presumably the Hasan bin Muhammad bin Ghaith who represented Hasan bin Rahma in the negotiations and signing of the provisional Anglo-Qasimi accord of October 1814.

76. Dep. Med. Storekeeper John McNeill, information collected from inhabitants of Qais and some of those from opposite shore, corroborated by shaikhs Harun and Yusuf, sons of Shaikh Barakat formerly of Charak, Feb. 1820, BA S 315/355–62.

77. One of two translated letters from Matar bin Rahma bin Rashid al-Qasimi to Rashid bin Rahma bin Rashid al-Qasimi, this one undated, the other dated 26 Ram. 1223/15 Nov. 1808, with Government decision on the same, entered under date 14 April 1809, BA P 327/3557–66.

78. Abu Hakima (ed.), Lam' al-Shihab, p. 177.

79. Samuel Manesty and Harford Jones, 'Report on the Commerce of Arabia and Persia', Basra 15 Aug. 1790, in Saldanha, Persian Gulf Précis, vol. 1, p. 433; cf. J. Malcolm's report of 1800, ibid., pp. 444, 452.

80. Ghassan's dates as per Wilkinson, Imamate Tradition, p. 10; see also pp. 44–7, 185–6, 332. Ibn Ruzaiq, Imams and Seyyids, pp. 12–15; Sirhan bin Sa'id al-Izkawi, Kashf al-Ghumma (Dilmun, Nicosia, 1985), pp. 257–9.

81. Muhammad bin Muhammad al-Idrisi, Kitab Nuzhat al-Mushtaq fi Ikhtiraq al-Afaq, 2 vols. (Alam al-Kutub, Beirut, 1989), vol. 1, pp. 156–7. Wilson, The Persian Gulf, chap. 7, pp. 92–109; V. Fiorani Piacentini, 'Siraf and Hormuz between East and West: Merchants and Merchandise in the Gulf', in Charles E. Davies, Global Interests in the Arab Gulf (University of Exeter Press, Exeter, 1992), pp. 1–28; J. Aubin, 'Les Princes d'Ormuz du XIIe au XVIe siècle', Journal Asiatique (1953), pp. 77–138, and 'Le Royaume d'Ormuz au début du XVIe siècle', Mare Luso-Indicum 2 (Geneva, 1972), pp. 77–179; Wilkinson, Imamate Tradition, pp. 41–7.

82. According to Seton, the Okha pirates had preyed on 'Arab', that is presumably in particular Muscat, shipping and seldom gave their victims quarter. Ibn Ruzaiq, Imams and Seyyids, pp. 170–1; David Seton, memorandum, annexed to J. Duncan's letter of 10 July 1804, BA S&P 158/2468–71.

83. Algerines refers of course to the Barbary Corsairs. Lorimer, Gazetteer, vol. 1, p. 79. Low, Indian Navy, vol. 1, chaps. 2 and 3; Wilkinson, Imamate Tradition, pp. 48–50, 218–225.

84. The sources used for this examination of the Ka'b and Bandar Rig include: Saldanha, Persian Gulf Précis, vol. 1, pp. 192–5, 215–18; 101–2, 107–10, 197, 224–5, 243–7, 268–73; and passim. Lorimer, Gazetteer, vol. 1, pp. 110–16, 128–33, 1627–44, 1776–830. Niebuhr, Voyage en Arabie, vol. 2, pp. 149–66, 186–93; Description de l'Arabie, pp. 276–82. Perry, Karim Khan, chap. 10, pp. 150–66. John R. Perry, 'Mir Muhanna and the Dutch: Patterns of Piracy in the Persian Gulf', Studia Iranica, vol. 2 (1973), pp. 79–95. Grummon, 'The Rise', pp. 61–119. Slot, The Arabs of the Gulf, pp. 352–77.

85. Date and name follow Perry: Niebuhr writes 'Soleiman' and 'Soliman', and so too Saldanha, Persian Gulf Précis, pp. 170, 215, which might otherwise have suggested Sulaiman as the correct form.

86. A Ka'b gallivat captured by the Eagle in 1775 measured 84 by 24 feet, carried 24 oars and ten six-pounders, was 'built forward like a London wherry, with a pink or lute stern', and had one tall mast, raking forward, supporting a large sail. Niebuhr writes 'kalbet' for gallivat; the Ka'b's smaller vessels were 'dauneks': he observes that Arab names for vessels varied greatly; in relation to Rig the second class of vessel, which could be armed when necessary and was smaller than the 'kalbet', was the 'batil'. Lorimer, Gazetteer, vol. 1, p. 1644; Niebuhr, Voyages en Arabie, vol. 2, pp. 186–7, note 152–3; Saldanha, Persian Gulf Précis, vol. 1, pp. 215–18.

87. The Ka'b also reportedly imposed tolls on river traffic: Slot, The Arabs of the Gulf, p. 352.

88. Saldanha, Persian Gulf Précis, vol. 1, pp. 193–5.

89. Saldanha, Persian Gulf Précis, vol. 1, pp. 101–2.

90. Niebuhr, *Travels through Arabia*, vol. 2, p. 147.

91. Francis Wood to Gombroon Agency, Bandar Rig 18 Nov. 1756, in Saldanha, *Persian Gulf Précis*, vol. 1, p. 108.

92. Saldanha, *Persian Gulf Précis*, vol. 1, p. 225.

93. Cf. 'The tribes upon the confines of Oman, and the shores of the Persian gulph, are also acquainted with these family wars, and more harrassed even than the Arabians by them. A great part of these tribes earn their subsistence by carrying coffee from Yemen to the Persian gulph, and by the pearl fishery; and, from this circumstance, parties at variance have more frequent opportunities of meeting and fighting at sea. Weak tribes are thus often obliged to quit their way of life, and fall into obscurity and misery.' Niebuhr, *Travels*, vol. 2, p. 203.

94. Bruce spoke of 'a force tyrannically exercised to the misfortune and affliction of those who groan beneath its oppressive weight', a point of view very much shared by his anonymous Arab informant ('ahl al-bahrain ... al-ra'aya al-qudama' fa-hum fi ghayat al-idtirar' etc. at the hands of their Utbi conquerors): W. Bruce, Resident, to Bombay, with enclosures, Bushire 26 Jan. 1817, BA Sel. 74/395–409, 416–17. For the later period see works such as Mahdi Abdalla al-Tajir, *Bahrain 1920–1945: Britain, the Shaikh and the Administration* (Croom Helm, London, 1987); and Fuad I. Khuri, *Tribe and State in Bahrain: the Transformation of Social and Political Authority in an Arab State* (University of Chicago, Chicago, 1980).

95. Kniphausen: Floor (trans.), 'A Description of the Persian Gulf and Its Inhabitants in 1756', pp. 176–7. Tammer, i.e. *tamr*. Text has 'sjeek', 'Catif'.

96. J. Malcolm, report on trade between Persia and India, Bushire 26 Feb. 1800, in Saldanha, *Persian Gulf Précis*, vol. 1, p. 451.

97. See Saldanha, *Persian Gulf Précis*, e.g. vol. 3, part 3, pp. 23–6; Abu Hakima (ed.), *Lam' al-Shihab*, p. 162.

98. With the partial exception of the category in the last paragraph.

99. Lorimer, *Gazetteer*, vol. 1, p. 204.

100. Saldanha, *Persian Gulf Précis*, vol. 5, part 3, pp. 83–5.

101. Saldanha, *Persian Gulf Précis*, vol. 3, part 3, pp. 27–8.

102. Saldanha, *Persian Gulf Précis*, vol. 1, pp. 184, 187–8, 225–30.

103. George Rentz, article under 'al-Kawasim', in E. van Donzel, C.E. Bosworth and others (eds), *Encyclopaedia of Islam*, new edition (E.J. Brill, Leiden, 1978), vol. 4, pp. 777–8.

104. This account is largely based upon Loane's own narrative, published by subscription presumably in Bombay and dedicated to Governor Johnathan Duncan: it was intended 'to warn the future travellers or navigators to, or near the inhospitable shores, on which my untoward fate so lately cast me, and from which I so providentially escaped, from similar misfortunes to my own', and thus recommended 'the necessity of arming their vessels sufficiently to repel any attack from these piratical barbarians'. Loane's publication, though destined to pass into obscurity perhaps even in the second decade, must initially have helped form attitudes to the Qawasim in Bombay: hence Morier's reference to it in 1808. To judge by Buckingham's unreliable, but dramatic, version, the story itself was already part of folklore in 1816. Loane's account accords with Bruce except in one detail: in Bruce's version, the captives were taken to Bukha, not Ajman. Were it not for Loane, one would assume that Bukha was correct and perhaps at this time under Qasimi control; but Loane's account is to be preferred. Loane's description of his captors, one section of the Qawasim, as 'Aza Arabs' is probably not significant: the term occurs in Bruce, as well as Seton's despatches, and if applied properly, as it is apparently not here, should refer to the Dubai Banu Yas under Shaikh Hazza' (presumably Hazza' bin Za'al who still ruled in 1814 and perhaps 1818, but had been succeeded by his son Muhammad, a minor, by January 1820). Loane was captured before Ras al-Khaima and the Qawasim became famous, hence in part this imprecision. R.W. Loane, *Authentic Narrative of the Late Fortunate Escape of Mr R.W. Loane etc.* (Ferris and Co., Bombay, 1805); W. Bruce, Acting Resident, to Bombay, 12 Jan. 1805, and to Manesty at Basra, Bushire 27 Nov. 1804, 5 Jan. 1805, BA S&P 164A/596–601, 610–14; Morier, *A Journey through Persia ... in 1808 and 1809*, pp. 43–4; Buckingham, *Travels in Assyria*, pp. 409–13.

105. Loane, *Authentic Narrative*, p. 3.
106. British sailors spoke of the Qawasim, which was pronounced Jawasim in the Gulf, and the Wahhabis as Joe Hassem and the War Bees. 'Egmaum bears about S.S.W. from Cape Musseldom, and nearly 70 miles distance, and about 25 miles from Roselkiem, where Joehassem, the chief of these rovers holds his place of residence and has his depôt of arms and ammunition; to him, the Sheik of Egmaum, and the places along this Coast are tributary, and furnish him whenever required with men and boats': place-names stand for Ajman, Musandam and Ras al-Khaima. Loane, *Authentic Narrative*, p. 28.
107. Loane, *Authentic Narrative*, pp. 6–7.
108. Loane, *Authentic Narrative*, pp. 7–8.
109. Loane, *Authentic Narrative*, pp. 9–11.
110. Loane, *Authentic Narrative*, pp. 11–12.
111. Loane, *Authentic Narrative*, pp. 14–15.
112. Loane, *Authentic Narrative*, p. 22.
113. Yule, *Hobson-Jobson*, pp. 367–9, says Gentoo could mean either a Hindu or, more specifically, a Telugu-speaking Hindu.
114. Loane, *Authentic Narrative*, p. 24.
115. Loane's recollection was of five weeks, but the known capture of the *Trimmer* on 1 December makes four the maximum.
116. Loane, *Authentic Narrative*, p. 36.
117. Charak was still being ransacked on 8 December. Loane, *Authentic Narrative*, p. 59.
118. Loane, *Authentic Narrative*, p. 43.
119. Loane, *Authentic Narrative*, p. 54.
120. W. Bruce to Bombay, Bushire 12 Jan. 1805, BA S&P 164A/596–9.
121. The fever descended on all the European part of the crew, possibly leaving the Indians unaffected, on one day at Nakhilu. It brought intermittent periods of delirium, debility and remission, which sounds like malaria. The condition of the Europeans worsened after they had sailed from Shaikh Shu'aib for Bushire, the Indians having been sent straight to Muscat, and both Youl and Simms died before their arrival: in the last stages, they had suffered violent spasms, convulsive fits and unrelieved hiccups, being, in Youl's case, unable to keep food down. Loane, *Authentic Narrative*, pp. 100–18.
122. Loane, *Authentic Narrative*, p. 68.
123. This discussion of bedouin activities relies mostly on the following: Burckhardt, *Notes*. Musil, *Rwala Bedouins*. H.R.P. Dickson, *The Arab of the Desert* (George Allen and Unwin, London, 1951). John Bagot Glubb, *War in the Desert* (Hodder and Stoughton, London, 1960). Saad Abdullah Sowayan, *Nabati Poetry: the Oral Poetry of Arabia* (Arab Gulf States Folklore Centre, Doha, 1985); and *The Arabian Oral Historical Narrative: an Ethnographic and Linguistic Analysis* (Otto Harrassowitz, Wiesbaden, 1992). Louise E. Sweet, 'Camel Raiding of North Arabian Bedouin: a Mechanism of Ecological Adaptation', chapter 14 in L.E. Sweet, *Peoples and Cultures of the Middle East, an Anthropological Reader* (Natural History Press, New York, 1970), vol. 1, pp. 265–89. Michael E. Meeker, *Literature and Violence in North Arabia* (Cambridge University Press, Cambridge, 1979).
124. Musil, *Rwala Bedouins*, p. 60.
125. The relationship of khuwa of course implied a formal incorporation of the client into the tribal system.
126. Musil, *Rwala Bedouins*, p. 540.
127. Charles Doughty, cited in Sweet, 'Camel raiding of North Arabian Bedouin', in Sweet, *Peoples and Cultures*, vol. 1, p. 267.
128. Example of Bedouin poetry, in Glubb, *War in the Desert*, p. 37.
129. Musil, *Rwala Bedouins*, p. 504.
130. Example of Bedouin poetry, in Musil, *Rwala Bedouins*, p. 537.
131. Burckhardt, *Notes*, vol. 1, pp. 157–75, 325–7.
132. See Saldanha, *Persian Gulf Précis*, vol. 5, part 3, pp. 78–127; vol. 4, part 2.
133. 'Seyhat' is near Qatif; the 'shooi' was often a small *sambuk*-like vessel. Saldanha, *Persian Gulf Précis*, vol. 5, part 3, p. 120; and, concerning 1878, p. 83.

134. Note in passing Rahma bin Jabir's angry vilification of the Banu Khalid ruler of Hasa Muhammad bin Urai'ir as 'a savage and a keeper of camels on the desert'; 'these jungle people are beddoos' etc. Rahma bin Jabir to Stannus, 7 Nov. 1825, in P. Tuson (ed.), *Records of Qatar, Primary Documents 1820–1960*, 8 vols. (Archive Editions, England, 1991), vol. 1, p. 205.

135. Note still, an isolated instance, the suggestion of chivalry in Rahma bin Jabir's last duel, which reportedly caused the Al Khalifa Shaikh Ahmad to take on Rahma's vessel one to one, without the aid of the Bahrain fleet. Tuson, *Records of Qatar*, vol. 1, pp. 234–6.

136. Three letters from Hasan bin Rahma to W. Bruce, Ras al-Khaima Nov. 1816, BA Sel. 72/93, 110, 116; cf. Abu Hakima (ed.), *Lam' al-Shihab*, pp. 79, 139.

137. The subject was the Sudan's boarding of a British baghla near Kharg in 1816. Muhammad bin Qadib to W. Bruce, Linga 20 Muh. 1232/10 Dec. 1816, BA Sel. 72/184A.

138. Three letters from Hasan bin Rahma to W. Bruce, Ras al-Khaima Nov. 1816, BA Sel. 72/93, 110, 116; Hasan bin Rahma to Abdullah bin Ahmad of Bahrain, sent on to Bushire where received 10 May 1819, BA Sel. 73/632A; Abu Hakima (ed.), *Lam' al-Shihab*, pp. 82, 139.

139. Abdullah bin Ahmad to W. Bruce, received 12 Jan. 1817, BA Sel. 72/437.

140. Sultan bin Saqr al-Qasimi to W. Bruce, 2 Safar 1232/22 Dec. 1816, BA Sel. 72/430; also Ibn Ruzaiq and Abu Hakima (ed.), *Lam' al-Shihab*, pp. 81–3.

141. As, Sowayan, *The Arabian Oral Historical Narrative*, pp. 288, 293, 245, 265, 286, 300; *Nabati Poetry*, p. 35: Musil, *Rwala Bedouins*, pp. 530, 623.

142. Anonymous report on the Qawasim and Bahrain, supplied to Bushire Resident W. Bruce, dated 22 Jan. 1817, BA Sel. 74/416–17.

143. Ibn Ruzaiq, *al-Fath al-Mubin*, p. 492.

144. Saldanha, *Persian Gulf Précis*, vol. 5, part 3, p. 81.

145. Colquhoun, Late Assistant-in-Charge Basra Residency, to Bombay Governor, Bombay 21 May 1819, BA S 312/973–81.

146. Brucks, *Account of the Survey*, pp. 86B–87A.

147. Capt. J. Cumming to Manesty, Basra 29 Dec. 1804, BA S&P 164A/439–43.

148. E.g. Loane's baghla in 1804, the *Ahmadi* in 1816, the *Darya Daulat* in January 1817.

149. Capt. J. Cumming to Manesty, Basra 29 Dec. 1804, BA S&P 164A/439–43, on a trading boat which 'making some resistance, the crew was put to death'; likewise, the fate of Captain Babcock of the *Shannon*.

150. As on the *Ahmadi*; cf. Saldanha, *Persian Gulf Précis*, vol. 5, part 3, p. 84.

151. Three letters from Hasan bin Rahma to W. Bruce, Ras al-Khaima Nov. 1816, BA Sel. 72/93, 110, 116. British vessels had committed shameful acts ('fi'l qabih') sufficient to annul the respect due to them under treaty: 72/110.

152. This was actually written by Thompson around late January, whereas he became chief officer at Ras al-Khaima on 5 February. Private memorandum from Capt. T.P. Thompson, Arabic Interpreter at Ras al-Khaima, to Capt. Marriott, recorded in Bombay Council Minutes under date 16 Feb. 1820, BA S 315/205–9.

153. T.P. Thompson to Bombay, Ras al-Khaima 7 May 1820, with enclosures, BA P 486/3927–58.

154. Purport of interview with Qasimi negotiator Hasan bin Muhammad bin Ghaith, reported by W. Bruce to Bombay, Bushire 11 Oct. 1814, BA P 419/122–30; (Saldanha, *Persian Gulf Précis*, vol. 2, p. 55).

155. This letter was written at Ras al-Khaima. When the author returned from the Khaur Fakkan campaign, he discovered that Salman had sold a dow, in which he had an interest, for 4,000 German Crowns: this was the sum of money he refers to in the letter. Salman bin Rahma was clearly a Qasimi and a close associate; one conjecture might be that he was the author's brother; his name appears in these letters as 'Sulman' and on two occasions as 'Suleman'. Two translated letters from Matar bin Rahma bin Rashid al-Qasimi to Rashid bin Rahma bin Rashid al-Qasimi at Bhavnagar, one dated 26 Ram. 1223/15 Nov. 1808, with Government decision on the same, entered under date 14 April 1809, BA P 327/3557–66.

Notes to Conclusion

1. Waring, A Tour to Sheeraz, p. 138; Morier, A Journey through Persia ... in 1808 and 1809, p. 6.
2. Villiers, 'Some aspects', in Sweet, Peoples and Cultures of the Middle East, vol. 1, p. 155; Anon, Oman, a Seafaring Nation, p. 170.
3. Sowayan, The Arabian Oral Historical Narrative, p. 87.
4. Tuson, Records of the Emirates, vol. 3, p. 173.
5. Capt. R. Mignan, cited in Winder, Saudi Arabia, pp. 39–40. Mignan employs dramatic licence: it seems, in fact, that the Bahrain vessel caught fire before she exploded, allowing her crew at least to escape. Kelly, Britain and the Persian Gulf, pp. 212–13, and Tuson, Records of Qatar, vol. 1, pp. 234–6.
6. Lorimer, Gazetteer, vol. 1, pp. 695–6.
7. This, according to Lorimer, Gazetteer, vol. 1, p. 719.
8. Or, to be precise, the murder of the Arab pilot who went ashore with the landing-party carrying the letter of protest, for whom he was to have acted as interpreter; the letter was in consequence not delivered.
9. Involvement was greatest at Muscat and Bahrain.
10. Lorimer, Gazetteer, vol. 1, p. 232.
11. Lorimer, Gazetteer, vol. 1, pp. 2638–9.
12. According to Philip Gosse, The History of Piracy (Longmans, London, 1932), pp. 260–3.
13. Brucks, 'Draft Chapters', pp. 33B–34A, 61B–62A, passim.

Notes to Afterword

1. Some parts of the analysis, particularly in respect to economic affairs, would probably benefit from further long, careful and thoughtful research.
2. See especially al-Qasimi, The Myth, as, pp. xv, 28, 31–2, 82.
3. Lorimer, Gazetteer, vol. 1, pp. 73–4.
4. Samuel Manesty and Harford Jones, Report on the Commerce of Arabia and Persia, Basra 15 Aug. 1790, Saldanha, Persian Gulf Précis, vol. 1, pp. 404–34, 431–2.
5. John Malcolm, Report on the State of Trade between Persia and India, Bushire 26 Feb. 1800, Saldanha, Persian Gulf Précis, pp. 442–55, 453. In this connection it is in fact positively reported in 1790 that Company cruisers regularly took glass and china from Bombay to Bushire: Saldanha, Persian Gulf Précis, vol. 1, p. 423.
6. These included the brig Viper (1797), the ship Mornington and the ketch Queen (1805), (the schooner Fury), the brig Nautilus and the schooners (Lively) and Sylph (1808), (the ketch Princess Augusta?) (1809), the ship Aurora (1816), the pattamar Darya Daulat (1817), and the brig Psyche and two troop-carrying pattamars (1818). Strictly speaking the Aurora and the Nautilus were held on the Bengal establishment. Warden also records the capture of the armed boat Turrarow in 1816: this could be a reference to the troop-carrying pattamar actually lost en route to Anjar in November 1818. BA, various reports; D. Seton, Resident, to Bombay, BA S&P 181/2399–402; Surgeon A. Jukes to Bombay, Bushire 26 Jan. 1809, BA P 323/1816–18; Thomas, Arabian Gulf Intelligence, p. 311; Moyse-Bartlett, The Pirates, p. 233.
7. The Ahmed Shah, Captain Herriman, was described as a native vessel; she had formerly belonged to the Persian Muhammad Nabi Khan.
8. The Company's vessels were understandably preferred in times of peace. The Committee estimated the annual cost of transmitting 24 packets directly between Bombay and Basra using four Company vessels full-time at 43,200 rupees, using country-vessels at 26,400 rupees, and using 'private ships navigated by Europeans' at 315,432 rupees. Report of Committee for

improving the channels of intercourse to Europe by the two Gulphs, Bombay 25 June, with comments by Nathan Crow, Minutes 22 Aug. 1797, BA S&P 57/1618–44.

9. Buckingham, *Travels in Assyria*, p. 511, cf. 384. The usual rates from Basra were 1 per cent to Bushire, 2 per cent to Muscat, 3 per cent to Bombay and 4 per cent to Bengal. In the few years following the first expedition, English private shipping was wont to receive this lucrative cargo at Muscat as a result, Buckingham says, of the Qasimi threat.

10. The merchants of Porbandar, in December 1818, offered 1 per cent for the possibility of entrusting treasure consigned to the coasts to the *Prince of Wales*: C.W. Elwood, Agent, to Governor Nepean, Porbandar 23 Dec. 1818, BA Sel. 73/249–52.

11. Saldanha, *Persian Gulf Précis*, vol. 1, pp. 411, 432–3. The report specifies 3 per cent duties and 2 per cent consulage payable at Basra and laments the decline in their total. Cf. Kelly, *Britain*, p. 57 records customs of 5 per cent and consulage of 2 per cent at Bushire.

12. John Malcolm, Commercial State of Persia, Basra 10 April 1801, in Charles Issawi (ed.), *The Economic History of Iran 1800–1914* (University of Chicago Press, Chicago, 1971), p. 264.

13. Perry, *Karim Khan*, p. 260: Perry suggests the figure of roughly one-fifth of such sales.

14. Issawi, *Economic History*, pp. 82–3: two bales appear to have weighed approximately one ton.

15. Grummon, 'The Rise', p. 201 note 51.

16. Lorimer, *Gazetteer*, vol. 1, pp. 185, 1955–8.

17. Buckingham, *Travels in Assyria*, pp. 352, 382.

18. Lorimer, *Gazetteer*, vol. 1, pp. 212–13, 1955–8. In late 1819 Warden noted that the commercial purpose of the Bushire Residency had ceased 'a few years back', when the Company substituted periodic sales at Bombay, in place of consignments to Bushire. Chief Secretary F. Warden to Keir, Minutes 19 Oct. 1819, BA S 313/1839–45.

19. Saldanha, *Persian Gulf Précis*, vol. 1, pp. 404–55; Grummon, 'The Rise', p. 174: viz. special reports commissioned by Government and drawn up by Watkins at Bushire (1788–9), Manesty and Jones at Basra and Baghdad (1790), Maister and Fawcett at Bombay (1799) and Malcolm on his visit to the Gulf (1800–1). For Charles Watkins' report on the imports and exports of Bushire, Bushire 15 Nov. 1789, see IOR L/MAR/C/891, pp. 108–16.

20. Saldanha, *Persian Gulf Précis*, vol. 1, pp. 340–2: 'The great object of your appointment is the extension of the Company's European imports into Persia, and the improvement to the highest possible degree of their selling prices, since those of late years have ... proved a loss to them'. It seems that Mehdi Ali Khan achieved some success: Lorimer, *Gazetteer*, vol. 1, pp. 1955–6.

21. See Kelly, *Britain*, pp. 72–3; Lorimer, *Gazetteer*, vol. 1, p. 1956; especially Saldanha, *Persian Gulf Précis*, vol. 1, pp. 386–90. The treaty renewed the Company's privileges with Iran and reduced duties payable on its staples.

22. This is clear from a comparison of the two aforementioned commercial reports: Manesty and Jones in 1790 still entertained some hopes of boosting the Company's trade, but Malcolm's report of 1800 in essence promotes the interests of the private merchant. In another report, of April 1801, Malcolm refers to the Company's trade as having a natural ceiling and being confined to its staples: Issawi, *Economic History*, pp. 263–4 (262–7). After Malcolm, resignation may almost have become the rule.

23. Buckingham, *Travels in Assyria*, pp. 352, 382.

24. A report for *c.* 1790 maintains that 'no trade can be carried on with those places from the sea without a regular establishment of persons constantly residing there, to cultivate the protection of those fluctuating arbitrary governments, by making presents, at times, to a considerable amount ... The Bombay cruisers are a great expense to the Company, but absolutely necessary ... from the vexations of pirates': Issawi, *Economic History*, p. 87; cf. Saldanha, *Persian Gulf Précis*, vol. 1, pp. 433–4.

25. Issawi, *Economic History*, pp. 85–9. It may be that these figures do not take account of consulage, but the basic lesson still holds. The number of cruisers visiting the Gulf naturally increased rapidly in the early nineteenth century in response to the perceived Qasimi threat, and also, more particularly in the first decade, as a result of the French wars. The cost of the Basra factory alone, put here at £4,276, was estimated by Buckingham at £5,000 per annum in 1816: Buckingham, *Travels in Assyria*, p. 382.

26. *Madras Courier*, 26 April 1792, in Yule, *Hobson-Jobson*, p. 267.
27. Cf. It has been guessed that in the later Safavid period Gulf and Indian merchants held 75 per cent of Gulf trade, the Company 15 per cent and other companies and private Europeans 10 per cent: Perry, *Karim Khan*, p. 256.
28. Saldanha, *Persian Gulf Précis*, p. 431. Manesty and Jones refer to 'the difficulty of procuring information relative to the commerce of the Red Sea, the incorrectness of the custom-house accounts at most of the ports of the Persian Gulf, the practice of smuggling prevailing at those ports, and the inability of some of the governors of those ports to afford the required communications'.
29. Viz. the report of 1790, Saldanha, *Persian Gulf Précis*, vol. 1, pp. 404–34, upon which the following account of the situation as it appeared in, and from, that year is based. See also Perry, *Karim Khan*, pp. 246–71.
30. Saldanha, *Persian Gulf Précis*, vol. 1, p. 412. A somewhat difficult point in this era, and indeed, even later, is the exact nature of what was termed a British vessel. For a short period, before being cautioned, the Company's Agent in Basra apparently simply auctioned the Company's pass: Lorimer, *Gazetteer*, vol. 1, pp. 160–1.
31. E.g. Saldanha, *Persian Gulf Précis*, vol. 1, p. 406.
32. Saldanha, *Persian Gulf Précis*, vol. 1, p. 432.
33. Ibid.
34. It is stated that a brief period of often lucrative British trade between Suez, Calcutta, Bombay and Surat came to an abrupt end in 1779. By 1790 British shipping had also ceased visiting Jeddah whose trade with India was now in the hands of Surat, Hudaida and Mocha vessels: Saldanha, *Persian Gulf Précis*, vol. 1, pp. 416–19.
35. Especially Saldanha, *Persian Gulf Précis*, vol. 1, pp. 416–19, 408, 406–7, 423, 410. Other Europeans sailing to Muscat (and Bushire) included the Dutch and the French.
36. This hypothetical English merchant is based on the assumption that the private views of Manesty (and perhaps also Jones), himself a merchant, shine through the report of 1790.
37. Saldanha, *Persian Gulf Précis*, vol. 1, pp. 442–55; and, Issawi, *Economic History*, pp. 262–7; cf. also, Maister and Fawcett, Report on the State of Trade between India and Persia, Bombay Castle 17 Dec. 1799, in Saldanha, *Persian Gulf Précis*, vol. 1, 435–40. Note that Malcolm's figures (see text) are only estimates and he himself soon revised them. They do not, it seems, include the, albeit small, Company imports. Cf. Grummon, 'The Rise', pp. 175–6.
38. Saldanha, *Persian Gulf Précis*, vol. 1, p. 445.
39. Saldanha, *Persian Gulf Précis*, vol. 1, p. 453.
40. Saldanha, *Persian Gulf Précis*, p. 445. This is alleged to have commenced c. 1798. It is possible this contributed to a growth in Bombay–Bushire shipping over the next two decades. This practice is also confirmed by Bogle at Muscat: Surgeon Bogle to Bombay, Muscat 2 April 1800, BA S&P 92/2626–33.
41. Waring, *A Tour to Sheeraz*, pp. 47–9, 76–80, 85–8.
42. See especially Bombay Commerce, Internal and External Reports, 1801/2–1824/5, IOR P/419/39–61 (and likewise ff.), (and Bombay Commercial Proceedings, IOR P/414/47–64, 1786/7–99); Grummon, 'The Rise', pp. 176–80; Kelly, *Britain*, pp. 137, 249–51; al-Qasimi, *The Myth*, tables pp. 230–1.
43. The total trade of the three Presidencies with the Gulf and the Red Sea is given as just over 112 lacs Rs in 1802–3 and 242 lacs Rs in 1817/18: Kelly, *Britain*, p. 137. The value of imports to Bombay from the Persian Gulf was 1,774,469 Rs in 1802–3 and 3,699,059 in 1817/18: Bombay Commerce, Internal and External Reports, IOR P/419/40 and 54.
44. The total trade of Bombay with the Persian Gulf was 2,899,607 rupees in 1801/2; 2,839,375 in 1813/14; 4,005,044 in 1814/15; and 7,247,263 in 1824/5. Bombay Commerce, Internal and External Reports, 1801/2–1824/5, IOR P/419/39–61.
45. Insurance paid at Bombay for the outward voyage to Basra was 5 per cent for most years 1803/4–1810/11, 4 per cent 1812/13–1815/16, 3 per cent 1816/17–1821/2, and 2½ per cent 1822/3–1823/4. Freight costs started falling in 1806/7, and despite years of extraordinary increase for certain categories of goods in the second decade, thereafter fell overall for two decades. Ibid.

46. Surat's total trade with the Persian Gulf was often between 300,000 and 500,000 rupees in the decade and a half before 1816/17, when it plummeted to 18,335 Rs, and did not rise above 40,837 Rs in the next eight years. Surat's trade with the Red Sea, however, was often as great or greater than Bombay's throughout these years. Ibid. Cf. Remarks on the trade of Surat, 29 June 1801, BA S&P 110/3199–210.

47. Buckingham, *Travels in Assyria*, pp. 509–10; cf. List of Gulf Shipping in Stannus to Willock, Bushire 3 June 1824, PRO FO 60/24. The latter is a list of the principal ships and trading boats in the Gulf. Of a total of 20 merchantmen, 6 belonged to Muscat, 4 to Bushire, 6 to Calcutta and 4 to Bombay. Of a total of 98 large trading-boats, all of which belonged to Gulf ports, 45 per cent belonged to Muscat. Nevertheless, in view of the fact that British vessels now went directly from Bombay to Bushire and Basra, a feature not observed by Malcolm in 1800, it seems likely that Muscat had indeed lost out proportionally over these two decades to British shipping, as well as to others such as Bushire (and the Utub) in the Indian trade. In 1823, in addition to her merchant ships, Muscat owned 4 ships-of-war; and there were, in addition to the 98 large, 157 small trading boats in the Gulf. This list includes the shipping at Bushire, Rig, Rudhilla, Tangistan, Dashti, Muscat, Bahrain and Kuwait, and excludes that of Kangan, Asalu, Bandar Abbas and the Arabian coast between Hasa and Musandam.

48. Buckingham, *Travels in Assyria*, p. 383.

49. W. Bruce to Bombay, Bushire 31 July 1816, BA S 312/1026–35. Bruce was alive to the potential market for imported goods in eastern Arabia, and the possible benefit which might accrue to Britain if it was developed in the right conditions: e.g. further, W. Bruce, Resident, to Bombay, Bushire 22 Aug. 1813, BA P 405/147–50; 26 Jan. 1817, BA Sel. 74/395–409.

50. Especially if Heude's experiences were representative: Heude, *A Voyage*, pp. 19, 47.

51. Buckingham, *Travels in Assyria*, pp. 509–10, also pp. 383–4. In addition to her ships, Muscat owned 40–50 dows and baghlas, which traded in the Gulf, to the Red Sea, and to Makran and Sind.

52. Heude, in 1816/17, *A Voyage*, pp. 47–8.

53. Report on the Foreign Trade of Bushire, Stannus to Willock, Bushire 3 June 1824, PRO FO 60/24. Of the goods brought into Bushire on British bottoms in 1817, 95 per cent came direct from India, 97 per cent being Indian and Chinese, 3 per cent European goods: the proportion of European goods was generally much higher over the next few years.

54. A significant part of this Arab shipping could have belonged to Muscat, but this is uncertain. Bombay Commerce, Internal and External Reports, 1801/2–1824/5, IOR P/419/39–61.

55. Residents at Basra seem to have been active in the private trade. Manesty, Resident for roughly two and a half decades (1784–1810), is the prime example, although others such as Harford Jones and Dr Gideon Colquhoun are known to have traded: as, Buckingham, *Travels in Assyria*, p. 385.

56. E.g. Masulipatnam (Guntur 1788), Malabar (1792), Ceylon (1796), N. and S. Kanara (1799), Madurai (1790–1801), Tinnevelly, S. Arcot, Trichi, Tanjore (1799), Orissa (1803), Gujarat (1800–18).

57. Statement of Surat Trade etc., Soper to Wellesley, Surat 6 Oct. 1802, BA S&P 129/6073–5.

58. Holden Furber, *John Company at Work* (Harvard, 1948: reprint, Octagon Books, New York, 1970), pp. 160–90 and *passim*. A list of free merchants and mariners at Bombay in 1749/50 records the names of 5 merchants, 16 'seafaring men' and 12 country-ships. A similar list for 1792 names 57 country-ships and 9 snows officered by 189 European seamen. In 1791/2 at least 70 British country-ships (or 27,000 tons of shipping) visited Cochin: this was double the size of six years before: Furber, *John Company*, pp. 224, 185. The *Cornwall* visited the Gulf in April–July 1819, taking on cargo at Muscat, unloading some at Bushire and delivering rice to Bahrain. Log of the Ship *Cornwall*, 9 November 1818 to 31 March 1821, National Library of Scotland MS 9661.

59. See also Chapters Twelve and Thirteen, section one.

60. E.g. in the account of the Qawasim supplied to W. Bruce at Bushire in January 1817 by his

anonymous Arab informant: Arabic report on Bahrain and the Qawasim, 22 Jan. 1817, BA Sel. 74/416–17, BA P 312/1064–72.

61. 'Trade cannot exist without a competition, nor competition without strangers are admitted to the market … The advantages of their trade to India in general far exceeds the loss it causes to individuals; they ought by no means to be excluded, but restricted from supplanting us in any branch of trade now exclusively possessed by us, in which light I can view the China trade only.' Remarks by David Seton, Muscat Resident, on report of Reporter General on External Commerce, 27 July 1804, IOR P/343/14, pp. 2875–84. Seton's view apparently coincided with that of Harford Jones, cited in Risso, *Oman*, p. 201.

62. There were, it is true, some such as Nepean, who was tempted prior to the second expedition to regard the Utub as pirates, or Warden, who tried to make out a case that Muscat had also been culpable, but these views were not of the same substance, were not translated into aggressive action and did not persist. At the risk of repetition, in the critical period 1808–19, the Qawasim were not considered traders: immediately before that, they were not considered significant traders; and there was no reason even then to suppose their commerce had attracted public or private notice in Bombay. In 1803–4, British merchants at Bombay had provoked much 'discussion and public complaint' on account of the recent progress of Muscat shipping, and even more that of the 'English Arabs', or those entitled to the British flag by virtue of their residence at Bombay, in the carrying trade with the Persian Gulf and with the east coast of India. Muscat shipping was believed to have expanded greatly, at the expense of British shipping, in the preceding decade, under Sultan bin Ahmad, on account of freight charges one third those of British vessels, assisted by the acquisition of European-style ships, and on account of the French menace; it was urged that discriminatory regulations be enforced to stanch this progress. Detailed records of shipping at Bombay commenced only in 1800/1, and showed that Arab shipping with the Persian Gulf increased sixfold over the next five years, whereas English tonnage fluctuated around a mean. The British merchants' jealousy was directed specifically and only at Muscat shipping: their complaints were answered by David Seton, who championed the cause of unrestricted Arab trade. This discontent dropped away after 1804/5, and no Government action or change of policy apparently resulted from it. Bombay Commerce, Internal and External Reports, 1801/2–1824/5, IOR P/419/39–61, especially 40–1; Letter from principal merchants of Bombay, Bombay 4 July 1804, with other papers July–Aug., IOR P/343/14, pp. 2380–94, 2860–88; another such letter, from Bruce, Fawcett and Co., Forbes and Co., and Alexander Adamson, recorded 25 Oct. 1804, IOR Home Misc. 333, pp. 663–80; (cf. IOR MSS Eur. D. 100, memorial, Calcutta 20 Nov. 1807).

63. See Kelly, *Britain*, p. 137, note 2; al-Qasimi, *The Myth*, p. 230. It is not at the least, it should be said, self-apparent that the figures do not reflect the supposed piracy; any useful judgement on the matter would require very careful consideration. (Observe also in passing Bombay Commerce, Internal and External Reports, 1804/5, IOR P/419/42, withdrawal of treasure from the Persian Gulf due to approach of Wahhabi 'freebooters'.)

64. It was not infrequently observed, for example at Muscat and off north-west India and south Arabia, that reported Qasimi activity nearby caused vessels to delay sailing. In 1814 local vessels could not be found at Bushire to make the voyage to Ras al-Khaima. In January 1820 Bruce observed, 'The effect the expedition has had in the Gulf is wonderful—before no boats would go about without being under convoy of our vessels, now you see craft of all kinds sailing about'. W. Bruce, Resident, to Warden, Bushire 22 March 1815, BA P 421/1059–60; C.W. Elwood to Warden, Porbandar 12 (18?) Nov. 1818, BA P 456/6147–9; Elwood to Warden, Porbandar 1 Feb. 1817, BA Sel. 72/235–6; Bruce to Willock, Bushire 30 Jan. 1820, PRO FO 248/38; Buckingham, *Travels in Assyria*, p. 511; and others.

65. The seizure of Arab vessels on the Mocha route not under the Company's pass was, according to Elwood, a blow for the whole merchant community of Porbandar on account of insurance: C.W. Elwood to Warden, Porbandar 3 July 1818, BA Sel. 72/554–5. On interest and insurance, Seton attested that in practice Muscat merchants, and presumably others too, 'give a premium on money advanced, and also insure their large vessels by means of their brokers': Remarks by David Seton, Muscat Resident, on report of Reporter General on External Commerce, 27 July 1804, IOR P/343/14, pp. 2875–84.

66. This was the year of the attacks upon the *Sylph* and the *Minerva*. Rates on the outward journey leapt to 6–8 per cent, from 4½ per cent in the previous year and 5 per cent in all others 1803/4–1811/12. Bombay Commerce, Internal and External Reports, 1801/2–1824/5, IOR P/419/39–61.

67. Buckingham, *Travels in Assyria*, pp. 509–11. The Bombay vessels had allegedly received the small coasting trade of Muscat for a time.

68. See above.

69. In 1765 Niebuhr had wryly observed, 'The whole coast from Bombay to Basra is inhabited by people addicted to piracy, such as the Malays, the Sangeries, the Kulis, the Arabs, with other petty nations. It might be easy for the English to exterminate these pirates ... But it is the Company's interest to leave those plunderers to scour the seas, and hinder other nations from sailing in the same latitudes. The English are therefore content with protecting their own trade'. Niebuhr, *Travels in Arabia*, vol. 2, p. 383.

70. Some had even argued against the second expedition for fear of this eventuality. There was an element of impressionism in the statements from Bushire that British shipping declined after 1819/20 since until 1823 there was no serious record of non-British shipping. In that year British shipping brought in only 35 per cent of imports at Bushire, whereas in 1817 Bruce had estimated imports on British vessels at roughly 75 per cent. In the years following 1819/20, for at least two decades, it continued to be stated that the suppression of piracy had had the long-term effect of increasing local at the comparative expense of British shipping in the Gulf: Robertson, in 1842, noted that Arab, and particularly Kuwait, vessels had especially benefited. Local shipping prospered since it was cheaper. With these changes also the indirect Muscat route for the trade of India with Bushire and Basra revived: in 1836, it was recorded that during October–March, 15 craft passed from Bushire to Muscat or Bombay, and during the remainder of the year, when monsoons prevented the sailing of local craft, 4 ships went to India; in the former period boats left Muscat for Bombay every 2½ days. Issawi, *Economic History*, pp. 89–91; Grummon, 'The Rise', pp. 178–80, 202–5; W. Bruce to Willock, Bushire 22 Sept. 1819, PRO FO 248/38; Robertson to Sheil, Bushire 23 July 1842, PRO FO 248/108; Hennell to McNeill, Bushire 15 Dec. 1836, PRO FO 248/85, (and 2 March 1837, PRO FO 248/85).

71. Petition of *c*. 36 native merchants of Bombay to Governor Nepean, Bombay 4 Nov. 1817, BA Sel. 72/448–50. Evan Nepean succeeded George Brown as Governor of Bombay in 1812, the latter having replaced Jonathan Duncan in 1811.

72. Cf. C.A. Bayly, *The New Cambridge History of India: II-1, Indian Society and the Making of the British Empire* (Cambridge University Press, Cambridge, 1988), pp. 63–4.

73. The most copious such reporting derived from the Porbandar Agent Captain C.W. Elwood.

74. 'In a pecuniary point of view some of the native merchants have suffered considerably': Governor Nepean to Hastings, Bombay 22 Sept. 1818, BA Sel. 74/4–19.

75. Governor Duncan wrote in 1797 that he 'would never have gone there had he known the state it was in': Duncan to Ross, 2 June 1797 cited in Percival Spear, *The Nabobs, a Study of the Social Life of the English in 18th Century India* (Oxford University Press, London, 1963), chap. 4, p. 71. For an evocation of social life at Bombay in 1809, see Maria Graham, *Journal of a Residence in India*, pp. 1–45, 28: 'The men are, in general, what a Hindoo would call of a higher caste than the women; and I generally find the merchants the most rational companions ... The civil servants to government being, in Bombay, for the most part young men, are so taken up with their own imaginary importance, that they disdain to learn, and have nothing to teach.'

76. Nightingale, *Trade and Empire*, chap. 4, pp. 73–127 and *passim*; Ashin Das Gupta, *Malabar in Asian Trade 1740–1800* (Cambridge University Press, Cambridge, 1967). Duncan, Governor of Bombay at the time of the first expedition, had, in fact, earlier been Commissioner in Malabar: Nightingale, *Trade and Empire*, pp. 94 ff.

77. Nightingale, *Trade and Empire*, p. 230.

78. Lorimer, *Gazetteer*, vol. 1, pp. 212–13.

79. But, according to Lorimer this was not the case at Muscat; if this was so, it did not apply to the Indian Brokers who often handled the Company's affairs there, including political

reporting, and who appear as merchants in their own right. In 1822 Bushire and Basra had at length to conform: Lorimer, *Gazetteer*, vol. 1, pp. 212–13. Dying only a few years after his spell as Bushire Resident (1780–5) before which he had served at Basra, John Beaumont, active in the country-trade, left a will which received probate on 6 February 1788 and comprised an estate worth at least £10,000: Furber, *John Company*, pp. 210–14.

80. 'The horses sent to Bengal are always of a finer kind and higher price. The greatest number of these are sent from here by the British Resident on his own private account': Buckingham, *Travels in Assyria*, p. 385.

81. Manesty wrote that 'with the bold and enterprising spirit of a British merchant he had carried on a trade with India, [Batavia], Arabia, Persia, Courdistan [Kurdistan], Medina, Syria, to the reciprocal benefit of those countries, and should ... have been one of the richest individuals in the Company's service, but for events which he could not control.' In September 1808, he valued all his property at under £12,000, less a debt from the Company. His export of horses had, he claimed, improved the breed in India. S. Manesty, memorial to Government, 27 Sept. 1808, with other material in IOR Home Misc. 81/637–730. Manesty had been appointed Writer in 1779, Basra Resident in 1786 (1784) and Senior Merchant in 1790. He was dismissed from his post at Basra on 30 August 1809, his 'proceedings and style', even once allowance had been made for length of service on an isolated station where excessive importance was attached to rank, having finally become insupportable. He reached England on 19 May 1812, and within two months had, probably, taken his own life. It was not until 1819 that the Company made provision for his greatly troubled family. Sprig Manesty, of Woodford in Essex, had been MP for Queenborough 1727–8.

82. The *Shannon* and *Trimmer*, plundered in 1804, and the *Minerva*, taken in 1809. Manesty lost at least one vessel to a French privateer, namely the *Pearl*, captured between Basra and Bombay on 7 October 1799; and his memorial also refers to losses incurred on another of his vessels upon Government service. Ibid.; Saldanha, *Persian Gulf Précis*, vol. 1, p. 366.

83. In slight contradiction, however, Manesty had earlier, in 1798, proposed a small naval force under his command to guarantee Gulf security. Nevertheless, in the next decade he himself assisted in the 1805–6 negotiations with the Qawasim and only lost confidence in the political solution in 1809. At certain times, in 1798 and 1805, Manesty was also an advocate of closing Indian ports to the Qawasim, and in 1810 he recommended the restriction of timber exports from India. In 1819 Colquhoun felt that the then prevailing situation would almost become acceptable if the Qawasim only spared their captives and learnt to 'content themselves with the plunder which their success might award them'. S. Manesty, Resident, to Bombay, Basra 12 April 1798, BA S&P 63/1612–20, and 20 March 1810, BA P 355/2045–50; G. Colquhoun, Bombay 21 May 1819, BA S 312/973–81.

84. Malcolm expected that the commercial success of such an establishment would equip Britain with a powerful political lever on neighbouring states, particularly Iran. The only merchants who he felt might lose out thereby would be those of Muscat: Saldanha, *Persian Gulf Précis*, vol. 1, p. 446 (442–55). Malcolm's views contrast with the more customary concerns expressed in the Company's instructions to Mehdi Ali Khan only two years before. In two decades time Warden was actively arguing in the Bombay Council that the protection of its Indian subjects was to be a major purpose of the second expedition and constituted the duty of Government: Saldanha, *Persian Gulf Précis*, vol. 1, pp. 340–2; Francis Warden, Minute, Bombay 12 Aug. 1819, BA Sel. 77/1–62, and Minute of 3 April 1819, BA Sel. 74/197–211.

85. Claimed by William Hickey to have been oft-heard repeated by Anjouan (Johanna) islanders, just north of Madagascar, in 1769: William Hickey, *Memoirs of William Hickey* (Century, London, 1984), pp. 97–8.

86. For the background and events of these years see Kelly, *Britain*, chap. 2, pp. 62–98.

87. In practice, such responsibilities usually devolved upon the Bombay Marine, rather than the Royal Navy, during these years.

88. Malcolm had noted Russian activity in northern Iran with alarm in 1800: Saldanha, *Persian Gulf Précis*, vol. 1, p. 448. Cf. Saldanha, *Persian Gulf Précis*, vol. 2, p. 16; and Kelly, *Britain*, pp. 96–7.

89. Lt Skinner visited Muscat two years before Mehdi Ali Khan negotiated the *Qaulnama*,

which was in turn confirmed by Malcolm in 1800. Before this, as indeed during the second decade of the century, the Company was represented at Muscat solely by an Indian Broker.

90. Bogle, Watts, Seton and Bunce all died at Muscat between 1800 and 1809. Smith left the station for health reasons in 1810 and his position was left vacant.

91. David Seton died in the Resident's country-house at Barka on 2 August 1809. He had returned to Muscat in February after an almost unbroken absence of over two years; he was on duty in connection with Cutch (and Kathiawar) in 1802–3, ordered to south Arabia in 1806 and to Sind in 1808. According to his will of October 1807, he had three children at Surat then aged two, seven and ten. In the event of his death, they were to be sent to the care of his mother Rebecca Seton Gelinerton near Edinburgh. He appears finally to have left 120,000 rupees in trust for his mother and children. Lt W. Eatwell to Bombay, HC brig *Vestal*, Barka 3 Aug. 1809, BA P 338/8079–81; other material 338/7990–8002, 339/8453–7; Wills and Administrations, Bombay, 19 Oct. 1809, IOR L/AG/34/29/343; Nightingale, *Trade and Empire*, pp. 200–1, 206, 213; Kelly, *Britain*, pp. 77, 110.

92. The orders to the commanders of the first expedition were founded on local information supplied by Seton, and note 'the unfortunate loss by death of Captain Seton at a period so critical as the present'. In the second decade of the century Francis Warden relied upon Seton as his prime source for an account, since published, of Muscat and Qawasim history. Chief Secretary to Government Francis Warden to Wainwright and Smith, Bombay Castle 7 Sept. 1809, BA P 339/8428–44; Thomas, *Arabian Gulf Intelligence*, pp. 55–60, 167–87, 299–312, 361–72, 427–36, 521–4.

93. See especially his historical, geographical and political sketches: D. Seton to Bombay, Surat 9 July 1802, BA S&P 126/4595–4612; Seton to Bombay, Baroda 2 July 1807, BA S&P 208/4937–4950; Seton, cited in Minutes for 10 Dec. 1808, BA S&P 255/14150–9; Seton, report, Muscat 19 Feb. 1809, BA P 325/2638–50.

94. Seton had accompanied Badr in his expedition to recover Minab and Bandar Abbas from the Banu Mu'in. Bruce was hard put to explain the situation to the Persian authorities: W. Bruce, Acting Resident, to Bombay, with enclosures and Council minute, Bushire 2 July 1805, BA S&P 170/4090–9; D. Seton, Resident, to Bombay, Muscat 25 July 1805, with relevant Council minute, BA S&P 170/4067–75; 171/4349–51, 173/5441–3. As to the more general point, note Seton's statement to the Banu Mu'in Shaikh that, 'I have entered into an agreement with Sayyid Badr that our peace and war should be one': Seton to Mulla Hasan of Qishm, 20 Oct. 1805, BA S&P 173/5688–90.

95. When Muscat was strong the Qawasim would 'sink into nothing and durst not show themselves': D. Seton to Bombay, Baroda 2 July 1807, BA S&P 208/4937–50.

96. In early 1808 Seton had described the condition of Muscat as one of 'degrading submission' to the Wahhabis: Kelly, *Britain*, pp. 109–10.

97. A somewhat liberal interpretation of affairs: D. Seton to Brig.-Gen. Malcolm, Muscat 19 and 20 Feb. 1809, BA P 325/2633–50.

98. Wainwright and Smith to Bombay, including substance of discussion with ruler, Muscat Dec. 1809, BA P 350/29–36.

99. The Supreme Government (Lord Minto and others) wrote in April 1809, 'the interest of the British government in the suppression of the pirates is not exclusively of a commercial nature ... the independence of the state of Muscat is of material importance to our interests and the preservation of that independence appears at the moment to turn upon the co-operation of the British power against the Qasimi pirates.' This was, of course, essentially Seton's reasoning, transmitted via Malcolm. Fort William to Rear Admiral Drury, 3 April 1809, BA P 329/4386–8.

100. Napoleon to Gardane, 10 May 1807, cited in Kelly, *Britain*, p. 82.

101. The secret Treaty of Finkenstein, signed on 4 May 1807, offered Iran French support over Persian claims to Georgia in return for a number of anti-British concessions. The Peace of Tilsit soon after represented an accommodation between France and Russia. Gardane reached Tehran in December 1807.

102. Two French officers would visit Bandar Abbas, Qishm and Hormuz in February 1808, before returning to Shiraz: N.H. Smith, Resident, to Fort William, enclosing two intercepted French letters, Bushire 11 March 1808, BA S&P 229/4150–4.

103. See Kelly, *Britain*, pp. 78–96; Saldanha, *Persian Gulf Précis*, vol. 2, pp. 9–21. It was later even stated, though the charge was not apparently pressed and did not, it seems, figure largely in British planning, that Sultan bin Saqr of Ras al-Khaima had been 'promised assistance by the French': al-Qasimi, 'Arab "Piracy"', Appendix 1, pp. 1, 4.

104. Malcolm referred to 'the fools at home … [and] their mischievous propensity to interfere with the local government': Kelly, *Britain*, p. 93. The East India Company's sphere of influence was destined to be limited to the Gulf, centring on Bushire, while Tehran fell to the Foreign Office.

105. Saldanha, *Persian Gulf Précis*, vol. 2, p. 16.

106. Kelly, *Britain*, pp. 92–3.

107. One account of the first expedition nevertheless includes amongst its supposed results the furtherance of the 'fame of the English power so as to be favourable to the political connection between Great Britain and Persia': al-Qasimi, 'Arab "Piracy"', Appendix 1.

108. Troops put on standby at Surat for the Kharg expedition were thus simply transferred to that against Ras al-Khaima: Moyse-Bartlett, *The Pirates*, p. 44.

109. Governor J. Duncan to ruler of Muscat, Bombay 30 March 1809, BA P 326/3147–54.

110. In consequence Sadleir was sent on his well-known mission to seek the goodwill and assistance of Ibrahim Pasha. The mission was, however, a miscalculation indicative of the measure of understanding Bombay then possessed of the politics of the peninsula.

111. Governor Nepean to Hastings, Bombay 22 Sept. 1818, BA Sel. 74/4–19.

112. Kelly argues that the assumption of the position of Mogul Admiral by the Commodore in 1759 could have brought with it a legal duty to protect Indian shipping. Kelly, *Britain*, pp. 57–61; Low, *Indian Navy*, vol. 1, pp. 150–1.

113. This account of the first expedition against Ras al-Khaima appears to have been written by Bombay for the benefit of the Court of Directors. al-Qasimi, 'Arab "Piracy"', Appendix 1, pp. 1–11.

114. See Nightingale, *Trade and Empire*, pp. 231–2, *passim*.

115. As opposed to the 'misconduct and atrocious acts' of the pirate: Governor J. Duncan to ruler of Muscat, Bombay 30 March 1809, BA P 326/3147–54.

116. The official instructions to the two commanders of the first expedition expressed the hope that success in the enterprise would be conducive to 'the general good and to the relief of the commercial world against these irreclaimable pests to the general prosperity': Chief Sec. to Government Francis Warden to Wainwright and Smith, Bombay Castle 7 Sept. 1809, BA P 339/8428–44.

117. In Taylor's history of Bahrain, following Governor Nepean to Hastings, Bombay 22 Sept. 1818, BA Sel. 74/40–50, 74–5; W. Bruce to Nepean, Bushire 20 Aug. 1819, BA Sel. 75/142–4.

118. Cf. one particularly stern, authoritative-sounding, almost apocalyptic account of the first expedition which makes claim, in relation to the alleged Qasimi piracy, that, 'It must be deemed an act of the soundest policy, as well as the most enlightened philanthropy, to crush in its bud an evil of such alarming magnitude': 'A Sketch of the Proceedings of the British Armament which Sailed from Bombay in September 1809 for the Purpose of Destroying the Vessels of the Jowasmee Pirates in the Gulph of Persia', al-Qasimi, 'Arab "Piracy"', Appendix 1, pp. 1–11.

119. E.g. the circumstances of Bahrain's admission to the General Treaty in 1820, and note, for example, Warden's comments in 1819: Minute by F. Warden, Bombay Council 16 July 1819, BA S 312/1102–3.

120. 'It is vain to expect any restitution or redress from these lawless banditti who show such little regard or respect to the laws established by all civilised communities': W. Bruce, Bushire Resident, to Bombay, Hanjam Sound 28 Nov. 1816, BA P 432/2435–40. Bruce frequently uses the term 'lawless' in respect of the Qawasim.

121. W. Bruce, reporting a conversation with Rahma bin Jabir, 'Piracy was what we meant and would not admit him or any other chieftain in the Gulf to commit [it]': W. Bruce to Bombay, Bushire 2 Feb. 1820, BA P 480/1701–3.

122. Adjectives such as 'ferocious and bloodthirsty' are not uncommon: Lt Davidson to Money, HCC *Fury*, Bushire Roads 22 Jan. 1809, BA P 323/1956–8.

123. Governor Nepean to Hastings, Bombay 22 Sept. 1818, BA Sel. 74. The legal justification for each of the two expeditions was the infraction of agreements by the Qawasim to respect the British flag: this placed them 'unequivocally in the condition of public enemies' and might also have been referable to the 'admitted principle of self-defence': Adam to Warden, Fort William 22 Feb. 1817, BA Sel. 74/380–6.

124. The instructions to the commanders of the first expedition refer to the *Sylph*, the *Darya Daulat* and the *Minerva*. Those of 1819 refer to the HC *Darya Daulat* and the troop-carrying pattamar lost in 1818. Fort William stressed the importance of the *Ahmadi* in the breakdown of relations in 1817.

125. As C.W. Elwood to Carnac, Porbandar 31 Jan. 1815, BA P 420/440–1.

126. G. Colquhoun, Bombay 21 May 1819, in Minutes for 21 July, BA S 312/973–81.

127. Heude, *A Voyage*, p. 39.

128. Malcolm: 'the late insulting and atrocious conduct of these freebooters'. Manesty: 'a very considerable degree of national dishonour attaches itself to the circumstances of Arabs having dared to retard the progress of an English vessel'. Bruce: 'atrocities which it would be impossible to overlook consistently with what is due to our national character and situation.' Cf. Wainwright of Sultan bin Saqr's having had 'the audacity to demand a tribute ... to allow British ships to navigate the Persian Gulph in safety'. Brig.-Gen. J. Malcolm to Warden, Bombay 15 Dec. 1808, BA S&P 255/14393–7; S. Manesty to Bombay, Basra 8 July 1797, BA S&P 57/1539–46; W. Bruce to Newnham, Bushire 25 May 1819, BA Sel. 73/558–63; Capt. J. Wainwright to Bombay, *La Chiffone*, off Muscat Khyma 14 Nov. 1809, BA P 347/11164–5.

129. President's Minute, 26 Sept. 1819, Minutes for 29 Sept. 1819, BA Sel. 75.

130. General orders of Lt Col. Smith, *La Chiffone*, Ras al-Khaima 14 Nov. 1809, BA P 347/11174–5.

131. Bruce uses phrases such as 'lawless freebooters', 'lawless plunderers', 'lawless predatory race of robbers', 'lawless vagabonds', 'lawless Asiatic Algerines', 'inhuman barbarians' and 'the bloody avaricious merchants of Ras al-Khaima', and claims they display 'perfidy and vice' and a 'contempt for moral principles'. Some of this bluster has an obvious nautical feel to it: W. Bruce to Hasan bin Rahma, November 1816, BA Sel. 72/99–104, and BA *passim*.

132. After the beating, Bruce and the crew were put ashore 'naked' on the island of Qais. Bruce had been bound for Bombay, in December 1800, carrying despatches from the Bushire Resident. W. Bruce to Bombay, Bushire 16 Nov. 1819, BA Sel. 73/195–9; D. Seton to Bombay, Muscat 29 Dec. 1800, BA S&P 105/189–94.

133. The former Agent, the latter Resident, at Basra.

134. Fort William, whilst admitting the inevitability of the outcome of this mission, still regretted the extreme nature of Bruce's rupture, fearing it might make matters still worse: Adam to Bombay, Fort William 22 Feb. 1817, BA Sel. 74/380–6. Bruce had also been offended by the seizure at Ras al-Khaima of his vessel in 1814, a vessel sent in the hope of reaching an agreement with the Qawasim.

135. For this the Basra Agency was censured by the Court of Directors, Lorimer, *Gazetteer*, vol. 1, pp. 160–1.

136. General orders of Lt Col. Smith, *La Chiffone*, Ras al-Khaima 14 Nov. 1809, BA P 347/11175–6.

137. S. Manesty, Resident, to Bombay, near Basra 4 Aug. 1802, BA S&P 127/5133–51 (5144). (Cf. The abrasive Samuel Gillett, Master of the *William Petrie* country-ship, who 'would see any officer damned first', before he would agree to lower the unauthorized St George's ensign his ship was flying, calling 'for his pistols and swearing he would shoot any person that attempted to haul down the colours'. Capt. F.E. Loch to Bombay, HMS *Eden*, Bushire Roads 1 May 1819, with enclosures, BA P 466/3153–64.)

138. N.H. Smith, Resident, to Bombay, Bushire 1 Nov. 1798, Saldanha, *Persian Gulf Précis*, vol. 1, pp. 350–1. N.H. Smith was the brother of Lt Col. Lionel Smith, joint commander of the first expedition.

139. 'The coolness of the pirates when within the range and fire of cannon, the excellence in engagement of their vessels, system and resolution, has surprised and called forth the

admiration of the naval commanders': C.W. Elwood to Warden, Porbandar 12 Jan. 1819, BA Sel. 73/294–9.

140. Referred to, for example, by Bruce, Smith (commander of the first expedition) and Taylor: as, Thomas, *Arabian Gulf Intelligence*, p. 38, BA Sel. 74/87; cf. Ibn Qurush, alluding to the same, in D. Seton to Bombay, Muscat 4 March 1806, BA S&P 181/2399–430.

141. Warden wrote that the prevalence of piracy in the Gulf 'may be attributed wholly and exclusively to the instigation of the Wahhabi tribe. Under that impression I feel disposed in some degree to advocate the cause even of the Joasmee tribe and to palliate their enormities': paragraph 20 of Warden's Minute of 12 Aug. 1819, Bombay, BA Sel. 77/1–62. The contrary argument, of course, tended to imply that there was something in their disposition that led them to piracy.

142. Warden: 'The result of my researches has established the important fact that piracy is not indigenous to the soil or the shores of the Persian Gulf, but of recent growth; on the contrary, every tribe is rather disposed to engage in commercial pursuits.' Cf. Nepean: contemporary naval and military officers, 'so far from thinking they are disposed to quit their present predatory habits ..., consider their present habits so deeply rooted that nothing but the strong hand of power will keep them down.' : paragraph 3 of F. Warden's Minute of 12 Aug. 1819, BA Sel. 77/1–62; Governor Nepean's Minute of 6 Sept. 1819, BA Sel. 75/96–9.

143. Saldanha, *Persian Gulf Précis*, vol. 1, pp. 268–73. Moore had previously, it seems, entertained a personal animosity towards Husain Khan of Rig's overlord, Karim Khan-i Zand. The specific cause of his anger was Husain Khan's seizure of British ships. From labelling him 'pirate', he proceeds to impugn his humanity and his morals, and claims that 'Husain Khan is most commonly intoxicated with liquor; ... his people are very poor and mutinous ... they constantly go armed and it is with great difficulty that he can keep them in order'.

144. 'From these troubles partly this Gulph is in great confusion. The Imam [of Muscat] continues at war with Shaikh Rashid [bin Matar of Ras al-Khaima]. Shaikh Abdullah of Hormuz is at war with the people of Charak, as is also Shaikh Saqr of [the] Al Haram with the Tamia[?] people, which latter place the former has burnt. The Zubara and Grain [Kuwait] people are at war with the Ka'b, and Bandar Rig was a few days ago accidentally consumed by fire': Saldanha, *Persian Gulf Précis*, vol. 1, pp. 315–16.

145. Cf. also the lessons of Manesty's earlier personal quarrel with the Jews of Basra which led to the brief withdrawal of the Residency to Kuwait in 1793: Saldanha, *Persian Gulf Précis*, vol. 1, pp. 328, 330–2.

146. Cf. the (unrealized) plans discussed by Nepean, Warden and the Bombay Council before the second expedition.

147. Thompson had apparently secured a stock of Arabic bibles. He also successfully secured the use of a mosque as a church whilst in charge of the temporary British garrison at Ras al-Khaima in 1820. Thompson was later especially proud of his having inserted the slaving clause in the General Treaty, 'the earliest declaration to that effect in point of time': Moyse-Bartlett, *The Pirates*, pp. 110–11, 102, 124–5. Thompson to Bombay, Ras al-Khaima 7 May 1820, with enclosures, BA P 486/3927–58.

148. Anne Thompson to her brother Revd Thomas Barker, Ras al-Khaima 25 April 1820, cited in Moyse-Bartlett, *The Pirates*, pp. 242–3. Mrs Thompson had been reading Moore's 'Lalla Rookh'.

149. Hasan bin Rahma to Bruce, Ras al-Khaima 26–7 Nov. 1816, BA P 432/2451–2, Sel. 72/116.

150. W. Bruce to Nepean, Bushire 25 Sept. 1819, BA Sel. 76/91–100.

Notes to Appendix A

1. David Seton, Muscat Resident, to Bombay, HMS *Albion* 30 March 1808, BA S&P 229/4181–4; Lt W. Maxfield to Major Alexander Walker, Baroda Resident, HCC *Sylph*, Mandvi Roads 14 April 1808 a.m., BA S&P 232/5613–15.

2. 'The inhabitants of this coast conceive the *Sylph*'s presence here a sort of protection against the Jasmi [Qasimi] pirates.'
3. 'The Jasmi [Qasimi] pirates belong to the Gulph of Persia'.
4. Capt. David Seton, Muscat Resident, to Brig.-Gen. John Malcolm, HCC *Ternate*, Muscat Cove 5 Feb. 1809, BA P 325/2622–8. (One imagines that the two men deemed too old to make good slaves, and consequently released by the Qawasim by early February 1809, who claimed to have witnessed the arrival at Ras al-Khaima of 'some boats ... as prizes, ... part of a Surat convoy', were, if to be credited, referring to captures not off India, but elsewhere such as south Arabia: Seton to Malcolm, Muscat 16 Feb. 1809, BA P 325/2629–33. A possibly oblique interpretation, conformable to known chronology and corroborative of the Indian captures in late 1808, may not be inconceivable.)
5. According to V.G. Dighe, *Descriptive Catalogue of the Secret and Political Department Series 1755–1820* (Government Publications, Bombay, 1954), p. 370, the petition of 1 December should be located at BA S&P 254/13953–7; unfortunately it has been passed over in the Exeter collection. Cf. Kelly, *Britain*, p. 114.
6. 'Remarks ... on the subject of the late piracies in the Gulph and the best means of repressing them' by D. Seton, in Bombay Council Minutes of 10 Dec. 1808, BA S&P 255/14150–60; Vishandass, Broker, to Bombay, Muscat 26 Oct. and 7 Nov. 1808, BA S&P 252/13089–92, 254/14027–8; cf. Seton to Malcolm, Muscat 6 March 1809, BA P 325/2692–701.
7. 'some time in the last year'.
8. Petition of Sunderjee Sewjee, Bombay merchant, to Bombay Governor, Bombay 23 Feb. 1809, BA P 323/1820–1. It might seem likely that this merchant was identical with the Company's Mandvi Agent, who went by the same name, but I am not quite assured that this was the case. Sunderjee Sewjee's brother, Bhimjee, occurs at Bombay in 1817 and in the same year his nephew is described as the Minister at Porbandar. Sunderjee Sewjee's petition of February 1809, principally concerned with the loss of the *Rampasa* in that month, also mentions the *Harsingar*, which was the subject of an earlier submission. On problems with the Bombay Sunderjee's identity, note the dates on the February 1809 letters, and the hypothetical difficulty raised by the name Khitree. Sunderjee Sewjee, Mandvi Agent, to Baroda Agent, Tankarra 28 Feb. 1808, BA P 324/2340–2; and Major A. Walker, Baroda Resident, to Bombay, 18 Dec. 1808, and to Lt Macdonald of the *Lively*, Baroda 17 Dec. 1808, BA S&P 257/15016–22; C.W. Elwood, Porbandar Agent, to Bombay, Porbandar 1 Feb. 1817, BA Sel. 72/235–6; Bhimjee Sewjee, brother to Sunderjee, to Government, Bombay 30 Oct. 1817, BA Sel. 72/429–30. (Seth Sunderjee Sewjee referred to in Hyderabad Agent to Bombay, 11 Nov. 1810, BA P 374/2601–30; Yule, *Hobson-Jobson*, p. 813.)
9. Petition of Jewraz Balloo Bhatia to Bombay Governor, Bombay 9 Feb. 1809, BA P 324/2213–18. Text has 'Wahaby', 'Russul Khayma'.
10. The Cranny was a ship's clerk or accountant, who also dispensed water: A. Jan Qaisar, 'From Port to Port: Life on Indian Ships in the Sixteenth and Seventeenth Centuries', in A. Das Gupta and M.N. Pearson (eds), *India and the Indian Ocean, 1500–1800* (Oxford University Press, Calcutta, 1987), pp. 331–49 (333, 336); Yule, *Hobson-Jobson*, pp. 273–4.
11. Zinc or pewter, according to Yule, *Hobson-Jobson*, pp. 932–3.
12. 'A light and glossy twilled stuff of wool', exported from England: Yule, *Hobson-Jobson*, p. 699.
13. Benzoin.
14. Equivalent to tugger?
15. Figures actually range from 10 to 14, but would appear to include prizes.
16. D. Seton, Resident, to Malcolm, Muscat 21 March 1809, BA P 326/3243–50: *ditto*, 9 March, 325/2702–7.
17. Assar pagoda, close to the town of that name, is eight miles north of Mandvi: Milburn, *Oriental Commerce*, vol. 1, p. 112.
18. Petition of Sunderjee Sewjee, Bombay merchant, to Bombay Governor, Bombay 23 Feb. 1809, BA P 323/1820–1.
19. The Banyan Hunsraj was the great rival of Fath Muhammad in the government of Cutch.

The former was at this time based at Mandvi, and the latter, it seems, at Bhuj, where he had control of the Raja. Fath Muhammad Jemadar had originally held the premier office of Dewan before Hunsraj. Fath/Fatih ('Futteh'). Nightingale, *Trade and Empire*, pp. 200–1, 207–8; Muhammad Ali Munshi to Baroda Resident, 6 Dec. 1804, BA S&P 164/317–19; Bombay to Court of Directors, paragraphs 5–8, Bombay Minutes for 25 Feb. 1807, BA S&P 199/1209–64; Bombay to Court of Directors, paragraphs 41–3, Bombay 20 Jan. 1808, BA P 320/775–847; etc.

20. Sunderjee Sewjee, Mandvi Agent, to Acting Baroda Resident Lt James Rivett Carnac, Tankarra 28 Feb. 1809, BA P 324/2340–2; Lt T. Harriott to Superintendent of Marine Money, HCC *Zephyr*, Bombay 5 March 1809, BA P 324/2343–59.

21. Lt T. Harriott to Supt of Marine Money, HCC *Zephyr*, Bombay 5 March 1809, BA P 324/2343–59. For Bombay's overall summary of Qasimi activity thus far, see, Bombay Council to Court of Directors, paragraphs 42–4, Bombay Castle 15 April 1809, BA P 327/3599–642.

22. D. Seton, Resident, to Malcolm, Muscat 22 March 1809, BA P 326/3210–12.

23. D. Seton, Resident, to Malcolm, Muscat 6 March (apparently a mistake; should perhaps read 16 April) 1809, BA P 329/4613–16; Seton to W.A. Montague of HMS *Cornwallis*, Muscat 10 March 1809, BA P 326/3250–1.

24. D. Seton, Resident, to Malcolm, Muscat 22 March 1809, BA P 326/3210–12.

25. 'The town of Karachi is 5 or 6 miles from the anchorage': Horsburgh, *India Directory*, in Cook, *Survey*, vol. 1, p. 252. Porbandar Agent to Bombay, transmitting letter from Sunderjee Sewjee at Mandvi 20 Nov., Porbandar 25 Nov. 1813, BA P 403/3693 ff.; Muhammad Yusuf Munshi, Native Agent in Sind, to Bombay, Hyderabad 27 Aug. 1814, BA P 415/4149–63.

26. She may also have represented a separate capture. Sewjee's description of the five supposed losses as all Cutch merchant boats, need not be taken as a rigid identification.

27. Veerchund Sunder's petition does not explicitly state to which port this botella belonged, under what flag she sailed or to whom she and her cargo belonged; unlike two other cases he brings to the notice of Government in the same petition. Nonetheless, it seems that he was expressing a personal interest in the case; he may therefore have been the owner. Regarding the two other cases in this petition, see the entry for late 1814. Petition of Veerchund Sunder, Bombay merchant, to Government, Bombay 4 Dec. 1814, BA P 417/4903–6.

28. Muhammad Yusuf Munshi, Native Agent in Sind, to Bombay, Hyderabad 27 Aug. 1814, BA P 415/4149–63. Dharajah lay at the mouth of the Indus.

29. Capt. C.W. Elwood, Porbandar Agent, to Bombay, Porbandar 22 Jan. 1814, IOR R/15/1/15 pp. 96–7.

30. Sent from Karachi on 14 January, she arrived at Porbandar on the 22nd.

31. C.W. Elwood, Agent, to Bombay, Porbandar 17 Aug. 1814, BA P 415/3788–91. A particularly cautious Sindi emissary is said to have delayed his departure from Karachi to Bombay, out of fear of the reported pirates, for up to two months, until the arrival of a Company cruiser at Karachi allayed his fears: Muhammad Yusuf Munshi, Native Agent in Sind, to Bombay, Hyderabad 27 Aug. 1814, BA P 415/4149–63. Text has 'Joasmees'.

32. Communications must have been restored before 27 February. Cassee Goolab, Broker, to Bombay, Muscat (3 Feb.), 27 Feb. 1814, BA P 408/1261–8.

33. 'Information was received that in consequence of the appearance of some Company's vessels, the communication by sea was again open, the pirates having withdrawn to their ports.' Whilst returning from Karachi at this time, Captain Davidson of the HCC *Ternate* claimed to have fallen in with 10 Qawasim and left them unmolested. Muhammad Yusuf Munshi, Native Agent in Sind, to Bombay, Hyderabad 27 Aug. 1814, BA P 415/4149–63; Davidson is cited in F. Warden to Capt. Eatwell, Bombay 27 Feb. 1814, IOR R/15/1/15 pp. 93–6.

34. Information provided by Rutton Sing, in Bombay Council Minutes, entry of 7 Dec. 1814, BA P 417/4898–902.

35. Kumbaha was a dependency of Navanagar in the Gulf of Cutch. It could correspond with modern Karumbhar, or, perhaps less likely, Khambhaaya inland to the south.

36. Text may read 'Kumusa'.

37. This is the name as it occurs in the owner's petition. Sing actually speaks of a dinghy called

'*Kilooree*', the property of one 'Veerchund Sunderance/ee'; but the case details in the two versions point to the same vessel.

38. Text may read 'Sugard'.

39. Apart from the name of one of the three vessels, Sing's account accords well with those given in the owners' petitions. Petition of Veerchund Sunder to Government, Bombay 4 Dec. 1814: petition of Dyal Moolaney to Government, Bombay 26 Nov. 1814: Luckah Madas to Porbandar Agent, C.W. Elwood, Porbandar 11 Dec. 1814; BA P 417/4903–7, 4909–11, 5003–5.

40. The word 'joys' was apparently used in Bombay as an equivalent of 'jewellery': Yule, *Hobson-Jobson*, p. 465.

41. or Luckmedass.

42. The Mehtar was subordinate to the Raja of Bhuj, who soon apparently ordered the vessel's release. Text reads 'Mehta'.

43. In his petition, Moolaney describes himself as a merchant and inhabitant of Bombay. Sing writes that he 'has a shop in Bombay kept by his brother', which seems to suggest that Moolaney himself may not have been permanently based there. Text has 'Joa[/u]smee'.

44. C.W. Elwood to Bombay, Porbandar 13 Dec. 1814, BA P 417/4998–5003.

45. The promises were those contained in the provisional Anglo–Qasimi agreement of 6 October 1814.

46. In May 1816, one Ali Quli Khan wrote that the Qawasim had plundered goods and property of his worth 300,000 rupees, noting that the matter had already been referred to the Bushire Resident. No further details of the incident are given. It could conceivably have fallen under one of the captures off India in early 1815, or at another time; or it may even have been the result of an act of plunder elsewhere, such as those of the *Omid* or *Salamat Savoy*. Nawab Ulee Koolee Khan of Patna to Bombay Governor, 5 May 1816, BA P 430/1375–6.

47. Henry Meriton, Supt of Marine, to Bombay Council, Bombay 4 Feb. 1815, and reply of Chief Secretary F. Warden, 28 Feb., BA P 420/427–30; cf. also, Bombay to Bushire Resident Lt W. Bruce, Bombay Castle 3 March 1815, BA P 420/448–50.

48. C.W. Elwood, Agent, to Bombay, Porbandar 25 Feb. 1815, BA P 420/510; cf. Elwood to Lt Maillard, Porbandar 21 March, BA P 420/665–6.

49. William Bruce, Resident, to Bombay, relaying news brought by a boat from Linga, Bushire 22 March 1815, BA P 421/1059–60.

50. Traffic resumed when the Mangrol merchants received their news.

51. It is not clear what this word, which does not however occur in the Broker's subsequent report, refers to. The strictest reading might suggest Omanis, rather than this being a reference to Yemenis or Ajman; conceivably, then, it intends such as the Suri Qawasim. Later in the same despatch, however, the Broker reports the capture of a baghla sailing from Bushire to Muscat by a group which could read the 'Enamees', and which in the context might suggest the Na'im, presumably of Ajman. Na'im would be the natural reading also of Imanees.

52. Goolab Anundass, Broker, to Bombay, Muscat 19 March 1815, and a slightly earlier report under entry 22 March, BA P 420/598–9, 746–7.

53. These two groups of Bahraini vessels passed through Muscat around the end of December and the start of January 1815/16. They were destined for Bombay and then Malabar, 'where the whole will be completely filled with rice, taking nothing else on board, that they may have a stock of provisions for two years and seek their own redress without standing in need of supplies.' This, at least, was the suspicion at Muscat, where it was believed that the Utub might soon break with the ruler. Muscat Broker to Bombay, Muscat 6 and 10 Jan. 1816, BA P 427/283–7.

54. Muscat Broker to Bombay, Muscat 6 and 10 Jan. 1816, BA P 427/283–7.

55. H. Meriton, Supt of Marine, to Governor Nepean, Bombay 30 Nov. 1816; C.W. Elwood, Agent, to Bombay, Porbandar 26 and 28 Dec. 1816; Deposition of Dewarjee, pilot of *Darya Daulat*, Porbandar 27 Feb. 1817; BA Sel. 72/65–6, 159–66, 285–9.

56. This was the judgement of Captain Macmurdo, Bhuj Resident. Capt. William Hill to Bombay, HMS *Towey*, off the Indus 20 Feb. 1817, BA P 435/614–15.

57. Sunderjee Sewjee's agent at Mandvi spoke on 15 January of 11 Qawasim; Macmurdo, also at Mandvi, reported on 30 January that there were 4–5 dows and a similar number of jymers, and, perhaps shortly afterwards, he talked of 6 sail; Govindjee writes that 4 Qawasim attacked the *Luckmee Pussaud*; the *Darya Daulat's* Serang apparently described the rendezvous of three baghlas with the 7 trankeys near Shahbandar. It is impossible to be certain how many, or what class, of vessels were involved, or even whether they truly formed or acted as one group. The Serang's is first-hand evidence of a sort, and Govindjee's is nearly so, being the report sent him by his crew from Lakhpat. Lower figures tend to look more convincing. Letter from Sunderjee Sewjee's agent at Mandvi, with another letter from Porbandar, 15 and 20 Jan. 1817, BA Sel. 72 /210–12; Capt. Macmurdo, Bhuj Resident, to Bombay 30 Jan. and ?Feb. 1817, /231–2, 241 ff.; Deposition of Sewjee Govindjee, Porbandar merchant, Porbandar 1 Feb., and petition of same to Governor, Bombay 5 Feb. 1817, /238–9, 228–9; C.W. Elwood, Agent, to Bombay, Porbandar 2 March 1817, /314–16.

58. On the cotia, or kotia, and other Indian craft, see Hawkins, *The Dhow*, pp. 91–125. Apropos Hawkins p. 92, note that in the material used for the present work, the term baghla, written bugla, buglah, bugalah etc., is almost certainly only used of Arab vessels: the sole unequivocal literal exception speaks of a Baluchi 'bugla' and this traded with Muscat. Text reads 'colliahs'.

59. This list was brought to Bushire by HMS *Towey* on 22 March. W. Bruce, Resident, to Bombay, Bushire 13 Feb. and 25 March 1817, BA Sel. 72/341–2, BA S 312/1083–4.

60. The date of the news of the Qawasim's departure seems too late; few of the captures listed seem potentially to match those otherwise recorded for January.

61. The possibility that all these accounts refer imperfectly to one series of events probably cannot be ruled out: the list of 18 supposed captures refers predominantly to Sind, whence intelligence of this kind might otherwise not have been forthcoming; some of these supposed captures could also perhaps be equated with those reportedly lost before February. The effect of this interpretation would be to increase the total list of alleged Qasimi prizes, in late 1816 and early 1817, by 11 or less, depending on the true accuracy of the locations given for the various attacks.

   The list of 18 captures arrived at Bushire on 22 March, by which time many of the Qawasim and their prizes were said to have returned to Ras al-Khaima. These dates suggest that the alleged captures had been made before March. Captain Hill, who brought this list to Bushire from Muscat, made no mention of these captures when he wrote from the Indus on 20 February; nor did the Porbandar Agent in a dispatch of 2 March. It seems that the list had been compiled from information collected by various cruiser commanders at Muscat and during recent their passage there via Sind and Makran. It is perhaps a mistake to make too much of it. Capt. William Hill to Bombay, HMS *Towey*, at sea off the Indus 20 Feb. 1817, BA P 435/614–15; C.W. Elwood, Agent, to Bombay, Porbandar 2 March 1817, BA P 435/ 647–8. Cf. W. Bruce, Resident, to Bombay, Bushire 14 May 1817, BA Sel. 72/410, which implies that the first official notification of the loss of the *Darya Daulat*, acknowledged in this despatch, went out to Bruce from Bombay on 10 March, suggesting that this news, at least, was not current in the Gulf until after 22 March.

62. The names appear to read: Konsoordass Ransordass, Mody Nager Herjee, Premjee Purtootum (?), Khoonjee Wastah, Nimchund Amichund, Nanjee Sheskron, Tucker Maujee Annundjee, Tucker Dyall Moolany, Jewraz Balloo, Guddoomul Terthaney, Tucker Bhanjee Rama, Mollyram Tazmuth, Sewjee Govindjee, Pragjee Purmanund, Tucker Annundjee Panhdum, Tucker Jaram Jevaney, Mauree Ranjee (?), Nathia Moosand, Bhemjee Jewaney, Pragjee Luckmedass, Pragjee Anundjee, Toolsardass Mathooradass, Jayehund Lallehund, Moorarjee Luckmadass, Amoorchund Khoonjee, Govoothan Verjar, Waljee Jeram, Moojee Balloo Sulleeran (?), Nanjee Dhamjee, Jawab Khotah, Poorjab Caryee (?), Burzorjee Byramjee, Memon Adjer Aboobaker, Shaikh Manahi bin Abd ?, and 2–3 others. Petition of *c.* 36 native merchants of Bombay to Governor Nepean, Bombay 4 Nov. 1817, BA Sel. 72/448–50.

63. C.W. Elwood to Bombay, Porbandar 21 Oct. 1817, BA Sel. 72/432–4; James Macmurdo, Resident in Cutch and Collector in Anjar, to Bombay, Anjar 25 Oct. 1817, BA Sel. 72/437–8.

64. C.W. Elwood, Agent, to Bombay, Porbandar 27 Oct. 1817, BA Sel. 72/441–2; Corjee Sewjee to Sunderjee Sewjee, Porbandar 21 Oct. 1817, BA Sel. 72/464; Portuguese Chief to British Acting Chief, Surat 20 Nov. 1817, BA Sel. 72/490; Portuguese Governor of Daman to Bombay Governor, Daman 16 Nov. 1817, BA P 439/2410–11.

65. Grant had entered the Bombay Marine as midshipman in 1810, and soon distinguished himself. He suffered a harrowing three months' confinement in the jungles of Kathiawar in 1820, but after a few years returned to active service, eventually being promoted to Senior Naval Officer on the Surat station. Ill health finally obliged him to retire to England in 1838, where he died in September 1874 at the age of 81. At the end of his life, Grant recalled his experience of captivity in 1820, at the hands of the noted Gujarati outlaw, or bahirwatia, Bawawalla: 'My sufferings during confinement were almost beyond endurance, and I used to pray in the evening that I might never see another morning ... I shall never forget the heavenly sensation of the hot bath and clean clothes I got in the tent of the Nawab of Joonughur's Dewan. The fever and ague then contracted continued on me for five years, and the ill effects still remain, my head being at times greatly troubled with giddiness, and I have severe fits of ague; my memory is also much affected, but I can never forget the foregoing incidents, though it is now upwards of fifty years since they occurred.' Low, *Indian Navy*, vol. 1, pp. 274–84.

66. C.W. Elwood to Bombay, Porbandar 14 Nov. 1817, BA Sel. 72/501–4; F.D Ballantine, Assistant, to Baroda Resident Capt. James Rivett Carnac, Camp Navanagar 26 Oct. 1817, BA Sel. 72/460–1.

67. Bombay Council Minutes of 6 and 10 Nov. 1817, BA Sel. 72/452–3, 466; Capt. W. Hill to Government, HMS *Towey*, Bombay 26 Nov. 1817, with reply of 28 Nov., BA Sel. 72/495–9; H. Meriton, Supt of Marine, to Government, Bombay 4 Dec. 1817, BA Sel. 72/512–13.

68. C.W. Elwood, Agent, to Bombay, Porbandar 4 Sept. 1817, BA Sel. 72/560–4; H. Meriton, Supt of Marine, to Government, 18 Sept. 1818, BA Sel. 72/567–9.

69. Portuguese Chief to British Acting Chief, Surat 20 Nov. 1817, BA Sel. 72/490; also Portuguese Governor of Daman to Bombay Governor, Daman 16 Nov. 1817, BA P 439/2410–11.

70. This refers to the Bombay merchant Khettoo Damjee, owner of the *Sacry Sallamly*: see text below.

71. Grant appears to have been the source of these reports; he passed the news on to the Governor of Diu, who then transmitted it to his colleagues at Surat and Daman.

72. Sewjee's information was conveyed in a letter to his brother at Bombay dated Mandvi 20 Oct., and was passed on to Government the day after it was received on 29 Oct.: Bhimjee Sewjee to Government, Bombay 30 Oct. 1817, BA Sel. 72/429–30.

73. Text reads 'Dyal Multany/ey'. The name also apparently occurs in the general petition of 4 November.

74. Petition of Dyal Multaney of Bombay, merchant, inhabitant, to Governor Nepean, Bombay 31 Oct. 1817, BA Sel. 72/444–6.

75. The estimated coss in Bengal was often about 2 miles, in Madras 2¼. Nevertheless the distance varied greatly in different parts. Yule, *Hobson-Jobson*, pp. 261–2, has values ranging from 1¼ to 3, or even, perhaps, 4 miles.

76. Text appears to read 'briat': breathe? break?

77. Petition of Khettoo Damjee to Governor Nepean, Bombay 12 Nov. 1817, BA Sel. 72/477–8.

78. Mir Muhammad Khan, Chief of Luz, to Bombay Governor, 31 January 1819, BA Sel. 73/614–17; Bombay Governor to Amirs of Sind, 10 Dec. 1818, BA Sel. 71/159–61. Text has 'Juwasimees'.

79. Extract of a letter from Lt Guy of the HCC *Psyche*, 10 Feb. 1819, BA P 462/1290–6.

80. Lt Thomas Tanner to Supt of Marine Meriton, HCC *Thetis*, off Mandvi 31 Oct. 1818, BA P 455/5890–6.

81. Examination and Depositions of Keywall, Supercargo or Banyan in boat one, and Parraree, Nakhuda of boat two, taken down before Lt J(/I). M. Guy of the HCC *Psyche* 26 Oct.; Deposition of Progjee, Mandvi merchant connected with Sulaiman, and of Abojee, native of Mandvi, taken before Tanner 30 Oct.; Lt R. Cogan to Tanner, Mandvi 30 Oct., with Tanner's list of arms found on board; BA P 455/5897–909.

82. The text reads 'bags, or baskets, of dates' and 'baskets for fish': it is tempting to hypothesize a copyist's error in the second phrase, and to read instead 'baskets *of* fish'.
83. or 'Kewall'.
84. Lt Cogan to Tanner, 30 Oct.
85. Parraree's deposition of 26 Oct.
86. Elwood in fact imagined the Qawasim's appearance off Kathiawar to have been the result of activity on the part of the Company's cruisers off Cutch and Sind: C.W. Elwood, Agent, to Bombay, Porbandar 7 Nov. 1818, BA Sel. 72/572–6.
87. Lt J(/I).M. Guy to Supt of Marine Meriton, HCC *Psyche*, Porbandar Roads 16 Nov. 1818, BA P 456/6138–45; J. Macmurdo, Cutch Resident, to Bombay, Anjar 9 Nov. 1818, BA P 456/6194–5.
88. Sunderjee Sewjee to Bombay Governor, Bombay 17 Nov. 1818, BA Sel. 72/578–9. Text has 'Joasmeas'.
89. Sunderjee Sewjee to Bombay Governor, Bombay 17 Nov. 1818; Capt. C.W. Elwood, Agent, to Bombay, Porbandar 7 Nov. 1818, BA Sel. 72/572–9.
90. Tanner had set sail from Porbandar to Mandvi on 4 November. Lt Thomas Tanner to Porbandar Agent Capt. Elwood, HCC *Thetis*, off Mandvi Roads 9 Nov. 1818, BA P 456/6134–5. (Also, H. Meriton to Governor, Bombay 25 Nov. 1818, with enclosures from Capt. G. Walker of the HCC *Teignmouth*, and Lt G. Grant, Com. of HH the Guicowar's pattamars, BA Sel. 71/238–45.) Muddie lay south of Dwarka. Text has 'Joassmee'.
91. or 'Rannah' (Rana).
92. The report of this occurrence may in fact refer to a very similar incident which took place on 11 November: see text, below.
93. C.W. Elwood, Agent, to Bombay, Porbandar 12 Nov. 1819, BA Sel. 71/222–5; Lt S. Powell cited in Moyse-Bartlett, *The Pirates*, p. 78.
94. Lt Guy to Meriton, HCC *Psyche*, Porbandar Roads 16 Nov. 1818; C.W. Elwood, Agent, to Bombay, Porbandar 17 Nov. 1818, BA P 456/6138–45, 6129–34.
95. Text reads 'Madopore'.
96. Seazkrun claims the Qawasim numbered about 8 or, with their prizes, 18 sail. Petition of Nanjee Seazkrun for Seazkrun Herjee the Company's Mocha Broker, to Bombay Governor, Bombay 18 November 1818, BA Sel. 71/186–7. Seazkrun's name appears the general petition of late 1817: see above, note. Elwood describes the owner of the dow taken at Mangrol as Nanjee Veerjee of Porbandar: C.W. Elwood, Agent, to Bombay, Porbandar 12 Nov. 1819, BA Sel. 71/222–5; regarding another of this merchant's vessels, see J. Macmurdo, Collector and Custom Master in Cutch, to Bombay, Anjar 18 Nov. 1818, BA P 456/6263–4.
97. A number of these names occur as signatories to the petition of 4 November 1817: see above, note.
98. Sunderjee Sewjee, petition to Bombay Governor, Bombay 12 July 1819, BA Sel. 73/661–2; also Sunderjee Sewjee to Bombay Governor, Bombay 29 December 1818, BA Sel. 71/182–3.
99. Could read '741'.
100. According to Yule, *Hobson-Jobson* pp. 688–9, the pawl was a small tent with two light poles and steep sloping sides.
101. According to Yule, *Hobson-Jobson* p. 325, doriya was a form of fabric, made originally of cotton and later of pure or mixed silk, whose characteristic pattern was stripes running in the warp threads.
102. or perhaps 'Rewarjoos'.
103. On Macmurdo, see Bird, James, 'Biographical Sketch of the Late Captain James M'Murdo', *Journal of the Royal Asiatic Society*, vol. 1 (London, 1834), pp. 123–7.
104. W. Bruce, Resident, to Bombay, Bushire 6 Feb. 1819; Capt. F.E. Loch to Bombay, HMS *Eden*, off Bahrain 17 Feb. 1819; Capt. D.D. Conyers to Loch, HCC *Mercury*, Muscat Cove 21 March 1819; extract of letter from Lt J. Arthur, HCC *Antelope* 22 March; BA Sel. 73/357–9, 418–23, 455–7, 460–3.
105. Text reads 'Korinar'.
106. C.W. Elwood, Agent, to Bombay, Porbandar 30 Nov. 1818, BA P 456/6337–8.
107. H. Meriton, Supt of Marine, to Bombay Governor, Bombay 23 November 1818, BA P 456/6136–8.

108. Cf. C.W. Elwood, Agent, to Bombay, Porbandar 12 Jan. 1819, BA Sel. 73/294–9.
109. 'On the 21st [Nov.] seventeen boats from Bombay and other ports arrived in the Porbandar Roads from the different creeks in which they had taken shelter from the Qawasim': H. Meriton to Governor, Bombay 1 Dec. 1818, BA P 456/6277–9. Text has 'Joassmees'.
110. C.W. Elwood to Bombay, Porbandar 24 Nov. 1818, BA Sel. 71/143B–152.
111. Muscat Broker to Bombay, Muscat 17 Nov. 1818, BA P 456/6232–6.
112. Powell presumably intends battils or baghlas.
113. Lt Powell cited in Moyse-Bartlett, *The Pirates*, p. 78; also C.W. Elwood, Agent, to Bombay, Porbandar 12 Nov. 1819, BA Sel. 71/222–5. Text has 'Joasmee'.
114. Conyers and Arthur, the officers involved in the release of the sepoys' wives, somewhat loosely, and presumably on the evidence of the women themselves, talk of the attack having happened four months before c. 21 March. They also locate the attack variously at Anjar, in the Gulf of Cutch, or (!) off Sind. Troop movements from Bombay to Cutch continued until the following spring, and an attack off southern Cutch or Kathiawar in the third week of December cannot be ruled out. November is nevertheless preferable, for the reasons cited in the text. D.D. Conyers to Loch, HCC *Mercury*, Muscat Cove 21 March 1819; Lt James Arthur to Meriton, HCC *Antelope*, 22 March 1819, BA Sel. 73/455–7, 460–3.
115. Captain Conyers implies that the women captives asserted the palanquin to have been taken on board their own pattamar. This is really impossible. Conceivably they meant to say that the palanquin was taken by the same boat that captured them. Clearly they knew about it from close at hand. D.D. Conyers to Loch, HCC *Mercury*, Muscat Cove 21 March 1819, BA Sel. 73/455–7.
116. The witness was a Banyan who had been released at Ras al-Khaima and travelled overland to Muscat; when his story reached Bushire, it actually spoke of the attack having happened 'about two months since'. W. Bruce, Resident, to Bombay, Bushire 18 May 1819, BA Sel. 73/627–33.
117. Extract of proceedings of the HCC *Thetis*, Lt T. Tanner, in H. Meriton to Governor, Bombay 16 Jan. 1819, BA Sel. 73/304–8.
118. Capt. C.W. Elwood, Agent, to Bombay, Porbandar 20 Dec. 1818, enclosing Handley to Elwood of 16 Dec., BA Sel. 73/259–62. Handley was at this time on service in Okha; he was first informed of the Qawasim's appearance by the Carcoon at Dwarka.
119. H. Meriton to Governor, Bombay 31 Dec. 1818, citing Lt Robson of the HCC *Prince of Wales*, BA Sel. 73/265–7.
120. J. Macmurdo, Cutch Resident, to Bombay, Anjar 22 Dec. 1818, BA Sel. 73/283–4.
121. C.W. Elwood, Agent, to Bombay, Porbandar 23 Dec. 1818, BA Sel. 73/249–52.
122. C.W. Elwood, Agent, to Bombay, Porbandar 23 Dec. 1818, BA Sel. 73/249–52.
123. Not including the Ormara incident.
124. ... 'but it must have been great.' C.W. Elwood, Agent, to Bombay, Porbandar 12 Jan. 1819, BA Sel. 73/294–9.
125. The first concerned two supposedly Qasimi battils towing a boat with a small cargo of cotton, which last was overtaken by the *Psyche*. See Chapter Eight.
126. F.E. Loch to Bombay, enclosing interrogation of captives, HMS *Eden*, Muscat 2 Jan. 1819, BA Sel. 73/320–6.
127. C.W. Elwood to Bombay, Porbandar 2 March 1819, BA Sel. 73/348–51.
128. C.W. Elwood, Agent, to Bombay, Porbandar 9 March 1819, BA P 464/2040–1.
129. Lt J.H. Grubb to Meriton, HC ketch *Chaeer*, Bombay harbour 14 March 1819; Lt George Robson to Meriton, HCC *Prince of Wales*, citing Lt Dominicetti, Porbandar 10 March 1819; BA P 464/2043–8.
130. Elwood could not recall any Qasimi appearance off these coasts so late as this.
131. Lt Grubb, cited in H. Meriton, Supt of Marine, to Governor, Bombay 16 March 1819, BA P 464/2042–3.
132. C.W. Elwood to Acting Baroda Resident James Williams, Porbandar 7 April 1819, BA Sel. 73/482–4. Text has 'Ras ul Khymun[?/a]', and earlier 'Ras ul Khyma'.
133. F.E. Loch to Bombay Governor, HMS *Eden*, off Muscat 3 Oct. 1819, BA Sel. 73/111.
134. C.W. Elwood, Agent, to Bombay, Porbandar 13 Oct. 1819, BA Sel. 73/130–4.

135. Information from lascar Samut of the *Bhuwanee* dinghy, arrived at Bombay from Cutch, in Bombay Council Minutes of 25 Oct. 1819, BA Sel. 73/108.
136. J. Macmurdo, Bhuj Resident, to Capt. Thomas Tanner, Camp Bhuj 16 Oct. 1819, BA Sel. 73/152–4.
137. This looks dubious, as does the precision of the number of matchlock-men.
138. C.W. Elwood, Agent, to Bombay, Porbandar 17 Nov. 1819, BA Sel. 73/156–8.
139. The nature of this cattle-raid also recalls a comment made by Elwood in December 1818 and cited above.

Notes to Appendix B

1. Or, less likely, conceivably Samun, just west of Saihut, at latitude 15°7′ N, longitude 50°55′ E.
2. It may, however, be worth noting that an unconnected translation from Gujarati by the translator of this report, uses the name 'Rasul' to describe an island in the Gulf near where Sayyid Sultan was killed: it may conceivably then have referred to Qishm or a neighbouring island, or to somewhere off the bar of Basra. Pudumul Judumul, EIC Broker, to Bombay, Muscat 21 and 24 Nov. 1804, BA S&P 162/4902–7. Cf. Thomas, *Arabian Gulf Intelligence*, p. 577 ('Rassul'); (the modern *Times Atlas of the World* shows a river Rasul inland north of Laft).
3. Conceivably Summana?
4. Dr Pringle to Bombay, Mocha 9 March 1804, with enclosures, including translated information from leading Banyan, BA S&P 157/1943–58. 'Barbara and Zugla'.
5. Perhaps the middle or later part of the month.
6. Seton argued that vessels coming from India to Mocha in March and April, and the Muscat dows that might return from Mocha at the start of May, were at risk.
7. Off Sharma. Horsburgh, *India Directory*, in Cook, *Survey*, vol. 1, p. 236.
8. The reading of this date may or may not be reliable; on the face of it, it looks a little soon. Events of this kind tended to have repercussions: on 1 May, 27 Utub sailed from Muscat up the Gulf: they were forced to expect action, since they had learnt of 10 Qawasim about Salama wa-Banatuha, and saw this as an opportunity for revenge; it may in fact be that nothing came of it. David Seton, Resident, to Bombay, Muscat 7 May 1809, BA P 329/4607–11.
9. Cf. 1810, concerning Mukalla. D. Seton, Resident, to Brig.-Gen. Malcolm, Muscat 9 and 30 March 1809, with another erroneously dated 6 March, which should perhaps read 16 or 26 April, and Seton's despatch of 7 May to Bombay, BA P 325/2702–7, 327/374(5)–9, 329/4607–16.
10. Capt. Henry Rudland to Henry Salt, Ambassador to Abyssinia, British Residency Mocha 1 Jan. 1810, BA P 358/2898–903.
11. The American was presumably a source for Rudland's view. Ibid.; Sundry papers written by A. Hammitt of Baltimore apparently dated Mocha 8 Feb. and 16 May 1807, and enclosed in Rudland to Bombay 25 Feb. 1810; Rudland to Bombay, Mocha 1 March 1810, with Bombay Council Minutes of 4 June: BA P 358/2898–903, 2916–23, 2976–84. (Cf. also Capt. Rudland's journal, Mocha 4 July 1811, BA P 379/4855–7.)
12. Text reads 'Kesh, in the Mohiah territories'.
13. 'Futteh ul Rehman'.
14. According to the report which reached Forbes, the only one to offer any dates. He observed that the activities of the Qawasim had caused great alarm in Mocha, and appeared to signify a resumption of their predatory pursuits.
15. According to Forbes, 'in cold blood'; the Muscat Broker recounts a feeble resistance of under two hours.
16. They may have put into Shuhair.

17. They had certainly left south Arabia before 14 April.
18. Further Declaration by Second Nakhuda of the *Ahmadi*, Bombay 26 Aug. 1816, BA Sel. 72/21–7. See Chapter Six, section three.
19. There is no indication where. The Naqib of Mukalla may possibly have had these in mind when he stated that 30 vessels had originally sailed from Ras al-Khaima, 10 of which then broke off and proceeded to south Arabia; the six active off Shihr were part of these 10, whilst the remaining 4, one infers, made for the Red Sea; these last could be identified with the squadron under Hazza', but this is uncertain. The name Hazza' is most obviously to be associated with Dubai, but this could be of no consequence: Hazza' (bin Za'al) still ruled Dubai in 1814, and perhaps 1818, but had been succeeded by his son Muhammad, a minor, by January 1820. One Shaikh Hazza', presumably a different man, was replaced by Sayyid Sa'id of Muscat as Governor of Shinas in December 1817, whereupon he fled to the Ras al-Khaima coast: Goolab Anundass, Broker, to Bombay, Muscat early–mid Jan. 1818, BA P 443/834–7.
20. Goolab Anundass, Broker, to Bombay, Muscat 10 April 1815 (?—Islamic dates wrongly converted: text reads 31 March), BA P 421/1036–8. Naqib of Mukalla to Bombay Governor, (c. late March?), in Minutes for 26 April, BA P 421/920–2; and subsequent letter of 14 April, BA P 422/1235–8. T. Forbes, Mocha Agent, to Bombay, Mocha 25 March 1815, BA P 422/1337–8.
21. These may, or may not, have been a separate party from those which had visited Shihr.
22. 'Dinjey'. Goolab Anundass, Broker, to Bombay, Muscat 10 April 1815 (?—Islamic dates wrongly converted: text reads 31 March), BA P 421/1036–8.
23. Ibid.
24. He had, on her outward journey, freighted her with 17 Company's horses taken by the Qawasim in the *Darabiya* and since restored.
25. I.e. presumably Faid Alam, Sulaiman Shah, Faid Rabbani.
26. Naqib of Mukalla to Bombay Governor, 5 May 1816, BA P 430/1310–13.
27. Termed 'Chieftain of Qatif'.
28. Text reads 'Suhood in the neighbourhood of Mukalla'. Two declarations on oath by Second Nakhuda of the *Ahmadi*, Abd al-Razzaq bin Abd al-Hayy, Bombay 24 and 26 Aug. 1816, BA Sel. 72/13–14 (11–27).
29. Text reads 'buttillas'.
30. 'Towree' bandar.
31. Elwood, Agent, to Bombay, Porbandar 23 July 1818, enclosing translated letter from Mocha to merchant Narjee Vurjee, BA P 453/4882–5.
32. Matching the two groups like this has an obvious seductive elegance; but although the general circumstances look compatible, the haziness of Chadayappah's narrative precludes further really comfortable speculation. See Chapter Five, section four.
33. Broker to Bombay, Muscat 1 March 1819, and following Bombay Council letter to commander of HMS *Orlando*, Bombay Castle 18 March 1819, with other similar material, BA P 464/2032–9, 2049–54.
34. Reported in Capt. G.F. Sadleir to Bombay, with enclosures, HCC *Mercury*, Muscat Cove 18 May 1819, BA Sel. 73/621–5, P 467/3259–62.
35. Sadleir described the cruise as an otherwise fruitless one on 15 May. Capt. G.F. Sadleir to Bombay, Muscat 15 May 1819, BA Sel. 74/281–303.
36. Text reads 'Deria Doulet/Dowlut'.
37. Junior Police Magistrate to Chief Secretary, Bombay 29 May 1819, BA Sel. 73/611–12.
38. Hinnawi/Hinawi?
39. Capt. G.F. Sadleir to Bombay, with enclosures, HCC *Mercury*, Muscat Cove 18 May 1819, BA Sel. 73/621–5, P 467/3259–62.
40. The eight crew members reached Muscat in or by mid-July. Gopal is the Gopal Mowjee whose baghla was attacked in May 1817. Goolab Anundass, Broker, to Bombay, undated (mid-July), under Minutes of 5 Aug. 1819, BA P 312/1136–8.
41. If so, the dates presumably make it possible that the descent on Berbera occurred either before or after the capture of *Darya Daulat*, though perhaps the earlier time looks rather easier.

42. Capt. G.F. Sadleir to Bombay, with enclosures, HCC *Mercury*, Muscat Cove 18 May 1819, BA Sel. 73/621–5, P 467/3259–62.
43. Sadleir to Bombay, Muscat 15 May 1819, BA Sel. 74/281–303.
44. Capt. Eatwell of the HCC *Benares*, reported in Supt of Marine Meriton to Council, Bombay 11 June 1819, BA Sel. 73/642–3.
45. It is not clear where the four vessels encountered by Loch on 10 May fit in: conceivably they were part of this apparent northern detachment of boats. Chadayappah states that before this encounter his vessel had been a long time out, and was then returning without having thus far met with any boats.
46. The implication may be that the vessel was taken by Qawasim on their way to the Red Sea. Capt. F.E. Loch to Bombay, HMS *Eden*, off Muscat 3 Oct. 1819, BA Sel. 73/111–12.
47. 'In consequence of the Ras al-Khaima pirates having intercepted the communication, no-one would venture out during the season, nor did anybody come here'. Naqib of Mukalla to Bombay Governor, 15 Sept. 1819, BA P 473/5676–9.

Notes to Appendix C

1. Lt W. Watts, Assistant to the Resident, to Bombay, Muscat 16 June 1808, BA S&P 238/8264–7.
2. This paragraph represents Watts's account, which circulated at Muscat and derived in part from Sayyid Sa'id. Lt W. Watts, Asst. Resident, to Bombay, Muscat 5 June 1808, BA S&P 236/7526–30; and 18 June, with enclosures, BA S&P 238/8293–310, 239/8311–18.
3. Where he was expected to remain for 5–6 weeks.
4. Lt W. Watts (reads 'Wastes') to Bombay, Barka 19 July and 4–6 Aug. 1808, BA S&P 243/9867–71, 9880–2.
5. 'In the country of Shinas and the creek of Mukbee[?]'.
6. Vishandass, Broker, to Bombay, Muscat 26 Oct. 1808, BA S&P 252/13089–92.
7. Vishandass, Broker, to Bombay, Muscat 7 Nov. 1808, BA S&P 254/14027–8.
8. This implies that Imam Sa'id had died before this. The text reads, 'Hummud ben Ahameed son of the last Emam of Rustag': presumably Seton has written 'Ahmad' for 'Sa'id', as the sense would require, rather than intending a grandson of the Imam Sa'id. (Cf., however, Ibn Ruzaiq, *Imams and Seyyids*, p. 325, not always a reliable source)
9. David Seton, Resident, to Brig.-Gen. Malcolm, Muscat 20 Feb. 1809, with enclosed report of 19 Feb., BA P 325/2633–50.
10. Abu Hakima (ed.), *Lam' al-Shihab*, pp. 87–8.
11. They also included Hirth and Banu Hasan: all Hinawi tribes of the south-east. Sayyid Sa'id also wrote to the Banu Harras of Jamma and to the Ya'ariba leader Malik bin Saif: both Ghafiri tribes of the Western Hajar.
12. Ibn Ruzaiq, *Imams and Seyyids*, pp. 293–5; *al-Fath al-Mubin*, pp. 491–4.
13. The author of the *Lam' al-Shihab* comments that in one exceptional year, which was not necessarily this year, Sayyid Sa'id reputedly paid as much as 100,000 riyals to Su'ud: Abu Hakima (ed.), *Lam' al-Shihab*, p. 88.
14. 1223 AH, to which Ibn Bishr here refers, lasted 28 Feb. 1808–15 Feb. 1809: Ibn Bishr, *Unwan al-Majd*, vol. 1, pp. 297–9.
15. Two other extracts, from this and an accompanying letter from Matar bin Rahma, are cited in Chapter Thirteen, sections two and three. The second letter is dated 15 Nov. 1808, and the first was presumably written about the same time, in mid–late November.
16. Chapter Six, section two, and Chapter Eight.
17. Lt Jacob Maughan of the HC ship *Benares* to Supt of Marine, 22 Dec. 1808, BA S&P 256/14695–703. The *Minerva* spoke the *Benares* off Bardistan during the afternoon of 26 November.
18. Lt Gowan to Supt of Marine Money, HC schooner *Fury*, Bombay 10 May 1808, with Council's orders, BA S&P 232/5669–72.
19. W. Watts, Asst. Resident, to Bombay, Barka 4–6 Aug. 1808, BA S&P 243/9867–72.

20. Remarks by David Seton, Muscat Resident, introduced by Governor, Bombay Castle 10 Dec. 1808, BA S&P 255/14150–8.
21. Conceivably this should have occurred in the preceding month or months, or have been less abrupt than Seton implies.
22. D. Seton, Resident, to Brig.-Gen. Malcolm, Muscat 20 Feb. 1809, with enclosed report of 19 Feb., BA P 325/2633–50.
23. D. Seton, Resident, to Brig.-Gen. Malcolm, Muscat 5, 16 and 20 Feb., with general report of 19th, BA P 325/2622–50.
24. He was reported in Muscat to have recovered Shinas, but this seems to have been mistaken.
25. D. Seton, Resident, to Brig.-Gen. Malcolm, Muscat 5, 16 and 20 Feb., with general report of 19th, BA P 325/2622–50.
26. As a consequence of this flight, Sayyid Sa'id visited the interior in early March. D. Seton to Brig.-Gen. Malcolm, Muscat 9 March 1809, BA P 325/2702–7.
27. Ibn Ruzaiq, *Imams and Seyyids*, p. 297.
28. D. Seton, Resident, to Brig.-Gen. Malcolm, Muscat 5, 16 and 20 Feb. 1809, with general report of 19th, BA P 325/2622–50.
29. D. Seton, Resident, to Brig.-Gen. Malcolm, Muscat 5, 16 and 20 Feb., with general report of 19th, BA P 325/2622–50.
30. D. Seton, Resident, to Brig.-Gen. Malcolm, Muscat 9 March 1809, BA P 325/2702–7.
31. D. Seton, Resident, to Brig.-Gen. Malcolm, Muscat 30 March 1809, 327/324(5)–9. The text may or may not read 'ten qadis': some copied pages are absent from the Bombay records at Exeter. Sultan bin Saqr presumably set off after Su'ud returned from pilgrimage, according to Seton in early March.
32. Sultan bin Saqr to commanders of the British expedition, dated Shawwal 1224/9 Nov.–7 Dec. 1809, written after 13 Nov., BA P 350/118–20.
33. Maurizi calls Sultan bin Saqr '[Sultan] Messaghe[/a]ra'. Maurizi, *Seyd Said*, p. 54; Ibn Ruzaiq, *Imams and Seyyids*, pp. 320–1.
34. Capt. Wainwright to Bombay, HMS *Chiffone*, off Ras al-Khaima 14 Nov. 1809, BA P 347/11164–5.
35. See below.
36. D. Seton, Resident, to Brig.-Gen. Malcolm, Muscat 30 March 1809, 327/324(5)–9.
37. The Utub could retire to Bahrain if pressed.
38. D. Seton, Resident, to Bombay, Muscat 7 May 1809, BA P 329/4607–11.
39. D. Seton, Muscat Resident, to Bombay, Barka 23 May 1809, enclosing Sayyid Muhammad bin Khalfan to Seton, Muscat 12 May, BA P 334/6478–88.
40. Text reads 'Ahmed ben Ahmed Moinee'. The reading 'Mu'ini' seems clear enough, though surprising.
41. I am not certain, though it seems not unlikely, that Hasan bin Ali himself belonged to this tribe. A poorly transcribed note in al-Qasimi, 'Arab "Piracy"', Appendix 23, describes Hasan bin Ali as the head of the Tanaij.
42. See above regarding the situation at Fujaira, and her overriding allegiance to Sultan bin Saqr, three months earlier.
43. D. Seton, Muscat Resident, to Bombay, Barka 23 May 1809, enclosing Sayyid Muhammad bin Khalfan to Seton, Muscat 12 May, BA P 334/6478–88.
44. Samuel Manesty to Bombay, Basra 8 July 1809, BA P 338/8088–93.
45. His could of course have been a temporary, or partial, demise.
46. Unofficial information cited in Bombay Council to Fort William, Bombay Castle 22 Nov. 1809, BA P 346/10962–6.
47. Sultan bin Saqr to commanders of the British expedition, dated Shawwal 1224/9 Nov.–7 Dec. 1809, written after 13 Nov., BA P 350/118–20.
48. Ibn Ruzaiq, *al-Fath al-Mubin*, p. 493.
49. Ibn Ruzaiq mentions this individual on two occasions, in separate and apparently unconsciously parallel passages. The longer of the two states that he was Governor at the time of the Omani–British attack in January 1810, and died during it, whilst on his way with reinforcements from Buraimi. It may be, then, that he had become Governor since late 1808,

and had perhaps increased his hold by taking over the fort still more recently in 1809. The other passage in Ibn Ruzaiq does not, however, readily accord with this, for it seems to suggest his appointment in January 1810 after the British had left Shinas. Ibn Ruzaiq is probably confused, but on the basis that in the first passage Muhammad bin Ahmad seems more integral to the story, one might, if forced to choose, opt for that version of events. Ibn Ruzaiq, *Imams and Seyyids*, pp. 298, 322; *al-Fath al-Mubin*, pp. 497, 518–19.

50. This date according to D. Seton, Muscat Resident, to Bombay, Baroda 2 July 1807, BA S&P 208/4937–50.
51. Abu Hakima (ed.), *Lam' al-Shihab*, pp. 81–2.
52. Note, earlier, the presence of an agent at Ras al-Khaima in July 1808, as attested by Fleming of the *Darya Daulat*. William Bruce, Resident, to Bombay, HMS *Curlew*, off Qais 14 Feb. 1820, BA S 315/362–73, BA P 480/1820–35; Bruce to Bombay, Bushire 27 Oct. 1819, BA Sel. 73/173–8.

Notes to Appendix D

1. ? Text may read 'Luradee Maiul situated about 40 miles from Burka'. This appears to be the sense rather than the fight having taken place at Barka.
2. Nicholas Hankey Smith, Bushire Resident, to Bombay, HCC *Mornington*, off Muscat 14 April 1810, BA P 355/2212–16.
3. Sayyid Sa'id to Bombay Governor, 26 March 1810, BA S 264/1287–91.
4. Fort William to Bombay, 11 Aug. 1810, BA P 361/4743–6. Bombay's consequent letter to Sayyid Sa'id was dated 13 Sept., 361/4770–1.
5. Letters from Rahma bin Jabir and Amir Su'ud, enclosed in Assistant-in-Charge Babington to Bombay, Bushire undated, in Bombay Council Minutes of 6 June 1810, BA P 358/3061–70. Bombay responded to Su'ud on Calcutta's instructions on 9 Aug.: BA P 360/3912–13, 4163–5.
6. Sayyid Sa'id of Muscat to Bombay Governor, 3 July 1810, BA P 359/3685–9.
7. Ibn Bishr, *Unwan al-Majd*, vol. 1, pp. 307–9. This episode seems to be passed over by Ibn Ruzaiq.
8. Ibn Bishr, *Unwan al-Majd*, vol. 1, pp. 305–7, suggests Abdullah bin Ufaisan reached Zubara four months before Su'ud returned from pilgrimage. 1 Muharram 1225 was equivalent to 6 February 1810. As well as Bahrain and Zubara, Ibn Ufaisan is said to have had charge of Qatif and all Qatar. Capt. N. Warren of HM 65th to N.H. Smith, Bushire 17 March 1810, BA P 355/2009–22; also Lt Eatwell to Capt. J. Jeakes, HCC *Vestal*, Bushire Roads 17 March 1810, with other material, BA P 355/1995–2036.
9. The *Lam' al-Shihab* claims that when Mutlaq al-Mutairi and Muhammad bin Nasir attacked Oman, and had reached the environs of Muscat, 30 Qasimi vessels spent six days trying to enter the port of Muscat, but were warded off with the assistance of 40 Utbi boats, then in harbour. This, according to the author, had provoked Su'ud's proceedings at Bahrain. On the face of it, if this incident, or something like it, did in fact occur, then it did so during the early months of 1810; but it may be that something of the kind had taken place earlier, since the autumn of 1808. Abu Hakima (ed.), *Lam' al-Shihab*, pp. 110–12.
10. Sayyid Sa'id of Muscat to Bombay Governor, 3 July 1810, BA P 359/3685–9. See also Ibn Ruzaiq's interesting depiction of the Persian embassy, in *Imams and Seyyids*, pp. 305–14.
11. Muhammad Yusuf Munshi, Native Agent Hyderabad, to Bombay, 27 July, 11 Nov., 17 Dec. 1810, BA P 374/2573–652, 2776–98. In October, Sayyid Sa'id reported to Bombay, 'with respect to the accursed tribe of Wahhabis, and what appertains to them, that they are daily falling off, and on the decline, and God willing they will be even worse than this': Sayyid Sa'id to Bombay Governor, undated, received 5 Nov. 1810, BA P 365/6111–13.
12. J. Malcolm to Bombay, camp near Bushire 30 March 1810, BA P 355/2201–4. Cf. al-Qasimi, 'Arab "Piracy"', Appendix 23.
13. Ibn Bishr, *Unwan al-Majd*, vol. 1, p. 306, under the year 1224 AH; Ibn Ruzaiq, *Imams and Seyyids*, pp. 298–305, 322–4.

14. The Dhawahir, inhabitants of Buraimi, are, unlike the other two named tribes, Hinawi.
15. Ibn Ruzaiq, *Imams and Seyyids*, pp. 297–9.
16. Besides Jadgal, Baluchis and slaves, Sayyid Sa'id's forces included Hajriyin, Banu Hasan, some of the Yemeni tribes of Sharqiya and Hirth; the Siyabiyin, a Ghafiri tribe, eventually also came over to his side; he and Azzan bin Qais, who is mentioned in connection with the Ma'awil, also raised forces from the Batina coast. Besides the Banu Jabir, Malik bin Saif al-Ya'rabi's men, and at first the Siyabiyin, the following tribes are included with Muhammad bin Nasir's forces: Banu Julanda, Awamir, Banu Hajir, Banu Mujallib, Banu Harras (?), Janaba and Duru'.
17. These December dates are cited as converted by the translator. The orthodox modern conversion would subtract one Christian day from each: i.e. 4 Dh.Q. 1225 AH becomes 1 Dec. 1810 AD etc.
18. Husain bin Hamad, agent of Sayyid Sa'id, to Bombay Governor, 10 April 1811, and Account by four escaped Russian prisoners-of-war, given at Muscat, in Bombay Council Minutes 12 April 1811, BA P 372/1741–6.
19. Ibn Bishr, *Unwan al-Majd*, vol. 1, p. 319; Ibn Ruzaiq, *Imams and Seyyids*, pp. 314–18.
20. The printed Arabic version differs from Badger's text, and may be slightly confused here: Ibn Ruzaiq, *al-Fath al-Mubin*, p. 514.
21. Maurizi gives the correct number. He puts the Muscat–Persian force at 10,000 *in toto*. Maurizi, *Seyd Said*, pp. 80–1.
22. The text (Husain bin Hamad) has him both sailing from, on 5 March, and returning to, the harbour at 'Lunjih', where one would have expected the name of an Omani port: it is easiest to assume this was a misreading, otherwise it assumes interest.
23. Text illegible. Husain bin Hamad, agent of Sayyid Sa'id, to Bombay Governor, 10 April 1811, and Account by four escaped Russian prisoners-of-war, given at Muscat, in Bombay Council Minutes 12 April 1811, BA P 372/1741–6.
24. Sayyid Sa'id to Governor Duncan, Muscat 20 May 1811, BA P 375/3095–102.
25. Maurizi, *Seyd Said*, pp. 79–86. The possibility that there was only one expedition, which took in the two places, cannot be ruled out. A Muscat expedition against Ras al-Khaima at the end of 1811 appears to be indicated in Edward Matson, of the *Moholar*, to Bombay, Bushire 9 Feb. 1812, BA P 383/394–6; Sayyid Sa'id of Muscat to his agent in Bombay, 22 Feb., April? (and 1 Sept.) 1812, BA P 389/2646–9.
26. Ibn Bishr, *Unwan al-Majd*, vol. 1, pp. 317–19; Ibn Ruzaiq, *Imams and Seyyids*, pp. 318–20.
27. Siyabiyin, Nadabiyin and Banu Rasib are also mentioned by Ibn Ruzaiq.
28. Presumably Jumada al-Aula is intended, though it is not specified.
29. Ibn Ruzaiq, *Imams and Seyyids*, p. 325; *al-Fath al-Mubin*, p. 521.
30. Thus some date later this year, or after that, cannot perhaps be ruled out. The other sources appear to omit this episode, and Mutlaq next appears in 1813. Ibn Ruzaiq, *Imams and Seyyids*, pp. 324–5; *al-Fath al-Mubin*, pp. 520–1.
31. Since, as noted, Bruce says he helped Ras al-Khaima to resist Sayyid Sa'id's expedition.
32. Ibn Ruzaiq, *Imams and Seyyids*, pp. 326–8; *al-Fath al-Mubin*, pp. 521–4: Ibn Bishr, *Unwan al-Majd*, vol. 1, p. 337; Maurizi, *Seyd Said*, pp. 86–8.

BIBLIOGRAPHY

A Manuscript Sources

1. Bombay Archives (BA): some 20,000 photocopied pages taken from the Bombay Record Office, of the Central Archival Agency of the Government of Maharashtra, India. This collection of photocopied documents is now housed in the Centre for Arab Gulf Studies, University of Exeter, England; it was the principal source for the present work. The collection consists of material relating to Arabia and the Persian Gulf, with an especial emphasis on maritime affairs and piracy, covering the period c. 1790–1820. It is taken from the Diaries of the East India Company's Government of Bombay, and is made up of incoming and outward despatches, together with the recorded deliberations of the Bombay Council. The most important part of the correspondence is that between Government and its political, Marine and other officers in the Gulf. The selected material at Exeter derives from the following series:

Secret and Political Department Diaries (S&P), Diaries 19A–258, 1778–1808.
Secret Department Diaries (S), Diaries 261–317, 1810–1820.
Political Department Diaries (P), Diaries 320–496, 1809–1820.

Complete copies of volumes entitled Selections on Piracy (Sel.), being mostly or entirely assemblies of original despatches connected with Qasimi piracy, part of it duplicated in copy in the Diaries, volumes 71 (1809–18), 72 (1816–18), 73 (1818–19), 74 (1815–19), 75, 76 and 77 (1819): these volumes are not apparently to be found in the India Office Library, London.

After 1820, new system of filing, Political Department, volumes 10/18, 14/34, 19/59, 42/366, 50/21: this material, relating to 1820–1 and 1829–30, was not employed for the present work.

See further, Ruth Butler, *Descriptive Listing of the Extracts from the Bombay Diaries Held at the Centre for Arab Gulf Studies* (Centre for Arab Gulf Studies, Exeter, 1989): note that this catalogue does not cover the most important part of the material relating to piracy and the Qawasim. V.G. Dighe, *Descriptive Catalogue of the Secret and Political Department Series 1755–1820* (Government Publications, Bombay, 1954). Sanjiv P. Desai, *The Hand Book of the Bombay Archives* (Dept of Archives, Government of Maharashtra, Bombay, 1978).

Exeter also holds microfilm copies from Bombay of the Basra Factory Diaries, volumes 193–212, 1763–1811. These yielded very little of use for the present study.

2. India Office Library and Records (IOR): the Bombay Archive material has been supplemented by a variety of material from the India Office Library in London. The most obviously useful of the documents there were the Gombroon Diaries, the Bushire

Residency files, and the Bombay commercial records. The following were amongst the records consulted:

Bandar Abbas (Gombroon) Diaries and Consultations 1708–1763, G/29/2–14. Various Gombroon and Basra material, 1704–1811, G/29/15–27; including G/29/27, ff. 555–600, H. Jones, remarks on Malcolm's trade report.

Bushire Residency Records, R/15/1/1–26 and 749, 1767–1822.

Bombay Commerce, Internal and External Reports, 1801/2–1824/5, P/419/39–61, and ff. Bombay Commercial Proceedings, P/414/47–64, 1786/7–99.

Home Miscellaneous, various. Including, Services in Persia 1804 etc., Outline of the Case of Mr Samuel Manesty, Home Misc. 81/637–730. Letter from principal merchants of Bombay, recorded 25 Oct. 1804, Home Misc. 333, pp. 663–80. Harford Jones, on Rahma bin Jabir and Wahhabi doctrine, Home Misc. 737, pp. 483–500.

MSS Eur., various. Including, Frederick Papers, Lt E. Frederick, 'A Trip to the Persian Gulf in 1802', MSS Eur. D. 109, pp. 40–58. Revd Henry Martyn to Revd Hitchins of Stoke, Bombay 19 Feb. 1811, MSS Eur. A. 87. Rich Collection, Maurizi's *Memorie di Seyd Saaid*, MSS Eur. D. 234, pp. 1–48. Lt James Macmurdo, record of a journey commencing Poseitra December 1809, Baroda 17 March 1810, MSS Eur. D. 637.

Personal Records, various. Including, biography of Samuel Manesty, O/6/6, pp. 339–405.

Wills and Administrations, Bombay, 8 Jan. 1810, IOR L/AG/34/29/343. Bombay Inventories, Register for Jan.–March 1813, IOR L/AG/34/27/389.

Marine Records, Charles Watkins' report on the imports and exports of Bushire, Bushire 15 Nov. 1789, L/MAR/C/891, pp. 108–16.

Military Department, Ras al-Khaima 1819/20, prize money, L/MIL/5/245.

Factory Records, Mocha, 1741–1815, G/17/3.

Bombay Public Proceedings, various. Including, letter from principal merchants of Bombay, Bombay 4 July 1804, with other papers July–Aug., P/343/14, pp. 2380–94, 2860–88.

3. Public Records Office, Kew (PRO): A small amount of material from the FO 248 and the FO 60 series.

4. British Library: Captain George Barnes Brucks, *Account of the Survey of the Persian Gulf, 1821–1835[/1837]*, Add. Ms. 14,383.

5. National Library of Scotland: Log of the Ship *Cornwall*, 9 November 1818 to 31 March 1821, MS 9661. Journal of a Voyage from Glasgow to Bombay and the Persian Gulf, 1828, MS 9594.

6. Scottish Record Office, Edinburgh: Captain F.E. Loch RN, *Diaries of Captain F.E. Loch, Compiled by him in 1835*, covering the period 19 March 1818–29 March 1821, GD1/633/1&2.

7. Brynmor Jones Library, University of Hull: Papers of Edith Thompson. Not consulted.

B Published Material

'Abdullāh, Muḥammad Mursī, *Imārat al-Sāhil wa-'Umān wal-Daula al-Su'ūdīya al-Ūlā 1793–1818* (al-Maktab al-Miṣrī al-Ḥadīth, Cairo, 1978).

Abdul Qadir, Khwaja, *Waqai-i Manazil-i Rum: Diary of a Journey to Constantinople*, ed. Mohibbul Hasan (Asia Publishing House, London, 1968).

al-'Ābid, Ṣāliḥ Muḥammad, *Daur al-Qawāsim fīl-Khalīj al-'Arabī 1747–1820* (Maṭba'at al-'Ānī, Baghdad, 1976).

Abū Ḥākima, Aḥmad Muṣṭafā (ed.), *Lam' al-Shihāb fī Sīrat Muḥammad bin 'Abd al-Wahhāb* (Dār al-Thaqāfa, Beirut, 1967).

Abu Hakima, Ahmad Mustafa, *History of Eastern Arabia 1750–1800: the Rise and Development of Bahrain and Kuwait* (Khayats, Beirut, 1965).

Abū Ḥākima, Aḥmad Muṣṭafā, *Ta'rīkh al-Kuwait* 2 vols. (Ḥukūmat al-Kuwait, Kuwait, 1970–3).

Aitchison, Charles Umpherston, *Treaties and Engagements Relating to Arabia and the Persian Gulf*, vol. 11 of *A Collection of Treaties etc.*, (Government of India, Delhi, 1933: reprint Archive Editions, England, 1987).

Alexander, Lt James Edward, *Travels from India to England* (Parbury, Allen, London, 1827).

Al Khalifa, Khalid Khalifa, 'Commerce and Conflict: the English East India Company Factories in the Gulf 1700–47', PhD thesis, University of Essex, 1988.

Allen, Calvin H., 'Sayyids, Shets and Sultans: Politics and Trade in Masqat under the Al Bu Sa'id, 1785–1914', PhD thesis, University of Washington, 1978.

Allen, Calvin H., 'The Indian Merchant Community of Masqat', *Bulletin of the School of Oriental and African Studies*, vol. 44 (1981), pp. 39–53.

Amin, Abdul Amir, *British Interests in the Persian Gulf* (E.J. Brill, Leiden, 1967).

Anon, *Oman, a Seafaring Nation* (Ministry of Information and Culture, Oman, 1979).

Asiatic Annual Register

Aubin, Jean, 'Le Royaume d'Ormuz au début du XVIe siècle', *Mare Luso-Indicum 2* (Geneva, 1972), pp. 77–179.

Aubin, Jean, 'Les Princes d'Ormuz du XIIe au XVIe siècle', *Journal Asiatique* (1953), pp. 77–138.

al-Azmeh, Aziz, 'Wahhabite Polity', in Ian Richard Netton, *Arabia and the Gulf: from Traditional Society to Modern States* (Croom Helm, London, 1986), pp. 75–90.

Bayly, Christopher Alan, *The New Cambridge History of India: II–1, Indian Society and the Making of the British Empire* (Cambridge University Press, Cambridge, 1988).

Belgrave, Charles, *Personal Column* (Hutchinson, London, 1960).

Belgrave, Sir Charles, *The Pirate Coast* (Librairie du Liban, Beirut, 1972).

Bhacker, M. Reda, 'Roots of Domination and Dependency: British Reaction towards the Development of Omani Commerce at Muscat and Zanzibar in the Nineteenth Century', DPhil thesis, St Antony's College, Oxford, 1988.

Bhacker, M. Reda, *Trade and Empire in Muscat and Zanzibar: Roots of British Domination* (Routledge, London, 1992).

Bibby, Geoffrey, *Looking for Dilmun* (Pelican, Harmondsworth, 1970).

Bidwell, Robin, 'Bibliographical Notes on European Accounts of Muscat 1500–1900', in *Arabian Studies* (Hurst, London, 1978), vol. 4, pp. 123–59.

Blackstone, Sir William, *Commentaries on the Laws of England* (Cadell and Davies, London, 1809).

BIBLIOGRAPHY.

Bombay Gazette

Brucks, George Barnes, 'Draft Chapters for an Unpublished Account of the Survey of the Persian Gulf' (1835/7) (chapters 1–2 of BL Add. Ms. 14,383), in A.S. Cook, *Survey*, vol. 1, pp. 1–28.

Brucks, George Barnes, 'Memoir Descriptive of the Navigation of the Gulf of Persia', in A.S. Cook, *Survey*, vol. 1, pp. 123–226; and R. Hughes Thomas, *Arabian Gulf Intelligence*, pp. 531–634.

Brydges, Sir Harford Jones, *An Account of the Transactions of His Majesty's Mission to the Court of Persia, in the Years 1807–11 . . . To which is appended a Brief History of the Wahauby* 2 vols. (James Bohn, London, 1834).

Buckingham, James Silk, *Travels in Assyria, Media, and Persia* (Henry Colburn, London 1829: reprint Gregg International, Farnborough, 1971).

Burckhardt, John Lewis, *Notes on the Bedouins and Wahabys, Collected during his Travels in the East*, 2 vols. (Colburn and Bentley, London 1831: reprint Johnson Reprint, New York, 1967).

Busse, see Fasā'ī.

Coleridge, Samuel Taylor, *Table Talk* (Routledge, London, 1884).

Cook, Andrew S. (ed.), *Survey of the Shores and Islands of the Persian Gulf 1820–1829*, 5 vols. (Archive Editions, England, 1990).

Cook, Michael, 'The Provenance of the Lam' al-Shihab fi Sirat Muhammad Ibn Abd al-Wahhab', *Journal of Turkish Studies*, 10 (1986), pp. 79–86.

Curzon, George Nathaniel, *Persia and the Persian Question*, 2 vols. (Longmans, London 1892: reprint Frank Cass, London, 1966).

Das Gupta, Ashin, and M.N. Pearson (eds), *India and the Indian Ocean, 1500–1800* (Oxford University Press, Calcutta, 1987).

Das Gupta, Ashin, *Indian Merchants and the Decline of Surat c. 1700–1750* (Franz Steiner Verlag, Wiesbaden, 1979).

Das Gupta, Ashin, *Malabar in Asian Trade 1740–1800* (Cambridge University Press, Cambridge, 1967).

Datta, S.K., and J.B. Nugent, 'Bahrain's Pearling Industry: how it was, why it was that way and its implications', in J.B. Nugent and T.H. Thomas (eds), *Bahrain and the Gulf* (Croom Helm, London, 1985), pp. 25–41.

Davies, Charles Edward, 'A History of the Province of Fars during the Later Nineteenth Century', DPhil thesis, St Antony's College, Oxford, 1985.

Dickson, Harold Richard Patrick, *The Arab of the Desert* (George Allen and Unwin, London, 1951).

Dubner, Barry Hart, *The Law of International Sea Piracy* (Martinus Nijhoff, The Hague, 1980).

Dubuisson, Patricia R., 'Qasimi Piracy and the General Treaty of Peace (1820)', in *Arabian Studies* (Hurst, London, 1978), vol. 4, pp. 47–57.

Edye, John, 'Description of the Various Classes of Vessels Constructed and Employed by the Natives of the Coasts of Coromandel, Malabar, and the Island of Ceylon, for their Coasting Navigation', *Journal of the Royal Asiatic Society of Great Britain and Ireland*, vol. 1 (London, 1834), pp. 1–14.

Fasā'ī, Mīrzā Ḥasan, *Fārsnāma-yi Nāṣirī*, translated by Heribert Busse as, *History of Persia under Qajar Rule* (Columbia University Press, New York, 1972).

Fenelon, Kevin G., *The United Arab Emirates: an Economic and Social Survey* (Longman, London, 1973).

Fiorani Piacentini, V., 'Siraf and Hormuz between East and West: Merchants and Merchandise in the Gulf', in Charles Edward Davies, *Global Interests in the Arab Gulf* (University of Exeter Press, Exeter, 1992), pp. 1–28.

Floor, Willem M., 'A Description of the Persian Gulf and Its Inhabitants in 1756', *Persica*, vol. 8 (1979), pp. 162–85.

Fraser, James Baillie, *Narrative of a Journey into Khorasan in the Years 1821 and 1822* (Longman, Hurst etc., London, 1825).

Furber, Holden, *Bombay Presidency in the Mid-Eighteenth Century* (Asia, London, 1965).

Furber, Holden, *John Company at Work* (Harvard, 1948: reprint, Octagon Books, New York, 1970).

Furber, Holden, *Rival Empires of Trade in the Orient 1600–1800* (University of Minnesota Press, Minneapolis and Oxford University Press, London, 1976).

Glubb, John Bagot, *War in the Desert* (Hodder and Stoughton, London, 1960).

Gosse, Philip, *The History of Piracy* (Longmans, London, 1932).

Graham, Maria, *Journal of a Residence in India* (Constable, Edinburgh and Longman, London, 1812).

Griffiths, Dr John, *Travels in Europe, Asia Minor and Arabia* (Cadell and Davies, London, 1805).

Grummon, Stephen Ray, 'The Rise and Fall of the Arab Shaykhdom of Bushire: 1750–1850', PhD thesis, Johns Hopkins University, 1985, (UMI, 1987).

Hall, J.A., *The Law of Naval Warfare* (Chapman and Hall, London, 1921).

Ḥandhal, Fāliḥ, *al-Mufaṣṣal fī Ta'rīkh al-Imārat al-'Arabīya al-Muttaḥida*, 2 vols. (Dār al-Fikr, Abu Dhabi, 1403/1983).

Hansman, John, *Julfar, an Arabian Port: its Settlement and Far Eastern Ceramic Trade from the 14th to the 18th Centuries* (Royal Asiatic Society, London, 1985).

Hawkins, Clifford W., *The Dhow: an Illustrated History of the Dhow and Its World* (Nautical Publishing, Lymington, 1977).

Heard-Bey, Frauke, *From Trucial States to United Arab Emirates: a Society in Transition* (Longman, London, 1982).

Helms, Christine Moss, *The Cohesion of Saudi Arabia: Evolution of Political Identity* (Croom Helm, London, 1981).

Heude, William, *A Voyage Up the Persian Gulf, and a Journey Overland from India to England in 1817* (Longman, Hurst etc., London, 1819).

Hickey, William, *Memoirs of William Hickey* (Century, London, 1984).

Holdsworth, William Searle, *A History of English Law* (Methuen, London, 1924).

Hopwood, Derek, 'The Ideological Basis: Ibn Abd al-Wahhab's Muslim Revivalism', in Tim Niblock, *State, Society and Economy in Saudi Arabia* (Croom Helm, London and Centre for Arab Gulf Studies, Exeter, 1982), pp. 23–35.

Horsburgh, James, *India Directory, or Directions for Sailing to and from the East Indies etc.* (4th ed. 1836), in A.S. Cook, *Survey*, vol. 1, pp. 229–305.

Houghton, Lt Michael, 'Account of Part of the Southern Coast or Arabian Side of the Persian Gulf between Ras Musandam and Dubai', dated 1822, in A.S. Cook, *Survey*, vol. 1, pp. 37–120.

Howarth, David, *Dhows* (Quartet, London, 1977).

Ibn Bishr, 'Uthmān bin 'Abdullāh, *'Unwān al-Majd fī Ta'rīkh Najd*, 2 vols. (Dārat al-Malik 'Abd al-'Azīz, Riyadh, 1982/1402).

Ibn Ruzaiq, Ḥumaid bin Muḥammad, *al-Fatḥ al-Mubīn fī Sīrat al-Bū Sa'īdyīn*, translated by George Percy Badger as, *History of the Imams and Seyyids of Oman* (Hakluyt Society, series 1, no. 44, 1871: reprint Burt Franklin, New York, 1970).

Ibn Ruzaiq, Ḥumaid bin Muḥammad, *al-Fatḥ al-Mubīn fī Sīrat al-Bū Saʿīdīyīn* (Wizārat al-Turāth, Oman, 1983/1403).

al-Idrīsī, Muḥammad bin Muḥammad, *Kitāb Nuzhat al-Mushtāq fī Ikhtirāq al-Āfāq*, 2 vols. ('Ālam al-Kutub, Beirut, 1989).

Ingrams, Edward, *Britain's Persian Connection 1798–1828: Prelude to the Great Game in Asia* (Oxford University Press, Oxford, 1992).

Issawi, Charles (ed.), *The Economic History of Iran 1800–1914* (University of Chicago Press, Chicago, 1971).

Ives, Dr Edward (EIC surgeon), *A Voyage from England to India ... Also, a Journey from Persia to England by an Unusual Route* (Dilly, London, 1773).

al-Izkawī, Sirḥān bin Saʿīd, *Kashf al-Ghumma* (Dilmūn, Nicosia, 1985).

al-Izkawī, Sirḥān bin Saʿīd, *Kashf al-Ghumma*, partially translated by E.C. Ross as *Annals of Oman to 1728* (Oleander Press, Cambridge, 1984).

Johnson, Captain Charles, *A General History of the Pyrates* (J.M. Dent, London, 1972).

Kelly, John Barrett, *Britain and the Persian Gulf 1795–1880* (Oxford University Press, Oxford, 1968).

Keppel, Captain Hon. George Thomas, *Personal Narrative of a Journey from India to England ... in the year 1824*, 2 vols. (H. Colburn, London, 1827).

Khuri, Fuad I., *Tribe and State in Bahrain: the Transformation of Social and Political Authority in an Arab State* (University of Chicago, Chicago, 1980).

Lienhardt, Peter, 'The Authority of Shaykhs in the Gulf: an Essay in Nineteenth-Century History', in *Arabian Studies* (Hurst, London, 1975), vol. 2, pp. 61–75.

Loane, R.W., *Authentic Narrative of the Late Fortunate Escape of Mr R.W. Loane etc.* (Ferris and Co., Bombay, 1805).

Lockhart, Laurence, *Nadir Shah* (1938: reprint Al-Irfan, Lahore, 1976).

Longrigg, Stephen Hemsley, *Four Centuries of Modern Iraq* (Oxford University Press, Oxford, 1925).

Lorimer, John Gordon, *Gazetteer of the Persian Gulf, Oman and Central Arabia*, 2 vols. (Superintendent Government Printing, Calcutta, 1915).

Low, Charles Rathbone, *History of the Indian Navy (1613–1863)*, 2 vols. (Richard Bentley, London, 1877).

Mackintosh, Sir James, *Memoirs of the Life of Sir James Mackintosh* 2 vols. (Edward Moxon, London, 1836).

Malcolm, Sir John, *Sketches of Persia*, 2 vols. (1815: republ. Cassell, London, 1888).

Martyn, Henry, *Journals and Letters of the Rev. Henry Martyn* (Seeley and Burnside, London, 1837).

al-Maʾthūrāt al-Shaʿbīya, no. 21, Jan. 1991.

Maurizi, Vincenzo, *History of Seyd Said, Sultan of Muscat* (John Booth, London, 1819: reprint Oleander, Cambridge, 1984).

McCluer, John, *An Account of the Navigation between India and the Gulph of Persia* (Alexander Dalrymple, London, 1786).

Meeker, Michael E., *Literature and Violence in North Arabia* (Cambridge University Press, Cambridge, 1979).

Mignan, Captain Robert, *A Winter Journey through Russia, the Caucasian Alps, and Georgia ... into Koordistaun* 2 vols. (Richard Bentley, London, 1839).

Milburn, William, *Oriental Commerce, or the East India Trader's Complete Guide*, 2 vols. (Kingsbury, Parbury and Allen, London, 1825).

Miles, Samuel Barrett, *The Countries and Tribes of the Persian Gulf* (Frank Cass, London, 1966).

Morier, James Justinian, *A Journey through Persia, Armenia, and Asia Minor to Constantinople in the Years 1808 and 1809; etc.* (Longman, Hurst etc., London, 1812).

Morier, James Justinian, *A Second Journey through Persia, Armenia and Asia Minor, to Constantinople, between the Years 1810 and 1816* (Longman, Hurst etc., London, 1818).

Moyse-Bartlett, Hubert, *The Pirates of Trucial Oman* (Macdonald, London, 1966).

Musil, Alois, *The Manners and Customs of the Rwala Bedouins* (American Geographical Society, New York 1928: reprint AMS, 1978).

Niebuhr, Carsten, *Description de l'Arabie* (S.J. Baalde, Amsterdam, 1774).

Niebuhr, Carsten, *Travels Through Arabia, and Other Countries in the East*, translated by Robert Heron, 2 vols. (Morison and son, Perth, etc., Edinburgh, 1792: reprint Librairie du Liban, Beirut *c*. 1968).

Niebuhr, Carsten, *Voyage en Arabie et en d'Autres Pays Circonvoisins*, 2 vols. (S.J. Baalde, Amsterdam, 1780).

Nightingale, Pamela, *Trade and Empire in Western India 1784–1806* (Cambridge University Press, Cambridge, 1970).

Owen, Captain William Fitzwilliam Wentworth, *Narrative of Voyages to Explore the Shores of Africa, Arabia, and Madagascar: Performed in HM Ships Leven and Barracouta* (Bentley, London, 1833).

Paris, François Edmond, *Essai sur la Construction Navale des Peuples Extra-européens ou Collection des Navires et Pirogues Construits par les Habitants de l'Asie, de la Malaisie, du Grand Océan et de l'Amérique Dessinés et Mesurés par M. Paris, Capitaine de Corvette, pendant les Voyages Autour du Monde de L'Astrolabe, La Favorite et L'Artémise* (Arthus Bertrand, Paris, 1841).

Parsons, Abraham, *Travels in Asia and Africa* (Longman, Hurst etc., London, 1808).

Pearson, Michael Naylor, *Coastal Western India* (Concept, New Delhi, 1981).

Pelly, Lt Col. Lewis, 'Report on a Journey to the Wahabee Capital of Riyadh in Central Arabia' (1866), in P. Tuson and A. Burdett (eds), *Records of Saudi Arabia, Primary Documents 1902–1960*, 10 vols. (Archive Editions, England, 1992), vol. 1, pp. 441–52.

Pelly, Lt Col. Lewis, 'Report on Tribes, Trade and Resources of Shoreline of Persian Gulf', Bushire 13 April 1863, in K. Bourne and D.C. Watt, *British Documents on Foreign Affairs: Reports and Papers from the Foreign Office Confidential Print*, part 1, series B, vol. 10 Persia 1856–1885 (University Publications of America), pp. 185–211.

Perry, John R., *Karim Khan Zand: a History of Iran, 1747–1779* (University of Chicago Press, Chicago, 1979).

Perry, John R., 'Mir Muhanna and the Dutch: Patterns of Piracy in the Persian Gulf', *Studia Iranica*, vol. 2 (1973), pp. 79–95.

Plaisted, Bartholomew, 'Narrative of a Journey from Basra to Aleppo in 1750', in Douglas Carruthers (ed.), *The Desert Route to India*, series 2, vol. 63 (Hakluyt Society, 1928: reprint Kraus Reprint, Nendeln, 1967).

al-Qasimi, Sultan Muhammad, 'Arab "Piracy" and the East India Company Encroachment in the Gulf 1797–1820', PhD thesis, University of Exeter, March 1985.

al-Qasimi, Sultan Muhammad, *The Myth of Arab Piracy in the Gulf* (Croom Helm, London, 1986).

al-Rashid, Zamil Muhammad, *Su'udi Relations with Eastern Arabia and 'Uman (1800–1871)* (Luzac, London, 1981).

Rentz, George, article under 'al-Kawasim', in E. van Donzel, C.E. Bosworth and others (eds), *Encyclopaedia of Islam*, new edition (E.J. Brill, Leiden, 1978), vol. 4, pp. 777–8.

Risso, Patricia, *Oman and Muscat: an Early Modern History* (Croom Helm, London, 1986).

Ruete, Emily (Salma bint Sa'id bin Sultan), *Memoirs of an Arabian Princess* (Ward and Downey, London, 1888).

Sadīd al-Salṭana, Muḥammad 'Alī, *Bandar 'Abbās wa Khalīj-i Fārs* (Dunyā-yi Kitāb, Tehran, 1368/1990).

Sadleir, George Forster (47th Regt), *Diary of a Journey Across Arabia (1819)* (Falcon Press, Naples and Oleander Press, New York, 1977).

Said Zahlan, Rosemarie, *The Making of the Modern Gulf States* (Unwin Hyman, London, 1989).

Sajadi, Jila, 'The East India Company's Trade with an Iranian Port at the End of the 18th and Beginning of the 19th Century: a Geographical Study', PhD thesis, University of Southampton, 1985.

Saldanha, Jerome Antony, *The Persian Gulf Précis*, 8 vols. (Superintendent Government Printing, Calcutta 1908: reprint Archive Editions, Gerrards Cross, 1986).

Savory, Roger, *Iran under the Safavids* (Cambridge University Press, Cambridge, 1980).

al-Shamlān, Saif Marzūq, *Ta'rīkh al-Ghaus 'alāl-Lu'lu' fīl-Kuwait wal-Khalīj al-'Arabī*, 2 vols. (Ḥukūmat al-Kuwait, Kuwait 1398/1978).

Slot, B.J., *The Arabs of the Gulf 1602–1784* (Leidschendam, 1993).

Slot, B.J., *The Origins of Kuwait* (E.J. Brill, Leiden, 1991).

Sowayan, Saad Abdullah, *Nabati Poetry: the Oral Poetry of Arabia* (Arab Gulf States Folklore Centre, Doha, 1985).

Sowayan, Saad Abdullah, *The Arabian Oral Historical Narrative: an Ethnographic and Linguistic Analysis* (Otto Harrassowitz, Wiesbaden, 1992).

Spear, Percival, *The Nabobs, a Study of the Social Life of the English in 18th Century India* (Oxford University Press, London, 1963).

Swann, Alfred J., *Fighting the Slave-Hunters in Central Africa* (1910: republ. Frank Cass, London, 1969).

Sweet, Louise E., 'Camel Raiding of North Arabian Bedouin: a Mechanism of Ecological Adaptation', in L.E. Sweet, *Peoples and Cultures*, vol. 1, pp. 265–89.

Sweet, Louise E., *Peoples and Cultures of the Middle East: an Anthropological Reader*, 2 vols. (The Natural History Press, New York, 1970).

al-Tajir, Mahdi Abdalla, *Bahrain 1920–1945: Britain, the Shaikh and the Administration* (Croom Helm, London, 1987).

Temple, R., *Sixteen Views of Places in the Persian Gulph Taken in the Years 1809–10, Illustrative of the Proceedings of the Forces Employed on the Expedition Sent from Bombay Under the Command of Lieutenant [Captain] Wainwright of HM Ship Chiffone, Lieutenant Colonel Smith of HM 65th Regiment Against the Arabian Pirates* (W. Haines, London, 1813).

The Aramco Reports on al-Hasa and Oman 1950–1955, 4 vols. (reprinted Archive Editions, England, 1990).

The Persian Gulf Administration Reports 1873–1947, 10 vols. (Archive Editions, Gerrards Cross, 1986).

Thomas, R. Hughes (ed.), *Arabian Gulf Intelligence: Selections from the Records of the Bombay Government* (Oleander Press, New York, 1985).

Tuson, Penelope (ed.), *Records of Qatar, Primary Documents 1820–1960*, 8 vols. (Archive Editions, England, 1991).

Tuson, Penelope (ed.), *Records of the Emirates, Primary Documents 1820–1960*, 12 vols. (Archive Editions, England, 1992).

Vassiliev, Alexei M., *Ta'rīkh al-'Arabīya al-Su'ūdīya* (Dār al-Taqaddum, Moscow, 1982).

Villiers, Alan, 'Some Aspects of the Arab Dhow Trade', in L.E. Sweet, *Peoples and Cultures*, vol. 1, pp. 155–72.

Vincent, William, *The Commerce and Navigation of the Ancients in the Indian Ocean* (Cadell and Davies, London, 1807).

Ward, Philip, *Travels in Oman: on the Track of the Early Explorers* (Oleander, Cambridge, 1987).

Waring, Edward Scott, *A Tour to Sheeraz by the Route of Kazroon and Feerozabad* (Cadell and Davies, London, 1807).

Wellsted, James Raymond, *Travels in Arabia*, 2 vols. (John Murray, London 1838: reprint Akademische Druck—u. Verlagsanstalt, Graz, 1978).

Wellsted, James Raymond, *Travels to the City of the Caliphs, along the Shores of the Persian Gulf and the Mediterranean*, 2 vols. (Colburn, London, 1840).

Whitelock, Lt H.H. IN, 'An Account of Arabs who inhabit the Coast between Ras-el Kheimah and Abothubee in the Gulf of Persia, generally called the Pirate Coast', *Transactions of the Bombay Geographical Society*, vol. 1 (1835–6), in A.S. Cook, *Survey*, vol. 1, pp. 325–47.

Wilkinson, John Craven, *The Imamate Tradition of Oman* (Cambridge University Press, Cambridge, 1987).

Wilkinson, John Craven, *Water and Tribal Settlement in South East Arabia: a Study of the Aflaj of Oman* (Clarendon Press, Oxford, 1977).

Wilson, Sir Arnold T., *The Persian Gulf: an Historical Sketch from the Earliest Times to the Beginning of the Twentieth Century* (1928: Allen and Unwin, London, 1954).

Wilson, N.F.J., *The Native Craft; a General Description of the Native Craft Visiting Bombay Harbour and Particulars as to their Survey, Registry, Measurement and Lighting* (Bombay Port Trust, Bombay, 1909).

Winder, R. Bayly, *Saudi Arabia in the Nineteenth Century* (Macmillan, London, 1965).

Yule, Henry, and Arthur Coke Burnell, *Hobson-Jobson* (1886: republ. Routledge & Kegan Paul, London, 1985).

INDEX

216–34; technology 27–8, 275; *see also* agriculture; alcohol; antimony; architecture; Banyans; beards; bedouin; cannibalism; citystate; clothes; coffee; culture; ecology; Europeans; fishing; food; furniture; gambling; health; henna; language; law; music; pearling; perception; Qasimi states, economy of; religion; ritual; seafaring; shaikhs; slaves; sport; tobacco; trade; tribes; women

Socotra Island: 89, 170, 319

Somalia: *see* Berbera

Sonmiani: 120, 161–2, 300, 304, 307, 367 n13

Sooleman Shah, Muscat vessel: 318

Soothree: 304, 307

sources: xii, xiii–xiv, 65–6, 67–8, 272, 370 n2; Arabic xiii–xiv, 131–3, 190, 266, 320–6, 327, 328–30, 356 n14, 385 n65; British xii, xiii, xiv, 5, 13, 18, 65–6, 67–8, 98–9, 102, 125, 137–8, 139, 145, 150, 151–63, 167, 178, 228, 257, 284, 287–8, 290, 292–3, 297–315, 321, 325, 328, 371 n6, 420–1; Dutch 172, 173–4, 178, 371 n6; European xii, 178, 256, 275–6, 329; Persian xiii, 134–5; Portuguese 306; *see also* Bombay, Government of: archives; history; Ibn Bishr; Ibn Ruzaiq; *Lam' al-Shihab*; Lorimer; Maurizi; Niebuhr

South Carolina: 64

Spain: seaports 36

sport: duck-shooting 72

steam: 275

Stephenson, Capt: 93

Stroker, Malcolm & Co, Bombay house: 310

Sublime Porte: 34

Sudan (Suwaidi) tribe: 77–8, 84–5, 180–1, 195, 197, 203, 219, 237–8, 256, 292, 365 n65

Suez: 287

Sufism: 40; at Ras al-Khaima 181, 248, 249; *see also* dervish

Sugand Pursad, Bombay botella: 302

Suhar: 48, 52, 53, 55, 56, 93, 173, 181, 183, 186, 187, 200, 320–3, 328, 330; *see also* Azzan bin Qais

Sulaiman, merchant: 308

Sulaiman Pasha: 35

Sultan of Muscat: 20th century 50

Sultan, Ottoman: 42, 193, 328

Sultan Bandar Riqi, British contact: 105, 138, 385 n65

Sultan bin Abdullah Marzuqi, vessel owner: 318

Sultan bin Ahmad, Al Bu Sa'id, ruler of Muscat: 92, 180–1, 238, 240–1, 253, *Figure 6* 225; commercial and Gulf policy 53–4, 77–8, 171, 174, 180–1, 237, 252–3, 273, 400 n62; killed 96–7, 182, 238, 261, 346 n26, 391 n73, 414 n2; reign 53–4, 55; *see also* Muscat

Sultan bin Saqr, Qasimi ruler: 83–4, 181–215, 347 n47, 374 n82, 375 n88, 375 n90, 378 n144; authority and tone 83–4, 192, 194, 195, 197, 198, 214; and Britain 76, 79–80, 82, 84–5, 96, 97, 99, 102, 104, 105, 184, 188, 189, 203–4, 206, 213–15, 222, 252, 273–4, 323, 324–5, 375 n91, 376 n98, 388 n15, 405 n128; death 84, 272–3; and France 217, 379 n5, 404 n103; hospitality 222; and Iran 136–7, 195, 203, 358 n35, 358 n39, 375 n91, 390 n52; marriages and relations 82, 84, 105, 182, 188, 205, 214, 215, 221, 372 n40, 373 n64, 375 n83, 375 n93, 385 n65, *Figures 3–6* 223–5; and Muscat 133, 182, 185–6, 187, 189, 192, 194, 205, 206–7, 320–5; and piracy 76, 79–80, 82, 84–5, 96, 97, 99, 102, 104, 131–2, 133, 188, 197, 213, 244, 303–4, 320–6; recovers power 206–15; ruler of Sharja only 83–4, 194–214; titles 185, 187, 247, 390 n52; trade and revenue 184, 207, 213, 221, 388 n15; and Wahhabis 80, 83–4, 99, 102, 104, 131–2, 136, 185–92, 194, 195, 206–7, 244, 245, 247, 249–50, 320–6, 373 n61; *see also* Dir'iya; Qasimi family; Qasimi states; Qawasim; Ras al-Khaima; Sharja

Sultan Muhammad al-Qasimi, Shaikh, modern ruler of Sharja: xiii, 65–6

Sultana, Basra baghla: 76, 80–1

Sumayil: 135, 321, 327, 328

Summana: 414 n3

Sunderjee Khitree, vessel owner: 297, 298

Sunderjee Sewjee, Bombay merchant: 87, 118, 298, 299, 301, 304, 306, 308–9, 310–12, 314, 407 n8; relative 305

superstition: *see* ritual

Supreme Government: 33, 104, 107, 118, 198, 289, 327, 403 n99

Sur: 50, 199, 229, 231, 318; fleet plundered 76–7, 78, 132, 169, 184, 236; Qawasim of 57, 76–7, 110, 184, 186, 218, 316–17, 342 n32; and south Arabia 316–17; vessels 54, 76–7, 78, 92, 115–16, 132, 169–70, 184, 231, 271, 316–17, 329